# Strategic Utilization of Information Systems in Small Business

M. Gordon Hunter
*The University of Lethbridge, Canada*

A volume in the Advances in Business Information Systems and Analytics (ABISA) Book Series

BUSINESS SCIENCE Reference
An Imprint of IGI Global

| | |
|---|---|
| Managing Director: | Lindsay Johnston |
| Managing Editor: | Austin DeMarco |
| Director of Intellectual Property & Contracts: | Jan Travers |
| Acquisitions Editor: | Kayla Wolfe |
| Production Editor: | Christina Henning |
| Development Editor: | Erin O'Dea |
| Typesetter: | Cody Page & Michael Brehm |
| Cover Design: | Jason Mull |

Published in the United States of America by
Business Science Reference (an imprint of IGI Global)
701 E. Chocolate Avenue
Hershey PA 17033
Tel: 717-533-8845
Fax: 717-533-8661
E-mail: cust@igi-global.com
Web site: http://www.igi-global.com



Library of Congress Cataloging-in-Publication Data

Strategic utilization of information systems in small business / by M. Gordon Hunter.
pages cm
Includes bibliographical references and index.
ISBN 978-1-4666-8708-0 (hardcover : alk. paper) -- ISBN 978-1-4666-8709-7 (ebook : alk. paper) 1. Small business--Information technology. 2. Management information systems. I. Hunter, M. Gordon.

HD62.7.S865 2015
658.4'038011--dc23

2015014828

This book is published in the IGI Global book series Advances in Business Information Systems and Analytics (ABISA) (ISSN: 2327-3275; eISSN: 2327-3283)

British Cataloguing in Publication Data
A Cataloguing in Publication record for this book is available from the British Library.

# Advances in Business Information Systems and Analytics (ABISA) Book Series

ISSN: 2327-3275
EISSN: 2327-3283

## Mission

The successful development and management of information systems and business analytics is crucial to the success of an organization. New technological developments and methods for data analysis have allowed organizations to not only improve their processes and allow for greater productivity, but have also provided businesses with a venue through which to cut costs, plan for the future, and maintain competitive advantage in the information age.

The **Advances in Business Information Systems and Analytics (ABISA) Book Series** aims to present diverse and timely research in the development, deployment, and management of business information systems and business analytics for continued organizational development and improved business value.

## Coverage

- Strategic Information Systems
- Data Strategy
- Legal information systems
- Data Governance
- Statistics
- Business intelligence
- Forecasting
- Decision support systems
- Data Management
- Geo-BIS

IGI Global is currently accepting manuscripts for publication within this series. To submit a proposal for a volume in this series, please contact our Acquisition Editors at Acquisitions@igi-global.com or visit: http://www.igi-global.com/publish/.

The Advances in Business Information Systems and Analytics (ABISA) Book Series (ISSN 2327-3275) is published by IGI Global, 701 E. Chocolate Avenue, Hershey, PA 17033-1240, USA, www.igi-global.com. This series is composed of titles available for purchase individually; each title is edited to be contextually exclusive from any other title within the series. For pricing and ordering information please visit http://www.igi-global.com/book-series/advances-business-information-systems-analytics/37155. Postmaster: Send all address changes to above address. 

## Titles in this Series

*For a list of additional titles in this series, please visit: www.igi-global.com*

*Improving Organizational Effectiveness with Enterprise Information Systems*
João Eduardo Varajão (University of Minho, Portugal) Maria Manuela Cruz-Cunha (Polytechnic Institute of Cávado and Ave, Portugal) and Ricardo Martinho (Polytechnic Institute of Leiria, Portugal)
Business Science Reference • copyright 2015 • 302pp • H/C (ISBN: 9781466683686) • US $195.00 (our price)

*Enterprise Management Strategies in the Era of Cloud Computing*
N. Raghavendra Rao (FINAIT Consultancy Services, India)
Business Science Reference • copyright 2015 • 359pp • H/C (ISBN: 9781466683396) • US $210.00 (our price)

*Handbook of Research on Organizational Transformations through Big Data Analytics*
Madjid Tavana (La Salle University, USA) and Kartikeya Puranam (La Salle University, USA)
Business Science Reference • copyright 2015 • 561pp • H/C (ISBN: 9781466672727) • US $245.00 (our price)

*Business Technologies in Contemporary Organizations Adoption, Assimilation, and Institutionalization*
Abrar Haider (University of South Australia, Australia)
Business Science Reference • copyright 2015 • 337pp • H/C (ISBN: 9781466666238) • US $205.00 (our price)

*Business Transformation and Sustainability through Cloud System Implementation*
Fawzy Soliman (University of Technology, Sydney, Australia)
Business Science Reference • copyright 2015 • 300pp • H/C (ISBN: 9781466664456) • US $200.00 (our price)

*Effects of IT on Enterprise Architecture, Governance, and Growth*
José Carlos Cavalcanti (Federal University of Pernambuco, Brazil)
Business Science Reference • copyright 2015 • 307pp • H/C (ISBN: 9781466664692) • US $195.00 (our price)

IGI GLOBAL
DISSEMINATOR OF KNOWLEDGE
www.igi-global.com

701 E. Chocolate Ave., Hershey, PA 17033
Order online at www.igi-global.com or call 717-533-8845 x100
To place a standing order for titles released in this series,
contact: cust@igi-global.com
Mon-Fri 8:00 am - 5:00 pm (est) or fax 24 hours a day 717-533-8661

*To my wife and best friend, Shirley, who helps me in so many ways with all of my projects.*

# Table of Contents

# Preface

This book is about Small Business and Information Systems.

The small business sector is an important part of an economy. Small business employs 48% of the total workforce in Canada (Industry Canada, 2010) and 50% in the USA (Michma & Bednarz, 2006). The contribution to GDP by small business is 29% in Canada and 30% in the USA. In order for small business to survive and prosper an innovative approach must be adopted. The main stay of any innovation is the effective adoption and use of technology, specifically information systems. The appropriate combination of information systems and the level of maturity of the management processes will create an effective environment to contribute to competitive advantage and the longevity of the small business through improved operations.

Small businesses, in general, may pass through a number of growth stages. To begin, a sole proprietor may form a home-based business. As production and sales volume increase a distinct location may be established for a micro-business. Further growth may necessitate the hiring of individuals to work in the business. Subsequently, expansion to a medium sized business will allow for the specialization of certain tasks and assignment to qualified individuals.

Each of the above stages may be described relative to the number of employees. The European Parliament (2002) defines a small business to include 10 to 50 employees. Industry Canada (2010) has two major categories for the definition of a small business. In the manufacturing sector a small business has 100 employees. In the service sector the number is 50 employees. In the United States a small business is defined as having fewer than 500 employees (Michma & Bednarz, 2006).

In the past small business success was associated with growth (Smallbone & Wyer, 2000). However, this is not necessarily the case. Dobbs and Hamilton (2007) and Tan et al (2009) determined that small business growth tends to slow after a certain size. Hunter and Kazakoff (2008) also identified this phenomenon when investigating multi-generation small business. They identified certain businesses which could grow with existing facilities such as automobile dealers and jewellers. However, home builders could not necessarily expand without incurring a significant increase in costs. Even a small increase in volume would require the addition of a complete set of sub-trades. Thus, the home builders considered themselves successful through longevity rather than growth.

As a small business exists for quite some time, the approach to conducting operations must necessarily mature along a continuum of three perspectives. One perspective relates to management processes. They will become more defined and easily replicated. Also, this maturing of management processes will promote efficiency, eventually effectiveness, and contribute to competitive advantage. Another perspective, E-commerce involves employing more advanced levels of web site functions. E-business represents the other perspective. Along this continuum more sophisticated functionality of administrative support will be employed through information system integration.

Small business adopts and uses information systems in innovative ways to improve operations and contribute to competitive advantage. This book provides a number of perspectives on the relationship between small business and information systems. As a small business matures more sophisticated information systems are employed involving more advanced technology. There are three major sections in the book.

## INTRODUCTION

An overview of the book is presented here along with definitions of major terms related to Small Business, Entrepreneurs, and Information Systems.

A business of any size needs information to function. Computer-based systems provide the necessary information to support the process of management. This book describes the relationship between information systems and small business. This chapter provides an overview of the book.

An overview description of the book is presented here. The term small business and the relationship with information systems is presented here. It includes a discussion of the importance of small business and the reasons and benefits for employing information systems. The format for the remainder of the book is presented.

*Chapter One: Small Business*, presents a description of small business.

This chapter presents a description of generic small business from a number of different perspectives. To begin, a definition for the term "small business" is discussed. There are many varied definitions used by government agencies and researchers. Thus, a contingency approach is usually taken with the investigator providing the adopted definition.

Next the importance of small business to a nation's economy is presented. The small business sector consists of a large proportion of overall employment and contributes a significant amount the national Gross Domestic Product (GDP).

Small business is not a small big business. Thus, small business managers take a different approach to making decisions than managers in large corporations. Mainly small business managers' decisions are affected by limited resources and the liabilities created by these limitations.

Many perspectives may be taken regarding what constitutes a small business. At a senior level there are alternative structures which facilitate policy decision making. At an operational level decisions are made relative to the resource limitations, experienced by all small business, concerning skills, time, and finances.

Small business will tend to focus on a small customer base because of the number which can be served. This approach entails risk regarding the loss of a few customers or a general down turn in the market.

Many small businesses must deal with the dynamics created by family member's involvement in the business. Initially family members may be employees. However, they may grow to become owners and decision makers, especially the children of the founding entrepreneur. Another issue revolves around participation versus non-participating family members.

There are intangible resources, such as culture and reputation that will contribute to the performance of a small business. Also, knowledge and skills of employees and managers; as well as the ability to pursue personal relationships both internally and externally will facilitate performance and contribute to competitive advantage.

Unfortunately, small businesses fail. The main contributing factor relates to poor management and the soft skills involved in dealing with employees and customers. Successful small businesses will initially make a profit. Then, the small business may grow. Although growth tends to lessen as the small business matures. A small business may be considered successful without growth if this is the objective of the small business manager. Another perspective of success is longevity, evidence of which is shown in multi-generation small business.

A major issue for small business is succession. The small business may be passed on from one generation to the next within the family or the business may be sold and continue under new management. A positive result for succession requires the current owner/manager to make a decision about their eventual cessation of involvement.

This chapter is organized as follows. The next section presents various definitions for small business. The importance of small business is related to employment and contribution to the economy. Then small business is differentiated from large companies. Various perspectives on policy and operational decision making are outlined. Then aspects which contribute to small business failure and success are compared. Issues regarding growth suggest this is a possible measure of success. But, so is longevity which leads to the final section of the chapter about succession.

*Chapter Two: Entrepreneurs*, describes the types and characteristics of individuals involved in small business. An entrepreneur willingly addresses relatively high risk situations which require making decisions about allocating scarce resources.

This chapter includes a description of the various types and characteristics of entrepreneurs involved in small business. The emphasis is on the individual who becomes an entrepreneur. A nascent entrepreneur is an individual who has not yet started a venture but has considered doing so and is in the process of forming a small business. The types of entrepreneur include novice, serial, and portfolio. Personality types influence the entrepreneur's approach to conducting business. Some entrepreneurs might be aggressive pursuing growth and expansion while others might take a more conservative approach.

Further, there is an obvious link between an entrepreneur and a small business. The characteristics and aptitude of an entrepreneur may apply to their involvement in a large corporation, but an entrepreneur is more obvious and indeed necessary in a small business. It is a difficult task to separate a discussion of the entrepreneur from the small business. However, the remainder of this chapter will focus on aspects related to entrepreneurs.

This chapter is organized as follows. The next section defines the types of entrepreneurs including novice, serial, and portfolio, including nascent. Another perspective considers manager, owner, technician, and crafts person. The following section presents descriptions of the characteristics of entrepreneurs. These characteristics include descriptions of cognitive style and the umbrella characteristics as displayed by "super achievers" and "small giants". Another perspective investigates the characteristics of the founding entrepreneur and the authentic leader. A differentiation is made between an entrepreneur and a small business owner. Further characteristics are explored from the perspective of traits, behaviors, and opportunity identification. This section also investigates the performance of entrepreneurs in relation to their human and social capital. Then entrepreneurship is explored through a discussion of the Theory of Entrepreneurship. The chapter concludes with the introduction of the entrepreneurial process, including creativity, innovation, and implementation, followed by a discussion of the dimensions involved in the entrepreneurial process including creativity, innovation, and implementation.

*Chapter Three: Information Systems*, provides a generic overview of this technology and how it may be employed to support small business.

This chapter describes information systems. In general, an information system turns data into information to support decision making. The information must be timely, complete, and accurate relative to the decisions which must be made.

There are many types of systems, such as the solar system or the nervous system. An information system is one type of system which supports various decision making activities within a business. Information systems may be manual or automated.

With a low volume of transactions and few data items a manual information system may suffice. However, as transaction volume increases along with the requirement for more data items an automated information system will become a necessity. This chapter focuses on aspects related to automated information systems.

This chapter is organized as follows. To begin, systems in general are described. Then, the terms "information technology" and "information system" are differentiated. The remainder of the chapter is focused on information systems. Next a general information systems diagram serves to explain the components of any information system and its relationship to the business environment. This diagram shows how data becomes information which, in turn, supports decision making. There are different types of information systems depending upon the management level in a business. Each type of information system is designed to address the requirements of decisions necessary at various management levels. The chapter includes a list of commonly used terms which might be encountered by the small business manager. Then an overview of research related to small business and information systems presents a description of small business readiness for the technology. A small business may use information systems to lower costs, increase profits, improve service, or achieve a competitive advantage. More specific research is presented in subsequent chapters. To conclude this chapter a sample investigation is included which outlines further considerations regarding the acquisition of information systems by small business. Project recommendations are made relative to a number of stakeholders as they relate to small business.

*Chapter Four: Theories for Investigations* reviews the plethora of conceptual and applied frameworks for investigating small business in general and more specifically the relationship between small business and information systems. It is concluded that currently there is not a generally accepted small business theory.

This chapter presents general theories, including models and frameworks, about small business and investigations related to information systems. Then a series of overviews describe approaches to information systems and small business. These overviews are presented in more detail in subsequent chapters in this section of the book.

*Chapter Five: Adoption* commences a series of chapters that relate small business and information systems via a specific aspect relating the two topics. In this chapter the idea of adopting the technology is explored from initially identifying an issue through to adopting a specific information system to address the issue.

This chapter addresses the issues involved in small business adoption of information systems. The adoption of technology in general will result in significant changes to the small business. It is not necessary that the technology is leading edge, just new to the small business. Pressure to adopt a new technology may come from external or internal sources. Externally, customers or suppliers may expect to interact with the small business via some form of technology. Internally, senior management of the small business may perceive that the adoption of a technology will provide a benefit to the business.

A specific form of technology involves information technology; those systems which provide input to management decision making. Small business adopts information technology to enhance the efficiency of daily operations. Previous experience will positively impact the adoption of traditional information systems; those functions which support normal business operations. The adoption of more current information systems, such as Internet based applications will be facilitated by an innovative approach to adopting a novel information technology.

Two theories have been employed to analyze the adoption of information systems by small business. The Resource-based View Theory suggests small business employ their internal resources to adopt information systems in a unique way to improve processes and potentially gain competitive advantage. The Technology-Organization-Environment (TOE) framework outlines the characteristics of information systems adoption relative to the specific context of the technology, the small business, and its environment.

The adoption of information systems may be considered a success of a failure. Successful adoption will result from user participation and the realization of the initially identified benefits. If there is no recognition of the impending change in the small business, the adoption may not be considered successful.

This chapter is organized as follows. The context of the adoption of information technology involves the acquisition of technology in general while taking an innovative approach. There are both internal and external pressures for the adoption of information systems. Previous experience will positively impact the adoption of traditional information systems. However, a more innovative attitude will facilitate the adoption of current technologies involving the Internet. Two theories are reviewed – Resource-based View and Technology-Organization-Environment (TOE). Then issues, related to adoption success and failure are reviewed. The chapter concludes with the presentation of an adoption project which, while completed, was not considered to be successful by the managers of a small business.

*Chapter Six: Use* describes how the information system is employed within a small business. An information system may be used to support deferent levels of management decision making. There may be issues in interacting with the information system which may impact user satisfaction.

This chapter presents an overview of the issues involved in the use of information systems by small business. Management of small business tends to make decisions based upon an informal approach to gathering information. Once adopted, an information system formalizes this approach and promotes a more structured process for decision making. From an external perspective the use of information systems by small business presents a positive image to customers, suppliers and other small businesses. Internally the responsibility resides with senior management to set a positive environment regarding the use of information systems.

Senior managers should take a strategic approach to determining how information systems can contribute to competitive advantage. They must be proactive in dealing with issues associated with the use of information systems. This is especially so for ensuring employees are sufficiently trained in the appropriate use of the information systems. The use of an information system should promote operational efficiency by providing timely information that accurately reflects what has transpired in the small business.

This chapter is organized as follows. To begin two theories are reviewed which provide the context for information systems use in small business. Then it is noted that information systems use will promote a positive image for the small business. Laggards and leaders are described regarding practices which facilitate the beneficial use of information systems. In general, a proactive attitude by management and employees will provide a positive environment. Once selected the information systems should be used effectively as well as efficiently. Operational efficiency will contribute to "doing things right". Effective information systems, providing timely and accurate information will contribute to management in their goal of "doing the right things". The chapter concludes with a presentation of the results based upon a series of projects which investigated small business use of information systems. There are issues to be addressed internally and those which arise externally that require a response.

*Chapter Seven: Strategy* explores the idea of how an information system may support strategic initiatives of small business.

Strategy involves planning for the future of the small business and considers both internal assets and external events which may impact the business. Small business may employ information systems in a strategic manner in order to attempt to gain competitive advantage. From an external perspective the small business will develop a strategy which proactively addresses the business environment. Continual scanning will provide information about the market and other small businesses in the same industry. Information systems related to websites and other Internet based applications will facilitate gathering important information.

Internally the focus is on skills and processes. The strategic use of information systems will improve employee skills and promote more sophisticated processes. The establishment of a learning environment will allow managers and employees to acquire knowledge about information technology. They will be encouraged to take novel initiatives in the application of information systems which may contribute to competitive advantage. In this environment the information technology knowledge of the owner/manager will promote investigations into the novel use of the technology to benefit the small business.

Overall, the strategic use of information systems will improve the performance of the small business. Physical assets such as equipment and machinery will be employed more productively. Intangible assets in the form of method and processes will lead to a more sophisticated approach to the management of the small business. Further, as the small business grows and matures informal processes will be replaced by formal processes supported by the adoption and use of information systems. Employee skills and a learning environment will facilitate the use of all of these assets to gain competitive advantage.

This chapter is organized as follows. To begin the generic term "strategy" is reviewed. Then for the remainder of the chapter strategy is related to information systems. Thus, it is suggested that the strategic use of information systems by small business will contribute to gaining competitive advantage. Next it is proposed that the information technology knowledge of the owner/manager and the creation of a learning environment within the small business will lead to a more sophisticated use of information technology and consequently competitive advantage. As the small business grows and matures more sophisticated and formalized processes are employed which are supported by information systems.

*Chapter Eight: Competitive Advantage* discusses the impact of information systems on the small business' interaction with the direct environment. This interaction involves both, relating to customers as well as identifying and reacting to competitors' initiatives.

Competitive advantage for a small business involves operating more efficiently and offering different products or services than competitors. A more efficient operation will result on lower costs and thus an advantage may be gained by establishing a lower market price. The advantage gained by offering different products or services must also take into account the needs of customers. That is, being different is not enough. There still must be a demand for the product or service.

A small business does not necessarily have to grow to attain competitive advantage. Indeed, just survival will suffice. In either case competent management is imperative. This relates to knowledgeable senior management and a positive learning environment for employees. The Theory of Constraints suggests that increased sales volume in conjunction with lower expenses will contribute to competitive advantage.

Information systems may be employed to contribute to the establishment of competitive advantage. The innovative adoption of technologies will support this initiative. Another theoretical perspective has been employed in this instance. The Resource-based View Theory, as presented in a previous chapter suggests the small business should employ its resources in a unique way from competitors.

This chapter is organized as follows. To begin, the term "competitive advantage" is described. Advantage may be gained through differentiation from competitors by having lower costs or different products or services that respond to a demand in the market. Next, competent management is presented as a factor contributing to competitive advantage. This factor involves knowledge of senior management and their ability to establish and maintain external networks. Then the Theory of Constraints suggests improved performance will result from increased sales and lower operating expenses. Three related issues are then presented which may contribute to competitive advantage. "Coopetition" is a term used to describe the conundrum of small businesses which are simultaneously cooperating and competing. The result is an increased market. "Family Capital" is another term which suggests the unique characteristics of a family business may contribute to competitive advantage. The last term is "luck". Here it is important to have a stimulating and open small business environment. Thus, when a situation arises which may be attributed to luck the small business will be in a position to take advantage. Finally, the Resource-based View theory provides the context for analyzing the unique information systems characteristics of small business which may contribute to competitive advantage. These characteristics include information systems infrastructure and information systems skills along with management knowledge and an integrated strategy to use information systems to facilitate competitive advantage.

*Chapter Nine: Management Processes* discusses how management of small business evolves over time as the business matures. In general, these processes become more formal and robust.

Management processes relate to a number of high level activities involved in small business operations. At the highest level management will set the direction for the small business in the form of a mission statement. Then, within the context of the mission statement goals may be used to give further direction to the small business. Goals, however, must be evaluated. This necessitates the development of objectives which possess measureable outcomes. These three initiatives relate to long range planning activities of the small business.

Management involves five functions. Irrespective of the level of management all five functions are necessary. The higher management levels involve more planning while the lower levels involve more controlling.

As a small business matures more sophisticated management processes are required. The continuum of sophistication relates to the stages of a small business – Genesis, Grounding, Growth, and Generations.

Management capabilities till promote growth of the small business. These capabilities are related to human resource activities, competency of managers, and the planning and control of management processes in an attempt to improve performance. Resources should be used to improve productivity. The core functional areas, marketing, fiancé, and human resources, should operate as efficiently as possible. The limited resources of a small business should be employed as productively as possible to gain maximum short-term and long-term advantage.

The personality characteristics and experience of a few senior managers in a small business are key aspects to the performance of the small business. These managers will provide direction and guidance to employees through establishing management processes and ensuring they continue to reflect the necessary operational functions of the small business.

This chapter is organized as follows. To begin the context for management processes is described relative to the sequence of planning related to mission, goals, and objectives. This sequence provides a path from general statements of direction to specific measureable activities. It is important to note that the specific activities should relate to the goals and respond to the mission. Next the five generic functions of management are reviewed. They relate to all levels of management with their emphasis changing depending upon the level within the hierarchy. Another perspective is presented with five themes of management which relate to the main operational area of a small business. Growth of a small business depends upon the characteristics and experience of the senior management. As small businesses grow management processes become more formalized. Information system support this formalization.

*Chapter Ten: E-commerce* also presents a maturity continuum for the use by the small business for Internet-based technology. This is a specific form of information system based upon current technology.

E-commerce involves the sale of products and services via the Internet. The unique properties of the Internet facilitate a variety of E-commerce models. The focus of this chapter is Business to Consumer (B2C). As a small business matures it will tend to incorporate more sophisticated aspects of E-commerce and pass through four stages – Presence, Portals, Transactions Integration, and Enterprises Integration.

E-commerce allows small business to be in virtual contact with any one from anywhere at any time. The customer relations component of the value chain is improved through using E-commerce. Sales may be completed faster. Post sales service may be related to the specific customer and their purchases.

Security concerns may be addressed by establishing specific user accounts with passwords. A response to telecommunications concerns could be the adoption of encryption techniques for data exchanged via communications networks.

Internet use and E-commerce is expanding. Small business adoption of E-commerce will be facilitated by three considerations. The goals of the small business should relate to the benefits created by using E-commerce. Senior management should be knowledgeable about E-commerce and enthusiastic about its adoption. Further, employees should possess sufficient knowledge to be able to implement and use a specific E-commerce application.

This chapter is organized as follows. To begin, the context of E-commerce is described. The Internet forms the base for any E-commerce application. The benefits of the Internet all businesses to be able to better communicate with the market in general and with specific customers. Then, the four stages of E-commerce use are described. These stages relate to the E-commerce dimension of the Balanced Maturity Framework described in more detail in Chapter Thirteen. Various categories of E-commerce are then presented. The focus of this chapter is on Business to Consumer (B2C). Next, advantages and disadvantages of E-commerce are listed. Not that the advantages far outweigh the disadvantages. Then the chapter reports on a series of projects which investigated various E-commerce issues. These issues range from increasing customers, improving customer service, pursuing a differentiation competitive strategy, and inhibiters of E-commerce adopt. Finally, organizational slack is identified as a positive contributor to the adoption of E-commerce. Organizational slack allows managers and employees the time to investigate alternative technologies and how they may be applied to the specific small business. Unfortunately, small businesses tend to not possess slack. Thus, small business will innovate within the restrictions imposed by limited resources of time, skills, and finances.

*Chapter Eleven: E-business* describes the third evolution component in the use of information systems by small business. This component relates to the more traditional use of information systems to support management processes and it also incorporates current technology.

E-business is a way of conducting business in an electronic form which employs the facilities of the Internet. Recall from Chapter Eleven – E-commerce that electronic commerce involves the sale of products and services on the Internet via the website of a business. E-business includes E-commerce. But, it goes beyond and extends E-commerce to both pre-sales and post-sales services. E-business puts the business in closer contact with its customers, through Customer Relationship Management systems, which improves customer service and loyalty as a consequence.

The other major initiative involved in E-business relates to Supply Chain Management. This facility allows a business to manage all processes involved in the acquisition and distribution of products. Again, it puts the business in closer contact with suppliers. Both Customer Relationship Management and Supply Chain Management promote interaction with external entities. This focus positively impacts performance through improved customer service and efficiencies in the supply chain.

This chapter is organized as follows. To start, the term E-business is defined along with various perspectives. In general, E-business involves internal management processes and external information systems based on the Internet. Next factors which facilitate the adoption and use of E-business are presented. These factors include the level of information systems knowledge in the business and the system's perceived usefulness. There are also organizational factors related to internal management processes. Then, benefits related to the adoption of E-business involve improved performance and contribution to competitive advantage. The chapter concludes with a presentation of the E-business stages which form one of the three dimensions on the Balanced Maturity framework discussed in Chapter Thirteen. The E-business stages include Basic, Silos, Internal Integration, and External Integration.

*Chapter Twelve: Balanced Maturity Framework* brings all of the previously presented material together by relating management processes, E-commerce, and E-business. The main thesis of the book is presented here in that as the three major components evolve they must do so in a relatively balanced manner.

The presentation of the Balanced Maturity Framework represents the culmination of this book. The framework consists of three dimensions. Management Processes include functions such as planning, organizing, staffing, directing, and controlling. All management levels include these functions. Each level will consist of a different mix of these functions. As a small business matures the management processes become more structured and more outward looking. Information for decision making will be more formalized. In support of the more structured management processes will be more sophisticated technology. E-commerce will support interaction with customers. More advanced E-business will allow communication with suppliers.

This chapter is organized as follows. To begin, growth and longevity are presented in association with success. The stages of growth are reviewed which were initially presented in Chapter Four – Theories for Investigation. Then E-commerce is related to stages of maturity. E-business follows with a progression over time. The small business life cycle stages are then related to information processing. The chapter then provides a description of some models the show how small businesses evolve. All of the previous descriptions here and the earlier chapters have provided the context for the Balanced Maturity Framework which is presented at the end of the chapter.

## CONCLUSION

This conclusion presents a summarized review of the book. The general context of information systems in small business is described in Chapters One through Three. This includes material on small business, entrepreneurs, and information systems. Chapter Four through Eight provide further detail. Each chapter includes a review of related theories along with an applied discussion of information systems aspects including adoption, use, strategy, and competitive advantage by small business. The three dimensions of the Balanced Maturity Framework are described in separate chapters. These dimensions include Management Processes, E-commerce, and E-business. The final chapter in this section presents a description of the Balanced Maturity Framework. The important aspect of the framework is the balanced approach to maturity.

## REFERENCES

Dobbs, M., & Hamilton, R. T. (2007). Small business growth: Recent evidence and new directions. *International Journal of Entrepreneurial Behaviour and Research, 13*(5), 296–322. doi:10.1108/13552550710780885

*European Parliament*. (2002). Retrieved from www.europarl.eu.int/dg4/factsheets/en/4_14_0.htm

Hunter, M. G., & Kazakoff, D. (2008). *Little Empires: Multi-Generation Small Business in Southern Alberta, Canada*. Melbourne, Australia: Heidelberg Press.

Industry Canada. (2010). *Key Small Business Statistics (Catalogue No. Iu186-1/2010-2E)*. Ottawa: Canadian Government Publishing Centre.

Michma, J., & Bednarz, L. M. (2006). Small business in the USA. *International Journal of Entrepreneurship and Innovation Management, 6*(1/2), 4–17. doi:10.1504/IJEIM.2006.008202

Smallbone, D., & Wyer, P. (2000). Growth and development in the small firm. In *Enterprise and small business*. Harlow, MA: Prentice Hall.

Tan, J., Fischer, E., Mitchell, R., & Phan, P. (2009). At the center of action: Innovation and technology strategy research in the small business setting. *Journal of Small Business Management, 47*(3), 233–262. doi:10.1111/j.1540-627X.2009.00270.x

# Acknowledgment

This book would not have been possible without the ongoing efforts of all the small business entrepreneurs and their innovative use of information systems.

# Introduction

## SMALL BUSINESS DEFINED

It is difficult to determine a generally accepted definition of a small business. A consensus does not exist about a definition even when a specific statistic is considered (Curran & Blackburn, 2001). Some definitions which have been considered include market share; whether the entity is owner-managed; and if it is not part of a larger corporation. These terms are relatively vague and subject to interpretation; and, therefore, have resulted in limited use. Another consideration relates to employing some internal financial aspect directly related to the entity, such as annual sales or revenue, or total assets. However, statistics related to these terms are difficult or impossible to obtain. Most small businesses are privately held entities and are not required to publically report such statistics. Also, small business owners may consider this data more of a personal nature and are reluctant to divulge it. Further, they may be concerned that the data could become available to competitors. It is also recognized that those individuals who manage small businesses tend not to use these statistics even when the numbers are readily available (Halabi et al, 2010). Their decision making process tends to be ad hoc and based more on intuition.

The statistic that tends to be used to identify a small business is number of employees (Longnecker et al, 1997). The reporting of this number is a requirement of government income tax agencies in most countries and is easily determined within the small business payroll system.

While the use of the number of employees is the most prevalent statistic to define a small business there are concerns about some of its inherent characteristics. For instance, what may be considered small in one particular industry, may be regarded as large in another industry. Further, it may be difficult to determine how to count the actual number of employees if the small business retains a number of part-time or casual staff members who only work a certain number of hours less than the normal work period.

When reporting national employment statistics governments have developed categories of business size based upon number of employees. In Canada the number is 100 employees for goods producing firms and 50 employees for service firms (Industry Canada, 2010). In the United States a small independent business is defined as having fewer than 500 employees (Michma & Bednarz, 2006). The most specific definition of small business is provided by the European Parliament (2002). They define micro businesses as having 0 – 10 employees. Small businesses include up to 50 employees, and medium sized businesses have up to 250 employees.

Researchers encounter similar difficulties in defining small business. Burgess (2003) surveyed a number of researchers to determine if they could agree on a definition for small business. Many responded that a common definition would be very helpful not only for conducting their own research but also to facilitate comparisons across investigations and between nations. Unfortunately, there was no consensus forthcoming regarding a common definition.

Currently, the most prevalent general approach to responding to this research problem is for the investigator, at the beginning of the research project, to develop a specific definition of what will be considered small within the investigation. Alternatively, some researchers will initially gather data from the small businesses willing to respond to their enquiry and then categorize the firms having adopted one of the definitions outlined above.

## IMPORTANCE OF SMALL BUSINESS

In many countries the small business sector is recognized as an important segment of the economy (Curran & Blackburn, 2001). Governments recognize the important contribution that small business makes to their country's economic growth (Balderson, 2000). Further, as technology becomes more affordable and thus pervasive, the adoption of business oriented information systems will provide the necessary support for all aspects of small business operations (Pugsley et al, 2000).

Statistics supporting the importance of small business to a nation's economy are similar. Small business contributes a significant portion of the national Gross Domestic Product (GDP) of many economies. For instance, in Canada small business contributes 29% (Industry Canada, 2010) toward GDP and in the United States the contribution is 30% (Astrachan & Shanker, 2003). Further, small business employs a large percentage of the total workforce as shown in Table 1.

## CHARACTERISTICS OF SMALL BUSINESS

Small businesses are unique. They are different than other businesses. Even within the small business sector they can be different from one another.

A small business is not the same as a large corporation. Small businesses are inflicted with resource poverty (Thong et al, 1994). This term involves having to deal with limited resources related to time, finances, and skills. Within this context, managers of small businesses tend to avoid taking a strategic perspective (Stevenson, 1999). Instead, they focus on resolving immediate issues making a minimum allocation of scares resources.

Because of their size small businesses may be significantly impacted by events in the environment. These events include actions by competitors, reactions by customers, response by suppliers, and general activity in the economy, such as a downturn in activity.

Within the small business sector the entities' characteristics vary. The small business could be in service or manufacturing; retail or commercial; or independent or franchise. A further factor for variability is whether the small business is in its first generation or has existed for quite some time and is in a multi-generation situation.

## ENTREPRENEURS

An entrepreneur requires many skills. But, an entrepreneurial perspective is more about a state of mind. That is, an entrepreneur will be more willing to take a risk than a small business manager. Further, an entrepreneur will tend to be more innovative in continually seeking out new opportunities. Eventually, however, the entrepreneur will move on to a new initiative; or to adopt the perspective of a small business manager. This chapter presents the evolving role of the entrepreneur's involvement in small business.

Beaver and Jennings (2005) provide a differentiation between entrepreneurs and owner-managers. An owner-manager is involved with a small business in order to pursue personal goals. An entrepreneur takes an innovative approach to creating profits and growing the small business.

## INFORMATION SYSTEMS

An information system translates data into information to support business decision making. Data, raw unorganized facts, are gathered relative to a business event. The resulting information, which has meaning in the hands of a user, must be complete and accurate in order to support timely decision making. The acquisition of an information system by a small business will be a relatively costly endeavour. The small business manager will tend to rely upon an internal individual or external organization for advice when acquiring and information system. Further, the information system will be employed to improve the efficiency of daily operations of a small business.

## SMALL BUSINESS AND INFORMATION SYSTEMS

Above, it was shown that small business is different than large corporations. Further, small business uses information systems in a different manner than large corporations. Small business has unique issues relating to availability of time, financial resources, and skills (Belich & Dubinsky, 1999; and Pollard & Hayne, 1998). Also, Taylor (1999) determined that small business managers had difficulty matching system capability to functional requirements. While this mismatch is prevalent in many businesses (Ewusi-Mensah, 1997; and Laudon & Laudon, 1998), the relative impact on small business can be significant especially with regards to the effect on available financial resources.

Further, small business tends to focus on using information systems to support daily operations (Bridge & Peel, 1999; and Hunter et al., 2002). There is not much evidence that small business uses information systems to respond to the competitive nature of their environment (Dandridge & Levenburg, 2000).

Hunter et al. (2002) determined that the adoption of information systems increased small business dependency on either an internal or external entity. The internal entity may be a resident champion of the information system. However, because of the highly technical skills required and relatively limited need, the internal champion tended to perform the necessary tasks more in an ancillary role. The concern then is that information system may not be recognized for its potential contribution to the operations of the small business. The external entity as determined by Hunter et al. (2002) could be a supplier or consultant. Also, the external entity could be a competitor or customer whose advice may influence the small business manager. While dependency, whether internal or external, does allow the small business manager to focus upon the particular niche of the business, it remains incumbent upon the small business manager to ensure adequate knowledge of information systems and how it may be productively applied for the benefit of the business.

## REFERENCES

Astrachan, J. H., & Shanker, M. C. (2003). Family businesses contributions to the US economy: A closer look. *Family Business Review*, *15*(3), 211–219.

Balderson, D. W. (2000). *Canadian Entrepreneurship and Small Business Management*. Toronto: McGraw-Hill Ryerson.

Beaver, G., & Jennings, P. (2005). Competitive advantage and entrepreneurial power: The dark side of entrepreneurship. *Journal of Small Business and Enterprise Development*, *12*(1), 9–23. doi:10.1108/14626000510579617

Belich, T. J., & Dubinsky, A. J. (1999). Information processing among exporters: An empirical examination of small firms. *Journal of Marketing Theory and Practice*, *7*(4), 45–58.

Bridge, J., & Peel, M. J. (1999). A study of computer usage and strategic planning in the SME sector. *International Small Business Journal*, *17*(4), 82–87. doi:10.1177/0266242699174005

Burgess, S. (2003). *A definition of small business*. Information Resources Management Association Special Research Cluster on Small Business and Information Technology. Retrieved from www.businessandlaw.vu.edu.au/sbirit/research_issue_Results.htm

Curran, J., & Blackburn, R. A. (2001). *Researching the Small Enterprise*. London: SAGE Publications.

Dandridge, T., & Levenburg, N. M. (2000). High-tech potential? An exploratory study of very small firms' usage of the Internet. *International Small Business Journal*, *18*(2), 81–91. doi:10.1177/0266242600182004

*European Parliament*. (2002). Retrieved from www.europarl.eu.int/dg4/factsheets/en/4_14_0.htm

Ewusi-Mensah, K. (1997). Critical issues in abondoned information systems development projects. *Communications of the ACM*, *40*(9), 74–80. doi:10.1145/260750.260775

*Federation of Small Businesses*. (2013). Retrieved from http://www.fsb.org.uk/stats

Halabi, A. K., Barrett, R., & Dyt, R. (2010). Understanding financial information used to assess small firm performance. *Qualitative Research in Accounting and Management*, *7*(2), 163–179.

Hunter, M. G., Diochon, M., Pugsley, D., & Wright, B. (2002). Unique challenges for small business adoption of information technology: The case of the Nova Scotia ten. In *Managing Information Technology in Small Business: Challenges and Solutions*. Hershey, PA: Idea Group Publishing. doi:10.4018/978-1-930708-35-8.ch006

Industry Canada. (2010). *Key Small Business Statistics (Catalogue No. Iu186-1/2010-2E)*. Ottawa: Canadian Government Publishing Centre.

Laudon, K. C., & Laudon, J. P. (1998). *Management Information Systems – New Approaches to Organization and Technology*. Upper Saddle River, NJ: Prentice Hall, Inc.

Longnecker, J., Moore, C., & Petty, J. (1997). *Small Business Management*. Cincinnati, OH: South-Western College Printing.

Michma, J., & Bednarz, L. M. (2006). Small business in the USA. *International Journal of Entrepreneurship and Innovation Management*, *6*(1/2), 4–17. doi:10.1504/IJEIM.2006.008202

Pollard, C., & Hayne, S. (1998). The changing faces of information systems issues in small firms. *International Small Business Journal*, *16*(3), 70–87. doi:10.1177/0266242698163004

Pugsley, D., Wright, B., Diochon, M., & Hunter, M. G. (2000). Information technology and small business: Listening to voices from the field. *Proceedings of the Administrative Sciences Association of Canada (ASAC) Conference*. Montreal, Canada: ASAC.

Small Business Administration. (2010). *SBA website*. Retrieved from www.sba.gov

Stevenson, H. H. (1999). A perspective of entrepreneurship. In *New Business Ventures and the Entrepreneur* (pp. 3–17). Boston: Irwin McGraw-Hill.

Taylor, J. (1999). Fitting enterprise software in smaller companies. *Management Accounting*, *80*(8), 36–39.

Thong, J., Yap, C., & Raman, K. (1994). Engagement of external expertise in information systems implementation. *Journal of Management Information Systems*, *11*(2), 209–223.

## ADDITIONAL READING

Curran, J., & Blackburn, R. A. (2001). *Researching the Small Enterprise*. London: SAGE Publications.

Laudon, K. C., & Laudon, J. P. (1998). *Management Information Systems – New Approaches to Organization and Technology*. Upper Saddle River, NJ: Prentice Hall, Inc.

Longnecker, J., Moore, C., & Petty, J. (1997). *Small Business Management*. Cincinnati, OH: South-Western College Printing.

## KEY TERMS AND DEFINITIONS

**Entrepreneur:** A business person who is innovative and willing to accept relatively high risk regarding business ventures.

**Information System:** A process to translate data into information to support decision making.

**Small Business:** Usually based upon the number of employees. But this will vary by country and even business sector.

# Chapter 1
# Small Business


## ABSTRACT

*Small businesses are quite unique in many ways. They make a major contribution to employment specifically and the economy in general. Decision making at all levels is affected by resource limitations. Many of the aspects of failure or success of the small business relate to management issues. When a small business is formed it may grow quickly. If they do not fail the growth may lessen. While this growth may be regarded as a success, longevity and the consequent multi-generation existence may also be a consideration for an interpretation of success. This chapter covers the gamut of small business perspectives.*


## INTRODUCTION

This chapter presents a description of generic small business from a number of different perspectives. To begin, a definition for the term "small business" is discussed. There are many varied definitions used by government agencies and researchers. Thus, a contingency approach is usually taken with the investigator providing the adopted definition.

Next the importance of small business to a nation's economy is presented. The small business sector consists of a large proportion of overall employment and contributes a significant amount the national Gross Domestic Product (GDP).

Small business is not a small big business. Thus, small business managers take a different approach to making decisions than managers in large corporations. Mainly small business managers' decisions are affected by limited resources and the liabilities created by these limitations.

DOI: 10.4018/978-1-4666-8708-0.ch001

Many perspectives may be taken regarding what constitutes a small business. At a senior level there are alternative structures which facilitate policy decision making. At an operational level decisions are made relative to the resource limitations, experienced by all small business, concerning skills, time, and finances.

Small business will tend to focus on a small customer base because of the number which can be served. This approach entails risk regarding the loss of a few customers or a general down turn in the market.

Many small businesses must deal with the dynamics created by family member's involvement in the business. Initially family members may be employees. However, they may grow to become owners and decision makers, especially the children of the founding entrepreneur. Another issue revolves around participation versus non-participating family members.

There are intangible resources, such as culture and reputation that will contribute to the performance of a small business. Also, knowledge and skills of employees and managers; as well as the ability to pursue personal relationships both internally and externally will facilitate performance and contribute to competitive advantage.

Unfortunately, small businesses fail. The main contributing factor relates to poor management and the soft skills involved in dealing with employees and customers. Successful small businesses will initially make a profit. Then, the small business may grow. Although growth tends to lessen as the small business matures. A small business may be considered successful without growth if this is the objective of the small business manager. Another perspective of success is longevity, evidence of which is shown in multi-generation small business.

A major issue for small business is succession. The small business may be passed on from one generation to the next within the family or the business may be sold and continue under new management. A positive result for succession requires the current owner/manager to make a decision about their eventual cessation of involvement.

This chapter is organized as follows. The next section presents various definitions for small business. The importance of small business is related to employment and contribution to the economy. Then small business is differentiated from large companies. Various perspectives on policy and operational decision making are outlined. Then aspects which contribute to small business failure and success are compared. Issues regarding growth suggest this is a possible measure of success. But, so is longevity which leads to the final section of the chapter about succession.

## SMALL BUSINESS DEFINED

The term "small business" may be interpreted in a number of different ways. There is, in fact, no consistency in defining the term. Indeed, within a specific interpretation of small business there exists a variety of definitions. The following paragraphs provide some perspectives on definitions of the term.

With a focus on decision making the Australian Wiltshire Committee developed the following definition:

*...a business in which one or two persons are required to make all the critical management decisions. Wiltshire Committee (1971, p.7)*

Other definitions have been related to financial aspects. These measures include total assets; net worth; total value of products; annual sales; or annual revenues. Unfortunately, when these measures are used there is no consistency in the threshold amounts for an interpretation of what constitutes a small business. Industry Canada (2010) has outlined more alternative definitions. The Canadian Bankers Association defines a small business via their loan authorization threshold of $250,000. The Export Development Corporation suggests a small business would have export sales of less the $1 Million. Unfortunately, again, not all small businesses require loans or export their products. Further, these measures are difficult to obtain. Many small businesses are privately held and therefore, are not required to report such information. Also, many small business managers are not prepared to divulge this information (even if it was available internally) because of the potential impact on their competitive environment. Further, recent research has determined that small business managers tend to rely more on informal sources of competitive information rather than on the above statistical measures. (Halabi et al, 2010).

Thus, the term small business tends to be defined based upon the number of employees (Longnecker et al, 1997). This measure is readily available due to the required reporting rules established by government agencies regulating payroll systems and the determination of income tax deductions. Most jurisdictions require the remittance of employee salary payment information along with income tax data.

In Canada the definition of small business depends upon the industry (Industry Canada, 2010). In the manufacturing sector a small business will have 100 or fewer employees. While in the service sector 50 or fewer employees will be used to define a small business. Medium sized businesses will employ fewer than 500 employees regardless of industry.

The European Parliament (2002) uses a range of numbers of employees to define different categories of businesses. So, a micro business has 0 – 10 employees. A small business will have 50 or fewer employees. Medium sized businesses will consist of up to 250 employees. There is no differentiation based upon the type of industry.

Finally, in the United States a small business will have fewer than 500 employees (Michma & Bednarz, 2006). Again, in the United States there is no differentiation based upon the type of industry.

The variety of small business definitions, even within the measure of number of employees, has lead researchers to take a contingency approach. Thus, for each project the definition which may be used could be the one generally accepted in the geographic location of the investigation as outlined above. While this approach will suffice for an individual project it becomes difficult to compare the results of international projects when different interpretations of measures have been used.

## IMPORTANCE OF SMALL BUSINESS

Small business contributes a significant portion of the national Gross Domestic Product (GDP) of many economies. For instance, in Canada small business contributes 29% toward GDP and employs 5 Million people representing 48% of the total work force in the private sector (Industry Canada, 2010). In the United States the contribution to GDP is 30% and employs 50% of the total work force (Michma & Bednarz, 2006). Further, small business employs a large percentage of the total workforce as shown in Table 1.

## SMALL BUSINESS VERSUS LARGE COMPANY

A small business is not a smaller version of a large company (Welsh & White, 1981). Small business managers take an approach to decision making that is different from large company administrators (Forsman, 2008). Stevenson (1999) determined that small business managers allocate their scarce resources to what are considered priority activities within a focus on the short term. The concept of scarce resources is known as "resource poverty" (Thong et al, 1994). When compared with large company administrators, small business managers lack time, finances, and skills. These limitations affect decision making and activities within a small business. Also, because of their lack of size small businesses may have limited market power and consequently will have a relatively few customers (Zontanos & Anderson, 2004). This situation may cause the small business to be dependent upon the actions of their customers. Also, because the small business will have few employees, they

*Table 1. Percentage employment of total workforce*

| Country | Percentage Employment of Total Workforce | Source |
|---|---|---|
| Canada | 48 | Industry Canada (2010) |
| United Kingdom | 47 | Department for Business Innovation and Skills (2013) |
| United States | 50 | Michma and Bednarz (2006) |

must be multi-skilled and prepared to perform many varied tasks. Further, when a small business is just starting out it is difficult to gain legitimacy and support from various stakeholders such as employees, customers, suppliers, and financial institutions (D'Intino et al, 2007). There are two types of liabilities that impact a small business. They are the liability of newness and the liability of smallness (Liao et al, 2008/2009). The liability of newness suggests that the small business has been formed relatively recently and does not have a track record dealing with external entities such as suppliers and financial institutions. The liability of smallness relates to the lack of resources in a similar way as the Thong et al (1994) concept of resource poverty.

## PERSPECTIVES OF SMALL BUSINESS

This section provides a more detailed description of what constitutes a small business. To begin a small business classification framework is presented (Deeks, 1973). Then two perspectives of small business characteristics are described. One involves the Thong et al (1994) concept of resource poverty. The other perspective describes small business managers' approach to business practice including a comparison with large company administrators (Stevenson, 1999). Ward and Lief (2005) present a further perspective with a comparison of family and non-family small business. This section concludes with a description of two perspectives on how individuals might participate in a small business. Gersick et al (1997) present a three circle static model and also a dynamic three dimensional developmental model.

Deeks (1973) developed a classification framework based upon the source of policy making decisions. The framework involves three types of structures as shown in Table 2. In all three structures those who are regarded as small business management will be responsible for carrying out the duties related to their specialist functions.

The Monocratic structure reflects the situation where one individual makes and implements policy decisions. The small business may be newly formed. An Oligarchic structure may evolve as the small business grows. Individuals become involved

*Table 2. Structure in terms of policy making decisions*

| Structure | Decision Maker | Management Staff |
|---|---|---|
| Monocratic | One owner/manager | • Not shareholders<br>• Not related to Decision Maker |
| Oligarchic | Two or more owner/managers | • All shareholders<br>• Not related to Decision Makers |
| Patrician | One owner/manager | • All shareholders<br>• All related to Decision Maker |

Adapted from: Deeks, 1973

in making policy decisions because they are shareholders. The small business may evolve into a Patrician structure whereby one individual makes policy decisions and is supported by management who are both shareholders and family members.

The organization structure which may evolve depends upon whether the small business management are shareholders and also whether there exists a family relationship. Also, because small business is small there is a relatively flat organization structure. Thus, communication is usually carried out face-to-face informally as the need arises (Vinten, 1999).

A perspective of small business characteristics is described by Stevenson (1999). Table 3 presents a continuum of approaches taken for business practice by small business managers and large company administrators. The continuum differentiates small business managers and large company administrators. The term "Promoter" is associated with small business managers and reflects a risk taking proactive and flexible approach to business practices. The large company administrator term is "Trustee". In this case the focus is on maintenance of existing assets through formal procedures.

Aspects along the continuum relate to strategic orientation and decision making which involves resource commitment and control decisions. The strategic orientation of small business managers suggests they will take an external focus in order to effectively capitalize on emerging opportunities. Alternatively, large company administrators will focus internally on making efficient use of existing resources. The decision making process is composed of two components. Initially, a resource commitment decision is made and then follow-up control decisions are made to respond to changes which may impact the revised situation. The small business manager will act in a very short time frame and attempt to make a minimum commitment of resources in multiple stages in order to maintain flexibility. When making resource commitment decisions the large company administrator will consider long term implications of a large scale allocation of resources at the outset of an initiative. The control decisions are made in response to changes in the business

*Table 3. Approaches to business practice*

| Aspects of Business Practice | Promoter Trustee<br>Small Business | Large Company |
|---|---|---|
| Strategic Orientation | Capitalize on an opportunity | Focus on efficient use of current resources to determine the greatest return |
| Resource Commitment Decisions | Act in a very short time frame | Long time frame, considering long term implications |
| | Multi-staged | One-time up-front commitment |
| | Minimum commitment of resources at each stage | Large scale commitment of resources at one stage |
| Control Decisions | Respond quickly to changes in competition, market, and technology | Formal procedures of analysis such as capital allocation systems |

Adapted from Stevenson, 1999

practice environment. The small business manager will react quickly to any changes in the environment. An assessment wil be made about impacts as a result of the competition, market, and technology. The large company administrator will follow formally established and repeatable procedures to analyze the situation and potential impacts on internal systems relating to financial and human capital.

Another perspective of small business involves the concept of "Resource Poverty" (Thong et al, 1994). This concept addresses the issue that small business managers lack important resources necessary to conduct operations. These resources relate to skills, time, and finances.

Small business, because of their limited size, employs only a few people. Thus, each person is required to perform a number of varied tasks. While being a generalist would be helpful there may be situations where the individual does not possess the necessary skill. Thus, because of the small number of employees not all of the appropriate skills may be available to support the entire business operation. Acquiring the necessary skills externally through outsourcing may be an alternative. Although the third component of Resource Poverty, finances, which is discussed below, may have a negative impact of this way of acquiring the necessary skills.

Another aspect of Resource Poverty relates to time. Small businesses possess fewer employees. Beyond the skill issue discussed above, having fewer employees means less time to devote to the necessary activities to carry out business operations. This lack of time relates to both the work level as well as management. Workers may not have sufficient time to carry out their duties. It may take longer than expected to build a product or provide a service. At the management level the lack of time for decision making may lead to poor decisions or the lack of recognition that a decision is necessary.

The final aspect of resource poverty relates to finances. As most small businesses are privately held, they tend to be similarly financed resulting in a limited supply of money. In general, small business has difficulty obtaining financing. Indeed, small business has more difficulty than large companies in accessing financial resources (Ang, 1991). Small business managers may take an informal approach generally described as the "3Fs" – Family, Friends, or Fools. This approach may prove difficult. Initially, the amount of finances available may be limited. Further, if repayment is delayed for some reason personal relationships may be negatively affected. A more formal approach would be to establish a business relationship with a lending institution (Cole & Wolken, 1996; Ang, 1992). However, because of the centralized nature of credit granting policies unique regional or industry sector aspects of small business operations may not be considered (Hunter, 2011; Boot, 2000; and Degryse & Van Cayseele, 2000).

Small businesses tend to focus on a relatively small customer base (Zontanos & Anderson, 2004). The focus is also within the local region (Weinrauch et al, 1991). The customer and regional focus are related to the fact that the business is small and lacks necessary resources to expand operations (Thong et al, 1994). This focus, however, creates a conundrum. It is incumbent upon the small business managers to work directly with their customers to provide a personalized service (Berry, 1983; McKenna, 1991; and Cardwell, 1994). Indeed, a long term relationship with customers will prove beneficial. However, this narrow focus could result in a negative financial impact upon the small business. A downturn in the local economy may lead to a slowing of operations in the small business customer base. This, in turn, will affect the small business. Further, relying on a few customers could also have a negative impact if even one or two customers cease operations of start dealing with another business. Note that one or two customers could represent a large percentage of a small customer base. Thus, it may be worth the effort required to establish a diversified customer base and regional operation which may contribute to reducing the risk of a more focused approach.

Ward and Lief (2005) outline the differences between the family firm and the non-family firm as shown in Table 4.

For the family firm the above table suggests a focus on continuity of family owned assets protected from risk through adaptation and incremental improvement to service customers and employees in a social environment. The non-family firm will attempt to maximize share price for investors through growth recognizing risk improves returns for shareholders even if the business is sold.

Further, the authors suggest,

*Table 4. Divergence on the basics*

| For the Family Firm | For the Non-Family Firm |
|---|---|
| The purpose is continuity | The purpose is maximizing near-term share price |
| The goal is to preserve the assets and reputation of the owning family | The goal is to meet institutional investor expectations |
| The fundamental belief is that the first priority is to protect downside risk | The fundamental belief is that more risk promises return |
| The strategic orientation is adaptation | The strategic orientation is constant growth |
| The management focus is continuous incremental improvement | The management focus is innovation |
| The most important stakeholders are customers and employees | The most important stakeholders are shareholders and management |
| The business is seen as a social institution | The business is seen as a disposable asset |
| Leadership is stewardship | Leadership is personal charisma |

Adapted from Ward and Lief, 2005:2

*To tap into their inherent strengths family enterprises must set off on a quest to recognize and appreciate their own DNA – what makes them what they are. With this greater awareness of self, combined with a welcoming attitude toward complexity and contradiction, family businesses can achieve holistic long-term success. (Ward & Lief, 2005, pp. 2-3)*

The Venn diagram presented in Figure 1 shows three independent but intersecting classifications of how individuals may relate to a small business. The three generic classifications are Family, Owner, and Business. The intersections create a total of seven unique classifications (Gersick et al, 1997)

Table 5 describes the seven unique classifications.

The Three-Circle Model shows the relationship between the individual and small business in a static form. That is, it shows the current relationship and does not reflect how the passage of time may change how an individual relates to the small business. An individual may become involved with the small business through birth, marriage, or employment. A departure may result from a resignation, retirement, or death. The following diagram, Three-Dimensional Developmental Model, also provided by Gersick et al (1997) shows the evolution of the three generic classifications of a small business over time.

Subsequent to their Three-Circle static model Gersick et al (1997) presented a dynamic model which reflects the passage of time. The Three-Dimensional Developmental Model is shown in Figure 2. Again, the three generic classifications are

*Figure 1. The three-circle model of small business*

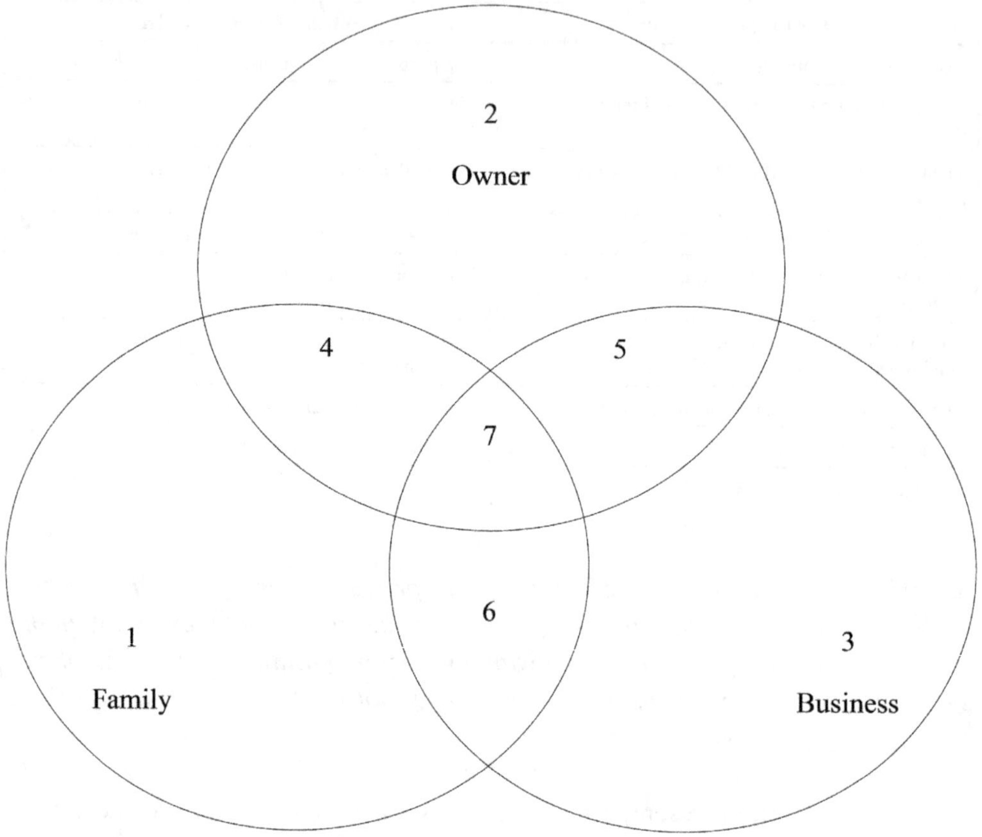


*Table 5. Individual – business classification*

| NUMBER | CLASSIFICATION | DESCRIPTION |
|---|---|---|
| 1 | Family | A spouse or child of the Family member |
| 2 | Owner | A shareholder who is not a Family member and not an employee |
| 3 | Business | An employee |
| 4 | Family – Owner | A Family member who is an owner but not an employee |
| 5 | Owner – Business | An owner who works in the business but is not a Family member |
| 6 | Family – Business | A Family member who is an employee but not an owner |
| 7 | Family – Owner – Business | A Family member who is an owner and an employee |

Adapted from Gersick et al (1997)

depicted along Family, Owner, and Business dimensions. However, in this case they are described along three separate axes. The passage of time is reflected in the progression along an axis from the centre through various stages towards the extremity.

Ward (2004) contributed detailed descriptions for each stage along the dimensions. Table 6 shows the combination of stages and descriptions.

The Business Dimension involves a progression of the small business from initial formation through to maturity.

In the "Start-up" stage the small business is officially formed and the focus is on survival. Initially, usually, one product or service is offered. As the small business normally involves only one person and perhaps another family member from the same generation there exists a very informal structure and approach to management.

In the "Expansion/Formalization" stage the small business is growing. The volumes of the initial product or service increases and perhaps new complementary products or services are added. Because of this expansion employees may be hired which increases the complexity of business operations. This increased complexity leads to the necessity to create a more formalized structure and approach to management. Employment contracts and job descriptions will be necessary. Some more specialized skills may be required.

The "Maturity" stage represents the third and final stage relative to the development of the small business. Products or services are now well established in the market place. Market share is relatively stable. Internally, management processes are consistent and adequately support the necessary business functions. Some small businesses may consider a major review of strategic focus and direction. This is a time to consider plans for renewal or dissolving the small business.

The Ownership Dimension presents the major considerations for ownership structures. This continuum represents progression from a single owner to an ownership structure involving individuals from subsequent generations.

In the "Controlling Owner" stage one individual retains control of the small business. In some instances a spouse or life partner may be involved in an equal or subordinate assistant role.

The "Sibling Partnership" stage involves individuals who are offspring of the Controlling Owner. Not all of the offspring could be involved in the small business so some form of sibling accommodation (Handler, 1991; Friedman, 1989; and Ward, 1987) will be necessary regarding participation in the equitable share of the family asset. In some situations the Controlling Owner may still participate in the operation of the small business but to a lesser extent.

The final stage along this dimension is "Cousin Consortium". Here the ownership structure is expanded beyond the Controlling Owner's direct offspring to include grandchildren who are, in effect, cousins. As the small business passes into subsequent generations and the ownership dimension evolves it becomes more complex.

*Figure 2. The three-dimensional developmental model*
*Adapted from Gersick et al (1997)*

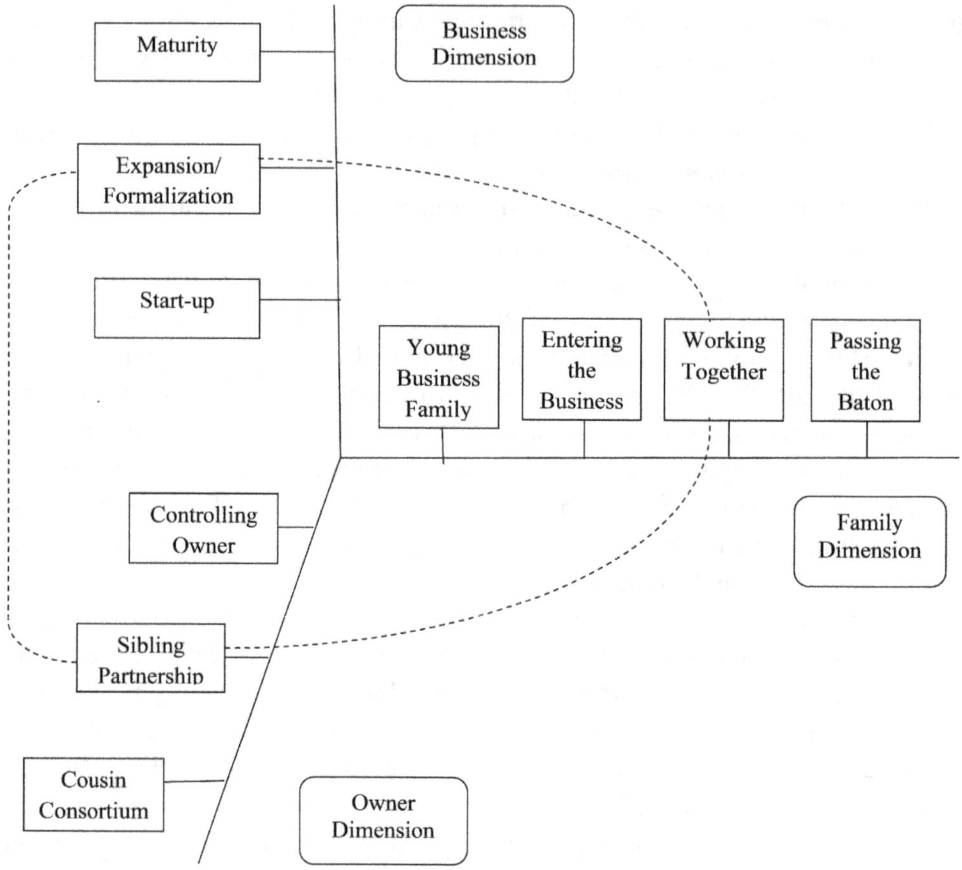


It is necessary to address the rights and responsibilities of both participating and non-participating family members.

The Family Dimension depicts the evolving status of the family entity involved in the small business.

In the "Young Business Family" the founding entrepreneur may take a spouse or life partner. These two individuals will establish their personal relationship as well as agreeing to a work/family balance.

The "Entering the Business" stage involves succession considerations. Offspring of the founding entrepreneur and perhaps individuals from subsequent generations may want to investigate options regarding their involvement in the business. In addition, at this time the founding entrepreneur may be reaching an age where life

*Table 6. Dimensional progression*

| Dimension | Stage | Description |
|---|---|---|
| Business | Start-up | The business is formed |
| | Expansion/Formalization | The business grows requiring a formalized structure |
| | Maturity | The products/services are established in the market |
| Ownership | Controlling Owner | The business is controlled by one owner |
| | Sibling Partnership | Siblings participate in the business |
| | Cousin Consortium | Subsequent generations participate in the business |
| Family | Young Business Family | The business owners are young |
| | Entering the Business | The business owners are middle aged |
| | Working Together | The next generation are involved in the business |
| | Passing the Baton | Control is passed to the next generation |

Adapted from Ward, 2004; and Gersick et al, 1997

style considerations may lead to the start of succession planning. This consideration could also result in an investigation into revising the business strategy in support of any succession plans.

In the "Working Together" stage the founding entrepreneur is adjusting to a revised and perhaps limited role within the business. The next generation is involved in the business and may be making decisions about its future direction. There is a potential at this time for conflict to arise regarding management of the business. Both the founding entrepreneur and the newly entering next generation family members are learning and adjusting to new roles. The founding entrepreneur may find it difficult to relinquish control. The younger family members may find it difficult to develop processes to take the business in what they consider to be a new and more beneficial direction.

The final stage along this dimension involves "Passing the Baton". The founding entrepreneur engages the succession plan and may withdraw from active participation in the business. Until the founding entrepreneur's death advice may be offered and may be accepted.

The profile of a specific small business may be depicted within this model by linking the current stage across the three dimensions. The dashed lines in Figure 2 represent the profile of a small business with sibling partnerships working together attempting expansion or the formalization of business processes.

The successful small business will pass through the stages of each of the three dimensions. The small business characteristics, as above, may affect how the stages of the model are operationalized. For instance, the Controlling Owner may retain more control over the small business and perhaps for a longer time. The Passing the Baton stage may be fraught with more emotional decisions because of the family dynamics in a relatively major component of family assets. Further, because the business is small the processes in the Expansion Formalization stage may be less formal resulting in relatively inconsistent management processes in the Maturity stage.

## PERFORMANCE OF SMALL BUSINESS

Huybrechts et al (2011) investigated the intangible aspects of small business through the lens of the resource-based view (Wernerfelt, 1984) which suggests that the level of performance of the small business is the result of its resources (Penrose, 1959) and how they are employed (Barney, 1991). The assessment of the intangible aspects as they relate to performance is presented in four categories in Table 7.

These four categories of intangible resources may contribute to competitive advantage. The following comments relate to the performance of small business and how these categories explain the competitive advantage obtained by family-base firms. The category of "Organizational Culture" may be considered by four dimensions. First, the family firm is group oriented. Employees interact altruistically (Lubatkin et al, 2005; Schulze et al, 2001; and Schulze et al, 2003). Thus, they tend to share knowledge and collaborate in an environment of trust (Zahra et al, 2004). Second, there is an internal focus regarding unique knowledge and expertise (Miller and Le Breton-Miller, 2006; and Zahra et al, 2004). Third, the influence of the founding entrepreneur is significant (Denison et al, 2004), even after relinquishing control of the business. Hunter and Kazakoff (2008) found further support for the continued influence of the founding entrepreneur even after his demise when they investigated multi-generation small business. Fourth, family firms tend to focus relatively more on the long term (James, 1999; and Ward & Aronoff, 1991). This long term perspective supports the pursuit of innovative strategies (Teece, 1992).

The "Reputation" of the small business may also contribute to competitive advantage. It is considered important to establish and maintain a positive reputation

*Table 7. Family firm intangible resources*

| Category | Description |
|---|---|
| Organizational Culture | "This collection of values, beliefs, assumptions and symbols (Barney, 1991) can influence employees in a way that is beneficial to financial performance." (Huybeechts et al, 2011, p. 272) |
| Reputation | "...a perceptual representation of a company's past actions and future prospects that describe the firm's overall appeal to all of its key constituents when compared with other leading rivals..." (Fombrun, 1996, p. 72) |
| Human Capital | "...the acquired knowledge, skills, and capabilities that enables persons to act in new ways..." (Coleman, 1988, p. 100) |
| Networks | "...personal relationships which transcend the requirements of organizational structure..." (Hall, 1992, p. 138) and include "...information, technologies, access to markets and complementary resources..." (Hitt et al, 2001) |

Adapted from Huybrechts et al, 2011

(Fombrun, 1996). The process of marketing the product or service brand should contribute to a unique image for the small business. Positive and on-going relationships with all stakeholders including the general public will contribute to a positive reputation and in turn competitive advantage (Fombrun, 1996).

"Human Capital" includes the knowledge and skills of employees of small business (Huybrechts et al, 2011). There is concern that the level of skill may be limited in small business because of the tendency to employ family members (Dunn, 1995; and Schulze, et al, 2001). However, there are positive aspects related to lower turnover (Miller & Le Breton-Miller, 2003); increased motivation (Tagiuri & Davis, 1996); and altruistic behaviour amongst employees (Voordeckers et al, 2010). Family members tend to be very committed to their job (Donnelly, 1964; and Horton, 1986) and are willing to make sacrifices for the good of the business (Dyer, 2006).

As an extension of the Human Capital Category various aspects of management may be considered including, the use of financial information, management practices, management capability, and management creativity.

Halabi et al (2010) investigated whether and how financial information is used in small businesses. They determined that small business managers possessed a very basic understanding of both accounting and finance and tended to rely upon an external accounting service for general business advice. This finding supports previous research (DeThomas & Fredenberger, 1985; Marriott & Marriott, 2000; and Argiles & Slof, 2003). When statistical performance information was available the managers seemed to prefer to consider a more informal assessment such the bank account. Again, this finding confirms prior investigations (Welsch & White, 1981; Khan & Rocha, 1982; Chaganti & Chaganti, 1983; Deakins et al, 2002; and Dyt & Halabi, 2007).

Floren (2006) investigated management practices in small businesses. He found that managers continually shifted their attention amongst many issues. Their work day is "...unplanned, informal, hectic and fragmented." (Floren, 2006, p. 281). Further, managers prefer informal communication and, as supported by Halabi et al (2010), tend to ignore formal information even when it is available.

Zinger et al (2001) investigated the impact of managerial capability on the performance of emerging small businesses and determined that sound marketing practices positively contributed to improved sales and earnings. This finding supports the contention by Pitt & Kannemeyer (2000) regarding the key role of a marketing strategy in an early stage enterprise.

Wyer et al (2010) suggest that owner manager creativity contributes positively to competitive advantage. They determined, among other findings, that attitudes towards flexibility and learning on the part of managers created a positive work environment which facilitated overall performance and, in turn competitive advantage.

Finally, "Networks", sometimes referred to as social capital (Nahapiet & Ghoshal, 1998), involve important personal relationships. In a small family run business family social capital relates to the relationships between family members (Huybrechts et al, 2011). Organizational social capital refers to the relationships with external entities (Arregle et al, 2007) such as banks, suppliers, or customers (Le Breton-Miller & Miller, 2006).

Poor small business performance due to a lack of managerial skills has been known for some time (Peterson et al, 1983; Baldwin et al, 1997; Chaganti & Chaganti, 1983; Chaston, 1997; Cochran, 1981; Fredland & Morris, 1976; and Theng & Boon, 1996). Konorti (2010) determined that employing professional managers contributed to the profitability of small business. He defined a professional manager as, "...a person who attended a post-secondary institution, who is a member of a professionally recognized institution in good standing, and who has practiced in his or her field for more than a year." Konorti, 2010, p. 14). Professional managers bring important skills and competence to a small business which, in general, are lacking in incumbent managers.

Alavi & Karami (2009) investigated the relationship between small business organizational performance and the existence of a formal mission statement. They adopted the Toftoy & Chatterjee (2004) definition of a mission statement as a document that, "...distinguishes its business from its peer firms, identifies its scope of operations, embodies its business philosophy and reflects the image it seeks to project (Alavi & Karami, 2009, p. 556). They determined that a mission statement was associated with improved performance. Further, performance also improved when non-management employees were involved in the development of the mission statement.

## SMALL BUSINESS FAILURE

To begin, this section reviews the various definitions of small business failure, which is the term adopted in this document. The term "entrepreneurial discontinuance" is then explored via theory related to the resource-based view of the firm. Further, terms related to liability are then presented. Subsequently, the issue of poor management and its potential contribution to small business failure is discussed. This section concludes with an overview of failure factors.

Table 8 presents a list of terms which have been employed to define small business failure.

The first four definitions result in either ceasing operations or the sale of small business assets. The fifth definition incorporates an assessment of the skills of a specific individual and implies that a deficiency in a certain skill set may contribute to small business failure. However, it is interesting to note that the closure of a small business may not be considered failure. For instance, Headd (2003) found that one third of start-ups that closed within four years were considered to have been successful by the owner.

Liao et al (2008/2009) further explored the term entrepreneurial discontinuance via the theory related to the resource-based view of the firm. This view incorporates terms related to financial, social, and human capital. Financial capital involves the ability to acquire the necessary funds to conduct operations. The pressure to address any lack of funds can be a distraction. The owner may not focus on other aspects of the business increasing the probability for failure. Social capital describes an individual's approach to relationships with others (Burt, 1997; and Nahapiet & Ghoshal, 1998). These relationships involve employees within the small business and external networks in the industry and the community. It has been determined that social capital plays a limited role in small business success but a lack of social capital may be a contributing factor to small business failure (Liao et al, 2008/2009). Thus social capital only comes into play in affecting a small business when it is not possessed.

Perhaps the most important component of the resource-based view of the firm is human capital which describes the characteristics, skills, and experience of an individual (Huybrechts et al, 2011). It has been determined that individuals with high human capital tend to be more productive in managing their current business operations; and better able to recognize business opportunities (Bruderl et al, 1992;

*Table 8. Definitions of small business failure*

| Term | Definition | Reference |
| --- | --- | --- |
| Discontinuance of Ownership | The business is sold to someone else | Bruderl et al (1992); Churchill (1952); Ganguly (1985); Hutchinson et al (1938); Phillips and Kirchoff (1989); Stewart and Gallagher (1986); and Watson and Everett (1999) |
| Discontinuance of Business | The business ceases operation | Bates (1995); Bates and Nucci (1989); Birley (1986); Cooper et al (1988); Dekimpe and Morrison (1991); Dunne et al (1989); Hamilton (1984); Price (1984); Reynolds (1987); Stanworth (1995); and Tauzell (1982) |
| Failure | The value of the business falls below the opportunity cost of continuing operation | Cressy (2006) |
| Bankruptcy | The formal process of liquidating business assets | Fredland and Morris (1976); Lowe et al (1991); and Watson and Everett (1999) |
| Entrepreneurial Discontinuance | Deficiency of education and management experience | Liao et al (2008/2009); Burt (1997); and Nahapiet and Ghoshal (1998); Bruderl et al (1992); Esteve-Perez and Manez-Castillejo (2008) |

and Bosma et al 2004). Further, deficiency in human capital, specifically education and management experience creates a situation where the small business becomes susceptible to failure. Also, possessing capabilities which aid in dealing with a competitive environment will increase small business survival rates (Esteve-Perez & Manez-Castillejo, 2008). These capabilities relate to the innovative development of advertising, and research and development initiatives.

Both of the terms "liability of newness" and "liability of smallness" may contribute to small business failure (Liao et al, 2008/2009). Liability of newness suggests the small business has not yet established efficient business processes and effective management structures (Mellahi & Wilkinson, 2004 and Honjo, 2000). The suggestion therefore is proffered that an emphasis be placed upon the internal management of the small business which will contribute to the increased potential for success. This emphasis does not preclude the necessity to also provide a quality product or service where there is demand. The term liability of smallness suggests the inability to attract necessary resources to the small business (Mellahi & Wilkinson, 2004). Earlier, Thong et al (1994) had employed the term "resource poverty" to describe the lack of time, finances, and skills within the small business. Thus, limited access to necessary resources will negatively impact the small business and eventually may lead to failure.

Poor management contributes to small business failure (Beaver, 2003; Dun & Bradstreet, 1991; Gibb & Webb, 1980; Lauzen, 1985; McNight, 1990). Further, when small business owners take a reactive approach to addressing situations as they arise the small business tends to fail (Van Gelder et al, 2007). They suggest a long term planning strategy and support an emphasis on generic business processes and consideration for future business opportunities (Bruderl et al, 1992).

Table 9 presents an overview of small business failure factors. There are ten factors which contribute to failure of they are either lacking or mismanaged. A review of these factors indicates they are mainly associated with "soft" skills. They range from communication; interpersonal relationships; adapting to change; teamwork; and the generic administrative functions of planning, organizing, staffing, directing, and controlling. Again, what is missing is a comment on the relative level of importance of these small business failure factors.

## SMALL BUSINESS SUCCESS

Table 10 presents an overview of small business success factors (Brown, 2007). These seven factors cover the complete range of potential issues which contribute to success. These factors range from managing financial and human resources; conducting efficient operations; keeping customer satisfied; and the effective management of administrative tasks. Unfortunately, this list is missing a measure of the relative importance of each success factor. That is, it would be helpful for the small business owner to not only know about all of these factors but also to know the factors upon which to focus.

There is also an issue regarding the decision of how to define a "successful" small business. Naturally, a small business must make a profit in order to survive. But beyond survival, how could the concept of "success" be incorporated? Some authors (Smallbone & Wyer, 2000; and Dobbs & Hamilton, 2007) propose growth as a measure of success. However, more recent research (Tan et al, 2009) has shown that the small business growth path may diverge. Hunter & Kazakoff (2008) found support for small business divergence. As discussed in Chapter 2, there are many different types of entrepreneurs (Westhead et al, 2005a, 2005b). Westhead and Wright (1999) determined there are differences in motivations of entrepreneurs. Some individuals at certain stages of the small business life are less growth oriented. They become satisfied with a certain level of performance and income. Their desire to maintain control leads them to a decision not to grow further. Support for this perspective was found by Hunter and Kazakoff (2008). Some of their research participants were content with the volume of their operations. Others realized that

*Table 9. Failure factors*

| Factor | Description |
|---|---|
| Ineffective communication skills/ practices | "Poor communication leaves employees in a cloud of uncertainty and stress that makes it difficult to make informed business decisions for managers and employees alike." (O'Connell, 2004, p. 27) |
| Poor work relationships and interpersonal skills | "The inability to foster effective working relationships isolates managers from the informal network of knowledge and resources that are necessary to cope with change." (O'Connell, 2004, p. 27) |
| Person job mismatch | "Changing roles and job descriptions put managers in challenging positions they are ill-equipped to fulfil resulting in poort performance for the managers and those who depend on their performance to get results." (O'Connell, 2004, p. 27) |
| Fail to clarify direction/ performance expectations | "Failing to provide a clear sense of direction and to clarify performance expectations hurts planning, motivation, resource allocation, and ultimately, the ability to navigate through uncertainty." (O'Connell, 2004, p. 27) |
| Delegation and empowerment breakdowns | "Ineffective delegation and empowerment practices contribute to confusion and immobilize staff and resources." (O'Connell, 2004, p. 27) |
| Failing to adapt and break old habits | "Failing to adapt and/or break old habits perpetuates behaviours and actions that are no longer valuable to the organization." (O'Connell, 2004, p. 27) |
| Unable to develop teamwork/ cooperation | "Without teamwork and cooperation, conflict and agendas of self-preservation will destroy collective performance." (O'Connell, 2004, p. 27) |
| Lack of personal integrity and trust | "A lack of integrity and trust negatively affects the managerial credibility that is essential for employees to buy-in to the change and move forward in the face of uncertainty." (O'Connell, 2004, p. 27) |
| Unable to lead/motivate others | "Failure to gain the commitment of employees leads to an attitude of minimal performance at a time when change requires extra effort." (O'Connell, 2004, p. 27) |
| Poor planning practices/ reactionary behaviour | "Poor planning practices and reactionary behaviour create disruptive crises that damage confidence, performance, and morale." (O'Connell, 2004, p. 27) |

Adapted from O'Connell (2004)

a small increase in the volume of output (house building) would lead to a significant increase in expenses (more sub-trades) which in turn, could financially ruin the small business.

*Table 10. Success factors*

| Factor | Description |
|---|---|
| Finance and Accounting | "...have an understanding of the process for raising capital, managing cash flow, and reading basic financial statements such as a balance sheet and an income statement." (Brown, 2007, p. 16) |
| Human Resources | "...issues...should be considered during the process of hiring, managing, and firing employees. [With] established policies beforehand [employers] will be able to better resolve conflict when it arises." (Brown, 2007, p. 17) |
| Operations and Production | "...source required raw materials, finished products, or other supplies. [Then] use these inputs to generate outputs such as sales revenue and profits." (Brown, 2007, p. 17) |
| Marketing and Sales | "Marketing involves everything that gets the customer through the door, makes the sale, and keeps the customer satisfied after the sale... it is also essential to understand your competition. Raising awareness is essentially advertising." (Brown, 2007, p. 17) |
| Customer Service | "Establishing a defined plan of action for customer interactions will help in dealing with any situation that could arise and will ensure better customer relations and satisfaction." (Brown, 2007, p. 18) |
| Information Management | "Information management is the function of managing the business's information resources, which includes creating the information stream necessary to support the business's operations. With the growing impact of computers in business, information technology is at the forefront of information management." (Brown, 2007, p. 18) |
| Administration | "Administration will plan, delegate, coordinate, control, and lead." (Brown, 2007, p. 18) |

Adapted from Brown (2007)

Beyond making a profit and creating growth, the following idea is proposed regarding defining a successful small business. De Geus (2002) investigated the common aspects of long-lived large companies. While he focused on large companies the general concept seems to apply to small business. He made the following comment:

*Companies die because their managers focus on the economic activity of producing goods and services, and they forget that their organizations' true nature is that of a community of humans. (De Geus, 2002, p. 3)*

Thus, a community of humans contributes to longevity and, as contended here, the success of the small business. The factors which help to establish and maintain the community of humans are discussed throughout this book. These factors are exemplified by those small businesses which exist for more than one generation. As they proceed beyond the first generation the small business will experience the crisis of succession and will indeed change. To be clear, a successful small business is considered to be a multi-generation small business. In all likelihood the small business will remain within the family. But this is not necessary for the determination of success. If a small business is going to exist for a long time there needs to be a focus on empowering employees and facilitating the development of a culture which promotes a learning environment (De Geus, 2002). Given this focus the small business will retain employees who will adopt an attitude of continuing to search for improvement. Burlingham (2006) identified individuals who rejected the opportunity for growth. These individuals did not necessarily want to do more. They were content with simply doing better. Note that this attitude does not discount taking an innovative approach to conducting business. This idea was supported by Hunter and Kazakoff (2008) in their study of multi-generation small business. They found that in these long-lived small businesses employees were treated in a positive way as family members and encouraged to adopt innovative approaches to operations.

Hunter and Kazakoff (2008) investigated various aspects of multi-generation small business. They suggest that a family owned small business could be considered successful if it has existed for more than two generations. Amongst a number of issues, they documented a small business approach to an interpretation of their business model. They determined that the successful small businesses would diversify within a focus. This seeming contradictory phrase has merit, especially in economic downturns when some aspects of the economy may be sluggish while others may be booming. So, for instance one automobile dealer, while focusing on automobiles, would diversify across manufacturers. Another automobile dealer would focus on a particular manufacturer but diversify geographically. In both cases it allowed the small business to respond positively to the recent economic crisis.

Further, Hunter and Kazakoff (2008) determined that the successful small businesses focused on developing a positive reputation within the community. Thus, they would strive to provide a superior product or an exceptional service. Further, they were prepared to participate in community activities such as serving as a member of the Chamber of Commerce or on the organizing committee of a social or sporting event. They also developed long term strategies rather than reacting to events as they occur (Van Gelder et al, 2007).

So, the business model and reason for existence are related to location. What makes small business unique is often location dependent. As above, small businesses exist because of a need in the local market and the response of an entrepreneur to an opportunity. There may be an industry of some kind close by. A regional hospital might dominate the local rural economy. There may be tourism facilities in the neighbourhood. All of these location-specific aspects impact the types of small businesses that exist in an area.

Lussier and Halabi (2010) employed the Lussier (1995) success versus failure prediction model to further understand the factors which contribute to small business outcomes. Table 11 explains the fifteen variables included in the model.

Lussier and Halabi (2010) were able to reduce the fifteen variables to 6 as highlighted in the above Table. So, "…if small businesses have adequate capital, maintain record keeping and financial control, have specific plans, make use of professional advice, have higher levels of education, and use marketing effectively, they will increase their chances of success." (Lussier & Halabi, 2010:368).

## GROWTH OF SMALL BUSINESS

Tan et al (2009) suggest that small business research "...has shifted towards the attributes and strategies that enable small business to grow, to contribute to economic value creation, and to flourish at the center of the innovation and technology-based calculus." (Tan et al, 2009, p. 234). The most common means for measuring growth is change in employment (Hoogstra & van Dijk, 2004; Chaganti et al, 2002; Smallbone et al, 1995; and Davidsson & Delmar, 1997) or change in sales (Kelley & Nakosteen, 2005; LeBrasseur et al, 2003; and McMahon, 2001). Dobbs and Hamilton (2007) investigated small business growth. Based upon 34 previous research studies they expanded upon four applicable categories, originally identified by Smallbone and Wyer (2000) relative to small business growth.

The following Table 12 documents these categories. In general, this table provides descriptions of the four categories. Growth will be related to management strategy. That is, to begin, a strategic decision is made that growth will be an objective. In conjunction with this decision is the character of the entrepreneur who must be motivated to exploit the opportunity to grow. The small business must be in a specific industry where the market provides the prospect for growth. Finally, the small business profile (size and age) will be other contributing factors to growth.

Kirkwood (2009) investigated growth aspirations in small businesses. Growth was defined by sales turnover and the number of employees. Growth in employees was hampered by availability of skilled personnel. However, sales growth was accomplished by those who intended to grow by diversifying, focusing on customer service, and the resulting development of a positive reputation.

An interesting research question posed by Tan et al (2009) relates to identifying the factors which contribute to the divergence of growth paths in small business.

*Table 11. Explanation of success versus failure variables*

| Variable | Description |
|---|---|
| Capital | Businesses that start undercapitalized have a greater chance of failure than firms that start with adequate capital |
| Record keeping and financial control | Businesses that do not keep update and accurate records and do not use adequate financial controls have a greater chance of failure than firms that do |
| Industry Experience | Businesses managed by people without prior industry experience have a greater chance of failure than firms managed by people with prior industry experience |
| Management Experience | Businesses managed by people without prior management experience have a greater chance of failure than firms managed by people with prior management experience |
| Planning | Businesses that do not develop specific business plans have a greater chance of failure than firms that do |
| Professional Advisors | Businesses that do not use professional advisors have a greater chance of failure than firms using professional advisors |
| Education | People without any college education who start a business have a greater chance of failing than people with one or more years of college education |
| Staffing | Businesses that cannot attract and retain quality employees have a greater chance of failure than firms that can |
| Product/Service Timing | Businesses that select products/services that are too new or too old have a greater chance of failure than firms that select products/services that are in the growth stage |
| Economic Timing | Businesses that start during a recession have a greater chance to fail that firms that start during expansion periods |
| Age | Younger people who start a business have a greater chance to fail than older people starting a business |
| Partners | A business started by one person has a greater chance of failure than a firm started by more than one person |
| Parents | Business owners whose parents did not own a business have a greater chance of failure than owners whose parents did own a business |
| Minority | Minorities have a greater chance of failure than non-minorities |
| Marketing | Business owners without marketing skills have a greater chance of failure than owners with marketing skills |

Adapted from Lussier and Halabi, 2010

Figure 3 depicts this divergence. This divergence in growth is supported by Dobbs and Hamilton (2007) who suggest that start-up firms tend to grow quickly until a certain size. Then, depending upon management strategies, growth tends to slow.

Hunter and Kazakoff (2008) found this divergence in growth when investigating multi-generation small business. They determined that most of the small busi-

*Table 12. Small business growth*

| Category | Factor | Description |
|---|---|---|
| Management Strategy | Growth Objective | Growth may not always be an objective. An owner's consideration of control, life style, and family desires will determine business goals. |
| | Employee Recruitment and Development | A growth oriented strategy will be affected by the business' ability to attract, develop and retain appropriate employees |
| | Product Market Development | Growth will be facilitated with an emphasis on product or service innovation and differentiation rather than on price. |
| | Financial Resources | A lack of financial resources may inhibit growth. Accepting external equity may impinge upon owner control. |
| | Internationalization and Business Collaboration | While most small businesses do not export, high growth businesses tend to do so. |
| Characteristics of the Entrepreneur | Motivation | Businesses established to exploit an opportunity will have a higher propensity to grow. |
| | Education | Educated individuals are more likely to grow their business. Education improves search skills, foresight, imagination, computational and communication skills. |
| | Experience | Management and industry experience will contribute to growth |
| | Size of the Founding Team | Larger teams possess more talent and resources which may contribute to growth if not affected by group conflict. |
| Environmental Industry specific Factors | Nature of the Market | High demand increases growth prospects. |
| | Role played by large companies | Sub-contracting and outsourcing policies of large companies can influence growth potential. |
| Characteristics of the business | Size | New small businesses have a higher growth rates. |
| | Age | Younger businesses have a higher growth rate. |

Adapted from Dobbs and Hamilton, 2007

nesses they investigated reported that an increase in sales could be addressed within existing facilities. More automobiles, cows, or watches could be sold. However, expansion was more complicated for a small business that was building houses. For instance, one small business home builder focused on entry level houses. They had established good working relationships with enough of the sub-trades (electrical, plumbing, roofing, etc.) to be able to build and sell an average of one house per week over one year. But even a small increase in volume would necessitate forming a working relationship with a completely new set of sub-trades.

*Figure 3. A higher versus lower growth comparison*
*Adapted from Tan et al, 2009*

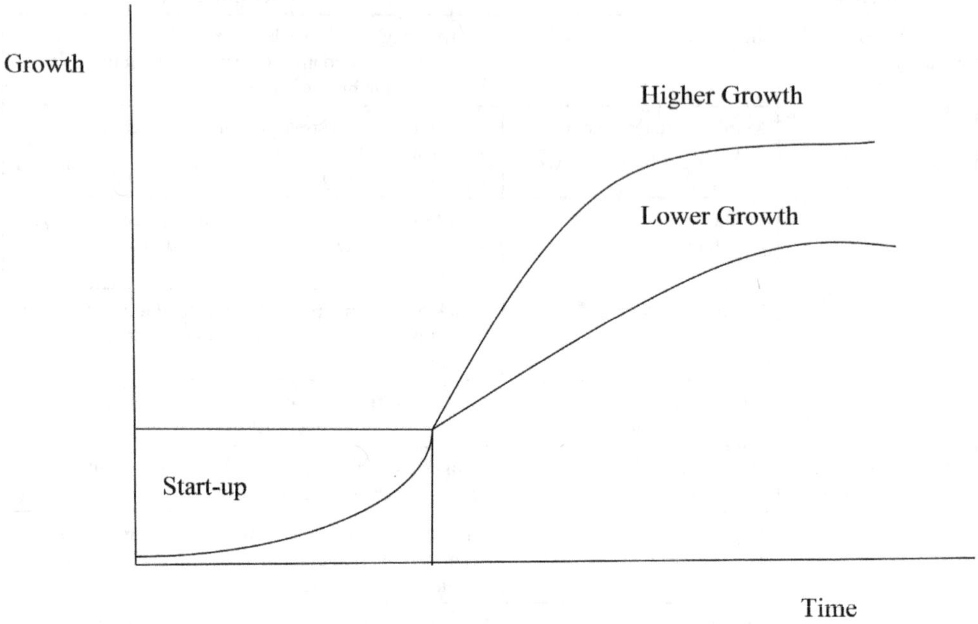


Also, for a period of time while volume continued to increase, this second set of sub-trades would only be necessary on a part-time basis. Usually, sub-trades do not find part-time associations beneficial.

Another factor that contributes to variance in growth is the small business approach to strategy. Examples of this factor were found in the business model of automobile dealers in Hunter and Kazakoff (2008). One dealer adopted a very conservative approach. Expansion plans involved a consideration for family involvement which resulted in a relatively lower growth path. Alternatively, another dealer took a more aggressive approach to growth. Expansion opportunities were investigated with the consideration of involving non-family members in management roles.

Where feasible all of the businesses considered the possibility of future expansion opportunities. Invariably, they emphasized a concern for continuing to provide quality products and services. They recognized the importance of loyal customer relationships and how this relationship could lead to new satisfied customers.

## SUCCESSION

Succession is an issue which has received much attention in small business investigations. The issue eventually arises as the founding entrepreneur ages and must decide about their future and that of the small business. If the small business is sold to a non-family member succession is not an issue. While this transaction may serve to indicate that the small business was a success in that someone was prepared to purchase the entity, it actually ceases as the entity which was originally formed by the founding entrepreneur. However, succession remains an issue if the small business is going to continue operation under the control of a family member.

Brun de Pontet et al (2007) suggest that succession involves both the transfer of ownership and management from one generation to the next. The transfer of management may be more or less informal. Indeed, the management transfer may start when the next generation becomes involved with the small business. Thus, management roles will evolve as the next generation gains experience and brings a new set of skills and perspective to the operation of the small business. Knowledge idiosyncrasy (Bjuggren & Sund, 2002) is a term which suggests that learning occurs by watching and doing. As the next generation works in the small business they learn from the founding entrepreneur. The intellectual assets (Choo & Bontis, 2002; and Sveiby, 2001) of knowledge are passed from the founding entrepreneur to the next generation in the form of written or explicit documentation. Perhaps more importantly tacit intangible knowledge (Huggins & Weir, 2007; and Watters et al, 2006) is passed from one generation to the next as they work together. This knowledge may go beyond direct aspects involved in business operations and include attitudes and ethics, all of which provide value to the small business (Garcia-Parra et al, 2009).

The transfer of ownership is a more formal transition which should be legally documented. A succession plan should facilitate the transfer (Manthey & Balhoff, 2002) and reflect the specific aspects of the small business (Barach et al, 1988). Each plan will be unique (Fiegner et al, 1996). The succession plan should attempt to provide a process for both parties to share all of the necessary information (Scholes et al, 2008). The plan should consider the implications of intergenerational tax (Narva, 2003). Also, the plan should address the required funds of the senior generation while not impinging upon the financial requirements of the small business. Further, as the small business is a family asset, there may be a requirement to respond to the needs of non-family members. This is known as sibling accommodation (Handler, 1991; Friedman, 1989; and Ward, 1987). Unfortunately, very few founding entrepreneurs have definite plans for succession. It seems that it is a difficult matter to consider that one day the owner will die (Brown & Coverley, 1999). Dealing with the issue of one's mortality tends to be ignored.

## CONCLUSION

This chapter has focused on aspects related to the small business as a unique entity. The various perspectives presented about small business serve to show how a small business may be categorized and how it may evolve. Each perspective provides a description of the management aspects involved in the evolution of a small business toward what may be considered a successful entity. The next chapter will focus on the individual entrepreneur.

## REFERENCES

Alavi, M. T., & Karami, A. (2009). Managers of small and medium enterprises: Mission statement and enhanced organizational performance. *Journal of Management Development*, *28*(6), 555–562. doi:10.1108/02621710910959729

Ang, J. (1991). Small business uniqueness and the theory of financial management. *The Journal of Small Business Finance*, *1*(1), 1–13.

Ang, J. (1992). On the theory of finance for privately held firms. *The Journal of Small Business Finance*, *1*(3), 185–203.

Argiles, J. M., & Slof, E. J. (2003). The use of financial accounting information and firm performance: An empirical quantification for farms. *Accounting and Business Review*, *33*(4), 251–273. doi:10.1080/00014788.2003.9729653

Arregle, J., Hitt, M. A., Sirmon, D. G., & Very, P. (2007). The development of organizational social capital: Attributes of family firms. *Journal of Management Studies*, *44*(1), 73–95. doi:10.1111/j.1467-6486.2007.00665.x

Baldwin, T. T., Danielson, C., & Wiggenhorn, W. (1997). The evolution of learning strategies in organizations: From employee development to business redefinition. *The Academy of Management Executive*, *11*(4), 47–58.

Barach, J. A., Gantisky, J., Carson, J. A., & Doochin, B. J. (1988). Entry of the next generation: Strategic challenge for family business. *Journal of Small Business Management*, *26*(2), 49–56.

Barney, J. (1991). Firm resources and sustained competitive advantage. *Journal of Management*, *17*(1), 99–120. doi:10.1177/014920639101700108

Bates, T. (1995). A comparison of franchise and independent small business survival rates. *Small Business Economics*, *7*(5), 377–388. doi:10.1007/BF01302738

Bates, T., & Nucci, A. (1989). An analysis of small business size and rate of discontinuance. *Journal of Small Business Management*, *27*(4), 1–7.

Beaver, G. (2003). Small business: Success and failure. *Strategic Change*, *12*(3), 115–122. doi:10.1002/jsc.624

Berry, L. L. (1983). Relationship marketing. Chapter. In L. L. Berry, G. L. Shostack, & G. D. Upah (Eds.), *Emerging Perspectives on Service Marketing*. Chicago, IL: American Marketing Association.

Birley, S. (1986). The role of new firms: Births, deaths, and job creation. *Strategic Management Journal*, *7*(4), 361–376. doi:10.1002/smj.4250070406

Bjuggren, P., & Sund, L. (2002). A transaction cost rationale for transition of the firm within the family. *Small Business Economics*, *19*(2), 123–134. doi:10.1023/A:1016289106477

Boot, A. (2000). Relationship banking: What do we know? *Journal of Financial Intermediation*, *9*(1), 7–25. doi:10.1006/jfin.2000.0282

Bosma, N., van Praag, M., Thurik, R., & de Wit, G. (2004). The value of human and social capital investments for the business performance of startups. *Small Business Economics*, *23*(3), 227–236. doi:10.1023/B:SBEJ.0000032032.21192.72

Brown, R. B., & Coverly, R. (1999). Succession planning in family businesses: A study from East Anglia, UK. *Journal of Small Business Management*, *37*(1), 93–97.

Brown, S. (2007). Seven Skills for the Aspiring Entrepreneur. *Business and Economic Review*, *53*(2), 16–18.

Bruderl, J., Preisendorfer, P., & Ziegler, R. (1992). Survival chances of newly founded business organizations. *American Sociological Review*, *57*(2), 227–242. doi:10.2307/2096207

Brun de Pontet, S., Wrosch, C., & Gagne, M. (2007). An exploration of the generational differences in levels of control held among family businesses approaching succession. *Family Business Review*, *20*(4), 337–354. doi:10.1111/j.1741-6248.2007.00103.x

Burlingham, B. (2006). In search of small giants. *Inc. Magazine*, *28*(2), 84–87.

Burt, R. S. (1997). The Contingent Value of Social Capital. *Administrative Science Quarterly*, *42*(2), 339–363. doi:10.2307/2393923

Cardwell, M. (1994). *Customer Care Strategy for the '90s*. Cheltenham, England: Thomas.

Chaganti, R. W., & Chaganti, R. (1983). A profile of profitable and not-so-profitable small businesses. *Journal of Small Business Management, 21*(3), 126–137.

Chaganti, R. W., Cook, R. G., & Smeltz, W. J. (2002). Effects of styles, strategies and systems on the growth of small businesses. *Journal of Developmental Entrepreneurship, 7*(2), 175–193.

Chaston, I. (1997). Small firm performance: Assessing the interaction between entrepreneurial style and organizational structure. *European Journal of Marketing, 31*(11/12), 814–831. doi:10.1108/03090569710190550

Choo, C. W., & Bontis, M. (2002). *Strategic Management of Intellectual Capital and Organizational Knowledge*. New York: Oxford University Press.

Churchill, B. C. (1952). Survival Patterns of the Postwar Business Population. *Survey of Current Business, 32*(12), 12–19.

Cochran, A. B. (1981). Small business mortality rates: A review of the literature. *Journal of Small Business Management, 19*(4), 50–59.

Cole, R. A., & Wolken, J. D. (1996). Bank and nonbank competition for small business credit: Evidence from the 1987 and 1993 national surveys of small business finances. *Federal Reserve Bulletin*, November, 983-995.

Coleman, J. S. (1988). Social capital in the creation of human capital. *American Journal of Sociology, 94*(s1), 95–120. doi:10.1086/228943

Cooper, A. C., Dunkelberg, W. C., & Woo, C. Y. (1988). Survival and Failure: A Longitudinal Study, Wellesley, MA, Frontiers of Entrepreneurship Research, Babson College.

Cressy, R. (2006). Why do most firms die young? *Small Business Economics, 26*(2), 103–116. doi:10.1007/s11187-004-7813-9

D'Intino, R. S., Goldsby, M. G., Houghton, J. D., & Neck, C. P. (2007). Self-leadership: A process for entrepreneurial success. *Journal of Leadership & Organizational Studies, 13*(4), 105–130. doi:10.1177/10717919070130040101

Davidsson, P., & Delmar, F. (1997). High-growth firms: Characteristics, job contribution and method observations. Paper presented at RENTXI Conference, Mannheim.

De Geus, A. (2002). *The Living Company: Habits for Survival in a Turbulent Environment*. Boston, MA: Harvard Business School Press.

Deakins, D., Morrison, A., & Galloway, L. (2002). Evolution, financial management and learning in the small firm. *Journal of Small Business and Enterprise Development*, *9*(1), 7–16. doi:10.1108/14626000210419446

Deeks, J. (1973). The small firm – asset or liability? *Journal of Management Studies*, *10*(1), 25–47. doi:10.1111/j.1467-6486.1973.tb00499.x

Degryse, H., & Van Cayseele, P. (2000). Relationship lending within a bank-based system: Evidence from European small business data. *Journal of Financial Intermediation*, *9*(1), 90–109. doi:10.1006/jfin.1999.0278

Dekimpe, M. G., & Morrison, D. G. (1991). A modeling framework for analyzing retail store durations. *Journal of Retailing*, *67*(1), 68–92.

Denison, D., Lief, C., & Ward, J. L. (2004). Culture in family-owned enterprises: Recognizing and leveraging unique strengths. *Family Business Review*, *17*(1), 61–70. doi:10.1111/j.1741-6248.2004.00004.x

Department for Business and Innovation Skills. (2013). *Small Business: Great Ambition. Business Population Estimates for the UK and Regions*. Retrieved from https://www.gov.uk/government/uploads/system/uploads/attachment_data/file/266212/bis-13-1313-small-business-great-ambition-FINAL.pdf. Retrieved January 8, 2014.

DeThomas, A. R., & Fredenberger, W. B. (1985). Account need of a very small business. *The CPA Journal*, *55*(10), 14–23.

Dobbs, M., & Hamilton, R. T. (2007). Small business growth: Recent evidence and new directions. *International Journal of Entrepreneurial Behaviour and Research*, *13*(5), 296–322. doi:10.1108/13552550710780885

Donnelly, R. (1964). The Family Business. *Harvard Business Review*, *42*(2), 93–105.

Dun & Bradstreet. (1991). Press Release June.

Dunn, B. (1995). Success themes in Scottish family enterprises: Philosophies and practices through the generations. *Family Business Review*, *8*(1), 17–28. doi:10.1111/j.1741-6248.1995.00017.x

Dunne, T., Roberts, M. J., & Samuelson, L. (1989). The growth and failure of U.S. manufacturing plants. *The Quarterly Journal of Economics*, *104*(4), 672–698. doi:10.2307/2937862

Dyer, W. G. (2006). Examining the 'family effect' on firm performance. *Family Business Review*, *19*(4), 253–273. doi:10.1111/j.1741-6248.2006.00074.x

Dyt, R., & Halabi, A. K. (2007). Empirical evidence examining the accounting information systems and accounting reports of small and micro business in Australia. *Small Enterprise Research, 15*(2), 1–9. doi:10.5172/ser.15.2.1

Esteve-Perez, S., & Manez-Castillejo, J. A. (2008). The resource-based theory of the firm and firm survival. *Small Business Economics, 30*(3), 231–249. doi:10.1007/s11187-006-9011-4

European Parliament. (2002). www.europarl.eu.int/dg4/factsheets/en/4_14_0.htm (07/06/2002).

Fiegener, M. K., Brown, B. M., Prince, R. A., & File, K. M. (1996). Passing on strategic vision: Favored modes of successor preparation by CEOs of family and non-family firms. *Journal of Small Business Management, 34*(3), 15–26.

Floren, H. (2006). Managerial work in small firms: Summarising what we know and sketching a research agenda. *International Journal of Entrepreneurial Behaviour and Research, 12*(5), 272–288. doi:10.1108/13552550610687646

Fombrun, C. J. (1996). *Reputation: Realizing Value from the Corporate Image*. Boston: Harvard Business School.

Forsman, H. (2008). Business development success in SMEs: A case study approach. *Journal of Small Business and Enterprise Development, 15*(3), 606–622. doi:10.1108/14626000810892382

Fredland, E. J., & Morris, C. E. (1976). A cross-section analysis of small business failure. *American Journal of Small Business, 1*(1), 7–18.

Friedman, S. (1989). Conflict inherited: Sibling rivalry in family firms. paper presented at the Academy of Management Meetings, Washington, DC.

Ganguly, P. (Ed.). (1985). *U.K. Small Business Statistics and International Comparisons*. London: Harper and Row.

Garcia-Parra, M., Simo, P., Sallan, J. M., & Mundet, J.Garcia-Parra. (2009). Intangible liabilities: Beyond models of intellectual assets. *Management Decision, 47*(5), 819–830. doi:10.1108/00251740910960141

Gersick, K. E., Davis, J. A., Hampton, M. M., & Lansberg, I. (1997). *Generation to Generation: Life Cycles of the Family Business*. Boston: Harvard Business School Press.

Gibb, A., & Webb, T. (1980). *Policy Issues in Small Business Research*. Andover: Teakfield.

Halabi, A. K., Barrett, R., & Dyt, R. (2010). Understanding financial information used to assess small firm performance. *Qualitative Research in Accounting and Management*, *7*(2), 163–179. doi:10.1108/11766091011050840

Hall, R. (1992). The strategic analysis of intangible resources. *Strategic Management Journal*, *13*(2), 135–144. doi:10.1002/smj.4250130205

Hamilton, B. (1984). Entry and exit of business in Scotland. In J. Lewis, J. Stanworth, & A. Gibb (Eds.), *Success and Failure in Small Business* (pp. 57–69). Aldershot, England: Gower.

Handler, W. C. (1991). Key interpersonal relationships of next-generation family members in family firms. *Journal of Small Business Management*, *29*(3), 21–32.

Headd, B. (2003). Redefining business success: Factors leading to surviving and closing successfully. *Small Business Economics*, *21*(1), 51–61. doi:10.1023/A:1024433630958

Hitt, M. A., Ireland, R. D., & Hoskisson, R. E. (2001). *Strategic Management: Competitiveness and Globalization*. Cincinnati, Ohio: South-Western College.

Honjo, Y. (2000). Business failure of new firms: An empirical analysis using a multiplicative hazards model. *International Journal of Industrial Organization*, *18*(4), 557–574. doi:10.1016/S0167-7187(98)00035-6

Hoogstra, G. J., & van Dijk, J. (2004). Explaining firm employment growth: Does location matter? *Small Business Economics*, *22*(3/4), 179–190. doi:10.1023/B:SBEJ.0000022218.66156.ac

Horton, T. P. (1986). Managing in a family way. *Management Review*, *75*(2), 3.

Huggins, R., & Weir, M. (2007). Intellectual assets and public policy. *Journal of Intellectual Capital*, *8*(4), 708–720. doi:10.1108/14691930710830855

Hunter, M. G. (2011). Small Business Orientation: A Preliminary Investigation into Variety in Canadian Small Business. Management Report prepared for The Monieson Centre, Queen's University School of Business.

Hunter, M. G., & Kazakoff, D. (2008). *Little Empires: Multi-Generation Small Business in Southern Alberta, CANADA*. Melbourne, Australia: Heidelberg Press.

Hutchinson, R. G., Hutchinson, A. R., & Newcomer, M. (1938). A study in business mortality. *The American Economic Review*, *28*(3), 497–514.

Huybrechts, J., Voordeckers, W., Lybaert, N., & Vandemaele, S. (2011). The distinctiveness of family-firm intangibles: A review and suggestions for future research. *Journal of Management & Organization*, *17*(2), 268–287. doi:10.5172/jmo.2011.17.2.268

Industry Canada. (2010). *Key Small Business Statistics*, (Catalogue No. Iu186-1/2010-2E), ISSN 1718-3456, Ottawa: Canadian Government Publishing Centre.

James, H. S. Jr. (1999). Owner as manager, extended horizons and the family firm. *International Journal of the Economics of Business*, *6*(1), 41–55. doi:10.1080/13571519984304

Kelley, D. J., & Nakosteen, R. A. (2005). Technology resources, alliances, and sustained growth in new, technology-based firms. *IEEE Transactions on Engineering Management*, *52*(3), 292–300. doi:10.1109/TEM.2005.851272

Khan, M. R., & Rocha, J. R. (1982). Recurring management problems in small business. *American Journal of Small Business*, *7*, 50–58.

Kirkwood, J. (2009). To grow or not? Growing small service firms. *Journal of Small Business and Enterprise Development*, *16*(3), 485–503. doi:10.1108/14626000910977189

Konorti, E. (2010). The relationship between wealth cration and professional management in small-medium enterprises. *The Journal of American Academy of Business*, *16*(1), 11–23.

Lauzen, L. (1985). Small business failures are controllable. *Corporate Accounting*, *3*(3), 34–38.

Le Breton-Miller, I., & Miller, D. (2006). Why do some family businesses outcompete? Governance, long-term orientations and sustainable capability. *Entrepreneurship: Theory and Practice*, *30*(6), 731–746.

LeBrassuer, R., Zanibbi, L., & Zinger, T. J. (2003). Growth momentum in early stages of small business start-ups. *International Small Business Journal*, *21*(3), 315–330. doi:10.1177/02662426030213004

Liao, J., Welsch, H., & Moutray, C. (2008/2009). Start-up resources and entrepreneurial discontinuance: The case of nascent entrepreneurs. *Journal of Small Business Strategy*, *19*(2), 1–15.

Longnecker, J., Moore, C., & Petty, J. (1997). *Small Business Management*. Cincinnati, OH: South-Western College Printing.

Lowe, J., McKenna, J., & Tibbits, G. (1991). Small firm growth and failure: Public policy issues and practical problems. *Economic Papers, 10*(2), 69–81. doi:10.1111/j.1759-3441.1991.tb00858.x

Lubatkin, M., Schulze, W., Ling, Y., & Dino, R. (2005). The effects of parental altruism on the governance of family-managed firms. *Journal of Organizational Behavior, 26*(3), 313–330. doi:10.1002/job.307

Lussier, R. N. (1995). A nonfinancial business success versus failure prediction model for young firms. *Journal of Small Business Management, 33*(1), 8–20.

Lussier, R. N., & Halabi, C. E. (2010). A three-country comparison of business success versus failure prediction model. *Journal of Small Business Management, 48*(3), 360–377. doi:10.1111/j.1540-627X.2010.00298.x

Manthey, R., & Balhoff, W. E. (2002). Pass the baton without missing a beat. *Journal of Accountancy, 193*(3), 43–48.

Marriott, N., & Marriott, P. (2000). Professional accountants and the development of a management accounting service for the small firm: Barriers and possibilities. *Management Accounting Research, 11*(4), 475–492. doi:10.1006/mare.2000.0142

McKenna, R. (1991). *Relationship Marketing: Successful Strategies for the Age of the Customer*. Reading, MA: Addison-Wesley.

McMahon, R. G. P. (2001). Business growth and performance and the financial reporting practices of Australian manufacturing SMEs. *Journal of Small Business Management, 39*(2), 152–165. doi:10.1111/1540-627X.00014

McNight, C. (1990). Business and bankruptcy: A review. *The Journal of Finance, 16*(3), 43–51.

Mellahi, K., & Wilkinson, A. (2004). Organizational failure: A critique of recent research and a proposed integrative framework. *International Journal of Management Reviews, 5-6*(1), 21–41. doi:10.1111/j.1460-8545.2004.00095.x

Michma, J., & Bednarz, L. M. (2006). Small Business in the USA. *International Journal of Entrepreneurship and Innovation Management, 6*(1/2), 4–17. doi:10.1504/IJEIM.2006.008202

Miller, D., & Le Breton-Miller, I. (2003). The challenges and advantages of family business. *Strategic Organization, 1*(1), 127–134. doi:10.1177/1476127003001001222

Miller, D., & Le Breton-Miller, I. (2006). Priorities, practices and strategies in successful and failing family businesses: An elaboration and test of the configuration perspective. *Strategic Organization*, *4*(4), 379–407. doi:10.1177/1476127006069575

Nahapiet, J., & Ghoshal, S. (1998). Social capital, intellectual capital, and the organizational advantage. *Journal of Corporate Finance*, *13*(5), 829–858.

Narva, R. L. (2003). Financing transitions: Managing capital and liquidity in the family business. *Family Business Review*, *16*(2), 153–154.

O'Connell, B. (2004). The FastTrac to Success – Why do some small businesses handle change better than others? *Baylor Business Review*, *22*(1), 26–27.

Penrose, E. T. (1959). *The Theory of the Growth of the Firm*. New York: John Wiley & Sons.

Peterson, R. A., Kozmetsky, G., & Ridgway, N. M. (1983). Perceived causes of small business failures: A research note. *American Journal of Small Business*, *8*(1), 15–19.

Phillips, B. D., & Kirchoff, B. A. (1989). Formation, growth and survival: Small firm dynamics in the U.S. economy. *Small Business Economics*, *1*(1), 65–74. doi:10.1007/BF00389917

Pitt, L. F., & Kannemeyer, R. (2000). The role of adaptation in microenterprise development: A marketing perspective. *Journal of Developmental Entrepreneurship*, *5*(2), 137–155.

Price, R. (1984). *Small Business Management for Small Business Owner/Managers*. Melbourne: Wadsworth.

Reynolds, P. D. (1987). New firms' societal contribution versus survival potential. *Journal of Business Venturing*, *2*(3), 231–246. doi:10.1016/0883-9026(87)90011-5

Scholes, L., Westhead, P., & Burrows, A. (2008). Family firm succession: The Management buy-out and buy-in routes. *Journal of Small Business and Enterprise Development*, *15*(1), 8–30. doi:10.1108/14626000810850829

Schulze, W. S., Lubatkin, M., & Dino, R. H. (2003). Exploring the agency consequences of ownership dispersion among the directors of private family firms. *Academy of Management Journal*, *46*(2), 179–194. doi:10.2307/30040613

Schulze, W. S., Lubatkin, M., Dino, R. H., & Buchholtz, A. K. (2001). Agency relationships in family firms: Theory and evidence. *Organization Science*, *12*(2), 99–116. doi:10.1287/orsc.12.2.99.10114

Smallbone, D., Leigh, R., & North, D. (1995). The characteristics and strategies of high growth SME's. *International Journal of Entrepreneurial Behaviour and Research, 1*(3), 44–62. doi:10.1108/13552559510100657

Smallbone, D., & Wyer, P. (2000). Growth and development in the small firm. Chapter in Carter, S. and D. James-Evans (Editors), Enterprise and Small Business. Harlow: Prentice Hall.

Stanworth, J. (1995). Penetrating the mists surrounding franchise failure rates: Some old lessons for new businesses. *International Small Business Journal, 13*(2), 59–63. doi:10.1177/0266242695132005

Stevenson, H. H. (1999). A perspective of entrepreneurship, in Stevenson, H. H., H. I. Grousebeck, M. J. Roberts and A. Bhide (Eds.). New Business Ventures and the Entrepreneur, 3-17. Boston: Irwin McGraw-Hill.

Stewart, H., & Gallagher, C. (1986). Business death and firm size in the U.K. *International Small Business Journal, 4*(1), 42–57. doi:10.1177/026624268500400104

Sveiby, K. E. (2001). A knowledge-based theory of the firm to guide in strategy formulation. *Journal of Intellectual Capital, 2*(4), 344–358. doi:10.1108/14691930110409651

Tagiuri, R., & Davis, J. A. (1996). Bivalent attributes of the family firm. *Family Business Review, 9*(2), 199–208. doi:10.1111/j.1741-6248.1996.00199.x

Tan, J., Fischer, E., Mitchell, R., & Phan, P. (2009). At the center of action: Innovation and technology strategy research in the small business setting. *Journal of Small Business Management, 47*(3), 233–262. doi:10.1111/j.1540-627X.2009.00270.x

Tauzell, J. (1982). Survival of Minnesota new businesses: 1977-1980. *Review of Labour and Economic Conditions, 9*(2), 10–17.

Teece, D. J. (1992). Foreign investment and technological development in Silicon Valley. *California Management Review, 34*(2), 88–106. doi:10.2307/41166695

Theng, L. G., & Boon, J. L. W. (1996). An exploratory study of factors affecting the failure of local small and medium enterprises. *Asia Pacific Journal of Management, 13*(2), 47–61. doi:10.1007/BF01733816

Thong, J., Yap, C., & Raman, K. (1994). Engagement of external expertise in information systems implementation. *Journal of Management Information Systems, 11*(2), 209–223.

Toftoy, C. N., & Chaterjee, J. (2004). Mission statements and the small business. *Business Strategy Journal, 15*(3), 41–44. doi:10.1111/j.0955-6419.2004.00326.x

Van Gelder, J.-L., de Vries, R. E., Frese, M., & Goutbeek, J.-P. (2007). Differences in psychological strategies of failed and operational business owners in the Fiji Islands. *Journal of Small Business Management*, *45*(3), 388–400. doi:10.1111/j.1540-627X.2007.00219.x

Vinten, G. (1999). Corporate communication in small and medium-sized enterprises. *Industrial and Commercial Training*, *31*(3), 112–119. doi:10.1108/00197859910269220

Voordeckers, W., Steijivers, T., & Peeters, L. (2010). The ownership-performance relationship: Agency issues in private family firms. paper presented at the Annual European Academy of Management, (EURAM) Conference, May 19-22, Rome Italy.

Ward, J. L. (1987). *Keeping the Family Business Healthy*. San Fransico: Jossey Boss.

Ward, J. L. (2004). *Perpetuating the Family Business*. New York: Palgrave MacMillan. doi:10.1057/9780230505995

Ward, J. L., & Aronoff, C. E. (1991). The power of patient capital. *Nation's Business*, *79*(9), 48–49.

Ward, J. L., & Lief, C. (2005). Unconventional wisdom: Counterintuitive insights for family business success. *Perspectives for Managers*, *120*, 1–4.

Watson, J., & Everett, J. E. (1999). Small business failure rates: Choice of definition and industry effects. *International Small Business Journal*, *17*(2), 33–49. doi:10.1177/0266242699172002

Watters, J., Jackson, F., & Russell, I. (2006). Capturing intangibles for improved IA management and benchmarking. *Journal of Intellectual Capital*, *7*(4), 549–567. doi:10.1108/14691930610709167

Weinrauch, J. D., Man, K., Robinson, P. A., & Pharr, J. (1991). Dealing with limited financial resources: A marketing challenge for small business. *Journal of Small Business Management*, *29*(4), 4–54.

Welsch, J. A., & White, J. F. (1981). A small business is not a little big business. *Harvard Business Review*, *59*(4), 18–32.

Wernerfelt, B. (1984). A resource-based view of the firm. *Strategic Management Journal*, *5*(2), 171–180. doi:10.1002/smj.4250050207

Westhead, P., Ucbasaran, D., & Wright, M. (2005a). Decisions, actions, and performance: Do novice, serial, and portfolio entrepreneurs differ? *Journal of Small Business Management*, *43*(4), 393–417. doi:10.1111/j.1540-627X.2005.00144.x

Westhead, P., Ucbasaran, D., Wright, M., & Binks, M. (2005b). Novice, serial, and portfolio entrepreneur behavior and contributions. *Small Business Economics*, *25*(2), 109–132. doi:10.1007/s11187-003-6461-9

Westhead, P., & Wright, M. (1999). Contributions of novice, portfolio and serial founders located in rural and urban areas. *Regional Studies*, *33*(2), 157–173.

Wiltshire Committee. (1971). *Report of the Committee on Small Business*. Canberra, Australia: The Government Printer of Australia.

Wyer, P., Donohue, S., & Matthews, P. (2010). Fostering strategic learning capability to enhance creativity in small service businesses. *Service Business*, *4*(1), 9–26. doi:10.1007/s11628-009-0086-2

Zahra, S. A., Hayton, J. C., & Salvato, C. (2004). Entrepreneurship in family vs. non-family firms: A resource-based analysis of the effect of organizational culture. *Entrepreneurship: Theory and Practice*, *28*(4), 363–381.

Zinger, J., LeBrasseur, T. R., & Zanibbi, L. R. (2001). Factors influencing early stage performance in Canadian microenterprises. *Journal of Developmental Entrepreneurship*, *6*(2), 129–150.

Zontanos, G., & Anderson, A. R. (2004). Relationships, marketing and small business: An exploration of links in theory and practice. *Qualitative Market Research*, *7*(3), 228–236. doi:10.1108/13522750410540236

## ADDITIONAL READING

Hunter, M. G., & Kazakoff, D. (2008). *Little Empires: Multi-Generation Small Business in Southern Alberta, CANADA*. Melbourne, Australia: Heidelberg Press.

Hunter, M. G., & Kazakoff, D. (2012). *Small Business: Journey to Success*. Redding, UK: Academic Publishing International, Curtis Farm, Kidmore End, Nr.

Longenecker, J. G., Petty, J. W., Palich, L. E., & Hoy, F. (2014). *Small Business Management*. Stamford, CT: Cnegage.

MacGregor, R., & Hodgkinson, A. T. (2007). *Small Business Clustering Technologies: Applications in Marketing, Management, IT and Economics*. Hershey, PA: IGI Global. doi:10.4018/978-1-59904-126-1

## KEY TERMS AND DEFINITIONS

**Culture:** The way people behave within a business including values, norms, and habits.

**Customer:** Recipient of a product or service obtained from a supplier.

**Decision Making:** The process of selecting a course of action.

**Decline:** Decrease in sales volume of a small business.

**Employee Skills:** Abilities of people in a small business.

**Existence:** A recently form small business.

**Family:** A group of people related through birth or marriage.

**Gross Domestic Product:** A measure of productive out at the national level.

**Innovation:** New ideas or processes that meet new requirements.

**Intangible Resources:** Assets that provide a benefit but lack physical substance.

**Manager:** Someone who works with or through others by coordinating their efforts.

**Operational:** The steps required to carry out a process.

**Policy:** A principle to guide decision making or a statement of intent.

**Poor management:** Lack of ability to coordinate others.

**Renewal:** Revision to management processes in a small business.

**Reputation:** Opinion about a small business held by the community.

**Small Business:** Usually based upon the number of employees. But this will vary by country and even business sector.

**Soft Skills:** Personality traits that facilitate relationships with other people.

**Succession:** Identifying and developing others to carry on the small business after the departure of the current leader.

**Survival:** Processes in a small business to ensure continued operation.

# Chapter 2
# Entrepreneurs


## ABSTRACT

*An entrepreneur requires many skills. But, an entrepreneurial perspective is more about a state of mind. That is, an entrepreneur will be more willing to take a risk than a small business manager. Further, an entrepreneur will tend to be more innovative in continually seeking out new opportunities. Eventually, however, the entrepreneur will move on to a new initiative; or to adopt the perspective of a small business manager. This chapter presents the evolving role of the entrepreneur's involvement in small business.*


## INTRODUCTION

This chapter includes a description of the various types and characteristics of entrepreneurs involved in small business. The emphasis is on the individual who becomes an entrepreneur. A nascent entrepreneur is an individual who has not yet started a venture but has considered doing so and is in the process of forming a small business. The types of entrepreneur include novice, serial, and portfolio. Personality types influence the entrepreneur's approach to conducting business. Some entrepreneurs might be aggressive pursuing growth and expansion while others might take a more conservative approach.

Further, there is an obvious link between an entrepreneur and a small business. The characteristics and aptitude of an entrepreneur may apply to their involvement in a large corporation, but an entrepreneur is more obvious and indeed necessary

DOI: 10.4018/978-1-4666-8708-0.ch002

in a small business. It is a difficult task to separate a discussion of the entrepreneur from the small business. However, the remainder of this chapter will focus on aspects related to entrepreneurs.

This chapter is organized as follows. The next section defines the types of entrepreneurs including novice, serial, and portfolio, including nascent. Another perspective considers manager, owner, technician, and crafts person. The following section presents descriptions of the characteristics of entrepreneurs. These characteristics include descriptions of cognitive style and the umbrella characteristics as displayed by "super achievers" and "small giants". Another perspective investigates the characteristics of the founding entrepreneur and the authentic leader. A differentiation is made between an entrepreneur and a small business owner. Further characteristics are explored from the perspective of traits, behaviors, and opportunity identification. This section also investigates the performance of entrepreneurs in relation to their human and social capital. Then entrepreneurship is explored through a discussion of the Theory of Entrepreneurship. The chapter concludes with the introduction of the entrepreneurial process, including creativity, innovation, and implementation, followed by a discussion of the dimensions involved in the entrepreneurial process including creativity, innovation, and implementation.

## TYPES OF ENTREPRENEURS

The origin of the term "entrepreneur" is derived from the French word "entreprende" which means "to undertake" (Brouwer, 2002).

It has been suggested that an entrepreneur is, "...someone who specialises in taking judgemental decisions about the coordination of scarce resources." (Casson, 2003, p. 225). This definition does not include a comment about the size of the business. An entrepreneur may be involved in a small business or a large company. The definition thus emphasizes an individual's approach to making decisions. Entrepreneurs, however, tend to be found more often in small business. This is the focus of this chapter. Because of the size of a small business and the lack of time, finances, and skills (Thong et al, 1994) these entrepreneurs will typically have to make decisions within the context of allocating scarce resources.

Birley (1996) suggested entrepreneurs tend to focus more on changing the current small business environment by implementing innovative management processes.

More recently, the term has been defined as, "...a person who has a financial stake in [a small business]; ...is involved in the production and sales of existing and innovative goods with the intent to maximize enterprise profits for personal benefit..." (Konorti, 2010, p. 14).

### *Entrepreneurs*

Entrepreneurs in general take a short term perspective when allocating scarce resources (Stevenson, 1999). At a more detailed level, there are differences in the types of entrepreneurs. A series of articles refers to the differing types of entrepreneurs. Westhead et al (2005a) describe three types of entrepreneurs. Table 1 describes the types as Novice, Serial, and Portfolio. A Novice entrepreneur is just starting out owning a small business and has no prior experience. A Serial entrepreneur will, over time, own a number of small businesses, but do so one after the other. A Portfolio entrepreneur will own multiple small businesses at the same time. The authors propose targeted support for the different types of entrepreneur. They suggest that novice entrepreneurs tend not to use as many sources of information as the more experienced serial and portfolio entrepreneurs (Westhead et al, 2005a and 2005b). The more experienced entrepreneurs' sources of information include people, print, and development agencies. It is interesting to note that serial entrepreneurs rely more on people such as customers, friends, and employees (Westhead et al, 2005c).

Earlier, Westhead and Wright (1999) compared the types of entrepreneurs located in urban versus rural locations. They determined that urban-located small business reported higher employment growth than new rural small businesses. Further, there was no difference in sales and reported profitability between urban and rural firms. Westhead and Wright (1999) also investigated motivations of individuals to form a small business. They noted two motives. First, over time,

*...some entrepreneurs become less growth focused and more risk averse once they have accumulated a certain degree of personal wealth. (Westhead & Wright, 1999, p. 160).*

*Table 1. Types of entrepreneurs*

| Type | Description |
|---|---|
| Novice | "...individuals with no prior minority or majority business ownership experience either as a business founder, an inheritor, or a purchaser of an independent business but who currently own a minority or majority equity stake in an independent business that is new, purchased, or inherited."<br>Westhead et al, 2005a, p. 394 |
| Serial | "...individuals who have sold/closed a business in which they had a minority or majority ownership stake, and they currently have a minority or majority ownership stake in a single independent business that is new, purchased, or inherited."<br>Westhead et al, 2005a, p. 394 |
| Portfolio | "...individuals who currently have minority or majority ownership stakes in two or more independent businesses that are new, purchased, or inherited."<br>Westhead et al, 2005a, p. 394 |

Adapted from Westhead et al (2005a)

This definition implies that mature entrepreneurs become more interested in addressing risk issues once they feel they are in a position to allocate financial resources to certain types of insurance. Second, small business in rural areas tends to be initiated as an expression of independence for the entrepreneur. Further, these entrepreneurs attempt to create multiple income streams. They may focus upon a particular niche or skill but attempt to apply it in alternative ways to create a continuous in-flow of income.

In conjunction with these three entrepreneur types, the term nascent entrepreneur has also been identified (Wagner, 2004). A nascent entrepreneur is an individual who has not yet started a new business (Delmar & Davidsson, 2000; and Rotefoss & Kolvereid, 2005). This definition suggests nascent entrepreneurs are about to become self-employed. These types of individuals seem to prefer to be self-employed rather than to work in a business for wages (Wagner, 2004; and Lazear, 2002). De Clercq et al (2009) investigated commitment of nascent entrepreneurs. They employed Expectancy Theory (Klein, 1991; and Vroom, 1964) which suggests an individual's level of effort applied to a task depends on their motivation. They determined that,

*...entrepreneurs should recognize ... the level of energy they are willing to devote to their start-up during the gestation phase will be influenced by their perceptions about their own capabilities and their personal preferences. (De Clercq et al, 2009, p. 135).*

Diochan et al (2008) pursued a slightly different perspective on nascent entrepreneurs. They employed Human Capital Theory to investigate the personal characteristics of nascent entrepreneurs as predictors of success (Becker, 1975; Davidsson & Honig, 2003; and Ucbasaran et al, 2008). It is noted that they defined success as the actual formation of a small business. As they state,

*...the challenge becomes one of identifying specific skills that might be associated with success in bringing a venture to fruition. (Diochan et al, 2008, p. 154).*

Their findings are edifying. Education and work experience were not related to a successful outcome in forming a business. This result has implications for trainers and educators. Thus, it is not necessarily what you know about business, it is more about who you are. Another finding determined that financial management capability (keeping and employing financial information directly related to the small business) played a role in the successful sustainability of the new venture. Thus it seems the focus for trainers and educators should be on aspects of financial management.

### *Entrepreneurs*

Carland et al (2000) studied multiple venture entrepreneurs. This is another term for serial entrepreneurs, which is described here in Table 1 (Westhead et al, 2005a). Carland et al (2000) determined that, compared to novice entrepreneurs,

*...serial entrepreneurs have stronger preferences for innovation, greater propensity for risk taking, and higher need for achievement, than do novice entrepreneurs. (Carland et al, 2000, p. 15).*

This finding supports the MacMillan (1986) conclusion that serial entrepreneurs are the truly successful ones.

Entrepreneurs vary with regards to their inclination to access information. This variety may be explained by the concepts expounded by Westhead et al (2005a, and 2005c). They presented descriptions of three types of entrepreneurs. See Table 1. Recall that they suggested novice entrepreneurs do not avail themselves of information sources as much as other types of entrepreneurs. The serial and portfolio entrepreneurs, possessing more experience, are more inclined to pursue various sources of information. This is an important difference between these groups of entrepreneurs. It suggests that different approaches should be taken to provide these entrepreneurs with valuable information about operating a small business. Novice entrepreneurs restrict their information sources. If they do seek information, they may tend to rely upon trusted entities or those that they are required to deal with. So, a source for the provision of information to novice entrepreneurs could be the local Economic Development organizations or the Chamber of Commerce. The more experienced serial and portfolio entrepreneurs pursue many sources of information. These individuals will possess knowledge about the information they might need and where it may be obtained. Thus, an entity wishing to provide information to serial and portfolio entrepreneurs might more effectively contact them directly.

Another perspective is provided by Boswell (1971) who identified four types of entrepreneurs, as shown in Table 2. These descriptions of entrepreneurs introduce the idea that some may be aggressive, favoring growth, while others are more conservative focusing on independence and survival.

Block and Wagner (2010) investigated the types of entrepreneur based upon definitions originally proposed in 2001 by the Global Entrepreneurship Monitor (GEM). (Reynolds et al, 2002; and Sternberg et al 2006). Block and Wagner (2010) suggest, "...a distinction should be made between entrepreneurship that reflects a voluntary pursuit of opportunity and entrepreneurship that reflects the necessity to engage in such activity in the absence of other employment opportunities". (Block & Wagner, 2010, p. 157). Thus, an opportunity entrepreneur is, "...a person [who] voluntarily leaves her paid job to set up a business..." (Block & Wagner, 2010, p. 157). A necessity entrepreneur is, "...a person who leaves her job involuntarily

*Table 2. Types of entrepreneurs*

| Entrepreneur | Description |
|---|---|
| Manager | "...is motivated towards self-realization, favors growth, and places less importance on financial and personal independence." |
| Owner | "...favors growth but is primarily interested in maintaining control and financial independence." |
| Technician | "...favors technical efficiency, productivity, and profitability over growth." |
| Crafts Person | "...aims at personal independence and survival. Working for himself or herself is more important than economic success." |

Adapted from Boswell, 1971

[because] she was pushed into entrepreneurship by external factors." (Block & Wagner, 2010, p. 157). Block and Wagner's (2010) investigation determined a number of findings, including the fact that opportunity entrepreneurs pursued more entrepreneurial ventures that resulted in more profit than did necessity entrepreneurs, and that opportunity entrepreneurs met with more financial success. These findings seem to be the result of opportunity entrepreneurs taking deliberate action for planning and skills acquisition.

## CHARACTERISTICS OF ENTREPRENEURS

To begin, Armstrong and Hird (2009) attempted to identify the potential of individuals to eventually become successful entrepreneurs. While they did not directly define "success" it is implied through their comparison of early stage entrepreneurs with entrepreneurs in more mature businesses. They reviewed the cognition of these two categories of entrepreneurs employing the Cognitive Style Index (Allinson & Hayes, 1996). As a framework, they also employed the concept of entrepreneurial drive (Carland et al, 2002), which suggests a continuum. At one end an entrepreneur may be highly driven with innovative ideas about creating new ventures. At the other end the entrepreneur may be content to simply manage a small business. Armstrong and Hird (2009) found support for the conclusions of Shaver and Scott (1991) which suggests the importance of cognitive style in contributing to the success of an entrepreneur. They also determined that entrepreneurs, "…tend to be more intuitive and less analytic than non-entrepreneurs." (Armstrong & Hird, 2009, p. 419). Further, they also found higher levels of entrepreneurial drive in those entrepreneurs who were more intuitive. Thus, investigating cognitive style may be a way to identify those individuals who may become successful entrepreneurs.

An earlier cognitive investigation was conducted by Carland and Carland (1992). They used the Myers-Briggs Type Indicator (Myers, 1962) to determine the cognitive typology of three different groups of individuals. The groups were defined as follows:

*"Manager: A manager holds a position of responsibility within an organization. This individual supervises employees or officers within the organization; has responsibility for use, protection or conservation of assets of the organization; has responsibility for performance of a unit of the organization; or has involvement in planning for the organization." (Carland & Carland, 1992, p. 59)*
*"Small Business Owner: A small business owner is an individual who establishes and/or manages a business for the principal purpose of furthering personal goals. The business must be his primary source of income and will consume the majority of his time and resources. The owner perceives the business as an extension of his or her personality, intricately bound with family needs and desires." (Carland & Carland, 1992, p. 61)*
*"Entrepreneur: An entrepreneur is an individual who establishes and manages a business for the principal purposes of profit and growth, is characterized principally by innovative behavior and will employ strategic management practices in the business." (Carland & Carland, 1992, p. 61)*

Beaver and Jennings (2005) support the above suggesting that managers participate in a small business for personal goals, while entrepreneurs take an innovative approach to generating profits and stimulating business growth.

The characteristics which help to identify the entrepreneur from the small business owner/managers are extroversion, intuition, and openness to spontaneity and novelty.

As shown in Chapter One small business performance will diverge over time into paths representing higher versus lower growth (Tan et al, 2009). These divergent paths may result from management strategies adopted by the entrepreneur. The entrepreneur may be either a "Super Achiever" (Anonymous, 2006) or a "Small Giant" (Burlingham, 2006).

Because of the uncertainty involved in starting and operating a small business entrepreneurs must commit a substantial amount of effort over a long period of time. Further, the entrepreneur will function in an ambiguous environment with limited resources (Shane & Venkataraman, 2000). Given these challenging circumstances individuals will tend to meet with entrepreneurial success if they are prepared to persevere.

The Super Achievers (Anonymous, 2006) outperformed other small business owners in a number of categories as shown in Table 3. They showed an innovative approach to adopting technology, consulting with advisors, structuring the business, networking, and education.

Small Giants (Burlingham, 2006) tended to reject growth opportunities and focus on doing better in the form of improving the quality of existing products and services, rather than through attempting to increase sales volume or introducing new products or services. Table 4 includes the common characteristics of Small Giants.

There are other characteristics of entrepreneurs which contribute to the potential success of small business. The following paragraphs include a presentation of the role these characteristics serve to further elaborate the description of an entrepreneur.

Some time ago Carland et al (1984) investigated the difference between the terms "entrepreneur" and "small business owner". They developed the following definitions:

*Table 3. "Super achievers" characteristics*

| Characteristic | Description |
|---|---|
| Technology | Small firms that are tech-savvy with a high level of Internet and wireless capabilities grew their revenues at 2.25 times the rate of those that are not Web connected |
| Exporting Internet Sales | Small businesses that export more than half of their Internet-based sales experienced 2.5 times the growth of their counterparts who didn't sell outside of Canada |
| Advisors | By nature, entrepreneurs tend to be super-optimists. Good professional advisors share a more realistic view of life. Owners who consulted advisors regularly tallied sales 76% higher than those who didn't |
| Incorporated | Small businesses that formed corporations increased revenues 40% more than sole proprietors who didn't incorporate |
| Outsourcing | Taking advantage of other companies' expertise can boost the bottom line. Firms that offered outsourcing work to other companies registered earnings 61% higher than those that didn't outsource contract work to third parties |
| Education | Small firms whose leaders have acquired some post-secondary education have experienced revenue growth 2.5 times greater than those whose leaders haven't done so |

Adapted from Anonymous, 2006

*Table 4. Characteristics of "small giants"*

| Characteristic | Description |
|---|---|
| Know yourself and what you want out of business | The Small Giants' owners and leaders are remarkable, first and foremost, for the clarity they have about their goals in business. They can decide not to go for maximum growth because they know what else they are looking for and why. |
| Love your business | The Small Giants' leaders are unusual for the passion they bring to their companies. They absolutely love whatever it is that the company does, and they care deeply about doing it as well as it can be done. |
| Be rooted in a community | Each of the Small Giants has a close connection with the local city, town, or county in which it does business – a relationship that goes beyond the usual concept of "giving back". While all of these companies are model corporate citizens, the relationship is very much a two-way street. The community also helps to mold the character of the business. |
| Cultivate relationships with employees, customers, and suppliers | With customers and suppliers, the Small Giants emphasize personal contact, one-on-one interaction, and mutual commitment to delivering on promises. The effect is to create a sense of community and common purpose. The companies treat their employees in the way that owners think people ought to be treated – with respect, dignity, integrity, fairness, kindness, and generosity. |
| Stay private and closely held | Finally, the owners are keenly aware of the need to keep ownership inside the company. Outside investors generally want the best return possible. Of course, Small Giants' owners also want a return, but it's not their paramount purpose. By keeping stock inside the company they are free to pursue other goals. |

Adapted from Burlingham, 2006

*...an entrepreneur is an individual who establishes and manages a business for the principal purposes of profit and growth. The entrepreneur is characterized principally by innovative behaviour and will employ strategic management practices in the business. (Carland et al 1984, p. 358)*
*A small business owner is an individual who establishes and manages a business for the principal purpose of furthering personal goals. The business must be the primary source of income and will consume the majority of one's time and resources. The owner perceives the business as an extension of his or her personality, intricately bound with family needs and desires. (Carland et al 1984, p. 358)*

They note, and support Brockhaus (1980), that risk is not a distinguishing characteristic of an entrepreneur. They suggest that innovation in a search for profits is what distinguishes an entrepreneur from a small business owner.

The founding entrepreneur plays a very important part in establishing a small business's identity, core beliefs, and overall purpose. (Denison et al, 2004). These aspects contribute to the culture of a small business. If a founding entrepreneur plays a dominant role early on in the life of a small business, then their values and motivations will result in the development of a unique culture, which may be one of the small business's greatest advantages (Barney, 1986). Further, subsequent family members may promote the founding entrepreneur's values by taking long term active roles within the business. Therefore, the culture developed by the founding entrepreneur may counteract the small business manager's focus on the near term (Stevenson, 1999) and contribute to the establishment of conditions for the existence of a multi-generation small business.

An authentic leader,

*...creates conditions for higher trust, which helps people to build on their strengths and be more positive, to broaden their thinking, to add value and a sense of what is right to their decisions, and to improve the overall performance of their organization over time." (Jensen & Luthans, 2006, p. 256).*

Jensen and Luthans (2006) further suggest that the authentic leader creates an atmosphere of respect and trust among employees by focussing on what is good for the small business rather than themselves. This approach is similar to the multi-generation hero as described by Hunter and Kazakoff (2008), who steps forward in a subsequent generation of a small business and treats the business as a family entity. Technology in general has allowed entrepreneurs to create a work situation that takes a more family orientation (Martin & Wright, 2005).

More recently, entrepreneurs have been viewed from three different perspectives. They are individual traits, behaviours, and identification of opportunities (Kobia & Sikalieh, 2010).

The first perspective suggests that individuals with certain traits will be more inclined to identify and exploit business opportunities (Frese, 2007; and Shane, 2007). These traits constitute need for achievement, locus of control, and risk taking. Thus, these individuals tend to have a high need for achievement (Stewart et al, 2003; and Collins, 2002). Stewart and Roth (2007) expand upon the achievement comment. They substantiate the difference between entrepreneurs and managers regarding their motivation for achievement. Further, they determined that achievement motivation difference is accentuated when the entrepreneur is the founder of the small business or has growth objectives for their existing small business. Also, individuals who possess an internal locus of control tend to associate with an entrepreneurial approach (Boone et al, 2000; Low & MacMillan, 2001; and Lee & Tsang, 2001). Note that locus of control theory involves two perspectives. So, an individual with an internal locus of control will believe that their behaviour will affect the outcome of an event. Alternatively, an individual with an external locus of control will attribute the outcome of an event to be beyond their control and subject to a chance occurrence of circumstances in their environment. Further, individuals with a high risk-taking trait are more likely to engage in entrepreneurial opportunities (Shane, 2007; and Van Praag & Cramer, 2001).

The second perspective on entrepreneurs relates to behaviours (Carland et al, 1988; and Gartner, 1989). Thus, entrepreneurs create businesses. This complex process involves social and economic change; the development of new products, services, and markets; and establishment of distribution channels (Bjerke, 2007).

The third perspective suggests entrepreneurial individuals readily identify opportunities that others may miss (Venkataraman, 1997). They are able to recognize the potential for future goods and series (Eckhardt & Shane, 2003; and Shane & Vankataraman, 2000). These individuals work at combining resources to create profitable entities (Shane, 2007).

Two personality traits of entrepreneurs relate to internal locus of control and need for achievement (Ong et al, 2010; Littunen, 2000; Rauch & Frese, 2000; Korunka et al, 2003; and Beugelsdijk, 2007). Internal locus of control determines the extent to which individuals feel responsible for outcomes (Beugelsdijk, 2007) and is based on Rotter's (1966) social learning theory. The need for achievement (McClelland, 1961) relates to individuals and their striving for excellence and eventually success. These individuals are proactive in setting and accomplishing goals (Beugelsdijk, 2007; Cromie, 2000; and McClelland, 1961). Both of the above traits are evident in entrepreneurs and play a significant role in their long-term success (Ong et al, 2010).

In summary, the above discussion of traits, behaviours, and opportunities serves to demonstrate that the subject of entrepreneurs which incorporates complex ideas involves many diverse disciplines.

Crick (2011) investigated the practices of enterprising individuals. He determined that they learn from past mistakes, which was previously identified as learning from failure (Shepherd et al, 2009). This contributes to the contention that experience is an important benefit to the success of entrepreneurs. The experience gained by serial entrepreneurs provides them with an advantage over novice entrepreneurs (Kirschenhofer & Lechner, 2012). The former had more of a chance to build effective networks (McKelvie & Cedere, 2001) and even develop teams with complementary skills (MacMillan, 1986).

Politis and Gabrielsson (2009) investigated why some entrepreneurs develop a positive attitude when their initiatives fail. They determined that entrepreneurs had a more positive attitude about failure if they had experience with previous start-up ventures. When analyzing their results in more detail they also determined that a valuable learning experience was gained when a small business was closed because of poor performance. Thus, failure may be regarded as a temporary phase in the entrepreneur's experience learning how to deal with risky and uncertain business situations.

Crick (2011) also determined that past successful partnerships may not lead to future success. Thus, it is more important that partnerships be established which provide the necessary skills in relation to the current venture. This was earlier identified by Hughes and Morgan (2008) who suggested that it was important to ensure an organization fit of resources to facilitate management decision making based upon the industry and type of business.

Markman and Baron (2003) identified the personal characteristics of entrepreneurs who were considered successful. Their definition of "successful" in relation to starting a new business includes matching supply and demand; and possessing the necessary stamina, knowledge, skills, and abilities. Based on this very general definition Markman and Baron (2003) provide four distinct descriptions of why some individuals tend to be considered more successful entrepreneurs. These descriptions include self-efficacy, opportunity recognition, perseverance, and social skills supported by human and social capital.

Self-efficacy suggests that individuals believe they can organize and carry out tasks which contribute to attaining goals (Bandura, 1997; and Chen et al, 1998). Individuals with high self-efficacy prefer challenging activities. This relates well to the entrepreneurial tasks of forming and operating a small business.

Opportunity recognition involves the ability to identify initiatives which have a high probability for success (Miller, 1996; and Kirzner, 1997). Further, entrepreneurs who can also take a proactive role to identify future potential obstacles will tend to meet with success and create superior small businesses.

Social skills involve social perception such as the ability to perceive others and social adaptation which includes the ability to interact with others (Baron & Markman, 2000). More specifically, the social skills of individuals are composed of human and social capital. In small business talent in the form of these skills is paramount. Human capital includes characteristics such as intelligence and personality; as well as acquired skills such as education and work experience. These characteristics and skills are personal and internal to the individual. Social capital is external and involves how the individual relates to the environment (Maman, 2000). Thus, social capital involves personal networks, contacts, and interactions with others. Positive social skills will enhance the performance of entrepreneurs and contribute to their potential success (Steier, 2000).

Mitchelmore and Rowley (2010) investigated entrepreneurial competencies. To begin they defined the terms "competency" and "competence".

- **Competency:** "...an underlying characteristic of a person which results in effective action and/or superior performance in a job." (Mitchelmore & Rowley, 2010, p. 93)
- **Competence:** "...something which a person who works in a given occupational area should be able to achieve..." (Mitchelmore & Rowley, 2010, p. 93)

So, competence represents a minimum standard of performance whole competency contributes to successful performance. (Mitchelmore & Rowley, 2010).

Further, according to Man et al (2002) entrepreneurial competencies facilitate starting a business, while managerial skills contribute to operating a business.

Management skills relate to a manager's attempt to minimize uncertainty through identifying internal weakness in business processes and by responding to external threats (Parnell & Lester, 2007).

Mitchelmore and Rowley (2010) present their interpretations of competent entrepreneurs suggesting they address more beneficial business opportunities and are able to develop superior strategies for small businesses.

## THEORY OF ENTREPRENEURSHIP

Drucker (1998) has suggested that entrepreneurship involves the practice of systematic innovation through establishing and maintaining economic potential in a business venture. Entrepreneurship is a creative process where there is a beginning (vision) and ending (living system) to the entrepreneurial act (Long, 1983; Long & McMullan, 1984; McMullan & Long, 1990). Small business and large companies are merely points reached during the process which begins with an abstract idea which the entrepreneur commits to as a structure for a business venture. Along the way, the entrepreneur makes strategic decisions to meet a series of structural challenges, and in so doing, shapes the venture. For example, an early strategic challenge relates to identifying, evaluating and committing to a particular opportunity. Once decided, the venture is delimited to a particular focal environment, i.e. industry/market and all that this entails. Successfully meeting each of these challenges brings the venture closer to the entrepreneurial goal of developing a self-sustaining living system with the in-built capacity to innovate and grow.

Many researchers have contributed to the development and evolution of Entrepreneurship Theory (Schumpeter, 1934; Shackle, 1962; Kirzner, 1973 and 1992; Herbert & Link, 1988 and 1989; Baron, 1998; and Shane & Venkataraman, 2000).

Perhaps the most well-known comment on entrepreneurship was made by Drucker (1998) who suggested entrepreneurship involves an innovative approach to establishing and maintaining the viability of a business.

An entrepreneur will continually seek out new and innovative opportunities (Pretorius et al, 2006). Someone who adopts this approach is described as an authentic leader (Jensen & Luthans, 2006). The interests of the organization are considered and placed before personal interests. Employees are treated with respect and mutual trust evolves. The entrepreneur is the focal point for the development of both business values and a positive operating culture (Denison et al, 2004).

While the entrepreneur or authentic leader will establish a positive *modus operandi* there will always be a consideration for further innovation and change. As the founding entrepreneur passes the business to a subsequent entrepreneur subsequent change will result.

Entrepreneurship is a long term creative process beginning with a vision of a business or process and culminating in a living system. This process is known as the entrepreneurial act (Long, 1983; Long & McMullan, 1984; McMullan & Long, 1990). Both small business and large companies are merely considered points reached on a continuum that includes a beginning with an abstract business idea that the founding entrepreneur resolves to pursue as a business venture. The business venture is shaped by strategic decisions made by the entrepreneur in response to environmental challenges. As an early start-up these challenges may relate to identifying, evaluating and pursuing a particular business opportunity. As these challenges are successfully addressed the business venture moves closer to the development of a self-sustaining living system that is capable of innovating and adapting to an ever changing environment.

Nielsen and Lassen (2012) present a framework, based upon past research, for categorizing the perspectives taken to investigate entrepreneurship. This framework is presented in Table 5.

The images presented in Table 5 above portray a multi-faceted subject area and allows researchers to select a framework to provide a perspective for their investigations about entrepreneurship.

## ENTREPRENEURIAL PROCESS

Taking an entrepreneurial approach means continually seeking growth and innovation in the pursuit of new business opportunities (Pretorius et al, 2006). An individual who tends to adopt this entrepreneurial attitude is referred to as an authentic leader (Jensen & Luthans, 2006). The authentic leader puts the interest of the organization ahead of self-interests. The leader develops trust in employees by treating them with

*Table 5. Five images of entrepreneurship*

| Images | Definition | Perception of Entrepreneur | Authors |
|---|---|---|---|
| Machines | Mechanical way of thinking of forming new organizations | Rational architect | Obloj et al (2010); Linton and Walsh (2008) |
| Evolution | Biological metaphor for environmental interaction and growth | Objective process that evolves | Davidsson et al (2006); Hung (2006); Fitzsimmons and Douglas (2011); Fairchild (2009); Ahlstrom and Bruton (2006); Haugh (2007) |
| Contingency | Entrepreneurial process is contingent upon complex conditions and changing situations | An open system | Read et al (2009); Brush et al (2008); Gundry and Welsch (2001); Haber and Reichel (2007); Bluedorn and Martin (2008); Lichtenstein et al (2006); Zerbinati and Souitaris (2005); Goel and Karri; (2006); Austin et al (2006); McKelvey (2004) |
| Mind | Inner mental state of humans | Cognitive processes | Westhead et al (2005b); Shepherd and Haynie (2009); Ardichivilli et al (2003); Verheul et al (2005); Ward (2004); Bryant (2009); York and Venkataraman (2010); Kickul et al (2009); Davidsson and Honig (2003); Kreuger et al (2000) |
| Social Becoming | Entrepreneurial process is socially formed by networks of heterogeneous actors | Unique interpretations by individuals | Jack et al (2008); Chiasson and Saunders (2005); Downing (2005) |

Adapted from Nielsen and Lassen (2012)

respect. The business culture and values are developed by the founding entrepreneur (Denison et al, 2004).

The innovative approach of the subsequent entrepreneur may result in a change in direction for the small business in future generations. Indeed, the business may be renewed in many creative entrepreneurial ways. Entrepreneurship Theory applies across all of the generations. It is incumbent upon the family members involved in a small business that they continually take an innovative approach to establishing and maintaining their small business operations.

The process followed by the entrepreneur is referred to as entrepreneurship, which involves the establishment and maintenance of a small business venture and the ongoing practice of systematic innovation (Drucker, 1998). A model of the entrepreneurial process is included here as Figure 1 (McMullan & Long, 1990). The result of this process is a small business entity.

This process may be summarized as follows:

*Figure 1. Modeling the entrepreneurial process*
*Adapted from McMullan and Long, 1990:135*

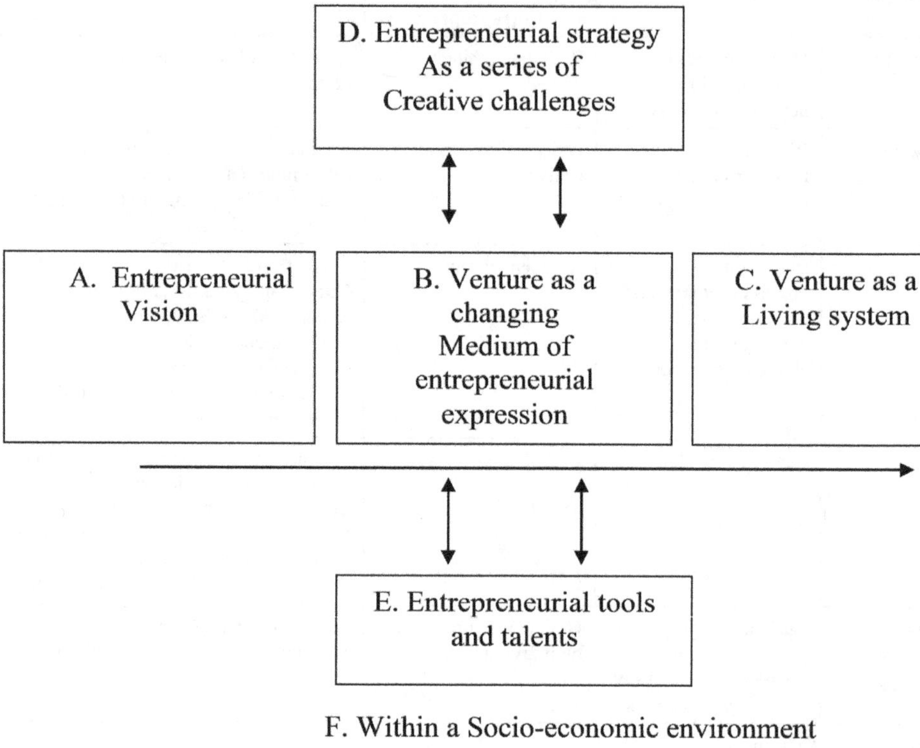


*The entrepreneurship process begins with a vision (A) of a business opportunity. Once a commitment is made to pursue the vision, the entrepreneur endeavors to build a self-sustaining living system (business venture) (C). The venture takes shape (B) as each strategic challenge (D) is addressed. The necessary tools and talents (E) are brought to the venture by the entrepreneur, through the commitment of members and may in part be acquired from independent consultants, or mentors. All of this takes place within and is influenced by a particular socio-economic environment (F). Part D (Figure 1) refers to a series of creative entrepreneurial challenges. There are ten of these challenges, each of which corresponds to a structural attribute of a living system (Table 5). As the strategic entrepreneurial challenges are reviewed, it is important to recognize that:*

1. *Their ordering is logically intuitive,*
2. *Each independent strategic decision makes a structural contribution to the business venture,*

3. *Structural components are dynamic and may be revisited, and*
4. *Each decision will build on those made previously and will affect those to come (Hunter & Kazakoff, 2008, pp. 7-8)*

Further, the entrepreneur undertakes strategic decisions in response to a series of challenges to developing the venture. Implementing these strategic decisions ultimately structures and defines the venture.

The components of the model may be described as follows in Table 6.

The theory goes on to suggest that, as shown in Figure 1, the entrepreneur is faced with ten organization building strategic challenges as the venture evolves from (A) vision, through (B) elaboration, to (C) a living system. These challenges are sorted into three broad groups (1) preparing the venture, (2) launching the venture and (3) growing the venture.

The entrepreneurship act (Long, 1983; Long & McMullan, 1984; and McMullan & Long, 1990) is a creative process which begins with a vision of an opportunity and culminates in a self-sustaining living system or ongoing venture. The initial vision may be an abstract idea or the realization of the potential for a business venture to provide a product or service. The functioning small business will require strategic responses to challenges such as those listed in Table 7. When these challenges have been successfully addressed the business venture will become a self-sustaining living system. The entrepreneurial process will have built into this system the capability to innovate and grow in response to an ever changing environment.

The above challenges could occur sequentially, although it may be necessary to conduct iterations of previously addressed challenges depending upon the issues encountered in an unpredictable future. The following comments are provided to more fully explain these challenges.

## Challenge 1: Identifying Realizable Opportunities

The founding entrepreneur must know himself or herself and have an appreciation for how the vision for a product or service may be accepted in the market place. A vision is a broad general concept while an opportunity is a specific course of action that is worthwhile pursuing.

## Challenge 2: Designing Feasible Products

The decision to implement the opportunity results in the creation of a product or service. This is the very reason the business exists. Products and services must enhance competitive advantage.

*Table 6. Entrepreneurial process component descriptions*

| Component | Description |
|---|---|
| H. Entrepreneurial Vision | The process commences with a vision of a desired venture outcome i.e. a business opportunity. |
| I. Venture as a Dynamic Medium of Expression | As an artist puts colour and form to the canvas to express his vision, the entrepreneur brings resources and people together who commit to a set of relationships in pursuit of the vision. The entrepreneur's action and the context of both the socio economic environment and the dynamics of the venture itself shape the venture. |
| J. Venture as a Living System | The above venture elaboration/structuring continues until it becomes a "living system no longer needing the entrepreneur's contribution to survive and prosper". (McMullan and Long, 1990, p.138) The vision is complete. |
| K. Self-Sustaining Organization or Living System | The organization is complete. The entrepreneur has succeeded in structuring the capacities common to living systems. The entrepreneurship process is complete. |
| L. Entrepreneurial Strategy | "The entrepreneur's strategies are in response to a series of creative challenges for developing a self-sustaining venture". (McMullan and Long, 1990:139). These strategies appropriately focus attention. |
| M. Entrepreneurial Tools and Talents | The entrepreneur must acquire the requisite skills and knowledge appropriate to the developmental tasks. |
| N. Socio Economic Environment | The venture must take into account both its macro and microenvironments. |

Adapted from McMullan and Long, 1990

## Challenge 3: Planning Resource Requirements

Resources in the form of human, material, financial, and intellectual capital must be identified. Then a plan may be developed as to how these resources will be sourced and how they will interact in support of business operations.

## Challenge 4: Negotiating Resource and Client Contracts

Once the resource requirements as outlined above are identified it will be necessary to determine the source. If the resource is not going to be supplied directly from the founding entrepreneur then the source may be the commonly referred "3Fs", Family, Friends, or Fools!

*Table 7. Challenges in developing an entrepreneurial venture*

| Entrepreneurial Challenge | Corresponding Living Systems Attribute |
|---|---|
| 11. Identifying realizable opportunities | All living systems have identifiable environments. |
| 12. Designing feasible products | All living systems have boundaries, which distinguish them from their environment. |
| 13. Planning resource requirements | All living systems are composed of interacting parts involving some functional differentiation and specialization. |
| 14. Negotiating resource and client contracts | All living systems must take in energy and information. |
| 15. Engineering efficient production | All living systems transform energy and information from one state to another. |
| 16. Regularizing sales revenue | All living systems export outputs into their environments. |
| 17. Standardizing operating performance | All living systems have cyclical patterns of changing activities within the system and within the environment. |
| 18. Expanding strategically and opportunistically | All living systems are characterized by homeostatic balance and governance mechanisms, evolving systematically to better fit their environment. |
| 19. Professionalizing middle management | All living systems become differentiated over time into more and more independent roles. |
| 20. Institutionalizing innovative capacity | All living systems are characterized by negative entropy. |

Adapted from McMullan and Long, 1990, p. 267

## Challenge 5: Engineering Efficient Production

The product or service must add value by efficiently converting raw material and other necessary inputs into the required outputs.

## Challenge 6: Regularizing Sales Revenue

Sales revenue is the life blood of a small business. Sales are proof that the vision is viable. More importantly, the product or service must be produced at a cost that results in a profit and encourages customers to make a positive purchase decision.

## Challenge 7: Standardizing Operating Performance

As sales grow the founding entrepreneur's attention will move to the management of functional issues. Accounting and financial records will provide input to decisions about efficiencies in operations of the business. As the processes are repeated perhaps more efficient approaches will be identified and implemented.

## Challenge 8: Expanding Strategically and Opportunistically

Over time the business must evolve in response to changes in the environment. This may mean growth, but growth is not necessary. But growth, if it is to occur, must be in concert with the environment. Further, the pace of growth may vary (Tan et al, 2009).

## Challenge 9: Professionalizing Middle Management

With growth it will be necessary to focus even more on management aspects. These aspects relate to organizational structure and the creation of a middle management level. Opportunities will arise to establish specialized management functions.

## Challenge 10: Institutionalizing Innovative Capability

The business was formed because of the innovative characteristic of the founding entrepreneur. Now it will be time for this characteristic to be transferred to the business. Evidence of a distinct innovative influence within a small business is shown by the establishment of a research and development function.

In Table 8, the ten strategic entrepreneurial challenges are restated in question form, and grouped into four broad categories. The first group of three challenges is preparatory and typically precedes the venture's launch. Second are those challenges that characterize the venture launch and search for market success and operational understanding. Some refer to this phase as the search for survival. Third are the critical challenges facing the venture's successful growth, and finally fourth is labelled Exiting meaning the attributes of a living system are in place including the capability for ongoing innovation. Exit does not imply the entrepreneur should leave the venture, rather it suggests the entrepreneurial act is complete and he/she may comfortably leave the venture with reasonable assurance of its continued survival and growth. Each broad grouping of challenges is briefly discussed below. It is important that IS researchers and consultants recognize the context of subject businesses. The discussion presents only abstract direction IS researchers might refer to in developing a contextual map.

It is also important to note that only a small proportion of the multitude of small businesses go beyond being "small to medium size", a large proportion of businesses do not survive beyond the first generation entrepreneur.

*Preparing:* The first three challenges are preparatory and involve (1) identifying and assessing the opportunity, (2) designing the product service offering, and (3) planning for the resources necessary to actually operate the business. Which markets to serve with what product/service package and with what business competencies

*Table 8. Evolving entrepreneurial challenges*

| Grouping | Entrepreneurial Challenges |
|---|---|
| Preparing | 11. What business will we be in<br>12. What products/services will we manufacture and sell<br>13. What is our operating strategy |
| Launching | 14. What resources will we employ<br>15. How will we produce<br>16. How will we sell and distribute our products |
| Growing | 17. How will operating efficiencies be improved<br>18. How will we expand<br>19. How and when will we professionalize management |
| Exiting | 20. How will we continue to innovate |

Adapted from McMullan and Long 1990, Chapters 5 and 7.

and structure are the major issues to be resolved. It behooves the entrepreneur to become fully knowledgeable of the industry, its practices, competitors, and markets. Planning skills are needed to articulate resource requirements and launch strategies. The entrepreneur may take advantage of the available business plan software as well as many archival and real time sources of market, supply and competitive information.

*Launching:* The next three challenges relate to (1) negotiating and acquiring the necessary financial and human resources to implement the launch strategy. It is of course critical to get customer commitment, and (2) to set up production at an appropriate scale, (3) accompanied by effective distribution. Once sales begin generating cash flow it is also critical to establish and implement adequate financial controls and mechanisms to ensure the launch is progressing within plan tolerances. The emerging firm will be faced with monitoring and assuring sufficient cash flow to accommodate growing product/service demand while learning the rudiments of operational activities. The chequebook is no longer adequate financial control and visually scanning inventories will soon require at least a rudimentary inventory control system.

*Growing:* In a sense the venture is now an operating prototype or small business. Whether the entrepreneur intends growth or wishes to remain small, will nevertheless require that he/she attend to (1) standardizing operations to achieve certain efficiencies and to facilitate responding to environmental change. If growth is the objective, then these systems should be designed with (2) expansion strategies in mind. Growth will necessitate structuring in (3) additional levels of management adding complexities to operating and strategic controls. As management is professionalized information system needs will become increasingly complex. Control will move from face-to-face to performance based. It will become more difficult to ensure the growing venture retains the entrepreneur's vision without consciously attending to the culture and building communication and feedback mechanisms. The linkages with customers and the distribution network must be tightly aligned and maintained. Formal information systems will be needed to replace what was daily face-to-face contact among members of the small firm team. Management development programs should be integrated with performance controls.

In short, the entrepreneur must be prepared for rapid growth and increasing leadership demands for leadership skills.

*Exiting:* In order to ensure growth potential, the entrepreneur needs to ensure the capacity to innovate is built into the venture. Effective new product development and broader R and D capacity will help to ensure continuance of the firm. The organization now exists as a professionally managed living system and the process of entrepreneurship as such is complete. The organization will now be capable of ongoing entrepreneurial behaviour as a self-sustaining living system, able to continually revisit and address the appropriateness of its structural configuration to profitably satisfying market needs and the goals of the firm. A number of alternatives exist for the founding entrepreneur from continued active involvement to complete liquidation of the venture. No matter what direction is taken, it is important to develop a succession plan with sufficient lead-time to accommodate a smooth withdrawal of the entrepreneur at the appropriate time.

Bosma et al (2004) investigated whether investments in human and social capital improved entrepreneurial performance. Human capital is generally regarded as education and experience. Bosma et al (2004) determined that both experience in business ownership and experience in a specific industry enhanced performance. However, while Bosma et al (2004) determined that education and experience made a positive contribution to on-going small business performance, Diochan et al (2008), as presented earlier in this chapter, found that education and experience was not related to the success of forming a small business. This apparent contradiction suggests that small businesses are formed as a result of the nascent founding entrepreneurs' passion for an idea. But education and experience become important once the small business is in operation. Bruderl et al (1992) found that successful small business managers with high human capital focused upon identifying business opportunities and were able to organize and manage appropriate business processes. Social capital involves a proclivity to network and it too was found to positively influence performance. Information gathering was enhanced through participating in established networks.

Zachary and Mishra (2010) call upon small business researchers to explore the aspects of sustainability through investigating the social context of the small business involving both family and community. It is not only the small business itself and the manager, but also the context within which the small business exists. This idea is explored further by Fitzgerald et al (2010) who suggest that socially responsible processes of the small business manager, along with the involvement of family, may contribute to resolving issues within the community.

## DIMENSIONS OF THE ENTREPRENEURIAL PROCESS

Pretorius et al (2006) suggest that entrepreneurship consists of three dimensions, including opportunity exploitation, venture creation, and venture growth. Opportunity exploitation involves identifying a potential opportunity (Hisrich & Peters, 2002) by actively seeking out opportunities (Wickham, 2001) and the implementing a process (Gibb, 1998) to take advantage of the opportunity. Venture creation relates to the establishment of an entity capable of supporting the above opportunity exploitation process (Pretorius et al, 2006). Not only are appropriate skills necessary but the entrepreneur must possess creativity when developing innovative processes (Pretorius et al, 2006). Venture growth implies a successful process implementation in response to an opportunity. The growth potential of a small business is related to the entrepreneur's inclination towards innovation (Pretorius et al, 2006). Krueger (2004) has suggested that the key ingredient among the dimensions is opportunity exploitation. Thus, Pretorius et al (2006) contend that an entrepreneur, "... constantly seeks growth and innovation and has the strategic objective of pursuing new opportunities. (Pretorius et al, 2006:3).

Figure 2 relates these three dimensions of the entrepreneurial process to creativity, innovation, and implementation. While a sequence is implied in the diagram, all three are necessary conditions for the creation of a successful entrepreneurial process.

Creativity within the entrepreneurial process, "...drives the thinking of the entrepreneur in finding alternative ways of doing business." (Preotius et al, 2006, p. 4). Innovation in the entrepreneurial process involves, "...having the idea and turning that idea into an opportunity through commercialization." (Ireland et al, 2001, p. 57). Thus creativity is the starting point for innovation. Further, "creativity without innovation does not produce results, and innovation without effective management does not produce marketable products, processes or services". (Beattie, 1999, p. 2). Implementation involves carrying out the creative idea and innovative plans. This is where the action takes place.

Carland et al (2002) determined a continuum of entrepreneurs in relation to drive or motivation. At one end of the continuum an entrepreneur is considered to be passionate about employing innovative ideas to create new and novel small businesses. Conversely, at the other end of the continuum an entrepreneur may be satisfied managing their current small business. Indeed, they will focus on the pro-

*Figure 2. Conceptual model of entrepreneurship and its relationship with creativity, innovation and implementation*
*Adapted from Pretorius et al, 2006*

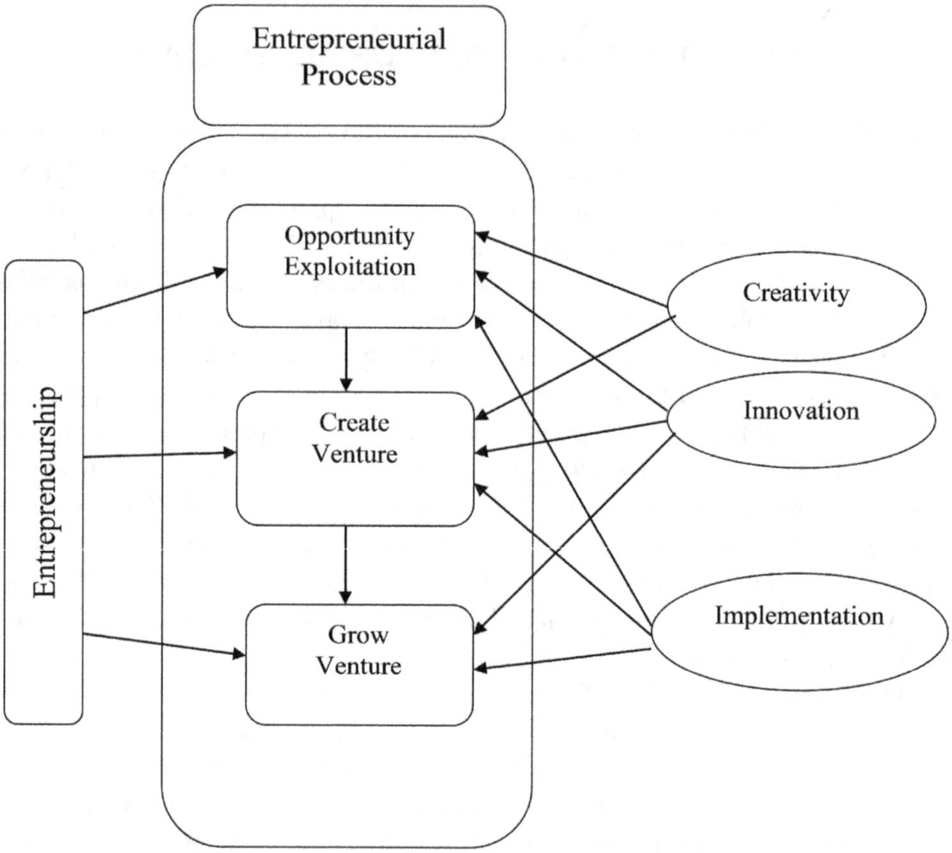


vision of quality product or service at their current volume of operation. Examples of entrepreneurs at both ends of the continuum were documented by Hunter and Kazakoff (2008). Some entrepreneurs continually search for new business opportunities, while others focus on current operations within a context of a work/life balance. Both types will take an innovative approach to operations. Also, both types are cautioned to remain focused upon the niche within which they have expertise. Further, Hunter and Kazakoff (2008) commented that both types of entrepreneurs considered themselves to be successful. This suggests that growth is not the only measure of success for a small business. As Hunter and Kazakoff (2008) investigated multi-generation small business longevity may also be considered a measure of success. Whether they focus on growth or the current level of operation they will employ an innovative approach (Drucker, 1998).

Huoivinen et al (2010) investigated the difference between entrepreneurial teams and management teams. To begin they define a team as, "...a small number of people with complementary skills who are committed to a common purpose, performance goals, and approach for which they hold themselves mutually accountable" (Huoivinen et al, 2010:437). Then they define a management team as, "...key people who give a firm its general direction and who specialize in running the business" (Huoivinen et al, 2010:438). An entrepreneurial team is, "...individuals [who] have common financial interests and goals, and who are both present during the founding stage and actively participating on the business" Huoivinen et al, 2010:438).

## CONCLUSION

This chapter has described the various perspectives on entrepreneurs, entrepreneurship, and the entrepreneurial process. Each perspective suggests individuals proceed through various stages in their on-going search for new opportunities or novel approaches to existing activities. The next chapter presents an introduction to the subject of information systems.

## REFERENCES

Ahlstrom, D., & Bruton, G. D. (2006). Venture capital in emerging economics: Network and institutional change. *Entrepreneurship Theory and Practice*, *30*(2), 299–320. doi:10.1111/j.1540-6520.2006.00122.x

Allison, C. W., & Hayes, J. (1996). The cognitive styles index: A measure of intuition-analysis for organizational research. *Journal of Management Studies*, *33*(1), 119–135. doi:10.1111/j.1467-6486.1996.tb00801.x

Anonymous, . (2006). How to succeed in small business. *Maclean's*, *119*(40), 9, 49–57.

Ardichivli, A., Cardozo, R., & Ray, S. (2003). A theory of entrepreneurial opportunity identification and development. *Journal of Business Venturing*, *18*(1), 105–123. doi:10.1016/S0883-9026(01)00068-4

Armstrong, S. J., & Hird, A. (2009). Cognitive style and entrepreneurial drive of new and mature business owner-managers. *Journal of Business and Psychology*, *24*(4), 419–430. doi:10.1007/s10869-009-9114-4

Austin, J., Stevenson, H., & Wei-Skillern, J. (2006). Social and commercial entrepreneurship: Same, different, or both? *Entrepreneurship Theory and Practice*, *30*(1), 1–22. doi:10.1111/j.1540-6520.2006.00107.x

Bandura, A. (1997). *Self-efficacy: The Exercise of Control*. New York: W. H. Freeman & Co.

Barney, J. (1986). Strategic factor markets: Expectations, luck, and business strategy. *Management Science*, *32*(10), 1231–1241. doi:10.1287/mnsc.32.10.1231

Baron, R. A. (1998). Cognitive mechanisms in entrepreneurship: Why and when entrepreneurs think differently than other people. *Journal of Business Venturing*, *13*(4), 275–294. doi:10.1016/S0883-9026(97)00031-1

Baron, R. A., & Markman, G. D. (2000). Beyond social capital: The role of social competence in entrepreneurs' success. *The Academy of Management Executive*, *14*(1), 106–116.

Beattie, R. (1999). The creative entrepreneur: A study of the entrepreneur's creative processes. www.babson.edu/entrep/fer/papers/99/III/III_B/IIIB%20Text.htm

Beaver, G., & Jennings, P. (2005). Competitive advantage and entrepreneurial power: The dark side of entrepreneurship. *Journal of Small Business and Enterprise Development*, *12*(1), 9–23. doi:10.1108/14626000510579617

Becker, G. S. (1975). *Human Capital* (2nd ed.). New York: Columbia University Press.

Beugelsdijk, S. (2007). Entrepreneurial culture, regional innovativeness and economic growth. *Journal of Evolutionary Economics*, *17*(2), 187–210. doi:10.1007/s00191-006-0048-y

Birley, S. (1996). The start-up. In P. Burns & J. Dewhurst (Eds.), *Small Business and Entrepreneurship*. Basingstoke: Macmillan.

Bjerke, B. (2007). *Understanding Entrepreneurship*. Cheltenham and Northampton, MA: Edward Elgar.

Block, J. H., & Wagner, M. (2010). Necessity and opportunity entrepreneurs in Germany: Characteristics and earnings differential. *Small Business Review*, *62*, 154–174.

Bluedorn, A. C., & Martin, G. (2008). The time frames of entrepreneurs. *Journal of Business Venturing*, *23*(1), 1–20. doi:10.1016/j.jbusvent.2006.05.005

Boone, C., de Brabander, B., & Hellemans, J. (2000). Research note: CEO locus of control and small firm performance. *Organization Studies*, *21*(3), 641–646. doi:10.1177/0170840600213007

Bosma, N., van Praag, M., Thurik, R., & de Wit, G. (2004). The value of human and social capital investments for the business performance of startups. *Small Business Economics, 23*(3), 227–236. doi:10.1023/B:SBEJ.0000032032.21192.72

Boswell, J. (1971). Corporate planning in small manufacturing firms. *Journal of Business Policy, 2*(1), 49–53.

Brockhaus, R. H. (1980). Risk taking propensity of entrepreneurs. *Academy of Management Journal, 23*(3), 509–520. doi:10.2307/255515

Brouwer, M. T. (2002). Weber, Schumpeter and Knoght on entrepreneurship and economic development. *Journal of Evolutionary Economics, 12*(1-2), 83–105. doi:10.1007/s00191-002-0104-1

Bruderl, J., Preisendorfer, P., & Ziegler, R. (1992). Survival chances of newly founded business organizations. *American Sociological Review, 57*(2), 227–242. doi:10.2307/2096207

Brush, C. G., Manolova, T. S., & Edelman, L. E. (2008). Properties of emerging organizations: An empirical test. *Journal of Business Venturing, 23*(5), 547–566. doi:10.1016/j.jbusvent.2007.09.002

Bryant, P. (2009). Self-regulation and moral awareness among entrepreneurs. *Journal of Business Venturing, 24*(6), 505–518. doi:10.1016/j.jbusvent.2008.04.005

Burlingham, B. (2006). In search of small giants. *Inc. Magazine, 28*(2), 84–87.

Carland, J. C., & Carland, J. W. (1992). Managers, small business owners and entrepreneurs: The cognitive dimension. *Journal of Business and Entrepreneurship, 4*(2), 55–66.

Carland, J. C., Carland, J. W., & Stewart, W. H. Jr. (2000). The indefatigable entrepreneur: A study of the dispositions of multiple venture founders. *Journal of Business and Entrepreneurship, 12*(1), 1–18.

Carland, J. W., Carland, J. C., & Ensley, M. (2002). Hunting the heffalump: The theoretical Basis and dimensionality of the Carland entrepreneurial index. *Academy of Entrepreneurship Journal, 7*(2), 51–84.

Carland, J. W., Hoy, F., Bolton, W. R., & Carland, J. A. (1984). Differentiating entrepreneurs from small business owners: A conceptualization. *Academy of Management Review, 9*(2), 354–359.

Carland, J. W., Hoy, F., & Carland, J. A. (1988). Who is an entrepreneur? Is a question worth asking. *American Journal of Small Business, 12*(4), 33–39.

Casson, M. (2003). Entrepreneurship, business culture and the theory of the firm, in Handbook of Entrepreneurship Research: An Interdisciplinary Survey and Introduction, Editors Acs, Z. J. & Audretch, D. B. Dordretch: Kluwer Academic Publishers, 223-246.

Chen, C. C., Greene, P. G., & Crick, A. (1998). Does entrepreneurial self-efficacy distinguish entrepreneurs from managers? *Journal of Business Venturing*, *13*(4), 295–316. doi:10.1016/S0883-9026(97)00029-3

Chiasson, M., & Saunders, C. (2005). Reconsiling diverse approaches to opportunity research using the structuration theory. *Journal of Business Venturing*, *20*(6), 747–767. doi:10.1016/j.jbusvent.2004.07.004

Collins, J. (2002). Chinese entrepreneurs: The Chinese diaspora in Australia. *International Journal of Entrepreneurial Behaviour & Research*, *8*(1/2), 113–133. doi:10.1108/13552550210423750

Crick, D. (2011). Enterprising individuals and entrepreneurial learning. *International Journal of Entrepreneurial Behaviour & Research*, *17*(2), 203–218. doi:10.1108/13552551111114941

Cromie, S. (2000). Assessing entrepreneurial inclinations: Some approaches and empirical evidence. *European Journal of Work and Organizational Psychology*, *9*(1), 7–30. doi:10.1080/135943200398030

Davidsson, P., & Honig, B. (2003). The role of social and human capital among nascent entrepreneurs. *Journal of Business Venturing*, *18*(3), 301–331. doi:10.1016/S0883-9026(02)00097-6

Davidsson, P., Hunter, E., & Klofsten, M. (2006). Institutional forces: The invisible hand that shapes venture ideas? *International Small Business Journal*, *24*(2), 115–131. doi:10.1177/0266242606061834

De Clercq, D., Menzies, T. V., Diochan, M., & Gasse, Y. (2009). Explaining nascent entrepreneurs' goal commitment: An exploratory study. *Journal of Small Business and Entrepreneurship*, *22*(2), 123–140. doi:10.1080/08276331.2009.10593446

Delmar, F., & Davidsson, P. (2000). Where do they come from? Prevalence and characteristics of nascent entrepreneurs. *Entrepreneurship and Regional Development*, *12*(1), 1–23. doi:10.1080/089856200283063

Denison, D., Lief, C., & Ward, J. L. (2004). Culture in family-owned enterprises: Recognizing and leveraging unique strengths. *Family Business Review*, *17*(1), 61–70. doi:10.1111/j.1741-6248.2004.00004.x

Diochan, M., Menzies, T. V., & Gasse, Y. (2008). Exploring the nature and impact of gestation-specific human capital among nascent entrepreneurs. *Journal of Developmental Entrepreneurship, 13*(2), 151–165. doi:10.1142/S1084946708000909

Downing, S. (2005). The social construction of entrepreneurship: Narratives and dramatic processes in the coproduction of organizations and identities. *Entrepreneurship Theory and Practice, 29*(2), 185–204. doi:10.1111/j.1540-6520.2005.00076.x

Drucker, P. F. (1998). The discipline of innovation. *Harvard Business Review, 76*(5), 143–159. PMID:10187245

Eckhardt, J., & Shane, S. (2003). The importance of opportunities to entrepreneurship. *Journal of Management, 29*(3), 333–349. doi:10.1016/S0149-2063(02)00225-8

Fairchild, G. B. (2009). Residential segregation influences on the likelihood of ethnic self-employment. *Entrepreneurship Theory and Practice, 33*(2), 373–395. doi:10.1111/j.1540-6520.2009.00295.x

Fitzgerald, M. A., Haynes, G. W., Schrank, H. L., & Danes, S. M. (2010). Socially responsible processes of small family business owners: Exploratory evidence from the national family businesss survey. *Journal of Small Business Management, 48*(4), 524–551. doi:10.1111/j.1540-627X.2010.00307.x

Fitzsimmons, J. R., & Douglas, E. J. (2011). Interaction between feasibility and desirability in the formation of entrepreneurial intentions. *Journal of Business Venturing, 26*(4), 431–440. doi:10.1016/j.jbusvent.2010.01.001

Frese, M. (2007). Towards a psychology of entrepreneurship: An action theory perspective. *Foundations and Trends in Entrepreneurship, 5*(6), 437–496. doi:10.1561/0300000028

Gartner, W. B. (1989). Who is an entrepreneur? Is the wrong question. *Entrepreneurship, Theory and Practice*, summer, 47-68.

Gibb, A. (1998). Entrepreneurial core capabilities, competitiveness and management development in the 21st Century. *8th Annual Conference of Internationalizing Entrepreneurship Education and Training, Schloss Reichartshausen Oestrich-Winkel*, Germany.

Goel, S., & Karri, R. (2006). Entrepreneurs, effectual logic, and over-trust. *Entrepreneurship Theory and Practice, 30*(4), 477–493. doi:10.1111/j.1540-6520.2006.00131.x

Grundry, L. K., & Welsch, H. P. (2001). The ambitious entrepreneur: High growth strategies of women-owned enterprises. *Journal of Business Venturing*, *16*(5), 453–470. doi:10.1016/S0883-9026(99)00059-2

Haber, S., & Reichel, A. (2007). The cumulative nature of the entrepreneurial process: The contribution of social capital, planning and environment resources to small venture performance. *Journal of Business Venturing*, *22*(1), 119–145. doi:10.1016/j.jbusvent.2005.09.005

Haugh, H. (2007). Community-led social venture creation. *Entrepreneurship Theory and Practice*, *31*(2), 161–182. doi:10.1111/j.1540-6520.2007.00168.x

Hebert, R. F., & Link, A. N. (1989). In search of the meaning of entrepreneurship. *Small Business Economics*, *1*(1), 39–49. doi:10.1007/BF00389915

Herbert, R. F., & Link, A. N. (1988). *The Entrepreneur – Mainstream Views and Radical Critiques*. New York: Praeger.

Hisrich, R. D., & Peters, M. P. (2002). *Entrepreneurship*. Boston Burr Ridge, IL: McGraw-Hill.

Hughes, P., & Morgan, R. E. (2008). Fitting strategic resources with product-market strategy: Performance implications. *Journal of Business Research*, *61*(4), 323–331. doi:10.1016/j.jbusres.2007.06.023

Hung, H. (2006). Formation and survival on new ventures. *International Small Business Journal*, *24*(4), 359–378. doi:10.1177/0266242606065508

Hunter, M. G., & Kazakoff, D. (2008). *Little Empires: Multi-Generation Small Business in Southern Alberta, CANADA*. Melbourne: Heidelberg Press.

Huoivinen, S., & Pasanen, M. (2010). Entrepreneurial and management teams: What makes the difference? *Journal of Management & Organization*, *16*(3), 436–453. doi:10.5172/jmo.16.3.436

Ireland, R. D., Hitt, M. A., Camp, S. M., & Sexton, D. L. (2001). Integrating entrepreneurship and strategic management actions to create firm wealth. *The Academy of Management Executive*, *15*(1), 49–64. doi:10.5465/AME.2001.4251393

Jack, S., Dodd, S. D., & Anderson, A. J. (2008). Change and the development of entrepreneurial networks over time: A processual perspective. *Entrepreneurship and Regional Development*, *20*(2), 125–159. doi:10.1080/08985620701645027

Jensen, M. C., & Luthans, F. (2006). Relationship between entrepreneurs' psychological capital and their authentic leadership. *Journal of Managerial Issues*, *18*(2), 254–273.

Kickul, J., Gundry, L. K., Barbosa, S. D., & Whitcanack. Intuition versus analysis? Testing differential models of cognitive style on entrepreneurial self-efficacy and the new venture creation. *Entrepreneurship Theory and Practice*, 33(2), 439-453.

Kirschenhofer, F., & Lechner, C. (2012). Performance drivers of serial entrepreneurs. *International Journal of Entrepreneurial Behaviour & Research*, *18*(3), 305–329. doi:10.1108/13552551211227693

Kirzner, I. (1973). *Competition and Entrepreneurship*. Chicago: Chicago University Press.

Kirzner, I. (1992). *The Meaning of the Market Process*. London: Routledge. doi:10.4324/9780203004456

Kirzner, I. (1997). Entrepreneurial discovery and the competitive market process: An Austrian approach. *Journal of Economic Literature*, *35*(1), 60–85.

Klein, H. (1991). Further evidence of the relationship between goal setting and expectancy theories. *Organizational Behavior and Human Decision Processes*, *49*(2), 230–257. doi:10.1016/0749-5978(91)90050-4

Kobia, M., & Sikalieh, D. (2010). Towards a search for the meaning of entrepreneurship. *Journal of European Industrial Training*, *34*(2), 110–127. doi:10.1108/03090591011023970

Konorti, E. (2010). The relationship between wealth creation and professional management in small-medium enterprises. *The Journal of American Academy of Business*, *16*(1), 11–23.

Korunka, C., Frank, H., Lueger, M., & Mugler, J. (2003). The entrepreneurial personality in the context of resources, environment, and the startup process – A configurational approach. *Entrepreneurship Theory and Practice*, *28*(1), 23–42. doi:10.1111/1540-8520.00030

Krueger, M. E. (2004). Creativity and innovation in the entrepreneurship domain. Unpublished PhD Thesis in Entrepreneurship, University of Pretoria, Pretoria.

Krueger, N. F., Reilly, M. D., & Carsrid, A. L. (2000). Competing models of entrepreneurial intentions. *Journal of Business Venturing*, *15*(5/6), 411–432. doi:10.1016/S0883-9026(98)00033-0

Lazear, E. P. (2002). Entrepreneurship. Working paper, National Bureau of Economic Research, Cambridge MA.

Lee, D. Y., & Tsang, E. W. K. (2001). The effects of entrepreneurial personality: Background and network activities on venture growth. *Journal of Management Studies, 38*(4), 583–602. doi:10.1111/1467-6486.00250

Lichtenstein, B. B., Dooley, K. J., & Lumpkin, G. T. (2006). Measuring emergence in the dynamics of new venture creation. *Journal of Business Venturing, 21*(2), 153–175. doi:10.1016/j.jbusvent.2005.04.002

Linton, D. J., & Walsh, S. T. (2008). Acceleration and extension of opportunity recognition for nanotechnologies and other emerging technologies. *International Small Business Journal, 26*(1), 83–99. doi:10.1177/0266242607084660

Littunen, H. (2000). Entrepreneurship and the characteristics of the entrepreneurial personality. *International Journal of Entrepreneurial Behaviour and Research, 6*(6), 295–309. doi:10.1108/13552550010362741

Long, W. A. (1983). The meaning of entrepreneurship. *American Journal of Small Business, 8*(2), 47–56.

Long, W. A., & McMullan, W. E. (1984). Mapping the opportunity identification process. In J. A. Hornaday et al. (Eds.), *Frontiers of Entrepreneurship Research*. Wellesley, MA: Babson College.

Low, M., & MacMillan, I. C. (2001). Entrepreneurship: Past research and future challenges. *Journal of Management, 14*(2), 139–161. doi:10.1177/014920638801400202

MacMillan, I. (1986). To really learn about entrepreneurship, let's study habitual entrepreneurs. *Journal of Business Venturing, 1*(3), 241–243. doi:10.1016/0883-9026(86)90001-7

Maman, D. (2000). Who accumulates directorships of big business firms in Israel? Organizational structure, social capital and human capital. *Human Relations, 53*(5), 603–630. doi:10.1177/0018726700535001

Man, T., Lau, T., & Chan, K. F. (2002). The competitiveness of small and medium enterprises: A conceptualization with focus on entrepreneurial competencies. *Journal of Business Venturing, 17*(2), 123–142. doi:10.1016/S0883-9026(00)00058-6

Markman, G. D., & Baron, R. A. (2003). Person – entrepreneurship fit: Why some people are more successful as entrepreneurs than others. *Human Resource Management Review, 13*(2), 281–301. doi:10.1016/S1053-4822(03)00018-4

Martin, L. M., & Wright, L. T. (2005). No gender in cyberspace? Women empowered in innovation and entrepreneurship by ICT. *International Journal of Entrepreneurship Behaviour & Research, 11*(2), 162–178. doi:10.1108/13552550510590563

McClelland, D. (1961). *The Achieving Society*. Princeton, New Jersey: Van Nostrand Reinhold. doi:10.1037/14359-000

McKelvie, A., & Cedere, A. (2001). Network pollination: Habitual entrepreneurship and incubators. Paper presented at BKERC 2001, Jonkoping.

McKelvie, B. (2004). Towards a complexity science of entrepreneurship. *Journal of Business Venturing, 19*(3), 313–341. doi:10.1016/S0883-9026(03)00034-X

McMullan, W. E., & Long, W. A. (1990). *Developing New Ventures: The Entrepreneurial Option*. San Diego, CA: Harcourt Brace Jovanovich, Publishers.

Miller, S. M. (1996). Monitoring and blunting of threatening information: Cognitive interference and facilitation in the coping process. In Sarason, I. G., Pierce, G. R., & Sarason, B. R. (Editors), Cognitive Interference: Theory, Methods, and Findings (175-190). Mahwahm NJ: Lawrence Erlbaum Associate Publishers.

Mitchelmore, S., & Rowley, J. (2010). Entrepreneurial competencies: A literature review and development agenda. *International Journal of Entrepreneurial behaviour & Research*, 16(2), 92-111.

Myers, I. B. (1962). *The Myers-Briggs Type Indicator*. Princeton, NJ: Educational Testing Service. doi:10.1037/14404-000

Nielsen, S. L., & Lassen, A. H. (2012). Images of entrepreneurship: Towards a new categorization of entrepreneurship. *The International Entrepreneurship and Management Journal, 8*(1), 35–53. doi:10.1007/s11365-010-0159-7

Obloj, T., Obloj, K., & Pratt, M. G. (2010). Dominant logic and entrepreneurial firms' performance in a transition economy. *Entrepreneurship Theory and Practice, 34*(1), 151–170. doi:10.1111/j.1540-6520.2009.00367.x

Ong, J. W., Ismail, H. B., & Goh, G. G. G. (2010). The competitive advantage of small and medium enterprises (SMEs): The role of entrepreneurship and luck. *Journal of Small Business and Entrepreneurship, 23*(3), 373–391. doi:10.1080/08276331.2010.10593491

Parnell, J. A., & Lester, D. L. (2007). Re-evaluating the entrepreneurship-management conundrum: Challenges and solutions. *Journal of Applied Management and Entrepreneurship, 12*(4), 74–88.

Politis, D., & Gabrielsson, J. (2009). Entrepreneurs' attitudes towards failure: An experiential learning approach. *International Journal of Entrepreneurial Behaviour & Research, 15*(4), 364–383. doi:10.1108/13552550910967921

Pretorius, M., Millard, S. M., & Kruger, M. E. (2006). The relationship between implementation, creativity and innovation in small business ventures. *Management Dynamics*, *15*(1), 2–13.

Rauch, A., & Frese, M. (2000). Psychological approach to entrepreneurial success: A general model and an overview of findings. In Cooper, C. L. & Robertson, I. T. (Editors), International review of Industrial and Organizational Psychology, 101-142. Chichester, Wiley.

Read, S., Song, M., & Smit, W. (2009). A meta-analytical review of effectuation and venture performance. *Journal of Business Venturing*, *24*(6), 573–587. doi:10.1016/j.jbusvent.2008.02.005

Reynolds, P., Camp, S. M., Bygrave, W. D., Autio, E., & Hay, M. (2002). *Global Entrepreneurship Monitor 2001 Executive Report. Babson Park/London*. Babson College and London Business School.

Rotefoss, B., & Kolvereid, L. (2005). Aspiring, nascent, and fledgling entrepreneurs: An investigation of the business start-up process. *Entrepreneurship and Regional Development*, *17*(2), 109–127. doi:10.1080/08985620500074049

Rotter, J. B. (1966). Generalized expectancies for internal versus external control of reinforcement. *Psychological Monographs*, *609*(80), 1–28. doi:10.1037/h0092976 PMID:5340840

Schumpeter, J. A. (1934). The Theory of Economic Development. New Brunswick, NP: Transaction Publishers.

Shackle, G. (1962). Concluding comment. Chapter in Carter, Meredith, C. G., & Shackle, G., (Editors), Uncertainty and Business Decisions, Liverpool: Liverpool University Press.

Shane, S. (2007). *A General Theory of Entrepreneurship: The Individual-Opportunity Nexus*. Aldershot: Edward Elgar.

Shane, S., & Venkataraman, S. (2000). The promise of entrepreneurship as a field of research. *Academy of Management Review*, *26*(1), 13–17. doi:10.5465/AMR.2001.27879269

Shaver, K. G., & Scott, L. R. (1991). Person, process, choice: The psychology of new venture creation. *Entrepreneurship Theory and Practice*, *16*(2), 23–45.

Shepherd, D., & Haynie, M. J. (2009). Family business, identity conflict and an expedited entrepreneurial process: A process of resolving identity conflict. *Entrepreneurship Theory and Practice*, *33*(6), 1245–1264. doi:10.1111/j.1540-6520.2009.00344.x

Shepherd, D. A., Wiklund, J., & Haynie, J. M. (2009). Moving forward: Balancing the financial and emotional costs of business failure. *Journal of Business Venturing*, *24*(2), 134–148. doi:10.1016/j.jbusvent.2007.10.002

Steier, L., & Greenwood, R. (2000). Entrepreneurship and the evolution of angel financial networks. *Organization Studies*, *21*(1), 163–192. doi:10.1177/0170840600211002

Sternberg, R., Brixy, U., & Schlapfner, J. F. (2006). *Global Entrepreneurship Monitor. Landerbericht Deutschland 2005*. Hanover, Bonn: University of Hanover and IAB.

Stevenson, H. H. (1999). A perspective of entrepreneurship. In H. H. Stevenson, I. Grousebeck, M. J. Roberts, & A. Bhide (Eds.), *New Business Ventures and the Entrepreneur* (pp. 3–17). Boston: Irwin McGraw-Hill.

Stewart, W. H. Jr, Carland, J. C., Carland, J. W., Watson, W. E., & Sweo, R. (2003). Entrepreneurial dispositions and goal orientations: A comparative exploration of United States and Russian entrepreneurs. *Journal of Small Business Management*, *14*(1), 27–46. doi:10.1111/1540-627X.00065

Stewart, W. H., & Roth, P. L. (2007). A meta-analysis of achievement motivation differences between entrepreneurs and managers. *Journal of Small Business Management*, *45*(4), 401–421. doi:10.1111/j.1540-627X.2007.00220.x

Tan, J., Fischer, E., Mitchell, R., & Phan, P. (2009). At the center of action: Innovation and technology strategy research in the small business setting. *Journal of Small Business Management*, *47*(3), 233–262. doi:10.1111/j.1540-627X.2009.00270.x

Thong, J., Yap, C., & Raman, K. (1994). Engagement of external expertise in information systems implementation. *Journal of Management Information Systems*, *11*(2), 209–223.

Ucbasaran, D., Westhead, P., & Wright, M. (2008). Opportunity identification and pursuit: Does an entrepreneur's human capital matter? *Small Business Economics*, *30*(2), 153–173. doi:10.1007/s11187-006-9020-3

Van Praag, C., & Cramer, J. (2001). The roots of entrepreneurship and labour demand: Individual ability and low risk aversion. *Economica*, *68*(269), 45–62. doi:10.1111/1468-0335.00232

Venkataraman, S. (1997). The distinctive domain of entrepreneurship research. *Entrepreneur Theory and Practice*, *4*(7), 34–45.

Verheul, I., Uhlaner, L., & Thurik, R. (2005). Business accomplishments, gender and entrepreneurial self-image. *Journal of Business Venturing*, *20*(4), 483–518. doi:10.1016/j.jbusvent.2004.03.002

Vroom, V. (1964). *Work and Motivation*. New York: Wiley.

Wagner, J. (2004). What a difference a Y makes – female and male nascent entrepreneurs in Germany. IZA Discussion Paper No. 1134, Institute for the Study of Labour, Bonn.

Ward, T. B. (2004). Cognition, creativity, and entrepreneurship. *Journal of Business Venturing*, *19*(2), 173–188. doi:10.1016/S0883-9026(03)00005-3

Westhead, P., Ucbasaran, D., & Wright, M. (2005a). Decisions, actions, and performance: Do novice, serial, and portfolio entrepreneurs differ? *Journal of Small Business Management*, *43*(4), 393–417. doi:10.1111/j.1540-627X.2005.00144.x

Westhead, P., Ucbasaran, D., & Wright, M. (2005b). Experience and Cognition: Do Novice, Serial and Portfolio Entrepreneurs Differ? *International Small Business Journal*, *23*(1), 72–98. doi:10.1177/0266242605049104

Westhead, P., Ucbasaran, D., Wright, M., & Binks, M. (2005c). Novice, serial, and portfolio entrepreneur behavior and contributions. *Small Business Economics*, *25*(2), 109–132. doi:10.1007/s11187-003-6461-9

Westhead, P., & Wright, M. (1999). Contributions of novice, portfolio and serial founders located in rural and urban areas. *Regional Studies*, *33*(2), 157–173.

Wickham, P. A. (2001). *Strategic Entrepreneurship: A Decision-Making Approach to New Venture Creation and Management*, 2nd Edition, London: Financial Times Pitman Publishing.

York, G. J., & Venkataraman, S. (2010). The entrepreneur-environment nexus: Uncertainty, innovation and allocation. *Journal of Business Venturing*, *25*(5), 449–463. doi:10.1016/j.jbusvent.2009.07.007

Zachary, R. K., & Mishra, C. S. (2010). Entrepreneurship research today and beyond: Hidden in plain sight. *Journal of Small Business Management*, *48*(4), 471–474. doi:10.1111/j.1540-627X.2010.00304.x

Zerbinati, S., & Souitaris, V. Entrepreneurship in the public sector: A framework of analysis in European local governments. *Entrepreneurship and Regional Development*, 17(1), 43-64.

## ADDITIONAL READING

Shane, S. (2007). *A General Theory of Entrepreneurship: The Individual-Opportunity Nexus*. Aldershot: Edward Elgar.

Wickham, P. A. (2001). *Strategic Entrepreneurship: A Decision-Making Approach to New Venture Creation and Management*, 2nd Edition. London: Financial Times Pitman Publishing.

Zhao, F. (2006). *Entrepreneurship and Innovation in E-Business: An Integrative Perspective*. Hershey, PA: IGI Global. doi:10.4018/978-1-59140-920-5

## KEY TERMS AND DEFINITIONS

**Authentic Leader:** Create positive conditions in the small business to improve overall performance.

**Creativity:** The phenomenon of creating something new and valuable.

**Entrepreneur:** A business person who is innovative and willing to accept relatively high risk regarding business ventures.

**Entrepreneurial Process:** Involves a series of activities from starting a business through to maintaining its continued operation.

**Human Capital:** Skills and abilities of a person.

**Innovation:** The application of a better solution to a business requirement.

**Manager:** A person who coordinates the work of others.

**Nascent:** Newly emerging or beginning to exist.

**Novice:** A person who is new to a field or activity.

**Portfolio:** A collection of assets, such as various small businesses owned by an entrepreneur.

**Serial:** Sequential or one after the other, such as an entrepreneur who may own a number of small businesses but one at a time.

**Small Giants:** Small business owners who reject growth in order to focus on improving the quality of current products or services.

**Social Capital:** A person's ability to work with other people.

**Super Achievers:** Outperform other small business owners.

**Theory of Entrepreneurship:** Involves an innovative approach to establishing and maintaining a viable business.

# Chapter 3
# Information Systems


## ABSTRACT

*An information system translates data into information to support business decision making. Data, raw unorganized facts, are gathered relative to a business event. The resulting information, which has meaning in the hands of a user, must be complete and accurate in order to support timely decision making. The acquisition of an information system by a small business will be a relatively costly endeavour. The small business manager will tend to rely upon an internal individual or external organization for advice when acquiring an information system. Further, the information system will be employed to improve the efficiency of daily operations of a small business. This chapter describes information systems. In general, an information system turns data into information to support decision making. The information must be timely, complete, and accurate relative to the decisions which must be made.*


## INTRODUCTION

There are many types of systems, such as the solar system or the nervous system. An information system is one type of system which supports various decision making activities within a business. Information systems may be manual or automated. With a low volume of transactions and few data items a manual information system may suffice. However, as transaction volume increases along with the requirement for more data items an automated information system will become a necessity. This chapter focuses on aspects related to automated information systems.

DOI: 10.4018/978-1-4666-8708-0.ch003

This chapter is organized as follows. To begin, systems in general are described. Then, the terms "information technology" and "information system" are differentiated. The remainder of the chapter is focused on information systems. Next a general information systems diagram serves to explain the components of any information system and its relationship to the business environment. This diagram shows how data becomes information which, in turn, supports decision making. There are different types of information systems depending upon the management level in a business. Each type of information system is designed to address the requirements of decisions necessary at various management levels. The chapter includes a list of commonly used terms which might be encountered by the small business manager. Then an overview of research related to small business and information systems presents a description of small business readiness for the technology. A small business may use information systems to lower costs, increase profits, improve service, or achieve a competitive advantage. More specific research is presented in subsequent chapters. To conclude this chapter a sample investigation is included which outlines further considerations regarding the acquisition of information systems by small business. Project recommendations are made relative to a number of stakeholders as they relate to small business.

## BASIC INFORMATION SYSTEMS

This section provides an overview introduction to the terms and concepts of information systems. There are many material sources on this subject which provide very extensive coverage. However, the goal of the material presented here is to provide an appreciation for information systems and to supply a context for the subsequent discussion of the relationship between small business and information systems.

To begin, a system is a set of components that interact to accomplish a goal. For example:

- The human nervous system contains a network of specialized cells which transmit signals to co-ordinate actions
- The economic system involves producing, distributing, and consuming goods and services along with the compensation for the exchanges
- The transportation system consists of entities (ie. planes, trains, and automobiles) involved in the movement of people
- The monetary system employs government policies and institutions to monitor and control the supply of money in order to affect economic activity.

Two common terms, Information Technology and Information System, tend to be used to mean the same thing. However, in the context presented here these terms will be described to relate to different aspects of computer-based technology. Figure 1 presents a way to differentiate the two terms.

Information Technology relates to the more technical aspects of computers. Thus, Information Technology is composed of Hardware; the Networks that allow computers to communicate with each other; and Systems Software which controls the Hardware and acts as an interface with the Application Software. The term Information Technology may also be referred to as the platform upon which rests the Information System.

Note, as depicted in Figure 1, that Information Technology is a sub-set of the term Information System. Further, this term involves more of the interaction between the computer and those individuals who work in the small business. Thus, People will employ manual Processes to prepare data to be entered into the Application Software. People will also carry out manual processes to ensure the availability of

*Figure 1. Information systems and information technology*

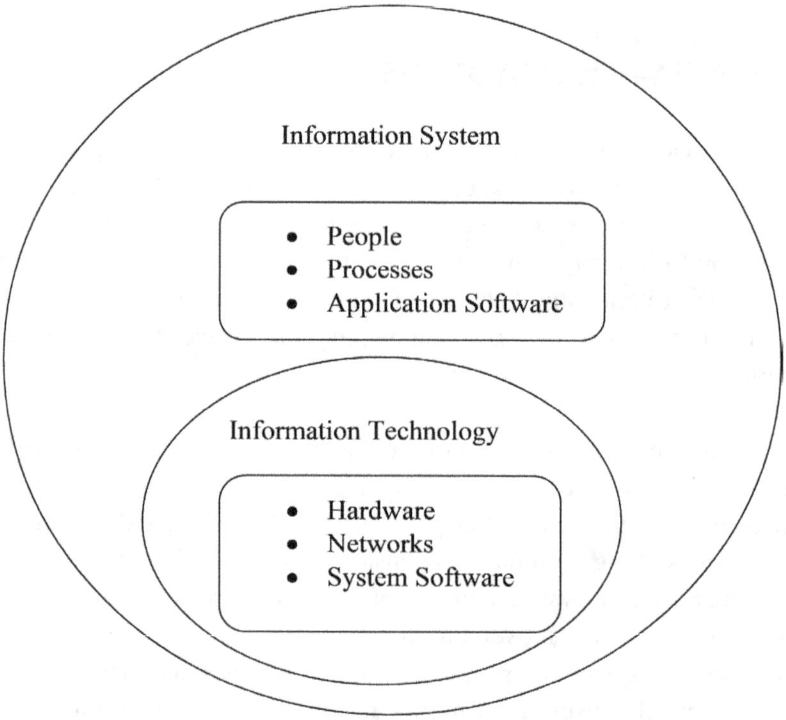

information received from the Application Software which will facilitate and support necessary management decision making. Thus, Information System is an enabler helping employees and management carry out their assigned duties.

In general, Information Systems must be employed to address the overall objectives of the small business. More specifically, Information Systems must support the small business plans. Indeed, the business plan must be developed in consort with the capabilities of the available Information Systems. New business ideas may be facilitated through the consideration and adoption of Information Systems. Further, the concepts of Information Systems may be employed to develop new business initiatives. This latter comment relates to computer literacy which represents an individual's knowledge of the capabilities of computer-based Information Systems along with Information Technology and the ways in which each component functions.

More specifically, an information system exists within a small business, which facilitates the operation of the small business. For a manufacturing business there will be a production system which takes raw material as input and produces finished goods as output. Also, various accounting systems will support the management of a small business. While there are many systems which support the operation of a small business, here are just two examples. An Accounts Payable system will take invoices as input and produce payment to supplies as output. A Payroll system will take time sheets as input and produce payment to employees as output. In both cases these systems will also produce information to support management decisions. Both systems will require funds to cover the expenditures. The information from the Accounts Payable system will allow the analysis of suppliers' volume of transactions. The Payroll systems will facilitate the analysis of labour costs.

Note in the above examples that some form of input must be gathered and processed into information to support management decisions. Examples of definitions of information systems include the following:

- A set of interrelated components that collect, manipulate, and store data, disseminate information, and provide feedback to monitor performance
- An organized combination of people, hardware, software, data, and communications networks that collect data, transform it, and disseminates information.

The second example definition introduces the aspects of technology to support the functions of an information system. While technology is not necessary, in general terms, for the operation of an information system its use is currently extensive. Indeed, while in the past the use of technology may have been considered a "trump card", it is currently regarded as "table stakes". That is, without technology the small business may simply be not in the game. Thus, throughout this book information systems supported by technology is considered to be a given relationship in supporting the operation of a small business.

The following narrative describes the generic information system diagram depicted in Figure 2.

**Data** are raw unorganized facts in the business environment. The data must be collected and organized so that it may be used within the information system. For example, a person's name may be organized by surname, first given name, and second given name. A date may be arranged in many formats depicting year, month, and day. But, the arrangement must coincide with that which is expected by the information system. The data may be gathered manually on a form (called a source document) or it may be collected via a computer screen. This dialogue may be controlled in a number of ways, such as: optical scanning; menu selection; prompts; or fill in the blanks.

Once gathered the data is passed over the threshold separating the business environment from the information system and becomes **Input**. Now it is expressed in the language of the information system and in a pre-determined format. In automated information systems the language (digital) is that of the computer. The input resides in the computer for immediate or future use.

*Figure 2. General information systems diagram*

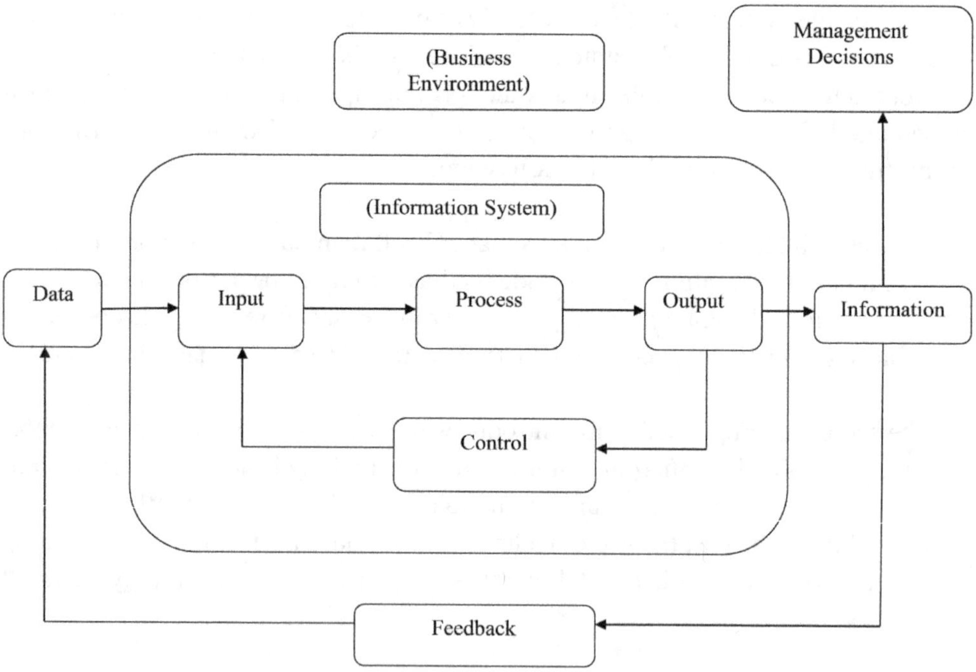

Data is transformed into information through various **processes** applied to the input. There are five generic processes:

- Calculate
- Compare
- Sort
- Classify
- Summarize

**Output** is the transformed input which resides within the information system until it is required by the user. Because the output remains within the information system it is still expressed in the language of the system. The output may be stored as fields and records within files; or as elements and structures in databases.

An internal **Control** loop ensures that the information system performs as it was designed. This loop may check to ensure that all name fields consist of alphabetical characters. It may also perform checks to highlight numeric fields that exceed a certain value. So, it may be decided that if the gross pay field exceeds a certain value the system will highlight that employee.

**Information** is data organized in a meaningful way for the user and is presented external to the information system back in the business environment. The information may be transmitted to the user on a computer display; on paper; or in audio. The information may be used for two purposes (Management Decisions and Feedback) as explained below.

An external **Feedback** loop will also ensure that the information system performs as it was designed. In this case the checks are performed outside the information system through manual processes. So, the given name field might be compared to the gender field for consistency.

Figure 3 depicts the types of decisions made at different levels of management and the information systems which support the managers in their decision making process. The triangle in the figure represents the management hierarchy in a business. There are four generic functions within a business. To begin (BUY) raw material must be purchased. Then, the material must be processed (MAKE) into finished product. Note that this may apply equally well, conceptually, to the acquisition and development of a service. Once completed the product must be distributed and sold (SELL). Finally, an administrative function is necessary to (KEEP TRACK) of the activities of the other three functions.

Decisions are made at the different levels of management. There is a continuum of decisions from structured to unstructured. In general, with structured decisions the decision variables and their values are known. Thus, the amount of an invoice should be paid if the goods have been received and the due date is soon. Unstructured

*Figure 3. Information systems in business*

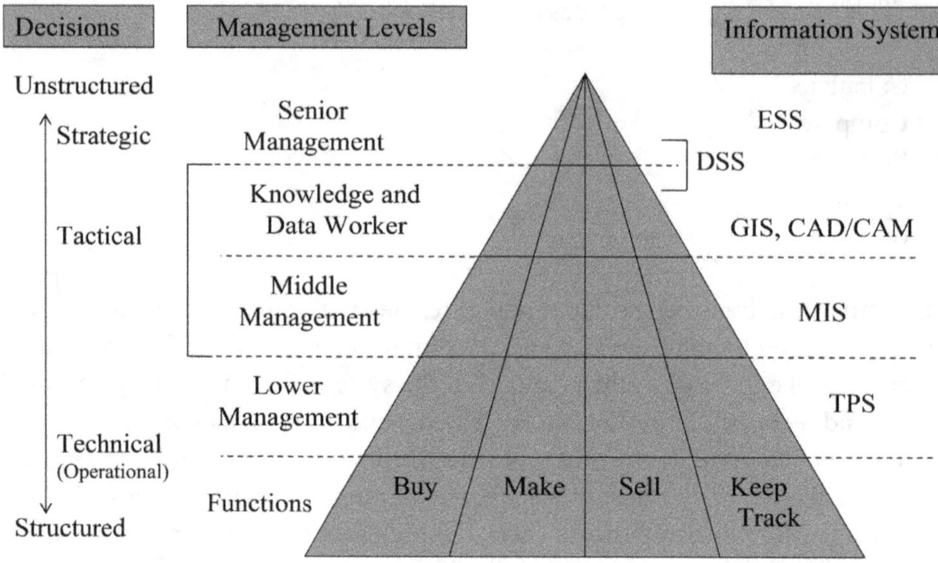


decisions are those where the decision variables are unknown or unclear. So, an example involves deciding whether a small business should venture into a new geographical area to sell a product or provide a service.

Lower Management make structured decisions which are technical or operational in nature. These decisions relate to the near term and are repetitive. The payment of an invoice, as explained above, is an example. Further, these types of decisions can be relatively easily incorporated into an information system. The general type of information system is a Transaction Processing System (TPS). These systems take as input the evidence of a business event (an invoice) and produce output (payment). This process is an accounts Payable information system. Also, information may be provided about amounts paid to specific suppliers or expenditures which should be expected based upon impending due dates of a number of invoices.

Middle Management and Knowledge and Data Workers make Tactical decisions. Note that Middle Management supervises Lower Management. Knowledge and Data Workers are experts in a specific area and may work on their own or with few support staff. Tactical decisions are longer range than Technical decisions and the decision variables are somewhat vague. So, Middle Management might make decisions about budgeting for specific programs or parts of the business. Management Information Systems (MIS) will support the further development of the budget and may incorporate relevant data external to the business such as the price of fuel or a necessary commodity. Knowledge and Data Workers make decisions relative to their area of expertise. Thus, geologists will make decisions in an oil exploration business about where to locate the next well. A Geographic Information Systems (GIS) will support this decision based upon seismic data and the location of existing oil wells. A design engineer will focus on the components of a new product and how it may be assembled. Computer Aided Design/Computer Aided Manufacture (CAD/CAM) systems will support the functions of this expert.

Senior Management makes strategic decisions which are unstructured and unique. They may decide to initiate a new program or develop a new product or service. The decisions only occur once and may have a major impact on the business. A Decision Support System (DSS) will provide some guidance but the final decision rests with the senior manager. Note that Decision Support Systems may also support the Knowledge and Data Worker.

Also, Senior Management may also be supported by Executive Support Systems (ESS). By design, information is pulled from all the other information systems. However, an Executive Information System is designed to push information to Senior Management. An example is an information system which notifies the senior manager when a stock price (the business' or a competitor) varies by a predetermined percentage.

Note that the four functions in the diagram depict fewer individuals in the higher levels of management. Also, the triangle shows what is referred to as "silos". That is, information in the business tends to be passed up and down the business functions. The information at the lower level is detailed while summary information is passed up the management hierarchy. There may be a limited amount of information exchanged across the functional areas. To improve this exchange integrated cross-functional information systems may be implemented. These systems are known as Enterprise Resource Planning (ERP). Figure 4 shows the generic components of a cross-functional information system.

To begin, note that the triangle in Figure 4 represents the same functions that are included in Figure 3. A large corporate-wide Data Warehouse will include all of the data necessary for the business. The cross-functional information system will have the capability of tracking people, products, and services across the major functions of the business. Data Marts, depicted by ovals within each of the four functions, provide function specific information. Thus, for BUY supplier trends may be included in the Data Mart. For MAKE productivity trends may be identified. For SELL geographic area sales information may be stored. A plethora of statistics may be stored for KEEP TRACK. These may include administrative expenses or asset depreciation amounts.

*Figure 4. Cross-functional information system*

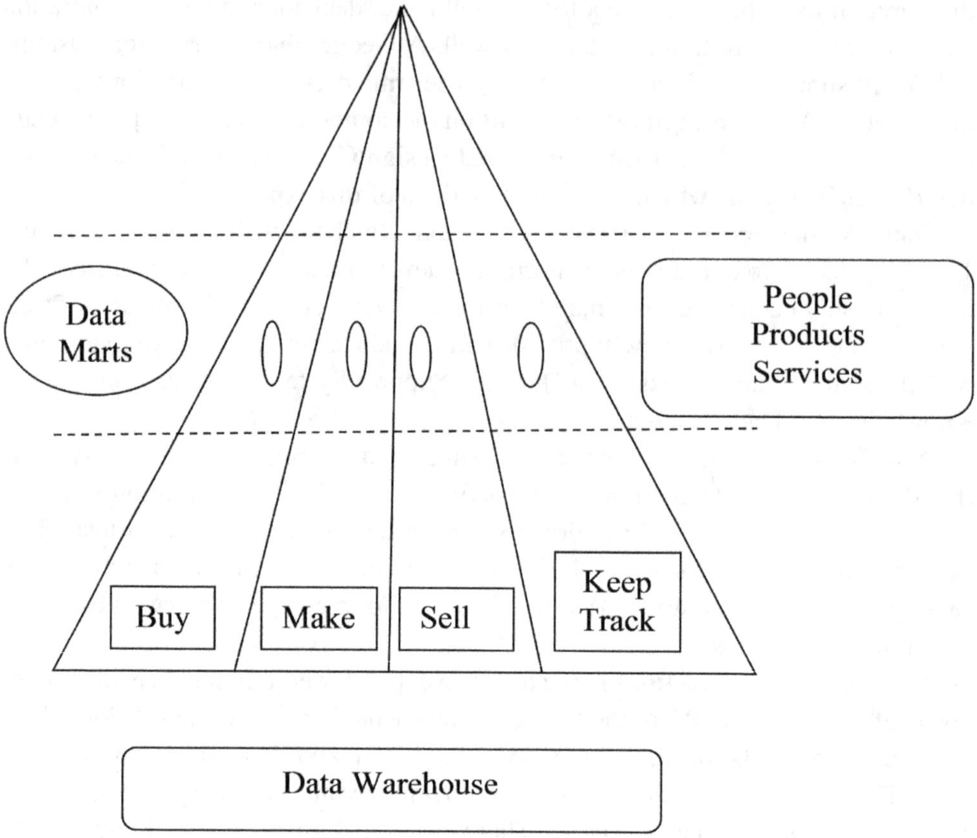


## OTHER TECHNOLOGY TERMS

The following list is meant to provide an overall understanding of terms that a small business manager may encounter. The terms are presented in alphabetical order.

- Backups
    - Copies of important files. These files for example may be about customers, products, or inventory. They should be stored in an off-site location. This is an important aspect related to business continuity. If something untoward transpires at the location of the main information system these off-site files may be employed to ensure continued operation of the small business.
- Client-Server

- A user's computer (Client) accesses programs and data via a host computer (Server). The objective is to balance the processing between the Client and the Server computers. In general, the Client is responsible for the user interface and the Server is where the data is stored. For larger applications there may be more than one Server in order to better balance the load of processing requirements.

- Cloud Computing
  - Location-independent computing services for hardware and software. The locations may be "public" which employs the Internet. Security is controlled through passwords and perhaps encryption of data. Alternatively, a "private" cloud environment may be established where only the one business has access to the cloud network and hardware. The benefits of Cloud computing relate to the model of pay per usage. Because of economies of scale Cloud computing may be cheaper than in-house processing. Further, if the business needs to run software more often, or requires a larger space for data this can be accomplished quite easily and there is simply an increase in costs.
- Computer Crime
  - The commission of illegal acts through the use of a computer or against a computer. Crimes against the computer involve the destruction of physical hardware. More commonly computers are used to commit a crime usually to perpetrate a fraud. Thus, data may be altered or finances may be absconded from accounts payable or payroll systems.
- Commercial Software
  - Pre-coded software for general business purposes or specific industry applications. Packaged software may be for general purposes or specific business functions. General purpose software would include word processors or spreadsheets where the user would develop a specific use. Packages for specific business functions would involve functions such as payroll or accounts payable. In this latter case it is important that the features of the package quite closely reflect the way the business carries out the function. For instance, while a payroll system should pay employees there might be a requirement to provide the option to pay weekly, bi-weekly or monthly. Another term is "Turnkey System" which usually involves a service which includes both hardware and software.
- Customer Relationship Management
  - Software that facilitates dealing with customers. Information about returning customers will aid in providing specific service. Previous purchases may be track and potential sales may be identified. Further, new customers may be contacted to increase sales.

- Database
  - A method of data storage that supports the grouping of data in a way that reflects how the business is run. In a small business a relational database may be employed. This type of data base will group data into tables that are related in some way to each other. Thus, for instance, there will be a customer table that is linked to a specific customer's orders. In turn, the orders will be related to the available products in the inventory of the small business.
- Firewall
  - Software and hardware that provides security by forcing all network transmissions through a control point. Security rules are enforced for all data entering or leaving the host computer. This is a good way to prevent viruses and worms from infecting the computers of businesses.
- Graphical User Interface (GUI)
  - Type of user – computer interface based on pictures which represent desired functions. So, instead of entering a command into the computer, a user simply clicks on a picture (also known as an icon) which initiates the processing of a specific function. GUI is the most common form of computer interface for users.
- Help Desk
  - A place where users can get answers about how to run hardware and software. A Help desk is the first level of support provided to users. Most issues are resolved at this level. If the issue cannot be resolved it may be elevated to a problem report and dealt with through training of the user or a system modification. This latter action may result in system maintenance.
- Internet
  - A global system of interconnected computer networks. The backbone is the main network connections and telecommunication lines. Many smaller networks are connected to this backbone to form the entire Internet. Within a business the concepts of the Internet may be employed between internal locations. This is referred to as an Intranet. If two or more businesses connect their Intranets this is known as an Extranet. Businesses which conduct a lot of transactions would employ a form of Extranet.
- Legacy System
  - Old but still functioning systems which may not be providing all of the necessary functions. For many reasons, usually related to finances,

management is not prepared to invest in updating these systems. Thus, an issue may arise regarding integration of these legacy systems with newer information systems.

- Local Area Network (LAN)
  - A network that connects computers and other hardware (printers) at a single location usually one building. Other types of networks include Metropolitan Area Network (MAN) and Wide Area Network (WAN). These networks represent a continuum of increased geographic space. Further, a Value added Network (VAN) provides the ability to communicate and also some information which may add value to network members, such as stock exchanges. In order to provide security some networks are restricted to individuals who register on the network and receive a user name and password. These networks are referred to as a Virtual Private Network (VPN).
- Network
  - A collection of interconnected computers. Bandwidth is a term which represents the transmission capacity of the network. It is measured in bits per second.
- Off-site storage
  - A remote location used to safeguard valuable data. This is where back files are stored. The location should be secure. It should also be in a different location from the main processing but easily accessed in the case of an emergency.
- Output Controls
  - Procedures to ensure information is not lost, misdirected, or corrupted and privacy is ensured. Information may be presented to users through computer screens or as printed reports. The decision about which to employ is based upon the users' need for a hard copy of the information. The users must receive the information within their decision-making time frame.
- Outsourcing
  - The process of hiring another organization to perform a service. The service could relate to hardware software, or project management. Offshore outsourcing relates to acquiring the services of a business in another country. The value of outsourcing is the accessing of skills that do not exist with the business. Alternatively, some suggest that a business should not outsource its core competence.
- Password
  - Secret code to allow users to gain access to a computer or data files. The code should be relatively complex and difficult for some to deter-

mine. Further, the code should be kept private and should be changed frequently. Passwords are just one form of authentication. Others include biometrics (physical characteristics) and voice recognition (vocal characteristics).

- Privacy
  - Ensure personal data is held in confidence. Most countries have privacy laws. These laws relate to an individual's right to determine what information may be gathered about them and with whom it may be shared.
- Supply Chain Management
  - Software that integrates inbound logistics of material used to produce products. The chain entails raw materials which flow into the production process to finished goods and distributed through warehouses to customers. Also included are all financial obligations which occur through the process.
- System Development Life Cycle (SDLC)
  - Process used to develop information systems. The process starts with the user identifying an issue or opportunity. Requirements are identified which will address the issue or opportunity. These requirements form the based for the design of an information system. The cycle is complete when the system is installed and turned over to the user.

## SMALL BUSINESS AND INFORMATION SYSTEMS RESEARCH

This section briefly outlines research about small business readiness to acquire information systems. Further, issues related to various stakeholders regarding small business and information systems are reviewed. Note that subsequent chapters provide more detail about small business and information systems. Chapter Four – Theories for Investigations presents general research theories about small business and information systems. Chapter Five – Adoption reports on the process of initially identifying an issue through to adopting an information system to respond to the issue. Chapter Six – Use describes how the information system is employed within a small business. An information system may be used to support deferent levels of management decision making. There may be issues in interacting with the information system which may impact user satisfaction. Chapter Seven – Strategy describes how small business may employ information systems in a strategic manner in order to gain competitive advantage. Chapter Eight – Competitive Advantage continues this discussion about how small business may improve operating efficiencies and offer different products or services than its competitors.

Haug et al (2011) investigated the readiness of small business to acquire information systems. Table 1 provides an outline of their framework. The framework identifies three categories of characteristics related to Company, Management, and employee.

The Company characteristics relate to pressure to change and willingness to accept risk. In both situations responses involve the application of information technology. Pressure to change is mainly external to the small business originating from competition, suppliers, customers, government, consultants, or vendors. A response here will involve the use of information technology to attempt to contribute to competitive advantage (Earl, 1989; Galliers & Sutherland, 1999; and Turban et al, 2003). Internally information technology may be applied in order to achieve more efficient processing of transactions in systems that support daily operations (Hollander et al, 2000). Risk involves the willingness to apply scarce resources of the small business to the implementation of information technology to address the above changes. Recall the term resource poverty (Thong, 1999). With limited resources the small business may hesitate to apply information technology because of the risk of failure (Agarwal & Prasad, 2000; and Love et al, 2001).

Management characteristics include knowledge of information technology and willingness to support information technology projects. Adequate knowledge of information technology, through education and experience, will contribute to the adoption of information technology (Venkatesh & Brown, 2001; Lewis & Cockrill, 2002; and Teo & Pian, 2003). Further, management will support information technology projects if they recognize that potential benefits will exceed the estimated costs. Project success is significantly impacted by management who support change through the application of information technology (Sharma & Rai, 2003; and Pitt et al, 2006).

The third characteristic for assessing information technology readiness relates to Employees including their skills and motivation. From the user's perspective, employees who interact directly with information technology, appropriate skills may be acquired through education and experience. Employee motivation will relate to how confident theyt feel about using the information technology and their future roll after implementation (Love et al, 2001; and Drew, 2003).

Haug et al (2011) further suggest that each of the three characteristics may be presented as a series of continua regarding information technology readiness. Thus, a small business may reflect information technology readiness if:

- The Company is pressured to change and is willing to accept risk
- Management is acquainted with information technology and willing to provide support
- Employees possess the necessary information technology skills and a positive attitude toward information technology implementation.

*Table 1. A framework for assessing the it readiness of SMES*

| Characteristics | Examples |
|---|---|
| *Company Characteristics* | |
| Pressure to change existing processes | • Technological abilities of competitors<br>• Ability to manage information internally<br>• Demands from customers and suppliers |
| Room for risk | • Profit ratio<br>• Net capital<br>• Banking relations |
| *Management Characteristics* | |
| IT acquaintance | • IT related education<br>• Experience from participation in IT projects<br>• Experience from using IT |
| IT project support | • Time for carrying out existing responsibilities<br>• Experience from IT projects<br>• Room for initiating risky projects |
| *Employee Characteristics* | |
| IT skills | • IT related education<br>• Experience from participation in IT projects<br>• Experience from using IT |
| IT project attitude | • Job development potential<br>• Multitude of employee abilities<br>• Relation to management |

Adapted from Haug et al, 2011

Pett and Wolff (2012) investigated differences in various sizes of small business. They identified a series of dimensions including entrepreneurial orientation, learning orientation, information technology competency, firm profitability, and growth. A comment about the information technology competency dimension is as follows:

*Top management teams that understand the importance of information technology and develop the competency to effectively us IT may be able to reap dividends on the profit performance end. (Pett & Wolff, 2012, p. 56)*

A higher level of IT competency may also be facilitated by advances in computing power along with lower costs per function, and improvements in the ease of use of computers for those with relatively little training (Pett & Wolff, 2012).

## A SAMPLE INVESTIGATION

The research described in this section presents the results of an investigation of how information systems are employed by small businesses in a small city in western Canada (Hunter, 2003). In general, information systems used by small businesses is an under-researched subject, as most investigations adopt a large business perspective. There are differences between large and small businesses in how they employ information systems. The data gathered in this project represents a continuation and expansion of investigations initiated by the researcher regarding the use of information systems by small businesses. The findings support previous research, which identified themes relating to "dependency" on a specific individual or another organization and "efficiency" of daily operations. Based upon the comments of the managers included in this research project, the results indicate that the current use of information systems follows a pattern that is very consistent with the way in which other resources are used by small business. While further research is needed, it may be suggested that the challenge associated with the adoption of information systems presents itself not only to the small business manager, but also to a series of stakeholders involved in the management of small businesses, including the managers of small businesses, and various external entities including information systems vendors, consultants, and administrators of government sponsored small business programs.

Information systems are creating a significant impact on the roles and work of individuals, and information system enabled change is revolutionizing businesses processes (Coghlan, 2001). There has been a consequent plethora of research into how business can best use information systems or adapt to information system precipitated change. While there has been considerable research into the way in which large businesses use this technology, there has been far less attention paid to the adoption of information systems among small businesses. This is surprising considering that the innovative capacity of a nation's economy to meet changing demands in the global economy has been linked to the flexibility and responsiveness of small businesses (Balderson, 2011).

This issue is important to several stakeholders. First, it is important to small businesses themselves that aim to use the technology to gain a competitive advantage. Second, it is important to consultants whose aim it is to help small businesses add value through the use of the technology. Third, it is important to vendors who aim to target this burgeoning market by being better able to service its needs. Finally, it is important to government policymakers in their effort to support the growth of the small business sector through use of technology.

As one of many resources a small business might use, information technology typically involves not only a significant investment of effort, time and capital it can also be a potentially high maintenance activity. On the one hand, when viewed in terms of a company's flexibility, such an investment could pose a serious constraint when it demands a permanent commitment to a certain technology or software. On the other hand, such an investment has tremendous potential to increase the speed at which business can respond to customers and market opportunities.

Research undertaken by Lin et al. (1993) determined that the deregulation of the telecommunications industry would allow more small businesses to compete with large businesses. It was felt that the impending wide spread use of the Internet would make E-commerce concepts more attractive to small business. Beyond these technologies, research (Berman, 1997; Canadian Federation of Independent Business, 1999) also found that momentum for the adoption of information technology by small businesses came from a number of sources. First, small businesses were reacting to actions of competition in adopting information technology. Second, because of the aforementioned deregulation and the prevalent use of information technology, the cost to implement was becoming within the reach of small businesses. Third, the technology was becoming more reliable and powerful. Fourth, small businesses started to see the adoption of information technology as a way to compete with larger companies (Timmons, 1999).

Although some studies (Bridge & Peel, 1999; Fuller, 1996) have found small and medium sized firms (SMEs) are using information technology mainly for operational and administrative tasks, others (Bennett & McCoshan, 1993; Chen & Williams, 1993; Pollard & Hayne, 1998; Timmons, 1999; Van de Ven, 1993) suggest the technology is playing a more strategic role. These somewhat conflicting results suggest that the extent to which small businesses are utilizing information technology for strategic purposes is unclear. Indeed, much of the research that has been conducted relates mainly to *plans* small businesses have with regard to information technology. For example, El Louadi (1998) found that small businesses were prepared to invest more resources in information technology. However, the nature of the actual investment is not clear. Thus, the research reported below investigates *how* the technology is currently being employed by small businesses.

The results of the above interviews and subsequent analysis of the data suggests the adoption of information technology by small businesses present many challenges. Two major themes emerged from the interview data: Dependency and Efficiency. The discussion that follows is not meant to indicate a relative level of importance of these two themes. Indeed, the relative importance would be contingent upon the situation unique to each small business.

## Theme 1: Dependency

The adoption of information technology increased dependency within the businesses. It was determined from the interview data that dependency related to either reliance on an internal individual (network administrator or information technology champion) or an external entity (consultants, customers, suppliers, competitors). The increase in dependency tends to increase the risk to the firm as noted in the discussion of the findings, which follow.

## 'Internal' Dependency

In most of the firms interviewed, an internal 'champion' or key information technology employee was responsible for the majority of information technology usage, upgrades and maintenance. Previous research (Montazami, 1988; Thong et al., 1994) has shown that internal expertise in information systems is preferred to external for small firms. However, respondents in the current study noted inhibitors such as high salaries and limited need for internal expertise to be problems. In the majority of the firms interviewed, the internal 'champion' tended to be an individual who took on the role as an ancillary task since a full time individual could not be justified. In one instance, an administrative assistant had taken some upgrading courses to allow performance of basic network administration while in another firm a full-time engineer would spend a day or more per week dealing with information technology issues and administration.

It may be surmised that information technology is seen as an ancillary task, related primarily to administration decisions. Consequently, it may receive sub-optimal attention by the small business owner in a busy work environment. This organizational structure may reduce the effectiveness of information technology in the firm but, as importantly, it makes the owner very dependent upon staff regarding the design and operation of the information system. The typical reliance on one individual (in our findings this was rarely the owner/manager) increases the risk to the firm if that individual were to leave. Being placed in this precarious position presents a challenge to the owner/manager's self-reliance. Much of the success enjoyed by small businesses stems from the owner/manager's knowledge, skills and/or abilities in the specific area of operation or activity. If information technology begins to play a key role in the operation of the business, it may mean that the owner/manager no longer has intimate knowledge of all aspects of the business.

## 'External' Dependency

In most instances, the decision regarding hardware or software applications tended to be based upon the advice or influence of a competitor, customer, supplier, or outside consultant. There was little evidence to indicate that a systematic assessment was made of how well the available offerings could meet the business's specific needs.

The use of a particular information technology application by a major competitor often made it necessary, as interpreted by the manager, for the small business to follow suit in order to retain the current customer base or potentially attract new business.

This illustrates a dependency on information technology, which can result in risky expenditures. Previous research has concluded that competitive forces had little effect on the adoption or extent of use of information technology in small firms (Thong et al., 1994). However, the research reported here suggests that in at least some small firm's competition is driving information technology adoption.

For many small firms, the adoption of information technology is perceived to be a necessity in order to maintain relations with suppliers. In several instances the firms had made significant capital expenditures in order to maintain supply chain relationships and not risk the loss of major customers.

Generally, there was little evidence that the key decision-makers were fully aware of the scope of products available and the extent to which product performance might vary in meeting a specific business need. Moreover, in no case was there any long-term information technology strategy. On the one hand, this could be viewed as a weakness but on the other it could be viewed as a way to increase the firm's capacity to respond to customer needs. Since small business owner/managers were found to either contract out or delegate responsibility for maintaining the information system or determining future requirements, they are very dependent upon the quality of the advice they receive from others. In some instances this advice may not lead to the optimal decision for the business.

Overall, dependency of small firms in relation to information technology seems to be widespread as discussed in this section. As stated, the dependency itself is not completely negative as it allows the small business to focus on its niche. However, failure to ensure adequate knowledge of information technology and at least some strategic vision does cause the risks inherent in these dependency relationships to become greater.

## Theme 2: Efficiency

Despite all the technological advances and calls for the strategic use of information technology by small business (Pollard & Hayne, 1998) it is still being employed primarily at the transactional/operational level. The findings of this research project suggest very little strategic use of information technology, as small business managers were primarily interested in using information technology as an operational tool. This term is referred to in this chapter as efficiency indicating that small businesses are still focused on getting things done as opposed to effectiveness or doing the right things. Information technology effectiveness is defined as the extent to which a given information system contributes to the achievement of organizational goals (Bridge & Peel, 1999; Thong et al, 1994).

For the majority of small businesses, the key benefit from information technology is the reduction of resources required to perform operational tasks – accounting, design, inventory management, invoicing, estimating and marketing/sales.

Alternatively, the general absence of strategic information technology deployment might be explained by the nature of resource commitments made in small firms. Arguably, if information technology were to be deployed to all functional areas of a firm, this would involve a large one-time commitment of financial and other resources (for example, training of personnel). While such an investment is consistent with the business practices of large firms, it is not characteristic of the way in which resource commitments are made by small firms. As indicated previously, our findings support the contention that small businesses tend to make minimal and multi-staged commitments. Arguably, large one-time commitments may make it difficult to use information technology strategically as the rapid changes in hardware and software applications could render incremental implementation virtually impossible. Moreover, it is possible that the current under-utilization of information technology for strategic advantage may result from owner/managers not having the experience or knowledge base to be able to fully recognize opportunities for doing so. Clearly, in order to shift from a focus on efficiency to that of effectiveness, the challenges associated with committing resources to information technology will need to be dealt with. The next section contains suggestions that attempt to address this situation.

The small business sector's current interest in the use of information technology is a fairly recent phenomenon. For example, in the mid 1980's Malone (1985) found that small businesses were not capitalizing on information technology. He attributed small businesses' failure to widely incorporate information technology into the firm to a lack of financial resources, an emphasis on a short-term decision making time frame, and a lack of formalized systems. Yet, if these factors are inherent aspects of small business practice as suggested in the previous section, they would not adequately explain the small business sector's current interest and momentum for taking advantage of information technology.

In noting a growing interest among small businesses in adopting information technology into operations during the early 1990's, research (Lin et al, 1993; Berman 1997; Canadian Federation of Independent Business 1999) indicated that the momentum for information technology has come from various sources. Firstly, small businesses were becoming concerned about the adoption of information technology by competition. Secondly, small businesses were considering the adoption of information technology because it was becoming more affordable, reliable and powerful. Thirdly, it was being perceived as a way to increase a firm's capacity to compete with large firms (Timmons 1999). For example, Lin et al (1993) reported that small business leaders felt that the deregulation of the telecommunications industry would enable small businesses to mask their size from external parties, thereby allowing them to compete on a level playing field with larger businesses. Finally, the recent widespread availability of the Internet has made e-commerce opportunities more attractive and viable.

In examining the use of information technology among small businesses, earlier research (Nickell & Seado, 1986) indicates that information technology mainly was being employed for accounting and administrative purposes. While small businesses seem to be well positioned to potentially capitalize on opportunities to use technology in responding to market changes in a timely and effective way (Berman 1997), there has been little research to determine the extent to which information technology is being used strategically. Although El Louadi (1998) found that small businesses are prepared to invest more resources in information technology, whether the role of information technology has shifted from that of supporting operational and administrative functions (Fuller, 1996) to a more strategic role in searching for and capitalizing on opportunities has yet to be determined. With the small business sector now recognized as being one of the fastest growing segments of the economy (Bennett & McCoshan 1993), and responsible for much of the innovation that now assumes such a strategic role in the global economy (Van de Ven, 1993; Timmons, 1999), it is important to determine the extent to which the small business sector is utilizing information technology for strategic purposes.

## Project Recommendations

In light of the emerging themes identified above, it is evident that the nature of small business practice presents some unique challenges in regard to the adoption of information technology. This section presents a number of recommendations for various stakeholders – small business managers, consultants, vendors, and government – intent on increasing the strategic use of information technology within the small business sector. These suggestions take into consideration the themes identified in this research project and data gleaned from other sources.

## Small Business Manager

In light of the characteristics of small business practice the following suggestions relate to making decisions and obtaining advice.

First, decision-making needs to be related to a long-term strategy. It is recognized that while small business managers tend not to engage in a formal strategic planning process, they usually have a future vision of what they want to accomplish. Therefore, the manager should at least be aware that quick decisions, made perhaps on a sales presentation, may not be in the best interests of achieving the long-term vision the owner/manager has for the firm. Thus due consideration should be given to decisions, especially those relating to the acquisition of information technology.

Second, the small business manager should establish a relationship with a specific individual regarding a source for advice. The following steps are suggested. To begin, the manager should "shop around' to find an individual with whom they may feel comfortable in working with and taking advice. In order to find this person the manager should rely upon his or her informal network. Thus individuals could be contacted who are in a similar business sector or who may be using the same technology. Then, it is important to ensure that those contacted in both the informal network and those who will provide the advice, do not have a vested interest in a particular product. That is, the small business manager should not rely upon hardware or software vendors for advice. The recommendation is for the manager to establish a relationship with someone who is independent of a specific solution and who will be prepared to play a strategic role taking a long-term perspective. Further, the small business manager must re-assess this relationship periodically. It is incumbent upon the manager to review the relationship to ensure that the recommendations being proffered are appropriately contributing to the long-term success of the firm. This advice is consistent with that of Stevenson and Sahlman (in Timmons 1999) who suggest doing two seemingly contradictory things when seeking to hire a consultant: seek out the best advisors, involving them early and more thoroughly than in the past. At the same time, be more sceptical of their credentials and their advice.

In addition, under the dependency theme, since the small firm is very focused on the 'bottom-line' it would be advisable to avoid being an early adopter of new hardware and/or software applications. Deferring adoption until the hardware and/or software has a proven performance capacity will help minimize financial risk. Unsuccessful forays into the information technology area can be expensive. A recent example, albeit a large company in Nova Scotia is Sobeys Inc. who abandoned an $89.1 million system due to incompatible application problems (Mearian and Songini, 2001). Thus small business owners may wish to wait to find out whether a particular information technology will add value or just add expense.

One final recommendation, to overcome the focus on efficiency exclusively, small business managers should take a more proactive approach toward the adoption of information technology. This would involve actively seeking out ways to leverage information technology to create or improve products or services offered to customers. While information technology in itself is not a source of competitive advantage, as it is readily available and easily duplicated, the way in which it is utilized may be difficult for other businesses to copy. For example, if the small business provides a very specialized service, it might use the web to collaborate with other firms that provide complementary services but who may be spread out across the country or the globe. By being able to 'bundle' their services, this 'virtual' firm now has a collective capacity to provide an offering that might be difficult for others to match in terms of quality or cost. Because no one firm has to develop and maintain multiple areas of expertise the overhead is lower and pricing competitive. What this would mean for the individual firm is that it would not be as dependent upon a single (or few) key customer. Such action, therefore, would increase efficiency and effectiveness, as well as the firm's capacity for flexibility and responsiveness to the needs and demands of the market.

## Consultant

In facing issues where expertise is lacking, such as those relating to the use of information technology, hiring a consultant is a common practice (Timmons, 1999). However, currently there is little evidence to suggest that consultants fully understand and consider the implications of how business practices vary between small and large firms. For example, Atlantic Progress (Strowbridge, 1999) prepared a feature article where two major consulting firms were commissioned to analyze the operations of two Atlantic Canadian small businesses and recommend technologies that could help the firms accomplish key business objectives. Indeed, their recommendations would require a large-scale commitment of resources at one point in time, which is akin to the resource commitments of corporations.

Clearly, it is important for consultants to recognize that in regard to the nature, timing and acquisition of resources, the small businessperson generally aims to minimize the amount of resources used at each stage of the firm's growth. As our findings indicate, the resources allocated for IT are consistent with this practice. Since small business people are concerned with being able to use a resource rather than owning it, this suggests that there may be opportunities for expanding currently available leasing options. Such an approach could reduce some of the risk in pursuing opportunities. For example, if less capital is required, the financial exposure and risk is reduced. Moreover, it could increase flexibility since commitment and de-commitment can be achieved quickly when a resource is not owned.

In aiming to meet the needs of the small business sector Timmons (1999:331) provides the following advice concerning the desirable qualities in a consultant: "a shirtsleeve approach to the problems, an understanding attitude toward the feelings of managers, a modest and truthful offer of services and an ability to produce results, a reasonable and realistic charge for services, and a willingness to maintain a continuous relationship".

Generally, consultants need to be able to provide opportunities for small businesses to 'phase in' information technology in stages. Doing so will accommodate small business practice and form the foundation for a potentially ongoing relationship.

## Vendors

In this context, vendors are regarded as those entities, which supply hardware and software to small businesses. The recommendations for this stakeholder group relate to commitment, functionality, and decisions.

The first suggestion is that vendors make a visible commitment to small business. Far too often vendors provide products or services based upon a geographic distribution. Vendors should consider the establishment of a more sector-oriented approach. Thus, the establishment of a division or even a separate entity specifically directed at small business is recommended. This act would address, to some extent, the concerns of the small business manager, regarding priority of service.

Second, vendors should develop solutions with the functionality of small business in mind. Software vendors must ensure that an application performs the necessary functions for small business. This requires the identification of what the small business does and the interpretation of that into the appropriate functionality of the application. Again, the important word here is "appropriate". Thus, it is incumbent upon the vendor to ensure the hardware or software addresses the appropriate functionality of the small business. A solution with too much capacity will not be helpful. A solution, which provides an unrequired capability, will also not be helpful.

Finally, the vendor representative should investigate who makes, or helps make the decisions in the small business. There will be, usually, one individual within the small business who has responsibility for IT decisions. But, as suggested above, there should also be an advisor (or consultant) who will provide input. Information about proposed solutions should also be supplied to this second individual. In deed in some cases this person may be the more important decision-maker.

## Government

Focusing on the research findings, if government aims to encourage the growth of the small business sector through the use of information technology they cannot ignore the financial constraints small business faces. Government can help overcome the resource poverty small businesses cope with by providing information technology advice to small business and by providing financial incentives.

While Canadian small businesses have been found to use outside professional services, many small businesses report that the fees for this service are excessive (Zinger et al, 1996). As securing advising relationships on information technology is important for the small business owner, providing specific, cost effective, information technology assistance would indeed be a valuable service.

As well, when faced with competing operational needs, tradeoffs are invariably required. If information technology is not perceived to be essential, it is unlikely opportunities to use information technology will be explored. Fundamentally, if government aims to encourage the growth and development of the small business sector, the role of tax and other financial incentives may need to be considered in encouraging both the use of information technology to improve how things are done (efficiency) and what things are done (effectiveness).

Finally, although there are a number of services which have been established to provide support to small business, often they are underutilized by small businesses (Zinger et al, 1996). Therefore, it is recommended that government services be provided on a more pro-active basis. By initiating relationships with small business managers, individuals representing government services can more effectively support these managers by tapping into their informal networks to provide and exchange required information.

While the findings of this research project indicate that information technology has increased the efficiency of various aspects of daily operations, they also indicate that the capacity of information technology to increase the business's effectiveness was being underutilized. Generally, the evidence suggests that information technology expenditures are being made in reaction to needs or problems.

Based on the in-depth experiences of ten businesses, the results of this investigation indicate that the current use of information technology follows a pattern that is very consistent with the way in which other resources are used by small businesses. There was little evidence of a willingness or ability to make a large one-time financial commitment to integrate information technology into all aspects of the firm. Arguably, even if a firm had the financial wherewithal to make such a commitment, doing so would compromise the flexibility and responsiveness that is the hallmark of the small business sector. While further research is needed before these results could be generalized, they do suggest that the greatest challenge associated with the adoption of information technology presents itself not to the small business sector, but to its constituents – consultants, vendors and government.

If the aim is to support the growth and development of the small business sector, then the onus is on others – for example, vendors to design software that can be adopted modularly - to provide products and/or services that are conducive to doing so. If the adoption of information technology would complement rather than conflict with small business practice, it is likely that it would be more enthusiastically embraced and strategically used by small businesses. Moreover, this would encourage small business owner/managers to seek out opportunities for leveraging information technology so that dependency situations could be minimized.

If the small business manager is pro-actively committed to capitalizing on information technology, he or she will be more likely to seek out opportunities for strategic impact. For example, by keeping abreast of information technology developments, managers can use this knowledge to determine ways of using information technology to add value by creating unique products or services. If multiple sources of reliable, objective information technology information are used as a basis for decision-making, there is a greater likelihood that the information technology adopted will be more suited to the needs of the firm. At a minimum, greater knowledge of information technology among small business managers will increase their ability to assess the quality of the advice or proposals they receive. Indeed, the respondents we interviewed seemed poised for learning about how to capitalize on the Internet.

In summary, this investigation has found that although there are some key differences in how information technology is used by small business, these differences are very much in keeping with how resource decisions are made by small businesses. In light of the increased dependency and the focus on efficiency, recommendations were proposed to address how various stakeholders might better meet the challenges associated with the adoption of information technology within the small business sector.

## CONCLUSION

This chapter has presented a generic description of information systems. Data, raw unorganized facts, are gathered relative to a business event. The resulting information, which has meaning in the hands of a user, must be complete and accurate in order to support timely decision making. The previous chapters have presented an overview of small business, entrepreneurs, and information systems. The next series of chapters provide more detail about information systems and small business. They begin by presenting an overview of theories about information systems and small business. Then models are presented about information systems and their adoption, use, strategy, and competitive advantage.

## REFERENCES

Agarwal, R., & Prasas, J. (2000). A field study of the adoption of software process innovations by information system professionals. *IEEE Transactions on Engineering Management*, *47*(3), 295–308. doi:10.1109/17.865899

Balderson, D. W. (2011). *Canadian Entrepreneurship and Small Business Management* (8th ed.). Toronto: McGraw-Hill Ryerson.

Bennett, R., & McCoshan, A. (1993). *Enterprise and Human Resource Development*. London: Paul Chapman Publishing Ltd.

Berman, P. (1997). *Small Business and Entrepreneurship*. Scarborough, Ontario: Prentice Hall.

Bridge, J., & Peel, M. (1999). Research note: A study of computer usage and strategic planning in the SME sector. *International Small Business Journal*, Jul-Sep, 82-87.

Canadian Federation of Independent Business. (1999). Results of members' opinion surveys #37-42, http://www.cfib.ca/research/98internet.asp

Chen, J. C., & Williams, B. C. (1993). The impact of microcomputer systems on small business: England, 10 years later. *Journal of Small Business Management*, (July): 96–102.

Coghlan, D. (2001). An intervals perspective of OD in IT enabled change. *Organization Development Journal*, *19*(1), 49–56.

Drew, S. (2003). Strategic uses of e-commerce by SMEs in the east of England. *European Management Journal*, *21*(1), 79–88. doi:10.1016/S0263-2373(02)00148-2

Earl, M. J. (1989). *Management strategies for information technology*. New York: Prentice-Hall.

El Louadi, M. (1998). The relationship among organizational structure, information technology and information processing in small Canadian firms. *Canadian Journal of Administrative Sciences*, *15*(2), 180–199. doi:10.1111/j.1936-4490.1998.tb00161.x

Fuller, T. (1996). Fulfilling IT needs in small businesses: A recursive learning model. *International Journal of Small Business*, *14*(4), 25–44. doi:10.1177/0266242696144002

Galliers, R. D., & Sutherland, A. R. (1999). Informaiton systems management and strategy formation: Applying and extending the "stages of growth" concept. In R. D. Galliers, D. E. Leidner, & D. S. H. Baker (Eds.), *Strategic information management: Challenges and strategies in managing information systems* (2nd ed.). Oxford: Butterworth-Heinemann.

Haug, A., Pedersen, S. G., & Arlbjorn, J. S. (2011). IT readiness in small and medium-sized enterprises. *Industrial Management & Data Systems*, *111*(4), 490–508. doi:10.1108/02635571111133515

Hollander, A. S., Cherrington, J. O., & Denna, E. L. (2000). *Accounting, Information Technology, and Business Solutions*. Boston, MA: McGraw-Hill.

Hunter, M. G. (2003). Information systems and small business: What's in the wind in L, A.? ISOneWorld, April 23-25, Las Vegas, NV.

Lewis, R., & Cockrill, A. (2002). Going global, remaining local: The impact of e-commerce on small retail firms in Wales. *Journal of International Information Management*, *22*(3), 195–215. doi:10.1016/S0268-4012(02)00005-1

Lin, B., Vassar, J., & Clack, L. (1993). Information technology strategies for small business. *Journal of Applied Business Research*, *9*(2), 25–29.

Love, P. E. D., Irani, Z., Li, H., Cheng, E. W. L., & Tse, R. Y. C. (2001). An empirical analysis of the barriers to implementing e-commerce in small-medium sized construction contractors in the state of Victoria, Australia. *Construction Innovation*, *1*(1), 31–41. doi:10.1108/14714170110814497

Malone, S. (1985). Computerizing small business information systems. *Journal of Small Business Management*, *23*(2), 10–16.

Montazami, A. R. (1998). Factors affecting information satisfaction in the context of small business environment. *Management Information Systems Quarterly*, *12*(2), 239–256. doi:10.2307/248849

Nickell, G., & Seado, P. (1986). The impact of attitudes and experiences on small business computer use. *American Journal of Small Business*, *10*(1), 37–48.

Pett, T. L., & Wolff, J. A. (2012). SME identity and homogeneity – are there meaningful differences between micro, small, and medium-sized enterprises? *Journal of Marketing Development and Competitiveness*, *6*(2), 48–59.

Pitt, L., Van der Merwe, R., Brethon, P., Salehi-Sanagari, E., & Barnes, B. R. (2006). Swedish biotech SMEs: The veiled values in online networks. *Technovation*, *26*(5/6), 553–560. doi:10.1016/j.technovation.2005.09.009

Pollard, C., & Hayne, S. (1998). The changing faces of information systems issues in small firms. *International Small Business Journal*, *16*(3), 70–87. doi:10.1177/0266242698163004

Sharma, S., & Rai, A. (2003). An assessment of the relationship between ISD leadership characteristics and IS innovation adoption in organizations. *Innovation & Management*, *40*(5), 391–401.

Strowbridge, L. (1999). Wired. *Atlantic Progress*, *6*(7), 41–50.

Teo, T. S. H., & Pian, Y. (2003). A contingency perspective on internet adoption and competitive advantage. *European Journal of Information Systems*, *12*(2), 78–92. doi:10.1057/palgrave.ejis.3000448

Thong, J. Y. L. (1999). An integrated model of information systems adoption in small businesses. *Journal of Management Information Systems*, *15*(4), 187–214.

Thong, J. Y. L., Yap, C., & Raman, K. (1994). Engagement of external expertise in information systems implementation. *Journal of Management Information Systems*, *11*(2), 209–223.

Timmons, J. A. (1999). *New Venture Creation* (5th ed.). Boston: Irwin McGraw-Hill.

Turban, E., MacLean, E., & Wetherbe, L. (2002). *Information Technology for Management: Transforming Business in the digital Economy*. New York: Wiley.

Van de Ven, H. (1993). The development of an infrastructure for entrepreneurship. *Journal of Business Venturing*, *8*(3), 211–230. doi:10.1016/0883-9026(93)90028-4

Venkatesh, V., & Brown, S. A. (2001). A longitudinal investigation of personal computers in homes: Adoption determinants and emerging challenges. *Management Information Systems Quarterly*, *25*(1), 71–102. doi:10.2307/3250959

Zinger, J. T., Huguette, B., Zanibbi, L., & Mount, J. (1996). An empirical study of the small business support network – the entrepreneurs' perspective. *Canadian Journal of Administrative Sciences*, *13*(4), 347–357. doi:10.1111/j.1936-4490.1996.tb00743.x

## ADDITIONAL READING

Balderson, D. W. (2011). *Canadian Entrepreneurship and Small Business Management* (8th ed.). Toronto: McGraw-Hill Ryerson.

Burgess, S. (2001). *Managing Information Technology in Small Business: Challenges and Solutions*. Hershey, PA: IGI Global.

Corbitt, B. J., & Al-Qirim, N. (2003). *E-Business, e_Government & Small and Medium-Size Enterprises: Opportunities and Challenges*. Hershey, PA: IGI Global.

Hollander, A. S., Cherrington, J. O., & Denna, E. L. (2000). *Accounting, Information Technology, and Business Solutions*. Boston, MA: McGraw-Hill.

Turban, E., MacLean, E., & Wetherbe, L. (2002). *Information Technology for Management: Transforming Business in the digital Economy*. New York: Wiley.

## KEY TERMS AND DEFINITIONS

**Back-Ups:** Copies of important files.

**Chief Information Officer:** The role of employing technology to support the current and future operations of the business.

**Client-Server:** A computer that performs the interface function between a user's computer and a network.

**Cloud:** The delivery of computing as a service.

**Commercial Software:** Computer programs which may be purchased.

**Computer Crime:** A process of breaking the law by using a computer.

**Database:** Formal computer file structure.

**Feedback:** A method to determine what has been sent has been received.

**Firewall:** Software that protects internal computers from external networks.

**Help Desk:** Individuals who provide immediate help to users regarding their computers.

**Information Systems:** Process of transforming data into information to support decision making.

**Information Technology:** The application of computers and telecommunication networks to manage data. Decision Making: the process of selecting a course of action. Low Cost: products that are produced as economically as possible. Profit: the amount by which revenue exceeds cost.

**Input:** Data that has been entered into an information systems and is expressed in the language of the system.

**Internet:** A telecommunications network that connects many computers using TCP/IP protocol.

**LAN:** Local Area Network, usually within one location of a business.

**Manual:** A process that is not supported by technology. Automated: a business process supported by information technology. Transactions: evidence of a business event. Data: raw unorganized facts. Information: data expressed in a meaningful way to the user.

**Network:** Technology that facilitates the communication between computers.

**Off-Site Storage:** A location not on the business premises.

**Output:** Information that is within the information system but is ready to be used as information.

**Outsourcing:** Acquiring an external source to perform a business function.

**Password:** A set of characters used to authenticate a user.

**Privacy:** The process of protecting the information about an individual.

**SDLC:** System Development Life Cycle, form the activities to be performed in the production of an information system.

**Service:** An intangible commodity provided to a customer. Competitive Advantage: the ability to perform better than the competition.

**Stakeholders:** A group that may affect or be affected by a business. Application Software: computer programs which support the major functions of a business. Hardware: the physical components of a computer.

**System Software:** The computer operating system which relates application software to the computer hardware.

# Chapter 4
# Theories for Investigations


## ABSTRACT

*While there are many theories about information systems and also about small business, there are few that relate to both topics. Some theories relate information systems to business in general, but not to small business specifically. Research in this area is becoming more rigorous. One helpful approach has been to map information systems research in small business onto the Stages Theory of Small business. Other research has employed Technology Acceptance Model (TAM) and Punctuated Equilibrium Theory. The result is the development of frameworks to facilitate investigations. These frameworks support the contention that new technologies may facilitate business transformation which, in turn, may improve performance and contribute to competitive advantage. This chapter presents general theories, including models and frameworks, about small business and investigations related to information systems. Then a series of overviews describe approaches to information systems and small business. These overviews are presented in more detail in subsequent chapters in this section of the book.*


## INTRODUCTION

*Chapter Five – Adoption* reviews a number of perspectives regarding how small business acquires the resource of information systems. In general, when a small business adopts an information system it represents a technological innovation. It is not necessary for the innovation to be representative of leading edge technology. It

DOI: 10.4018/978-1-4666-8708-0.ch004

is simply a matter of adopting a technology that is new to the small business. Thus, the small business may experience a radical change in how it carries out business operations.

Innovative technologies may involve traditional information systems or some form of Internet application. Traditional information systems are described in more detail in Chapter Eleven – E-business. A discussion of Internet applications is included in Chapter Ten – E-commerce.

Internal sources of adoption relate to perceptions and knowledge of owner/managers and employees. External sources of adoption may include customers or suppliers requesting technology based services. Further, the competitive environment may drive the requirement for a response by the small business. Thus, information technology may be adopted because of perceived benefits or as a response to perceived competitive advantage. Inhibitors to information technology adoption relate to a lack of resources. The small business may lack financial capability, size, or in-house expertise leading to the inability to adopt information technology.

One theory relates to the Technology-Organization-Environment (TOE) Framework which suggests that small business adoption of information technology will be facilitated by three components. One is the perceived benefits of adopting the technology. Another is the small business must be ready and capable of adopting the technology. Also, there will be pressure from the small business environment to adopt the technology.

The final topic covered in Chapter Five – Adoption is the resource-based view of the firm which suggests that small business will adopt information technology based upon their resource endowments. This view suggests that small business resources are unique and they are difficult to copy by the competition.

*Chapter Six – Use* discusses the use of information systems by small business. Use may be differentiated by small business terms of "laggards" and "leaders". Laggards may use information systems but only to the extent deemed necessary. No new opportunities are explored. Leaders regard information systems as providing competitive advantage and regularly explore new initiatives which may contribute to improvements in operations.

Again in this chapter, Resource-based Theory is employed to investigate use of information systems. Successful use depends upon both positive attitudes and capabilities to use information systems.

Absorptive Capacity Theory describes the ability of a small business to identify, assimilate, and exploit knowledge. Given these abilities small business will benefit from the use of information systems.

The dependency theme re-occurs in this chapter with regards to information system use. Within the small business employees will depend upon their skills of a few others to demonstrate the use of information systems. External dependency may take the form of a consultant or vendor who will be employed to demonstrate how to use an acquired information systems.

In general, most small businesses focus their use of information on efficiency. Thus, daily operations may be supported by an information system. Little or no strategic perspective is taken. Although Chapter Seven proposes that some strategic initiatives would be beneficial.

*Chapter Seven – Strategy.* This chapter combines the closely related topics of strategy and competitive advantage.

The first major section of this chapter relates small business strategy to information systems. Mainly, information systems are used by small business to support daily operations with little or no initiatives regarding strategy or competitive advantage. However, as a small business grows there is an increased need for more sophisticated information systems. This tends to lead to a more strategic approach to employing information systems.

It becomes important to align both information systems and business strategy. Some suggest the information system strategy should support the business strategy. Others propose the establishment of the strategies in concert with each other.

When information systems become integral to the small business strategy overall performance will improve. This, in turn, will have a positive impact on competitive advantage. This leads to the second major section of this chapter, namely competitive advantage.

Small business must move from an efficiency perspective to one of effectiveness. It must be determined what innovation in information systems will lead to competitive advantage.

In order to improve performance via information systems a small business should possess infrastructure, skills, and a customer orientation. However, for competitive advantage to be attained these components must be integrated in a way that is unique to the small business. One approach would be to employ information systems to acquire information about customers, suppliers, and competitors.

Long term successful small businesses focus on people related issues rather than just technical aspects. While the technology is important, it becomes valuable in the hands of skilled and knowledgeable people.

Luck may play a part in gaining competitive advantage. But, it is the open and stimulating environment that sets the stage for the role of luck in the small business.

## BACKGROUND

The subject area of the application of information systems to small business is a thoroughly interesting, yet relatively under researched topic.

There are three major roles that information systems play in a business (Schein, 1992 and Zuboff, 1988).

*The automate role refers to mere replacement of labor processes by technology. In the informate role, IS provides data and information that empowers different levels of management and organizational employees. In the transformational role, IS helps to fundamentally redefine and alter the business processes and business relationships. (Sharma & Bhagwat, 2006)*

An example of automate could be the computerization of a manual information system. An informate role example could be a budget system that provides details to lower management and summary information to more senior level management. A transformational role example could be the result of sharing production plans with a supplier and the creation of Just-In-Time inventory system along with automatic payments associated with the arrival of material from the supplier.

Recent research has supported the contention that the use of information systems by small business represents a unique approach. For instance Belich and Dubinsky (1999), and Pollard and Hayne (1998) determined that the issues being faced by small business managers (lack of time, skills, and financial resources) are different than those faced by large business managers. Further, Taylor (1999) investigated the implementation of enterprise software in small businesses and found that neither the businesses themselves, nor the software vendors were fully cognizant of the unique problems (matching system capability to functional requirements) encountered by small business managers. Finally, Hunter et al (2002) identified two major themes regarding small business use of information systems. These themes are "dependency" and "efficiency". The authors suggest that the adoption of information systems increased the small business' dependency on an internal champion, and a series of external stakeholders, including consultants and suppliers. Hunter et al (2002) suggest this increased dependency results from the approaches to business (Stevenson, 1999) taken by the manager and the concept of resource poverty (Thong et al, 1994). The efficiency theme suggests that small business managers primarily use information systems as an operational tool to help complete daily activities.

Earlier research (Nickell & Seado, 1986) determined that small business was mainly using information systems for accounting and administrative purposes. Research conducted in the 1990s (Lin et al, 1993; Fuller, 1996; Berman, 1997; Canadian Federation of Independent Business, 1999; and Timmons, 1999) noted a growing interest by small business in employing information systems for daily operations. While small business has been more than prepared to exploit the use of information systems to support daily operations (El Louadi, 1998), there exists little evidence that they are prepared to employ the technology in a strategic manner (Berman, 1997). Bridge and Peel (1999) determined that small businesses employed computers mainly to support daily operations and tended not to use them to support decision making or long term planning. Current research suggests this situation has not changed. For instance, Dandridge and Levenburg (2000) found that information systems were being employed for daily operations and there was little use of computerization for competitiveness aspects such as accessing the Internet.

Hunter et al (2002) support the conclusion that small business focus on efficiency gains when implementing information systems rather than a contribution to improve effectiveness. So, the focus is on carrying out existing processes faster rather than identifying new more productive processes.

## RESEARCH METHODS

Mullen et al (2009) reviewed the research methods employed to investigate small business and entrepreneurship in academic journals from 2001 to 2008. They note that Chandler & Lyon (2001) had called for methodological sophistication to provide a base for the lack of theory development in this area. Mullen et al (2009) note an improvement in the rigour of methods. However, they suggest further improvements are needed in such areas a sampling (size and bias); construct validity (reliability, and convergent and discriminant validity); and internal and external validity.

Dobbs and Hamilton (2007) conducted an extensive review of contributions to the literature of small business growth. They concluded there was an absence of an overall unifying theory. However, they did suggest that there exist six conceptual framework categories. Table 1 presents an overview of these categories.

The diversity of the above frameworks suggests that with no unifying theory small business growth prospects are specific to each unique situation. (Davidsson & Klofsten, 2003).

Tan et al (2009) also offer perspectives on small business research. They suggest that research is moving away from describing small business and their importance. The emphasis has shifted towards identifying aspects which contribute to growth, the creation of economic value, and innovation.

Nicholson (2008) proposes evolutionary psychology (EP) in response to the lack of generally accepted theory for conducting research into family firms.

*Table 1. Small business growth frameworks*

| Category | Description | Authors |
|---|---|---|
| Stochastic | The depiction of future growth is not dependent on past growth | McMahon, 1998; Gibrat, 1931 |
| Descriptive | Necessary internal changes to continue growth | Steinmetz, 1969; Filley and House, 1969; Greiner, 1972, 1998; Churchill and Lewis, 1983; Scott & Bruce, 1987 |
| Evolutionary | Circumstances unique to each business result in growth | Aldrich, 1999 |
| Resource-based | To facilitate growth management must be able to identify opportunities, maintain current operations, and take the time to plan | Pensrose, 1959; Orser et al, 2000 |
| Learning | Knowledge acquired by the decision makers will lead to potential growth | Deakins and Freel, 1998; Dalley and Hamilton, 2000 |
| Deterministic | Identify the causes of growth | Olson and Bokor, 1995; Barkham, 1994; Barringer and Jones, 2004; Davidsson, 1991; Kangasharju, 2000; Lin, 1998; Montserrat, 2002; Hoogstra and van Dijk, 2004; O'Gorman, 2001; Wiklund and Shepard, 2003; Rutherford et al, 2001 |

Adapted from Dobbs and Hamilton, 2007

*From an EP perspective, the family firm endures as an appealing form because it is uniquely close to our evolutionary origins through the extreme overlap of family and work, the intergenerational transmission of responsibility for the economic unit of the family, and its capacity to generate binding community commitments and cooperation between kin and non-kin. Nicholson (2008, p. 106)*

He then proceeds to relate EP to family firms through a description of motives, goals, and cognition; social relationships, and communal living; and individual differences. He concludes that family firms are unique and uniquely vulnerable. Returning to EP he suggests that, "… firms that have weathered and overcome difficulties have enhanced survival qualities and capabilities." (Nicholson, 2008, p. 114). This comment reflects those aspects of evolution as espoused by the Darwinian perspective.

Floren (2006) reviewed previous investigations into the behaviour of managers in small business. He identified three basic characteristics of managerial activities and managers. They are time allocation; interaction and communication; and roles.

The first characteristic relates to how managers allocate their time. It is noted that their work day is long and not routine. The day is unplanned and there are many interruptions. Activities are short and fragmented. Interruptions involve others who are either providing information or asking for direction. Managers tend to react immediately to these interruptions. An explanation for this result was provided by Choran (1969) who suggested the necessity for a wide range of fragmented activities relates to both the lack of available resources and a formal structure in a small business. Further, O'Gorman et al (2005) support this suggestion and add that managers prefer to work with others rather than alone.

This comment leads to the second characteristic of interaction and communication. O'Gorman et al (2005) suggest managers of small business prefer forms of informal communication. They also prefer informal information over that which may be more statistically reliable. These two comments provide some insight into their potential avoidance of formal computer-based information systems. Lack of time has been given as a reason to avoid these management tools (Muir & Langford, 1994).

The third characteristic describes elements of the managers' job. They play many roles which continually change throughout the work day. They must perform the role as a manager. Also, in some cases they may be a member of a project team. Further, they may have to "roll up their sleeves" and perform a task as a substitute operator. As an extension to this roll responsibility, Floren (2006) suggests managers tend to spend time on activities they enjoy and have the ability to do. They avoid other tasks. This can become an issue of the avoidance of tasks impacts the performance of the small business.

Table 2 adapted from Scott and Bruce (1987), provides an outline of issues that must be addressed as a small business transitions through five stages to become a mature and viable operation. Each transition requires change. A proactive approach to identifying the issues involved in each stage will facilitate the transition and contribute to the on-going viability of small business.

The model developed by Scott and Bruce (1987) presents a number of comments relating to small business growth. The third issue in Table 2 refers to one of these aspects, Systems and Controls. This entry in the table serves to show the movement toward more formal information systems as the small business matures. This idea forms the basis, and is expanded upon, of the discussion in Chapter Thirteen regarding a balanced approach to maturity on a small business.

While large corporations may employ information systems for strategic purposes, small business tends to emphasize the use of information systems to support daily operations. (Berman, 1997; Bridge & Peel, 1999; El Louadi, 1998; Fuller, 1996; Lin et al, 1993; Timmons, 1999). Further, Hunter et al (2002) found that small business emphasized efficiency gains in employing information systems versus considering effectiveness improvements.

*Table 2. Stages of growth in small business*

| Issues | Stage 1 Inception | Stage 2 Survival | Stage 3 Growth | Stage 4 Expansion | Stage 5 Maturity |
|---|---|---|---|---|---|
| **Features** | Developing a product and establishing a place in the market | Develop credibility with financial institutions and suppliers | Develop an organization structure based on major functions | Develop budgetary control and consider equity partners | Develop long term plans for continuation |
| **Focus** | Establishing and maintaining positive cash flow<br>Developing formal systems and record keeping<br>Establish an organization structure to facilitate delegation | Control growth<br>Respond to competition<br>Expand customer base<br>Acquire new skills | Decide to compete on price or differentiation<br>Expand into new markets or new products<br>Manage an expanded and diverse operation | Founder becomes a manager<br>Focus on customers | Expense control<br>Productivity<br>Growth opportunities |
| **Systems and Controls** | Simple bookkeeping | Simple bookkeeping | Simple control reports | Budgeting<br>Regular sales and production reports | Formal systems to report on objectives |

Adapted from Scott and Bruce, 1987

Punctuated Equilibrium Theory (Gersick, 1991; Romanelli & Tushman, 1994; and Tushman & Romanelli, 1985) has been employed to analyze change in business. Adopted from evolutionary biology the theory characterizes three concepts. Thus, periods of evolutionary change are "punctuated" by periods of revolutionary change. The response to the revolutionary change results in structural changes in the business. For a small business the implementation of an information system, to facilitate growth, represents a revolutionary change which will impact the organization structure of the small business (Street & Meister, 2004). A more formalized structure as a result of the implementation of an information system will have further impacts. Communication will become more formalized. Information emanating from an information system will be more structured. The more formalized information and reporting structures may lead to less transparency as the small business grows. It becomes important that managers in small businesses are aware of these changes as the business transitions into more formalized information systems.

Hayes (2012) explored the use of TAM (Technology Acceptance Model) to explain the adoption of information technology by small business. In general, TAM demonstrates the relationship between acceptance of a technology and an individual's attitude toward the technology. Attitude is dependent upon the individual's perception of the technology relative to its usefulness and ease of use. Hayes (2012) extended TAM to include a diagram which represents an individual's mental model of the technology. This extension proved beneficial to small business. First, the mental model provided a better understanding of the usefulness of the technology. This is important to small business because of the relatively high cost of implementing the technology. Second, because of this better understanding the technology appeared easy to use. For a small business this result may lead to the successful adoption of the technology.

Lester et al (2003) proposed a five stage organizational life cycle which is presented in Table 3. Knowledge of the stage of the small business will aid managers in determining how to improve performance and develop a competitive strategy.

Lester et al (2008) provide a further elaboration of the five life cycle stages in the table above. They investigated the relationship between strategy and performance. Their literature review is presented in relation to the five life cycle stages.

## Existence

*Stage one is existence (Churchill & Lewis, 1983). Labeled the entrepreneurial (Quinn & Cameron, 1983) or birth stage (Lippitt & Schmidt, 1967), it is characterized by a firm's struggle to achieve viability. Decision-making is in the hands of one or a few members, while ownership is concentrated. Structure is simple, as most firms are quite small in terms of revenues and number of employees. (Lester et al, 2008, p. 315).*

*Firms in the existence (Churchill & Lewis, 1983) stage tend to enact (Bedeian, 1990) their environments, creating something different than the accepted status quo. They are characterized by bold, intuitive decision making, focusing on innovation and bringing new ideas to market with speed. The first mover strategy (Parnell & Carraher, 2002), which seeks high margins through innovation, reflects a predicted fit for the existence life cycle stage. (Lester et al, 2008, p. 319).*

## Survival

*Stage two is survival. Growth (Adizes, 1979; and Downs, 1967) is the primary goal for many firms in this stage. Organizations move from a simple structure to one*

*Table 3. Five stage organizational life cycle*

| Stage | Description |
|---|---|
| Existence | "Known as the entrepreneurial (Quinn & Cameron, 1983) or birth stage (Lippitt & Schmidt, 1967), Existence (Churchill & Lewis, 1983) marks the beginning of organizational development. The focus is on viability, or simply identifying a sufficient number of customers to support the existence of the organization. Decision-making and ownership are in the hands of one, or a few, and the environment is considered to be unanalyzable (Daft & Weick, 1984). Organizations in this stage tend to enact or create (Bedeian, 1990) their own environments." (Lester et al, 2003, p. 342) |
| Survival | "As firms move into the Survival stage they seek to grow (Adizes, 1979; Downs, 1967), develop some formalization of structure (Quinn & Cameron, 1983), and establish their own distinctive competencies (Miller & Friesen, 1984). Goals are formulated routinely in this stage, with the primary goal being the generation of enough revenue to continue operations and finance sufficient growth to stay competitive (Churchill & Lewis, 1983). The Survival stage provides several interesting alternatives: Some organizations grow large and prosper well enough to enter stage three, some "hit and miss," earning marginal returns in some fiscal cycles, and others fail to generate sufficient revenue to survive. Most organizations in this stage view the environment as analyzable (Daft & Wcick, 1984)." (Lester et al, 2003, p. 342) |
| Success | "Commonly called maturity (Adizes, 1979), the Success stage represents an organizational form where formalization and control through bureaucracy are the norm (Quinn & Cameron, 1983). A common problem in this stage is what American businesses have long referred to as "red tape" (Miller & Friesen, 1984), a condition of wading through layers of organizational structure to get anything accomplished. Job descriptions, policies and procedures, and hierarchical reporting relationships have become much more formal. Such organizations have passed the survival test, growing to a point that they may seek to protect what they have gained instead of targeting new territory. The top management team focuses on planning and strategy, leaving daily operations to middle managers. The environment is viewed as analyzable (Daft & Weick, 1984)." (Lester et al, 2003, p. 343) |
| Renewal | "The renewing organization displays a desire to return to a leaner time (Miller & Friesen, 1984) where collaboration and teamwork foster innovation and creativity. This creativity is sometimes facilitated through the use of a matrix structure, and decision-making is very much decentralized. The organization is still large and bureaucratic, but organizational members are encouraged to work within the bureaucracy without adding to it. The needs of customers are placed above those of organizational members." (Lester et al, 2003, p. 343) |
| Decline | "Although firms may exit the life cycle at any stage, the Decline stage can trigger the demise. The Decline stage is characterized by politics and power (Mintzberg, 1984), as organizational members become more concerned with personal goals than they are with organizational goals. For some organizations, the inability to meet the external demands of a former stage has led them to a period of decline where they experience a lack of profit and a loss of market share (Miller & Friesen, 1984). Control and decision-making tend to return to a handful of people, as the desire for power and influence in earlier stages has eroded the viability of the organization." (Lester et al, 2003, p. 343) |

Adapted from Lester et al, 2003

*that emphasizes the role of managers and promotes division of labor. Fast-growing firms are striving to become large enough to achieve economies of scale. However, Churchill & Lewis (1983) indicated that some organizations never move beyond the beginnings of this stage by not becoming successful, but not being so unsuccessful as to go out of business. (Lester et al, 2008, p. 315).*

*Survival (Churchill & Lewis, 1983) organizations tend to analyze the market to find opportunities that have been opened up by first movers. Survival firms are larger, have more resources, and are focused on growth (Adizes, 1979; Baird & Meshoulam, 1988; Downs, 1967). Their initial successes have given them an established market where they can pick and choose new segments to exploit through product innovation and expert marketing. Second movers (Parnell & Carraher, 2002) tend to match the profile of survival organizations as they allow first movers to encounter the early difficulties of new market penetration, while they lag somewhat (Miles & Snow, 1978). They bring speed, resources, and expert marketing ability to these new growth markets. In a similar vein, perceived uniqueness firms attempt to differentiate from their competitors through effective product research and development and marketing expertise. (Lester et al, 2008, p. 319).*

## Success

Stage three is success. This stage is commonly referred to as maturity (Adizes, 1979). Firms develop more formal organizational structures with job descriptions, hierarchical reporting relationships, and policies and procedures that remove much of the flexibility enjoyed in earlier stages of the organization. Success is characterized by large firms that operate bureaucratically (Miller & Friesen, 1984)." (Lester et al, 2008, p. 315).

*Mature firms (Smith, et al, 1985) in the success (Lester et al, 2003) stage are characterized by formalization and control (Quinn & Cameron, 1983). Information processing is sophisticated, management is professional, and an overarching goal is to avoid risk. The segment control strategy provides a match for the success firm due to the emphasis on cost control and production efficiency (Miles & Snow, 1978). Likewise, the production/distribution efficiency (Parnell & Carraher, 2002) strategy is similarly a good match when one considers the effective process research and development focus, efficient production processes, and cost containment culture that dominate this strategic type. (Lester et al, 2008, pp. 319-320).*

## Renewal

Stage four is renewal. Renewal firms reflect the desire of mature organizations to return to leaner times (Quinn & Cameron, 1983) without the loss of built-up economies. There is a pressing need to cut the "red tape" of the success stage and focus on collaboration and teamwork. Decision-making is decentralized in an effort to get close to the customer and put the customers' needs first. A matrix organizational structure is sometimes employed to achieve this decentralization." (Lester et al, 2008, p. 315).

The renewing organization exhibits a desire to return to leaner times through collaboration (Greiner, 1972) and teamwork (Quinn & Cameron, 1983). The goal is to grow and diversify without adding to the bureaucracy. This goal is often facilitated through the use of a matrix structure (Miller & Friesen, 1984). Decision-making is more participatory and the use of task forces can be prevalent. The first mover (Parnell & Carraher, 2002) strategy is a match for this life cycle stage, as firms seek to create or discover new markets to add to their existing stable of markets served. The product/service breadth strategy is also a match for this stage due to the nature of most renewal firms to be large in size, operating in heterogeneous environments, and focusing on diversification." (Lester et al, 2008, p. 320).

## DECLINE

*Stage five is decline. During this stage the needs of customers diminish as organizational members engage in fierce political power struggles (Mintzberg, 1984). Emphasis shifts from a focus on the customer to a focus on the personal objectives of employees as they put their individual goals ahead of what might be best for the organization. The result is decreased or no innovation with a subsequent loss of market share and a decline in profitability that can eventually lead to a firm's demise. (Lester et al, 2008, pp. 315-317).*

*Organizations in decline (Miller & Friesen, 1984) tend to focus inward with a narrow scope. Communication is poor, power is centralized (Mintzberg, 1984), information processing is unsophisticated, structure is bureaucratic (Hanks, 1990), and decision-making is through coalition building. Miles & Snow (1978) might label these organizations as reactors, but they also acknowledge that the reactor is, in reality, not really a strategy. This stage is an unfertile field for any strategy because none will be successful in the long-term as long as conditions within the organization remains as described. The key to a successful recovery is turnaround (Hanks, 1990). (Lester et al, 2008, pp. 320-321).*

The second factor in Table 4 describes how information is used in relation to the five stages in the life cycle of a small business. It is interesting to note that the use of information passes through an informal stage through to a sophisticated approach supported by current technology to contribute to competitive advantage. Unfortunately, in the Decline life cycle stage information may be used negatively simply to maintain internal personal power.

As a small business proceeds through the five life cycle stages they may be described by four differentiating factors, situation, structure, decision making, and strategy (Lester & Parnell, 2008). Situation involves aspects of the small business such as size, number of employees, ownership, and market. Structure relates to reporting relationships which may include departments versus divisions; and centralized versus decentralized. Decision making may be focused on one person or open and participative among a group of individuals. Strategy relates to setting the direction for the small business. In the early life cycle stages growth and innovation are the main focus. In the later stages there is more of a focus on developing efficient operations.

Rogers (1983) suggested an innovation is new. Poutsma et al (1987) further explained that the practice or object only has to be perceived as new to be considered an innovation. Thus, an approach may be innovative even if an existing technology is applied for the first time in a specific small business.

Innovation may be characterized by the continua of four dimensions (Poutsma et al, 1987). The dimensions of the first continuum are process versus product. A process innovation involves the adoption of a new method. A product innovation results in a new capital good. The second continuum is represented by radical versus incremental innovations. A radical innovation represents a fundamental change in how business is conducted. This is reflected in the concept of Business Process

*Table 4. Life cycle stages of small business*

| Factor | Stage One Existence | Stage two Survival | Stage three Success | Stage four Renewal | Stage five Decline |
|---|---|---|---|---|---|
| **Focus** | Viability<br>Finding customers | Formal structure<br>Revenue generation | Job descriptions<br>Policies and procedure | Collaboration and teamwork<br>Foster innovation and creativity | More concern for personal goals |
| **Information** | Informal | More sophisticated | Viewed as a necessary burden<br>May hamper operations | Current technology<br>Competitive advantage | Used for internal power |

Adapted from Lester and Parnell, 2006

Re-Engineering. An incremental innovation involves a minor improvement which is similar to the evolutionary approach to improvement proffered by Total Quality Management. The third continuum involves technology-push versus market-pull. A technology-push innovation involves the development of a new product which may result in a change in how business is conducted. A market-pull is created through a demand for a new product. The fourth continuum distinguishes a planned versus incidental innovation. A planned innovation results from a specific business initiative relating to the innovation. An incidental innovation results from a business initiative but is not specifically related to the initiative.

In general, the acquisition of an information system or any technological innovation involves three stages (Pierce & Delbecq, 1977; and Thompson, 1969). First, in the Initiative Stage, information about the innovation must be gathered and evaluated. Second, in the Adoption Stage, the technology is acquired. Third, in the implementation Stage, the technology is installed throughout the business. Thong (1999) investigated the applicability of this three-stage process to technological innovation in small business. In order to assess both the likelihood and extent of information system adoption by small business Thong (1999) developed the framework documented in Table 5.

In the framework in Table 5 (Thong, 1999) the first characteristic is composed of two elements, the CEO's innovativeness and IS Knowledge. Innovativeness involves either doing things better (adopting) or doing things differently (innovating) (Kirton, 1976). In both cases success depends upon the senior individual's will to innovate. Little change will result without the requisite will to do so. IS Knowledge may lead to adoption of an innovation through a better understanding of the technology and how it may be beneficially applied in the business.

The second characteristic relates to Information Systems and includes relative advantage, compatibility, and complexity (Tornatzky & Klein, 1982). Thus, a positive attitude to adopt a technology may be formed if it will improve the business situation; is consistent with current the values within the business; and is not overly difficult to use (Rogers, 1983).

The third characteristic relates to the organization and includes Business Size, Employees' IS Knowledge, and Information Intensity. Larger businesses possess more resources to support the adoption of an innovation (Dewar & Dutton, 1986). Smaller businesses experience resource poverty (Thong et al, 1994). In conjunction with senior management information system knowledge, the level of employee information systems knowledge will impact the adoption of an innovation (Ettlie, 1990). Also, if a business is in an industry that is more information based an innovative technology will be more easily adopted (Galbraith, 1973).

*Table 5. Information systems adoption framework for small business*

| Characteristics | Description |
|---|---|
| **CEO Characteristics** | |
| CEO's Innovation | Willingness to adopt technology to promote change |
| CEO's IS Knowledge | Understanding of the benefits of information systems |
| **IS Characteristics** | |
| Relative Advantage of IS | The information system may improve the business relative to those in the same industry |
| Compatibility of IS | The information system relates to the current culture of the business |
| Complexity of IS | The information system is easy to use |
| **Organizational Characteristics** | |
| Business Size | The number of employees |
| Employees' IS Knowledge | Understanding of the benefits of information systems |
| Information Intensity | Some industries provide an information serve rather than a capital good |
| **Environmental Characteristics** | |
| Competition | Technology adoption practices of other businesses in the industry |

Adapted from Thong, 1999

The fourth characteristic relates to the environment of the business. An innovative technology will be adopted if a business' competition is actively adopting technology (Link & Bozeman, 1991).

A positive response from all of the elements of the four characteristics will result in an increase on the likelihood of information systems adoption as well as the extent of the information systems adoption (Thong, 1999). The most significant factors, as identified by Thong (1999) relate to size and employees' IS Knowledge, both of which relate to having available the necessary resources to adopt an innovative technology.

Lee and Runge (2001) supported Rogers (1983) suggestion that an innovation does not have to relate to the adoption of a new invention of a product or process, but just new to the business. Lee and Runge (2001) propose a model for small business adoption of information technology. The model is composed of three factors. First, Relative Advantage means the new product or process is better than the existing one. Adoption of the new idea in a small business is facilitated with the support from internal relative experts and those who allocate resources of the business. Second, Social Expectations suggest that individuals may act based on their perceptions of the expectations of others. Thus, a small business may adopt an innovation because it is perceived to be beneficial by customers or even competitors. Third, Innovativeness posits that those who have experience adopting innovations will tend to more easily behave in an innovative manner.

Lee and Runge (2001) findings suggest Relative Advantage and Innovativeness will facilitate the adoption of information technology. Further, they determined a difference in the adoption of certain kinds of information technology. Internet adoption is more related to Relative Advantage. But, traditional information systems adoption is more related to Innovativeness. This result suggests that the more traditional adoptions are considered to be a necessity in order to conduct business.

Tippins and Sohi (2003) contend that the ability to effectively manage information will contribute to providing support for competitive advantage. Table 6 presents the factors relating to information technology competency and organizational learning.

In general, the presentation in Table 5 (Tippins & Sohi, 2003) suggests that information technology does not positively impact the performance of a business in a direct manner. However, when information technology is related to and supported by organizational learning positive performance results may be expected.

Information technology, currently a necessity within a business, can be employed to contribute to competitive advantage. However, any advantage may be fleeting because information technology can be acquired and easily imitated (Clemons & Row, 1991). However, to initially gain an advantage the concepts of "complementarity" and "co-specialization" apply (Powell & Dent-Micallef, 1997). Complementarity suggests the value of one resource increases if it is employed in conjunction with another resource (Powell & Dent-Micallef, 1997). Thus, the use of information technology for payroll does not enhance another resource. However, the use of information technology to develop an understanding of customers' preferences and buying habits will contribute to improving the performance of marketing initiatives. The concept of co-specialization suggests the opposite. That is, a resource may have no value if it is not associated with another resource (Clemons & Row, 1991). Certain types of information technology may have no value if the business does not employ individuals with the necessary skills. So it may be impossible to develop an application for radio frequency identification (RFID) tags if no one in the business understands their capability.

Small business success is usually associated with growth (Hay & Kamshad, 1994). However, some individuals become involved in a small business for the life style advantages and are not necessarily interested in growth (Levy et al, 2002).

Levy et al (2001) proposed a framework which supports the potential for small business to obtain value from information systems. Table 7 provides a description of their framework.

*Table 6. Factors relating information technology to firm performance*

| Factor | Description |
|---|---|
| **IT Competency** | "…the extent to which a firm is knowledgeable about and effectively utilizes IT to manage information within the firm." (Tippins & Sohi, 2003, p. 748) |
| IT Knowledge | "…the extent to which a firm possesses a body of technical knowledge about objects such as computer based systems." (Tippins & Sohi, 2003, p. 748) |
| IT Operations | "…the extent to which a firm utilizes IT to manage market and customer information. (Tippins & Sohi, 2003, p. 748) |
| IT Objects | "…computer-based hardware, software, and support personnel." (Tippins & Sohi, 2003, p. 749) |
| **Organizational Learning** | "…the process by which new knowledge or insights are developed by a firm (Slater & Narver, 1995)." (Tippins & Sohi, 2003, p. 749) |
| Information Acquisition | "…the process by which firms actively seek out and gather useable information (Kohli & Jaworski, 1990)." (Tippins & Sohi, 2003, p. 749) |
| Information Dissemination | "…the extent to which the information that is obtained by an organization is shared between its functional units through formal and informal channels (Maltz & Kohli, 1996; and Slater & Narver, 1995)." (Tippins & Sohi, 2003, p. 749) |
| Shared Interpretation | "…the presence of consensus among organizational members with regard to the meaning of information (Slater & Narver, 1996)." (Tippins & Sohi, 2003, p. 749) |
| Declarative Memory | "…knowledge of facts and events." (Tippins & Sohi, 2003, p. 749) |
| Procedural Memory | "…knowledge about routines, processes, and procedures." (Tippins & Sohi, 2003, p. 750) |

Adapted from Tippins and Sohi, (2003)

Levy et al (2002) further expanded upon their theoretical framework in order to describe how small business may gain advantage through employing information systems. The above figure consists of two dimensions, Strategic Focus and Customer Dominance.

The Strategic Focus for information systems adoption could either be for cost reduction or adding value to the small business. If a cost reduction focus is adopted then information systems will be employed to support the traditional business

*Table 7. The focus-dominance model*

| | | | |
|---|---|---|---|
| **CUSTOMER** | LOW | Co-ordination | Innovation |
| **DOMINANCE** | HIGH | Efficiency | Collaboration |
| | | COST | VALUE ADDED |
| | | **STRATEGIC** | **FOCUS** |

Adopted from Levy et al, 2001

processes (Hashmi & Cuddy, 1990 and Blili & Raymond, 1993). Alternatively, a value added focus will lead the small business to identify how information systems may be employed to create a competitive advantage (Yetton et al, 1994 and Levy & Powell, 2000).

Customer Dominance is the second dimension of the above framework. The small business may have a few customers or many. As the customer base grows, individual customers will have less dominance over the small business.

The framework includes four quadrants.

- Efficiency: "…reflects the position of many start-up firms and those that effectively exploit simple systems to run their businesses efficiently (Naylor & Williams (1994). These firms usually have basic accounting and word processing systems." (Levy et al, 2002, p. 342).
- Co-ordination: "…recognizes the needs of growing firms to manage their increasing customer base, often through the addition of a database. Internal networking of systems may begin here." (Levy et al, 2002, p. 342).
- Collaboration: "…incorporation of emerging technologies, with the introduction of EDI to manage relationships with customers. While this is mainly driven by customer push, there are benefits to SMEs in planning and managing production as well as developing a more collaborative relationship." (Levy et al, 2002, p. 342).
- Innovation: "…proactive introduction of IS/IT by SMEs. The owners recognise that the competitive market demands different ways of working and that IS/IT may provide the requisite tools. The Internet is a potential tool to exploit here. These firms contemplate growth and look to invest in IS to drive it." (Levy et al, 2002, pp. 342-343).

Currently, most small businesses are situated in the Efficiency quadrant, where they are employing basic technology. The majority of movement from this quadrant is either to Co-ordination to increase market share or to Collaboration to manage customer relationships. Unfortunately, there was very little movement to the Innovation quadrant to actively seek out and adopt technologies to support achieving competitive advantage.

## CONCLUSION

This chapter has presented a description of research into the relationship between information systems and small business. The Small Business Stages Theory has been employed in a number of investigations to show the growth pattern of small business and issues related to information systems at each stage of growth. The chapter includes some frameworks which may be used to describe how information systems may be employed in small business. Subsequent chapters in this section provide more detail about research into specific relationships between information systems and small business. The next chapter reviews a number of perspectives on small business adoption of information systems.

## REFERENCES

Adizes, I. (1979). Organizational passages: Diagnosing and treating life cycle problems in organizations. *Organizational Dynamics*, *8*(1), 3–24. doi:10.1016/0090-2616(79)90001-9

Aldrich, H. (1999). *Evolving Organizations*. London: Sage Publications.

Baird, L., & Meshoulam, I. (1988). Managing two fits of strategic human resource management. *Academy of Management Review*, *13*(1), 116–126.

Barkham, R. J. (1994). Entrepreneurial characteristics and the size of the new firm: A model and an econometric test. *Small Business Economics*, *6*(2), 117–126. doi:10.1007/BF01065184

Barringer, B. R., & Jones, F. F. (2004). Achieving rapid growth – revisiting the managerial capacity problem. *Journal of Developmental Entrepreneurship*, *9*(1), 73–87.

Bedeian, A. (1990). Choice and determination: A comment. *Strategic Management Journal*, *11*(7), 571–573. doi:10.1002/smj.4250110707

Belich, T. J., & Dubinsky, A. J. (1999). Information processing among exporters: An empirical examination of small firms. *Journal of Marketing Theory and Practice*, *7*(4), 45–58.

Berman, P. (1997). *Small Business and Entrepreneurship*. Scarborough, Ontario: Prentice Hall.

Blili, S., & Raymond, L. (1993). IT: Threats and opportunities for SMEs. *International Journal of Information Management*, *13*, 439–448. doi:10.1016/0268-4012(93)90060-H

Bridge, J., & Peel, M. J. (1999). A study of computer usage and strategic planning in the SME sector. *International Small Business Journal*, *17*(4), 82–87. doi:10.1177/0266242699174005

Canadian Federation of Independent Business. (1999). Results of Members' Opinion Surveys #37-42, http://www.cfib.ca/research/98internet.asp (August 29, 2000).

Chandler, G. N., & Lyon, D. W. (2001). Issues of research design and construct measurement in entrepreneurship research. *Entrepreneurship Theory and Practice*, *25*(4), 101–113.

Choran, I. (1969). *The Manager of a Small Company*, unpublished MBA thesis, Montreal, Quebec: McGill University.

Churchill, N. C., & Lewis, V. L. (1983). The five stages of small business growth. *Harvard Business Review*, *61*(3), 30–50.

Clemons, E. K., & Row, M. C. (1991). Sustaining IT advantage: The role of structural differences. *Management Information Systems Quarterly*, *15*(3), 275–294. doi:10.2307/249639

Daft, R., & Weick, K. (1984). Toward a model of organizations as interpretations systems. *Academy of Management Review*, *9*(2), 284–295.

Dalley, J., & Hamilton, R. T. (2000). Knowledge, context and learning in the small business. *International Small Business Journal*, *18*(3), 51–59. doi:10.1177/0266242600183003

Dandrige, T., & Levenburg, N. M. (2000). High-tech potential? An exploratory study of very small firms' usage of the internet. *International Small Business Journal*, *18*(2), 81–91. doi:10.1177/0266242600182004

Davidsson, P. (1991). Continued Entrepreneurship: Ability, need, and opportunity as determinants of small firm growth. *Journal of Business Venturing*, *6*(6), 405–429. doi:10.1016/0883-9026(91)90028-C

Davidsson, P., & Klofsten, M. (2003). The business platform: Developing an instrument to gauge and to assist the development of young firms. *Journal of Small Business Management*, *41*(1), 1–26. doi:10.1111/1540-627X.00064

Deakins, D., & Freel, M. (1998). Entrepreneurial learning and growth processes in SMEs. *The Learning Organization*, *5*(3), 144–156. doi:10.1108/09696479810223428

Dewar, R. D., & Dutton, J. E. (1986). The adoption of radical and incremental innovations: An empirical analysis. *Management Science*, *32*(11), 1422–1433. doi:10.1287/mnsc.32.11.1422

Dobbs, M., & Hamilton, R. T. (2007). Small business growth: Recent evidence and new directions. *International Journal of Entrepreneurial Behaviour & Research, 13*(5), 296–322. doi:10.1108/13552550710780885

Downs, A. (1967). The life cycle of bureaus. In A. Downs (Ed.), *Inside Bureaucracy*. San Francisco, CA: Little Brown & Co. and Rand Corporation.

El Louadi, M. (1998). The relationship among organizational structure, information technology and information processing in small Canadian firms. *Canadian Journal of Administrative Sciences, 15*(2), 180–199. doi:10.1111/j.1936-4490.1998.tb00161.x

Ettlie, J. E. (1990). What makes a manufacturing firm innovative? *The Academy of Management Executive, 4*(4), 7–20. doi:10.5465/AME.1990.4277195

Filley, A. C., & House, R. J. (1969). Managerial process and organisational behaviour. Glenview, Il: Scott Foresman and Company.

Floren, H. (2006). Managerial work in small firms: Summarising what we know and sketching a research agenda. *International Journal of Entrepreneurial Behaviour & Research, 12*(5), 272–288. doi:10.1108/13552550610687646

Fuller, T. (1996). Fulfilling IT needs in small businesses: A recursive learning model. *International Journal of Small Business, 14*(4), 25–44. doi:10.1177/0266242696144002

Galbraith, J. R. (1973). *Designing complex organizations*. Reading, MA: Addison-Wesley.

Gersick, C. (1991). Revolutionary change theories: A multilevel exploration of the punctuated equilibrium paradigm. *Academy of Management Review, 16*(1), 10–36.

Gibrat, R. (1931). *Les Inegalites Economiques*. Paris: Librairie du Recueil.

Greiner, L. E. (1972). Evolution and revolution as organizations grow. *Harvard Business Review, 76*(3), 55–68. PMID:10179654

Hanks, S. (1990). Am empirical examination of the organizaitonal life cycle in high technology firms. Doctoral dissertation, University of Utah: Salt Lake City, Utah.

Hashmi, M., & Cuddy, J. (1990). Strategic initiatives for introducing CIM technologies. In Faria, L. (Editor), *Computer Integrated Manufacturing – Proceedings of the 6th CIM-Europe Conference*, Lisbon: Spring Verlag.

Hay, M., & Kamshad, K. (1994). Small firm growth: Intentions, implementation and impediments. *Business Strategy Review, 5*(3), 49–68. doi:10.1111/j.1467-8616.1994.tb00166.x

Hayes, T. P. (2012). Predicting information technology adoption in small businesses: An extension of the technology acceptance model. *Academy of Information and Management Sciences Journal*, *15*(1), 37–46.

Hoogstra, G. J., & van Dijk, J. (2004). Explaining firm employment growth: Does location matter? *Small Business Economics*, *22*(3/4), 179–190. doi:10.1023/B:SBEJ.0000022218.66156.ac

Hunter, M. G., Diochon, M., Pugsley, D., & Wright, B. (2002). Unique challenges for small business adoption of information technology: The case of the Nova Scotia ten. In S. Burgess (Ed.), *Managing Information Technology in Small Business: Challenges and Solutions*. Hershey, PA: Idea Group Publishing. doi:10.4018/978-1-930708-35-8.ch006

Kangasharju, A. (2000). Growth of the smallest: Determinants of small firm growth during strong macroeconomic fluctuations. *International Small Business Journal*, *19*(1), 28–43. doi:10.1177/0266242600191002

Kirton, M. J. (1976). Adaptors and innovators: A description and measure. *The Journal of Applied Psychology*, *61*(5), 622–629. doi:10.1037/0021-9010.61.5.622

Kohli, A. K., & Jaworski, B. J. (1990). Market orientation: The construct, research propositions, and managerial implications. *Journal of Marketing*, *54*(2), 1–18. doi:10.2307/1251866

Lee, J., & Runge, J. (2001). Adoption of information technology in small business: Testing drivers of adoption for entrepreneurs. *Journal of Computer Information Systems*, *42*(1), 44–57.

Lester, D. L., & Parnell, J. A. (2006). The complete life cycle of a family business. *Journal of Applied Management and Entrepreneurship*, *11*(3), 3–22.

Lester, D. L., & Parnell, J. A. (2008). Firm size and environmental scanning pursuits across organizational life cycle stages. *Journal of Small Business and Enterprise Development*, *15*(3), 540–554. doi:10.1108/14626000810892337

Lester, D. L., Parnell, J. A., & Carraher, S. (2003). Organizational life cycle: A five-stage empirical scale. *The International Journal of Organizational Analysis*, *11*(4), 339–354. doi:10.1108/eb028979

Lester, D. L., Parnell, J. A., Crandall, W. R., & Menefee, M. L. (2008). Organizational life cycle and performance among SMEs: Generic strategies for high and low performers. *International Journal of Commerce and Management*, *18*(4), 313–330. doi:10.1108/10569210810921942

Levy, M., & Powell, P. (2000). Information systems strategy for small and medium sized enterprises: An organisational perspective. *The Journal of Strategic Information Systems*, *9*(1), 63–84. doi:10.1016/S0963-8687(00)00028-7

Levy, M., Powell, P., & Yelton, P. (2002). The dynamics of SME information systems. *Small Business Economics*, *19*(4), 341–354. doi:10.1023/A:1019654030019

Levy, M., Powell, P., & Yetton, P. (2001). SMEs: Aligning IS and the strategic context. *Journal of Information Technology*, *16*(3), 133–144. doi:10.1080/02683960110063672

Lin, B., Vassar, J., & Clark, L. (1993). Information technology strategies for small business. *Journal of Applied Business Research*, *9*(2), 25–29.

Lin, C. Y. Y. (1998). Success factors of small and medium sized enterprises in Taiwan: An analysis of cases. *Journal of Small Business Management*, *36*(4), 43–57.

Link, A. N., & Bozeman, B. (1991). Innovative behavior in small-sized firms. *Small Business Economics*, *3*(3), 179–184. doi:10.1007/BF00400023

Lippitt, G., & Schmidt, W. (1967). Crises in developing organizations. *Harvard Business Review*, *45*(6), 102–112.

Maltz, E., & Kohli, A. K. (1996). Market intelligence dissemination across functional boundaries. *JMR, Journal of Marketing Research*, *33*(1), 177–201. doi:10.2307/3152012

McMahon, R. G. P. (1998). Stage models of SME growth reconsidered. *Small Business Research: The Journal of SEAANZ*, *6*(2), 20–35.

Miles, R., & Snow, C. (1978). *Organizational Strategy, Structure, and Process*. New York, NY: McGraw-Hill.

Miller, D., & Friesen, P. (1984). A longitudinal study of corporate life. *Management Science*, *30*(10), 1161–1183. doi:10.1287/mnsc.30.10.1161

Mintzberg, H. (1984). Power and organization life cycles. *Academy of Management Review*, *9*(2), 207–224.

Montserrat, E. (2002). The impact of the alignment of strategy and managerial characteristics on Spanish SMEs. *Journal of Small Business Management*, *40*(3), 260–271. doi:10.1111/1540-627X.00056

Muir, I., & Langford, D. (1994). Managerial behaviour in two small construction organizations. *International Journal of Project Management*, *12*(4), 244–253. doi:10.1016/0263-7863(94)90049-3

Mullen, M. R., Budeva, D. G., & Doney, P. M. (2009). Research methods in the leading small business – entrepreneursip journals: A critical review with recommendations for future research. *Journal of Small Business Management, 47*(3), 287–307. doi:10.1111/j.1540-627X.2009.00272.x

Naylor, J., & Williams, J. (1994). Successful use of IT in SMEs. *European Journal of IS, 3*(1), 48–56.

Nicholson, N. (2008). Evolutionary psychology and family business: A new synthesis for theory, research, and practice. *Family Business Review, 21*(1), 103–118. doi:10.1111/j.1741-6248.2007.00111.x

Nickell, G., & Seado, P. (1986). The impact of attitudes and experiences on small business computer use. *American Journal of Small Business, 10*(1), 37–48.

O'Gorman, C. (2001). The sustainability of growth in small and medium sized enterprises. *International Journal of Entrepreneurship Behaviour & Research, 7*(2), 60–71. doi:10.1108/13552550110396095

O'Gorman, C., Bourke, S., & Murray, J. A. (2005). The nature of managerial work in small growth-oriented small businesses. *Small Business Economics, 25*(1), 1–16. doi:10.1007/s11187-005-4254-z

Olson, P. D., & Bokor, D. W. (1995). Strategy process-content interaction: Effects on growth performance in small start-up firms. *Journal of Small Business Management, 33*(1), 34–44.

Orser, B. J., Hogarth-Scott, S., & Riding, A. L. (2000). Performance, firm size, and management problem solving. *Journal of Small Business Management, 38*(4), 42–58.

Parnell, J., & Carraher, S. (2002). The role of effective resource utilization in strategy's impact on performance. *International Journal of Commerce and Management, 13*(3), 1–34.

Penrose, E. T. (1959). *The Theory of the Growth of the Firm*. Oxford: Basil Blackwell.

Pierce, J. L., & Delbecq, A. L. (1977). Organizational structure, individual attitudes and innovation. *Academy of Management Review, 2*(1), 27–37.

Pollard, C., & Hayne, S. (1998). The changing faces of information systems issues in small firms. *International Small Business Journal, 16*(3), 70–87. doi:10.1177/0266242698163004

Poutsma, E. F., Van Uxem, F. W., & Walravens, A. H. C. M. (1987). *Process Innovation and Automation in Small and Medium Sized Business*. Delft, Netherlands: Delft University Press.

Powell, T. C., & Dent-Micallef, A. (1997). Information technology as competitive advantage: The role of human, business, and technology resources. *Strategic Management Journal, 18*(5), 375–405. doi:10.1002/(SICI)1097-0266(199705)18:5<375::AID-SMJ876>3.0.CO;2-7

Quinn, R., & Cameron, K. (1983). Organizational life cycles and shifting criteria of effectiveness: Some preliminary evidence. *Management Science, 29*(1), 33–41. doi:10.1287/mnsc.29.1.33

Rogers, E. M. (1983). *Diffusion of Innovations 3rd*. New York: Free Press.

Romanelli, E., & Tushman, M. L. (1994). Organizational transformation as punctuated equilibrium: An empirical test. *Academy of Management Journal, 37*(5), 1141–1166. doi:10.2307/256669

Rutherford, M. W., McMullen, P., & Oswald, S. (2001). Examining the issue of size and the small business: A self-organising map approach. *The Journal of Business and Economic Studies, 7*(2), 64–81.

Schein, E. H. (1992). The role of the CEO in the management of change: The case of information technology. In T. A. Kochan & M. Useem (Eds.), *Transforming Organizations*. Oxford: Oxford University Press.

Scott, M., & Bruce, R. (1987). Five stages of growth in small business. *Long Range Planning, 20*(3), 45–52. doi:10.1016/0024-6301(87)90071-9

Sharma, M. K., & Bhagwat, R. (2006). Performance measurements in the implementation of information systems in small and medium-sized enterprises: A framework and empirical analysis. *Measuring Business Excellence, 10*(4), 8–21. doi:10.1108/13683040610719245

Slater, S. F., & Narver, J. C. (1995). Market orientation and the learning organization. *Journal of Marketing, 59*(3), 63–74. doi:10.2307/1252120

Smith, K., Mitchell, T., & Summer, C. (1985). Top level management priorities in different stages of the organizational life cycle. *Academy of Management Journal, 28*(4), 799–820. doi:10.2307/256238

Steinmetz, L. L. (1969). Critical stages of small business growth: When they occur and how to survive them. *Business Horizons, 12*(1), 29–36. doi:10.1016/0007-6813(69)90107-4

Stevenson, H. H. (1999). A perspective of entrepreneurship. In H. H. Stevenson, H. I. Grousebeck, M. J. Roberts, & A. Bhide (Eds.), *New Business Ventures and the Entrepreneur*. Boston: Irwin McGraw-Hill.

Street, C. T., & Meister, D. B. (2004). Small business growth and internal transparency: The role of information systems. *Management Information Systems Quarterly*, *28*(3), 473–506.

Tan, J., Fischer, E., Mitchell, R., & Phan, P. (2009). At the center of the action: Innovation and technology strategy research in the small business setting. *Journal of Small Business Management*, *47*(3), 233–262. doi:10.1111/j.1540-627X.2009.00270.x

Taylor, J. (1999). Fitting enterprise software in smaller companies. *Management Accounting*, *80*(8), 36–39.

Thompson, V. A. (1969). *Bureaucracy and Innovation*. Huntsville: University of Alabama Press.

Thong, J. Y. L. (1999). An integrated model of information systems adoption in small businesses. *Journal of Management Information Systems*, *15*(4), 187–214.

Thong, J. Y. L., Yap, C. S., & Raman, K. S. (1994). Engagement of external expertise in information systems implementation. *Journal of Management Information Systems*, *11*(2), 209–231.

Timmons, J. A. (1999). *New Venture Creation* (5th ed.). Boston: Irwin McGraw-Hill.

Tippins, M. J., & Sohi, R. S. (2003). IT competency and firm performance: Is organizational learning a missing link? *Strategic Management Journal*, *24*(8), 745–761. doi:10.1002/smj.337

Tornatzky, L. G., & Klein, K. J. (1982). Innovation characteristics and innovation adoption implementation: A meta-analysis of findings. *IEEE Transactions on Engineering Management*, *29*(1), 28–45. doi:10.1109/TEM.1982.6447463

Tushman, M. L., & Romanelli, E. (1985). Organizational evolution: A metamorphosis model of convergence and reorientation. In B. M. Shaw (Ed.), *Research in Organizational Behavior* (Vol. 7, pp. 171–222). Greenwich, CT: JSL Press.

Wiklund, L., & Shepherd, D. (2003). Aspiring for, and achieving growth: The moderating role of resources and opportunities. *Journal of Management Studies*, *40*(8), 1919–1941. doi:10.1046/j.1467-6486.2003.00406.x

Yetton, P., Johnston, K., & Craig, J. (1994). Computer-aided architects: A case study of IT and strategic change. *Sloan Management Review*, *35*(4).

Zuboff, S. (1988). *In the Age of Smart Machine: The Future of Work and Power*. New York, NY: Basic Books.

## ADDITIONAL READING

Cassell, C., & Lee, B. (2001). *Challenges and Controversies in Management Research*. New York, NY: Routledge.

Clegg, S. (2002). *Central Currents in Organization Theory*. London: Sage. doi:10.4135/9781446260982

Krogstie, J. (2013). *Frameworks for Developing Efficient Information Systems: Models, Theory, and Practice*. Hershey, PA: IGI-Global. doi:10.4018/978-1-4666-4161-7

Pettigrew, A., Thomas, H., & Whittington, R. (2002). *Handbook of strategy and Management*. London: Sage.

## KEY TERMS AND DEFINITIONS

**Absorptive Capacity:** The ability of a small business to identify, assimilate, and exploit knowledge.

**Adoption:** The acquisition of a process. Innovation: the application of a better solution to a business requirement.

**Competitive Advantage:** The ability to perform better than the competition.

**Frameworks:** An abstract description of a generic function.

**Life Cycle:** Small businesses pass through birth, growth, maturity, and demise or rebirth.

**Models:** Concepts which represent an actual process.

**Punctuated Equilibrium Theory:** Small businesses pass through periods of slow change punctuated by periods of revolutionary change.

**Resource-based View:** The successful adoption of information systems relies upon positive attitudes and capabilities of individuals within the small business.

**Skills:** Learned abilities. Customer Orientation: the process of focusing on customers' needs and wants. Luck: an unpredictable, positive consequence.

**Stages of Growth:** Phases through which a small business passes as it expands.

**Success:** Achievement of a goal. Infrastructure: facilities that support the business function.

**Technology-Organization-Environment (TOE):** These three components facilitate the adoption of information technology by a small business.

# Chapter 5
# Adoption

## ABSTRACT

*The adoption of information systems by small business requires an innovative approach to the acquisition of technology. There are external pressures from the environment, such as customer and supplier expectations regarding interacting with the small business. However, it is incumbent upon management and employees form within to be open to considerations for change that will result in the small business. Further, a successful adoption will be facilitated through participation of everyone who will be affected by the adoption. The overall goal is improvement in processes which will positively impact the competitive advantage of the small business. This chapter addresses the issues involved in small business adoption of information systems. The adoption of technology in general will result in significant changes to the small business. It is not necessary that the technology is leading edge, just new to the small business. Pressure to adopt a new technology may come from external or internal sources. Externally, customers or suppliers may expect to interact with the small business via some form of technology. Internally, senior management of the small business may perceive that the adoption of a technology will provide a benefit to the business.*

## INTRODUCTION

A specific form of technology involves information technology; those systems which provide input to management decision making. Small business adopts information technology to enhance the efficiency of daily operations. Previous experience will positively impact the adoption of traditional information systems; those functions

DOI: 10.4018/978-1-4666-8708-0.ch005

which support normal business operations. The adoption of more current information systems, such as Internet based applications will be facilitated by an innovative approach to adopting a novel information technology.

Two theories have been employed to analyze the adoption of information systems by small business. The Resource-based View Theory suggests small business employ their internal resources to adopt information systems in a unique way to improve processes and potentially gain competitive advantage. The Technology-Organization-Environment (TOE) framework outlines the characteristics of information systems adoption relative to the specific context of the technology, the small business, and its environment.

The adoption of information systems may be considered a success of a failure. Successful adoption will result from user participation and the realization of the initially identified benefits. If there is no recognition of the impending change in the small business, the adoption may not be considered successful.

This chapter is organized as follows. The context of the adoption of information technology involves the acquisition of technology in general while taking an innovative approach. There are both internal and external pressures for the adoption of information systems. Previous experience will positively impact the adoption of traditional information systems. However, a more innovative attitude will facilitate the adoption of current technologies involving the Internet. Two theories are reviewed – Resource-based View and Technology-Organization-Environment (TOE). Then issues, related to adoption success and failure are reviewed. The chapter concludes with the presentation of an adoption project which, while completed, was not considered to be successful by the managers of a small business.

## INFORMATION SYSTEMS ADOPTION MODELS

Technological innovation involves a sequence of three stages (Pierce & Delbecq, 1977; and Thompson, 1969). The first stage, initiation, involves gathering and evaluating relevant information about the specific innovation. In the second stage, adoption, a decision is made to acquire the innovation. The third stage, implementation, relates to the installation and use of the innovation.

A recognized authority of Innovation Theory, Rogers (1983) has defined an innovation as an idea, practice, or object which is perceived by the adopting individual or work unit as new. Thus, the innovation itself may have existed for some time. But, its adoption in a specific situation is new and novel for the small business (Zaltman et al, 1973).

In general, an innovation is composed of four dimensions (Poutsma et al, 1987). First, an innovation may be a process or a product. A process innovation may improve and administrative or production activity. A product innovation involves the development and dissemination of a physical entity. A second dimension of an innovation relates to revolutionary versus evolutionary. A revolutionary innovation results in a radical change. An evolutionary innovation involves an incremental change. Third, the innovation may result from a technology-push or market-pull. A technology-push innovation suggests that as technology evolves its adoption is considered necessary. A market-pull innovation results from the demand for the technology. The fourth dimension is planned versus incidental. Planned innovations result from specific actions by an entity to implement a change. An incidental innovation occurs as a reaction to a market demand.

Chibelushi (2008) investigated issues surrounding the adoption of new technologies by small business. Initiatives to adopt new technologies emanated from within the small business. These initiatives were facilitated when the owner-manager possessed knowledge of information technology obtained through education. The adoption of new technologies may enhance both efficiency and effectiveness. More specifically new technologies may facilitate business transformation which, in turn, may contribute to competitive advantage.

Wernerfelt (1984) proposed a resource perspective rather than a product perspective for analyzing performance of a business. The "resource-based view of the firm" suggests that businesses assess their resource endowments and then attempt to exploit where they are different than their competitors in order to gain an advantage. This perspective has been taken by researchers investigating the use of information technology by small business.

It should be noted that small business face different challenges that large corporations when adopting information technology. For instance, the term resource poverty (Thong, 1999) applies to small business. The term suggests that small business does not possess resources related to time, finances, and skills. Thus, it is difficult to afford the necessary information technology champion to lead the adoption process. Further, it falls to the owner to lead the adoption of information technology. Thus, the small business owner must take an innovative approach in order for any adoption to be successful.

Qureshil et al (2009) suggest the resource-based view of the firm may be employed to support the development of strategies to address cost reduction or product differentiation with the goal of creating value for the business.

Small business adopts information technology to enhance the efficiency of daily operations (Blili & Raymond, 1993; Foong, 1999; Levy & Powell, 1998; and Poon & Swatman, 1999). Some small businesses adopt information technology to improve their relationship with customers (Porter, 1980; Reid & Jacobsen, 1988;

Lefebvre & Lefebvre, 1993). Small business will rely on a small customer base. Thus, a few relatively larger customers may be able to exert a great deal of power in this relationship.

In general, sustained competitive advantage may be attained through two major concepts (Mata et al, 1995). "Resource heterogeneity" suggests that the resources and capabilities of competing businesses will vary. "Resource immobility" suggests that the resources and capabilities differ between competing businesses and may continue for some time. Thus, Mata et al (1995) conclude that the only source of sustained information technology competitive advantage involves the management skills of information technology staff. Chao and Chandra (2012) support this contention suggesting that the small business owner's know of information technology is a significant predictor of the adoption of both traditional information technologies as well as internet technologies.

Lee and Runge (2001) investigated the adoption of information technology by small independent retailers. They suggested that information technology adoption would be influenced by the following:

1. *The owner's perception of the relative advantage of information technology use,*
2. *Social expectations of information technology use, and*
3. *The owner's innovativeness in managing their own business. (Lee & Runge, 2001, p. 44)*

They determined that the adoption of traditional information systems was influenced by the innovative approach taken by the owner. However, more current technology such as the internet was adopted mainly as a result of the owner's perception of the relative advantage to be gained by adopting the technology.

This finding suggests that adoption of traditional information systems depends more on previous experience. But, Internet adoption is more related to attempting to gain competitive advantage by taking an innovative approach to acquiring a novel information technology. Consequently, the adoption of new technology suggests that the small business owner is responding in a strategic manner.

Winston and Dologite (2002) investigated how the attitude of small business owners affects the adoption of information technology. They determined that an entrepreneurial approach was a positive influence on adoption and eventual successful implementation. This approach will help the small business owner overcome the frustration of dealing with technical issues and organizational changes precipitated by the adoption (Harrison et al, 1997; and Quinn, 1979).

It is suggested, "...the results of a high-quality IT implementation process include increased internal organizational performance and efficiency, better customer service, and a higher quality working life within the organization…" (Winston & Dologite, 2002, p. 17). This contention is supported by several researchers (Doukidis et al, 1994; Julien, 1995; Schafer, 1995; and Serwer, 1994) who suggest the small business will eventually accrue increased financial aspects of profits, market share, and return on investment.

Pressure to adopt new technologies may come from external or internal sources. Externally customers or suppliers may impact on adoption decisions in order to facilitate the business relationship (Kirbey & Turner, 1993; and Yap et al, 1992).

Internal pressures to adopt new technologies arise from many sources. The education and experience with adopting new technologies by the senior individuals in the small business will create a positive environment for innovative adoption (Barringer & Jones, 2004; and Marvel & Lumpkin, 2007). Further, top management support (Jeyaraj et al, 2006) will support this positive environment for employees to explore adoption of new technologies (Winston & Dologite, 2002). Also, top management will be more inclined to adopt new technologies if they perceive there are benefits to do so (Kirbey & Turner, 1993; and Thong & Yap, 1995). The more information technology literate top managers will make positive adoption decisions (Jullien & Raymond, 1994: and Harrison et al, 1997).

Nguyen (2007) suggested that information technology adoption by small business is affected by both internal and external sources. Figure 1 depicts the sources.

External drivers are related to market-pull which involves the small business reacting proactively (Laudon & Laudon, 2007) to industry standards (Romano et al, 2001). Technology-push relates to the small business adopting a technology and developing a market (Andries & Debackere, 2006).

The internal driver of life cycle suggests that small businesses progress through various stages and may adopt technology to facilitate any necessary changes (Siggelkow & Levinthal, 2005). Maturity relates to the knowledge of information technology possessed by individuals within the business (Liao et al, 2003).

Information technology may be employed to improve business processes (Acar et al, 2005; Burca et al, 2005; and Levy et al, 2001). These improved business processes may lead to lower production and labour costs, and improved products and services which in turn will contribute to competitive advantage (Corso et al, 2003; Levy et al, 2001, Nguyen et al, 2007; and Premkumar, 2003).

Kannabiran (2012) investigated the influences on small businesses in India to adopt information technology. The results suggest enablers include perceived benefits and perceived competitive pressure. Inhibiters included lack of financial capacity, small scale operation, and lack of in-house IT expertise. Table 6.1 provides the details of the framework used for this investigation.

Thong (1999) developed an integrated model of information systems adoption by small businesses. He investigated the likelihood and extent of adoption and

*Figure 1. Drivers of information technology adoption*
*Adapted from Nguyen, 2007*

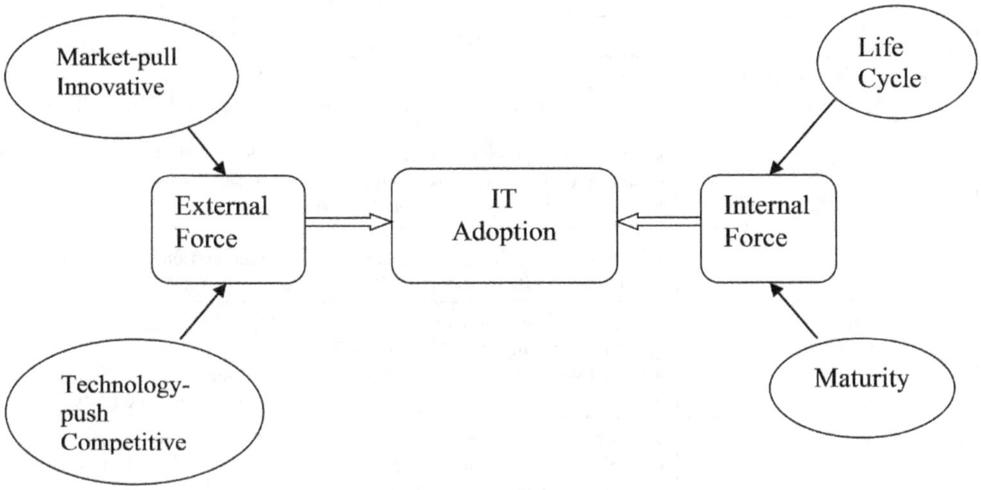


determined the following results. First, the extent of information systems adoption is related to business size. Thus, the larger the size of the business the more resources are available to adopt the technology. Second, employee knowledge of information systems also contributes to its adoption. Thus, the more familiar employees are with technology in general, and information systems specifically the more they will accept the innovation. Third, if the product or service is related to the provision of information there will be an increased extent of adoption of an information system. Again, individuals within the small business will be familiar with the aspects of information systems because of the similarity with the product or service they provide.

Ifinedo (2011) explored the adoption of Internet and e-business technologies (IEBT) by small business in the eastern region of Canada. He determined that the major predictors for adoption include perceived benefits, management commitment, and external pressure. The theoretical foundation employed to support this investigation is known as the Technology-Organization-Environment (TOE) framework. Table 2 describes the components of the TOE framework applied by Ifinedo. Other research that has employed the TOE framework include (Kendall et al, 2001; Love & Irani, 2004; Wade et al, 2004; Van der Deen, 2005; Davis & Vladica, 2006; Mustaffa & Beaumont, 2004; Chong & Pervan, 2007; and Chau & Hui, 2001).

Ramdani et al (2009) employed the TOE framework to explore the adoption of enterprise systems by small and medium-sized enterprises. They determined that,

*Table 1. Factors that influence adoption of information technology*

| Factor | Description |
| --- | --- |
| **Enablers** | |
| Perceived benefits of the use of information technology | • Anticipated advantages that will benefit the business (Mehrtens et al, 2001; Seyal et al, 2004; Apulu & Latham, 2011; Lai et al, 2007; Alshawi, 2010)<br>• Improve competitiveness (Alberto & Fernando, 2007)<br>• Reduce costs and increase productivity (Lymer et al, 1997)<br>• Efficiency in daily operations (Ongori & Migiro, 2010)<br>• Reduce operating costs (Al-Qirim, 2007)<br>• Manufacturing flexibility, increased systems integration, and improved product and process innovation (Raymond & Bergeron, 2008) |
| Changes in business environment | • Small businesses adopt information technology as a result of globalization (Ongori & Migiro, 2010)<br>• Global value chains impact business partners (Decker et al, 2006)<br>• Business must consider the big picture (Mendo & Fitzgerald (2005) |
| IT experience of owner | • Experience with information technology will facilitate its adoption<br>• Involvement assists identifying information technology goals, business information needs, allocating necessary financial resources, and managing implementation (Somuyiwa & Adewoye, 2010; and Windrum & de Beranger, 2003)<br>• Information system knowledge (Wainwright et al, 2005; Hashim, 2007; Mirchandani & Motwani, 2001; Dholakia & Kshetri, 2004; Sabherwal et al, 2006; Tan et al, 2009) |
| Increased external information linkages | Adoption decisions may be affected by customers, vendors, or suppliers (Bharati & Chaudhury, 2010; Hinson & Sorensen, 2006; Pires & Stanton, 2005; Wymer & Regan, 2005). |
| Perceived competitive pressure | IT adoption by competitors may influence business adoption (Cragg et al, 2002; Bharati & Chaudhury, 2010; Dholakia & Kshetri, 2004; and Zhu et al, 2003) |
| **Inhibiters** | |
| Lack of financial capacity | Initial set-up and operating costs of IT are high relative to the resources of a small business (Somuyiwa & Adebayo, 2011; Duncombe & Heeks, 2001; Seyal et al, 2007; and Dixon et al, 2002) |
| Lack of in-house IT expertise | IT adoption requires both human skills and technical knowledge (Packalen, 2010; MacGregor, 2004; Levy et al, 2001; Wainwright et al, 2005; Hashim, 2007; and Kartiwi & MacGregor, 2007) |
| Small scale operation | Firm size affects IT adoption (Yulong Li, 2011; Dixit & Prakash, 2011; Dholakia & Kshetri, 2004; Brown & Kaewkitipong, 2009) |
| Lack of IT infrastructure | Small businesses need the supporting technology and services (Johnson, 2010; Mpofu & Watkins-Mathys, 2011; Tan & Eze, 2008; and Todd & Javalgi, 2007) |
| Lack of information security | A legal framework is necessary to support business adopting IT (Koshy, 2011; Grandon & Pearson, 2004b; Jeon et al, 2006; Ratnasingam, 2001; and Love et al, 2001) |

Adapted from Kannabiran, 2012

*Table 2. Technology-orgainzation-environment (TOE) framework*

| Characteristic | Description |
|---|---|
| **Technological Context** | |
| Perceived Benefits | Relative advantage to be gained by the small business adoption of IEBT (Rogers, 2003, Premkumar & Roberts, 1999; Chwelos et al, 2001; Mehrtens et al, 2001; Chau & Jim, 2002; Gunasekaran & Ngai, 2005; Al-Qirim, 2007; and Chong & Pervan, 2007) |
| **Organizational Context** | |
| Management Commitment and Support | Involvement, enthusiasm, motivation, and encouragement provided by management regarding adoption of IEBT (Thong et al, 1996; Chatterjee et al, 2002; Al-Qirim, 2007; Ramdani et al, 2009; and Jeyaraj, 2006) |
| Organizational IT Competence | Level of technical expertise within the small business (Raymond, 2001; Zhu et al, 2006; Chircu & Kauffman, 2000; Cragg & King, 1993; Chwelos et al, 2001; Mehrtens et al, 2001; Raymond, 2001; Caldeira & Ward, 2002; and Pflughoeft et al, 2003) |
| **Environmental Context** | |
| External Pressure | Influences on a small business from competitors, suppliers, and customers (Hart & Saunders, 1998; Chau & Jim, 2002; Kula & Tatoglu, 2003; Chong et al, 2009;Looi, 2005; Jeyaraj et al, 2006; Chong & Pervan, 2007; Huang et al, 2008; Raymond, 2001; and Hadaya, 2006) |
| IS Vendor Support and Pressure | (De Guinea et al, 2005; Ramdani et al, 2009; Al-Qirim, 2007; McDonagh & Prothero, 2000; Scupola, 2003; and Simpson & Doherty, 2004) |
| Financial Resources Availability | Ability to obtain necessary financial reosurces (Walczuch et al, 2000; Tan & Wu, 2003; Lawson et al, 2003; Grandon & Pearson, 2004a; Cragg et al, 2001; Dongen et al 2002; and Simpson & Doherty, 2004) |

Adapted from Ifinedo, 2011

*...it can be predicted that SMEs with a greater perceived relative advantage, a greater ability to experiment with ES [enterprise systems] before adoption, greater top management support, greater organisational readiness and a larger size are more likely to become adopters of ES. (Ramdani et al, 2009, p. 21)*

## ADOPTION SUCCESS vs. FAILURE

When is an information system adoption considered a success, and when is it considered a failure? What factors contribute to a conclusion of either success or failure? How does the situation arise to create the environment, which contributes to the above conclusions? Generally, an information system is considered a success when it does what it is supposed to and/or the user is satisfied with the system's performance in support of the information providing and decision making responsibilities. Naturally, this area is fraught with the problems inherent in divergent interpretations of "what it is supposed to do", "satisfaction", and "systems performance". Suffice it to say, when the systems developer and user are in positive agreement about these interpretations, the information system development outcome may be considered successful.

Negative information system adoption can be classified as either "completed" or "abandoned" projects. First, "completed" projects result in the implementation of an information system but either the information system fails to attain initially stated goals or attains the goals after the expenditure of more time and effort. According to Laudon and Laudon (2007) 51 percent of all corporate software development projects result in costs of two to three times more than the initial budget amount, and eventually may require up to three times longer than originally estimated to complete. Ewusi-Mensah (1997) reports similar statistics, suggesting, as reported in a study by the Standish Group that almost one third of all information system projects are terminated before completion. As well, "... 52.7% of the projects completed are 189% over budget..." (Ewusi-Mensah, 1997, p. 74). Thus, is the project a failure, or was the original estimation simply in error? Should these outcomes be regarded as failures or eventual successes? The answer seems to depend upon the perspective taken by the decision-maker. User satisfaction has been employed to provide a relative measure of an interpretation of success or failure as perceived by users. Second "abandoned" projects are those projects, which are never completed. Unfortunately, while they do not even result in the implementation of an information system, they are the cause of the ineffective consumption of company resources.

Research into information system adoption can be categorized as relating to Users, Systems Analysts, or the interaction between the two groups. First, a series of research projects is reported on, which have attempted to identify factors contributing to successful information system development outcomes. Then a series of projects is presented, which discuss aspects leading to negative outcomes.

The research described in the following paragraphs, investigated successful information system development outcomes. The identified factors relate to some aspect of users and their relationship to the information system development project.

Barki and Hartwick (1994) investigated the relationships among user participation, user involvement, and user attitude, and their contribution to the development of successful information system. To conduct their research into user – information system relationship, the authors have developed the following definitions:

## User Participation

*...refers to the assignment, activities and behaviors that users ... perform during the systems development process. (Barki and Hartwick, 1994, p. 60).*

## User Involvement

*...a psychological state reflecting the importance and personal relevance of a new system to the user. (Barki and Hartwick, 1994, p. 62).*

## User Attitude

*...a psychological state reflecting the reflective or evaluative feelings concerning a new system. (Barki and Hartwick, 1994, p. 62).*

They determined that user participation influenced both involvement and attitude, and all three contribute to the development of successful information system.

Robey et al (1993) investigated the relationships among participation, influence, and conflict resolution during information system development, with success as an outcome variable. They found, among other factors, that conflict resolution leads to project success. They suggest that, "... the success of a project is largely dependent on the extent to which incompatible goals are resolved by consensus among project members." (Robey et al, 1993, pp. 135-136). They also discovered that user participation did not contribute as much to project success as did influence and conflict resolution. Relevant definitions in this case are as follows:

## Participation

*...extent to which members of an organization are engaged in activities related to system development. (Robey et al, 1993, p. 125).*

## Influence

*...extent to which members affect decisions related to the final design of an information system. (Robey et al, 1993, p. 125).*

## Conflict

*...Manifest disagreement among group members [which] implies incompatible goals among group members. (Robey et al, 1993, p. 125).*

It is interesting to note that while Robey et al (1993) have used the same definition for "participation" as Barki and Hartwick (1994), the concept of "involvement", as defined by Barki and Hartwick (1994), has not been included as a differentiating aspect of the User – information system relationship.

Byers and Blume (1994) investigated the relationship between critical success factors (CSF) and information system development. They suggest the process of identifying CSFs leads to increased user involvement and a better understanding of the business functions on the part of information system personnel. These two factors lead to the creation of a partnership between information system development staff and the functional area, which supports the focus on those aspects critical to the business.

In general then the above research suggests that information system development outcomes will tend to be considered successful with the existence of increased user participation or user involvement; and some mechanism, which may be employed for conflict resolution. The following paragraphs describe unsuccessful information system development outcomes. The factors identified here relate to project management and organizational context of the information system development project.

Using Cognitive Dissonance Theory, Szajna and Scamell (1993) investigated the ability to predict information system failures based upon an assessment of user expectations. They determined the existence of an association between realistic user expectations and their perceptions. However, they were unable to establish a relationship between expectations and perceptions, and users' actual performance.

Negative adoption outcomes may result if small business owners do not understand the strategic impact of information technology (Cragg & King, 1993; and Delone, 1988).

Keil and Mixon (1993) investigated the concept of "escalating commitment" to runaway information system development projects. While the authors have considered several theories such as self-justification theory, and the sunk cost effect of prospect theory, they have developed their research program through studies grounded in escalation theory as a framework to attempt to explain why decision makers tend to delay project cancellation decisions. They have adapted Brockner's (1992) concept of "escalating commitment to a failing course of action" to attempt to explain runaway projects. This concept suggests that individuals will remain committed to a prior decision in spite of information, which suggests the decision was incorrect. They discuss some theories (self-justification theory, prospect theory, and escalation theory) as a framework to attempt to explain why decision-makers tend to delay project cancellation decisions.

Ewusi-Mensah and Przasnyski (1991) discuss development project abandonment as one aspect of information system failure. Survey results indicate project abandonment was a complex issue relating to a combination of factors such as cost overrun, schedule slippage, technological inadequacies, as well as issues related to behavioral, political, and organizational factors, which emerged from the research as the most dominant. Ewusi-Mensah (1997) confirmed the earlier results obtained by Ewusi-Mensah and Przasnyski (1991) and suggested factors contributing to the cancellation of projects relate to project goals, project management and control, technical know-how, infrastructure, senior management involvement, and escalating cost and time.

Lederer and Nath (1991) suggest information system failures are the result of the individuals involved not sufficiently recognizing that information system development actually represents organizational change. They suggest that systems developers consider, "… such commonly practiced organizational change activities as the redesign of worker responsibilities to improve efficiency, the instituting of new management styles, the restructuring of management reporting relationships, or the reduction of interpersonal conflict …" (Lederer & Nath, 1991, p. 23) as a means to put in context the development process. They suggest a framework, which promotes developer - user interaction and includes such components as cultivation of a project champion, recognition of resistance to change, resolution of conflict, recognition of human sub-system issues, collaboration, and team building. Unfortunately, the article does not include a detailed discussion of the operationalization of the framework and its components. It does, however, serve to support the contention of the importance of the human aspects of information system development practices and their impact on outcomes.

Davis et al (1992) provide a diagnostic framework and interpretative process for analyzing information system failures. Based upon one episode of an information system failure they have developed the social and technical dimensions of their framework. Each dimension is divided into four characteristics creating sixteen components, which highlight useful considerations for analyzing information systems failures. The framework is proposed, as a model to be used when approaching the analysis of a specific information system failure. While taking an individual information system perspective, this framework seems to be more related to, and thus, more appropriate for the investigation of information system development outcomes in larger organizations.

The next research reported on here presents a framework, which emphasizes the interaction between stakeholders. For this reason (stakeholder interaction), this framework seems to be an appropriate method for analyzing the case discussed here, because of the focus upon individuals performing within the context of a small business.

This framework also incorporates factors determined by other researchers, which were presented earlier in this section. Factors contributing to successful information system development outcomes include user participation and involvement (Barki & Hartwick, 1994); participation, influence, and conflict (Robey et al, 1993); and involvement and understanding (Byers and Blume, 1994). Factors contributing to unsuccessful information system development outcomes include user expectations (Szajna and Scamell, 1993); escalating commitment (Keil and Mixon, 1993); organizational change (Lederer and Nath, 1991); and a series of issues relating to costs, schedule, technological in adequacies, project goals, project management, infrastructure, and senior management involvement (Ewusi-Mensah and Przasnyski, 1991 and Ewusi-Mensah, 1997). Also, the framework proposed by Davis et al (1992) provides further support for the use of the McComb and Smith (1991) framework. While Davis et al (1992) proposed a framework with similar dimensions to the McComb and Smith (1991) framework the Davis et al (1992) proposal seems to relate more to the environment encountered in larger organizations. As presented later in the Results and Discussion section, the McComb and Smith (1991) framework presents dimensions of information system outcomes more suited to the environment encountered by small business.

McComb and Smith (1991) identified patterns within less successful information system development projects. They identified two categories relating to planning and executing, and two factors within each category of human and technical. Based on their findings they propose an analytical framework to assist in the identification of potential problems, which may contribute to the prevention of project failures. Figure 2 presents the McComb and Smith (1991) system failure risk framework.

McComb and Smith (1991) suggest that Figure 2, "… provides an analytical framework for linking observed systems failures to behavioral factors. Common planning and execution behaviors are traceable to both the technical and human sides of systems development that have resulted in systems failures. Any given project may be traceable to one or more of these factors." (McComb & Smith, 1991, pp. 25-26).

Thus, the authors organize their framework along two continua. The first continuum, the Planning - Executing dimension differentiates factors relative to deciding what to do (Planning) and then carrying out the activities (Executing). The Planning dimension includes such factors as estimating (developing time and costs resource requirements) and compression (deciding whether to apply additional time and monetary resources). The Executing dimension includes change management (methods employed to monitor and control modification to specifications during

*Figure 2. System failure framework*
*Adapted from McComb and Smith, 1991*

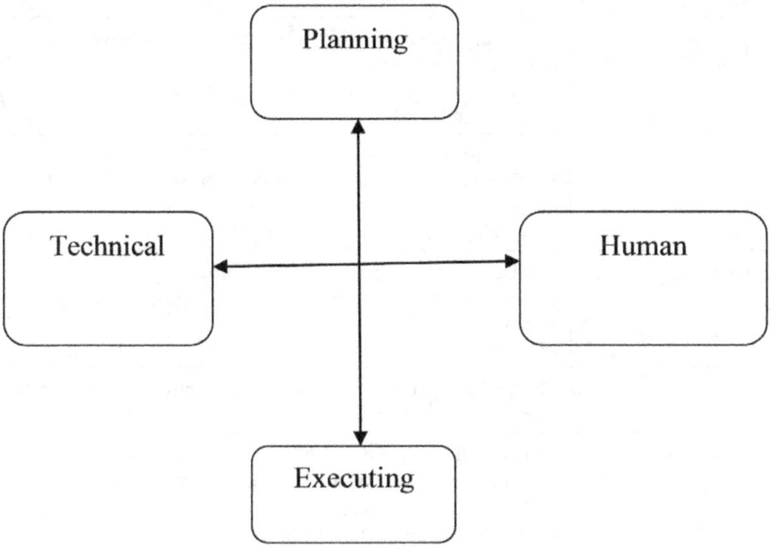


system development) and workarounds (innovative methods used to resolve inconsistencies between planned and actual activities).

The second continuum, the Technical - Human dimension serves to differentiate the factors relative to the physical components (Technical) of an information system rather than the personal (Human) components. The Technical dimension includes such aspects as ensuring data accuracy and system reliability, response time, and ensuring current technology is appropriate, or investigating the application of new technology. The Human dimension revolves around aspects relating to interpersonal relations and includes staffing, feedback, motivation, and involvement.

A further description of each factor is included here in Table 3.

These factors are discussed later in this document with specific reference to the case reported on in the next section.

In summary, small business adoption of information technology may be unsuccessful for a number of reasons. The three main contributors to failure may include one or all of the following. First, management may not understand the process of adopting information technology (Levy et al, 2001; and Southern & Tilley, 2000). Second, management may not understand how information technology can help the business (Bull, 2003; Carson & Gilmore, 2000). Third, small businesses lack necessary resources, such as finances, to adopt information technology (Bhagwat & Sharma, 2007).

*Table 3. Interpretation of framework factors*

| Factor | Interpretation |
|---|---|
| Planning | Estimating: independent of the method used, the more accurate the estimate the less risk<br>Compression: adding staff to complete a task may actually increase the time required |
| Planning – Human | Bid Strategy: methods use to acquire and assess external services<br>Staffing: assigning and retaining the appropriate skills of those involved in the project<br>Scheduling: the logical sequencing of activities |
| Executing – Human | Feedback: unbiased reporting of performance<br>User Involvement: participation in the design and training related to the system<br>Motivation: commitment of those involved to solving the problem |
| Executing | Change Management: methods used to control specification modification<br>Workarounds: ingenious ways to resolve inconsistencies |
| Executing – Technical | Vendor: reliability and credibility of external service organization<br>Control: methods for ensuring accuracy of data and reliability of the system<br>Performance: system response time |
| Planning – Technical | Experimenting with new technology: attempt to use unproven physical components<br>Technical architecture: ensure the physical components address functional requirements |

Adapted from McComb and Smith, 1991

## A SAMPLE INVESTIGATION

This section analyses an information systems development project, which is considered by the users to be "completed" yet, unsuccessful. Initially, the literature available in the area is presented and reviewed. The McComb and Smith (1991) system failure risk framework has been adopted as a means of analysing the case presented in this section. Then the specific situation is presented with a description of the project and the results. This section concludes with a discussion of how the framework may be useful in understanding information system success or failure within a small business context.

A case study research approach was employed to investigate the specific situation of adopting an integrated information system for a small sheet music store, which will be referred to as Song Book Music. As Yin (1994) suggests, case studies are appropriate when investigating contemporary events where the researcher does not have control of the events, which transpire within the area of investigation. More specifically, research projects, which ask, "How and why questions are likely to favour the use of case studies …" (Yin, 1994, p. 7). Also, Stake (1994) suggests,

"... a particular case is examined to provide insight into an issue or refinement of theory." (Stake, 1995, p. 237). Further, more specifically related to the study of information systems, Galliers (1994) has suggested that case studies provide an opportunity for capturing reality in detail in order to describe existing relationships. Thus, case studies allow researchers to investigate an information system in its natural setting. This approach permits the researcher to thoroughly investigate the nature and complexity of the existing process, and the interactions among stakeholders. The data gathering process employed the Narrative Inquiry method, which documents for subsequent analysis research participants' interpretations of personal experiences from an event or series of events. The interviews gathered comments from the research participants about the major events, which transpired in the planning and adoption of a specific information system.

The following paragraphs present a brief overview of the company and the adoption project.

In the summer of 1994, Ruth and Ellen (fictitious names) purchased Song Book Music from the absentee owner. Ruth, a music teacher, had managed the store since September 1993. Ellen, who had an Administration degree, brought small business accounting experience to the partnership. The two ladies had known each other socially since 1972 when their husbands were in university.

For the first few years, the new owners continued operations as before. Eventually, they decided it would be necessary to implement a more effective inventory control system. This decision was made in response to problems concerning knowing what inventory was on-hand, what had to be ordered, and where to acquire both existing and new items. The inventory problem was also creating poor customer service because product might not be available or it could be difficult to process special orders. The owners also thought it would be helpful to include order entry and sales processes into an integrated inventory control system.

Initially, the owners investigated various alternatives. They interviewed a ski shop owner and attended a seminar presentation of an accounting system, which included an inventory control module. They determined in each case that the systems did not meet their needs.

Because most of the owners' time was taken up in managing and running the store, they decided to acquire the services of a consultant to help them resolve this business problem. So, they contacted Buck, the sole proprietor of Buffalo Consulting. Buck not only developed custom software, he built his own computers. He had been working as an independent consultant with local industry for quite some time. Buck provided the owners with a very impressive list of former clients. As stated by the owners, because the list was so impressive, they did not consider contacting any of the former clients. They also concluded that no other bids would be necessary, again because of the names of former clients. The owners accepted this list as fact. However, they discovered later that, while it was a list of former clients, the services provided were not related to the information system development effort to be acquired, in this instance, by the owners.

The owners met with Buck and explained their situation to him in detail. After two or three subsequent visits Buck made a verbal proposal and presented a bill for $240 for consulting services. Buck suggested a custom designed system, which he would develop. The system would include software developed by him and two networked computers entirely constructed by him. It was the owners' interpretation that the system would be completely developed and implemented within two months. However, there was never a written document exchanged regarding these dates.

Thus, Phase 1, software development and hardware construction was to be carried out over the first two weeks. Phase 2, system testing, would be conducted during the third week. Over the next few weeks the system would be implemented, as Phase 3. This is the period of time when all product data would be entered into the system. By the end of the second month Phase 3 would be completed with the installation of the system. This was the plan however, what transpired was quite different.

The owners were not involved in Phase 1. During this time Buck spent his time constructing the hardware and developing the software according to his interpretation of the requirements of the system as outlined by the owners. There was very little interaction between the owners and Buck. When queried, his response was invariably polite with an indication that all was proceeding, as it should.

During Phase 2, system testing, some problems started to arise. At this time, not all of the system was available to test. It was still being developed. Also, the part, which was available, could not handle all of the required data elements.

Early in the second month the situation began to deteriorate drastically. Even though the system was not completely installed, Buck began to demand full payment for his services. The Song Book Music's lawyer recommended withholding payment. Buck began to behave unprofessionally, regularly missing appointments. Data entry proceeded very slowly. It had to be re-started in the fifth month because of a system crash with no back up in place. Testing was eventually completed in the eighth month and a physical inventory was taken. Thus, the project, which had been planned to be complete in two months, actually took eight months.

At that time Buck was paid in full at the recommendation of Song Book Music's lawyer and he was informed his services were no longer required. The husband of one of the owner's currently is carrying out maintenance of the system. While the system is being used, it regularly causes problems and must be reprogrammed when errors are discovered. The overall reaction of the owners to the experience is negative. They are not satisfied and classify the system as a failure. They feel it is simply a matter of time before they will replace the system.

## Project Discussion

The literature reviewed earlier in this chapter suggests aspects contributing to negative information system development outcomes can be related to technical and human-oriented factors.

First, several technical factors contributed to the negative outcome at Song Book Music. The most significant was the schedule overrun. Originally, it was expected that the project would be completed in two months. However, the project actually took eight months. While no cost overruns were generated, the timing of the delivery of the information system functional components and the "demand" for payment did not match. This situation increased the Users' frustration with the overall process and the information system specifically. There was no conflict resolution mechanism in place which Robey et al (1993) suggest would have contributed to the potential for a successful information system development outcome. Another technical factor related to technological inadequacies. Both users are not technical experts. Indeed, they recognized this fact with the decision to obtain the services of a consultant. The consultant, however, was also found lacking in this aspect. Buck experienced problems with his knowledge of the software and understanding its capability regarding the development of the required functionality. He also encountered problems with the hardware. He assembled the computers himself. The construction process was not the best. This caused the machines to operate inconsistently. He had a great deal of trouble trying to have the two machines communicate with each other.

Second, a number of human-oriented aspects also contributed to the negative information system adoption. Both users felt that they participated and were involved in the development process. However, their participation was limited to data entry and their involvement was, at best, a superficial interaction with Buck regarding the current status of the project. Perhaps the more important factors relate to expectations and commitment. There seems to be a major difference in the interpretation of the expectations for the functionality of the information system. Both parties seemed to not understand the others' description of the information system requirements. This situation was even further confounded by the lack of written documentation. Also, the users reported a feeling of escalating commitment to the project even though they thought the process was not going to produce the kind of information system they expected. The users felt that they had committed the greater portion of available funds to the project too early in its existence. Their interpretation was that it would have been difficult or impossible to extricate them from the situation.

All of these factors lead to deterioration in the interaction between Buck and the users. By the end of the project the two parties were even having difficulty discussing aspects of the information system.

In this case, perhaps the most important factor contributing to the negative information system development outcome relates to the fact that both parties are involved in the operation of relatively small companies. This fact creates a unique situation with regards to the development and implementation of an information system to support the business functions. In the following paragraphs the Song Book Music case is discussed relative to the McComb and Smith (1991) framework, presented in Figure 2 and Table 3.

Small business managers tend to be action oriented and would then fall closer to the "Executing" than the "Planning" continuum. In this case both the Songbook owners and Buck would tend to converge toward the "Executing" end. Thus, both parties would subsequently tend to ignore those aspects associated with Planning. This would create a potential for risk with regards to the unsuccessful completion of the information system project. This was indeed the situation here. There was little evidence of planning, especially in relation to what should have been conducted relative to the early stages of a system development life cycle.

Further, the two parties involved can be associated with different ends of the continuum relative to "Technical" versus "Human". Buck is obviously technically oriented. His education and work experience was specifically related to the more technical aspects of computers. His interpersonal skills were also lacking as indicated earlier when the project started to deteriorate. The two owners, on the other hand, are more "Human" oriented. They possess excellent interpersonal skills. They work in a people-oriented business. The technical aspects of computers and information systems are of little interest. This divergent situation would tend to create difficulties in the relationship between these two groups, which would result in another area where the information system would be more susceptible to failure.

## Project Epilogue

Approximately eighteen months after the initial case study, reported above, was documented, another interview was conducted with Ruth and Ellen in order to determine their current interpretation of the outcome of adopting the information system.

Since the initial contact the business has grown. Revenues have increased and the geographical market place has become more extensive. Indeed, potential customers from other countries have contacted Song Book Music.

With regards to the information system, many changes have been made. New, faster computers have been installed. Some program logic has been revised mainly in order to correct mistakes. A number of new programs have been added which provide more reporting capability regarding invoices, payments, and un-reconciled inventory. Overall, about another 300 hours have been spent resolving the above problems and adding the new reporting capability. Fortunately, this work has been carried out, in effect, for free by Ruth's husband who works as a systems analyst for a large company.

So, the owners feel the system is 'useable', but they retain a very negative impression of the information system and the overall experience. In general, they are satisfied. They will continue to use the information system only because they cannot find anything better. In its current form the system supports the owner's information requirements. They both now know how to interact with the system.

## Project Conclusion

This section has reported a case of two small organizations attempting to develop and implement an information system. The result of the project has been interpreted by the users as negative. The outcome of this project has been affected by technical factors such as schedule overrun and technological inadequacies of the parties involved. Also, human-oriented factors, such as, user expectations and commitment, have negatively affected the outcome. Perhaps the most important factor affecting this specific case relates to the small business perspective of the parties involved.

In general, individuals running small businesses (with the exception of information system development firms) will tend to associate more easily with the "Executing - Human" ends of the McComb and Smith (1991) continua. Thus, they will be more susceptible to potential system failure from aspects relating to Planning and Technical factors. It is therefore incumbent upon small business managers who intend to develop and implement information systems to respond to these factors. From a technical perspective, they must at least know the capabilities of computers and related communications facilities. Further, small business managers must ensure that time is taken early in an information system development project to devote to planning.

Small business information system development firms, however, will more easily associate with "Executing - Technical" ends of the McComb and Smith (1991) continua. Thus, Planning and Human factors will tend to contribute to an interpretation of information system failure. In responding to these factors, information system development firms must address communication in general through concentrating on user involvement, motivation, and feedback. Further, extensive planning early in the project will contribute to both a better understanding of what has to be done and an improved estimate of how long it will take to complete the task.

Finally, these are the areas where small businesses are most susceptible to negative information system development outcomes. Concentrating on these factors will increase the potential for a successful information system development outcome.

## CONCLUSION

This chapter has presented the issues related to the adoption of information systems by small business. It is important to take an innovative approach to the adoption of information systems. Management and employees must realize that processes change and they need to respond appropriately. The goal is improved operations and the consequent positive contribution to competitive advantage. The next chapter presents a review of the use of information systems by small business.

## REFERENCES

Acar, E., Kocak, L., Sey, Y., & Arditi, D. (2005). Use of information and communication technologies by small and medium-sized enterprises (SMEs) in building construction. *Construction Management and Economics*, *23*(7), 713–722. doi:10.1080/01446190500127112

Al-Qirim, N. (2007). The adoption of e-commerce communications and applications technologies in small business in New Zealand. *Electronic Commerce Research and Applications: Intelligent Agents in E-services*, *6*(4), 462–473. doi:10.1016/j.elerap.2007.02.012

Albertao, B. M., & Fernando, L. L. (2007). A firm-level analysis of determinants of ICT adoption in Spain. *Technovation*, *27*(6/7), 352–366.

Alshawi, S., Missi, F., & Irani, Z. (2010). Organizational, technical and data quality factors in CRM adoption: SMEs perspective. *Industrial Marketing Management*, *40*(3), 376–383. doi:10.1016/j.indmarman.2010.08.006

Andries, P., & Debackere, K. (2006). Adoption of new technology-based ventures: Insights at the company level. *International Journal of Management Reviews*, *8*(2), 91–112. doi:10.1111/j.1468-2370.2006.00122.x

Apulu, I., & Latham, A. (2011). Drivers for information and communication technology adoption: A case study of Nigerian small and medium sized enterprises. *International Journal of Business and Management*, *6*(5), 51–60. doi:10.5539/ijbm.v6n5p51

Barki, H., & Hartwick, J. (1994). Measuring User Participation, User Involvement, and User Attitude. *Management Information Systems Quarterly*, *18*(1), 59–82. doi:10.2307/249610

Barringer, B. R., & Jones, F. F. (2004). Achieving rapid growth: Revisiting the managerial capacity problem. *Journal of Developmental Entrepreneurship*, *9*(1), 73–86.

Bhagwat, R., & Sharma, M. K. (2007). Information system architecture: A framework for a cluster of small and medium-sized enterprises (SMEs). *Production Planning and Control*, *18*(4), 283–296. doi:10.1080/09537280701248578

Bharati, P., & Chaudhury, A. (2010). IT adoption in small and medium-sized enterprises: The role of knowledge acquisition. *Proceedings of Americas Conference on Information Systems*, Lima, August, 12-15.

Blili, S., & Raymond, L. (1993). Information technology: Threats and opportunities for small and medium-sized enterprises. *International Journal of Information Management*, *13*(6), 439–448. doi:10.1016/0268-4012(93)90060-H

Brockner, J. (1992). The Escalation of Commitment to a failing Course of Action: Toward Theoretical Progress. *Academy of Management Review*, *17*(1), 39–61.

Brown, D. H., & Kaewkitipong, L. (2009). Relative size and complexity: E-business use in small and medium sized tourism enterprises in Thailand. *Journal of Enterprise Information Management*, *22*(1/2), 212–231. doi:10.1108/17410390910932849

Bull, C. (2003). Strategic issues in customer relationship management (CRM) implementation. *Business Process Management Journal*, *9*(5), 592–602. doi:10.1108/14637150310496703

Burca, S., Fynes, B., & Marshall, D. (2005). Strategic technology adoption: Extending ERP across the supply chain. *Journal of Enterprise Information Management*, *18*(4), 427–440. doi:10.1108/17410390510609581

Byers, C. R., & Blume, D. (1994). Tying Critical Success Factors to Systems Development. *Information & Management*, *26*(1), 51–61. doi:10.1016/0378-7206(94)90006-X

Caldeira, M. M., & Ward, J. M. (2002). Understanding the successful adoption and use of IS/IT in SMEs: An explanation for Portuguese manufacturing industries. *Information Systems Journal*, *12*(2), 121–152. doi:10.1046/j.1365-2575.2002.00119.x

Carson, D., & Gilmore, A. (2000). SME marketing management competencies. *International Business Review*, *9*(3), 363–382. doi:10.1016/S0969-5931(00)00006-8

Chao, C. A., & Chandra, A. (2012). Impact of owner's knowledge of information technology (IT) on strategic alignment and IT adoption in US small firms. *Journal of Small Business and Enterprise Development, 19*(1), 114–131. doi:10.1108/14626001211196433

Chatterjee, D., Grewal, R., & Sambamurthy, C. (2002). Shaping up for e-commerce: Institutional enablers of the organizational assimilation of web technologies. *Management Information Systems Quarterly, 26*(2), 65–89. doi:10.2307/4132321

Chau, P. Y. K., & Hui, K. L. (2001). Determinants of small business EDI adoption: An empirical investigation. *Journal of Organizational Computing and Electronic Commerce, 11*(4), 229–252. doi:10.1207/S15327744JOCE1104_02

Chau, Y. K., & Jim, C. F. (2002). Adoption of electronic data interchange in small and medium enterprises. *Journal of Global Information Management, 10*(4), 61–85. doi:10.4018/jgim.2002100104

Chibelushi, C. (2008). Learning the hard way? Issues in the adoption of new technology in small technology oriented firms. *Education + Training*, 50(8/9), 725-736.

Chircu, A. M., & Kauffman, R. J. (2000). Limits to value in electronic commerce-related IT investments. *Journal of Management Information Systems, 17*(2), 59–80.

Chong, A. Y.-L., Ooi, K.-B., Lin, B., & Tang, S. Y. (2009). Influence of interorganizational relationships on SMEs' e-business adoption. *Internet Research, 19*(30), 313–331. doi:10.1108/10662240910965379

Chong, S., & Pervan, G. (2007). Factors influencing the extent of deployment of electronic commerce for small and medium-sized enterprises. *Journal of Electronic Commerce in Organizations, 5*(10), 1–29. doi:10.4018/jeco.2007010101

Chwelos, P., Benbasat, I., & Dexter, A. S. (2001). Empirical test of an EDI adoption model. *Information Systems Research, 12*(3), 304–321. doi:10.1287/isre.12.3.304.9708

Corso, M., Martini, A., Pellegrini, L., & Paolucci, E. (2003). Technological and organizational tools for knowledge management: In search of configurations. *Small Business Economics, 21*(4), 397–408. doi:10.1023/A:1026123322900

Cragg, P., Mehrtens, J., & Mills, A. (2001). A model of internet adoption by SMEs. *Information & Management, 39*(3), 165–176. doi:10.1016/S0378-7206(01)00086-6

Cragg, P. B., & King, M. (1993). Small-firm computing: Motivators and inhibitors. *Management Information Systems Quarterly, 17*(1), 47–60. doi:10.2307/249509

Cragg, P. B., King, M., & Hussin, H. (2002). IT alignment and performance in small manufacturing firms. *The Journal of Strategic Information Systems, 11*(2), 109–132. doi:10.1016/S0963-8687(02)00007-0

Davis, C. H., & Vladica, F. (2006). Use of internet technologies and e-business solutions: A structural model of sources of business value among Canadian micro-enterprises. *Proceedings of the 39th Annual HICCS Conference*, Hawaii. doi:10.1109/HICSS.2006.519

Davis, G. B., Lee, A. S., Nickles, K. R., Chatterjee, S., Hartung, R., & Wu, Y. (1992). Diagnosis of an information system failure - a framework and interpretive process. *Information & Management, 23*(5), 293–318. doi:10.1016/0378-7206(92)90059-O

De Guinea, O. A., Kelly, H., & Hunter, M. G. (2005). Information systems effectiveness: Extending a Singapore model in Canada. *Journal of Global Information Management, 13*(2), 55–79. doi:10.4018/jgim.2005070104

Decker, M., Schiefer, G., & Bulander, R. (2006). Specific challenges for small and medium-sized enterprises in m-business: A SME-suitable framework for mobile services. *Proceedings of the International Conference on E-Business*, 169-174.

Delone, W. H. (1988). Determinants of success for computer usage in small business. *Management Information Systems Quarterly, 12*(1), 51–61. doi:10.2307/248803

Dholakia, R. R., & Kshetri, N. (2004). Factors impacting the adoption of the internet among SMEs. *Small Business Economics, 23*(4), 311–322. doi:10.1023/B:SBEJ.0000032036.90353.1f

Dixit, A. K., & Prakash, O. (2011). A study of issues affecting ERP implementation in SMEs. *International Refereed Research Journal, 2*(2), 77–85.

Dixon, T., Thompson, B., & McAllister, P. (2002). *The value of ICT for SMEs in the UK: A critical review of literature. Report for the Small Business Research Programme*. Reading: The College of Estate Management.

Dongen, J., Maitland, C., & Sadowski, B. (2002). Strategic use of the internet by small and medium-sized companies: An exploratory study. *Information Economics and Policy, 14*(1), 75–93. doi:10.1016/S0167-6245(01)00054-3

Doukidis, G. L., Smithson, S., & Lybereas, T. (1994). Trends in information technology in small businesses. *Journal of End User Computing, 6*(4), 15–25.

Duncombe, R. A., & Heeks, R. B. (2001). Information and communication technologies and small enterprise development in Africa: Lessons from Botswana. *Institute for Development Policy and Management, 16*, 66–87.

Ewusi-Mensah, K. (1997). Critical Issues in Abandoned Information Systems Development Projects. *Communications of the ACM*, *40*(9), 74–80. doi:10.1145/260750.260775

Ewusi-Mensah, K., & Przasnyski, Z. H. (1991). On Information Systems Project Abandonment: An Exploratory Study of Organizational Practices. *Management Information Systems Quarterly*, *15*(1), 67–86. doi:10.2307/249437

Foong, S. Y. (1999). Effect of end user personal and systems attributes on computer based information systems success in Malaysian SMEs. *Journal of Small Business Management*, *37*(3), 81–87.

Galliers, R. (1994). Choosing Information Systems Research Approaches. In Information Systems Research - Issues, Methods and Practical Guidelines. Henley-on-Thames, UK: Alfred Waller Ltd.

Grandon, E., & Pearson, J. (2004a). E-commerce adoption: Perceptions of managers/owners of small and medium-sized firms in Chile. *Communications of the Association for Information Systems*, *13*, 81–102.

Grandon, E., & Pearson, J. (2004b). Electronic commerce adoption: An empirical study of small and medium US businesses. *Information & Management*, *42*(97), 216.

Gunasekaran, A., & Ngai, E. W. T. (2005). E-commerce in Hong Kong: An empirical perspective and analysis. *Internet Research*, *15*(2), 141–159. doi:10.1108/10662240510590333

Hadaya, P. (2006). Determinants of the future level of use of electronic marketplaces: The case of Canadian firms. *Electronic Commerce Research*, *6*(2), 173–185. doi:10.1007/s10660-006-6956-y

Harrison, D. A., Mykytyn, P. P., & Rienenschneider, C. K. (1997). Executive decisions about IT adoption in small business: Theory and empirical tests. *Information Systems Research*, *8*(2), 171–195. doi:10.1287/isre.8.2.171

Hart, P. J., & Saunders, C. S. (1998). Emerging electronic partnerships: Antecedents and dimensions of EDI use from the supplier's perspective. *Journal of Management Information Systems*, *14*(4), 87–111.

Hashim, J. (2007). Information technology adoption among small and medium enterprise owners in Malaysia. *The International Journal of Business and Information*, *2*(2), 221–240.

Hinson, R., & Sorenson, O. (2006). E-business and small Ghanaian exporters: Preliminary micro firm explorations in the light of a digital divide. *Online Information Review*, *30*(2), 116–138. doi:10.1108/14684520610659166

Huang, Z., Janz, B. D., & Frolick, M. N. (2008). A comprehensive examination of internet-eDI adoption. *Information Systems Management*, *25*(3), 273–286. doi:10.1080/10580530802151228

Ifinedo, P. (2011). Internet/e-business technologies acceptance in Canada's SMEs: An exploratory investigation. *Internet Research*, *21*(3), 255–281. doi:10.1108/10662241111139309

Jeon, B. N., Han, K. S., & Lee, M. J. (2006). Determining factors for the adoption of e-business: The case of SMEs in Korea. *Applied Economics*, *38*(16), 1905–1916. doi:10.1080/00036840500427262

Jeyaraj, A., Rottman, J. W., & Lacity, M. C. (2006). A review of the predictors, linkages, and biases in IT innovation adoption research. *Journal of Information Technology*, *21*(1), 1–23. doi:10.1057/palgrave.jit.2000056

Johnson, M. (2010). Barriers to innovation adoption: A study of e-markets. *Industrial Management & Data Systems*, *110*(2), 157–174. doi:10.1108/02635571011020287

Julien, P. (1995). New technologies and technological information in small businesses. *Journal ofBusiness Venturing*, *10*(6), 459–475. doi:10.1016/0883-9026(95)00084-L

Julien, P., & Raymond, L. (1994). Factors of new technology adoption in the retail sector. *Entrepreneurship Theory and Practice*, Summer, 79-90.

Kannabiran, G., & Dharmalingam, P. (2012). Enablers and inhibitors of advanced information technologies adoption by SMEs: An empirical study of auto ancillaries in India. *Journal of Enterprise Information Management*, *25*(2), 186–209. doi:10.1108/17410391211204419

Kartiwi, M., & MacGregor, R. C. (2007). Electronic commerce adoption barriers in small to medium-sized enterprises in developed and developing countries: A cross-country comparison. *Journal ofElectronic Commerce in Organizations*, *5*(3), 35–51. doi:10.4018/jeco.2007070103

Keil, M., & Mixon, R. (1993). Laboratory Studies of IS Failures as Escalating Commitment to a Failing Course of Action: Overcoming the Obstacles", *Proceedings ofthe Fourteenth International Conference on Information Systems*, DegrossJ.I.BostromR. P.RobeyD. (Editors), New York: ACM.

Kendall, J. D., Tung, L. L., Chua, K. H., Hong, C., Ng, D., & Tan, S. M. (2001, September). (20010. Receptivity of Singapore's SMEs to electronic commerce adoption. *The Journal of Strategic Information Systems*, *10*(3), 223–242. doi:10.1016/S0963-8687(01)00048-8

Kirbey, D., & Turner, M. (1993). IT and the small retail business. *International Journal of Retail & Distribution Management*, *21*(7), 20–27.

Koshy, P. (2011). *Adoption of information and communications technology in rural micro and small enterprises. Paper 2, Institute for Development Studies and Enterprise Research.* Kerala: Samadhan Foundation.

Kula, V., & Tatoglu, E. (2003). An exploratory study of internet adoption by SMEs in an emerging market economy. *European Business Review*, *15*(5), 324–333. doi:10.1108/09555340310493045

Lai, F., Wang, J., Hsieh, C. T., & Chen, J. C. V. (2007). On network external, e-business adoption and information asymmetry. *Industrial Management & Data Systems*, *107*(5), 728–746. doi:10.1108/02635570710750453

Laudon, K., & Laudon, J. (2007). *Essentials of Business Information Systems* (7th ed.). Englewood Cliffs, NJ: Prentice-Hall.

Lawson, R., Alcock, C., Cooper, J., & Burgess, L. (2003). Factors affecting adoption of electronic commerce technologies by SMEs: An Australian study. *The Electronic Journal on Information Systems in Developing Countries*, *14*(1), 1–9.

Lederer, A. L., & Nath, R. (1991). Managing Organizational Issues in Information Systems Development. *Journal of Systems Management*, *42*(11), 23–39.

Lee, J., & Runge, J. (2001). Adoption of information technology in small business: Testing drivers of adoption for entrepreneurs. *Journal of Computer Information Systems*, *42*(1), 44–57.

Lefebvre, L. A., & Lefebvre, E. (1993). Competitive positioning and innovative efforts in SMEs. *Journal of Small Business Economics*, *5*(4), 297–305. doi:10.1007/BF01516250

Levy, M., & Powell, P. (1998). SME flexibility and the role of information systems. *Journal of Small Business Economics*, *11*(2), 183–196. doi:10.1023/A:1007912714741

Levy, M., Powell, P., & Yetton, P. (2001). SMEs: Aligning IS and the strategic context. *Journal of Information Technology*, *16*(3), 133–144. doi:10.1080/02683960110063672

Liao, J., Welsch, H., & Stoica, M. (2003). Organizaitonal obsorptive capacity and responsiveness: An empirical investigation of growth-oriented SMEs. *Entrepreneurship Theory and Practice*, *28*(1), 133–144. doi:10.1111/1540-8520.00032

Looi, H. C. (2005). E-commerce adoption in Brunei Darussalam: A quantitative analysis of factors influencing its adoption. *Communications of the Association for Information Systems*, *15*(3), 61–81.

Love, P. E. D., & Irani, Z. (2004). An exploratory study of information technology evaluation and benefits management practices of SMEs in the construction industry. *Information & Management*, *42*(1), 227–242. doi:10.1016/j.im.2003.12.011

Love, P. E. D., Irani, Z., Li, H., Cheng, E. W. L., & Tse, R. Y. C. (2001). An empirical analysis of the barriers to implementing e-commerce in small-medium sized construction contractors in the state of Victoria. *Construction Innovation*, *1*(1), 31–41. doi:10.1108/14714170110814497

Lymer, A., Johnson, R., & Baldwin, A. (1997). The internet and small businesses: A study of impacts. *Fifth European Conference on Information Systems*, Cork Publishing, Cork. 145-163.

MacGregor, R. C. (2004). Factors associated with formal networking in regional small business: Some findings from a study of Swedish SMEs. *Journal of Small Business and Enterprise Development*, *11*(1), 60–74. doi:10.1108/14626000410519100

Marvel, M. R., & Lumpkin, G. T. (2007). Technology entrepreneurs' human capital and its effects on innovation radicalness. *Entrepreneurship Theory and Practice*, *31*(6), 807–828. doi:10.1111/j.1540-6520.2007.00209.x

Mata, F. J., Fuerst, W. L., & Barney, J. B. (1995). Information technology and sustained competitive advantage: A resource-based analysis. *Management Information Systems Quarterly*, *19*(4), 487–507. doi:10.2307/249630

McComb, D., & Smith, J. Y. (1991). System Project Failure: The Heuristics of Risk. *Journal of Information Systems Management*, *8*(1), 25–34. doi:10.1080/07399019108964967

McDonagh, P., & Prothero, A. (2000). Euroclicking and the Irish SME: Prepared for e-commerce and the single currency. *Irish Marketing Review*, *13*(1), 21–33.

Mehrtens, J., Cragg, P. B., & Mills, A. M. (2001). A model of internet adoption by SMEs. *Information & Management*, *39*(3), 165–176. doi:10.1016/S0378-7206(01)00086-6

Mendo, F. A., & Fitzgerald, G. (2005). A multidimensional framework for SME e-business progression. *Journal of Enterprise Information Management, 18*(15), 678–696. doi:10.1108/17410390510628382

Mirchandani, A. A., & Motwani, J. (2001). Understanding small business electronic commerce adoption: An empirical analysis. *Journal of Computer Information Systems, 41*(3), 70–73.

Mpufu, C., & Watkins-Mathys, L. (2011). Understanding ICT adoption in the small firm sector in southern Africa. *Journal of Systems and Information Technology, 13*(2), 179–199. doi:10.1108/13287261111136007

Mustaffa, S., & Beaumont, N. (2004). The effect of electronic commerce on small Australian enterprises. *Technovation, 24*(2), 85–95. doi:10.1016/S0166-4972(02)00039-1

Nguyen, T., Sherif, J., & Newby, M. (2007). Strategies for successful CRM implementation. *Information Management & Computer Security, 15*(2), 102–115. doi:10.1108/09685220710748001

Ongori, H., & Migiro, S. O. (2010). Information and communication technology adoption in SMEs: A literature review. *Journal of Chinese Entrepreneurship, 2*(1), 93–104. doi:10.1108/17561391011019041

Packalen, K. (2010). ICT capabilities and possibilities in micro-firms: A study of micro-firms in the Aland Islands archipelago. 23rd Bled e-Conference on e-Trust, Slovenia.

Pflughoeft, K., Ramamurthy, K., Soofi, E., Yasai-Ardekani, M., & Zahedi, F. (2003). Multiple conceptualizations of small business web use and benefit. *Decision Sciences, 34*(3), 467–512. doi:10.1111/j.1540-5414.2003.02539.x

Pierce, J. L., & Delbecq, A. L. (1977). Organizational structure: Individual attitudes and innovation. *Academy of Management Review, 2*(1), 27–37.

Pires, G. D., & Stanton, J. (2005). A research framework for the electronic procurement adoption process: Drawing from Australian evidence. *Journal of Global Business and Technology, 1*(2), 12–20.

Poon, S., & Swatman, P. (1999). An exploratory study of small business internet commerce issues. *Information & Management, 35*(1), 9–18. doi:10.1016/S0378-7206(98)00079-2

Porter, M. E. (1980). *Competitive Strategy: Techniques for Analyzing Industries and Competitors*. New York: Free Press.

Poutsma, E. F., Van Uxem, F. W., & Walravens, A. H. C. M. (1987). *Process Innovation and Automation in Small and Medium Sized Business*. Delft, Netherlands: Delft University Press.

Premkumar, G. (2003). A meta-analysis of research on information technology implementation in small business. *Journal of Organizational Computing and Electronic Commerce*, *13*(2), 91–121. doi:10.1207/S15327744JOCE1302_2

Premkumar, G., & Roberts, M. (1999). Adoption of new information technologies in rural small businesses. *Omega: International Journal of Management Science*, *27*(4), 467–484. doi:10.1016/S0305-0483(98)00071-1

Quinn, J. B. (1979). Technological innovation, ownership, and strategy. *Sloan Management Review*, *20*(2), 19–30.

Qureshil, S., Kamal, M., & Wolcott, P. (2009). Information technology interventions for growth and competiveness in micro-enterprises. *International Journal of E-Business Research*, *5*(1), 117–139. doi:10.4018/jebr.2009010106

Ramdani, B., Kawalek, P., & Lorenzo, O. (2009). Predicting SMEs' adoption of enterprise systems. *Journal of Enterprise Information Management*, *22*(1/2), 10–24. doi:10.1108/17410390910922796

Ratnasingam, P. (2001). Electronic commerce adoption in Australia and New Zealand. *Malaysian Journal of Computer Sciences*, *4*, 223–242.

Raymond, L. (2001). Determinants of web site implementation in small businesses. *Internet Research*, *11*(5), 411–422. doi:10.1108/10662240110410363

Raymond, L., & Bergeron, F. (2008). Enabling the business strategy on SMEs through e-business capabilities: A strategic alignment perspective. *Industrial Management & Data Systems*, *108*(5), 577–595. doi:10.1108/02635570810876723

Reid, G., & Jacobsen, C. (1988). *The Small Entrepreneurial Firm*. Aberdeen: Aberdeen University Press.

Robey, D., Smith, L. A., & Vijayasarathy, L. R. (1993). Perceptions of Conflict and Success in Information Systems Development Projects. *Journal of Management Information Systems*, *10*(1), 123–139.

Rogers, E. M. (1983). *Diffusion of Innovation* (3rd ed.). New York: Free Press.

Rogers, E. M. (2003). *Diffusion of Innovation* (5th ed.). New York: Free Press.

Romano, A., Passiante, G., & Elia, V. (2001). New sources of clustering in the digital economy. *Journal of Small Business and Enterprise Development*, *8*(1), 19–27. doi:10.1108/EUM0000000006813

Sabherwal, R., Jeyaraj, A., & Chowa, C. (2006). Information system success: Individual and organizational determinants. *Management Science*, *52*(12), 849–864. doi:10.1287/mnsc.1060.0583

Schafer, S. (1995). How information technology is leveling the playing field. *Inc. Technology (Elmsford, N.Y.)*, *17*(4), 92–96.

Scupola, A. (2003). The adoption of internet commerce by SMEs in the south of Italy: An environmental, technological and organizational perspective. *Journal of Global Information Technology Management*, *6*(1), 52–71. doi:10.1080/1097198X.2003.10856343

Serwer, A. E. (1995). Paths to wealth: In the new economy. *Fortune*, (20), February, 57-62.

Seyal, A. H., Awais, M. M., Shamail, S., & Abbas, A. (2004). Determinants of electronic commerce in Pakistan: Preliminary evidence from small and medium enterprises. *Electronic Markets*, *14*(4), 372–387. doi:10.1080/10196780412331311801

Seyal, A. H., Noah Abd Rahman, M., & Awg Yussof Hj Awg Mohammad, H. (2007). A quantitative analysis of factors contributing electronic data interchange adoption among Bruneian SMEs. *Business Process Management Journal*, *13*(5), 728–746. doi:10.1108/14637150710823183

Siggelkow, N., & Leventhal, D. (2005). Escaping real (non-benign) competency trap: Linking the dynamics of organizational structure to the dynamics of search. *Strategic Organization*, *3*(1), 85–115. doi:10.1177/1476127005050521

Simpson, M., & Doherty, A. J. (2004). E-commerce adoption support and advice for UK SMEs. *Journal of Small Business and Enterprise Development*, *11*(3), 315–328. doi:10.1108/14626000410551573

Somuyiwa, A., & Adebayo, T. (2011). Analysis of information and communication technologies (ICT) usage on logistics activities of manufacturing companies in Southwestern Nigeria. *Journal of Emerging Trends in Economics and Management Science*, *2*(1), 68–74.

Somuyiwa, A. O., & Adewoye, J. O. (2010). Managing logistics information system: Theoretical underpinnings. *Asian Journal of Business Management*, *2*(2), 41–47.

Southern, A., & Tilley, F. (2000). Small firms and information and communication technologies (ICTs): Toward a typology of ICTs usage. *New Technology, Work and Employment*, *15*(2), 138–154. doi:10.1111/1468-005X.00070

Stake, R. E. (1994). Case Studies. In N. K. Denzin & Y. S. Lincoln (Eds.), *Handbook of Qualitative Research*. Thousand Oaks, USA: Sage Publications, Inc.

Szajna, B., & Scamell, R. W. (1993). The Effects of Information System User Expectations on Their Performance and Perceptions. *Management Information Systems Quarterly*, *17*(4), 493–516. doi:10.2307/249589

Tan, K. S., Chong, S., Lin, B., & Eze, U. (2009). Internet-based ICT adoption: Evidence from Malaysian SMEs. *Industrial Management & Data Systems*, *109*(2), 224–244. doi:10.1108/02635570910930118

Tan, K. S., & Eze, U. (2008). An empirical study of internet-based ICT adoption among Malaysian SMEs. *Communications of IBIMA Malaysia*, *1*(1), 1–12.

Tan, Z., & Wu, Q. (2003). Globalization and e-commerce I: Factors affecting e-commerce diffusion in China. *Communications of the Association for Information Systems*, *10*(2), 25–35.

Thompson, V. A. (1969). *Bureaucracy and Innovation*. Huntsville, Alabama: University of Alabama Press.

Thong, J. Y. L. (1999). An integrated model of information systems adoption in small businesses. *Journal of Management Information Systems*, *15*(4), 187–214.

Thong, J. Y. L., & Yap, C. S. (1995). CEO characteristics, organizational characteristics, and information technology adoption in small business. *Omega*, *23*(4), 429–442. doi:10.1016/0305-0483(95)00017-I

Thong, J. Y. L., Yap, C. S., & Raman, K. S. (1996). Top management support, external expertise and information systems implementation in small business. *Information Systems Research*, *7*(2), 248–267. doi:10.1287/isre.7.2.248

Todd, P. R., & Javalgi, R. (2007). Internationalization of SMEs in India. Fostering entrepreneurship by leveraging information technology. *International Journal of Emerging Markets*, *2*(2), 160–188.

Van der Deen, M. (2005). Measuring e-business adoption in SMEs. In W. During, R. Oakley, & S. Kauser (Eds.), *New technology-based Firms in the New Millennium* (Vol. 5). Amsterdam: Elsevier.

Wade, M., Johnston, D., & McClean, R. (2004). Exploring the net impact of internet business solution adoption of SME performance. *International Journal of Electronic Business, 2*(4), 336–350. doi:10.1504/IJEB.2004.005637

Wainwright, D., Green, G., Mitchell, E., & Yarrow, D. (2005). Toward a framework for benchmarking ICT practice, competence and performance in small firms. *The International Journal for Library and Information Sciences, 6*(1), 39–52.

Walczuch, R., van Braven, G., & Lundgran, H. (2000). Internet adoption barriers for small firms in The Netherlands. *European Management Journal, 18*(5), 561–572. doi:10.1016/S0263-2373(00)00045-1

Wernerfelt, B. (1984). A resource-based view of the firm. *Strategic Management Journal, 5*(2), 171–180. doi:10.1002/smj.4250050207

Windrum, P., & de Berranger, P. (2003). *Factors affecting the adoption of intranets and extranets by SMEs: A UK study. Research Memoranda.* Maastricht: Maastricht Economic Research Institute on Innovation and Technology.

Winston, E., & Dologite, D. (2002). How does attitude impact IT implementation: A study of small business owners. *Journal of End User Computing, 14*(2), 16–29. doi:10.4018/joeuc.2002040102

Wymer, S., & Regan, E. (2005). Factors influencing e-commerce adoption and use by small and medium businesses. *Electronic Markets, 15*(4), 412–438. doi:10.1080/10196780500303151

Yap, C., Soh, C., & Raman, K. (1992). Information systems success factors in small business. *Omega, 20*(5-6), 597–609. doi:10.1016/0305-0483(92)90005-R

Yin, R. K. (1994). *Case Study Research – Design and Methods.* Thousand Oaks, USA: Sage Publications, Inc.

Yulong, L. (2001). ERP adoption in Chinese small enterprise: An exploratory case study. *Journal of Manufacturing Technology Management, 22*(4), 489–505.

Zaltman, G., Duncan, R., & Holbek, J. (1973). *Innovations and Organizations.* New York: John Wiley.

Zhu, K., Kraemer, K., & Xu, S. (2003). Electronic business adoption by European firms: A cross-country assessment of the facilitators and inhibitors. *European Journal of Information Systems, 12*(4), 251–268. doi:10.1057/palgrave.ejis.3000475

Zhu, K., Kraemer, K., & Xu, S. (2006). The process of innovation assimilation by firms in different countries: A technology diffusion perspective on e-business. *Management Science*, *52*(10), 1557–1576. doi:10.1287/mnsc.1050.0487

## ADDITIONAL READING

Hunter, M. G., & Dhanda, K. K. (2004). *Information systems: Exploring Applications in Business and Government*. Las Vegas, NV: The Information Institute.

Rogers, E. M. (2003). *Diffusion of Innovation* (5th ed.). New York: Free Press.

## KEY TERMS AND DEFINITIONS

**Adoption Models:** Conceptual representation of process acquisitions.

**Adoption:** The acquisition of a process.

**Cognitive Dissonance:** Discomfort caused by contradictions.

**Critical Success Factors:** Elements related to the success or failure of a project or process.

**Escalating Commitment:** Justification of further involvement based upon past involvement.

**Evolutionary:** Slow.

**Innovation Theory:** The adoption of a process new to the small business.

**Market-Pull:** The adoption of a new process because of requests from customers.

**Perceived Benefits:** Anticipated positive results.

**Resource Heterogeneity:** The resources and capabilities of competing small businesses will be different.

**Resource Immobility:** The resources and capabilities of a small business will be consistent for some time.

**Revolutionary:** Radical.

**System Failure:** A process does not function as it should or not at all.

**Technology-Push:** The adoption of a new process because of changes in technology.

**User Attitude:** Perceptions of users in a revised process.

**User Participation:** Involvement of users in the development of a process for their use.

# Chapter 6
# Use


## ABSTRACT

*A positive environment will contribute to the beneficial use of information systems by small business. It is incumbent upon senior management to take a proactive approach to the strategic use of information systems. Employees must be trained with the appropriate skills. New processes should be explored regularly both with current information systems and new systems that could potentially provide an improvement in performance. Information systems should be sued in a way that contributes to both efficiency and effectiveness to support operational decision making and eventually the competitive advantage of small business. This chapter presents an overview of the issues involved in the use of information systems by small business. Management of small business tends to make decisions based upon an informal approach to gathering information. Once adopted, an information system formalizes this approach and promotes a more structured process for decision making. From an external perspective the use of information systems by small business presents a positive image to customers, suppliers and other small businesses. Internally the responsibility resides with senior management to set a positive environment regarding the use of information systems.*


## INTRODUCTION

Senior managers should take a strategic approach to determining how information systems can contribute to competitive advantage. They must be proactive in dealing with issues associated with the use of information systems. This is especially so for ensuring employees are sufficiently trained in the appropriate use of the information

DOI: 10.4018/978-1-4666-8708-0.ch006

systems. The use of an information system should promote operational efficiency by providing timely information that accurately reflects what has transpired in the small business.

This chapter is organized as follows. To begin two theories are reviewed which provide the context for information systems use in small business. Then it is noted that information systems use will promote a positive image for the small business. Laggards and leaders are described regarding practices which facilitate the beneficial use of information systems. In general, a proactive attitude by management and employees will provide a positive environment. Once selected the information systems should be used effectively as well as efficiently. Operational efficiency will contribute to "doing things right". Effective information systems, providing timely and accurate information will contribute to management in their goal of "doing the right things". The chapter concludes with a presentation of the results based upon a series of projects which investigated small business use of information systems. There are issues to be addressed internally and those which arise externally that require a response.

## INFORMATION SYSTEM USE FRAMEWORKS

If information system use is different in small business versus large companies, how does this use evolve as a small business grows and matures? The answer to this question will be addressed in Chapter Thirteen which presents a maturity framework for small business use of information systems. The following paragraphs provide the basic description of information system use within small business.

Briefly, two theories, reported here, have been employed to provide a context for information use in small business. These theories are the Resource-based View of the firm Theory and the Theory of Absorptive Capacity. Caldeira and Ward (2003) employed Resource-based View Theory to attempt to explain small business success with the use of information systems. Factors associated with success were related to internal aspects of the business. One factor involved positive management perspectives and attitudes toward the use of information systems. The other internal aspect involved the development of capabilities to use information systems.

Francalanci and Morabito (2008) employed Absorptive Capacity Theory to analyze how the use of information technology facilitates the performance of small business. The Theory of Absorptive Capacity (Cohen & Levinthal, 1990; and Zahra & George, 2002) relates to a small business' ability to uniquely identify, assimilate, and exploit knowledge from external sources (Cohen & Levinthal, 1990). Francalanci & Morabito (2008) determined that absorptive capacity facilitates information system integration which promotes maturity and quality in the use of information systems.

Winter et al (2009) determined that the impression held by customers and other firms of a small business' legitimacy is facilitated through the use of information systems. A positive image may influence purchase decisions which in turn, may contribute to survival and competitive advantage.

It is important that small business managers chose the appropriate information system for their purposes. The acquisition of an information system represents a relatively large investment which must provide a benefit (Delvecchio & Anselmi, 2006) for its subsequent use.

Cragg and Mills (2011) found that few small business employed information systems to support two strategically important processes which are facilitating the delivery of products and services and managing customer service.

Earlier, Cragg (2002) had investigated information technology use in small business. He developed a framework which differentiates laggards and leaders in the use of information technology and is included here as Table1.

The findings suggest that small businesses which are considered leaders of information technology use are sure to involve senior management and possess employees with technical capabilities. Thus managers provide leadership and display a willingness to consider new opportunities to use information technology. Employee technical capability is developed through a preference for relying on internal skills for system customization and development (Cragg, 2002).

While Laggards use information systems there is little initiative to be proactive and take an innovative approach. Senior management rarely explore new uses and tend to ignore addressing issues until they arise. Employees lack the necessary training and skills.

Ortiz de Guinea et al (2005) replicated the Thong et al (1996) model of information system effectiveness for small business. The original model was developed based on Singapore small business. The replication was conducted on small business in western Canada. The findings, which support the earlier results, suggest that managerial and vendor support will contribute to the effective use of information systems.

Sharma and Bhagwat (2006) measured information systems performance in SMEs from six different perspectives, as follows:

- Operational efficiency of the information system function
    - *...SMEs who have implemented IS have achieved a great improvement in the operational efficiency of the IS function. Implementation of IS drastically reduces bottlenecks in the decision making from design to sale, and from order to shipment, and WIP [work in progress] inventory, and increase the manufacturing capabilities, product and service quality, and overall business performance. (Sharma & Bhagwat, 2006, p. 15)*

***Use***

*Table 1. Laggards and leaders information technology practices*

| Practice | It Laggards | | It Leaders |
|---|---|---|---|
| Role of IT within the business | IT assists with many processes but provides no or little advantage over competitors | Most IT provides value to the firm and some advantage over competitors | IT is viewed as strategic and provides considerable advantage over competitors |
| Senior management commitment to IT | Some senior managers prefer to ignore IT issues unless in a crisis | Some, but not all, senior managers are enthusiastic about IT | All senior managers are enthusiastic about IT, regularly discuss IT issues, and share responsibility for IT projects when necessary |
| Seeking out new uses for IT | Managers rarely explore possible new uses for IT | Managers occasionally explore new uses for IT | Managers regularly explore new issues for IT through discussions within and outside the firm, and at exhibitors and seminars, as part of the firm's commitment to continuous improvement |
| Customisation of new IT systems | Packaged systems are purchased and undergo no or little customisation | Packaged systems are purchased and undergo some customisation | Either bespoke systems are developed or packaged systems are purchased and undergo considerable customisation |
| IT specialist | An employee with no formal IT training manages IT on a daily basis. IT problems are usually fixed by technical experts from another firm | Staff have developed sufficient technical expertise to fix most IT problems and manage most IT projects, but occasionally need to seek help from external experts | The firm employs an IT specialist with years of formal IT training. This makes the firm relatively independent of IT service providers |
| IT development skills | No one within the firm can develop small systems with either database or spreadsheet software | We have sufficient hands-on skills to develop small databases and spreadsheets | Our system development skills allow us to customise new systems and build significant systems with database and spreadsheet software |

Adapted from Cragg, 2002

- Down time of information systems
    - *The ability of IS consistently to provide right kind of information at right time in any organization will influence decision-making in day-to-day business. Hence, down time of IS is an undesirable situation for SMEs business operations and adequate measures should be taken to make it as minimal as possible. (Sharma & Bhagwat, 2006, p. 15)*

- Responsiveness of the information system
    - *...responsiveness to its operational demands is a vital measure of how a business is progressing. In general, SMEs that have implemented IS have seen certain impact on there is responsiveness... (Sharma & Bhagwat, 2006, p. 16)*
- Timeliness of information
    - *The information about products, processes, and market potential can be made more accessible and usable by integrated computer-based systems. Overall, the SMEs that have implemented IS have achieved a very significant improvement in the timeliness of information that help them to take decisions much faster... (Sharma & Bhagwat, 2006, p. 16)*
- Accuracy of information
    - *...SMEs have achieved significant improvement in quality of information flow in terms of the accuracy particularly in the areas of product development, manufacturing, purchasing, shipping, customer care and sales. (Sharma & Bhagwat, 2006, p. 17)*
- Overall competitive position
    - *SMEs that have implemented IS have seen certain impact on their overall competitive advantage... (Sharma & Bhagwat, 2006, p. 17)*

The findings suggest that businesses which have implemented information systems have experienced improvement in all of the aspects investigated. Further, Smith and Simon (2009) found that systems which integrate data from multiple sources improve decision making for small business.

## SAMPLE PROJECT

The description in this section is based upon a series of projects (Hunter, 2003; Hunter, 2005; and Hunter, 2008) which investigated the use of information systems by small business.

While it is recognized that the time available to the small business manager is limited, it is suggested that the individual consider gaining an understanding of the capability of information systems. While it is not necessary to know the details of how to develop an information system, the small business manager should know how the information system may be employed to add value to the functioning of the business. In response to the "dependency" theme, the small business manager should seek to establish a long-term relationship with a knowledgeable individual for advice about information systems. The manager would best be served through a mentor-type relationship rather than one where the advisor had a vested interest in the consequences of a decision.

External entities should recognize the approach to decisions by the small business manager, which is relatively informal. Also, recall that Stevenson (1999) has suggested the small business manager prefers to make multi-staged decisions with a minimum of commitment at each instance. Thus, perhaps leasing versus buying will address this issue somewhat. Further, while a long-term strategic plan for adoption of an information system is generally considered wise, it should be noted that the small business manager will focus on the requirements for the near term immediate decisions.

Also, Hunter et al (2002) identified two major themes regarding small business use of information systems. These themes are "dependency" and "efficiency". The authors suggest that the adoption of information systems increased the small business' dependency on an internal champion, and a series of external stakeholders, including consultants and suppliers. This increased dependency, Hunter et al (2002) suggest, results from the approaches to business (Stevenson, 1999) taken by the manager and the concept of resource poverty (Thong et al, 1994). The efficiency theme suggests that information systems are primarily used by small business managers as an operational tool to help complete daily activities. Further, Dandridge and Levenburg (2000) determined that while IS were being employed for daily operations, there was little use of computerization for competitiveness aspects.

The above presentation shows there are differences when comparing the information systems needs of small versus medium and large businesses. Also, small business has yet to take advantage of the ability of information systems to support competitive and strategic initiatives. The next section describes a project which attempts to further investigate this issue.

Other research has supported the contention that the use of information systems by small business represents a unique approach. For instance, Pollard and Hayne (1998) investigated the information systems issues identified by small business managers across Canada. Their results indicate that the issues being faced by small business managers are different than those faced by large business managers. Also, in the area of information systems the issues are in a continual state of change. Also, Belich and Dubinsky (1999) applied information theory to investigate the information processing among a group of small business exporters. They determined that information processing of the small businesses was not the same as that found in larger firms. Further, Taylor (1999) investigated the implementation of enterprise software in small businesses and found that neither the businesses themselves, nor the software vendors are fully cognizant of the unique problems encountered by small business managers. Finally, Hunter et al (2002) identified two major themes regarding small business use of IS. These themes are "dependency" and "efficiency". The authors suggest that the adoption of information systems increased the small business' dependency on an internal champion, and a series of external stakeholders, including consultants and suppliers. This increased dependency, Hunter et al (2002) suggest, results from the approaches to business (Stevenson, 1999) taken by the manager and the concept of resource poverty (Thong et al, 1994). The efficiency theme suggests that information systems are primarily used by small business managers as an operational tool to help complete daily activities.

Earlier research (Nickell & Seado, 1986) determined that small business was mainly using information systems for accounting and administrative purposes. Research conducted in the 1990s (Lin et al, 1993; Fuller, 1996; Berman, 1997; Canadian Federation of Independent Business, 1999; and Timmons, 1999) noted a growing interest by small business in employing information systems in daily operations. The impetus for this growing interest originated from various sources. First, small business was becoming concerned about the adoption of information systems by competition. The small business manager did not want to be left behind the competition regarding the use of technology. Second, the technology was becoming more affordable, reliable, and powerful. These trends were allowing the small business manager to make decisions about the technology, which fit the general decision-making profile of the small business manager. Third, information systems were starting to be recognized as a means for the small business to attempt to compete with larger business. Fourth, the widespread use of the Internet facilitated the identification and implementation of E-commerce opportunities.

While small business has been more than prepared to exploit the use of information systems to support daily operations (El Louadi, 1998), there exists little evidence that they are prepared to employ the technology in a strategic manner (Berman, 1997). Further, Bridge and Peel (1999) also determined that small businesses employed computers mainly to support daily operations and tended not to use them to support decision-making or long term planning.

Another area of investigation relates to the use of the Internet by small business. Burgess and Trethowan (2002) examined the use of web sites by small businesses, represented by general practitioners, in Australia. They found that, while there was reasonably high use of computers, to improve efficiency and lower costs, there was not much use of computers for web sites. Those who had web sites mainly employed them to provide basic information and contact details. Dandridge and Levenburg (2000) investigated Internet use by small (fewer than 25 employees) businesses. They determined that very few small businesses were moving to this next step in the use of IS. While they found that IS were being employed for daily operations, there was little use of computerization for competitiveness aspects. Other research projects have identified that small businesses have not adopted Internet use because of lack of knowledge and experience (Iacovou et al, 1995; Damsgaard and Lyytinen, 1998; and Kuan and Chau, 2001), or the lack of personnel and time (Bennett et al, 1999). Even when time and personnel are available, there seems to be reluctance by small businesses to investigate the use of the Internet (Chapman et al, 2000).

To summarize the discussion to this point, it is clear that no single template exists to prescribe the information systems needs of a business. Clearly small and large businesses are different. Stevenson's (1999) model (presented in Table 3 in Chapter One) suggests differing approaches to business practices between entrepreneurs (promoter) and managers (trustee). They are pursuing different goals and responding to different constraints and strictures, for example, resource poor business owners versus large businesses rich in both financial and human resources. Further, it is generally known that many small business owners initiate information systems use in their businesses more to facilitate daily operations and not so much for competitive and strategic reasons. Stevenson (1999) determined differences in the strategic orientation of managers of large business versus managers of small business. He found that managers of large business focus on efficient use of resources; they take the time to follow formal procedures to make a one-time decision regarding a long-term commitment. However, small business managers tend to emphasize responding to opportunities with a minimum commitment of resources in a multi-staged approach (i.e. numerous small commitments over a period of time). Unfortunately, the deployment of information systems requires the development of a long-term plan and a large one-time commitment of both financial and human resources, which is an approach to resource commitment that is the opposite from that normally taken by small business managers.

## Project Recommendations

This section presents a number of recommendations for various stakeholders' intent on increasing the use of information systems within the small business sector. These recommendations represent suggestions for the future and reflect a synthesis of available literature, presented in the previous section, in the area in conjunction with, and in the specific context of, previous research (Hunter & Long, 2003; Hunter, 2002; and Hunter et al, 2002).

### Small Business Manager

To overcome the limitations of being dependent upon other's expertise, managers need to gain an understanding of the capabilities of information systems. While managers do not need to know how to design or develop information systems, they do need to understand how technology might be used as a key resource in adding value to the firm's core business products or services.

Further, the small business manager should establish a relationship with a specific individual regarding a source for advice. The recommendation is for the manager to establish a relationship with someone who is independent of a specific solution and who will be prepared to play a strategic role taking a long-term perspective. It is incumbent upon the manager to review the relationship to ensure that the recommendations being proffered are appropriately contributing to the long-term success of the firm.

Also, managers should take a proactive approach toward the adoption of information systems. This would involve actively seeking out ways to leverage information systems to create or improve products or services offered to customers. However, the manager should avoid being an early adopter of new hardware and/or software applications.

## Consultant

It is important for consultants to recognize that in regard to the nature, timing and acquisition of resources, the small business manager generally aims to minimize the amount of resources used at each stage of the firm's growth. Generally, consultants need to be able to provide opportunities for small businesses to 'phase in' information systems in stages. Doing so will accommodate small business practice and form the foundation for a mutually beneficial ongoing relationship.

## Vendor

Vendors should make a visible commitment to small business through the establishment of an entity specifically directed at small business. The small business sector is a large and important one thus target marketing this sector makes good business sense. Also, software vendors must ensure that an application performs the necessary functions for small business. It is incumbent upon the vendor to ensure the hardware or software addresses the appropriate functionality of the small business.

## Government

Government can help overcome resource poverty by providing advice and financial incentives to small business. By initiating relationships with small business managers, individuals representing government services can more effectively support these managers by tapping into their informal networks to exchange required information. The role of tax and other financial incentives may be employed to encourage the expanded use of information systems.

### Project Conclusion

Information systems have increased the efficiency of daily operations for small business.

Generally, evidence suggests that information systems expenditures are being made in reaction to needs or problems, rather than as a result of a long term coordinated plan. The suggestions included here should contribute to more effective use of information systems by small business.

## CONCLUSION

This chapter has presented the issues involved in the use of information systems by small business. The main contributing factor to the beneficial use of information systems is a positive environment in the small business. This environment can created by senior management taking a proactive approach to addressing issues in the use of information systems and ensuring employees have access to the necessary training and possess the necessary skills. The next chapter presents a review of factors associated with information systems and strategy within the small business.

## REFERENCES

Belich, T. J., & Dubinsky, A. J. (1999). Information processing among exporters: An empirical examination of small firms. *Journal of Marketing Theory and Practice*, *7*(4), 45–58.

Bennett, J., Polkinghorne, M., Pearce, J., & Hudson, M. (1999). Technology transfer for SMEs. *Engineering Management Journal*, (April): 75–80.

Berman, P. (1997). *Small business and entrepreneurship*. Scarborough, Ontario: Prentice Hall.

Bridge, J., & Peel, M. J. (1999). A study of computer usage and strategic planning in the SME sector. *International Small Business Journal*, *17*(4), 82–87. doi:10.1177/0266242699174005

Burgess, S., & Trethowan, P. (2002). GP's and their web sites in Australia: Doctors as small businesses. *Proceedings of ISOneWorld Conference, Las Vegas, Nevada.*

Caldeira, M. M., & Ward, J. M. (2003). Using resource-based theory to interpret the successful adoption and use of information systems and technology in manufacturing small and medium-sized enterprises. *European Journal of Information Systems*, *12*(2), 127–141. doi:10.1057/palgrave.ejis.3000454

Canadian Federation of Independent Business. (1999). Results of members' opinion surveys #37-42, http://www.cfib.ca/research/98internet.asp (August 29, 2000).

Chapman, P., James-Moore, M., Szczygiel, M., & Thompson, D. (2000). Building internet capabilities in SMEs. *Logistics Information Management*, *13*(6), 353–361. doi:10.1108/09576050010355662

Cohen, W., & Levinthal, D. (1990). Absorptive capacity: A new perspective on learning and innovation. *Administrative Science Quarterly*, *35*(1), 128–152. doi:10.2307/2393553

Cragg, P. B. (2002). Benchmarking information technology practices in small firms. *European Journal of Information Systems*, *11*(4), 267–282. doi:10.1057/palgrave.ejis.3000430

Cragg, P. B., & Mills, A. (2011). IT support for business processes in SMEs. *Business Process Management Journal*, *17*(5), 697–710. doi:10.1108/14637151111166141

Damsgaard, J., & Lyytinen, K. (1998). Contours of diffusion of electronic data interchange in Finland: Overcoming technological barriers and collaborating to make it happen. *The Journal of Strategic Information Systems*, *7*(4), 275–297. doi:10.1016/S0963-8687(98)00032-8

Dandrige, T., & Levenburg, N. M. (2000). High-tech potential? An exploratory study of very small firms' usage of the internet. *International Small Business Journal*, *18*(2), 81–91. doi:10.1177/0266242600182004

Delvecchio, S., & Anselmi, K. (2006). Sales force automation tools for small business. *Journal of Small Business Strategy*, *16*(2), 15–27.

El Louadi, M. (1998). The relationship among organizational structure, information technology and information processing in small Canadian firms. *Canadian Journal of Administrative Sciences*, *15*(2), 180–199. doi:10.1111/j.1936-4490.1998.tb00161.x

Francalanci, C., & Morabito, V. (2008). IS integration and business performance: The mediation effect of organizational absorptive capacity in SMEs. *Journal of Information Technology, 23*(4), 297–312. doi:10.1057/jit.2008.18

Fuller, T. (1996). Fulfilling IT needs in small businesses: A recursive learning model. *International Journal of Small Business, 14*(4), 25–44. doi:10.1177/0266242696144002

Hunter, M. G. (2002). Information systems development outcomes: The case of song book music. In S. Burgess (Ed.), *Managing Information Technology in Small Business: Challenges and Solutions*. Hershey, PA: Idea Group Publishing. doi:10.4018/978-1-930708-35-8.ch003

Hunter, M. G. (2003). Information systems and small business: What's in the wind in L, A.? ISOneWorld, April 23-25, Las Vegas, Nevada.

Hunter, M. G. (2005). International information systems and small business project: A western Canadian perspective, Chapter 5 in Hunter, M. G., Burgess, S. & Wenn. A. (Editors). Small Business and Information Technology: Research Issues and International Case Studies, Heidelberg Press, Melbourne, Australia. ISBN: 1-920889-04

Hunter, M. G. (2008). Information systems and small business, Chapter in Khosrow-Pour, M. (Editor). Encyclopedia of Information Science and Technology, Volume I-V, Idea Group Publishing, Hershey, PA.

Hunter, M. G., Diochon, M., Pugsley, D., & Wright, B. (2002). Unique challenges for small business adoption of information technology: The case of the Nova Scotia ten. In S. Burgess (Ed.), *Managing Information Technology in Small Business: Challenges and Solutions*. Hershey, PA: Idea Group Publishing. doi:10.4018/978-1-930708-35-8.ch006

Hunter, M. G., & Long, W. A. (2003). Adopting the Entrepreneurial Process in the Study of Information Systems and Small Business. In G. Gingrich (Ed.), *Managing Information Technology in Government, Business, and Communities*. Hershey, PA: IRM Press.

Iacovou, C., Benbasat, I., & Dexter, A. (1995). Electronic data interchange and small organizations: Adoption and impact of technology. *Management Information Systems Quarterly, 19*(4), 465–485. doi:10.2307/249629

Kuan, K., & Chau, P. Y. K. (2001). A perception-based model for EDI adoption in small businesses using a technology-organized environment framework. *Information & Management, 38*(8), 507–521. doi:10.1016/S0378-7206(01)00073-8

Lin, B., Vassar, J., & Clack, L. (1993). Information technology strategies for small business. *Journal of Applied Business Research*, *9*(2), 25–29.

Nickell, G., & Seado, P. (1986). The impact of attitudes and experiences on small business computer use. *American Journal of Small Business*, *10*(1), 37–48.

Ortiz de Guinea, A., Kelly, H., & Hunter, M. G. (2005). Information systems effectiveness in small business: Extending a Singaporean model in Canada. *Journal of Global Information Management*, *13*(3), 55–79. doi:10.4018/jgim.2005070104

Pollard, C., & Hayne, S. (1998). The changing faces of information systems issues in small firms. *International Small Business Journal*, *16*(3), 70–87. doi:10.1177/0266242698163004

Sharma, M. K., & Bhagwat, R. (2006). Performance measurements in the implementation of information systems in small and medium-sized enterprises: A framework and empirical analysis. *Measuring Business Excellence*, *10*(4), 8–21. doi:10.1108/13683040610719245

Smith, B., & Simon, M. (2009). How data integration systems affect strategic decision making in small firms. *Journal of Small Business Strategy*, *20*(1), 35–51.

Stevenson, H. H. (1999). A perspective of entrepreneurship. In H. H. Stevenson, H. I. Grousebeck, M. J. Roberts, & A. Bhide (Eds.), *New Business Ventures and the Entrepreneur* (pp. 3–17). Boston: Irwin McGraw-Hill.

Taylor, J. (1999). Fitting enterprise software in smaller companies. *Management Accounting*, *80*(8), 36–39.

Thong, J., Yap, C., & Raman, K. (1994). Engagement of external expertise in information systems implementation. *Journal of Management Information Systems*, *11*(2), 209–223.

Thong, J. Y. L., Yap, C. S., & Raman, K. S. (1996). Top management support, external expertise and information systems implementation in small business. *Information Systems Research*, *7*(2), 248–267. doi:10.1287/isre.7.2.248

Timmons, J. A. (1999). *New Venture Creation* (5th ed.). Boston: Irwin McGraw-Hill.

Winter, S. J., Gaglio, C. M., & Rajagopalan, H. K. (2009). The value of information systems to small and medium-sized enterprises: Information and communications technologies as signal and symbol of legitimacy and competitiveness. *International Journal of E-Business Research*, *5*(1), 65–91. doi:10.4018/jebr.2009010104

Zahra, S. A., & George, G. (2002). Absorptive capacity: A review, reconceptualization, and extension. *Academy of Management Review*, *27*(2), 185–203.

## ADDITIONAL READING

DeLooff, L. A. (1997). *Information System Outsourcing Decision Making: A Managerial Approach*. Hershey, PA: IGI-Global. doi:10.4018/978-1-878289-40-7

Hunter, M. G., Burgess, S., & Wenn, A. (Editors). (2005). Small Business and Information Technology: Research Issues and International Case Studies. Melbourne, Australia: Heidelberg Press

Khosrow-Pour, M. (Ed.). (2008). *Encyclopedia of Information Science and Technology* (Vol. I-V). Hershey, PA: Idea Group Publishing.

Pankowska, M. (2010). *Infonomics for Distributed Business and Decision-Making Environments: Creating Information System Ecology*. Hershey, PA: IGI-Global. doi:10.4018/978-1-60566-890-1

Portela, I. M., & Almeida, F. (2014). *Organizational, Legal, and Technological Dimensions of Information System Administration*. Hershey, PA: IGI-Global. doi:10.4018/978-1-4666-4526-4

## KEY TERMS AND DEFINITIONS

**Accuracy:** Level of correctness.
**Consultant:** Functional expert external to the business.
**Dependency:** When the performance of one function relates to another function.
**Down Time:** A period of time when a process or function is not available.
**Laggards:** Those who are slow to adopt an innovation.
**Leaders:** Those who initiate the adoption of an innovation.
**Operational Efficiency:** Ability to perform a function with few resources.
**Positive Image:** Performance reputation which is recognized by others.
**Responsiveness:** Speed of responding to a request.
**Timeliness:** Responding to a request within a specific period.
**Use:** Method of employing a process to carry out a business function.
**Vendor:** An entity which sells a product or service.

# Chapter 7
# Strategy


## ABSTRACT

*Small business tends not to take a strategic approach to planning and operations. The focus tends to be on efficient operations in the near term. Thus, it is incumbent upon senior management in a small business to take a longer term perspective to strategically address how to gain and sustain competitive advantage. This chapter discusses how the use of information systems will promote the necessary internal environment which, in turn, will facilitate responding to the external environment. The strategic use of information systems will lead to more sophisticated and formal processes. A learning environment will support creative initiatives where information systems will improve performance and contribute to competitive advantage.*


## INTRODUCTION

Strategy involves planning for the future of the small business and considers both internal assets and external events which may impact the business. Small business may employ information systems in a strategic manner in order to attempt to gain competitive advantage. From an external perspective the small business will develop a strategy which proactively addresses the business environment. Continual scanning will provide information about the market and other small businesses in the same industry. Information systems related to websites and other Internet based applications will facilitate gathering important information.

DOI: 10.4018/978-1-4666-8708-0.ch007

Internally the focus is on skills and processes. The strategic use of information systems will improve employee skills and promote more sophisticated processes. The establishment of a learning environment will allow managers and employees to acquire knowledge about information technology. They will be encouraged to take novel initiatives in the application of information systems which may contribute to competitive advantage. In this environment the information technology knowledge of the owner/manager will promote investigations into the novel use of the technology to benefit the small business.

Overall, the strategic use of information systems will improve the performance of the small business. Physical assets such as equipment and machinery will be employed more productively. Intangible assets in the form of method and processes will lead to a more sophisticated approach to the management of the small business. Further, as the small business grows and matures informal processes will be replaced by formal processes supported by the adoption and use of information systems. Employee skills and a learning environment will facilitate the use of all of these assets to gain competitive advantage.

This chapter is organized as follows. To begin the generic term "strategy" is reviewed. Then for the remainder of the chapter strategy is related to information systems. Thus, it is suggested that the strategic use of information systems by small business will contribute to gaining competitive advantage. Next it is proposed that the information technology knowledge of the owner/manager and the creation of a learning environment within the small business will lead to a more sophisticated use of information technology and consequently competitive advantage. As the small business grows and matures more sophisticated and formalized processes are employed which are supported by information systems.

## INFORMATION SYSTEMS AND STRATEGY

Generally, information systems support the efficiency of internal operations for a small business. The strategic use of information systems will contribute to achieving competitive advantage through improved relationships with customers and suppliers. Further, strategic use of information systems will allow the small business to more effectively compete with other small businesses within the industry.

Early investigations into the use of information systems by small business suggested the technology was mainly used to support daily operations (Rivard et al, 1988). Later Pollard and Hayne (1998) identified a shift towards a more strategic use of information systems by small business in an attempt to gain competitive advantage. Kagan et al (1990) supported this finding concluding that as a small business grows there is an increased need for more sophisticated information. As a consequence information systems become employed at a more strategic level within the small business as it grows.

Strategic entrepreneurship is a relatively recently emerging topic at the intersection of strategic management and entrepreneurship (Hitt et al, 2001; Ireland et al, 2003; Zahra & Dess, 2001; Venkataraman & Sarasyathy, 2001; and Kuratko et al, 2005). In general, entrepreneurship identifies opportunities (Shane & Venkataraman, 2000; McCline et al, 2000; Davidsson et al, 2002; Hitt et al, 2002; and Thompson, 1999) and strategic management transforms the opportunities in attempting to contribute sustained competitive advantage (Ireland et al, 2003; Ramachandran et al, 2006; Duncan et al, 1998; Prahalad & Hamel, 1990; Porter, 1985; Wernerfelt, 1984; and Barney, 1991).

An entrepreneurial opportunity involves identifying new goods, services, raw materials, and operating methods which create value (Companys & McMullen, 2007). Exploiting these opportunities is strategically important (Hitt et al, 2001) because of the potential to gain competitive advantage (Ahuja & Katila, 2004) through innovative development of goods and services which will result in increased wealth (Schumpeter, 1934 and Kirzner, 1997).

Roberts and Wood (2001) proposed a framework from which to view the perspectives of information systems in small business. They described two perspectives, functionality and benefit. Functionality relates to specific tasks such as payroll or inventory. Benefit relates to advantages and includes efficiency, effectiveness, and strategic. Efficiency benefits relate to carrying out activities correctly. They focus on conducting operations as currently designed but with fewer resources. A benefit is effective if it supports new activities or results in the elimination of old activities; both of which contribute value to the small business. Strategic benefits may facilitate the approach taken by a small business to competing with other businesses within its industry. This competitive advantage may be sustained if other small businesses are not able to easily replicate the process which created the benefit.

In the late 1990s there were a number of investigations into information technology and business strategic alignment (Chan et al, 1997; Raymond et al, 1995; Reich & Benbasat, 1996; and Luftman et al, 1999). Unfortunately, in the early 2000s there remained few investigations into the strategic use of information technology by small business (Hussin et al, 2002).

The small business owner/manager's knowledge of information technology will positively impact strategic business and information technology alignment (Chan et al, 1997; and Hussin et al, 2002); and consequently adoption of both traditional information technology and Internet technologies (Chao & Chandra, 2012). Further, the small business owner/manager often assumes responsibility for both business and information technology strategic planning. This further supports the contention of the importance of the owner/managers' information technology knowledge (Kyobe, 2004 and Lee & Runge, 2001). Small business owner/managers who do not understand information technology will generally avoid making information technology investments (Cragg & King, 1993). Small business strategies will impact information technology use. If the business strategy is low cost the information technology is considered a peripheral initiative and is used mainly for efficiencies (Lesjak & Lynn, 2000). If information technology is considered integral to business performance then it tends to garner strategic benefits such as value added differentiation with a customer emphasis (Levy et al, 2001).

Hussin et al (2002) determined that alignment of information technology strategy and business strategy depended upon the small business level of maturity and the senior manager's software knowledge. They suggest that small business maturity involves a learning environment about the sophisticated use of information technology as well as the development of more advanced management processes. This learning environment results from several years of successful operation of the small business. Senior manager's software knowledge facilitated communication with information technology specialists and contributed to a positive attitude towards information technology. The consequent commitment to information technology leads to an acknowledgement of the necessity to align the strategic plans for information technology and the business.

In order to improve performance, small business should focus on two aspects of internal capabilities (Man et al, 2002; and Vargas & Rangel, 2007). One aspect relates to equipment and machinery which should be employed in an innovative way regarding the use of raw material. The other aspect involves the development of efficient and effective methods and processes. Taken together, these aspects will support strategic initiatives for on-going improvement of operations through innovation and the ability to respond to new situations.

When developing a strategy small business should be flexible (Singh et al, 2006). With a focus on the small business niche products and services should be innovative (Corbett & Campbell-Hunt, 2002). This focus will be facilitated through improved skills and competencies (Fuller-Love, 2006). An external orientation regarding the market and competition will support growth strategies (O'Regan et al, 2006a & 2006b). Small business that takes a strategic perspective tends to outperform their competition (Singh et al, 2008).

Leitner and Guldenberg (2010) compared the approach taken by small business regarding generic strategies. They compared the use of traditional strategies related to either cost efficiency or product differentiation with a strategy that combines both of the above initiatives. That is, traditionally small business has been encouraged to adopt either a cost efficiency perspective or a product differentiation approach – but not both. However, a hybrid approach addressing both perspectives may lead to long term improved performance and competitive advantage (Spanos et al, 2004; Parnell, 2005; and Thornhill & White, 2007). Leitner and Guldenberg (2010) determined that a combination strategy lead to long term profitability and growth. This strategy was facilitated by the use of modern technology and an advanced approach to quality management and flexible production.

Street and Meister (2004) investigated how a small business employed information systems to promote growth. They employed Punctuated Equilibrium Theory to analyze the change precipitated by the installation of an information system. They determined that as small business grows the formal communication process becomes important replacing to some degree the informal processes because of the increasingly complex business structure.

Mazzarol et al (2009) investigated how small business owner-managers carried out strategic management and whether the practice contributed to growth. They determined the following:

*The possession of a formal business plan may not directly improve business performance, but the process of developing such a document is likely to require the owner-manager to review their firm's vision, mission and external market environment and outlook. It will also require them to consider their internal and external critical information and the key information that allows them to monitor their financial performance. The possession of good information technology systems that collect and report such information is highly desirable. Owner-managers are also likely to benefit from establishing strong external support networks, as well as forming strong organisational cultures that make employees feel more like partners. (Mazzarol et al, 2009, p. 338)*

Thus, it is recognized that most small business owner-managers tend to take an intuitive approach to planning.

Singh et al (2008) investigated the relationship between small business strategy development and competitive advantage. They suggest that small business should take a longer term perspective when developing strategic goals which may contribute further to competitive advantage.

Joyce and Woods (2003) investigated formal strategic systems and their contribution to competitive advantage. They determined that the existence of an internal strategic system supported decision making and contributed to the small business growth objectives. Further, planning, in the form of a strategic system facilitated innovation and the ability to respond to changes.

## CONCLUSION

This chapter has presented a brief overview of how small business may employ information systems strategically. With a learning environment and knowledge of how to employ information technology the small business may gain competitive advantage. As the small business grows and matures information systems will support more sophisticated and formalized management processes. The next chapter describes the relationship between information systems and competitive advantage.

## REFERENCES

Ahuja, G., & Katila, R. (2004). Where do resources come from? The role of idiosyncratic situations. *Strategic Management Journal*, *25*(89), 887–904. doi:10.1002/smj.401

Barney, J. (1991). Firm resources and sustained competitive advantage. *Journal of Management*, *17*(1), 99–120. doi:10.1177/014920639101700108

Chan, Y. E., Huff, S. L., Barclay, D. W., & Copeland, D. G. (1997). Business strategic orientation, information systems orientation and strategic alignment. *Information Systems Research*, *8*(2), 125–150. doi:10.1287/isre.8.2.125

Chao, C. A., & Chandra, A. (2012). Impact of owner's knowledge of information technology (IT) on strategic alignment and IT adoption in US small firms. *Journal of Small Business and Enterprise Development*, *19*(1), 114–131. doi:10.1108/14626001211196433

Companys, Y. E., & McMullen, J. S. (2007). Strategic entrepreneurs at work: The nature, discovery, and exploitation of entrepreneurial opportunities. *Small Business Economics*, *28*(4), 301–322. doi:10.1007/s11187-006-9034-x

Corbett, L. M., & Campbell-Hunt, C. (2002). Grappling with a gusher! Manufacturing's response to business success in small and medium enterprises. *Journal of Operations Management*, *20*(5), 495–517. doi:10.1016/S0272-6963(02)00026-8

Cragg, P. B., & King, M. (1993). Small-firm computing: Motivators and inhibitors. *Management Information Systems Quarterly*, *17*(1), 47–60. doi:10.2307/249509

Davidsson, P., Delmar, F., & Wiklund, J. (2002). Entrepreneurship as growth: Growth as entrepreneurship. In M. A. Hitt, R. D. Ireland, S. M. Camp, & D. L. Sexton (Eds.), *Strategic Entrepreneurhsip: Creating a New Mindset* (pp. 328–340). Oxford: Blackwell.

Duncan, W. J., Ginter, P. M., & Swayne, L. E. (1998). Competitive advantage and internal organizational assessment. *The Academy of Management Executive, 12*(3), 6–16.

Fuller-Love, N. (2006). Management development in small firms. *International Journal of Management Reviews, 8*(3), 175–190. doi:10.1111/j.1468-2370.2006.00125.x

Hitt, M. A., Ireland, R. D., Camp, M. S., & Sexton, D. L. (2001). Special introduction to the special issue on strategic entrepreneurship: Entrepreneurial strategies for wealth creation. *Strategic Management Journal, 22*(6-7), 479–491. doi:10.1002/smj.196

Hitt, M. A., Ireland, R. D., Camp, M. S., & Sexton, D. L. (2002). Strategic entrepreneurship: Integrating entrepreneurial and strategic management perspectives. In M. Hitt, R. Ireland, M. Camp, & D. Sexton (Eds.), *Strategic Entrepreneurship: Creating a New Mindset* (pp. 1–13). Oxford: Blackwell. doi:10.1111/b.9780631234104.2002.00015.x

Hitt, M. A., Ireland, R. D., & Hoskisson, R. E. (2001). *Strategic Management: Competitiveness and Globalization*. Cincinnati, Ohio: South-Western College.

Hussin, H., King, M., & Cragg, P. (2002). IT alignment in small firms. *European Journal of Information Systems, 11*(2), 108–127. doi:10.1057/palgrave/ejis/3000422

Ireland, R. D., Hitt, M. A., & Simon, D. G. (2003). A model of strategic entrepreneurship: The construct and its dimensions. *Journal of Management, 29*(6), 963–989. doi:10.1016/S0149-2063(03)00086-2

Joyce, P., & Woods, A. (2003). Managing for growth: Decision making, planning, and making changes. *Journal of Small Business and Enterprise Development, 10*(2), 144–151. doi:10.1108/14626000310473175

Kagan, A., Lau, K., & Nusgart, K. R. (1990). Information system usage within small business firms. *Entrepreneurship Theory and Practice*, Spring, 25-37.

Kirzner, I. M. (1997). Entrepreneurial discovery and the competitive market process: An Austrian approach. *Journal of Economic Literature, 35*(1), 60–85.

Kuratko, D. F., Ireland, R. D., Covin, J. G., & Hornsby, J. S. (2005). A model of middle-level managers' entrepreneurial behavior. *Entrepreneurship Theory & Practice, 29*(6), 699–716. doi:10.1111/j.1540-6520.2005.00104.x

Kyobe, M. (2004). Investigating the strategic utilization of IT resources in small and medium-sized firms of the Eastern Free State Province. *International Small Business Journal, 22*(2), 131–158. doi:10.1177/0266242604041311

Lee, J., & Runge, J. (2001). Adoption of information technology in small business: Testing drivers of adoption for entrepreneurs. *Journal of Computer Information Systems*, *42*(1), 44–57.

Leitner, K. H., & Guldenberg, S. (2010). Generic strategies and firm performance in SMEs: A longitudinal study of Austrian SMEs. *Small Business Economics*, *35*(2), 169–189. doi:10.1007/s11187-009-9239-x

Lesjak, D., & Lynn, M. (2000). Small Slovene firms and strategic information technology usage. *Proceedings of the Eighth European Conference on Information Systems*, 63-70.

Levy, M., Powell, P., & Yetton, P. (2001). SMEs: Aligning IS and the strategic context. *Journal of Information Technology*, *16*(3), 133–144. doi:10.1080/02683960110063672

Luftman, J. N., Papp, R., & Brier, T. (1999). Enablers and inhibitors of business-IT alignment. *Communications of the Association for Information Systems*, *1*(11), 1–32.

Man, T. W. Y., Lau, T., & Chan, K. F. (2002). The competitiveness of small and medium enterprises: A conceptualization with focus on entrepreneurial competencies. *Journal of Business Venturing*, *17*(2), 123–142. doi:10.1016/S0883-9026(00)00058-6

Mazzarol, T., Reboud, S., & Soutar, G. N. (2009). Strategic planning in growth oriented small firms. *International Journal of Entrepreneurial Behaviour & Research*, *15*(4), 320–345. doi:10.1108/13552550910967912

McCline, R. L., Bhat, S., & Baj, P. (2000). Opportunity recognition: An exploratory investigation of a component of the entrepreneurial process in the context of the health care industry. *Entrepreneurship Theory & Practice*, *25*(2), 81–94.

O'Regan, N., Ghobadian, A., & Gallear, D. (2006a). In search of the drivers of high growth in manufacturing SMEs. *Technovation*, *26*(1), 30–41. doi:10.1016/j.technovation.2005.05.004

O'Regan, N., Ghobadian, A., & Sims, M. (2006b). Fast tracking innovation in manufacturing SMEs. *Technovation*, *26*(2), 251–261. doi:10.1016/j.technovation.2005.01.003

Parnell, J. A. (2005). Managing paradoxes in strategic decision-making. *International Journal of Management and Decision Making*, *7*(6), 708–724. doi:10.1504/IJMDM.2006.011078

Pollard, C. E., & Hayne, S. E. (1998). The changing face of information systems issues in small firms. *International Small Business Journal, 16*(3), 70–87. doi:10.1177/0266242698163004

Porter, M. E. (1985). *Competitive Advantage: Creating and Sustaining Superior Performance*. New York, NY: The Free Press.

Prahalad, C. K., & Hamel, G. (1990). The core competence of the corporation. *Harvard Business Review, 68*(3), 79–91.

Ramachandran, J., Mukherji, S., & Sud, M. (2006). Strategic entrepreneurship in a globalising economy: Evidence from emerging economies. *IIMB Management Review, 28*(3), 291–302.

Raymond, L., Pare, G., & Bergeron, F. (1995). Matching information technology and organizational structure: An empirical study with implications for performance. *European Journal of Information Systems, 4*(1), 3–16. doi:10.1057/ejis.1995.2

Reich, B. H., & Benbasat, I. (1996). Measuring the linkage between business and information technology objectives. *Management Information Systems Quarterly, 20*(1), 3–16. doi:10.2307/249542

Rivard, S., Boisvert, C., & Talbot, J. (1988). Key management issues in IS: A comparative analysis. *Proceedings of the Annual Conference of the ASAC*.

Roberts, M., & Wood, M. (2001). The strategic use of computerised information systems by a micro enterprise. *Logistics Information Management, 15*(1/2), 115–125.

Schumpeter, J. A. (1934). *The Theory of Economic Development*. Cambridge, MA: Harvard University Press.

Shane, S., & Venkataraman, S. (2000). The promise of entrepreneurship as a field of research. *Academy of Management Review, 25*(1), 217–226.

Singh, R. K., Garg, S. K., & Deshmukh, S. G. (2006). Strategy development by Indian SMEs in plastic sector: An empirical study. *Singapore Management Review, 28*(2), 65–83.

Singh, R. K., Garg, S. K., & Deshmukh, S. G. (2008). Strategy development by SMEs for competitiveness: A review. *Benchmarking: An International Journal, 15*(5), 525–547. doi:10.1108/14635770810903132

Spanos, Y. E., Zaralis, G., & Lioukas, S. (2004). Strategy and industry effects on profitability: Evidence from Greece. *Strategic Management Journal*, *25*(2), 139–165. doi:10.1002/smj.369

Street, C. T., & Meister, D. B. (2004). Small business growth and internal transparency: The role of information systems. *Management Information Systems Quarterly*, *28*(3), 473–506.

Thompson, J. L. (1999). A strategic perspective of entrepreneurship. *International Journal of Entrepreneurial Behavior & Research*, *5*(6), 279–296. doi:10.1108/13552559910306105

Thornhill, S., & White, R. E. (2007, May). (20070. Strategic purity: A multi-industry evaluation of pure vs. hybrid business strategies. *Strategic Management Journal*, *28*(5), 553–561. doi:10.1002/smj.606

Vargas, D. M., & Rangel, R. G. T. (2007). Development of internal resources and capabilities as sources of differentiation of SME under increased global competition: A field study in Mexico. *Technological Forecasting and Social Change*, *74*(1), 90–99. doi:10.1016/j.techfore.2005.09.007

Venkataraman, S., & Sarasvathy, S. D. (2001). Strategy and entrepreneurship: Outlines of an untold story. In M. A. Hitt, E. Freeman, & J. S. Harrison (Eds.), *Handbook of Strategic Management* (pp. 650–668). Oxford: Blackwell. doi:10.2139/ssrn.275186

Wernerfelt, B. (1984). A resource-based view of the firm. *Strategic Management Journal*, *5*(2), 171–180. doi:10.1002/smj.4250050207

Zahra, S., & Dess, G. G. (2001). Entrepreneurship as a field of research: Encouraging dialogue and debate. *Academy of Management Review*, *26*(1), 8–10. doi:10.5465/AMR.2001.4011916

## ADDITIONAL READING

Hunter, M. G. (2009). *Selected Readings in Strategic Information Systems*. Hershey, PA: Information Science Reference. doi:10.4018/978-1-60566-090-5

Khosrow-Pour, M. (2009). *Best Practices and Conceptual Innovations in Information Resources Management: Utilizing Technologies to Enable Global Progressions*. Hershey, PA: Information Science Reference. doi:10.4018/978-1-60566-128-5

Weinman, J. (2012). *Cloudonomics: The Business Value of Cloud Computing*. Hoboken, NJ: Wiley.

## KEY TERMS AND DEFINITIONS

**Business Performance:** Conducting operations leading to objectives.

**Business Structure:** A method of assigning duties to employees.

**Competition:** Those businesses which provide the same products or services in the same geographic area.

**Cost Efficiency:** Ensuring resources required in the production process are minimized.

**Growth:** Expansion of revenues requiring the addition of more employees.

**Internal Capabilities:** Skills of employees.

**Learning Environment:** The acquisition of skills is promoted.

**Market:** Potential customers.

**Physical Assets:** Resources that can be touched.

**Product Differentiation:** Incorporating components into a product that creates uniqueness.

**Strategic Alignment:** Ensuring that processes support the high level plan.

**Strategic Entrepreneurship:** A plan to adopt innovative processes or businesses.

**Strategy:** High level plan to achieve a goal. Internal assets: resources of the small business.

# Chapter 8
# Competitive Advantage


## ABSTRACT

*If a small business is going to survive it must be competitive. Internally, efficient operations will contribute to lower costs. A positive environment will allow employees to gain and apply the necessary skills. Management knowledge of information systems will provide leadership. Externally, the establishment of knowledge acquisition networks will facilitate the novel use of information systems. This chapter discusses how a strategy which integrates all of the small business resources, especially those related to information systems, will improve performance. An overall customer orientation applying internal resources and accessing external knowledge will contribute to competitive advantage.*


## INTRODUCTION

Competitive advantage for a small business involves operating more efficiently and offering different products or services than competitors. A more efficient operation will result on lower costs and thus an advantage may be gained by establishing a lower market price. The advantage gained by offering different products or services must also take into account the needs of customers. That is, being different is not enough. There still must be a demand for the product or service.

A small business does not necessarily have to grow to attain competitive advantage. Indeed, just survival will suffice. In either case competent management is imperative. This relates to knowledgeable senior management and a positive learning environment for employees. The Theory of Constraints suggests that increased sales volume in conjunction with lower expenses will contribute to competitive advantage.

DOI: 10.4018/978-1-4666-8708-0.ch008

Information systems may be employed to contribute to the establishment of competitive advantage. The innovative adoption of technologies will support this initiative. Another theoretical perspective has been employed in this instance. The Resource-based View Theory, as presented in a previous chapter suggests the small business should employ its resources in a unique way from competitors.

This chapter is organized as follows. To begin, the term "competitive advantage" is described. Advantage may be gained through differentiation from competitors by having lower costs or different products or services that respond to a demand in the market. Next, competent management is presented as a factor contributing to competitive advantage. This factor involves knowledge of senior management and their ability to establish and maintain external networks. Then the Theory of Constraints suggests improved performance will result from increased sales and lower operating expenses. Three related issues are then presented which may contribute to competitive advantage. "Coopetition" is a term used to describe the conundrum of small businesses which are simultaneously cooperating and competing. The result is an increased market. "Family Capital" is another term which suggests the unique characteristics of a family business may contribute to competitive advantage. The last term is "luck". Here it is important to have a stimulating and open small business environment. Thus, when a situation arises which may be attributed to luck the small business will be in a position to take advantage. Finally, the Resource-based View theory provides the context for analyzing the unique information systems characteristics of small business which may contribute to competitive advantage. These characteristics include information systems infrastructure and information systems skills along with management knowledge and an integrated strategy to use information systems to facilitate competitive advantage.

## INFORMATION SYSTEMS AND COMPETITIVE ADVANTAGE

A competitive advantage is gained when a small business, relative to other small businesses, becomes more efficient or acquires increased bargaining power over it competition. Researchers have investigated how information technology can contribute to competitive advantage (Bakos & Treacy, 1986).

Porter (1985 and 1998) suggested that competitive advantage may be achieved through a strategy of having lower costs or being different than other small businesses. Lower costs mean the small business is relatively more efficient than competitors and thus is better able to produce quality goods and/or services at prices which prevail in the market. A differentiation strategy means the small business can produce goods and services which are unique or superior resulting in the ability to charge a premium price creating higher profits.

Feindt et al (2002) suggest that most small businesses do not grow. They reported that only 3% of small businesses grow beyond the first few years after start-up.

There are many factors that contribute to small business success.

*Successful SMEs place greater emphasis on soft issues (people) than hard issues (technology, structure). The management skills and concepts of the founders are deemed much more important than their technical skills. Employee skills are of crucial concern and can be most effectively developed in a nurturing working environment. Nevertheless the impact of business founders on organisational success remains the leading factor.(Feindt et al, 2002, p. 53)*

Littunen and Niittykangas (2010) investigated factors related to high growth in small business. Their novel approach was to divide the firms included in the project into two age categories. One group included those small businesses in their first four years of operation. The other group included the five to eight years of small business age. They determined two important factors contributing to high growth. First, across both age categories, the knowledge of the entrepreneur contributed positively to growth.

The second factor involved entrepreneurial networks. In general, networks involve establishing and maintaining personal relationships. An informal network consists of, "...personal relationships, families, and business contacts." (Littunen & Niittykangas, 2010:13). A formal network includes, "...venture capitalists, banks, accountants, creditors, lawyers, and trade associations." (Littunen & Niittykangas, 2010:13). In both cases these networks are external to the small business and provide the entrepreneur with a window to the environment.

Littunen and Niittykangas (2010) determined that these external networks were a positive influence on growth of the small business in the first four years of operation. They provided opportunities for competitive advantage, innovations, and efficiency. However, during year's five to eight internal networks became a more important contributing factor to growth. The internal networks involve interactions with employees. The external networks remain an important contributor. However, the internal networks become relatively more important. Thus, the entrepreneur becomes more of a manager interacting with individuals on the team. This is a consequence of growth and the resulting increase in the number of individuals employed by the small business.

Grandy and Wicks (2008) investigated competitive advantage in small business. It is noted that competitive advantage for small business is more related to survival than growth (Beaver & Prince, 2004). To gain competitive advantage a small business should focus on adding value to products and services and then passing that value on to customers (Jones, 2003). Sustained competitive advantage necessitates value creation through applying resources appropriately (Adner & Zemsky, 2006). They suggest the following initiatives:

- Reduce production costs
- Improve performance
- Be a market leader
- Be an early adopter of technology

In order to create on-going competitive advantage it is necessary to have competent management (Kickul, 2001). This contention is supported by Konorti (2010) who suggests that small business acquire the services of professional managers who would complement the skills of the small business manager.

Kohli and Gupta (2010) suggest the Theory of Constraints (Goldratt, 1994; and Breen et al, 2002) for aiding small business managers to create and sustain competitive advantage. The theory focuses on issues that could cause problems for small business and, more importantly, if addressed positively, could contribute to competitive advantage. Thus, the theory consists of three specific performance measures.

- Throughput: "…the rate at which the system generates money through sales."
- Inventory: "…all the money invested in purchasing the things the system intends to sell."
- Operating Expenses: "…all the money the system spends in turning inventory to throughput." (Kohli & Gupta, 2010, p. 39)

The objective of the small business manager is to increase throughput while reducing inventory and operating expenses to create competitive advantage.

The term "coopetition" (Walley, 2007) has been further explored by Thomason et al (2013) which is a multi-business strategy to expand the potential market by developing new products and services. The term suggests, "…competitors simultaneously cooperate and compete with each other to create value." (Thomason et al, 2013:16). Thus small business working together may reduce costs and provide better customer service thereby increasing their market.

Hoffman et al (2006) introduced the term "family capital" as, "…the basic characteristic that distinguishes family from other businesses is the influence of family relationships on the business." (Hoffman et al, 2006, p. 136). The term is similar to "social capital" (Adler & Kwon, 1999; Burt, 1992; Coleman, 1988; Nahapiet & Ghoshal, 1998: and Putnam, 1993) which involves the value created by the relationships among people associated with a small business. However, because of the nucleus of family member relationships, family businesses do not require the extensive effort to develop social capital. Hoffman et al (2006) conclude that family capital provides a significant advantage over non-family small business and contributes to sustained competitive advantage (Barney, 1986, 1991, 1995, 1996; Derickx & Cool, 1989; Hunt, 1999; Penrose, 1959; Porter, 1980; and Rumelt, 1984).

Ma (2002) investigated the role "luck" plays in gaining competitive advantage. A typology of luck is presented in Table 1.

The source of the luck can be exogenous, arising from outside the small business; or endogenous, occurring as a result of internal processes from within the small business. The approach taken by the small business may be proactive with management seeking opportunities; or reactive with management passively responding to serendipitous events.

Each quadrant of the table may be described as follows:

- **Pure Luck:** "...factors [external] to the firm give rise to competitive advantage spontaneously..." (Ma, 2002, p. 526)
- **Prepared Luck:** "...managers [are] always on the alert for potential opportunities and act proactively." (Ma, 2002, p. 527)
- **Useful Weeds:** "...serendipity within the firm from its often seemingly accidental innovation and creativity." (Ma, 2002, p. 527)
- **Skunk Works**: "...individuals or working groups – often temporary of informal ones – within an organization work voluntarily and secretively on their own initiative to tackle entrepreneurial, technical, or organizational challenges which will likely lead to innovative practice and beneficial results to the formal organization." (Ma, 2002, pp. 527-528)

The important comment by Ma (2002) is that small business should maintain a stimulating and open environment in order to be able to respond to any situation which may descend upon the small business or occur from within.

*Table 1. Luck and competitive advantage*

| | | | |
|---|---|---|---|
| | | **Source** | |
| | | **Exogenous** | **Endogenous** |
| **Approach** | **Proactive** | Prepared Luck | Skunk Works |
| | **Reactive** | Pure Luck | Useful Weeds |

Adapted from Ma, 2002

Subsequently, Parnell & Dent (2009) further explored the concept of luck and how it relates to competitive advantage. They suggest that managers are more likely to perceive that luck affects outcomes, relating to competitive advantage, the higher their position in the business.

Some time ago it was suggested that information systems could be employed to establish competitive advantage. Bergeron and Raymond (1992) investigated how information systems provided a competitive edge for small business. They suggested that "Information Systems for Competitive Advantage" (ISCA) create this edge by facilitating added value to the products or services provided by the small business. They concluded that in general information technology may be used strategically for a small business to establish and maintain a competitive advantage.

As presented in Chapter Five, Levy et al (2001) proposed a focus-dominance model to examine how small business may employ their information technology capabilities to gain competitive advantage. The framework is presented here again in Table 2.

Currently, most small businesses are situated in the Efficiency quadrant, where they are employing basic technology. The majority of movement from this quadrant is either to Co-ordination to increase market share or to Collaboration to manage customer relationships. Unfortunately, there was very little movement to the Innovation quadrant to actively seek out and adopt technologies to support achieving competitive advantage. This situation may be explained by the following investigation conducted by Qureshil et al (2009).

Qureshil et al (2009) employed the Resource-based View of the firm to investigate how small business employs information technology to achieve competitive advantage. They concluded that small business lacks the skills necessary to understand and apply information technology. Thus, they suggested that an external entity may be necessary to acquire the kind of knowledge that is necessary to adopt information technology to facilitate competitive advantage.

*Table 2. The focus-dominance model*

| | | | |
|---|---|---|---|
| **Customer** | LOW | Co-ordination | Innovation |
| **Dominance** | HIGH | Efficiency | Collaboration |
| | | COST | VALUE ADDED |
| | | **Strategic** | **Focus** |

Adapted from Levy et al, 2001

Further, Avram and Kuhne (2008) employed the framework outlined in Table 2 to evaluate small business approach to corporate social responsibility. They proposed that responsible business behaviour should be incorporated into the strategy of small business which would lead eventually to competitive advantage.

Information systems support the knowledge base of small business (Alavi & Leidner, 2001). The adoption of information systems represents a tool to gain market share and operational efficiency (BarNir et al, 2003; Bharadwaj & Soni, 2007; and Johnston et al, 2007). These improvements are further facilitated by enterprise-wide systems (Li et al, 2009).

There are three types of information technology based resources that may be employed to improve the performance of small business (Bharadwaj, 2000). Table 3 presents a description of these resources.

Bharadwaj (2000) also suggests that the small business capability is not the result of specific information technology functions. The capability results from the integration of the information technology resources. Further, the integration results in a unique advantage that is difficult for other small businesses to emulate. Thus, the competitive advantage may be sustained because of the unique environment created by a small business.

Information technology capabilities contribute indirectly to improved performance and ultimately facilitate gaining competitive advantage for small business. One perspective suggests that information technology capabilities may be employed to develop knowledge management processes which will contribute to improved performance (Patrakosol & Lee, 2009; and Perez-Lopez & Alegra, 2012).

Sustainable competitive advantage may be gained through the on-going acquisition of environment information about customer, suppliers, and competitors (Lai et al, 2006).

In general, information technology refers fundamentally to the various components of software, hardware, and telecommunications. Then, information technology competency relates to the use of these components to respond to the information

*Table 3. Information technology based resources*

| Resource | Description |
|---|---|
| Tangible information technology infrastructure | Hardware, software, and telecommunications |
| Human information technology skills | Information technology skills of employees and managers |
| Intangible assets | Knowledge base and customer orientation |

Adapted from Bharadwaj, 2000

requirements of small business (Mithas et al, 2011). Another more recent perspective of information technology competency may be represented by three dimensions described in Table 4.

Competitive advantage is gained through how these dimensions are uniquely employed within a small business to contribute to knowledge management. For instance, information technology infrastructure provides access to information to support collaboration and decision making (Choi et al, 2010; Ho, 2009; King, 2005; and Migdadi, 2008). Information technology operations support business processes (Crawford et al, 2011) and the ability to implement knowledge management processes (Nfuka & Rusu, 2011). Information technology knowledge facilitates the assimilation of external information and the sharing of this information internally (Bhatt & Grover, 2005).

Research has shown that information technology is mainly a facilitator of business processes. It may support the development of new products (Pavlou & Elsawy, 2006); dealing with customers (Ray et al, 2005); and the complete re-design of business processes (Albadvi et al, 2007; and Lee et al, 2011). Consequently, these improved business processes will lead to the achievement of a competitive advantage (Pavlou & El Sawy, 2006; Zhang et al, 2009; and Yao et al, 2010).

Perez-Arostegui et al (2012) suggest that information technology competence will indirectly contribute to competitive advantage through improved quality management (Jenkins, 2010; Sanchez-Rodriquez & Martinez-Lorente, 2011) and leadership (Kaynak, 2003).

Quality management is a major enabler of competitive advantage (Willcocks et al, 2007). In general, quality management represents an evolutionary approach to continuously attempt to improve all business processes through a culture of innovation and knowledge sharing. This culture is developed and maintained through dedicated leadership (Kaynak, 2003). Leadership also facilitates the adoption of information technology (Waldman et al, 2001).

*Table 4. Information technology competency*

| Dimension | Description |
|---|---|
| Infrastructure | Resources, including hardware, software and employees, that contribute to the acquisition, processing, storage, dissemination and use of information |
| Operations | Methods, processes, and techniques which support the improvement of decision making and the creation of value |
| Knowledge | The degree to which individuals within the business understand the capabilities of current and emerging technologies |

Adapted from Perez-Lopez and Alegre, 2012

Various resources are combined to represent information technology competence. Table 5 defines these resources.

As above, these resources in combination will contribute to quality management and along with the appropriate leadership will contribute positively to creating and maintaining competitive advantage.

Tables 3, 4, and 5 outline various resources of small business which contribute to information technology competence in support of competitive advantage. In Table 3 Bharadwaj (2000) list infrastructure, skills, and intangible assets in the form of knowledge and a customer orientation. Perez-Lopez & Alegre (2012) in Table 4 repeats infrastructure and knowledge; and adds operations involving methods and techniques to improve decision making and add value. Consequently, Perez-Arostegui et al (2012) provide a consolidation of the resources in the previous two tables highlighting infrastructure, knowledge, both technical and managerial. The term strategy integration encompasses the use of information technology to facilitate strategic initiatives involving decision making and performance.

## CONCLUSION

This chapter has presented a brief overview of how small business may employ information systems to contribute to attaining and sustaining competitive advantage. The base of information systems involves infrastructure including adequate hardware, software, and telecommunications. Given this base the information systems skills of employees and management will promote beneficial use of the infrastructure. An integrative strategy of these resources will contribute to competitive advantage. The next chapter forms the start of section C which involves the main thesis of the book regarding a balanced approach to the mature use of information systems by small business.

*Table 5. Information technology competence resources*

| Resource | Description |
|---|---|
| Infrastructure | Hardware, software, and telecommunications |
| Technical Knowledge | Experience with operating systems and communication protocols |
| Managerial Knowledge | Project management, resource allocation, and team supervision |
| Strategy Integration | Ensure that the use of information technology facilitates strategic initiatives |

Adapted from Perez-Arostegui et al, 2012

## REFERENCES

Adler, P., & Kwon, S. (1999). Social capital: The good, the bad, and the ugly. In E. L. Lesser (Ed.), *Knowledge and Social Capital*. Boston, MA: Butterworth-Heinemann. doi:10.2139/ssrn.186928

Adner, R., & Zemsky, P. (2006). A demand-based perspective on sustainable competitive advantage. *Strategic Management Journal*, *27*(3), 215–239. doi:10.1002/smj.513

Alavi, M., & Leidner, D. E. (2001). Review: Knowledge management and knowledge management systems: Conceptual foundations and research issues. *Management Information Systems Quarterly*, *25*(1), 107–136. doi:10.2307/3250961

Albadvi, A., Keramati, A., & Razmi, J. (2007). Assessing the impact of information technology on firm performance considering the role of intervening variables: Organizational infrastructures and business processes reengineering. *International Journal of Production Research*, *45*(12), 2697–2734. doi:10.1080/00207540600767780

Avram, D. O., & Kuhne, S. (2008). Implementing responsible business behavior from a strategic management perspective: Developing a framework for Austrian SMEs. *Journal of Business Ethics*, *82*(2), 463–475. doi:10.1007/s10551-008-9897-7

Bakos, J. Y., & Treacy, M. E. (1986). Information technology and corporate strategy: A research perspective. *Management Information Systems Quarterly*, *10*(2), 107–119. doi:10.2307/249029

Barney, J. B. (1986). Strategic factor markets: Expectations, luck, and business strategy. *Management Science*, *32*(10), 1231–1241. doi:10.1287/mnsc.32.10.1231

Barney, J. B. (1991). Firm resources and sustained competitive advantage. *Journal of Management*, *17*(1), 99–120. doi:10.1177/014920639101700108

Barney, J. B. (1995). Looking inside for competitive advantage. *The Academy of Management Executive*, *9*(4), 49–61.

Barney, J. B. (1996). The resource-based theory of the firm. *Organization Science*, *7*(5), 469. doi:10.1287/orsc.7.5.469

BarNir, A., Gallaugher, J. M., & Auger, P.BarNir. (2003). Business process digitization, strategy, and the impact of firm age and size: The case of the magazine publishing company. *Journal of Business Venturing*, *18*(6), 789–814. doi:10.1016/S0883-9026(03)00030-2

Beaver, G., & Prince, C. (2004). Management, strategy and policy in UK small business sector: A critical review. *Journal of Small Business and Enterprise Development*, *11*(1), 34–49. doi:10.1108/14626000410519083

Bergeron, F., & Raymond, L. (19920. Planning of information systems to gain a competitive advantage. *Journal of Small Business Management*, *30*(1), 21–26.

Bharadwaj, A. S. (2000). A resource-based perspective on information technology capability and firm performance: An empirical investigation. *Management Information Systems Quarterly*, *24*(1), 169–196. doi:10.2307/3250983

Bharadwaj, A. S., & Soni, R. G. (2007). E-commerce usage and perception of e-commerce issues among small firms: Results and implications from an empirical study. *Journal of Small Business Management*, *45*(4), 501–521. doi:10.1111/j.1540-627X.2007.00225.x

Bhatt, G. D., & Grover, V. (2005). Types of information technology capabilities and their role in competitive advantage: An empirical study. *Journal of Management Information Systems*, *22*(2), 253–277.

Breen, A., Burton-Houle, T., & Aron, C. (2002). Applying the theory of constraints in health care: Part 1 – the philosophy. *Quality Management in Health Care*, *10*(3), 40–46. doi:10.1097/00019514-200210030-00010 PMID:12512464

Burt, R. S. (1992). *Structural Holes: The Social Structure of Competition*. Cambridge: Harvard University Press.

Choi, S. Y., Lee, H., & Yoo, Y. (2010). The impact of information technology and transitive memory systems on knowledge sharing, application and team performance: A field study. *Management Information Systems Quarterly*, *34*(4), 855–870.

Coleman, J. S. (1988). Social capital in the creation of human capital. *American Journal of Sociology*, *94*(s1), 95–120. doi:10.1086/228943

Crawford, J., Leonard, L. N. K., & Jones, K. (2011). The human resource's influence in shaping IT competence. *Industrial Management & Data Systems*, *111*(2), 164–183. doi:10.1108/02635571111115128

Derickx, L., & Cool, K. (1989). Asset stock accumulation and the sustainability of competitive advantage. *Management Science*, *35*(12), 1504–1511. doi:10.1287/mnsc.35.12.1504

Feindt, S., Jeffcoate, J., & Chappell, C. (2002). Identifying success factors for rapid growth in SME E-commerce. *Small Business Economics*, *19*(1), 51–62. doi:10.1023/A:1016165825476

Goldratt, E. M. (1994). *It's not luck, Croton-on-Hudson*. New York: North River Press, Inc.

Grandy, G., & Wicks, D. (2008). Competitive advantage as a legitimacy-creating process. *Qualitative Research in Organizations and Management*, *3*(1), 21–41. doi:10.1108/17465640810870373

Ho, C. T. (2009). The relationship between knowledge management enablers and performance. *Industrial Management & Data Systems*, *109*(1), 98–117. doi:10.1108/02635570910926618

Hoffman, J., Hoelscher, M., & Sorenson, R. (2006). Achieving sustained competitive advantage: A family capital theory. *Family Business Review*, *19*(2), 135–145. doi:10.1111/j.1741-6248.2006.00065.x

Hunt, S. D. (1999). The strategic imperative and sustainable competitive advantage: Public policy implications of resource-advantage theory. *Journal of the Academy of Marketing Science*, *27*(2), 144–159. doi:10.1177/0092070399272003

Jenkins, M. (2010). Technological discontinuities and competitive advantage: A historical perspective on Formula 1 motor racing 1950-2006. *Journal of Management Studies*, *47*(5), 884–910. doi:10.1111/j.1467-6486.2010.00928.x

Johnston, D. A., Wade, M., & McClean, R. (2007). Does e-business matter to SMEs? A comparison of the financial impacts of internet business solutions on European and North American SMEs. *Journal of Small Business Management*, *45*(3), 354–361. doi:10.1111/j.1540-627X.2007.00217.x

Jones, O. (2003). Competitive advantage in SMEs: Towards a conceptual framework. In O. Jones & F. Tilley (Eds.), *Competitive Advantage in SMEs: Organising for Innovation and Change* (pp. 15–33). Chichester: Wiley.

Kaynak, H. (2003). The relationship between total quality management practices and their effects on firm performance. *Journal of Operations Management*, *21*(4), 405–435. doi:10.1016/S0272-6963(03)00004-4

Kickul, J. (2001). Promises made, promises broken: An explanation of employee attraction and retention practices in small business. *Journal of Small Business Management*, *39*(4), 320–335. doi:10.1111/0447-2778.00029

King, W. R. (2005). Communication and information processing as a critical success factor in the effective knowledge organization. *International Journal of Business Information Systems*, *1*(1/2), 31–52. doi:10.1504/IJBIS.2005.007399

Kohli, A. S., & Gupta, M. (2010). Improving operations strategy: Application of TOC principles in a small business. *Journal of Business & Economics Research*, *8*(4), 37–45.

Konorti, E. (2010). The relationship between wealth creation and professional management in small-medium enterprises. *The Journal of American Academy of Business*, *16*(1), 11–23.

Lai, F., Zhao, X., & Wang, Q. (2006). The impact of information technology on the competitive advantage of logistics firms in China. *Industrial Management & Data Systems*, *106*(9), 1249–1263. doi:10.1108/02635570610712564

Lee, Y. C., Chu, P. Y., & Tseng, H. T. (2011). Corporate performance of ICT-enabled business process re-engineering. *Industrial Management & Data Systems*, *111*(5), 735–754. doi:10.1108/02635571111137287

Levy, M., Powell, P., & Yetton, P. (2001). SMEs: Aligning IS and the strategic context. *Journal of Information Technology*, *16*(3), 133–144. doi:10.1080/02683960110063672

Li, J., Merenda, M., & Venkatachalam, A. R. (2009). Business process digitization and new product development: An empirical study of small and medium-sized manufacturers. *International Journal of E-Business Research*, *5*(1), 49–64. doi:10.4018/jebr.2009010103

Littunen, H., & Niittykangas, H. (2010). The rapid growth of young firms during various stages of entrepreneurship. *Journal of Small Business and Enterprise Development*, *17*(1), 8–31. doi:10.1108/14626001011019107

Ma, H. (2002). Competitive advantage: What's luck got to do with it? *Management Decision*, *40*(6), 525–536. doi:10.1108/00251740210433927

Migdadi, M. (2008). Knowledge management enablers and outcomes in the small-and-medium sized enterprises. *Industrial Management & Data Systems*, *109*(6), 840–858. doi:10.1108/02635570910968072

Mithas, S., Ramsubbu, N., & Sambamurthy, V. (2011). How information management capability influences firm performance. *Management Information Systems Quarterly*, *35*(1), 237–256.

Nahapiet, J., & Ghoshal, S. (1998). Social capital, intellectual capital, and the organizational advantage. Academy of Management Review, 23(20, 242-266.

Nfuka, E. N., & Rusu, L. (2011). The effect of critical success factors on IT governance performance. *Industrial Management & Data Systems*, *111*(9), 1418–1448. doi:10.1108/02635571111182773

Parnell, J. A., & Dent, E. B. (2009). The role of luck in the strategy-performance relationship. *Management Decision*, *47*(6), 1000–1021. doi:10.1108/00251740910966703

Patrakosol, B., & Lee, S. (2009). IT capabilities, interfirm performance and the state of economic development. *Industrial Management & Data Systems*, *109*(9), 1231–1247. doi:10.1108/02635570911002298

Pavlou, P. A., & El Sawy, O. A. (2006). From IT leveraging competence to competitive advantage in turbulent environments: The case of new product development. *Information Systems Research*, *17*(3), 198–227. doi:10.1287/isre.1060.0094

Penrose, E. (1959). *The Theory of the Growth of the Firm*. New York: Wiley.

Perez-Arostegui, M. N., Benitez-Amado, J., & Tamayo-Torres, J. (2012). Information technology-enabled quality performance: An exploratory study. *Industrial Management & Data Systems*, *112*(3), 502–518. doi:10.1108/02635571211210095

Perez-Lopez, S., & Alegre, J. (2012). Information technology competency, knowledge processes and firm performance. *Industrial Management & Data Systems*, *112*(4), 644–662. doi:10.1108/02635571211225521

Porter, M. E. (1980). *Competitive strategy: Techniques for Analyzing Industries and Competitors*. New York: Macmillan Publishing Co.

Porter, M. E. (1985). *Competitive Advantage*. New York: The Free Press.

Porter, M. E. (1998). *The Competitive Advantage of the Nation*. New York: The Free Press.

Putnam, R. D. (1993). The prosperous community: Social capital and public life. *The American Prospect*, *13*, 35–42.

Qureshil, S., Kamal, M., & Wolcott, P. (2009). Information technology interventions for growth and competiveness in micro-enterprises. *International Journal of E-Business Research*, *5*(1), 117–139. doi:10.4018/jebr.2009010106

Ray, G., Muhanna, W., & Barney, J. B. (2005). Information technology and the performance of the customer service process: A resource-based analysis. *Management Information Systems Quarterly*, *29*(4), 625–652.

Rumelt, R. P. (1984). Towards a strategic theory of the firm. In R. R. Lamb (Ed.), *Competitive Strategic Management*. Upper Saddle River, NJ: Prentice Hall.

Sanchez-Rodriquez, C., & Martinez-Lorente, A. R. (2011). Effect of IT and quality management on performance. *Industrial Management & Data Systems*, *111*(6), 830–848. doi:10.1108/02635571111144937

Thomason, S. J., Simendinger, E., & Kiernan, D. (2013). Several determinants of successful coopetition in small business. *Journal of Small Business and Entrepreneurship*, *26*(1), 15–28. doi:10.1080/08276331.2012.761800

Waldman, D. A., Ramirez, G. G., House, R. J., & Puranam, P. (2001). Does leadership matter? CEO leadership attributes and profitability under conditions of perceived environmental uncertainty. *Academy of Management Journal*, *44*(1), 134–143. doi:10.2307/3069341

Walley, K. (2007). Coopetition: An introduction to the subject and an agenda for research. *International Studies of Management & Organization*, *37*(2), 11–31. doi:10.2753/IMO0020-8825370201

Willcocks, L., Reynolds, P., & Feeny, D. (2007). Evolving IS capabilities to leverage the external IT services market. *MIS Quarterly Executive*, *6*, 127–145.

Yao, L. j., Sutton, S. G., & Chan, S. H. (2010). Wealth creation from information technology investments using the eva. *Journal of Computer Information Systems*, *50*, 42–48.

Zhang, K., Li, H., & Ziegelmayer, J. L. (2009). Resource or capability? A dissection of SMEs' IT infrastructure flexibility and its relationship with IT responsiveness. *Journal of Computer Information Systems*, *50*, 46–53.

## ADDITIONAL READING

Carr, N. G. (2004). *Does IT Matter? Information technology and the Corrosion of Competitive Advantage*. Boston: Harvard Business School Press.

Chilton, M. A., & Bloodgood, J. M. (2014). *Knowledge Management and Competitive Advantage: Issues and Potential Solutions*. Hershey, PA: Information Science Research. doi:10.4018/978-1-4666-4679-7

Murmann, J. P. (2003). *Knowledge and Competitive Advantage: The Coevolution of Firms, Technology and National Institutions*. Cambridge, NY: Cambridge University Press. doi:10.1017/CBO9780511510953

Narayanan, V. K. (2001). Managing Technology and Innovation for Competitive Advantage. Upper Saddle River, NNJ: Prentice Hall.

## KEY TERMS AND DEFINITIONS

**Adding Value:** Contribution to the worthiness of a product or service.

**Competitive Advantage:** Offering better products and services than others in the market.

**Coopetition:** Simultaneous cooperation and competition.

**Customers:** Potential entities to acquire products or services.

**Demand:** Willingness to acquire a product or service.

**Efficient Operation:** Conducting business functions with minimum use of resources.

**Entrepreneurial Networks:** Groups of fellow business managers with similar attitudes.

**Family Capital:** Aspects that separate a family business from other businesses.

**Market leader:** A business that introduces new or revised products or services before competitors.

**Skunk Works:** Temporary informal working groups assigned to resolve a specific challenge.

**Survival:** Continued existence.

**Theory of Constraints:** Small business problems could result from performance issues related to throughput, inventory, and operating expenses.

**Throughput:** The rate of moving materials through the production process.

**Useful Weeds:** Accidental innovation.

# Chapter 9
# Management Processes


## ABSTRACT

*On a daily basis small businesses carry out the basic operations of the venture. These management processes must support the general direction set by the small business in its long-term mission statement and goals and objective plans. But the small business must also address the short term functional requirements. As the small business grows and matures the management processes must expand and change to support the larger business. More formal and structured processes will be facilitated through the adoption and use of information systems. These processes are presented in this chapter.*


## INTRODUCTION

Management processes relate to a number of high level activities involved in small business operations. At the highest level management will set the direction for the small business in the form of a mission statement. Then, within the context of the mission statement goals may be used to give further direction to the small business. Goals, however, must be evaluated. This necessitates the development of objectives which possess measureable outcomes. These three initiatives relate to long range planning activities of the small business.

Management involves five functions. Irrespective of the level of management all five functions are necessary. The higher management levels involve more planning while the lower levels involve more controlling.

DOI: 10.4018/978-1-4666-8708-0.ch009

As a small business matures more sophisticated management processes are required. The continuum of sophistication relates to the stages of a small business – Genesis, Grounding, Growth, and Generations.

Management capabilities till promote growth of the small business. These capabilities are related to human resource activities, competency of managers, and the planning and control of management processes in an attempt to improve performance. Resources should be used to improve productivity. The core functional areas, marketing, finances, and human resources, should operate as efficiently as possible. The limited resources of a small business should be employed as productively as possible to gain maximum short-term and long-term advantage.

The personality characteristics and experience of a few senior managers in a small business are key aspects to the performance of the small business. These managers will provide direction and guidance to employees through establishing management processes and ensuring they continue to reflect the necessary operational functions of the small business.

This chapter is organized as follows. To begin the context for management processes is described relative to the sequence of planning related to mission, goals, and objectives. This sequence provides a path from general statements of direction to specific measureable activities. It is important to note that the specific activities should relate to the goals and respond to the mission. Next the five generic functions of management are reviewed. They relate to all levels of management with their emphasis changing depending upon the level within the hierarchy. Another perspective is presented with five themes of management which relate to the main operational area of a small business. Growth of a small business depends upon the characteristics and experience of the senior management. As small businesses grow management processes become more formalized. Information systems support this formalization.

## GENERIC MANAGEMENT PROCESSES

There is a hierarchy of long range planning for a business. To begin the mission of the business is documented. The mission is states the purpose of the business. Then within the context of the mission statement various goals can be developed. A goal is a general statement of activity. Further objectives will be established for the goals. Objectives are measureable outcomes against which performance may be evaluated.

Robbins et al (2012) outline the general steps in setting goals as follows:

1. "Review the organization's mission. The mission is the purpose of the organization. The broad statement of what the organization's purpose is and what it hopes to accomplish provides an overall guide to what organizational members think is important.
2. Evaluate available resources. Even though goals should be challenging they should be realistic.
3. Determine the goals individually or with input from others. These goals reflect desired outcomes and should be consistent with the organization's mission and goals in other organizational areas.
4. Write down the goals and communicate them to all who need to know.
5. Review results and whether goals are being met. If goals are not being met, make changes to the goals as needed, and in some cases make changes to the plan based on the new information at hand." (Robbins et al, 2012, pp. 192-193)

Thus, within the context of the above established goals specific performance objectives may be set. The objectives may be set by the managers or preferably in conjunction with employees. This second alternative will contribute to a beneficial manager – employee relationship. Employees will tend to feel more committed to performing a task if they have participated in the establishment of the duties and how their performance will be measured.

Independent of the management level there are five functions that managers perform. The level in the management hierarchy will determine the extent of each function performed. The five functions are Planning, Organizing, Staffing, Directing, and Controlling.

The following definitions for the five management functions have been gleaned from Robbins et al (2012).

*Planning: "...involves defining goals, establishing an overall strategy for achieving those goals, and developing a comprehensive set of plans to integrate and coordinate the work needed to achieve the goals. It's concerned with both the ends (what's to be done) and means (how it's to be done)." (Robbins et al, 2012, p. 185)*
*Organizing: "...determine what tasks are to be done, who is to do them, how the tasks are to be grouped, who reports to whom (that, they define authority relationships), and where decisions are to be made." (Robbins et al, 2012, p. 7)*
*Staffing: "The process by which managers ensure that they have the right number and kinds of people in the right places, and at the right times, who are capable of effectively and efficiently performing assigned tasks." (Robbins et al, 2012, p. 327)*
*Directing: "...involves motivating subordinates, directing the work of individuals or teams, selecting the most effective communication channels, and resolving employee behaviour issues." (Robbins et al, 2012, p. 7)*

*Controlling: "...involves monitoring actual performance, comparing actual performance to a standard, and taking corrective action when necessary." (Robbins et al, 2012, p. 7)*

In Chapter Twelve the Balanced Maturity Framework will be presented. The framework consists of three dimensions, Management Processes, E-commerce, and E-business. This section of this chapter presents a description of the Management Processes dimension. As a small business matures it will tend to pass through four stages of Management Processes. They are Genesis, Grounding, Growth, and Generations

## Genesis

An entrepreneur has an idea about a product or service and decides to create a business to respond to a perceived market need. Armed with a business plan potential funding sources will be identified and pursued. Given the viability of the product or service and access to adequate funding a small business is launched.

*"Only after these start-up activities have been completed is the entrepreneur ready to actually launch the venture. This involves setting goals and strategies, as well as establishing the technology operations methods, marketing plans, information systems, financial accounting systems, and cash flow management systems.*
*When the entrepreneurial venture is up and running, the entrepreneur's attention switches to managing it. An important activity of managing the entrepreneurial venture is managing the various processes that are part of every business: making decisions, establishing action plans, analyzing external and internal environments, measuring and evaluating performance, and making needed changes. Also the entrepreneur must perform activities associated with managing people, including selecting and hiring, appraising and training, motivating, managing conflict, delegating tasks, and being an effective leader." (Robbins et al, 2012, p. 99)*

## Grounding

As the small business establishes itself and perhaps grows the management processes will become more formal. Information systems will support this more formal approach to management. Job description may be developed to help employees to carry out their assigned tasks. Specific policy decisions will be make which will further formalize daily operations.

## Growth

As the small business meets with success it will grow. Sales volumes will increase and more employees will be hired. Further, growth will mean an expansion of products or services with the consequent increase in the necessity for access to financial resources. All of this will lead to more formal management processes along with more sophisticated information systems to support these expanded processes.

It is important that the small business which does grow that it focus on the inherent expertise. That is the focus should remain on whatever is the niche product or service. Hunter and Kazakoff (2008) determined for instance that a small farm services business continued to focus on the land while expanding into seed growing and cleaning, a feedlot, and a gravel pit operation. There was diversification but within the expertise of the small business management.

Further, the small business may decide that having reached a certain size it will not continue to grow. The growth of most small firms tends to lessen over time. The owner/manager may make a life style choice that the current size is sufficient. Also, the owner/manager may want to keep control of the business and further expansion is not possible within this context. Another reason for little or no growth relates to the large incremental increase in cost with only a slight increase in sales volume. Again, Hunter and Kazakoff (2008) found this situation with a home builder. The builder could build on average one house per week over the year. Only a small increase in home building would cause a significant increase in the requirement for further trades' personnel. This, in effect, would take a viable small business into a financial loss situation.

## Generations

The issue of succession arises when the founding entrepreneur ages requiring a decision about their personal future and that of the small business. Thus, the small business will pass to a subsequent generation. Individuals taking over the small business may or may not be members of the founding entrepreneur's family or extended family. In either case new ideas and experiences will be introduced into the small business. A younger generation may be able to take the small business in new directions. Again, it will be incumbent upon new management to focus operations on their relative expertise. Also, the younger generation, in general, can better relate to and understand the capabilities of information technology. This may result in yet another expansion in the novel use of information systems to support business operations and the continued formalization of management processes.

These management practices relate to five themes which have been identified in a number of research projects. These themes are management development; financial management; human resource management; marketing; and planning and control. They are described in the following sub-sections.

## 1. Management Development

Initially, an entrepreneur's management skills and experience will contribute to the maturity and growth of a small business (Gibb & Davies, 1990; Smallbone et al, 1995; Jennings & Beaver, 1997; and Beaver & Jennings, 2005). However, sustained growth will necessitate the migration from an entrepreneurial approach to a more professionally oriented style of management (Churchill & Lewis, 1983; Gibb & Davies, 1990; Storey, 1994; Dyer, 1997; Packham, 2002). This professional style is outlined in the presentation of the following themes related to financial management, human resource management, marketing, and planning and control. In general, the approach will become for formal which will be supported by the adoption and use of structured information systems.

## 2. Financial Management

Establishing and maintaining financial control will contribute to achieving necessary profits and ultimately facilitating growth (Storey, 1994; Smallbone et al, 1995; Hankinson et al, 1997; Balje & Waasdorp, 1999; Thomson & Gray, 1999). Further, Hunter & Kazakoff (2012) provide support for this theme as described in the following.

*"The recent financial crisis spanned the period of mid-2008 to late-2009, and was characterized by a sharp economic downturn, world-wide financial markets collapse, and significant job losses. The goal of this project was to identify the aspects related to how multi-generation small businesses reacted to the recent financial crisis. Multi-generation small businesses are considered successful mainly because of their long term survival beyond the normal tenure of a small business. The project thus provides lessons for all small businesses regarding responses to the recent financial crisis. The lessons learned will serve to contribute to reducing the large number of small business failures as shown in the above statistics." (Hunter & Kazakoff, 2012, pp. 37-38)*

They conclude with the following comments.

*"When asked about the future a clear ray of optimism shone through the comments of all research participants. They saw an opportunity to improve their approach to management. They were prepared to adopt a customer focus. Some were investigating revisions to the performance metrics with a concentration on margins. If price changes were not possible then the cost of goods sold were reviewed in an attempt to maintain or increase margins.*
*Growth was a common consideration for the future. This translated into opportunities for employees to advance within the business. Some plans were also being developed for the inclusion of non-family members and the next generation of family in the management and participation in ownership of the small business. As these growth opportunities were reviewed, a willingness to accept more risk in future endeavours was expressed. Participants quickly added that increased risk would be considered from a very financially conservative perspective. (Hunter & Kazakoff, 2012, p. 47)*

## 3. Human Resource Management

Generally, individuals are recruited to fill a specific role. This practice is even more prevalent in small business where the role is filled by someone who can meet a current and specific need rather than by a trainee who may require time to develop the skills necessary to perform the role. Thus, it is suggested (Packham et al, 2005) that rather than addressing a current requirement growth oriented small business should consider investing strategically in human resource development practices. These skills could be developed in-house through professional development programs or through a recruitment program which addresses responding to anticipated needs as the small business grows and matures. Further, it is incumbent upon senior management to establish an open and learning environment within the small business. This will promote consideration for new ideas by employees. It will also foster employee commitment to the small business.

## 4. Marketing

It is commonly known that marketing is about obtaining correct and current information about customers and competitors. Sourcing this information in a small business may be quite informal. However, as the small business grows and matures it becomes necessary to introduce more formal marketing information systems and to regularly conduct market and competitor analyses (Packham et al, 2005). The decision to be made relates to the number of customers. That is, the small business may decide to focus on a few customers in order to provide excellent service. However, this focus may result in financial issues if some of the few customers move on or reduce their purchases because of a down turn in the economy.

## 5. Planning and Control

At the commencement of a small business a business plan will be necessary to identify what the business will do and to acquire any necessary external finances. Then, on an on-going basis, an operating plan may be employed to identify potential sales of products or the provision of services and the necessary associated inputs. Growth oriented small business take the next step in the development and implementation of a strategic plan which outlines the future direction of the business. Along with this plan a control mechanism is also established to provide feedback about whether or not current objectives and future goals are being addressed. Aspects related to planning and controls were presented above (Robbins et al, 2012).

Managerial capabilities will facilitate the development of strategies that promote growth (Graves & Thomas, 2006). There are three components of managerial capabilities. They are management capacity, management expertise, and management process (Graves & Thomas, 2006). Management capacity involves human resource activities related to growth and the consequent necessity for role specialization and increased management levels. Management expertise relates to manager's competencies resulting from education and experience. Management process involves planning and control activities that contribute to improved performance.

High growth small businesses tend to adopt professional management processes in order to improve performance (Smallbone et al, 1995). The entrepreneur's skill and experience contribute to growth (Gibb & Davies, 1990; Smallbone et al, 1995; Jennings & Beaver, 1997; and Sirmon & Hitt, 2003). However, sustained growth results from the introduction and on-going capability of management (O'Farrell & Hitchens, 1988; and Penrose, 1995).

*"Thus, [while] entrepreneurial behaviour is conducive to initial entrepreneurial success, growth, in the medium to long term, is dependent upon the ability of the owner-manager to manage the small firm effectively at both the operational and strategic level." (Packham et al, 2005, p. 482)*

The performance of a small business will depend upon the resources it has available to be productively employed. However, sustained advantage, as suggested by the resource-based view of the firm, will result from how the resources are uniquely managed (Sirmon & Hitt, 2003). It is important that the resources be managed in a way that competitors will find it difficult to impossible to replicate (Barney, 2001).

A common theme amongst successful small businesses is management competence in core functional area such as marketing, finance, human resources, and strategic planning (Balderson, 2003). It is also important for management to have the ability to identify issues as they arise and to develop a resolution within the context of their small business (Koontz Traverso, 2001; Hisrich, 2004; Cohen, 2006; and Giroux, 2009).

Beaver annd Jennings (2005) investigated the management processes of small business. They suggest the following:

*"...management in the smaller firm is primarily an adaptive process concerned with adjusting a limited amount of resources usually in order to gain the maximum immediate and short-term advantage. In the small firm efforts are concentrated not on predicting but on reacting to the operating environment, adapting as quickly as possible to the changing demands of that environment and devising suitable tactics for mitigating the consequences of any changes which occur." (Beaver & Jennings, 2005, p. 12)*

Further:

*"The small firm management process cannot be separated from the personality set and experience of the key role player or players. Anther characteristic is the closeness of the key players to the operating personnel and activities being undertaken. This provides the key role players with extraordinary opportunity to influence these operatives and activities directly. However, these relationships are often informal, there being no precise definition of rights and obligations, duties and responsibilities. Appointment and promotion are often made on the basis of birth or personal friendship rather than on the basis of educational and technical qualifications. Organisation structures in so far as they exist, are likely to develop around the interests and abilities of the key role players. Such organisation structures are likely to be organic and loosely structured rather than mechanistic and high formalised. Thus, the management process in the small firm is seldom a readily visible process. It often has an abstract rather than concrete form." (Beaver & Jennings, 2005, pp. 12-13)*

Kelliher and Reinl (2009) documented the management practices of small business. They identified five factors which influence management practices as shown in Table 1.

They also suggest direct contact with customers, suppliers, and employees as a strategic advantage for a small business (Kelliher & Reinl, 2009).

Also, the small business must be prepared and able to adjust faster than changes in the business environment (Barney et al, 2001; and Hamel & Prahad, 1994).

*Table 1. Factors which impact management practices*

| Factor | Description |
|---|---|
| Business Strategy | • Conservative strategic perspective and incremental change (Storey & Cressy, 1996)<br>• Few formal strategic plans (Hall, 1995)<br>• Informal tacit plans (Kuratko et al, 1999; Wyer, 1997; and Phillipson et al, 2004) |
| Organization Structure | • Flat organization with centralized authority (Dutta & Evrard, 1999; Palvia et al, 1994; and Simpson, 2001)<br>• Minimal internal management levels (Brady & Voss, 1995) |
| Decision Process | • Decisions made by owner (Palvia et al, 1994)<br>• Use informal decision models (Rice & Hamilton, 1979)<br>• Owner must possess vast knowledge (Kelliher & Henderson, 2006) |
| Business Culture | • Extension of owner's personality (Kelliher & Reinl, 2009)<br>• Informal communication (Penn et al, 1999)<br>• Inherently collaborative (Matlay, 1999)<br>• Regular contact with employees (Storey & Cressy, 1996) |
| Business Environment | • Limited competitive influence (Dutta & Evrard, 1999; Simpson, 2001; and Storey & Cressy, 1996)<br>• Overly sensitive to market changes (Whaley, 2003) |

Adapted from Kelliher and Reinl, 2009

## CONCLUSION

This chapter has presented a brief overview of management processes. Daily operations are facilitated by processes established by management. Within the context of mission statements and goals processes are established to support the operation of the small business. As the small business grows and matures these management processes become more formal and structure supported by the adoption and use of information systems. The next chapter presents a description of E-commerce. The current technology allows the small business to interact in a more effective way with customers. This leading edge technology improves the small business performance and contributed to competitive advantage.

## REFERENCES


Balderson, D. W. (2003). *Canadian Entrepreneurship and Small Business Management* (5th ed.). Toronto: McGraw-Hill Ryerson.

Balje, S. H., & Waasdorp, P. M. (1999). High growth companies in The Netherlands. In B. C. M. Alder (Ed.), *The Formula for High Growth Companies: A Question of Smart Competition? TNO Report STB-98-32*.

Barney, J. (2001). Resource-based theories of competitive advantage: A ten-year retrospective on the resource-based view. *Journal of Management*, *27*(6), 643–650. doi:10.1177/014920630102700602

Barney, J., Wright, M., & Ketchen, D. J. (2001). The resource-based view of the firm: Ten years after 1991. *Journal of Management*, *27*(6), 625–641. doi:10.1177/014920630102700601

Beaver, G., & Jennings, P. (2005). Competitive advantage and entrepreneurial power: The dark side of entrepreneurship. *Journal of Small Business and Enterprise Development*, *12*(1), 9–23. doi:10.1108/14626000510579617

Brady, A., & Voss, B. (1995). Small is as small does. *The Journal of Business Strategy*, *16*(2), 44–52. doi:10.1108/eb039690

Churchill, N. C., & Lewis, V. L. (1983). The five stages of small business growth. *Harvard Business Review*, *61*(3), 30–50.

Cohen, W. (2006). *The entrepreneur and Small Business Problem Solver* (2nd ed.). Hoboken, NJ: John Wiley & Sons.

Dutta, S., & Evrard, P. (1999). Information technology and organisation within European small enterprises. *European Management Journal*, *17*(3), 239–251. doi:10.1016/S0263-2373(99)00003-1

Dyer, W. G. Jr. (1997). Organisation development in the entrepreneurial firm. *The Journal of Applied Behavioral Science*, *33*(2), 190–208. doi:10.1177/0021886397332008

Gibb, A. A., & Davies, L. (1990). Pursuit of frameworks for the development of growth models of the small business. *International Small Business Journal*, *9*(1), 15–31.

Giroux, I. (2009). Problem solving in small firms: An interpretive study. *Journal of Small Business and Enterprise Development*, *16*(1), 167–184. doi:10.1108/14626000910932944

Graves, C., & Thomas, J. (2006). Internationalization of Australian family businesses: A managerial capabilities perspective. *Family Business Review*, *19*(3), 207–224. doi:10.1111/j.1741-6248.2006.00066.x

Hall, G. (1995). *Surviving and Prospering in the Small Firm Sector*. London: Routledge.

Hamel, G., & Prahalad, C. K. (1994). *Competing on the Future*. Boston, MA: Harvard Business School Press.

Hankinson, A., Bartlett, D., & Ducheneaut, B. (1997). The key factors in the small profiles of small-medium enterprise owner-managers that influence business performance. The UK (Rennes) SME survey 1995-97: An international research project survey. *International Journal of Entrepreneurial Behaviour and Research*, *3*(3), 168–175. doi:10.1108/13552559710190421

Hisrich, R. (2004). *Small Business Solutions*. New York, NY: McGraw-Hill.

Hunter, M. G., & Kazakoff, D. (2008). *Little Empires: Multi-Generation Small Business in Southern Alberta, CANADA*. Melbourne, Australia: Heidelberg Press.

Hunter, M. G., & Kazakoff, D. (2012). Multi-generation small business response to the recent financial crisis. *Journal of Applied Management and Entrepreneurship*, *17*(1), 37–51.

Jennings, P. A., & Beaver, G. (1997). The performance and competitive advantage of small firms: A management perspective. *International Small Business Journal*, *15*(2), 63–75. doi:10.1177/0266242697152004

Kelliher, F., & Henderson, J. B. (2006). A learning framework for the small business environment. *Journal of European Industrial Training*, *30*(7), 512–528. doi:10.1108/03090590610704385

Kelliher, F., & Reinl, L. (2009). A resource-based view of micro-firm management practice. *Journal of Small Business and Enterprise Development*, *16*(3), 521–532. doi:10.1108/14626000910977206

Koontz Traverso. (2001). *The Small Business Owner's Guide to a Good Night's Sleep: Preventing and Solving Chronic and Costly Problems*. Princeton, NJ: Bloomberg Press.

Kuratko, D. F., Hornsby, J. S., & Naffziger, D. (1993). The adverse impact of public policy on micro-enterprises: An exploratory study of owners' perceptions. *Journal of Developmental Entrepreneurship*, *4*(1), 81–92.

Matlay, H. (1999). Employee relations in small firms: A micro-business perspective. *Employee Relations, 21*(3), 285–295. doi:10.1108/01425459910273125

O'Farrell, P. N., & Hitchens, D. M. W. N. (1988). Alternative theories of small firm growth: A critical review. *Environment & Planning, 20*(3), 1365–1383. doi:10.1068/a201365

Packham, G. (2002). Competitive advantage and growth: The challenge for small firms. *International Journal of Management and decision Making*, 3(2), 165-179.

Packham, G., Brooksbank, D., Miller, C., & Thomas, B. (2005). Climbing the mountain: Management practice adoption in growth oriented firms in Wales. *Journal of Small Business and Enterprise Development, 12*(4), 482–497. doi:10.1108/14626000510628171

Palvia, P., Mearns, D. B. Jr, & Jackson, W. M. (1994). Determinants of computing in very small businesses. *Information & Management, 27*(3), 161–174. doi:10.1016/0378-7206(94)90044-2

Penn, D. W., Angiwa, W., Forster, R., Heydon, G., & Rishardson, S. J. (1998). Learning in small organisations. *The Learning Organization, 5*(3), 128–137. doi:10.1108/09696479810223400

Penrose, E. (1995). *The Theory of the Growth of the Firm.* Oxford, UK: Oxford University Press. doi:10.1093/0198289774.001.0001

Phillipson, J., Bennett, K., Lowe, P., & Raley, M. (2004). Adaptive responses and asset strategies: The experience of rural micro-firms and foot and mouth disease. *Journal of Rural Studies, 20*(2), 227–243. doi:10.1016/j.jrurstud.2003.08.006

Rice, G. H., & Hamilton, R. E. (1979). Decision theory and the small business. *American Journal of Small Business, 6*(4), 1–9.

Robbins, S. P., Coulter, M., Leach, E., & Kilfoil, M. (2012). *Management* (10th Canadian Edition). Don Mills, Ontario: Pearson, Canada, Inc.

Simpson, B. (2001). Innovation and the micro-enterprise. *Internàtional Journal of Services Technology and Management, 2*(3/4), 377–387. doi:10.1504/IJSTM.2001.001610

Sirmon, D. G., & Hitt, M. (2003). Managing resources: Linking unique resources, management and wealth creation in family firms. *Entrepreneurship Theory and Practice, 27*(4), 339–358. doi:10.1111/1540-8520.t01-1-00013

Smallbone, D., Leigh, R., & North, D. (1995). The characteristics and strategies of high growth firms. *International Journal of Entrepreneurial Behaviour and Research*, *1*(3), 44–62. doi:10.1108/13552559510100657

Storey, D. J. (1994). *Understanding the Small Business Sector*. London: Routledge.

Storey, D. J., & Cressy, R. (1996). Small business risk – a firm bank perspective. Working paper: The Centre for Small & Medium-sized Enterprises (CSME), Warwick Business School, 39, 1-16.

Thomson, A., & Gray, C. (1999). Determinants of management development in small businesses. *Journal of Small Business and Enterprise Development*, *6*(2), 113–127. doi:10.1108/EUM0000000006676

Whaley, A. M. (2003). Study of information systems integration into micro-enterprises. *Proceedings of the Fourth Conference in the Department of Computing*, University of central Lancashire, Preston.

Wyer, P. (1997). Small business integration with the external operating environment – the role of strategic management and planning in the small business. Paper presented at Small Business and Enterprise Development Conference, Sheffield.

## ADDITIONAL READING

Balderson, D. W. (2003). *Canadian Entrepreneurship and Small Business Management* (5th ed.). Toronto: McGraw-Hill Ryerson.

Harnish, V. (2012). *The Greatest Business Decisions of all Time*. New York, NY: Fortune Books.

Hisrich, R. (2004). *Small Business Solutions*. New York, NY: McGraw-Hill.

Hunter, M. G., & Kazakoff, D. (2008). *Little Empires: Multi-Generation Small Business in Southern Alberta, CANADA*. Melbourne, Australia: Heidelberg Press.

Hunter, M. G., & Kazakoff, D. (2012). Multi-generation small business response to the recent financial crisis. *Journal of Applied Management and Entrepreneurship*, *17*(1), 37–51.

## KEY TERMS AND DEFINITIONS

**Controlling:** Monitoring actual performance.

**Directing:** Ensure individuals know what is to be accomplished.

**Financial Management:** Establishing and maintaining control over monetary resources.

**Generations:** The passing of the small business to off-spring of the founder.

**Genesis:** The start of an initiative.

**Goals:** General description of initiatives which contribute to the business mission.

**Grounding:** The formalization of management processes.

**Growth:** Increase in sales volume and the consequent addition of more employees.

**Human Resources:** Skills of employees in the small business.

**Management Processes:** Activities which support the daily operations of a business.

**Marketing:** Obtaining correct and current information about customers and competitors.

**Mission:** High level direction of a business.

**Objectives:** Description of tasks which possess measurable outcomes.

**Organizing:** Defining work to be accomplished.

**Planning:** Defining goals and objectives of the small business.

**Staffing:** Assigning individuals to specific tasks.

# Chapter 10
# E-Commerce


## Abstract

*There are many ways for a small business to interact with current or potential customers. E-commerce represents the most current communications channel which is supported by leading edge technology in the form of the Internet. The communication between a business and customer is referred to as Business to Customer (B2C). This communication may occur at various levels of interaction. At a very basic level a business web site may simply present a description of its products and services in the form of an electronic catalogue. More sophisticated E-commerce applications will conduct sales and provide follow-up services for customers. The advantages of implementing E-commerce outweigh the disadvantages. However, small business adoption may be restricted due to limitations of resources such as time, skills, and finances. The focus of this chapter is Business to Consumer (B2C). As a small business matures it will tend to incorporate more sophisticated aspects of E-commerce and pass through four stages – Presence, Portals, Transactions Integration, and Enterprises Integration.*


## INTRODUCTION

E-commerce involves the sale of products and services via the Internet. The unique properties of the Internet facilitate a variety of E-commerce models.

E-commerce allows small business to be in virtual contact with any one from anywhere at any time. The customer relations component of the value chain is improved through using E-commerce. Sales may be completed faster. Post sales service may be related to the specific customer and their purchases.

DOI: 10.4018/978-1-4666-8708-0.ch010

Security concerns may be addressed by establishing specific user accounts with passwords. A response to telecommunications concerns could be the adoption of encryption techniques for data exchanged via communications networks.

Internet use and E-commerce is expanding. Small business adoption of E-commerce will be facilitated by three considerations. The goals of the small business should relate to the benefits created by using E-commerce. Senior management should be knowledgeable about E-commerce and enthusiastic about its adoption. Further, employees should possess sufficient knowledge to be able to implement and use a specific E-commerce application.

This chapter is organized as follows. To begin, the context of E-commerce is described. The Internet forms the base for any E-commerce application. The benefits of the Internet all businesses to be able to better communicate with the market in general and with specific customers. Then, the four stages of E-commerce use are described. These stages relate to the E-commerce dimension of the Balanced Maturity Framework described in more detail in Chapter Thirteen. Various categories of E-commerce are then presented. The focus of this chapter is on Business to Consumer (B2C). Next, advantages and disadvantages of E-commerce are listed. Not that the advantages far outweigh the disadvantages. Then the chapter reports on a series of projects which investigated various E-commerce issues. These issues range from increasing customers, improving customer service, pursuing a differentiation competitive strategy, and inhibiters of E-commerce adopt. Finally, organizational slack is identified as a positive contributor to the adoption of E-commerce. Organizational slack allows managers and employees the time to investigate alternative technologies and how they may be applied to the specific small business. Unfortunately, small businesses tend to not possess slack. Thus, small business will innovate within the restrictions imposed by limited resources of time, skills, and finances.

## ELECTRONIC COMMERCE

The Internet is an extensive network of computer networks. Computers on local business networks can be connected to the Internet.

*"The computers and organizational nodes on the Internet can be of different types and makes. They are connected to one another by data communications lines of different speeds. The primary network connections and telecommunications lines that link the nodes are referred to as the backbones. For the Internet, the backbone is a fibre-optic network that is operated primarily by large telecommunications companies.*

*As a network of networks, the Internet enabled people to access data in other organizations and to communicate, collaborate, and exchange information seamlessly around the world, quickly and inexpensively. Thus, the Internet has become a necessity for modern business." (Rainer et al, 2014, p. 113)*

Table 1. presents a list of many valuable properties of the Internet. Overall, the Internet creates a positive environment for businesses to extend their reach to more new customers in disparate geographical markets or to better serve current customers by providing extensive information about products and services.

The Internet facilitates adding value to business, as follows:

- Generate new revenue streams
- Reduce costs
- Attract new customers
- Increase the loyalty of current customers
- Develop new distribution channels for existing products
- Develop new information based products

The terms "E-commerce" and "E-business" tend to be used inter-changeably. Here, however, the terms will be employed to represent different aspects of working on-line and employing the Internet. Thus, E-commerce is interpreted as buying and selling of goods and services via the Internet. Then, E-business, which is discussed in more detail in Chapter Eleven, includes the components of E-commerce plus all the supporting technologies involved in business operations. These technolo-

*Table 1. Properties of the Internet*

| Property | Description |
|---|---|
| Mediating Technology | Connects many individuals |
| Universality | Engages the world – anyone, anywhere |
| Network Externalities | More users increases the value |
| Distribution Channel | Can better serve current customers or new customers |
| Time Moderator | Instant 24 hour access |
| Information Asymmetry | Both parties to a transaction have equal access to information |
| Infinite Virtual Capacity | Ability to serve customers seems infinite |
| Low Cost Standard | Development costs have been underwritten |
| Creative Modifiers | Facilitates the old giving way to the (superior) new |
| Transaction Cost Reducer | Reduces cost per transaction |

gies support internal operations such accounts Payable, Accounts Receivable, and Payroll. External activities such as Supply Chain Management, Sales Support, and Customer Service are also involved in E-business.

Other terms include:

- M-commerce: the ability to purchase goods and services through wireless Internet-enable hand-held devices
- Pure play: a retailer that is solely based on the Internet with no physical store
- Clicks and bricks: a retailer who possesses both a physical store and a web site

Chapter Twelve presents the Balanced Maturity Framework. The framework consists of three dimensions, Management Processes, E-commerce, and E-business. This section of this chapter presents a description of the E-commerce dimension. As a small business matures it will tend to pass through four stages in the use of E-commerce. These stages are Presence, Portals, Transactions Integration, and Enterprises Integration. These stages are based on the research model of Rao et al (2003) and a subsequent replication and extension by Zhu et al (2009).

## Presence

*"The company has an established website to exhibit information (e.g. product descriptions) to anyone surfing the Internet. One-way communication is used. Namely, information flows solely from the site to browsers." (Zhu et al, 2009, p. 287)*

Portals

*"Not only is information displayed on the site, but two-way communication is established. Namely, information flows between the business and Internet users in both directions. This stage includes creating customer profiles and cookies, email functionality, and the option to place orders online." (Zhu et al, 2009, p. 287)*

Transactions Integration

*"On-line monetary transactions between the business and its customers are a benchmark of this stage. The payment function is facilitated either by the vendor's own website or by a third party. Money is transferred electronically through a website and customers can finish the entire purchase without help from the selling company. (Zhu et al, 2009, p. 287)*

Enterprises Integration

*"Full integration of Customer Relationship Management (CRM), Value Chain Management (VCM) and Supply Chain Management (SCM) tools are used at this stage. Traditional offline enterprises and modern e-businesses become indistinguishable at this point due to the successful marriage of front-office and back-office tasks." (Zhu et al, 2009, pp. 287-288)*

Table 2. presents the different categories of E-commerce. The focus of this chapter is the Business to Consumer (B2C) category where businesses sell products and services to customers.

Table 3. presents some unique aspects of E-commerce. These aspects promote the use of E-commerce on the Internet and businesses may reach or be reached by any one from anywhere at any time.

E-commerce can be employed to support the Value Chain, which is a series of activities that add value to the products and services provided by a business (Porter, 1985).

According to Bidgoli (2013);

*"E-commerce can enhance a value chain by offering new ways to reduce costs or improve operations, including the following:*

- *Using e-mail rather than regular mail to notify customers of upcoming sales can reduce costs.*
- *Selling to customers via the company web site can generate new sources of revenue, particularly from customers who live far away from the company's headquarters or physical store.*

*Table 2. Categories of e-commerce*

| Category | Description |
|---|---|
| Business to Consumer (B2C) | Selling products and services directly to Customers |
| Business to Business (B2B) | Links between businesses for material acquisition and payment |
| Consumer to Consumer (C2C) | Individuals exchange products and services |
| Government to Citizen (G2C) | Tax filing and payments and voter registration |
| Government to Business (G2B) | Business license and acquisition of products and services |
| Government to Government (G2G) | Transfer payments between different levels of government |

*Table 3. Unique aspects of e-commerce*

| Aspect | Description |
|---|---|
| Ubiquity | Available anywhere, anytime, given access to the Internet |
| Global Reach | Convenient to conduct international transactions |
| Richness of Information | The business message may include text, audio, or video |
| Interactivity | Consumer and merchant can communicate |
| Information Density | Information is current, accurate, and timely |
| Personalization | Message can be directed to specific individual groups based on specific demographic characteristics |

Adapted from Laudon et al, 2015

- *Offering online customer service can make products or services more appealing to customers." (Bidgoli, 2013, p. 155)*

Advantages of E-commerce include the following:

- *"Creating better relationships with suppliers, customers, and business partners*
- *Creating "price transparency", meaning all market participants can trade at the same price*
- *Being able to operate around the clock and around the globe*
- *Gathering more information about potential customers*
- *Increasing customer involvement (ie. Offering a feedback section on the company web site)*
- *Improving customer service*
- *Increasing flexibility and ease of shopping*
- *Increasing the number of customers*
- *Increasing opportunities for collaboration with business partners*
- *Increasing return on investment because inventory needs are reduced*
- *Offering personalized services and product customization*
- *Reducing administrative and transaction costs" (Bidgoli, 2013, p. 156)*

Disadvantages of E-commerce include the following:

- *"bandwidth capacity problems (in certain parts of the world)*
- *Security issues*
- *Accessibility (not everybody is connected to the Web yet)*
- *Acceptance (not everybody accepts this technology) (Bidgoli, 2013, p. 156)*

There are two perspectives regarding security. From the consumer's perspective the issue of security relates to the information provided to consummate a transaction. Thus, the consumer would want to be satisfied that personal information will be held in confidence and that payment would result in the acquisition of the product or service. From the business perspective the concern is that a valid customer is initiating the transaction. This issue is addressed through the registration (including user ID and password) of an individual before a transaction is processed and the establishment of challenge questions.

Internet use and E-commerce is expanding at a remarkable rate (Karakaya & Stahl, 2009). This is an international phenomenon (Internetworldstats.com, 2007). This expansion includes both retail (eMarketer, 2005) and Business-to-Business (E-Commerce Times, 2008).

Some time ago Mirchandani and Motwani (2001) identified the issues that affected the adoption of E-commerce by small business. They determined that adopting small businesses displayed the following characteristics. The business had an enthusiastic leader. The adoption of E-commerce supported the goals of the small business. The system would provide an advantage for the small business over competitors. The employees possessed sufficient knowledge to assess and implement an E-commerce application.

Bricks and mortar small businesses adopt E-commerce in order to address the issues related to size and location (Karagozoglu & Lindell, 2004). On the internet these issues become relatively irrelevant.

Small businesses tend to adopt E-commerce to facilitate an increase in the number of customers, to improve customer service, and to improve the management of their purchasing process (Sekhar, 2001; Kienan, 2000; and Calkins et al, 2000). An expanded customer base is achieved through such marketing initiatives as providing product or service information; employing advertising to build a brand; and consummating online sales (Sekhar, 2001; and Rosen, 2000). Customer service involves providing warranty information, return policy and procedures, and the ability to ask questions and get answers (Korper & Ellis, 2001; and Schneider & Perry, 2000). Purchasing costs are reduced when the implementation of E-commerce creates a low transaction cost environment (Karagozoglu & Lindell, 2004).

Porter (1980) suggested that a competitive strategy may be based on differentiation or cost leadership. Small businesses tend to focus on differentiation simply because their size is an impediment to competing based on lower cost. E-commerce provides a further opportunity for small business to develop a competitive strategy based on differentiation (Kienan, 2000; and Reynolds, 2000).

An effective web site must be easy to use for customers (Pavlou, 2003). Ease of use is determined by the ease of navigation throughout the web site; efficient access to pages; and fast response to enquiries (Korper & Ellis, 2001).

*E-Commerce*

A number of researchers determined that the use of e-commerce by small business is relatively low (Goode, 2002; Jutla et al, 2002; Korchak & Rodman, 2001; Lewis & Cockrill, 2002; Poon & Swatman, 1999; and Stokes, 2000). More recently, Chong (2008) determined that small businesses were recognizing the promise of E-commerce to communicate with customers and business partners; and contribute to the overall improvement in business operations. This is especially so for small businesses which consider E-commerce an essential part of the overall business strategy.

Perhaps analyzing the adoption of E-commerce by small business is inhibited by regarding too broad of a category. Hence Stockdale and Standing (2006) proposed a classification scheme to describe small business motivation to adopt E-commerce. Table 4 provides a description of the five categories.

Quaddus and Hofmeyer (2007) investigated the adoption of business to business (B2B) trading exchanges by small business. They determined that there is significant influence by vendors on the awareness of the benefits of B2B involvement by small business. Once awareness is established it is possible for a positive attitude to develop on the part of the small business manager regarding intention to adopt B2B applications. Thus, if the supply chain environment mainly controlled by vendors, involves B2B exchange the small business will experience pressure to participate. This is an example of information technology, in general, moving from a "trump card" to "table stakes". That is, information technology is now necessary just to be in the game. How it is used will contribute to competitive advantage.

*"Electronic Commerce is first and foremost Commerce and ...the Electronic component is merely one of the means of serving the commercial ends." (Chong, 2008, p. 470)*

*Table 4. Small business e-commerce adoption*

| Category | Description |
|---|---|
| Landlubber | Small business has no intention of adopting E-commerce |
| Toe Dippers | Small business has no desire to grow and possesses an innate distrust of information technology |
| Paddlers | Small business may possess an internet connection and use email but use them infrequently |
| Waders | Small business may have been forced by trading partners to use E-commerce |
| Swimmers | Small business plans to grow and is willing to take advantage of E-commerce |

Adapted from Stockdale and Standing (2006)

The adoption of E-commerce may be inhibited by a number of factors including cost, skills, and lack of system integration, financial resources, and top management commitment (Dholakia & Kshetri, 2004; Grandon & Pearson, 2003; and Stockdale & Standing, 2004).

Trading partners (Grandon & Pearson, 2003; Iacovou et al, 1995; Stockdale & Standing, 2004; Thong, 2001; and Wagner et al, 2003) and competition (Grandon & Pearson, 2003; Iacovou et al, 1995; and Wagner et al, 2003) are a positive influence on the adoption of E-commerce.

The successful implementation of an E-commerce application will lead to many benefits for a small business. Improvements may be expected in sales, profitability, productivity, and service through reduced costs in supply chain components of procurement, inventory levels, and distribution (Campbell, 1998; Dholakia & Kshetri, 2004; Grandon & Pearson, 2003; Purao & Campbell, 1998; Stockdale & Standing, 2004; and Whiteley, 2000).

Childers and Offstein (2007) combined the resource-based view (RBV) of the firm and transaction cost economics (TCE) to demonstrate how E-commerce can be employed to generate competitive advantage. Recall that RBV suggests that unique capabilities of the small business may be used to improve performance resulting in competitive advantage. TCE was employed to demonstrate that the use of E-commerce can reduce the cost of transactions which improves customer relationships, again resulting in competitive advantage.

Bahaddad et al, (2012) investigated E-commerce adoption by SMEs. Their review of the available literature identified a number of factors which influenced E-commerce adoption by SMEs. They categorized the factors into three groups. One group which did not affect the adoption was tradition and culture. Another group included factors relating to people and the small business. The important adoption factors identified were previous IT experience and educational background. The third group included factors related to technology. Here factors internal to the small business included the website and its security, payment methods, and consequent delivery procedures. External to the small business the factor of telecommunications infrastructure became important.

Franquesa and Brandyberry (2009) investigated organizational financial resources slack and the propensity of small business to innovate through the use of information technology. They define innovation of information technology in two ways. E-commerce, "…is present when a firm engages in any level of sales of products and/or services via the Internet." (Franquesa & Brandyberry, 2009:27). Computerized core, "…relates to the adoption of computer systems that contribute directly to the firm's primary business activity." (Franquesa & Brandyberry, 2009:27).

They also identify two types of slack (Franquesa & Brandyberry, 2009). Available slack represents internal financial resources that may be used innovatively. Potential slack involves additional financial resources that may be accessed externally. It is noted that in both cases the concept of resource poverty applies (Thong et al, 1994). That is, because of the fact that the business is small both available and potential slack perhaps will not exist. Internally, small business operates on fumes (Winborg & Landstrom, 2001). That is, time, skills and financial resources will be limited. Externally, access to finances will be limited and explained by liabilities of newness and small ness (Freeman et al, 1983). Given these limitations Franquesa & Brandyberry (2009) conclude that small business will innovate within the confines of the financial resources, in the form of available and potential slack, that exist or can be acquired.

## CONCLUSION

This chapter has presented a brief overview of E-commerce. Situated on the Internet E-commerce allows interaction between the business and any one, from anywhere, at any time. E-commerce represents a leading edge technology based marketing and sales channel. It allows the business to interact with current customers on an individualized basis and to attempt to identify new markets and new customers. Small business will adopt E-commerce within the limitations imposed by the generic lack of time, skills, and finances. The next chapter presents the specific aspects of E-business. These are the many information systems which support internal daily operations and external relations with suppliers and other entities throughout the supply chain.

## REFERENCES

Bahaddad, A. A., AlGhamdi, R., & Houghton, L. (2012). To what extent would e-mall enable SMEs to adopt E-commerce? *International Journal of Business and Management*, *7*(22), 123–132. doi:10.5539/ijbm.v7n22p123

Bidgoli, H. (2013). *MIS3*. Boston, MA: Course Technology, Cengage Learning.

Calkins, J. D., Farello, M. J., & Shi, C. S. (2000). From retailing to e-tailing. *The McKinsey Quarterly*, *1*, 4–11.

Campbell, A. J. (1998). Embracing electronic data interchange now will keep your company in step with the competition. *Business America*, *119*(6), 28–30.

Childers, J. S., & Offstein, E. (2007). Building entrepreneurial E-commerce competitive advantage: A blending of theory and practice. *Advances in Competitiveness Research*, *15*(1/2), 41–53.

Chong, S. (2008). Success in electronic commerce implementation: A cross-country study of small and medium-sized enterprises. *Journal of Enterprise Information Management*, *21*(5), 469–492. doi:10.1108/17410390810904247

Dholakia, R. R., & Kshetri, N. (2004). Factors impacting the adoption of the internet among SMEs. *Small Business Economics*, *23*(4), 311–322. doi:10.1023/B:SBEJ.0000032036.90353.1f

E-Commerce Times. (2008). US B2B to Reach $6 Trillion by 2005. www.ecommercetimes.com

eMarketer. (2005). E-Commerce in the US. www.eMarketer.com

Franquesa, J., & Brandyberry, A. (2009). Organizaitonal slack and information technology innovation adoption in SMEs. *International Journal of E-Business Research*, *5*(1), 25–48. doi:10.4018/jebr.2009010102

Freeman, J., Caroll, G. R., & Hannan, M. T. (1983). The liability of newness: Age dependence in organizational death rates. *American Sociological Review*, *48*(5), 692–710. doi:10.2307/2094928

Goode, S. (2002). Management attitudes towards the world wide web in Australian small business. *Information Systems Management*, *19*(1), 45–48. doi:10.1201/1078/43199.19.1.20020101/31475.6

Grandon, E., & Pearson, J. M. (2003). Strategic value and adoption of electronic commerce: An empirical study of Chilean small and medium businesses. *Journal of Global Information Technology Management*, *6*(3), 22–43. doi:10.1080/1097198X.2003.10856354

Iacovou, C., Benbasat, I., & Dexter, A. (1995). Electronic data interchange and small organizations: Adoption and impact of technology. *Management Information Systems Quarterly*, *19*(4), 465–485. doi:10.2307/249629

Internetworldstats.com. (2007). Internet users by world region. www.internetworldstats.com

Jutla, D., Bodorik, P., & Dhaliqal, J. (2002). Supporting the e-business readiness of small and medium-sized enterprises: Approaches and metrics. *Internet Research: Electronic Networking Applications and Policy*, *12*(2), 139–164. doi:10.1108/10662240210422512

Karagozoglu, N., & Lindell, M. (2004). Electronic commerce strategy, operations, and performance in small and medium-sized enterprises. *Journal of Small Business and Enterprise Development*, *11*(3), 290–301. doi:10.1108/14626000410551555

Karakaya, F., & Stahl, M. J. (2009). After market entry barriers in E-commerce markets. *Journal of Electronic Commerce Research*, *10*(3), 130–143.

Kienan, B. (2000). *Small Business Solutions: E-Commerce*. Redmond, WA: Microsoft Press.

Korchak, R., & Rodman, R. (2001). Ebusiness adoption among US small manufacturers and the role of manufacturing extension. *Economic Development Review (Schiller Park, Ill.)*, *17*(3), 20–25.

Korper, S., & Ellis, J. (2001). *The E-Commerce Book*. San Diego, CA: Academic Press.

Laudon, K. C., Laudon, J. P., & Brabston, M. E. (2015). *Management Information Systems* (7th Canadian Edition). Don Mills, Ontario: Pearson Canada Inc.

Lewis, R., & Cockrill, A. (2002). Going global – remaining local: The impact of e-commerce on small retail firms in Wales. *International Journal of Information Management*, *22*(3), 195–209. doi:10.1016/S0268-4012(02)00005-1

Mirchandani, D. A., & Motwani, J. (2001). Understanding small business electronic commerce adoption: An empirical analysis. *Journal of Computer Information Systems*, *41*(3), 70–73.

Pavlou, P. A. (2003). Consumer acceptance of electronic commerce: Integrating trust and risk with the technological acceptance model. *International Journal of Electronic Commerce*, *7*(3), 101–134.

Poon, S., & Swatman, P. (1999). An exploratory study of small business internet commerce issues. *Information & Management*, *35*(1), 9–18. doi:10.1016/S0378-7206(98)00079-2

Porter, M. (1980). *Competitive Strategy*. New York, NY: Free Press.

Porter, M. (1985). *Competitive Advantage: Creating and Sustaining Superior Performance*. New York, NY: Free Press.

Purao, S., & Campbell, S. (1998). Critical concerns for small business electronic commerce: Some reflections based on interviews of small business owners. *Proceedings of the AIS Conference*, Baltimore, MD.

Quaddus, M., & Hofmeyer, G. (2007). An investigation into the factors influencing the adoption of B2B trading exchanges in small businesses. *European Journal of Information Systems*, *16*(3), 202–215. doi:10.1057/palgrave.ejis.3000671

Reynolds, J. (2000). *The Complete E-Commerce Book*. Berkley, CA: Publishers Group West.

Rosen, A. (2000). *The Commerce: A Survival Guide for Business Managers*. New York, NY: AMA Publishers.

Schneider, G. P., & Perry, J. T. (2000). *Electronic Commerce*. Cambridge, MA: Course Technology.

Sekhar, S. C. (2001). E-commerce and two popular business-level typologies: A competitive analysis. *Global Competitiveness*, *9*(1), 525–543.

Stockdale, R., & Standing, C. (2004). Benefits and barriers of electronic marketplace participation: An SME perspective. *Journal of Enterprise Information Management*, *17*(4), 301–311. doi:10.1108/17410390410548715

Stockdale, R., & Standing, C. (2006). A classification model to support SME e-commerce adoption initiatives. *Journal of Small Business and Enterprise Development*, *13*(3), 381–394. doi:10.1108/14626000610680262

Stokes, A. (2000). Small and medium-sized enterprises and the environment: Business imperatives. *International Small Business Journal*, *19*(1), 100–102. doi:10.1177/0266242600191007

Thong, J. (2001). Resource constraints and information system implementation in Singaporean small businesses. *OMEGA International Journal of Management science*, 29(2), 143-156.

Thong, J., Yap, C., & Raman, K. (1994). Engagement of external expertise in information systems implementation. *Journal of Management Information Systems*, *11*(2), 209–223.

Wagner, B., Fillis, I., & Johansson, U. (2003). An empirical investigation into e-business adoption in the Scottish smaller firm. *International Journal of Electronic Business*, *1*(4), 408–422. doi:10.1504/IJEB.2003.004113

Whiteley, D. (2000). *E-commerce – Strategy, Technologies and Applications*. Maidenhead: McGraw-Hill Publishing Company.

Winborg, J., & Landstrom, H. (2001). Financial bootstrapping in small businesses: Examining small business managers' resource acquisition behaviors. *Journal of Business Venturing*, *16*(3), 235–254. doi:10.1016/S0883-9026(99)00055-5

Zhu, Y., Basil, D. Z., & Hunter, M. G. (2009). The extended website stage model: A study of Canadian winery websites. *Canadian Journal of Administrative Sciences*, *26*(4), 286–300. doi:10.1002/cjas.118

## ADDITIONAL READING

Bidgoli, H. (2013). *MIS3*. Boston, MA: Course Technology, Cengage Learning.

Kienan, B. (2000). *Small Business Solutions: E-Commerce*. Redmond, WA: Microsoft Press.

Laudon, K. C., Laudon, J. P., & Brabston, M. E. (2015). *Management Information Systems* (7th Canadian Edition). Don Mills, Ontario: Pearson Canada Inc.

Reynolds, J. (2000). *The Complete E-Commerce Book*. Berkley, CA: Publishers Group West.

Rosen, A. (2000). *The Commerce: A Survival Guide for Business Managers*. New York, NY: AMA Publishers.

Thomas, B., & Simmons, G. (2010). *E-Commerce adoption and Small Business in the Global Marketplace: Tools for Optimization*. Hershey, PA: IGI Global. doi:10.4018/978-1-60566-998-4

## KEY TERMS AND DEFINITIONS

**Customer Relations:** Working with customers before, during, and after the sales event.

**E-Commerce:** The sale of products and services via the Internet.

**Enterprises Integration:** A website which incorporates the ability to work with customers and suppliers beyond the sales event.

**Infinite Virtual Capacity:** The size of the Internet seems to be unlimited.

**Information Asymmetry:** Both parties to a transaction do not have equal access to information about the transaction.

**Landlubber:** A small business with no intention of adopting E-Commerce.

**M-commerce:** Conducting E-Commerce on mobile devices.

**Mediating Technology:** Connects individuals via the Internet.

**Network Externalities:** A network becomes more valuable as more individuals become involved.

**Paddler:** A small business which has a website and uses email.

**Portals:** A website which provides links to other websites.

**Presence:** The establishment of a website which only exhibits information about products and services.

**Swimmers:** A small business which takes advantage of E-Commerce.

**Time Moderator:** Access to the Internet is quick and always available.

**Toe Dipper:** A small business which may investigate E-Commerce.

**Transaction Cost Reducer:** The Internet reduces the cost per transaction.

**Transactions Integration:** A website that can carry out business events for products and services.

**Universality:** Given an Internet connections individuals can connect with anyone, anywhere.

**Waders:** A small business which may have been forced to use E-Commerce because of trading partners.

# Chapter 11
# E-Business


## Abstract

*The management of a small business requires many processes which promote a smooth and efficient operation. Internally, these processes relate to inventory, accounts payable, accounts receivable, and payroll. Externally, there are processes which support the small business interaction with customers and suppliers. As a small business matures so should the management processes. Sophisticated technology, such as the Internet, will add further benefits to applying e-business to the management processes. This chapter discusses the benefits of this application.*


## INTRODUCTION

E-business is a way of conducting business in an electronic form which employs the facilities of the Internet. Recall from Chapter Eleven – E-commerce that electronic commerce involves the sale of products and services on the Internet via the website of a business. E-business includes E-commerce. But, it goes beyond and extends E-commerce to both pre-sales and post-sales services. E-business puts the business in closer contact with its customers, through Customer Relationship Management systems, which improves customer service and loyalty as a consequence.

The other major initiative involved in E-business relates to Supply Chain Management. This facility allows a business to manage all processes involved in the acquisition and distribution of products. Again, it puts the business in closer contact

DOI: 10.4018/978-1-4666-8708-0.ch011

with suppliers. Both Customer Relationship Management and Supply Chain Management promote interaction with external entities. This focus positively impacts performance through improved customer service and efficiencies in the supply chain.

This chapter is organized as follows. To start, the term E-business is defined along with various perspectives. In general, E-business involves internal management processes and external information systems based on the Internet. Next factors which facilitate the adoption and use of E-business are presented. These factors include the level of information systems knowledge in the business and the system's perceived usefulness. There are also organizational factors related to internal management processes. Then, benefits related to the adoption of E-business involve improved performance and contribution to competitive advantage. The chapter concludes with a presentation of the E-business stages which form one of the three dimensions on the Balanced Maturity framework discussed in Chapter Twelve. The E-business stages include Basic, Silos, Internal Integration, and External Integration.

## ELECTRONIC BUSINESS

Van Hooft & Stegwee (2001) define E-business as follows:

*A secure, flexible and integrated approach to delivering differentiated business value by combining the systems and processes that run core business operations with the simplicity and reach made possible by Internet technology. (Van Hooft & Stegwee, 2001, p. 44)*

Schlenkar and Crocker (2003) investigated how the Internet could contribute to increased value for small business. Good use of technology will support current operations of the small business and contribute to its long-term success (Schlenkar & Crocker, 2003). They defined the following terms:

- Information Technology: "...the use of management and processing of information, traditionally within the confines of a company or institution." (Schlenkar & Crocker, 2003, p. 9)
- Internet Technology: "...the use of both public and private telecommunications networks to extend and interconnect information technologies inside the organization and out." (Schlenkar & Crocker, 2003, p. 10)
- E-business: "...the use of Internet technologies to produce business value. (Schlenkar & Crocker, 2003, p. 10)

A closer look at these definitions shows that E-business encompasses both of the other terms. Thus, overall E-business relates to how employees can improve business processes and provide information to meet customer needs (Schlenkar & Crocker, 2003).

Another definition of E-business suggests it involves business transactions or exchanges of information which employs the Internet (Moodley, 2003). The available information is more timely and accurate. This facilitates internal decision-making and external relationships with business partners and customers (Zhuang & Lederer, 2003). E-business positively affects management processes within the business and with other partner businesses (Ash & Burn, 2003). Adoption of E-business, considered valuable technological innovation, contributes to small business competitive advantage (Martin & Matlay, 2003).

Brown and Lockett (2004) suggested that prior to the inception of the Internet only large corporations could afford the cost of conducting business via proprietary networks. Thus, the Internet has provided low cost infrastructure for small business to identify new markets or to improve how customers are served in current markets. Further, Brown & Lockett (2004) define E-business as, "…the use of inter-organisational electronic networks to transact, process, and collaborate in business markets…" (Brown & Lockett, 2004, p. 22).

"…e-business systems adoption can be considered a technical innovation (Kendall et al, 2001; Jackson & Harris, 2003; and Patterson et al, 2003), which offers firm's opportunities to establish interactive relationships with business partners (such as suppliers, logistics providers, wholesalers, distributors, service providers, and end customers), improve operating efficiency and extend their reach, all at a very low cost (Ash & Burn, 2003). E-business systems enable firms to execute electronic transactions with any business partner along the value chain. E-business thus significantly impact business process change, diffusion of innovation, and even business transformation." (Lin & Lee, 2005, pp. 172-173).

Many business processes may now be conducted using computer-based information systems.

*E-business (electronic business) is a way of doing business that relies on electronic (Internet-based) linkages with employees, managers, customers, clients, suppliers, and partners to efficiently and effectively achieve goals. E-business includes e-commerce (electronic commerce) which is essentially the sales and marketing component of e-business. (Robbins et al, 2012, p. 15)*

"Using the Internet, companies have, for instance,

1. Created knowledge bases that employees can tap into anytime, anywhere;
2. Turned customers into collaborative partners who help design, test, and launch new products;
3. Become virtually paperless in specific tasks such as purchasing and filing expense reports;
4. Managed logistics in real time; and
5. Changed the nature of numerous work tasks throughout the organization." (Robbins et al, 2012, p. 225)

Recall in Chapter Nine – Competitive Advantage that a small business may attempt to gain an advantage over competitors through lower costs (cost leader) or by being different (Porter 1985 and 1998). A small business can attain lower costs by being more efficient than its competitors and passing on some of the savings to customers. A small business can be different by producing unique or superior products.

*"Using e-business techniques, managers can formulate strategies that contribute to the development of a sustainable competitive advantage. A cost leader can use e-business techniques to reduce costs in a variety of ways. It might use online bidding and order processing to eliminate the need for sales calls and to decrease sales force expenses; it could use web-based inventory control systems that reduce storage costs; or it might use online testing and evaluation of job applicants.*
*The differentiator might use Internet-based knowledge systems to shorten customer response times; provide rapid online responses to service requests; or automate purchasing and payment systems so that customers have detailed status reports and purchasing histories." (Robbins et al, 2012, p. 225)*

Dembla et al (2007) investigated factors which facilitate small business adoption of transaction processing systems based on the Internet. These systems facilitate all aspects of the supply chain (Pflughoeft et al, 2003). Further, small business is able to penetrate new markets and improve customer service through Internet adoption (Dembla et al, 2007). Figure 1 represents their model.

The components of this model are explained as follows:

## Environmental Uncertainty

*"...is a consequence of dynamic and hostile (i.e., competitive) environment and heterogeneity. The more dynamic and hostile the environment, the greater the need for innovation and the more likely it is that firms will be innovative (Miller & Freisen, 1982)." (Dembla et al, 2007, p. 4)*

*Figure 1. Factors affecting adoption of web-based transaction processing*
*Adapted from Dembla et al, 2007*

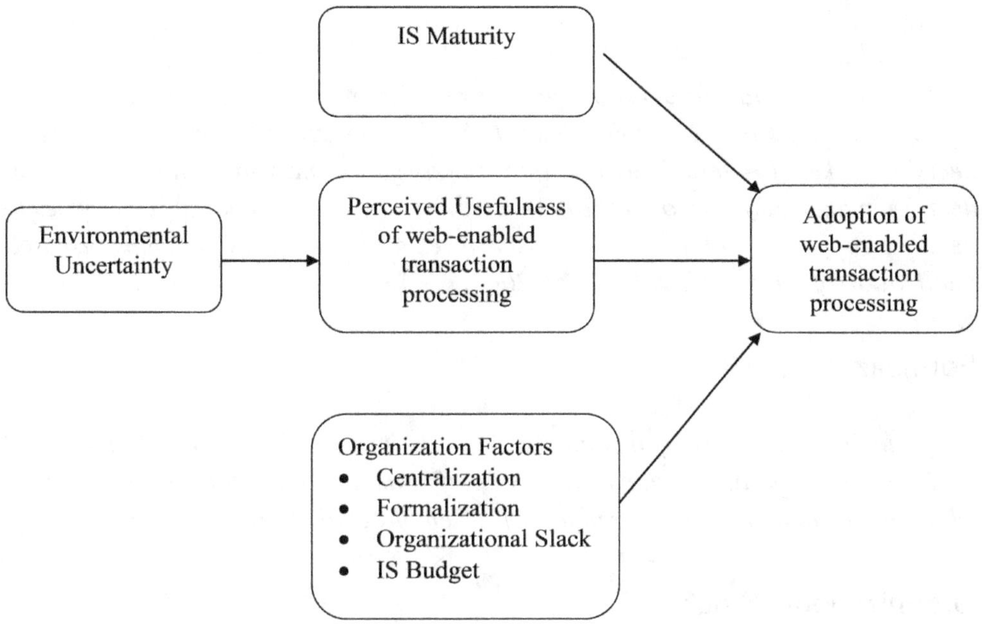


## IS Maturity

*"...a greater IS sophistication or maturity may provide the organization with the knowledge base to integrate new technologies. Organizations with a mature IS group tend to be more proactive in evaluating the advantages of web-enabled services and implementing them. Simply put, they are more likely to adopt new innovations (Shim & Min, 2002). Studies of adoption and use of IT have shown that top management support and enthusiasm is a key motivator of adoption and use of new information technologies (Delone, 1988; and Thong, 1999). At the same time, these businesses are more likely to perceive the usefulness of web-enabled services for transaction processing and adopt them." (Dembla et al, 2007, p. 4)*

## Perceived Usefulness

*"...the degree to which an individual in the organization believes that using a particular system enhances the performance of the organization. If a particular technology is deemed useful to the organization, it is expected that it will be helpful." (Dembla et al, 2007, pp. 3-4)*

## Organizational Factors

### Centralization

*"...the concentration of decision-making activity increases the predictability of outcomes of decisions (Hage & Aitken, 1967). In a centralized structure, top-level decision makers are less likely to differ in their goals and values than lower level decision makers (Jarzabkowski, 2002). Centralization can encourage employees to be more cooperative about sharing discoveries and techniques, reducing risk and duplication of effort." (Dembla et al, 2007, p. 5)*

### Formalization

*"...the use of rules in an organization (Hage and Aiken, 1967). Leaders cannot spend all their time making decisions, so they codify past decisions into rules to specify what job occupants are supposed to do." (Dembla et al, 2007, p. 5)*

### Organizational Slack

*"...the extra resources available in excess of what is required for the normal operation of an organization...innovation is more likely in the presence of organizational slack because it buffers organizations from downside risk and because the legitimacy of experimenting is less likely to be questioned (Thompson, 1969; [and] Singh, 1986)." (Dembla et al, 2007, p. 5)*

### IS Budget

*"A higher IS budget allows the organization the flexibility to adopt new innovations. Greater investment in resources not only help reduce IS knowledge barriers, but may also reflect a firms' financial position and the top management's support and enthusiasm for information technologies." (Dembla et al, 2007, p. 6)*

An interesting relationship was identified by Dembla et al (2007). They determined that "organizational slack" was positively related to Internet adoption. In general, organizational slack facilitates the ability to explore new ideas and to act as a buffer when considering the adoption of innovative processes (Dembla et al, 2007).

Schlemmer and Webb (2009) determined that small business may be able to employ the Internet to leverage their resources to positively impact performance and consequently create competitive advantage. Two important business resources involve the external relationships with suppliers and customers. The use of the Internet is now imperative when participating in the supply chain. Co-ordination activities and communication skills, carried out via the Internet will support on-going and financially via relationships with suppliers. Excellence in customer relationships will be furthered by adopting the Internet. This is especially so in the digital age where more individuals are accustomed to interacting electronically with small businesses.

Ifinedo (2011) determined that the adoption of Internet and E-business technologies by small business was mainly related to perceived benefits of those technologies. This finding supports previous investigations into the adoption of technological innovations (Iacovou et al, 1995; Chwelos et al, 2001: Mehrtens et al, 2001; Premkumar & Roberts, 1999; Kuan & Chau, 2001; Gibbs & Kramer, 2004; Grandon & Pearson, 2004; and Looi, 2005).

Currently, small businesses tend to not have developed an effective web site (Lin et al, 2011). Small businesses are constrained regarding the adoption of the Internet for Business–to-Business (B2B) purposes because of a lack of technical expertise and financial resources (Chircu & Kauffman, 2000; and Mehrtens et al, 2001). However, small businesses are pressured to adopt Internet based processes (Lin et al, 2008; and Standing & Lin, 2007). It is important that small business recognize that technology investments are not directly related to benefits for the business. These investments promote novel and innovative management processes and practices (Carr, 2003). The indirect result may be improved business processes which may indirectly provide benefits.

Another approach which may be taken by small business is to interact with the government via E-business applications. Thompson et al (2005) investigated how small business profits from e-government. To begin, they adopt a definition of e-government as, "...government's use of IT applications to enhance the access and delivery of government information and service to citizens, business partners, employees, other agencies and government entities (McClure, 2000)." (Thompson et al, 2005, p. 386)

They determined that small business benefit from dealing with e-government through increased revenues and decreased costs. Revenues expand as a result of identifying new markets and providing improved customer service. Decreased costs mainly result from time savings and more efficient interaction with government regarding compliance with regulations and submitting required information (Thompson et al, 2005).

Chapter Twelve presents the Balanced Maturity Framework. The framework consists of three dimensions, Management Processes, E-commerce, and E-business. This section of this chapter presents a description of the E-business dimension. In conjunction with the other two dimensions, as a small business grows and matures it will adopt more sophisticated technology. The E-business dimension consists of four stages. They are Basic, Silos, Internal Integration, and External Integration.

## Basic

When a small business is initially formed it will not have many information systems to support management. There may be some automated systems in the creation of a product. However, management systems will be very simple. Sales may be recorded on a cash register. Perhaps credit sales will be outsourced to a credit card company. If credit sales are managed internally some form of Accounts Receivable system may be developed which is based on an elementary spreadsheet. Purchases made by the small business may also be recorded on a spreadsheet based information system. A management process is required to ensure valid invoices are paid to the correct suppliers. It is also important to pay invoices "on time". There are a myriad of interpretations of on time ranging from when the invoice terms allow a discount to when an interest surcharge will be applied to the invoice amount.

If a small business is a manufacturer then inventory must be tracked. There will be the receipt of raw material as input to the production process. Then work-in-process will allow the small business to determine the status during the production process. The final inventory category relates to finished products. These items will be held in the small business until they are sold.

Payroll is another basic business process. Initially the information system may be manual. However, it is usually converted to an automated system soon after the small business is formed. One approach to an automated payroll system could be to outsource the process to a financial institution. A number of services may be provided by one financial institution and payroll may be bundled with other banking resources. It is also possible to purchase and install a payroll software information system. The generic management processes involved in payroll are easily replicated in software packages. The reporting requirements of government agencies regarding payroll will be reflected in internal management processes and the resulting software system.

Unfortunately, the information systems that support these major processes do not communicate. The necessary form of communication takes place in the next stage.

## Silos

In Chapter Three – Information Systems a management hierarchy was presented and is replicated here in Figure 2.

*Figure 2. Management hierarchy*

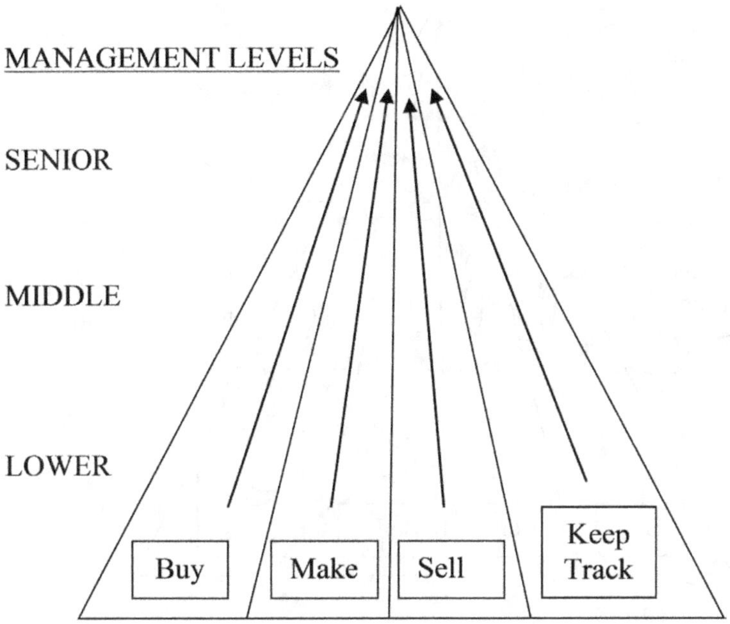


At this stage more sophisticated information systems will be employed. These systems will reflect the requirements to generate information that is timely and accurate in order to provide support for more formal decision making processes.

As Figure 2 depicts there are different levels in the management hierarchy. These levels require a different amount of detailed information to support decision making. At the LOWER level of management, information must be presented in very detailed and structured way in order to support more operationally oriented near term decision making. The higher or SENIOR level managers make long range strategically oriented decisions. Information requirements at this level are summarized and are oriented towards overall trends. The more generic management processes may be supported by software packages as described above.

This stage is named "Silos" because the information is passed up each major functional area with little or no exchange of information between the areas.

## Internal Integration

In this stage the information systems within each silo are enabled to exchange data. This ability allows a cross-functional process. This concept was first presented in Chapter Four – Information Systems and is replicated here as Figure 3.

*Figure 3. Cross-functional information system*

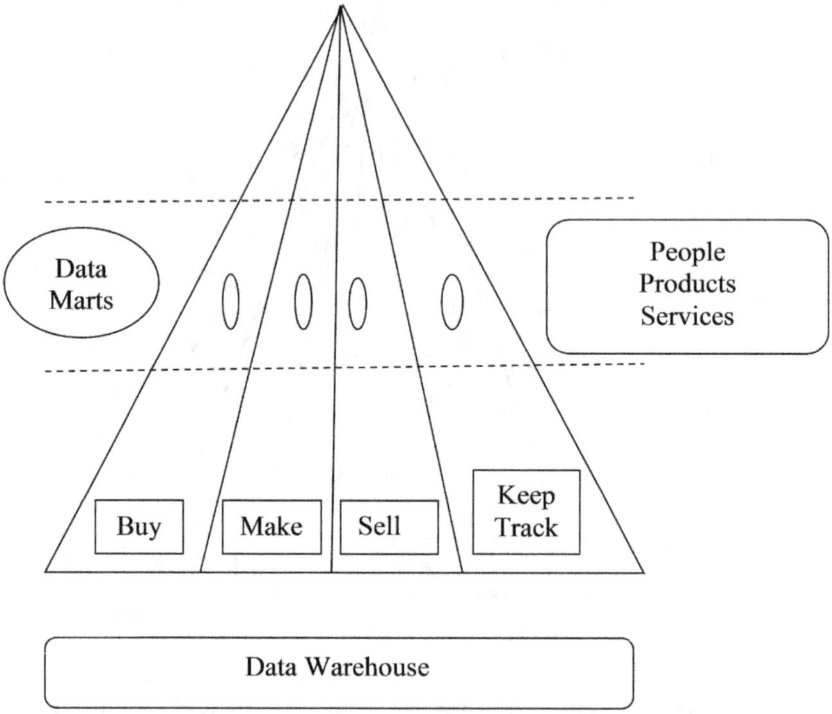


A system which facilitates the cross-functional approach is titled Enterprise Resource Planning (ERP). Internally, this type of system allows the integration of all of the management processes that are supported by computer-based software – referred to here as E-business.

*"Enterprise resource planning (ERP) integrates all departments and functions throughout an organization into a single information system (or integrated set of information systems) so that employees can make decisions by viewing enterprise-wide data on all business operations." (Baltzan et al, 2011, p. 115)*

Beyond this form of internal integration more sophisticated management processes are initiated in this stage. Because of the cross functional ability it becomes possible to implement the complete scheduling of transforming raw material through work-in-progress to finished products. Also, corporate level planning may be initiated which will incorporate all initiatives across the business.

Other functional areas may also be automated. The finances of the business, such as acquisition and management of financial resources are one area that will benefit from automation. Human Resources systems may be employed to document employee skills and track individualized training programs. Basic internal marketing processes may be implemented to keep track of product development and sales.

## External Integration

At this most sophisticated stage of E-business information systems facilitate interaction with external entities including customers and suppliers. The small business may employ social media to gather market data beyond their immediate customers. Comments may be gathered about potential customers' purchase intentions or their impressions of the image of the small business. This stage focuses on business oriented information systems such as Customer Relationship Management and Supply Chain Management.

Customer Relationship Management facilitates all interactions with customers.

*"Customer relationship management (CRM) involves managing all aspects of a customer's relationship with an organization to increase customer loyalty and retention and profitability for the organization. CRM components provide an integrated view of customer data and interactions, allowing organizations to work more effectively with customers and be more responsive to their needs. CRM components typically include contact centres, sales force automation, and marketing functions. These improve the customer experience while identifying a company's most (and least) valuable customers to better allocate resources." (Baltzan et al, 2011, p. 124)*

The supply chain represents all activities involved in the acquisition of raw material from suppliers through to the distribution of finished products to customers. Supply Chain Management attempts to make the process as efficient and effective as possible.

*"Supply chain management (SCM) involves managing data flows between and among stages in the supply chain to maximize total supply chain effectiveness and profitability. SCM components help an organization plan, schedule, control, and optimize the supply chain from its acquisition of raw materials to the receipt of finished goods by customers." (Baltzan et al, 2011, p. 124)*

## CONCLUSION

This chapter has presented a brief overview of E-business. A major component of E-business is E-commerce, discussed in Chapter eleven, which involves sales via the Internet. But, E-bisoness involves more internal and external management processes. Internally, a more sophisticated approach will be taken to the traditional administrative functions. Externally, E-business will facilitate Customer Relationship Management and Supply Chain Management which will contribute to performance efficiencies and the ability to interact effectively with customers and suppliers. The next chapter presents the main thesis of the book, as a small business matures in its use of management processes more sophisticated information systems should be applied to E-commerce and E-business. Further, the maturity and sophistication should proceed in a balanced manner.

## REFERENCES

Ash, C. G., & Burn, J. M. (2003). A strategic framework for the management of ERP enabled e-business change. *European Journal of Operational Research*, *146*(2), 374–387. doi:10.1016/S0377-2217(02)00556-8

Baltzan, P., Phillips, A., & Detlor, B. (2011). *Business Driven Information Systems* (2nd Canadian Edition). Toronto, Ontario: McGraw-Hill Ryerson.

Brown, D. H., & Lockett, N. (2004). Potential of critical e-applications for engaging SMEs in e-business: A provider perspective. *European Journal of Information Systems*, *13*(1), 21–34. doi:10.1057/palgrave.ejis.3000480

Carr, N. G. (2003). IT doesn't matter. *Harvard Business Review*, *81*(5), 41–49. PMID:12747161

Chircu, A. M., & Kauffman, R. J. (2000). Limits to value in electronic commerce-related IT investments. *Journal of Management Information Systems*, 17(20), 59-80.

Chwelos, P., Benbasat, I., & Dexter, A. S. (2001). Empirical test of an EDI adoption model. *Information Systems Research*, *12*(3), 302–321. doi:10.1287/isre.12.3.304.9708

DeLone, W. H. (1988). Determinants of success of computer usage in small business. *Management Information Systems Quarterly*, *12*(1), 51–61. doi:10.2307/248803

Dembla, P., Palvia, P., & Krishnan, B. (2007). Understanding the adoption of web-enabled transaction processing by small business. *Journal of Electronic Commerce Research*, *8*(1), 1–17.

Gibbs, J. L., & Kramer, K. L. (2004). A cross-country investigation of the determinants of scope of e-commerce use: An institutional approach. *Electronic Markets*, *14*(2), 124–137. doi:10.1080/10196780410001675077

Grandon, E. E., & Pearson, J. (2004, December). Electronic commerce adoption: An empirical study of small and medium US businesses. *Information & Management*, *42*(1), 197–216. doi:10.1016/j.im.2003.12.010

Hage, J., & Aiken, M. (1967). Relationship of centralization to other structural properties. *Administrative Science Quarterly*, *12*(1), 72–93. doi:10.2307/2391213

Iacovou, C. L., Benbasat, I., & Dexter, A. S. (1995). Electronic data interchange and small organizations: Adoption and impact of technology. *Management Information Systems Quarterly*, *19*(4), 465–485. doi:10.2307/249629

Ifinedo, P. (2011). Internet/e-business technologies acceptance in Canada's SMEs: An exploratory investigation. *Internet Research*, *21*(3), 255–281. doi:10.1108/10662241111139309

Jackson, P., & Harris, L. (2003). E-business and organizational change. *Journal of Organizational Change Management*, *16*(5), 497–511. doi:10.1108/09534810310494900

Jarzabkowski, P. (2002). Centralized or decentralized? Strategic implications of resource allocation models. *Higher Education Quarterly*, *56*(1), 5–32. doi:10.1111/1468-2273.00200

Kendall, J. D., Tung, L. L., Chau, K. H., Ng, C. H., & Tan, S. M. (2001). Receptivity of Singapore's SMEs to electronic commerce adoption. *The Journal of Strategic Information Systems*, *10*(3), 223–242. doi:10.1016/S0963-8687(01)00048-8

Kuan, K., & Chau, P. (2001). A perception-based model for EDI adoption in small businesses using a technology-organization-environment framework. *Information & Management*, *38*(8), 507–521. doi:10.1016/S0378-7206(01)00073-8

Lin, C., Huang, Y. A., & Stockdale, R. (2011). Developing a B2B web site effectiveness model for SMEs. *Internet Research*, *21*(3), 304–325. doi:10.1108/10662241111139327

Lin, C., Pervan, G., Lin, H. C., & Tsao, H. (2008). An investigation into business-to-business electronic commerce organizations. *Journal of Research and Practices in Information Technology*, *40*(1), 3–18.

Lin, H. F., & Lee, G. G. (2005). Impact of organizational learning and knowledge management factors on e-business adoption. *Management Decision*, *43*(2), 171–188. doi:10.1108/00251740510581902

Looi, H. C. (2005). E-commerce adoption in Brunei Darussalam: A quantitative analysis of factors influencing its adoption. *Communications of the Association for Information Systems*, *15*(3), 61–81.

Martin, L. M., & Matlay, H. (2003). Innovative use of the internet in established small firms: The impact of knowledge management and organizational learning in assessing new opportunities. *Qualitative Market Research: An International Journal*, *6*(1), 18–26. doi:10.1108/13522750310457348

McClure, D. L. (2000). Statement of David L. McClure, US General Accounting Office, before the Subcommittee on Government Reform, House of representatives, www.gao.gov

Mehrtens, J., Cragg, P. B., & Mills, A. M. (2001). A model of internet adoption by SMEs. *Information & Management*, *39*(3), 165–176. doi:10.1016/S0378-7206(01)00086-6

Miller, D., & Freisen, P. H. (1982). Innovation in conservation and entrepreneurial firms. *Strategic Management Journal*, *3*(1), 1–25. doi:10.1002/smj.4250030102

Moodley, S. (2003). The challenge of e-business for South African apparel sector. *Technovation*, *23*(7), 557–570. doi:10.1016/S0166-4972(02)00002-0

Patterson, K. A., Grimm, C. M., & Corsi, T. M. (2003). Adopting new technologies for supply chain management. *Transportation Research Part E, Logistics and Transportation Review*, *39*(2), 95–121. doi:10.1016/S1366-5545(02)00041-8

Pflughoeft, K. A., Ramamurthy, K., Soofi, E. S., Yasai-Ardekani, M., & Zahedi, F. (2003). Multiple conceptualizations of small business web use and benefit. *Decision Sciences*, *34*(3), 467–512. doi:10.1111/j.1540-5414.2003.02539.x

Porter, M. E. (1985). *Competitive Advantage*. New York: The Free Press.

Porter, M. E. (1998). *The Competitive Advantage of the Nation*. New York: The Free Press.

Premkumar, G., & Roberts, M. (1999). Adoption of new information technologies in rural small businesses. *Omega: International Journal of Management Science*, *27*(4), 467–484. doi:10.1016/S0305-0483(98)00071-1

Robbins, S. P., Coulter, M., Leach, E., & Kilfoil, M. (2012). *Management* (10th Canadian Edition). Don Mills, Ontario: Pearson, Canada, Inc.

Schlemmer, F., & Webb, B. (2009). The internet as a complementary resource for SMEs: The interaction effect of strategic assets and the internet. *International Journal of E-Business Research*, *5*(1), 1–24. doi:10.4018/jebr.2009010101

Schlenkar, L., & Crocker, N. (2003). Building an e-business scenario for small business: The IBM SME Gateway project. *Qualitative Market Research*, *6*(1), 7–17. doi:10.1108/13522750310457339

Shim, J. S., & Min, B. K. (2002). Organizational factors associated with expert systems implementation. *Journal of Computer Information Systems*, *42*(4), 71–76.

Singh, J. V. (1986). Performance, slack, and risk taking in organizational decision making. *Academy of Management Journal*, *29*(4), 562–585. doi:10.2307/256224

Standing, C., & Lin, C. (2007). Organizational evaluation of the benefits, constaints and satisfaction with business-to-business electronic commerce. *International Journal of Electronic Commerce*, *11*(3), 107–153. doi:10.2753/JEC1086-4415110304

Thompson, D. V., & Rust, R. T. (2005). The business of value of e-government for small firms. *International Journal of Service Industry Management*, *16*(4), 385–407. doi:10.1108/09564230510614022

Thompson, V. A. (1969). *Bureaucracy and Innovation*. Huntsville: University of Alabama.

Thong, J. Y. L. (1999). An integrated model of information systems adoption in small businesses. *Journal of Management Information Systems*, *15*(4), 187–214.

Van Hooft, F. P. C., & Stegwee, R. A. (2001). E-business strategy: How to benefit from a hype. *Logistics Information Management*, *14*(1/2), 44–53. doi:10.1108/09576050110360223

Zhuang, Y., & Lederer, A. L. (2003). An instrument for measuring the business benefits of e-commerce retailing. *International Journal of Electronic Commerce*, *7*(3), 65–99.

## ADDITIONAL READING

Baltzan, P., Phillips, A., & Detlor, B. (2011). *Business Driven Information Systems* (2nd Canadian Edition). Toronto, Ontario: McGraw-Hill Ryerson.

Cruz-Cunha, M. M., & Varajao, J. (2011). *E-Business Issues, Challenges and Opportunities for SMEs: Driving Competitiveness*. Hershey, PA: IGI-Global. doi:10.4018/978-1-61692-880-3

Lee, I. (2011). *E-Business Applications for Product Development and Competitive Growth: Emerging Technologies*. Hershey, PA: IGI-Global. doi:10.4018/978-1-60960-132-4

Robbins, S. P., Coulter, M., Leach, E., & Kilfoil, M. (2012). *Management* (10th Canadian Edition). Don Mills, Ontario: Pearson, Canada, Inc.

Sounderpandian, J., & Sinha, T. (2007). *E-Business Process Management: Technologies and Solutions*. Hershey, PA: IGI-Global. doi:10.4018/978-1-59904-204-6

## KEY TERMS AND DEFINITIONS

**Basic:** Lowest, but necessary level of performance.

**Cross Functional:** Communication across the major business activities.

**Customer Relationship Management:** Activities involved in working with customers.

**Customer Service:** Activities conducted before, during, and after a transaction in an attempt to increase loyalty.

**Data Marts:** Subset of a database which may contain calculated data.

**E-Business:** Includes E-Commerce and pre-sales and post-sales services.

**External Integration:** Technology which facilitates communication with entities outside of the small business.

**Information Systems Maturity:** The process of transforming data into information becomes more sophisticated.

**Internal Integration:** Communication within and across silos within the small business.

**Loyalty:** The commitment of a customer to return to a small business.

**Organizational Slack:** Extra resources beyond normal operations which support the consideration of innovative processes.

**Perceived Usefulness:** Belief by an individual that a product or service would be beneficial.

**Post-Sales:** Activities involved after the transaction is consummated.

**Pre-Sales:** Activities involved before a transaction is commenced.

**Silos:** Focus solely on functional areas in a business with little cross functional communication.

**Supply Chain Management:** Activities involved in working with vendors.

# Chapter 12
# Balanced Maturity Framework


## ABSTRACT

*Entrepreneurs form businesses to be successful. To begin, a small business must make a profit. But then success may be measured in growth or longevity. In either case the small business will mature over time. The management processes will become more structured as decision making is formalized and the necessity for information expands beyond the boundary of the small business. To support this structured approach technology must be more sophisticated. More extensive E-commerce will facilitate improved interaction with customers via Customer Relationship management systems. Advanced E-business will promote more efficient and effective Supply Chain management and relations with suppliers. A balanced approach to maturity, as proposed in this chapter, will improve performance of the small business and contribute to competitive advantage.*


## INTRODUCTION

The presentation of the Balanced Maturity Framework represents the culmination of this book. The framework consists of three dimensions. Management Processes include functions such as planning, organizing, staffing, directing, and controlling. All management levels include these functions. Each level will consist of a different mix of these functions. As a small business matures the management processes become more structured and more outward looking. Information for decision making

DOI: 10.4018/978-1-4666-8708-0.ch012

will be more formalized. In support of the more structured management processes will be more sophisticated technology. E-commerce will support interaction with customers. More advanced E-business will allow communication with suppliers.

This chapter is organized as follows. To begin, growth and longevity are presented in association with success. The stages of growth are reviewed which were initially presented in Chapter Four – Theories for Investigation. Then E-commerce is related to stages of maturity. E-business follows with a progression over time. The small business life cycle stages are then related to information processing. The chapter then provides a description of some models the show how small businesses evolve. All of the previous descriptions here and the earlier chapters have provided the context for the Balanced Maturity Framework which is presented at the end of the chapter.

## GROWTH AND LONGEVITY

Sustainable growth is considered important for small business (Laurence, 2001; O'Gorman, 2001; and Watson et al, 1998). Some consider growth to be a measure of success (O'Gorman, 2001). Others define success by including family aspects or personal life style consideration (Curran, 1986; and Stanworth & Curran, 1986). This suggests longevity as a measure of success (Hunter & Kazakoff, 2008).

Feindt et al (2002) suggested that very few small businesses grow beyond the first few years after start-up. While growth slows or becomes non-existent these small businesses consider themselves successful mainly due to their continued existence (Hunter & Kazakoff, 2008). Indeed, growth may not be pursued due to the owner/manager's attitude (Feindt et al, 2002) or in consideration of the significant increase in costs resulting from even the smallest increase in production (Hunter & Kazakoff, 2008).

Thus, as proposed by Feindt et al (2002),

*"Successful SMEs place greater emphasis on soft issues (people) than hard issues (technology, structure). The management skills and concepts of the founders are deemed much more important than their technical skills. Employee skills are of crucial concern and can be most effectively developed in a nurturing working environment. Nevertheless the impact of business founders on organisational success remains a leading factor." (Feindt et al, 2002, p. 53)*

Salojarvi et al (2005) investigated the relationship between knowledge management and growth in sales in small business. They determined a direct link between knowledge management and long-term sustained growth. They adopted the following definition for knowledge management, "...the art of creating value by leveraging intangible assets." (Svieby, 1997). Further, they incorporated the following aspects for intangible assets: (Edvinsson & Malone, 1997; Roos et al, 1997; and Sveiby, 1997).

- Human capital
    - Employees' competencies and commitments
- External capital
    - Image
    - Customer relations
    - Other external relationships
- Organisational capital
    - Internal processes and management of the company

In Chapter Five – Theories for Investigations the Scott & Bruce (1987) framework for stages of growth in small business was introduced. The framework is repeated here in Table 1.

Progress through the stages will uniquely relate to each individual small business. Scott and Bruce (1987) suggest that the small business may fail at any of the stages. They further suggest that the transition points from one stage to the other represent crisis points for the small business. It is at these times that there is an increased chance that the small business will fail. They conclude as follows:

*"It is the anticipation of these crises and the successful management of the change that they cause that ensures the survival of the growing small business." (Scott & Bruce, 1987, p. 51)*

One of the many issues relates to the adoption and use of information systems. Advanced technology may improve management and business processes. However, it may also create problems related to change and developing an understanding of how to interact with the technology and employ it productively.

## E-COMMERCE

Karagozoglu and Lindell (2004) explored E-commerce use by small business. They suggest that,

*"Small companies' interest in e-commerce is not surprising in light of the advantages that make their small size and location irrelevant to compete effectively while increasing their adaptiveness through opportunities for richer customer feedback." (Karagozoglu & Lindell, 2004, p. 290)*

*Table 1. Stages of growth in small business*

| Issues | Stage 1 Inception | Stage 2 Survival | Stage 3 Growth | Stage 4 Expansion | Stage 5 Maturity |
|---|---|---|---|---|---|
| **Features** | Developing a product and establishing a place in the market | Develop credibility with financial institutions and suppliers | Develop an organization structure based on major functions | Develop budgetary control and consider equity partners | Develop long term plans for continuation |
| **Focus** | Establishing and maintaining positive cash flow<br>Developing formal systems and record keeping<br>Establish an organization structure to facilitate delegation | Control growth<br>Respond to competition<br>Expand customer base<br>Acquire new skills | Decide to compete on price or differentiation<br>Expand into new markets or new products<br>Manage an expanded and diverse operation | Founder becomes a manager<br>Focus on customers | Expense control<br>Productivity<br>Growth opportunities |
| **Systems and Controls** | Simple bookkeeping | Simple bookkeeping | Simple control reports | Budgeting<br>Regular sales and production reports | Formal systems to report on objectives |

Adapted from: Scott and Bruce, 1987

Further, they report on the Straub and Klein (2001) levels of E-commerce strategies as follows:

*"An empirical study by Straub and Klein (2001) identified three progressive levels to which companies evolve in their attempts to pursue e-commerce strategies. At the initial level, the focus is mainly on cutting costs and/or raising productivity. At the next level the focus shifts to the use of e-commerce to access new customers and markets. The third level builds upon gains at the previous levels companies seek sustainable competitive advantage by attempting to achieve a company integration of e-commerce into the company's overall business strategy. Most large companies advance to the third objectives whereas SMEs focus on the first and second levels. Third level objectives reflect greater complexity and risk (Straub & Klein, 2001) and SMEs are less likely to pursue these objectives, at the present stage [of] the learning curve, due to their relatively limited access to slack resources to absorb the risks. Also, more sophisticated e-commerce features such as personalization for customer specific content may be more affordable to larger companies (Korper and Ellis, 2001)." (Straub & Klein, 2001, p. 291)*

Rao et al (2003) developed a stages model to depict the maturing use of E-commerce by small business. The four stages are described in Table 2.

Based upon the above comments Karagozoglu and Lindell (2004) suggest that small business will employ E-commerce to attempt to expand their customer base.

## E-BUSINESS

E-business is now just as necessary for small business as a telephone (Waters, 2000). It is necessary for basic operations and as a vehicle to provide competitive advantage (Rodgers et al, 2002). However, while many small businesses are adopting Internet technologies they are slow to incorporate E-business (DTI, 2003). Indeed, information technology does not have a direct effect of the performance of small business (Makadok, 2001; and Powell & Dent-Micallef, 1997).

The concept of E-business extends beyond the technology to allow a small business to focus on customers and their needs. The Internet provides the supporting technology to facilitate the exchange of information. Basic business operations are improved because of faster processing and fewer errors (Pavic et al, 2007). E-business connects suppliers, employees, and customers with the information they need via the systems within the small business (Van Hooft & Stegwee, 2001: Rodgers et al,

*Table 2. E-commerce stages of maturity*

| Stage | Description |
|---|---|
| PRESENCE | "The company has an established website to exhibit information (e.g., product descriptions) to anyone surfing the Internet. One-way communication is used. Namely, information flows solely from the site to browsers." (Zhu et al, 2009, p. 287) |
| PORTALS | "Not only is information displayed on the site, but two-way communication is established. Namely, information flows between the business and Internet users in both directions. This stage includes creating customer profiles and cookies, email functionality, and the option to place orders online." (Zhu et al, 2009, p. 287) |
| TRANSACTIONS INTEGRATION | "Online monetary transactions between the business and its customers are a benchmark of this stage. The payment function is facilitated either by the vendor's own website or by a third party. Money is transferred electronically through a website and customers can finish the entire purchase without help from the selling company." (Zhu et al, 2009, p. 287) |
| ENTERPRISES INTEGRATION | "Full integration of Customer Relationship Management (CRM), Value Chain Management (VCM), and Supply Chain Management (SCM) tools are used at this stage. Traditional offline enterprises and modern e-businesses become indistinguishable at this point due to the successful marriage of front-office and back-office tasks." (Zhu et al, 2009, pp. 287-288) |

Adapted from Zhu et al, 2009

2002; and Koh & Maguire, 2004). The technological advances of E-business allow small business to compete with large corporations. Firms of any size are able to more easily interact internally with employees and externally with suppliers and customers (Pavic et al, 2007).

So, E-business facilitates the acquisition of knowledge about suppliers and customers; and consequently contributes to competitive advantage (Maiga & Jacobs, 2009). Devaraj et al (2007) suggested that small business which employs E-business to integrate processes related to both suppliers and customers tend to outperform rivals. Thus, E-business should be employed to facilitate the entire supply chain (input) and final product distribution (output). Progression in the use of E-business is shown in Figure 1 (United Nations, 2004). The figure shows the increase in maturity in the use of technology starting from email through to fully integrated business processes which represents the concept of E-business.

## INNOVATION

Kmieciak et al (2012) investigated how small business innovativeness is facilitated by information technology capability. They suggest that information technology should be employed to leverage small business resources, such as internal communications and employee information technology skills, in order to positively affect performance. Information technology alone cannot create competitive advantage (Huang & Liu, 2005; Mata et al, 1995; Tippins & Sohi, 2003). Thus information technology should be employed to create resources unique to the small business (Bharadwaj, 2000).

Bharadwaj (2000) determined that the integration of three information technology based resources contribute to competitive advantage. The resources are as follows:

- Physical information technology infrastructure
    - Hardware
    - Software
- Human information technology skills
    - Employees
    - Managers
- Information technology enabled intangible assets
    - Customer orientation
    - Knowledge management

*Figure 1. E-business progression*
*Adapted from United Nations, 2004*

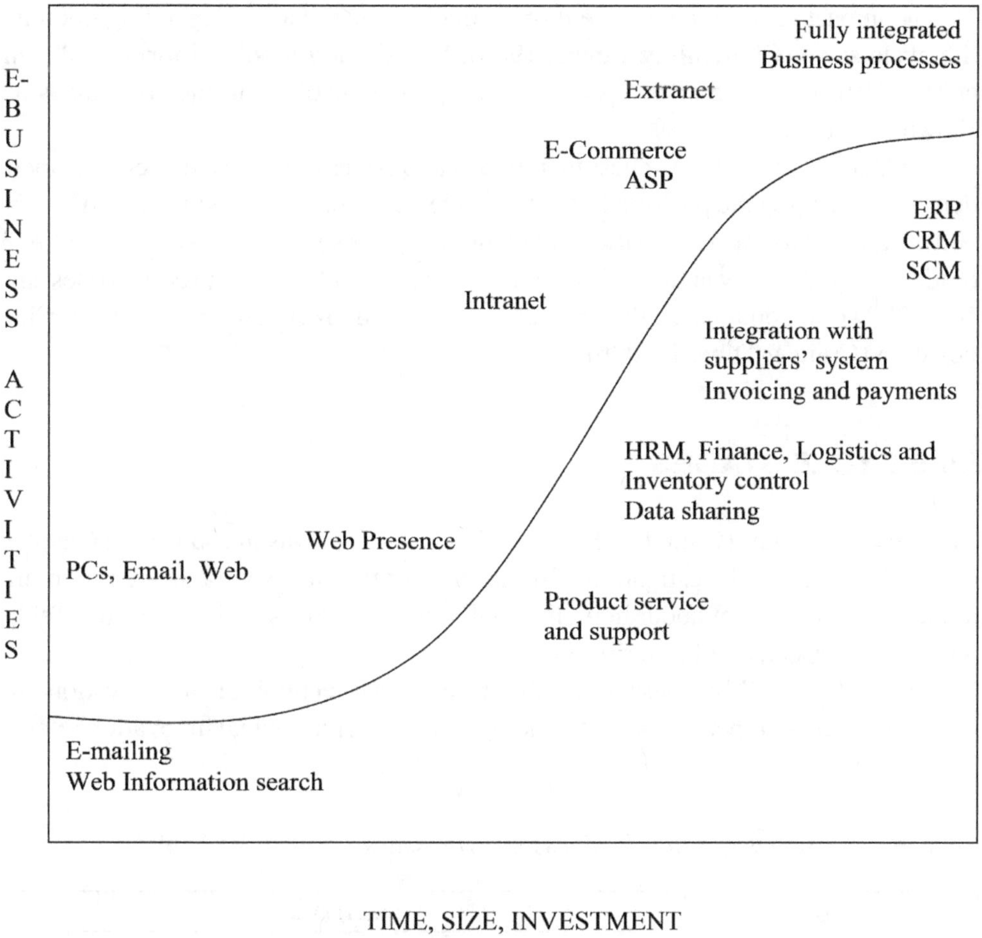


Each resource alone does not contribute to competitive advantage because they are easily replicated by other businesses. It is the unique integration of these resources which is difficult for rivals to replicate that contributes to competitive advantage.

Clark (2010) determined that product and service innovations dominate high performing small business. Further, it is important to possess management processes to support these innovative initiatives. Not only should the small business be well organized, it should acquire the necessary employee skills and adequate finances. All of these resources will promote small business innovation.

McAdam et al (2010) investigated the effect of critical incidents on the innovative capacity of small business. Examples of critical incidents include, "…market collapse, new entrant competition and developments in technology…" (McAdam et al, 2010, pp. 438-439).

The impact of a critical incident on a small business varies depending upon its life cycle stage (Churchill & Lewis, 1983). In a slightly modified form McAdam et al (2010) present their perspective of the issues involved in the five stages as shown in Table 3.

McAdam et al (2010) suggest that the small business response to a critical incident depends upon the position in the life cycle stage. In general, small business are better prepared to survive a critical incident if they possess an "innovative pipeline" of ideas related to new and existing markets and new and existing products (Bessant et al, 2004). In some cases the critical incident will create an opportunity for innovation (Craig & Dibrell, 2006).

## LIFE CYCLE STAGES

The life cycle stages (Churchill & Lewis, 1983) concept was introduced in Chapter Four – Theories for Investigations. In this chapter the stages are repeated with the addition of a comment about how the small business processes information. Table 4 presents this extended description.

Successful small businesses are able to integrate technological innovations in order to sustain competitiveness (Carneiro, 2007). Technological innovation relates

*Table 3. Five stages of small business growth issues*

| Stages | Description |
|---|---|
| Existence | "…the main problems of the business are obtaining customers and delivering the product or service." (McAdam et al, 2010:440) |
| Survival | "The company has now developed and has sufficient customers and satisfies them sufficiently with its products or services." (McAdam et al, 2010:440) |
| Success | "The decision facing owners at this stage is whether to exploit the company's accomplishments and expand or to keep the company stable and profitable, providing a base for alternative owner activities." (McAdam et al, 2010:440) |
| Take-Off | "…the key problems are how to grow rapidly and how to finance the growth." (McAdam et al, 2010:440) |
| Resource Maturity | "Challenges at this stage are, first, to consolidate and control the financial gains brought on by rapid growth and second to retain the advantages of small size, including flexibility." (McAdam et al, 2010:440) |

Adapted from McAdam et al, 2010

*Table 4. Life cycle stages and information processing*

| Stage | Definition | Information Processing Description |
|---|---|---|
| Existence | "…the beginning of organizational development. The focus is on viability, finding enough customers to support the existence of the organization. Decision-making, ownership, and power are in the hands of one, or a few, and organizational structure is quite simple." (Lester & Parnell, 2006, p. 5) | "Information processing is informal, with some documentation being hand-written. (Lester & Parnell, 2006, p. 5) |
| Survival | "…firms…seek to grow (Adizes, 1979: Downs, 1967), develop some formalization of structure (Quinn & Cameron, 1983), and establish their own distinctive competencies (Miller & Friesen, 1984). The primary goal is to generate enough revenue to continue operations and finance sufficient growth to stay competitive (Churchill & Lewis, 1983)." (Lester & Parnell, 2006, p. 5) | "Information processing becomes more sophisticated in keeping with the need for more formalization to facilitate growth." (Lester & Parnell, 2006, p. 5) |
| Success | "…represents an organizational form where formalization and control through bureaucracy are the norm (Quinn & Cameron, 1983). Job descriptions, policies and procedures, and hierarchical reporting relationships are all very formal. Decision making is decentralized as top managers focus on planning and strategy, leaving daily operations to middle managers." (Lester & Parnell, 2006, p. 6) | "Information processing systems mature to the point that they are viewed as a necessary burden, in many ways hampering operations." (Lester & Parnell, 2006, p. 6) |
| Renewal | "The…organization desires to return to a leaner time (Miller & Friesen, 1984), allowing collaboration and teamwork to foster innovation and creativity. This creativity can be facilitated through the use of a matrix structure, and decision-making is very much decentralized. The needs of customers are…placed above those of organizational members." (Lester & Parnell, 2006, p. 6) | "Information processing systems are totally state of the art technologically, providing their users with sharp competitive weapons." (Lester & Parnell, 2006, p. 6) |
| Decline | "Organizational members become more concerned with personal goals than organizational goals. For some organizations…they experience a lack of profit and a loss of market share (Miller & Friesen, 1984)." (Lester & Parnell, 2006, p. 6) | Information processing supports personal goals |

Adapted from Lester & Parnell, 2006

to improvements in all aspects of the value chain including supplier relationships, production of goods and services, and distribution to customers. Underlying all of these processes is the need for appropriate information.

*"The success of SMEs depends on using advanced technologies in an integrated manner, being aware of changing client's needs, producing quality goods and services, enhancing profits by reducing costs, and reaching new markets within a competitive perspective and a wide-open mentality. Reducing production and distribution costs while improving the features of products/services are the main operational problems for managers seeking to compete effectively in multinational markets." (Carneiro, 2007, pp. 52-53)*

The use of information technology is an important component in the competitive landscape for small business.

*"For SMEs, four factors found to have a profound influence on IT investments are: the perceived cost savings and income generation benefits; external pressure from rivals, suppliers, and buyers; organizational readiness; and perceived ease of use (Grandon & Pearson, 2004; and Mehrtens et al, 2001). IT investment in SMEs differs from IT investment in large firms because a smaller number of people have decision-making responsibility, standard procedures are not instituted, long-term planning is limited, and there is more reliance on external IT experts in SMEs (Prekumar, 2003). Nonetheless, IT capabilities may enable the long term survival of SMEs in a number of ways. They provide access to external knowledge and financial resources, create trust and legitimacy through widespread information dissemination, and generate more social network ties (Morse et al, 2007)." (Lester & Tran, 2008, p. 75)*

Information Technology capabilities may support small business owner/managers to respond to the crises which emerge as the business transitions form on life cycle stage to the next. Table 5 provides some suggestions and is based on Kazanjian (1988) life cycle model.

## MANAGEMENT PROCESSES

Recall from Chapter Ten – Management Processes that they consist of the daily activities involved in small business operaitons. A small business requires processes related to finances, employees, customers, and suppliers. Management of these processes includes functions such as planning, organizing, staffing, directing, and

*Table 5. Information technology capability suggestions*

| Life Cycle Stage | Problem Factors | Information Technology Capabiity Suggestions |
|---|---|---|
| Concept and Development | • Product development<br>• Resource acquisition<br>• Sales/Marketing | • Creativity – Open source collaboration; Website<br>• Connectivity – Website, E-mail<br>• Design – CAD/CAM |
| Commercialization | • Strategic positioning<br>• Recruitment and training | • Flexibility – Project planning and scheduling software; Inventory management system<br>• Training – Online recruitment and training system<br>• Communication – Web-linked value chain activities |
| Growth | • Sales/Marketing<br>• Internal control | • Customer relations – CRM software<br>• Market responsiveness – Blogs; E-mail; Text messaging<br>• Marketing – Website; Social networking site |
| Stability | • Profitability<br>• Internal Control<br>• Future growth | • Efficient Production – Web-linked value chain activities<br>• Back-office support – Automaiton software for accounting, payroll, purchasing, travel<br>• Collaboration – Website |

Adapted from Lester and Tran, 2008

controlling. As the small business matures these processes and functions will become more structured and will involve a more sophisticated use of technology.

Parrott et al (2010) suggest that small business will focus more on sales than on marketing. A sale represents a short term perspective in the delivery of a product or service. Marketing takes a longer term perspective in identifying potential customer needs and developing initiatives to respond to those needs.

Further, small business managers must also manage their human resources.

*"...the most commonly found HRM {Human Resource Management] practices in small firms reflect operational needs and pragmatic concerns: record keeping; staffing activities, such as recruiting and selecting staff; and, to a lesser extent, motivation and retention activities such as compensation and reward practices (Deshpande & Golhar, 1994; Duberley and Walley, 1995; Heneman & Berkely, 1999; Hornsby & Kuratko, 2003; Kotey & Sheridan, 2001; and McEvoy, 1984)." (Barrett & Mayson, 2007, p. 308)*

## MODELS OF THE EVOLVING SMALL BUSINESS

This section presents a series of models which describes aspects of change as the small business evolves and matures.

The Three-Dimensional Development Model by Gersick et al (1997) represents the passage of time along three dimensions. The Business Dimension represents the progression of the small business entity from start-up to maturity. The Ownership Dimension depicts various ownership structures from one person to multiple family members. The Family Dimension, which seems very applicable to small business, presents changing status as family members become involved in the small business. Note that there is a difference between Ownership and Family involvement such that the Family Dimension relates to management of the small business while the other dimension involves official ownership of the small business.

A further adaptation of this model is shown in Figure 2 where the three theories (Entrepreneurship, Agency, and Stewardship) are highlighted. Thus, Entrepreneurship Theory is applicable when the start-up business is controlled by one owner involving a young family. Drucker (1998) proposed Entrepreneurship Theory to involve an innovative approach to accepting risk in order to establish and maintain a viable business venture. As time progresses Agency Theory becomes applicable when the small business expands and the one owner involves more employees or family members. As Agency Theory suggests the relationship between the owner and employees is formally established via an employment contract. Agency Theory entails the formal relationship between a principal (owner) and an agent (employee). This formal relationship is established through an employment contract which generally involves a job description of the duties to be performed. Performance within an Agency Theory relationship involves extrinsic rewards, such as tangible assets which represent material wealth. Eventually, Stewardship Theory relates to a mature small business which includes many family members some of whom may have an ownership status. Stewardship Theory involves a more informal relationship which suggests intrinsic rewards such as, socialization, esteem, and self-actualization will guide the performance of the steward towards dong what is best for the firm.

It is important to note that while the initial model implies a progression along the three dimensions, the theoretical perspectives involve a change in emphasis. This concept is presented more clearly in Figure 5.

The individual entrepreneur evolves along a continuum as depicted in Figure 3. A nascent entrepreneur is about to start a small business (Wagner, 2004, Delmar and Davidsson, 2000, Rotefoss and Kolvereid, 2005; and Diochon et al, 2008). Novice entrepreneurs have newly acquired ownership of a small business (Westhead et al, 2005a and 2005b). Over time the entrepreneur will become experienced in dealing with the variety of small business issues. Two types of individuals will be identified as the entrepreneurial process continues. A serial entrepreneur will move from one small business to another. A portfolio entrepreneur will possess multiple small businesses at the same time. These individuals are referred to as "habitual" entrepreneurs because of their on-going entrepreneurial activities and a desire to

*Figure 2. The three-dimensional developmental model*
*Adapted from Gersick et al 1997*

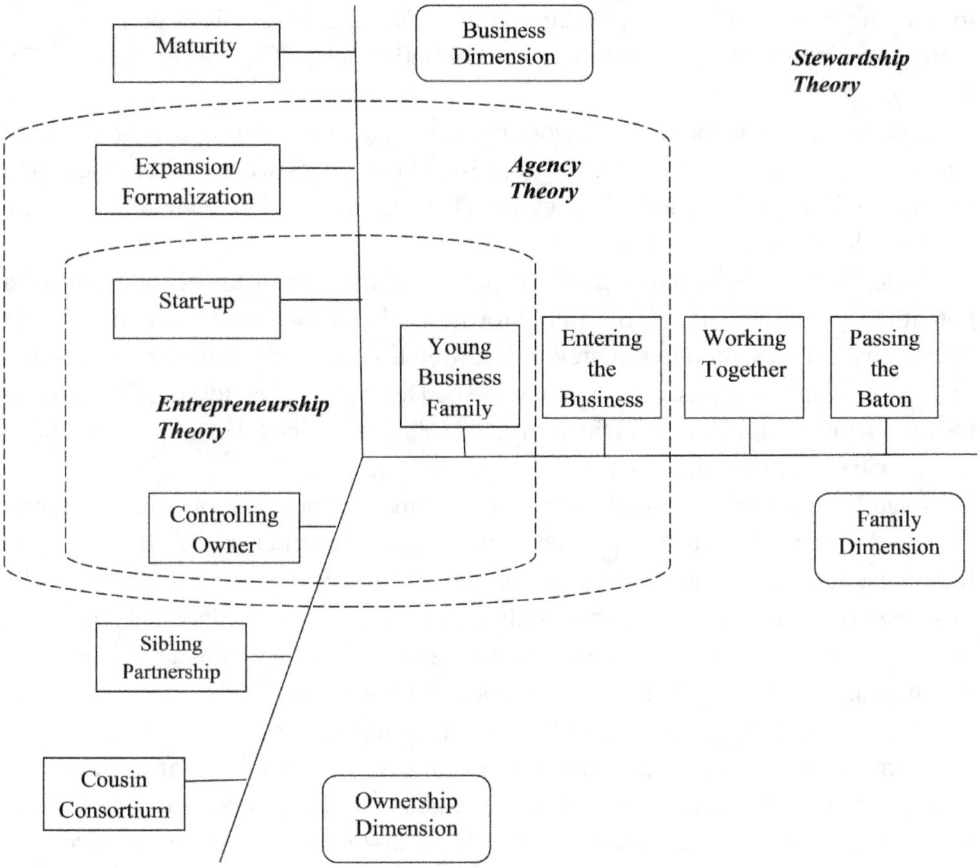


*Figure 3. The entrepreneur continuum*

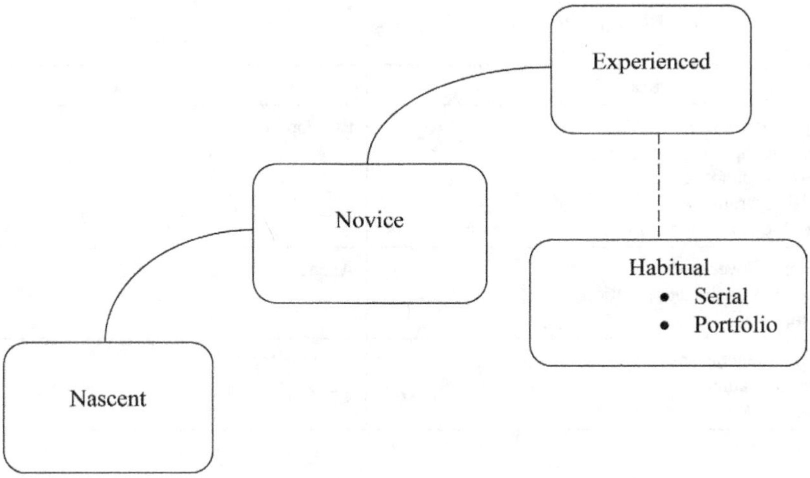

search out new opportunities. Another perspective suggests that the individual will remain involved in one small business and will focus upon management issues formalizing business processes (Carland and Carland, 1992). This perspective is represented in the emphasis of the concepts of both Agency Theory and Stewardship Theory.

Table 6 Small Business Framework presents four stages through which a small business might pass on its journey to success. These stages were initially presented in Chapter Ten – Management Processes. They are reviewed here and related to an evolving emphasis of theories.

Stage One: Genesis represents that period of time from the recognition of a potential idea for a business to actually forming a business entity and commencing operations. As presented in the previous section this stage involves the progression of an individual from nascent (Wagner, 2004, Delmar and Davidsson, 2000, Rotefoss and Kolvereid, 2005; and Diochon et al, 2008) to novice (Westhead et al, 2005a and 2005b) entrepreneur.

Stage Two: Grounding involves the establishment of business operations including the delivery of front line products and services. Further, back office support functions, such as accounting are developed. The period of time represented by this stage is fraught with danger regarding the continuation of the small business. Statistics show that this is when most businesses fail (Industry Canada, 2010; Small Business administration, 2010; and Zantanos and Anderson, 2004). These two stages may be viewed through the lens of Entrepreneurship Theory.

Stage Three: Governance represents the formalization of business functions. The operations which facilitate conducting business are developed to a point where they are consistent and repeatable. In this form the processes may be used to support expansion if this is the goal of the small business. Further, with expansion will come the necessity to hire employees because of increased sales volumes, or

*Table 6. Small business framework*

| Stages | Theories |
|---|---|
| Stage One: Genesis<br>• Idea to start-up<br>Stage Two: Grounding<br>• Establish operations<br>• Survive the period when most fail or cease operations | Entrepreneurship |
| Stage Three: Governance<br>• Expand or consolidate operations<br>• Hire employees | Agency |
| Stage Four: Generations<br>• Succession planning<br>• Establish and maintain entity | Stewardship |

to acquire necessary skills. These formalized activities may be analyzed in relation to Agency Theory (Ross, 1973; and Jensen & Meckling, 1976). The entrepreneur will establish a formal relationship with employees to promote alignment of objectives. The alignment process will, in turn, facilitate the development of repeatable business functions.

Finally, Stage Four: Generations represents the evolution of the small business into an on-going thriving entity which will exist beyond the tenure of the founding entrepreneur. It wil be necessary to develop plans for succession. Usually, these plans involve passing the small business from one generation to the next within a family. However, this does not necessarily have to be the case. Indeed, the small business may be sold to a non-family member. In either case this transition represents the success of the small business as it proceeds to subsequent generations. Stewardship Theory applies in the case of passing the small business to the next generation, whether it is to a family or non-family member. The non-family member will recognize the value of the entity through the decision to purchase the business. They will act as a steward in order to maintain the valuable asset.

A family member will act in a similar manner. However, there will be two differences. First, as determined by Hunter and Kazakoff (2008) a family member must voluntarily step forward to take over the small business from the previous generation. Hunter and Kazakoff (2008) coined the term "Multi-Generation Hero" (MGH) for this individual because this person recognizes the value of the family asset and is prepared to work toward maintaining the small business within the family. Second, the multi-generation hero also recognizes that the small business is a family asset that must be maintained for all family members, even those who do not participate in the business.

Figure 4 the Small Business Continuum presents the framework material from Table 6 in the form of a continuum, again depicting the small business journey to success. The continuum includes further elaboration of the factors for each of the stages.

Recall that Stage One: Genesis involves the evolution of the nascent entrepreneur's idea through to start-up of the small business. Early in the existence of the small business the entrepreneur is considered a novice who is learning the functions required in operating a small business. Stage Two: Grounding necessitates the development of repeatable business processes regarding delivery of the primary product or service as well as secondary support functions. In this stage the entrepreneur, gaining experience, will transition into performing the administration of the small business. In general, the administration function involves the performance of business operations. The focus is on efficiency. Thus, given a business process the entrepreneur will attempt to complete the task through minimal effort. Stage Three: Governance involves a separation from "doing" to "supervising". The small

*Figure 4. Small business continuum*

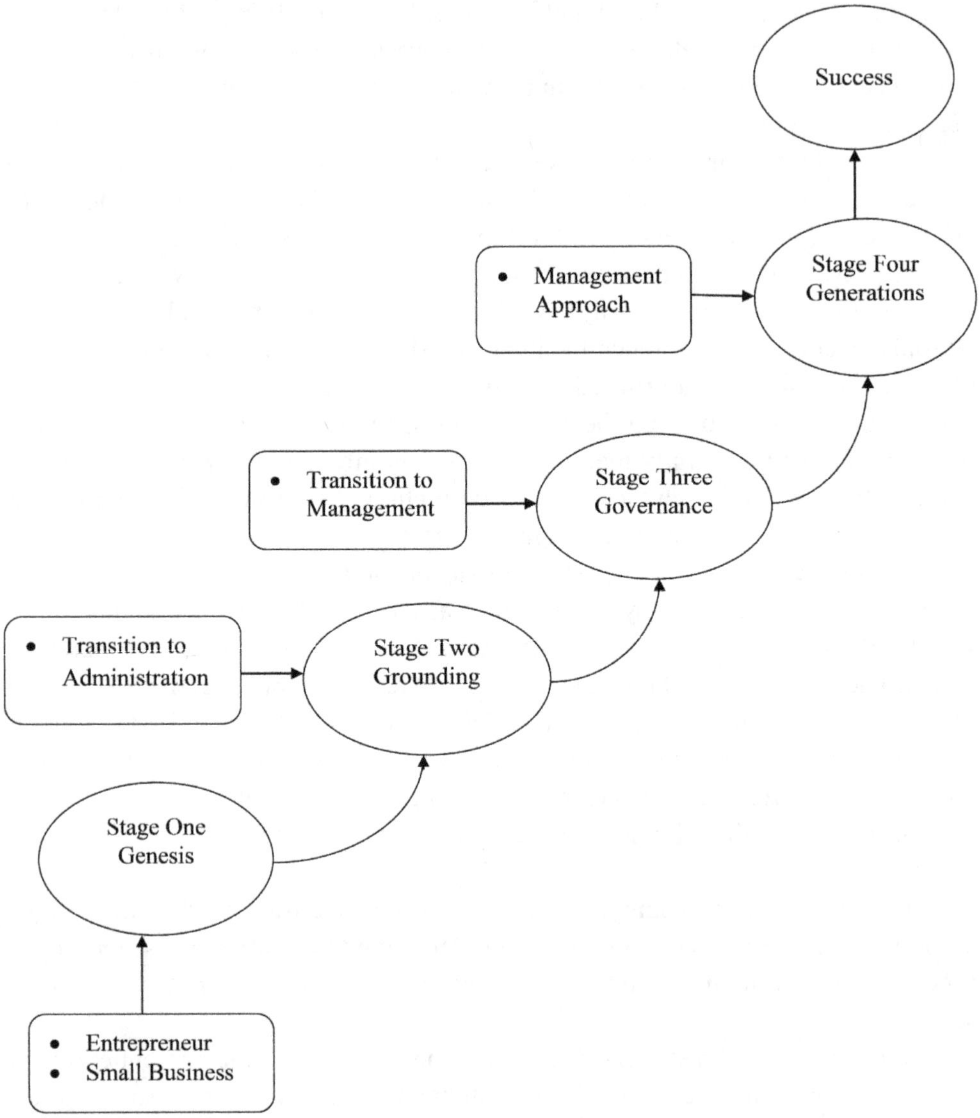


business grows in sales volume necessitating the acquisition further skills through hiring employees. The entrepreneur steps away from hands-on activities and transitions into the management of the small business. In general, management involves providing direction and guidance to individuals who perform the necessary tasks. Also, during and after completion of the task, control, in the form of supervision, must exist to ensure the task is carried out correctly and is completed in the appropriate manner. Thus, the entrepreneur, through management, will set general goals for employees and objectives relating to performing tasks. The focus here shifts to effectiveness. This represents a change from Stage Three. Rather than attempting to complete a task with minimal effort (efficiency) the objective or outcome of the task is considered which leads to more effective performance. Stage Four: Generations leads to a more long term management approach. The small business is now considered an on-going entity which may exist beyond the tenure of the founding entrepreneur. An example of taking a long term perspective involves succession planning. This plan could involve passing the small business to a subsequent generation family member or the sale of the business to a non-family member. In either, case the small business will continue and will be considered successful.

Another perspective on the small business journey to success is presented in Figure 5, the Evolution of Emphasis. This figure shows that the series of three theo-

*Figure 5. Evolution of emphasis*
*Adapted from Hunter and Kazakoff, 2008:184*

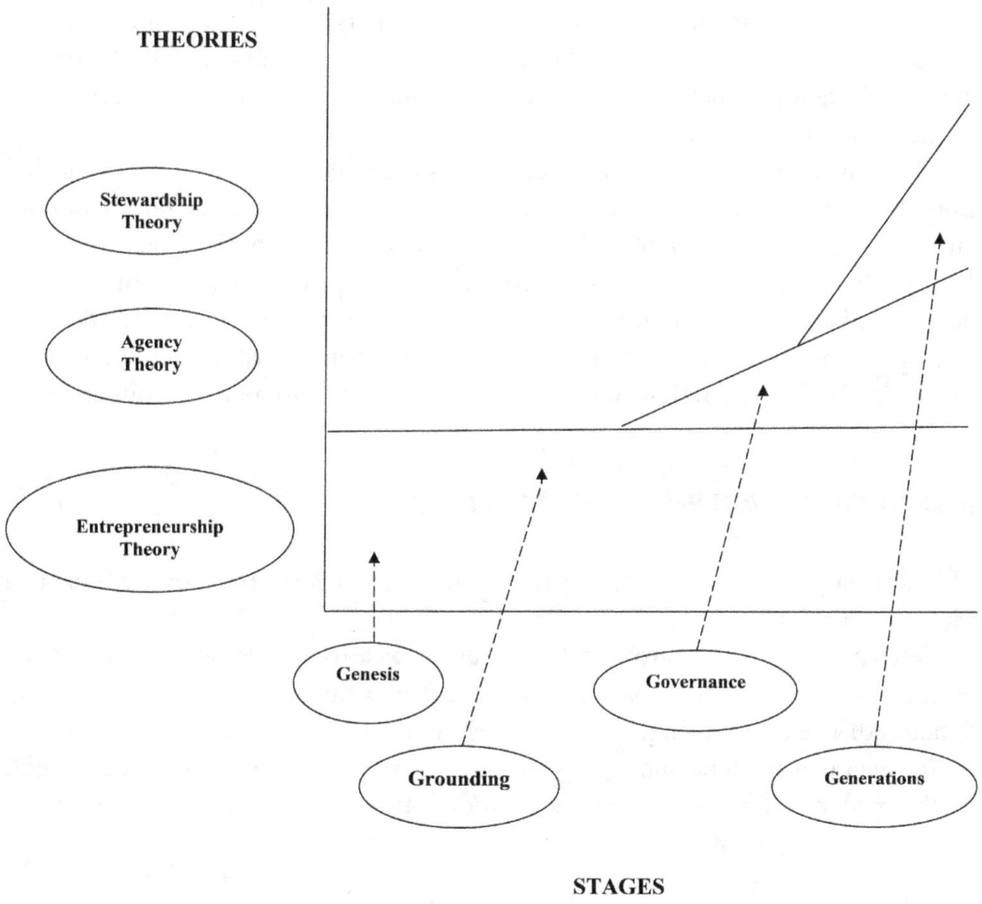

ries is not a distinct sequential process but, as the title suggests, is meant to imply an evolutionary change of emphasis from the founding entrepreneur who initiates the small business; through grounding; potential growth requiring governance; to the eventual recognition of a valuable asset as the small business exists beyond the tenure of the founding entrepreneur.

The stages labelled Genesis and grounding relate to Entrepreneurship Theory where the small business is formed and operations are established. The founding entrepreneur takes an innovative approach to identifying a business opportunity; forms an entity to address the opportunity; and establishes a viable operation. Figure 5 shows that the entrepreneurial approach carries on throughout the life of the small business. Subsequent owners, whether family of non-family members, may change the direction of the small business. It is, however, the entrepreneurial approach which will continue to form the base and support the on-going operation of the small business.

In the Governance stage the small business grows and/or new skills become required. Non-family members may be hired or family members brought into the business in management positions, but not necessarily ownership positions. As an approach to ensure the goals of these new individuals are aligned with the founding entrepreneur Agency Theory applies. An employment contract represents the method to ensure this alignment.

The final stage in Figure 5 is Generations. In this stage ownership is transferred from the founding entrepreneur. The recipient of ownership may be family or non-family; and may also be an individual or a group. If the small business is recognized as a valuable asset and if the resource is going to continue stewardship Theory applies. For a small business to continue it is necessary for a steward to emerge who will make decisions which consider issues beyond the operation of the small business. The term "Multi-Generation Hero" (MGH) has emerged to represent this steward.

## BALANCED MATURITY FRAMEWORK

This section provides a brief review of the context and description of the Balanced Maturity Framework.

Few small businesses grow and even fewer exist for any length of time. However, a small business does mature. The basic management functions become more structured. The use of technology becomes more sophisticated.

In general, a small business progresses at its own rate through a series of stages. As the small business matures the use of information becomes more formalized into computer-based systems. Further, the small business shifts from an internal emphasis to one of dealing with external entities such as customers and suppliers. Neither ceases, there is just a change in emphasis. This shift contributes to the attempt by the small business to create and maintain competitive advantage.

Internally, a series of three theories depicts the evolution of the small business. At the start of a small business Entrepreneurship Theory applies. It relates how the establishment of a small business involves an individual (Entrepreneur) accepting risk and taking an innovative approach to providing a product or service. Next is Agency Theory. As the small business hires people to work in the business there is a need to ensure they perform in a manner expected by the entrepreneur. As the principle the entrepreneur will ensure the employee (agent) performs the necessary task. This is the start of the entrepreneur moving from a doer to a supervisor. This supervision may be accomplished informally or more formally through a job description. Eventually, the entrepreneur will move on. This may be to pursue other ventures or it may relate to the age of the entrepreneur and their desire to retire. Someone will step forward to take over the small business. In this case Stewardship Theory applies. This takeover may or may not involve a family member. If it does the term used is multi-generation hero (MGH).

Externally, as the small business matures the emphasis will shift to customers and suppliers and other entities outside the business. In order to accomplish this more sophisticated management processes will be necessary supported by information systems.

The Balanced Maturity Framework in Figure 6 outlines three dimensions which facilitate the evolution of the small business and its maturing approach to near-term and long-term operations. The framework depicts a balanced approach to the evolution of the small business. A balance will ensure that at each stage of the dimensions there is support. As there is a shift in focus from internal processes to relationships with external entities an appropriate level of sophistication is required in the technology and information systems.

## CONCLUSION

This chapter culminates the description of context information in support of the Balanced Maturity Framework. Small business will mature. The management processes will become more structured and the technology will become more sophisticated in support of the processes. A balanced approach will ensure the appropriate level

*Figure 6. Balanced maturity framework*

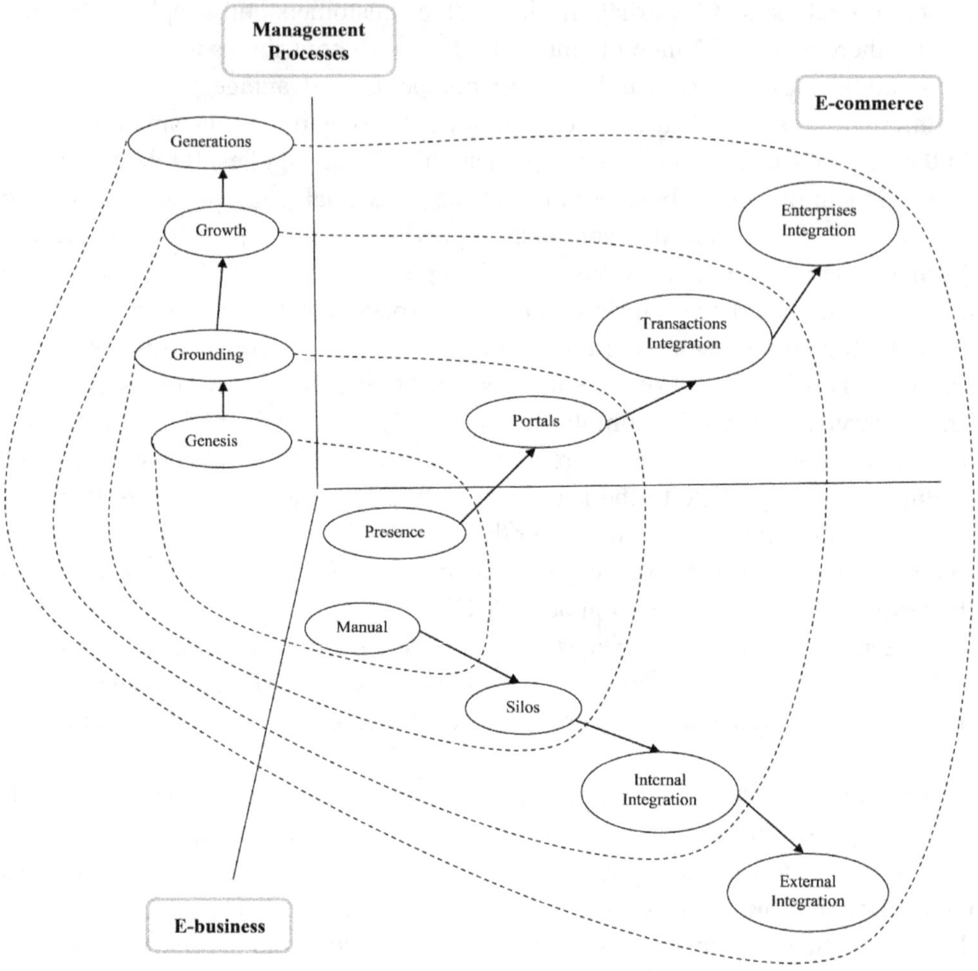


of technology will support the necessary management processes. With all of these dimensions in the Balanced Maturity Framework working together performance of the small business will improve and it will be possible to create and maintain competitive advantage.

## REFERENCES

Adizes, I. (1979). Organizational passages: Diagnosing and treating life cycle problems in organizations. *Organizational Dynamics*, *8*(1), 3–24. doi:10.1016/0090-2616(79)90001-9

Ang, J., Cole, R., & Lin, J. (2000). Agency costs and ownership structure. *The Journal of Finance*, *55*(1), 81–106. doi:10.1111/0022-1082.00201

Barrett, R., & Mayson, S. (2007). Human resource management in growing small firms. *Journal of Small Business and Enterprise Development*, *14*(2), 307–320. doi:10.1108/14626000710746727

Bessant, J., Burkinshaw, J., & Delbridge, R. (20040. Innovation as usual. *Business Strategy Review*, 15(3), 32-35.

Bharadwaj, A. S. (2000). A resource-based perspective on information technology capability and firm performance, an empirical investigation. *Management Information Systems Quarterly*, *24*(1), 169–196. doi:10.2307/3250983

Block, J. H., & Wagner, M. (2010). Necessity and opportunity entrepreneurs in Germany: Characteristics and earnings differential. *Small Business Review*, *62*, 154–174.

Carland, J. C., & Carland, J. W. (1992). Managers, small business owners and entrepreneurs: The cognitive dimension. *Journal of Business and Entrepreneurship*, *4*(2), 55–66.

Carland, J. W., Hoy, F., Bolton, W. R., & Carland, J. A. (1984). Differentiating entrepreneurs from small business owners: A conceptualization. *Academy of Management Review*, *9*, 354–359.

Carneiro, A. (2007). What is required for growth? *Business Strategy Series*, *8*(1), 51–57. doi:10.1108/17515630710686888

Casson, M. (2003). Entrepreneurship, business culture and the theory of the firm, in Handbook of Entrepreneurship Research: An Interdisciplinary Survey and Introduction, Editors Acs, Z. J. & Audretch, D. B. Dordretch: Kluwer Academic Publishers, 223-246.

Chrisman, J. J., Chua, J. H., & Litz, R. A. (2004). Comparing the agency costs of family and non-family firms: Conceptual issues and exploratory evidence. *Entrepreneurship Theory and Practice*, *28*(4), 335–354. doi:10.1111/j.1540-6520.2004.00049.x

Churchill, N., & Lewis, V. (1983). The five stages of small business growth. *Harvard Business Review*, *61*(3), 30–50.

Clark, D. N. (2010). Innovation management in SMEs: Active innovators in New Zealand. *Journal of Small Business and Entrepreneurship*, *23*(4), 601–619. doi:10.1080/08276331.2010.10593504

Craig, J., & Dibrell, C. (2006). The natural environment, and firm performance: A comparative study. *Family Business Review, 19*(4), 275–288. doi:10.1111/j.1741-6248.2006.00075.x

Curran, J. (1986). *Bolton 15 Years on: A Review and Analysis of Small Business Research in Britain 1977-1986*. London: Small Business Research Trust.

Davis, J. H., Schoorman, F. D., & Donaldson, L. (1997). Toward a stewardship theory of management. *Academy of Management Review, 22*(1), 20–47.

Delmar, F., & Davidsson, P. (2000). Where do they come from? Prevalence and characteristics of nascent entrepreneurs. *Entrepreneurship and Regional Development, 12*(1), 1–23. doi:10.1080/089856200283063

Deshpande, S., & Golhar, D. (1994). HRM practices in large and small manufacturing firms: A comparative study. *Journal of Small Business Management, 32*(2), 49–56.

Devaraj, S., Krajewski, L., & Wei, J. C. (2007). Impact of e-business technologies on operational performance: The role of production information integration in the supply chain. *Journal of Operations Management, 25*(6), 1199–1216. doi:10.1016/j.jom.2007.01.002

Diochan, M., Menzies, T. V., & Gasse, Y. (2008). Exploring the nature and impact of gestation-specific human capital among nascent entrepreneurs. *Journal of Developmental Entrepreneurship, 13*(2), 151–165. doi:10.1142/S1084946708000909

Donaldson, L., & Davis, J. H. (1989). CEO governance and shareholder returns: Agency theory and stewardship theory. Academy of Management Annual Meeting, Washington, DC.

Donaldson, L., & Davis, J. H. (1991). Stewardship theory or agency theory: CEO governance and shareholder returns. *Australian Journal of Management, 16*(1), 49–64. doi:10.1177/031289629101600103

Downs, A. (1967). The life cycle of bureaus. In A. Downs (Ed.), *Inside Bureaucracy*. San Francisco: Little Brown & Co. and Rand Corporation.

Drucker, P. F. (1998). The discipline of innovation. *Harvard Business Review, 76*(5), 143–159. PMID:10187245

DTI. (2003). *The Small Business Services; National Statistics*, Department of Trade and Industry. www.sbs.gov.uk

Duberley, J., & Walley, P. (1995). Assessing the adoption of HRM by small and medium sized manufacturing organizations. *International Journal of Human Resource Management*, *6*(4), 891–909. doi:10.1080/09585199500000052

Edvinsson, L., & Malone, M. S. (1997). *Intellectual Capital: Realizing Your Company's True Value by Finding its Hidden Brainpower*. New York, NY: Harper Collins Business.

Fama, E. F., & Jensen, M. C. (1983). Agency problems and residual claims. *The Journal of Law & Economics*, *26*(2), 327–349. doi:10.1086/467038

Feindt, S., Jeffcoate, J., & Chapell, C. (2002). Identifying success factors for rapid growth in SME e-commerce. *Small Business Economics*, *19*(1), 51–62. doi:10.1023/A:1016165825476

Friedman, S. (1989). Conflict inherited: Sibling rivalry in family firms. Paper presented at the Academy of Management Meetings, Washington, DC.

Gersick, K. E., Davis, J. A., Hampton, M. M., & Lansberg, I. (1997). *Generation to Generation: Life Cycles of the Family Business*. Boston: Harvard Business School Press.

Grandon, E. E., & Pearson, J. M. (2004). Electronic commerce adoption: An empirical study of small and medium US businesses. *Information & Management*, *42*(1), 197–216. doi:10.1016/j.im.2003.12.010

Handler, W. C. (1991). Key interpersonal relationships of next-generation family members in family firms. *Journal of Small Business Management*, *29*(3), 21–32.

Heneman, H., & Berkley, R. (1999). Applicant attraction practices and outcomes among small businesses. *Journal of Small Business Management*, *37*(1), 53–74.

Hornsby, J., & Kuratko, D. (2003). Human resource management in US small business: A replication and extension. *Journal of Developmental Entrepreneurship*, *8*(1), 73–92.

Huang, C. J., & Liu, C. J. (2005). Exploraiton for the relationship between innovation, IT and performance. *Journal of Intellectual Capital*, *6*(2), 237–252. doi:10.1108/14691930510592825

Hunter, M. G., & Kazakoff, D. (2008). *Little Empires: Multi-Generation Small Business in Southern Alberta, CANADA*. Melbourne: Heidelberg Press.

Industry Canada. (2010). *Key Small Business Statistics*, (Catalogue No. Iu186-1/2010-2E), ISSN 1718-3456, Ottawa: Canadian Government Publishing Centre.

Jensen, M. C., & Luthans, F. (2006). Relationship between entrepreneurs' psychological capital and their authentic leadership. *Journal of Managerial Issues, 18*(2), 254–273.

Jensen, M. C., & Meckling, W. (1976). The theory of the firm: Managerial behaviour, agency costs, and ownership structure. *Journal of Financial Economics, 3*(4), 305–360. doi:10.1016/0304-405X(76)90026-X

Karagozoglu, N., & Lindell, M. (2004). Electronic commerce strategy, operations, and performance in small and medium-sized enterprises. *Journal of Small Business and Enterprise Development, 11*(3), 290–301. doi:10.1108/14626000410551555

Kazanjian, R. (1988). Relation of dominant problems to stages of growth in technology-based new ventures. *Academy of Management Journal, 31*(2), 257–279. doi:10.2307/256548

Kirzner, I. (1973). *Competition and Entrepreneurship*. Chicago: Chicago University Press.

Kmieciak, R., Michna, A., & Meczynska, A. (2012). Innovativeness, empowerment and IT capability: Evidence from SMEs. *Industrial Management & Data Systems, 112*(5), 707–728. doi:10.1108/02635571211232280

Koh, S. C. L., & Maguire, S. (2004). Identifying the adoption of e-business and knowledge management within SMEs. *Journal of Small Business and Enterprise Development, 11*(3), 338–348. doi:10.1108/14626000410551591

Korper, S., & Ellis, J. (2001). *The E-Commerce Book*. San Diego, CA: Academic Press.

Kotey, B., & Sheridan, A. (2001). Gender and the practice of HRM in small business. *Asia Pacific Journal of Human Resources, 39*(3), 23–40. doi:10.1177/103841110103900303

Laurence, G. (2001). *Fast Growth: How to Attain it, How to Sustain it*. Chicago, IL: Kaplan Professional Company.

Lester, D. L., & Parnell, J. A. (2006). The complete life cycle of a family business. *Journal of Applied Management and Entrepreneurship, 11*(3), 3–22.

Lester, D. L., & Tran, T. T. (2008). Information technology capabilities: Suggestions for SME growth. Institute of Behavioral and Applied Management, 72-88.

Maiga, A. S., & Jacobs, F. A. (2009). Performance impacts of extent of information technology usage. *Journal of International Technology and Information Management, 18*(3/4), 277–298.

Makadok, R. (2001). Toward a synthesis of the resource-based and dynamic-capability views of rent creation. *Strategic Management Journal, 22*(5), 387–401. doi:10.1002/smj.158

Mata, F. J., Fuerst, W. L., & Barney, J. B. (1995). Information technology and sustained competitive advantage, a resource-based analysis. *Management Information Systems Quarterly, 19*(4), 487–505. doi:10.2307/249630

McAdam, R., Reid, R., & Mitchell, N. (2010). Longitudinal development of innovation implementation in family-based SMEs: The effects of critical incidents. *International Journal of Entrepreneurial Behaviour & Research*, 437-456.

McEvoy, G. (1984). Small Business personnel practices. *Journal of Small Business Management, 22*(4), 1–8.

Mehrtens, J., Cragg, P. B., & Mills, A. M. (2001). A model of internet adoption by SMEs. *Information & Management, 39*(3), 165–176. doi:10.1016/S0378-7206(01)00086-6

Miller, D., & Friesen, P. (1984). A longitudinal study of the corporate life cycle. *Management Science, 30*(10), 1161–1183. doi:10.1287/mnsc.30.10.1161

Morse, E. A., Fowler, S. W., & Lawrence, T. B. (2007). The impact of virtual embeddedness on new venture survival: Overcoming the liabilities of newness. *Entrepreneurship Theory & Practice, 31*(2), 139–159. doi:10.1111/j.1540-6520.2007.00167.x

Mowday, R., Porter, L., & Steers, R. (1982). *Organizational Linkages: The Psychology of Commitment, Absenteeism, and Turnover*. New York: Academic Press.

O'Gorman, C. (2001). The sustainability of growth in small and medium-sized enterprises. *International Journal of Entrepreneurial Behaviour & Research, 7*(2), 60–75. doi:10.1108/13552550110396095

O'Reilly, C., & Chatman, J. (1986). Organizational commitment and psychological attachment: The effects of compliance, identification, and internalization on prosocial behavior. *The Journal of Applied Psychology, 71*(3), 492–499. doi:10.1037/0021-9010.71.3.492

Parrott, G., Roomi, M. A., & Holliman, D. (2010). An analysis of marketing programmes adopted by regional small and medium-sized enterprises. *Journal of Small Business and Enterprise Development, 17*(2), 184–203. doi:10.1108/14626001011041201

Pavic, S., Koh, S. C. L., Simpson, M., & Padmore, J. (2007). Could e-business create a competitive advantage in UK SMEs? *Benchmarking: An International Journal, 14*(3), 320–351. doi:10.1108/14635770710753112

Powell, T. C., & Dent-Micallef, A. (1997). Information technology as competitive advantage: The role of human, business, and technology resources. *Strategic Management Journal, 18*(5), 375–405. doi:10.1002/(SICI)1097-0266(199705)18:5<375::AID-SMJ876>3.0.CO;2-7

Premkumar, G. (2003). A meta-analysis of research on information technology implementation in small business. *Journal of Organizational Computing and Electronic Commerce, 13*(2), 91–121. doi:10.1207/S15327744JOCE1302_2

Pretorius, M., Millard, S. M., & Kruger, M. E. (2006). The relationship between implementation, creativity and innovation in small business ventures. *Management Dynamics, 15*(1), 2–13.

Quinn, R., & Cameron, K. (1983). Organizational life cycles and shifting criteria of effectiveness: Some preliminary evidence. *Management Science, 29*(1), 33–41. doi:10.1287/mnsc.29.1.33

Rao, S. S., Metts, G., & Mora-Monge, C. A. (2003). Electronic commerce development in small and medium sized enterprises; A stage model and its implications. *Business Process Management Journal, 9*(1), 11–32. doi:10.1108/14637150310461378

Rodgers, J. A., Yen, D. C., & Chou, D. C. (2002). Developing e-business: A strategic approach. *Information Management & Computer Security, 10*(4), 184–192. doi:10.1108/09685220210436985

Roos, J., Roos, G., Dragonetti, N. C., & Edvinsson, L. (1997). *Intellectual capital: Navigating the New Business Landscape*. London: Macmillan Press.

Ross, S. A. (1973). The economic theory of agency: The principal's problem. *The American Economic Review, 63*(2), 134–139.

Rotefoss, B., & Kolvereid, L. (2005). Aspiring, nascent, and fledgling entrepreneurs: An investigation of the business start-up process. *Entrepreneurship and Regional Development, 17*(2), 109–127. doi:10.1080/08985620500074049

Salojarvi, S., Furu, P., & Sveiby, K. E. (2005). Knowledge management and growth in Finnish SMEs. *Journal of Knowledge Management, 9*(2), 103–122. doi:10.1108/13673270510590254

Schulze, W. S., Lubatkin, M., Dina, R., & Buchholtz, A. (2001). Agency relationships in family firms: Theory and evidence. *Organization Science*, *12*(2), 99–116. doi:10.1287/orsc.12.2.99.10114

Schumpeter, J. A. (1934). The Theory of Economic Development. New Brunswick, NP: Transaction Publishers.

Scott, M., & Bruce, R. (1987). Five stages of growth in small business. *Long Range Planning*, *20*(3), 45–52. doi:10.1016/0024-6301(87)90071-9

Shleifer, A., & Vishny, R. W. (1997). A survey of corporate governance. *The Journal of Finance*, *52*(2), 759–783. doi:10.1111/j.1540-6261.1997.tb04820.x

Small Business Administration. (2010). SBA website www.sba.gov, retrieved July 19, 2011.

Smith, C. A., Organ, D., & Near, J. (1983). Organizational citizenship behavior: Its nature and antecedents. *The Journal of Applied Psychology*, *68*(4), 653–663. doi:10.1037/0021-9010.68.4.653

Smith, M. J. (2004). Steward leadership in the public sector. *Global Virtue Ethics Review*, *5*(3), 120–150.

Stanworth, J., & Curran, J. (1986). Growth and the small firm. In J. Curran, J. Stanworth, & D. Watkins (Eds.), *The Survival of the Small Firm* (Vol. 2). Aldershot: Gower.

Straub, D., & Klein, R. (2001). E-competitive transformations. *Business Horizons*, *44*(3), 3–12. doi:10.1016/S0007-6813(01)80029-X

Sveiby, K. E. (1997). *The New Organizational Wealth: Managing and Measuring Knowledge Based Assets*. San Francisco, CA: Berrett-Koehler.

Thong, J., Yap, C., & Raman, K. (1994). Engagement of external expertise in information systems implementation. *Journal of Management Information Systems*, *11*(2), 209–223.

Tippins, M. J., & Sohi, R. S. (2003). IT competency and firm performance, is organizational learning a missing link? *Strategic Management Journal*, *24*(8), 745–761. doi:10.1002/smj.337

United Nations. (2004). *E-Commerce and Development Report*. Geneva: United Nations.

Villalonga, B., & Amit, R. (2006). How do family ownership, control and management affect firm value? *Journal of Financial Economics*, *80*(2), 385–417. doi:10.1016/j.jfineco.2004.12.005

Wagner, J. (2004). What a difference a Y makes – female and male nascent entrepreneurs in Germany. IZA Discussion Paper No. 1134, Bonn: Institute for the Study of Labour.

Ward, J. L. (1987). *Keeping the family business healthy*. San Fransico: Jossey Boss.

Waters, J. (2000). Living in the world 24x7. *Software Magazine*, *20*(1), 53–57.

Watson, K., Hogarth-Scott, S., & Wilson, N. (1998). Small business start-ups: Success factors and support implications. *International Journal of Entrepreneurial Behaviour & Research*, *4*(3), 217–238. doi:10.1108/13552559810235510

Westhead, P., Ucbasaran, D., & Wright, M. (2005a). Decisions, actions, and performance: Do novice, serial, and portfolio entrepreneurs differ? *Journal of Small Business Management*, *43*(4), 393–417. doi:10.1111/j.1540-627X.2005.00144.x

Westhead, P., Ucbasaran, D., Wright, M., & Binks, M. (2005b). Novice, serial, and portfolio entrepreneur behavior and contributions. *Small Business Economics*, *25*(2), 109–132. doi:10.1007/s11187-003-6461-9

Zhu, Y., Basil, D. Z., & Hunter, M. G. (2009). The extended website stage model: A study of Canadian winery websites. *Canadian Journal of Administrative Sciences*, *26*(4), 286–300. doi:10.1002/cjas.118

Zontanos, G., & Anderson, A. R. (2004). Relationships, marketing and small business: An exploration of links in theory and practice. *Qualitative Market Research*, *7*(3), 228–236. doi:10.1108/13522750410540236

## ADDITIONAL READING

Hunter, M. G., & Kazakoff, D. (2008). *Little Empires: Multi-Generation Small Business in Southern Alberta, CANADA*. Melbourne: Heidelberg Press.

Laurence, G. (2001). *Fast Growth: How to Attain it, How to Sustain it*. Chicago, IL: Kaplan Professional Company.

## KEY TERMS AND DEFINITIONS

**Balanced Maturity Framework:** Small business functions should advance in sophistication in concert.

**Customer Orientation:** A focus on needs of current and potential customers.

**Expansion:** Growth of a small business.

**External Capital:** Relationships external to the small business including image and customer relations.

**Growth:** Increase in sales volume resulting in requirement for more employees.

**Hard Skills:** Technical abilities related to a functional area.

**Human Capital:** Skills and abilities of individuals within the small business.

**Inception:** The commencement of a small business.

**Innovation:** The adoption of processes unique and new to the small business.

**Knowledge Management:** Process of capturing, developing, and sharing information to achieve small business goals.

**Life Cycle Stages:** Major phases through which a small business will pass over time.

**Longevity:** Emphasis on continued existence and less so on growth.

**Maturity:** Management processes of the small business become more sophisticated.

**Multi-Generation Hero:** Someone within a family who steps forward to take on the task of running a small business.

**Organisational Capital:** Internal processes and management of the small business.

**Soft Skills:** Interpersonal abilities.

**Success:** meeting expectations.

**Survival:** continued existence of a small business.

# Conclusion

## INTRODUCTION

This chapter presents a summarized review of the book. The general context of information systems in small business is described in Chapters One, Two, and Three. This includes material on small business, entrepreneurs, and information systems. Chapters Four, Five, Six, Seven, and Eight provide further detail. Each chapter includes a review of related theories along with an applied discussion of information systems aspects including adoption, use, strategy, and competitive advantage by small business. The culmination of this book is presented in Chapters Nine, Ten, Eleven, and Twelve. The three dimensions of the Balanced Maturity Framework are described in separate chapters. These dimensions include Management Processes, E-commerce, and E-business. The final chapter in this book presents a description of the Balanced Maturity Framework. The important aspect of the framework is the balanced approach to maturity.

## REVIEW OF EACH CHAPTER

### Chapter One: Small Business

This chapter presented a detailed description of various aspects of small business. There are many definitions for the term small business. Usually, the definition is based upon the number of employees. But, even this definition varies across government jurisdictions and by business sector within nations. A small business is not a little big business. Small business decisions are affected by limited resources. Further, these limited resources necessitate a focus on a small number of customers. While this focus will support quality personalized service, it may create issues related to external market fluctuations. Small business, of necessity, tends to rely upon family members for various resources, mainly skills. Eventually, however, issues surrounding succession will arise. This major transition requires long term planning in consideration for unique family dynamics. Competitive advantage for a small business is gained through providing quality service at a market oriented price.

This advantage will be maintained internally by a positive culture and externally by a generally recognized reputation throughout the community. Many small businesses fail, mainly due to poor management. To begin, a small business must make a profit. Then success may be demonstrated through growth. Eventually, however, growth may lessen. The market may limit further growth. The small business owner may want to maintain control or may want a revised work/life balance. Thus, another perspective on success is longevity.

## Chapter Two: Entrepreneurs

This chapter introduced the term entrepreneur and described the various types. Entrepreneurs willingly accept risk in their business ventures. Some aggressively pursue growth and expansion. Others take a more conservative approach to their business ventures. The entrepreneurial process involves creativity and innovation. Entrepreneurs tend to be found in small businesses. The attitude and approach may also be discovered in some large companies.

## Chapter Three: Information Systems

This chapter described the components of generic information systems and how data is transformed into information to support decision making by the management of a small business. The transformation process starts by recording transactions related to conducting business. These transactions may relate to invoices, receipts, or time sheets for employees. If there is a low volume of transactions then a manual information system may suffice. However, as the volume increases an automated system becomes appropriate. This chapter focused on automated information systems. Different types of information systems support the various levels of management decision making. Lower level management functions require information systems that support daily operations and making short term decisions. More senior level management functions, while relying upon internal historical data, must also consider external market data to make more long term decisions which will affect the future direction of the small business.

In summary, the stage is set in this section for a more detailed discussion, in subsequent sections, about the use of information systems by small business. This section represents the start of the description of the components of the Balanced Maturity Framework presented later in the book.

## Chapter Four: Theories

This chapter presented general theories, in the form of models and frameworks, employed to conduct research into information systems in small business. There is an absence of a unifying theory but many perspectives have been employed to investigate this topic. Many projects adopt a stages approach to investigate small business use of information systems over time. Also, a life cycle approach has been employed. The following theories have have been used:

- Absorptive Capacity Theory
- Resource-based View Theory
- Theory of Constraints
- Punctuated Equilibrium Theory
- Technology-Organization-Environment Framework
- Relative Advantage and Innovativeness Framework
- Technology Acceptance Model
- Focus-Dominance Model

## Chapter Five: Adoption

This chapter presented a discussion of issues related to adopting information systems in small business. Pressure to adopt information systems will come from external stakeholders and internally due to the perceived benefits. Adopting information systems will lead to significant changes in the management of a small business. More information will be available and the ability to make decisions will be improved.

## Chapter Six: Use

This chapter described how information systems are employed within small business. Lower level management roles use information systems to facilitate short term structured decisions. This relates to payment of invoices, payroll, and other accounting processes. Higher level management roles employ information systems from a strategic perspective to help make long term unstructured decisions. The processes involved in these types of decisions may relate to budgeting, planning, and deciding on the future direction of the small business within the competitive market place.

## Chapter Seven: Strategy

This chapter explored how information systems may be used to support the strategic initiatives in small business. Information systems may be employed to monitor external events. The external business environment may be continuously scanned to identify opportunities or competitive threats. Internally, information systems may be used to assess and improve employee skills as well as promote more sophisticated management processes.

## Chapter Eight: Competitive Advantage

This chapter described how information systems in small business may be employed to address issues in the competitive environment in order to attempt to gain an advantage. An internal focus on processes and on external concentration on the market will contribute to competitive advantage. Thus, information systems in small business could be employed to lower expenses and to increase sales volumes.

In summary, this section provided more detail about the functions of information systems in small business. This discussion further supports the main thesis of the book which is presented in the following section.

## Chapter Nine: Management Processes

This chapter discussed how management of small business evolves over time as the business matures. In general, these processes become more formal and robust. As a small business matures more sophisticated management processes are required. The Framework continuum of sophistication relates to the stages of a small business – Genesis, Grounding, Growth, and Generations.

## Chapter Ten: E-Commerce

This chapter also presented a maturity continuum for the use by the small business for Internet-based technology. This is a specific form of information system based upon current technology. E-commerce involves the sale of products and services via the Internet. The unique properties of the Internet facilitate a variety of E-commerce models. The focus of this chapter is Business to Consumer (B2C). As a small business matures it will tend to incorporate more sophisticated aspects of E-commerce and pass through four stages – Presence, Portals, Transactions Integration, and Enterprises Integration.

## Chapter Eleven: E-Business

This chapter described the third evolution component in the use of information systems by small business. This component relates to the more traditional use of information systems to support management processes and it also incorporates current technology. E-business is a way of conducting business in an electronic form which employs the facilities of the Internet. Recall from Chapter Eleven – E-commerce that electronic commerce involves the sale of products and services on the Internet via the website of a business. E-business includes E-commerce. But, it goes beyond and extends E-commerce to both pre-sales and post-sales services. E-business puts the business in closer contact with its customers, through Customer Relationship Management systems, which improves customer service and loyalty as a consequence.

### Chapter Twelve: Balanced Maturity Framework

This chapter brought all of the previously presented material together by relating management processes, E-commerce, and E-business. The main thesis of the book is presented here in that as the three major components evolve they must do so in a relatively balanced manner.

The presentation of the Balanced Maturity Framework represents the culmination of this book. The framework consists of three dimensions. Management Processes include functions such as planning, organizing, staffing, directing, and controlling. All management levels include these functions. Each level will consist of a different mix of these functions. As a small business matures the Management Processes become more structured and more outward looking. Information for decision making will be more formalized. In support of the more structured Management Processes will be more sophisticated technology. E-commerce will support interaction with customers. More advanced E-business will allow communication with suppliers and support for internal processes.

## CONCLUSION

This chapter has presented a review of the book. It has been suggested that as a small business matures the management processes will become more formal and the supporting technology must, in concert with this formalization, become more sophisticated.

# Related References


Abdullah, M., Ahmad, R., Peck, L. S., Kasirun, Z. M., & Alshammari, F. (2014). Benefits of CMM and CMMI-based software process improvement. In *Software design and development: Concepts, methodologies, tools, and applications* (pp. 1385–1400). Hershey, PA: Information Science Reference; doi:10.4018/978-1-4666-4301-7.ch067

Abu-Shanab, E., & Ghaleb, O. (2012). Adoption of mobile commerce technology: An involvement of trust and risk concerns. *International Journal of Technology Diffusion*, *3*(2), 36–49. doi:10.4018/jtd.2012040104

Adapa, S. (2013). Electronic retailing of prepared food in Australia. In K. Tarnay, S. Imre, & L. Xu (Eds.), *Research and development in e-business through service-oriented solutions* (pp. 280–292). Hershey, PA: Business Science Reference; doi:10.4018/978-1-4666-4181-5.ch014

Aklouf, Y., & Drias, H. (2011). An adaptive e-commerce architecture for enterprise information exchange. In *Enterprise information systems: Concepts, methodologies, tools and applications* (pp. 329–345). Hershey, PA: Business Science Reference; doi:10.4018/978-1-61692-852-0.ch202

Al-Nawayseh, M. K., Alnabhan, M. M., Al-Debei, M. M., & Balachandran, W. (2013). An adaptive decision support system for last mile logistics in e-commerce: A study on online grocery shopping. *International Journal of Decision Support System Technology*, *5*(1), 40–65. doi:10.4018/jdsst.2013010103

Al-Somali, S. A., Clegg, B., & Gholami, R. (2013). An investigation into the adoption and implementation of electronic commerce in Saudi Arabian small and medium enterprises. In *Small and medium enterprises: Concepts, methodologies, tools, and applications* (pp. 816–839). Hershey, PA: Business Science Reference; doi:10.4018/978-1-4666-3886-0.ch040

Al-Somali, S. A., Gholami, R., & Clegg, B. (2013). An investigation into the adoption of electronic commerce among Saudi Arabian SMEs. In M. Khosrow-Pour (Ed.), *E-commerce for organizational development and competitive advantage* (pp. 126–150). Hershey, PA: Business Science Reference; doi:10.4018/978-1-4666-3622-4.ch007

Alavi, S. (2013). Collaborative customer relationship management-co-creation and collaboration through online communities. *International Journal of Virtual Communities and Social Networking*, *5*(1), 1–18. doi:10.4018/jvcsn.2013010101

Alavi, S., & Ahuja, V. (2013). E-commerce in a web 2.0 world: Using online business communities to impact consumer price sensitivity. *International Journal of Online Marketing*, *3*(2), 38–55. doi:10.4018/ijom.2013040103

Alawneh, A., Al-Refai, H., & Batiha, K. (2011). E-business adoption by Jordanian banks: An exploratory study of the key factors and performance indicators. In A. Tatnall (Ed.), *Actor-network theory and technology innovation: Advancements and new concepts* (pp. 113–128). Hershey, PA: Information Science Reference; doi:10.4018/978-1-60960-197-3.ch008

Albuquerque, S. L., & Gondim, P. R. (2012). Applying continuous authentication to protect electronic transactions. In T. Chou (Ed.), *Information assurance and security technologies for risk assessment and threat management: Advances* (pp. 134–161). Hershey, PA: Information Science Reference; doi:10.4018/978-1-61350-507-6.ch005

Alfahl, H., Sanzogni, L., & Houghton, L. (2012). Mobile commerce adoption in organizations: A literature review and future research directions. *Journal of Electronic Commerce in Organizations*, *10*(2), 61–78. doi:10.4018/jeco.2012040104

Aloini, D., Dulmin, R., & Mininno, V. (2013). E-procurement: What really matters in B2B e-reverse auctions. In P. Ordóñez de Pablos, J. Lovelle, J. Gayo, & R. Tennyson (Eds.), *E-procurement management for successful electronic government systems* (pp. 87–113). Hershey, PA: Information Science Reference; doi:10.4018/978-1-4666-2119-0.ch006

Amer, M., & Gómez, J. M. (2010). Measuring B2C quality of electronic service: Towards a common consensus. In I. Lee (Ed.), *Encyclopedia of e-business development and management in the global economy* (pp. 135–143). Hershey, PA: Business Science Reference; doi:10.4018/978-1-61520-611-7.ch014

Amer, M., & Gómez, J. M. (2012). Measuring quality of electronic services: Moving from business-to-consumer into business-to-business marketplace. In E. Kajan, F. Dorloff, & I. Bedini (Eds.), *Handbook of research on e-business standards and protocols: Documents, data and advanced web technologies* (pp. 637–654). Hershey, PA: Business Science Reference; doi:10.4018/978-1-4666-0146-8.ch029

Andriole, S. J. (2010). Business technology strategy for an energy information company. *Journal of Information Technology Research*, *3*(3), 19–42. doi::10.4018/jitr.2010070103

Andriole, S. J. (2010). Templates for the development of business technology strategies. *Journal of Information Technology Research*, *3*(3), 1–10. doi:10.4018/jitr.2010070101

Archer, N. (2010). Electronic marketplace support for B2B business transactions. In *Electronic services: Concepts, methodologies, tools and applications* (pp. 85–93). Hershey, PA: Information Science Reference; doi:10.4018/978-1-61520-967-5.ch007

Archer, N. (2010). Management considerations for B2B online exchanges. In *Business information systems: Concepts, methodologies, tools and applications* (pp. 1740–1747). Hershey, PA: Business Science Reference; doi:10.4018/978-1-61520-969-9.ch105

Arduini, D., Nascia, L., & Zanfei, A. (2012). Complementary approaches to the diffusion of innovation: Empirical evidence on e-services adoption in Italy. *International Journal of E-Services and Mobile Applications*, *4*(3), 42–64. doi:10.4018/jesma.2012070103

Arh, T., Dimovski, V., & Blažic, B. J. (2011). ICT and web 2.0 technologies as a determinant of business performance. In M. Al-Mutairi & L. Mohammed (Eds.), *Cases on ICT utilization, practice and solutions: Tools for managing day-to-day issues* (pp. 59–77). Hershey, PA: Information Science Reference; doi:10.4018/978-1-60960-015-0.ch005

Arikpo, I., Osofisan, A., & Eteng, I. E. (2012). Enhancing trust in e-commerce in developing IT environments: A feedback-based perspective. In A. Usoro, G. Majewski, P. Ifinedo, & I. Arikpo (Eds.), *Leveraging developing economies with the use of information technology: Trends and tools* (pp. 193–203). Hershey, PA: Information Science Reference; doi:10.4018/978-1-4666-1637-0.ch011

Aryanto, V. D., & Chrismastuti, A. A. (2013). Model for digital economy in Indonesia. In I. Oncioiu (Ed.), *Business innovation, development, and advancement in the digital economy* (pp. 60–77). Hershey, PA: Business Science Reference; doi:10.4018/978-1-4666-2934-9.ch005

Asim, M., & Petkovic, M. (2012). Fundamental building blocks for security interoperability in e-business. In E. Kajan, F. Dorloff, & I. Bedini (Eds.), *Handbook of research on e-business standards and protocols: documents, data and advanced web technologies* (pp. 269–292). Hershey, PA: Business Science Reference; doi:10.4018/978-1-4666-0146-8.ch013

Askool, S., Jacobs, A., & Nakata, K. (2013). A method of analysing the use of social networking sites in business. In *IT policy and ethics: Concepts, methodologies, tools, and applications* (pp. 794–813). Hershey, PA: Information Science Reference; doi:10.4018/978-1-4666-2919-6.ch036

Association, I. R. (2013). Enterprise resource planning: Concepts, methodologies, tools, and applications (Vols. 1–3). Hershey, PA: IGI Global; doi:10.4018/978-1-4666-4153-2

Azab, N., & Khalifa, N. (2013). Web 2.0 and opportunities for entrepreneurs: How Egyptian entrepreneurs perceive and exploit web 2.0 technologies. In N. Azab (Ed.), *Cases on web 2.0 in developing countries: Studies on implementation, application, and use* (pp. 1–32). Hershey, PA: Information Science Reference; doi:10.4018/978-1-4666-2515-0.ch001

Azevedo, S. G., & Carvalho, H. (2012). RFID technology in the fashion supply chain: An exploratory analysis. In T. Choi (Ed.), *Fashion supply chain management: Industry and business analysis* (pp. 303–326). Hershey, PA: Information Science Reference; doi:10.4018/978-1-60960-756-2.ch017

Baporikar, N. (2013). ICT challenge for ebusiness in SMEs. *International Journal of Strategic Information Technology and Applications*, *4*(1), 15–26. doi:10.4018/jsita.2013010102

Barbin Laurindo, F. J., Monteiro de Carvalho, M., & Shimizu, T. (2010). Strategic alignment between business and information technology. In M. Hunter (Ed.), *Strategic information systems: Concepts, methodologies, tools, and applications* (pp. 20–28). Hershey, PA: Information Science Reference; doi:10.4018/978-1-60566-677-8.ch002

Barjis, J. (2012). Software engineering security based on business process modeling. In K. Khan (Ed.), *Security-aware systems applications and software development methods* (pp. 52–68). Hershey, PA: Information Science Reference; doi:10.4018/978-1-4666-1580-9.ch004

Barnes, D., & Hinton, M. (2011). The benefits of an e-business performance measurement system. In N. Shi & G. Silvius (Eds.), *Enterprise IT governance, business value and performance measurement* (pp. 158–169). Hershey, PA: Information Science Reference; doi:10.4018/978-1-60566-346-3.ch011

Bask, A., Lipponen, M., & Tinnilä, M. (2012). E-commerce logistics: A literature research review and topics for future research. *International Journal of E-Services and Mobile Applications*, *4*(3), 1–22. doi:10.4018/jesma.2012070101

Bask, A., & Tinnilä, M. (2013). Impact of product characteristics on supply chains: An analytical literature review. *International Journal of Applied Logistics*, *4*(1), 35–59. doi:10.4018/jal.2013010103

Basu, S. (2012). Direct taxation and e-commerce: Possibility and desirability. In E. Druicã (Ed.), *Digital economy innovations and impacts on society* (pp. 26–48). Hershey, PA: Information Science Reference; doi:10.4018/978-1-4666-1556-4.ch003

Beckinsale, M. (2010). E-business among ethnic minority businesses: The case of ethnic entrepreneurs. In B. Thomas & G. Simmons (Eds.), *E-commerce adoption and small business in the global marketplace: Tools for optimization* (pp. 187–207). Hershey, PA: Business Science Reference; doi:10.4018/978-1-60566-998-4.ch010

Beckinsale, M. (2011). eBusiness among ethnic minority businesses: Ethnic entrepreneurs' ICT adoption and readiness. In S. Sharma (Ed.), E-adoption and socio-economic impacts: Emerging infrastructural effects (pp. 168-189). Hershey, PA: Information Science Reference. doi::10.4018/978-1-60960-597-1.ch009

Bedini, I., Gardarin, G., & Nguyen, B. (2011). Semantic technologies and e-business. In E. Kajan (Ed.), *Electronic business interoperability: Concepts, opportunities and challenges* (pp. 243–278). Hershey, PA: Business Science Reference; doi:10.4018/978-1-60960-485-1.ch011

Beedle, J., & Wang, S. (2013). Roles of a technology leader. In S. Wang & T. Hartsell (Eds.), *Technology integration and foundations for effective leadership* (pp. 228–241). Hershey, PA: Information Science Reference; doi:10.4018/978-1-4666-2656-0.ch013

Belhajjame, K., & Brambilla, M. (2013). Ontological description and similarity-based discovery of business process models. In J. Krogstie (Ed.), *Frameworks for developing efficient information systems: Models, theory, and practice* (pp. 30–50). Hershey, PA: Engineering Science Reference; doi:10.4018/978-1-4666-4161-7.ch002

Benou, P., & Bitos, V. (2010). Developing mobile commerce applications. In M. Khosrow-Pour (Ed.), *E-commerce trends for organizational advancement: New applications and methods* (pp. 1–15). Hershey, PA: Information Science Reference; doi:10.4018/978-1-60566-964-9.ch001

Berisha-Namani, M. (2013). Information systems usage in business and management. In I. Oncioiu (Ed.), *Business innovation, development, and advancement in the digital economy* (pp. 48–59). Hershey, PA: Business Science Reference; doi:10.4018/978-1-4666-2934-9.ch004

Bermúdez, G. M., & Rojas, L. A. (2013). Model-driven engineering for electronic commerce. In V. Díaz, J. Lovelle, B. García-Bustelo, & O. Martínez (Eds.), *Progressions and innovations in model-driven software engineering* (pp. 196–208). Hershey, PA: Engineering Science Reference; doi:10.4018/978-1-4666-4217-1.ch007

Bernardino, J. (2013). Open business intelligence for better decision-making. *International Journal of Information Communication Technologies and Human Development*, *5*(2), 20–36. doi:10.4018/jicthd.2013040102

Berzins, M. (2012). Scams and the Australian e-business environment. In K. Mohammed Rezaul (Ed.), *Strategic and pragmatic e-business: Implications for future business practices* (pp. 156–175). Hershey, PA: Business Science Reference; doi:10.4018/978-1-4666-1619-6.ch007

Binsaleh, M., & Hassan, S. (2011). Systems development methodology for mobile commerce applications. *International Journal of Mobile Computing and Multimedia Communications*, *3*(4), 36–52. doi:10.4018/jmcmc.2011100103

Binsaleh, M., & Hassan, S. (2013). Systems development methodology for mobile commerce applications. In I. Khalil & E. Weippl (Eds.), *Contemporary challenges and solutions for mobile and multimedia technologies* (pp. 146–162). Hershey, PA: Information Science Reference; doi:10.4018/978-1-4666-2163-3.ch009

Blake, R., Gordon, S., & Shankaranarayanan, G. (2013). The role of case-based research in information technology and systems. In P. Isaias & M. Baptista Nunes (Eds.), *Information systems research and exploring social artifacts: approaches and methodologies* (pp. 200–220). Hershey, PA: Information Science Reference; doi:10.4018/978-1-4666-2491-7.ch011

### *Related References*


Boateng, R., Heeks, R., Molla, A., & Hinson, R. (2013). Advancing e-commerce beyond readiness in a developing country: Experiences of Ghanaian firms. In M. Khosrow-Pour (Ed.), *E-commerce for organizational development and competitive advantage* (pp. 1–17). Hershey, PA: Business Science Reference; doi:10.4018/978-1-4666-3622-4.ch001

Bonfatti, F., Monari, P. D., & Martinelli, L. (2011). Business document exchange between small companies. In E. Kajan (Ed.), *Electronic business interoperability: Concepts, opportunities and challenges* (pp. 482–510). Hershey, PA: Business Science Reference; doi:10.4018/978-1-60960-485-1.ch020

Boucadair, M., & Binet, D. (2014). Issues with current internet architecture. In M. Boucadair & D. Binet (Eds.), *Solutions for sustaining scalability in internet growth* (pp. 1–16). Hershey, PA: Information Science Reference; doi:10.4018/978-1-4666-4305-5.ch001

Bouras, A., Gouvas, P., & Mentzas, G. (2009). A semantic service-oriented architecture for business process fusion. In I. Lee (Ed.), *Electronic business: Concepts, methodologies, tools, and applications* (pp. 504–532). Hershey, PA: Information Science Reference; doi:10.4018/978-1-60566-056-1.ch032

Braun, P. (2011). Advancing women in the digital economy: eLearning opportunities for meta-competency skilling. In *Global business: Concepts, methodologies, tools and applications* (pp. 1978–1990). Hershey, PA: Business Science Reference; doi:10.4018/978-1-60960-587-2.ch708

Brown, M., & Garson, G. (2013). Organization behavior and organization theory. In *Public information management and e-government: Policy and issues* (pp. 160–195). Hershey, PA: Information Science Reference; doi:10.4018/978-1-4666-3003-1.ch007

Brown, M., & Garson, G. (2013). The information technology business model. In *Public information management and e-government: Policy and issues* (pp. 76–98). Hershey, PA: Information Science Reference; doi:10.4018/978-1-4666-3003-1.ch004

Burete, R., Badica, A., Badica, C., & Moraru, F. (2011). Enhanced reputation model with forgiveness for e-business agents. *International Journal of Agent Technologies and Systems, 3*(1), 11–26. doi:10.4018/jats.2011010102

Business Research and Case Center. (2011). *Cases on business and management in the MENA region: New trends and opportunities*. Hershey, PA: IGI Global; doi:10.4018/978-1-60960-583-4

Bwalya, K. J. (2011). E-commerce penetration in the SADC region: Consolidating and moving forward. In M. Cruz-Cunha & J. Varajão (Eds.), *E-business managerial aspects, solutions and case studies* (pp. 235–253). Hershey, PA: Business Science Reference; doi:10.4018/978-1-60960-463-9.ch014

Charbaji, R., Rebeiz, K., & Sidani, Y. (2010). Antecedents and consequences of the risk taking behavior of mobile commerce adoption in Lebanon. In H. Rahman (Ed.), *Handbook of research on e-government readiness for information and service exchange: Utilizing progressive information communication technologies* (pp. 354–380). Hershey, PA: Information Science Reference; doi:10.4018/978-1-60566-671-6.ch018

Chaturvedi, N. (2013). Collaborative web for natural resources industries. In *Supply chain management: Concepts, methodologies, tools, and applications* (pp. 601–614). Hershey, PA: Business Science Reference; doi:10.4018/978-1-4666-2625-6.ch035

Chen, C., & Yang, S. C. (2008). E-commerce and mobile commerce application adoptions. In A. Becker (Ed.), *Electronic commerce: Concepts, methodologies, tools, and applications* (pp. 826–836). Hershey, PA: Information Science Reference; doi:10.4018/978-1-59904-943-4.ch068

Chen, Q., & Zhang, N. (2013). IT-supported business performance and e-commerce application in SMEs. *Journal of Electronic Commerce in Organizations*, *11*(2), 41–52. doi:10.4018/jeco.2013040104

Chen, T. F. (2011). Emerging business models: Value drivers in e-business 2.0 and towards enterprise 2.0. In T. Chen (Ed.), *Implementing new business models in for-profit and non-profit organizations: Technologies and applications* (pp. 1–28). Hershey, PA: Information Science Reference; doi:10.4018/978-1-60960-129-4.ch001

Chen, T. F. (2011). The critical success factors and integrated model for implementing e-business in Taiwan's SMEs. In *Global business: Concepts, methodologies, tools and applications* (pp. 1109–1133). Hershey, PA: Business Science Reference; doi:10.4018/978-1-60960-587-2.ch416

Chew, E., & Gottschalk, P. (2013). Critical success factors of IT strategy. In *Knowledge driven service innovation and management: IT strategies for business alignment and value creation* (pp. 185–220). Hershey, PA: Business Science Reference; doi:10.4018/978-1-4666-2512-9.ch006

Chew, E., & Gottschalk, P. (2013). Strategic alignment and IT-enabled value creation. In *Knowledge driven service innovation and management: IT strategies for business alignment and value creation* (pp. 141–184). Hershey, PA: Business Science Reference; doi:10.4018/978-1-4666-2512-9.ch005

Chew, E., & Gottschalk, P. (2013). Theories and models of service-oriented firms. In *Knowledge driven service innovation and management: IT strategies for business alignment and value creation* (pp. 1–34). Hershey, PA: Business Science Reference; doi:10.4018/978-1-4666-2512-9.ch001

Chiang, L. (2010). Digital confidence in business: A perspective of information ethics. In M. Pankowska (Ed.), *Infonomics for distributed business and decision-making environments: Creating information system ecology* (pp. 288–300). Hershey, PA: Business Science Reference; doi:10.4018/978-1-60566-890-1.ch017

Chugh, R., & Gupta, P. (2011). A unified view of enablers, barriers, and readiness of small to medium enterprises for e-business adoption. In M. Cruz-Cunha & J. Varajão (Eds.), *E-business issues, challenges and opportunities for SMEs: Driving competitiveness* (pp. 291–312). Hershey, PA: Business Science Reference; doi:10.4018/978-1-61692-880-3.ch017

Clear, F., Woods, A., & Dickson, K. (2013). SME adoption and use of ICT for networked trading purposes: The influence of sector, size and age of firm. In *Small and medium enterprises: Concepts, methodologies, tools, and applications* (pp. 774–791). Hershey, PA: Business Science Reference; doi:10.4018/978-1-4666-3886-0.ch038

Connolly, R. (2013). eCommerce trust beliefs: Examining the role of national culture. In P. Isaias & M. Baptista Nunes (Eds.), Information systems research and exploring social artifacts: Approaches and methodologies (pp. 20-42). Hershey, PA: Information Science Reference. doi::10.4018/978-1-4666-2491-7.ch002

Cormican, K. (2013). Collaborative networks: Challenges for SMEs. In *Small and medium enterprises: Concepts, methodologies, tools, and applications* (pp. 1638–1653). Hershey, PA: Business Science Reference; doi:10.4018/978-1-4666-3886-0.ch083

Costante, E., Petkovic, M., & den Hartog, J. (2013). Trust management and user's trust perception in e-business. In *IT policy and ethics: Concepts, methodologies, tools, and applications* (pp. 64–83). Hershey, PA: Information Science Reference; doi:10.4018/978-1-4666-2919-6.ch004

Costin, Y. (2012). Adopting ICT in the mompreneurs business: A strategy for growth? In C. Romm Livermore (Ed.), *Gender and social computing: Interactions, differences and relationships* (pp. 17–34). Hershey, PA: Information Science Publishing; doi:10.4018/978-1-60960-759-3.ch002

Cox, S. (2013). E-business planning in morphing organizations: Maturity models of business transformation. In E. Li, S. Loh, C. Evans, & F. Lorenzi (Eds.), *Organizations and social networking: Utilizing social media to engage consumers* (pp. 286–312). Hershey, PA: Business Science Reference; doi:10.4018/978-1-4666-4026-9.ch015

Cruz-Cunha, M. M., Moreira, F., & Varajão, J. (2014). *Handbook of research on enterprise 2.0: Technological, social, and organizational dimensions*. Hershey, PA: IGI Global; doi:10.4018/978-1-4666-4373-4

D'Aubeterre, F., Iyer, L. S., Ehrhardt, R., & Singh, R. (2011). Discovery process in a B2B emarketplace: A semantic matchmaking approach. In V. Sugumaran (Ed.), *Intelligent, adaptive and reasoning technologies: New developments and applications* (pp. 80–103). Hershey, PA: Information Science Reference; doi:10.4018/978-1-60960-595-7.ch005

Dabbagh, R. A. (2011). E-business: Concepts and context with illustrative examples of e-business and e-commerce in education. In A. Al Ajeeli & Y. Al-Bastaki (Eds.), *Handbook of research on e-services in the public sector: E-government strategies and advancements* (pp. 450–462). Hershey, PA: Information Science Reference; doi:10.4018/978-1-61520-789-3.ch033

Demirkan, H., & Spohrer, J. C. (2012). Servitized enterprises for distributed collaborative commerce. In S. Galup (Ed.), *Technological applications and advancements in service science, management, and engineering* (pp. 70–83). Hershey, PA: Business Science Reference; doi:10.4018/978-1-4666-1583-0.ch005

Denno, P. (2013). Trade collaboration systems. In *Supply chain management: Concepts, methodologies, tools, and applications* (pp. 615–633). Hershey, PA: Business Science Reference; doi:10.4018/978-1-4666-2625-6.ch036

Djoleto, W. (2011). E-business efficacious consequences the etiquettes and the business decision making. In O. Bak & N. Stair (Eds.), *Impact of e-business technologies on public and private organizations: Industry comparisons and perspectives* (pp. 278–295). Hershey, PA: Business Science Reference; doi:10.4018/978-1-60960-501-8.ch017

Djoleto, W. (2013). Information technology and organisational leadership. In *Electronic commerce and organizational leadership: Perspectives and methodologies*. Hershey, PA: IGI Global; doi:10.4018/978-1-4666-2982-0.ch003

Djoleto, W. (2013). Cloud computing and ecommerce or ebusiness: "The now it way" – An overview. In *Electronic commerce and organizational leadership: Perspectives and methodologies* (pp. 239–254). Hershey, PA: Business Science Reference; doi:10.4018/978-1-4666-2982-0.ch010

Djoleto, W. (2013). eCommerce and organisational leadership. In Electronic commerce and organizational leadership: Perspectives and methodologies (pp. 99-121). Hershey, PA: Business Science Reference. doi::10.4018/978-1-4666-2982-0.ch005

Djoleto, W. (2013). eCommerce: An overview. In Electronic commerce and organizational leadership: Perspectives and methodologies (pp. 74-98). Hershey, PA: Business Science Reference. doi::10.4018/978-1-4666-2982-0.ch004

Djoleto, W. (2013). Empirical analyses of ecommerce: The findings – A mixed methodology perspective. In *Electronic commerce and organizational leadership: Perspectives and methodologies* (pp. 150–189). Hershey, PA: Business Science Reference; doi:10.4018/978-1-4666-2982-0.ch007

Djoleto, W. (2013). Future endeavours. In *Electronic commerce and organizational leadership: Perspectives and methodologies* (pp. 269–280). Hershey, PA: Business Science Reference; doi:10.4018/978-1-4666-2982-0.ch012

Djoleto, W. (2013). Information technology: The journey. In *Electronic commerce and organizational leadership: Perspectives and methodologies* (pp. 32–54). Hershey, PA: Business Science Reference; doi:10.4018/978-1-4666-2982-0.ch002

Doolin, B., & Ali, E. I. (2012). Mobile technology adoption in the supply chain. In *Wireless technologies: Concepts, methodologies, tools and applications* (pp. 1553–1573). Hershey, PA: Information Science Reference; doi:10.4018/978-1-61350-101-6.ch603

Duin, H., & Thoben, K. (2011). Enhancing the preparedness of SMEs for e-business opportunities by collaborative networks. In M. Cruz-Cunha & J. Varajão (Eds.), *E-business issues, challenges and opportunities for SMEs: Driving competitiveness* (pp. 30–45). Hershey, PA: Business Science Reference; doi:10.4018/978-1-61692-880-3.ch003

Dulai, T., Jaskó, S., & Tarnay, K. (2013). IOTP and payments protocols. In K. Tarnay, S. Imre, & L. Xu (Eds.), *Research and development in e-business through service-oriented solutions* (pp. 20–56). Hershey, PA: Business Science Reference; doi:10.4018/978-1-4666-4181-5.ch002

Dza, M., Fisher, R., & Gapp, R. (2013). Service-dominant logic and supply network management: An efficient business mix? In N. Ndubisi & S. Nwankwo (Eds.), *Enterprise development in SMEs and entrepreneurial firms: Dynamic processes* (pp. 376–389). Hershey, PA: Business Science Reference; doi:10.4018/978-1-4666-2952-3.ch021

Ehsani, E. (2011). Defining e-novation in action. In H. Pattinson & D. Low (Eds.), *E-novation for competitive advantage in collaborative globalization: Technologies for emerging e-business strategies* (pp. 58–74). Hershey, PA: Business Science Reference; doi:10.4018/978-1-60566-394-4.ch005

Ekong, U. O., Ifinedo, P., Ayo, C. K., & Ifinedo, A. (2013). E-commerce adoption in Nigerian businesses: An analysis using the technology-organization-environmental framework. In *Small and medium enterprises: Concepts, methodologies, tools, and applications* (pp. 840–861). Hershey, PA: Business Science Reference; doi:10.4018/978-1-4666-3886-0.ch041

Emens, S. (2010). The new paradigm of business on the internet and its ethical implications. In D. Palmer (Ed.), *Ethical issues in e-business: Models and frameworks* (pp. 15–27). Hershey, PA: Business Science Reference; doi:10.4018/978-1-61520-615-5.ch002

Eriksson, P., Henttonen, E., & Meriläinen, S. (2011). Managing client contacts of small KIBS companies: Turning technology into business. *International Journal of Innovation in the Digital Economy*, *2*(3), 1–10. doi:10.4018/jide.2011070101

Escofet, E., Rodríguez-Fórtiz, M. J., Garrido, J. L., & Chung, L. (2012). Strategic e-business/ IT alignment for SME competitiveness. In *Computer engineering: Concepts, methodologies, tools and applications* (pp. 1427–1445). Hershey, PA: Engineering Science Reference; doi:10.4018/978-1-61350-456-7.ch604

Eze, U. C., & Poong, Y. S. (2013). Consumers' intention to use mobile commerce and the moderating roles of gender and income. In I. Lee (Ed.), *Strategy, adoption, and competitive advantage of mobile services in the global economy* (pp. 127–148). Hershey, PA: Information Science Reference; doi:10.4018/978-1-4666-1939-5.ch007

Eze, U. C., & Poong, Y. S. (2013). The moderating roles of income and age in mobile commerce application. *Journal of Electronic Commerce in Organizations*, *11*(3), 46–67. doi:10.4018/jeco.2013070103

Fehér, P. (2012). Integrating and measuring business and technology services in the context of enterprise architecture. In V. Shankararaman, J. Zhao, & J. Lee (Eds.), *Business enterprise, process, and technology management: Models and applications* (pp. 148–163). Hershey, PA: Business Science Reference; doi:10.4018/978-1-4666-0249-6.ch008

Feja, S., Witt, S., & Speck, A. (2014). Tool based integration of requirements modeling and validation into business process modeling. In *Software design and development: Concepts, methodologies, tools, and applications* (pp. 285–309). Hershey, PA: Information Science Reference; doi:10.4018/978-1-4666-4301-7.ch016

Fengel, J. (2012). Semantic alignment of e-business standards and legacy models. In E. Kajan, F. Dorloff, & I. Bedini (Eds.), *Handbook of research on e-business standards and protocols: Documents, data and advanced web technologies* (pp. 676–704). Hershey, PA: Business Science Reference; doi:10.4018/978-1-4666-0146-8.ch031

Ferreira, M. P. (2013). SMEs and e-business: Implementation, strategies and policy. In *Small and medium enterprises: Concepts, methodologies, tools, and applications* (pp. 97–117). Hershey, PA: Business Science Reference; doi:10.4018/978-1-4666-3886-0.ch006

Fluvià, M., & Rigall-I-Torrent, R. (2013). Public sector transformation and the design of public policies for electronic commerce and the new economy: Tax and antitrust policies. In N. Pomazalová (Ed.), *Public sector transformation processes and internet public procurement: Decision support systems* (pp. 32–57). Hershey, PA: Engineering Science Reference; doi:10.4018/978-1-4666-2665-2.ch003

Franquesa, J., & Brandyberry, A. (2011). Organizational slack and information technology innovation adoption in SMEs. In I. Lee (Ed.), *E-business applications for product development and competitive growth: emerging technologies* (pp. 25–48). Hershey, PA: Business Science Reference; doi:10.4018/978-1-60960-132-4.ch002

Fries, T. P. (2014). Reengineering structured legacy system documentation to UML object-oriented artifacts. In *Software design and development: Concepts, methodologies, tools, and applications* (pp. 749–771). Hershey, PA: Information Science Reference; doi:10.4018/978-1-4666-4301-7.ch036

Galinski, C., & Beckmann, H. (2014). Concepts for enhancing content quality and eaccessibility: In general and in the field of eprocurement. In *Assistive technologies: Concepts, methodologies, tools, and applications* (pp. 180–197). Hershey, PA: Information Science Reference; doi:10.4018/978-1-4666-4422-9.ch010

Gan, J., & Gutiérrez, J. A. (2011). Viable business models for m-commerce: The key components. In M. Cruz-Cunha & F. Moreira (Eds.), *Handbook of research on mobility and computing: Evolving technologies and ubiquitous impacts* (pp. 837–852). Hershey, PA: Information Science Reference; doi:10.4018/978-1-60960-042-6.ch052

Garito, M. (2012). Mobile business and mobile TV: Available technologies, future opportunities and new marketing trends. In E-marketing: Concepts, methodologies, tools, and applications (pp. 1240-1251). Hershey, PA: Business Science Reference. doi::10.4018/978-1-4666-1598-4.ch072

Ghobakhloo, M., & Zulkifli, N. (2013). Adoption of mobile commerce: The impact of end user satisfaction on system acceptance. *International Journal of E-Services and Mobile Applications*, *5*(1), 26–50. doi:10.4018/jesma.2013010102

Gill, A. Q., & Bunker, D. (2014). SaaS requirements engineering for agile development. In *Software design and development: Concepts, methodologies, tools, and applications* (pp. 351–380). Hershey, PA: Information Science Reference; doi:10.4018/978-1-4666-4301-7.ch019

Gimenez, J. (2014). Reflections of professional practice: Using electronic discourse analysis networks (EDANs) to examine embedded business emails. In H. Lim & F. Sudweeks (Eds.), *Innovative methods and technologies for electronic discourse analysis* (pp. 327–345). Hershey, PA: Information Science Reference; doi:10.4018/978-1-4666-4426-7.ch015

Gionis, G. A., Schroth, C., & Janner, T. (2011). Advancing interoperability for agile cross-organisational collaboration: A rule-based approach. In Y. Charalabidis (Ed.), *Interoperability in digital public services and administration: Bridging e-government and e-business* (pp. 238–253). Hershey, PA: Information Science Reference; doi:10.4018/978-1-61520-887-6.ch013

Gnoni, M. G., & Rollo, A. (2011). A content analysis for evaluating RFID applications in supply network management. In I. Mahdavi, S. Mohebbi, & N. Cho (Eds.), *Electronic supply network coordination in intelligent and dynamic environments: Modeling and implementation* (pp. 93–112). Hershey, PA: Business Science Reference; doi:10.4018/978-1-60566-808-6.ch004

Gonçalves, A., Serra, N., Serra, J., & Sousa, P. (2011). How to use information technology effectively to achieve business objectives. In M. Cruz-Cunha & J. Varajao (Eds.), *Enterprise information systems design, implementation and management: Organizational applications* (pp. 21–37). Hershey, PA: Information Science Reference; doi:10.4018/978-1-61692-020-3.ch002

Gordini, N., & Veglio, V. (2014). Customer relationship management and data mining: A classification decision tree to predict customer purchasing behavior in global market. In P. Vasant (Ed.), *Handbook of research on novel soft computing intelligent algorithms: Theory and practical applications* (pp. 1–40). Hershey, PA: Information Science Reference; doi:10.4018/978-1-4666-4450-2.ch001

Gottschalk, P. (2007). The CIO developing e-business. In P. Gottschalk (Ed.), *CIO and corporate strategic management: Changing role of CIO to CEO* (pp. 148–185). Hershey, PA: Idea Group Publishing; doi:10.4018/978-1-59904-423-1.ch007

Goutam, S. (2010). Analysis of speedy uptake of electronic and digital signatures in digital economy with special reference to India. In E. Adomi (Ed.), *Frameworks for ICT policy: Government, social and legal issues* (pp. 76–88). Hershey, PA: Information Science Reference; doi:10.4018/978-1-61692-012-8.ch005

Grieger, M., Hartmann, E., & Kotzab, H. (2011). E-markets as meta-enterprise information e systems. In *Enterprise information systems: Concepts, methodologies, tools and applications* (pp. 638–647). Hershey, PA: Business Science Reference; doi:10.4018/978-1-61692-852-0.ch306

grzonkowski, s., ensor, b. d., & mcdaniel, b. (2013). applied cryptography in Electronic Commerce. In *IT policy and ethics: Concepts, methodologies, tools, and applications* (pp. 368-388). Hershey, PA: Information Science Reference. doi:10.4018/978-1-4666-2919-6.ch017

Ha, H. (2012). Online security and consumer protection in ecommerce an Australian case. In K. Mohammed Rezaul (Ed.), *Strategic and pragmatic e-business: Implications for future business practices* (pp. 217–243). Hershey, PA: Business Science Reference; doi:10.4018/978-1-4666-1619-6.ch010

Ha, H., Coghill, K., & Maharaj, E. A. (2012). Current measures to protect e-consumers' privacy in Australia. In *Cyber crime: Concepts, methodologies, tools and applications* (pp. 1728–1755). Hershey, PA: Information Science Reference; doi:10.4018/978-1-61350-323-2.ch806

Halas, H., & Klobucar, T. (2011). Business models and organizational processes changes. In *Global business: Concepts, methodologies, tools and applications* (pp. 192–205). Hershey, PA: Business Science Reference; doi:10.4018/978-1-60960-587-2.ch113

Han, B. (2012). I play, I pay? An investigation of the user's willingness to pay on hedonic social network sites. *International Journal of Virtual Communities and Social Networking*, *4*(1), 19–31. doi:10.4018/jvcsn.2012010102

Harnesk, D. (2011). Convergence of information security in B2B networks. In E. Kajan (Ed.), *Electronic business interoperability: Concepts, opportunities and challenges* (pp. 571–595). Hershey, PA: Business Science Reference; doi:10.4018/978-1-60960-485-1.ch023

Harwood, T. (2012). Emergence of gamified commerce: Turning virtual to real. *Journal of Electronic Commerce in Organizations*, *10*(2), 16–39. doi:10.4018/jeco.2012040102

Heravi, B. R., & Lycett, M. (2012). Semantically enriched e-business standards development: The case of ebXML business process specification schema. In E. Kajan, F. Dorloff, & I. Bedini (Eds.), *Handbook of research on e-business standards and protocols: Documents, data and advanced web technologies* (pp. 655–675). Hershey, PA: Business Science Reference; doi:10.4018/978-1-4666-0146-8.ch030

Hill, D. S. (2012). An examination of standardized product identification and business benefit. In E. Kajan, F. Dorloff, & I. Bedini (Eds.), *Handbook of research on e-business standards and protocols: Documents, data and advanced web technologies* (pp. 387–411). Hershey, PA: Business Science Reference; doi:10.4018/978-1-4666-0146-8.ch018

Hoops, D. S. (2011). Legal issues in the virtual world and e-commerce. In B. Ciaramitaro (Ed.), *Virtual worlds and e-commerce: Technologies and applications for building customer relationships* (pp. 186–204). Hershey, PA: Business Science Reference; doi:10.4018/978-1-61692-808-7.ch010

Hu, W., Zuo, Y., Kaabouch, N., & Chen, L. (2010). A technological perspective of mobile and electronic commerce systems. In M. Khosrow-Pour (Ed.), *E-commerce trends for organizational advancement: New applications and methods* (pp. 16–35). Hershey, PA: Information Science Reference; doi:10.4018/978-1-60566-964-9.ch002

Hua, G. B. (2013). *Implementing IT business strategy in the construction industry*. Hershey, PA: IGI Global; doi:10.4018/978-1-4666-4185-3

Hua, S. C., Rajesh, M. J., & Theng, L. B. (2011). Determinants of e-commerce adoption among small and medium-sized enterprises in Malaysia. In S. Sharma (Ed.), *E-adoption and socio-economic impacts: Emerging infrastructural effects* (pp. 71–89). Hershey, PA: Information Science Reference; doi:10.4018/978-1-60960-597-1.ch005

Huang, J., & Dang, J. (2011). Context-sensitive ontology matching in electronic business. In E. Kajan (Ed.), *Electronic business interoperability: Concepts, opportunities and challenges* (pp. 279–301). Hershey, PA: Business Science Reference; doi:10.4018/978-1-60960-485-1.ch012

Hunaiti, Z., Tairo, D., Sedoyeka, E., & Elgazzar, S. (2010). Factors facing mobile commerce deployment in United Kingdom. In W. Hu & Y. Zuo (Eds.), *Handheld computing for mobile commerce: Applications, concepts and technologies* (pp. 109–123). Hershey, PA: Information Science Reference; doi:10.4018/978-1-61520-761-9.ch007

Hung, W. J., Tsai, C., Hung, S., McQueen, R., & Jou, J. (2011). Evaluating web site support capabilities in sell-side B2B transaction processes: A longitudinal study of two industries in New Zealand and Taiwan. *Journal of Global Information Management, 19*(1), 51–79. doi:10.4018/jgim.2011010103

Hunter, M. G. (2013). The duality of information technology roles: A case study. In C. Howard (Ed.), *Strategic adoption of technological innovations* (pp. 38–49). Hershey, PA: Information Science Reference; doi:10.4018/978-1-4666-2782-6.ch003

Huq, N., Shah, S. M., & Mihailescu, D. (2012). Why select an open source ERP over proprietary ERP? A focus on SMEs and supplier's perspective. In R. Atem de Carvalho & B. Johansson (Eds.), *Free and open source enterprise resource planning: Systems and strategies* (pp. 33–55). Hershey, PA: Business Science Reference; doi:10.4018/978-1-61350-486-4.ch003

Ingvaldsen, J., & Gulla, J. (2010). Semantic business process mining of SAP transactions. In M. Wang & Z. Sun (Eds.), *Handbook of research on complex dynamic process management: Techniques for adaptability in turbulent environments* (pp. 416–429). Hershey, PA: Business Science Reference; doi:10.4018/978-1-60566-669-3.ch017

Ingvaldsen, J., & Gulla, J. (2011). Semantic business process mining of SAP transactions. In *Enterprise information systems: Concepts, methodologies, tools and applications* (pp. 866–878). Hershey, PA: Business Science Reference; doi:10.4018/978-1-61692-852-0.ch320

Ioannou, M. (2013). Customer relationship management (CRM): A one-size-fits-all philosophy? In H. Kaufmann & M. Panni (Eds.), *Customer-centric marketing strategies: Tools for building organizational performance* (pp. 150–170). Hershey, PA: Business Science Reference; doi:10.4018/978-1-4666-2524-2.ch008

Islam, M. S., & Scupola, A. (2013). E-service research trends in the domain of e-government: A contemporary study. In A. Scupola (Ed.), *Mobile opportunities and applications for e-service innovations* (pp. 152–169). Hershey, PA: Information Science Reference; doi:10.4018/978-1-4666-2654-6.ch009

Jailani, N., Patel, A., Mukhtar, M., Abdullah, S., & Yahya, Y. (2010). Concept of an agent-based electronic marketplace. In I. Lee (Ed.), *Encyclopedia of e-business development and management in the global economy* (pp. 239–251). Hershey, PA: Business Science Reference; doi:10.4018/978-1-61520-611-7.ch024

Johns, R. (2011). Technology, trust and B2B relationships: A banking perspective. In O. Bak & N. Stair (Eds.), *Impact of e-business technologies on public and private organizations: Industry comparisons and perspectives* (pp. 79–96). Hershey, PA: Business Science Reference; doi:10.4018/978-1-60960-501-8.ch005

Joshi, S. (2013). E-supply chain collaboration and integration: Implementation issues and challenges. In D. Graham, I. Manikas, & D. Folinas (Eds.), *E-logistics and e-supply chain management: Applications for evolving business* (pp. 9–26). Hershey, PA: Business Science Reference; doi:10.4018/978-1-4666-3914-0.ch002

Kamal, M., Qureshil, S., & Wolcott, P. (2013). Promoting competitive advantage in micro-enterprises through information technology interventions. In *Small and medium enterprises: Concepts, methodologies, tools, and applications* (pp. 581–606). Hershey, PA: Business Science Reference; doi:10.4018/978-1-4666-3886-0.ch030

Kamel, S. (2012). Electronic commerce prospects in emerging economies: Lessons from Egypt. In *Regional development: Concepts, methodologies, tools, and applications* (pp. 1104–1115). Hershey, PA: Information Science Reference; doi:10.4018/978-1-4666-0882-5.ch604

Kamoun, F., & Halaweh, M. (2012). User interface design and e-commerce security perception: An empirical study. *International Journal of E-Business Research, 8*(2), 15–32. doi:10.4018/jebr.2012040102

Karakaya, F. (2012). Business-to-consumers ecommerce: How companies use the internet in marketing products and services to consumers. In N. Delener (Ed.), *Service science research, strategy and innovation: Dynamic knowledge management methods* (pp. 227–244). Hershey, PA: Business Science. doi:10.4018/978-1-4666-0077-5.ch014

Karakaya, F. (2013). B2B ecommerce: Current practices. In *Supply chain management: Concepts, methodologies, tools, and applications* (pp. 497–510). Hershey, PA: Business Science Reference; doi:10.4018/978-1-4666-2625-6.ch029

Karimov, F. P. (2013). Factors influencing e-commerce growth: A comparative study of central Asian transition economies. In S. Sharma (Ed.), *Adoption of virtual technologies for business, educational, and governmental advancements* (pp. 1–17). Hershey, PA: Information Science Reference; doi:10.4018/978-1-4666-2053-7.ch001

Kart, F., Moser, L. E., & Melliar-Smith, P. M. (2010). An automated supply chain management system and its performance evaluation. *International Journal of Information Systems and Supply Chain Management, 3*(2), 84–107. doi:10.4018/jisscm.2010040105

Kelarev, A. V., Brown, S., Watters, P., Wu, X., & Dazeley, R. (2011). Establishing reasoning communities of security experts for internet commerce security. In J. Yearwood & A. Stranieri (Eds.), *Technologies for supporting reasoning communities and collaborative decision making: Cooperative approaches* (pp. 380–396). Hershey, PA: Information Science Reference; doi:10.4018/978-1-60960-091-4.ch020

Kerr, D., Gammack, J. G., & Boddington, R. (2011). Overview of digital business security issues. In D. Kerr, J. Gammack, & K. Bryant (Eds.), *Digital business security development: Management technologies* (pp. 1–36). Hershey, PA: Business Science Reference; doi:10.4018/978-1-60566-806-2.ch001

Kerr, D., Gammack, J. G., & Bryant, K. (2011). *Digital business security development: Management technologies*. Hershey, PA: IGI Global; doi:10.4018/978-1-60566-806-2

Kett, H. (2013). A business model approach for service engineering in the internet of services. In P. Ordóñez de Pablos & R. Tennyson (Eds.), *Best practices and new perspectives in service science and management* (pp. 228–236). Hershey, PA: Business Science Reference; doi:10.4018/978-1-4666-3894-5.ch013

Khurana, R., & Aggarwal, R. (2013). *Interdisciplinary perspectives on business convergence, computing, and legality*. Hershey, PA: IGI Global; doi:10.4018/978-1-4666-4209-6

Kim, G., & Suh, Y. (2012). Building semantic business process space for agile and efficient business processes management: Ontology-based approach. In V. Shankararaman, J. Zhao, & J. Lee (Eds.), *Business enterprise, process, and technology management: Models and applications* (pp. 51–73). Hershey, PA: Business Science Reference; doi:10.4018/978-1-4666-0249-6.ch004

King, K. P., & Foley, J. J. (2012). 21st century learning opportunities for SME success: Maximizing technology tools and lifelong learning for innovation and impact. In *Human resources management: Concepts, methodologies, tools, and applications* (pp. 731–752). Hershey, PA: Business Science Reference; doi:10.4018/978-1-4666-1601-1.ch045

Kipp, A., & Schubert, L. (2011). E-business interoperability and collaboration. In E. Kajan (Ed.), *Electronic business interoperability: Concepts, opportunities and challenges* (pp. 153–184). Hershey, PA: Business Science Reference; doi:10.4018/978-1-60960-485-1.ch008

Klink, S., & Weiß, P. (2011). Social impact of collaborative services to maintain electronic business relationships. In *Virtual communities: Concepts, methodologies, tools and applications* (pp. 2011–2040). Hershey, PA: Information Science Reference; doi:10.4018/978-1-60960-100-3.ch609

Koumpis, A., & Protogeros, N. (2010). Doing business on the globalised networked economy: Technology and business challenges for accounting information systems. In M. Cruz-Cunha (Ed.), *Social, managerial, and organizational dimensions of enterprise information systems* (pp. 81–92). Hershey, PA: Business Science Reference; doi:10.4018/978-1-60566-856-7.ch004

Kritchanchai, D., Tan, A. W., & Hosie, P. (2010). An empirical investigation of third party logistics providers in Thailand: Barriers, motivation and usage of information technologies. *International Journal of Information Systems and Supply Chain Management*, *3*(2), 68–83. doi:10.4018/jisscm.2010040104

Kritchanchai, D., Tan, A. W., & Hosie, P. (2012). An empirical investigation of third party logistics providers in Thailand: Barriers, motivation and usage of information technologies. In J. Wang (Ed.), *Information technologies, methods, and techniques of supply chain management* (pp. 272–288). Hershey, PA: Business Science Reference; doi:10.4018/978-1-4666-0918-1.ch016

Kumar, M. (2011). Role of web interface in building trust in B2B e-exchanges. In S. Chhabra & H. Rahman (Eds.), *Human development and global advancements through information communication technologies: New initiatives* (pp. 63–74). Hershey, PA: Information Science Reference; doi:10.4018/978-1-60960-497-4.ch005

Kumar, M., & Sareen, M. (2012). Trust theories and models of e-commerce. In *Trust and technology in B2B e-commerce: Practices and strategies for assurance* (pp. 58–77). Hershey, PA: Business Science Reference; doi:10.4018/978-1-61350-353-9.ch003

Kumar, M., Sareen, M., & Chhabra, S. (2013). Technology related trust issues in SME B2B e-commerce. In S. Chhabra (Ed.), *ICT influences on human development, interaction, and collaboration* (pp. 243–259). Hershey, PA: Information Science Reference; doi:10.4018/978-1-4666-1957-9.ch015

Kung, M. T., & Zhang, Y. (2011). Creating competitive markets for small businesses with new media and e-business strategy. *International Journal of E-Business Research*, *7*(4), 31–49. doi:10.4018/jebr.2011100103

Kuo, D., Wong, D., Gao, J., & Chang, L. (2013). A 2D barcode validation system for mobile commerce. In W. Hu & S. Mousavinezhad (Eds.), *Mobile and handheld computing solutions for organizations and end-users* (pp. 1–19). Hershey, PA: Information Science Reference; doi:10.4018/978-1-4666-2785-7.ch001

Kyobe, M. (2010). E-crime and non-compliance with government regulations on e-commerce: Barriers to e-commerce optimization in South African SMEs. In B. Thomas & G. Simmons (Eds.), *E-commerce adoption and small business in the global marketplace: Tools for optimization* (pp. 47–66). Hershey, PA: Business Science Reference; doi:10.4018/978-1-60566-998-4.ch003

Lawrence, J. E. (2011). The growth of e-commerce in developing countries: An exploratory study of opportunities and challenges for SMEs. *International Journal of ICT Research and Development in Africa*, *2*(1), 15–28. doi:10.4018/jictrda.2011010102

Lawrence, J. E. (2013). Barriers hindering ecommerce adoption: A case study of Kurdistan region of Iraq. In A. Zolait (Ed.), *Technology diffusion and adoption: Global complexity, global innovation* (pp. 152–165). Hershey, PA: Information Science Reference; doi:10.4018/978-1-4666-2791-8.ch010

Lee, I. (2012). B2B e-commerce, online auction, supply chain management, and e-collaboration. In *Electronic commerce management for business activities and global enterprises: Competitive advantages* (pp. 249–299). Hershey, PA: Business Science Reference; doi:10.4018/978-1-4666-1800-8.ch007

Lee, I. (2012). B2C online consumer behavior. In *Electronic commerce management for business activities and global enterprises: competitive advantages* (pp. 166–201). Hershey, PA: Business Science Reference; doi:10.4018/978-1-4666-1800-8.ch005

Lee, I. (2012). Introduction to e-commerce in the global economy. In *Electronic commerce management for business activities and global enterprises: Competitive advantages* (pp. 1–46). Hershey, PA: Business Science Reference; doi:10.4018/978-1-4666-1800-8.ch001

Lee, I. (2012). Mobile commerce. In *Electronic commerce management for business activities and global enterprises: Competitive advantages* (pp. 300–338). Hershey, PA: Business Science Reference; doi:10.4018/978-1-4666-1800-8.ch008

Lee, I. (2012). Online payment systems. In *Electronic commerce management for business activities and global enterprises: Competitive advantages* (pp. 340–365). Hershey, PA: Business Science Reference; doi:10.4018/978-1-4666-1800-8.ch009

Leonard, L. N. (2010). C2C mobile commerce: Acceptance factors. In I. Lee (Ed.), *Encyclopedia of e-business development and management in the global economy* (pp. 759–767). Hershey, PA: Business Science Reference; doi:10.4018/978-1-61520-611-7.ch076

Lertpittayapoom, N., & Paul, S. (2010). The roles of online intermediaries in collective memory-supported electronic negotiation. In *Electronic services: Concepts, methodologies, tools and applications* (pp. 1831–1847). Hershey, PA: Information Science Reference; doi:10.4018/978-1-61520-967-5.ch112

Li, L., Liu, C., Zhao, X., & Wang, J. (2011). Transactional properties of complex web services. In H. Leung, D. Chiu, & P. Hung (Eds.), *Service intelligence and service science: Evolutionary technologies and challenges* (pp. 21–34). Hershey, PA: Information Science Reference; doi:10.4018/978-1-61520-819-7.ch002

Li, X., & Lin, J. (2011). Call u back: An agent-based infrastructure for mobile commerce. *International Journal of E-Entrepreneurship and Innovation, 2*(2), 1–13. doi:10.4018/jeei.2011040101

Liao, Q., Luo, X., & Gurung, A. (2011). Trust restoration in electronic commerce. In S. Clarke & A. Dwivedi (Eds.), *Organizational and end-user interactions: New explorations* (pp. 72–88). Hershey, PA: Information Science Reference; doi:10.4018/978-1-60960-577-3.ch003

Liberato, N. A., Varajão, J. E., Correia, E. S., & Bessa, M. E. (2011). Location based e-commerce system: An architecture. In M. Cruz-Cunha & F. Moreira (Eds.), *Handbook of research on mobility and computing: Evolving technologies and ubiquitous impacts* (pp. 881–892). Hershey, PA: Information Science Reference; doi:10.4018/978-1-60960-042-6.ch055

Lim, S. Y., & Wong, S. F. (2012). Impact of applying aggregate query processing in mobile commerce. *International Journal of Business Data Communications and Networking, 8*(2), 1–17. doi:10.4018/jbdcn.2012040101

Lin, C., & Jalleh, G. (2013). Key issues and challenges for managing and evaluating B2B e-commerce projects within the Australian pharmaceutical supply chain. In *Supply chain management: Concepts, methodologies, tools, and applications* (pp. 1083–1100). Hershey, PA: Business Science Reference; doi:10.4018/978-1-4666-2625-6.ch064

Lin, C., Jalleh, G., & Huang, Y. (2013). E-business investment evaluation and outsourcing practices in Australian and Taiwanese hospitals: A comparative study. In K. Tarnay, S. Imre, & L. Xu (Eds.), *Research and development in e-business through service-oriented solutions* (pp. 244–266). Hershey, PA: Business Science Reference; doi:10.4018/978-1-4666-4181-5.ch012

Lin, C., Lin, H. K., Jalleh, G., & Huang, Y. (2011). Key adoption challenges and issues of B2B e-commerce in the healthcare sector. In M. Cruz-Cunha & F. Moreira (Eds.), *Handbook of research on mobility and computing: Evolving technologies and ubiquitous impacts* (pp. 175–187). Hershey, PA: Information Science Reference; doi:10.4018/978-1-60960-042-6.ch011

Liyanage, J. P. (2011). Copying with dynamic change: Collaborative business interfacing for SMEs under intergated eoperations. In M. Cruz-Cunha & J. Varajão (Eds.), *E-business managerial aspects, solutions and case studies* (pp. 136–147). Hershey, PA: Business Science Reference; doi:10.4018/978-1-60960-463-9.ch008

Liyanage, J. P. (2012). Hybrid intelligence through business socialization and networking: Managing complexities in the digital era. In M. Cruz-Cunha, P. Gonçalves, N. Lopes, E. Miranda, & G. Putnik (Eds.), *Handbook of research on business social networking: organizational, managerial, and technological dimensions* (pp. 567–582). Hershey, PA: Business Science Reference; doi:10.4018/978-1-61350-168-9.ch030

Loeser, F., Erek, K., & Zarnekow, R. (2013). Green IT strategies: A conceptual framework for the alignment of information technology and corporate sustainability strategy. In P. Ordóñez de Pablos (Ed.), *Green technologies and business practices: An IT approach* (pp. 58–95). Hershey, PA: Information Science Reference; doi:10.4018/978-1-4666-1972-2.ch004

Maamar, Z., Faci, N., Mostéfaoui, S. K., & Akhter, F. (2011). Towards a framework for weaving social networks into mobile commerce. *International Journal of Systems and Service-Oriented Engineering*, *2*(3), 32–46. doi:10.4018/jssoe.2011070103

Mahmood, M. A., Gemoets, L., Hall, L. L., & López, F. J. (2011). Building business value in e-commerce enabled organizations: An empirical study. In *Global business: Concepts, methodologies, tools and applications* (pp. 229–253). Hershey, PA: Business Science Reference; doi:10.4018/978-1-60960-587-2.ch201

Mahran, A. F., & Enaba, H. M. (2013). Exploring determinants influencing the intention to use mobile payment service. In R. Eid (Ed.), *Managing customer trust, satisfaction, and loyalty through information communication technologies* (pp. 288–309). Hershey, PA: Business Science Reference; doi:10.4018/978-1-4666-3631-6.ch017

Marimuthu, M., Omar, A., Ramayah, T., & Mohamad, O. (2013). Readiness to adopt e-business among SMEs in Malaysia: Antecedents and consequence. In S. Sharma (Ed.), *Adoption of virtual technologies for business, educational, and governmental advancements* (pp. 18–36). Hershey, PA: Information Science Reference; doi:10.4018/978-1-4666-2053-7.ch002

Mayes, P. (2014). Interactive advertising: Displays of identity and stance on YouTube. In H. Lim & F. Sudweeks (Eds.), *Innovative methods and technologies for electronic discourse analysis* (pp. 260–284). Hershey, PA: Information Science Reference; doi:10.4018/978-1-4666-4426-7.ch012

McGrath, T. (2012). The reality of using standards for electronic business document formats. In E. Kajan, F. Dorloff, & I. Bedini (Eds.), *Handbook of research on e-business standards and protocols: Documents, data and advanced web technologies* (pp. 21–32). Hershey, PA: Business Science Reference; doi:10.4018/978-1-4666-0146-8.ch002

Meredith, J., & Potter, J. (2014). Conversation analysis and electronic interactions: Methodological, analytic and technical considerations. In H. Lim & F. Sudweeks (Eds.), *Innovative methods and technologies for electronic discourse analysis* (pp. 370–393). Hershey, PA: Information Science Reference; doi:10.4018/978-1-4666-4426-7.ch017

Millman, C., & El-Gohary, H. (2011). New digital media marketing and micro business: A UK perspective. *International Journal of Online Marketing*, *1*(1), 41–62. doi:10.4018/ijom.2011010104

Mishra, B., & Shukla, K. K. (2014). Data mining techniques for software quality prediction. In *Software design and development: Concepts, methodologies, tools, and applications* (pp. 401–428). Hershey, PA: Information Science Reference; doi:10.4018/978-1-4666-4301-7.ch021

Misra, H., & Rahman, H. (2013). *Managing enterprise information technology acquisitions: Assessing organizational preparedness*. Hershey, PA: IGI Global; doi:10.4018/978-1-4666-4201-0

Mohammadi, S., Golara, S., & Mousavi, N. (2012). Selecting adequate security mechanisms in e-business processes using fuzzy TOPSIS. *International Journal of Fuzzy System Applications*, *2*(1), 35–53. doi:10.4018/ijfsa.2012010103

Möhlenbruch, D., Dölling, S., & Ritschel, F. (2010). Interactive customer retention management for mobile commerce. In K. Pousttchi & D. Wiedemann (Eds.), *Handbook of research on mobile marketing management* (pp. 437–456). Hershey, PA: Business Science Reference; doi:10.4018/978-1-60566-074-5.ch023

Molla, A., & Peszynski, K. (2013). E-business in agribusiness: Investigating the e-readiness of Australian horticulture firms. In S. Chhabra (Ed.), *ICT influences on human development, interaction, and collaboration* (pp. 78–96). Hershey, PA: Information Science Reference; doi:10.4018/978-1-4666-1957-9.ch004

Monsanto, C., & Andriole, S. J. (2010). Business technology strategy for a major real estate and mortgage brokerage company. *Journal of Information Technology Research*, *3*(3), 43–53. doi:10.4018/jitr.2010070104

Montes, J. A., Gutiérrez, A. C., Fernández, E. M., & Romeo, A. (2013). Reality mining, location based services, and e-business opportunities: The case of city analytics. In S. Nasir (Ed.), *Modern entrepreneurship and e-business innovations* (pp. 87–99). Hershey, PA: Business Science Reference; doi:10.4018/978-1-4666-2946-2.ch007

Moqbel, A., Yani-De-Soriano, M., & Yousafzai, S. (2012). Mobile commerce use among UK mobile users: An experimental approach based on a proposed mobile network utilization framework. In A. Zolait (Ed.), *Knowledge and technology adoption, diffusion, and transfer: International perspectives* (pp. 78–111). Hershey, PA: Information Science Reference; doi:10.4018/978-1-4666-1752-0.ch007

Movahedi, B. M., Lavassani, K. M., & Kumar, V. (2012). E-marketplace emergence: Evolution, developments and classification. *Journal of Electronic Commerce in Organizations*, *10*(1), 14–32. doi:10.4018/jeco.2012010102

Mugge, R., & Schoormans, J. P. (2010). Optimizing consumer responses to mass customization. In C. Mourlas & P. Germanakos (Eds.), *Mass customization for personalized communication environments: Integrating human factors* (pp. 10–22). Hershey, PA: Information Science Reference; doi:10.4018/978-1-60566-260-2.ch002

Musso, F. (2012). Technology in marketing channels: Present and future drivers of innovation. *International Journal of Applied Behavioral Economics*, *1*(2), 41–51. doi:10.4018/ijabe.2012040104

Mutula, S. M. (2010). Digital economy components. In S. Mutula (Ed.), *Digital economies: SMEs and e-readiness* (pp. 29–38). Hershey, PA: Business Science Reference; doi:10.4018/978-1-60566-420-0.ch003

Mutula, S. M. (2010). Trends and best practices in the digital economy. In S. Mutula (Ed.), *Digital economies: SMEs and e-readiness* (pp. 283–301). Hershey, PA: Business Science Reference; doi:10.4018/978-1-60566-420-0.ch017

Nachtigal, S. (2011). E-business: Definition and characteristics. In O. Bak & N. Stair (Eds.), *Impact of e-business technologies on public and private organizations: Industry comparisons and perspectives* (pp. 233–248). Hershey, PA: Business Science Reference; doi:10.4018/978-1-60960-501-8.ch014

Nah, F. F., Hong, W., Chen, L., & Lee, H. (2012). Information search patterns in e-commerce product comparison services. In K. Siau (Ed.), *Cross-disciplinary models and applications of database management: Advancing approaches* (pp. 131–145). Hershey, PA: Information Science Reference; doi:10.4018/978-1-61350-471-0.ch006

Nair, P. R. (2010). Benefits of information technology implementations for supply chain management: An explorative study of progressive Indian companies. In S. Parthasarathy (Ed.), *Enterprise information systems and implementing IT infrastructures: Challenges and issues* (pp. 323–343). Hershey, PA: Business Science Reference; doi:10.4018/978-1-61520-625-4.ch021

Ndou, V., Del Vecchio, P., Passiante, G., & Schina, L. (2013). Web-based services and future business models. In P. Papajorgji, A. Guimarães, & M. Guarracino (Eds.), *Enterprise business modeling, optimization techniques, and flexible information systems* (pp. 1–13). Hershey, PA: Business Science Reference; doi:10.4018/978-1-4666-3946-1.ch001

Ndou, V., & Sadguy, N. (2013). Digital marketplaces as a viable model for SME networking. In *Supply chain management: Concepts, methodologies, tools, and applications* (pp. 275–288). Hershey, PA: Business Science Reference; doi:10.4018/978-1-4666-2625-6.ch016

Ochara, N. M., & Krauss, K. (2012). Towards a collaborative e-business vision for Africa. In K. Mohammed Rezaul (Ed.), *Strategic and pragmatic e-business: Implications for future business practices* (pp. 396–414). Hershey, PA: Business Science Reference; doi:10.4018/978-1-4666-1619-6.ch018

Oncioiu, I. (2013). *Business innovation, development, and advancement in the digital economy*. Hershey, PA: IGI Global; doi:10.4018/978-1-4666-2934-9

Ondimu, K. O., Muketha, G. M., & Ondago, C. O. (2013). E-business adoption framework in the hospitality industry: The case of Kenyan coast. In K. Tarnay, S. Imre, & L. Xu (Eds.), *Research and development in e-business through service-oriented solutions* (pp. 225–243). Hershey, PA: Business Science Reference; doi:10.4018/978-1-4666-4181-5.ch011

Ovaskainen, M., & Tinnilä, M. (2013). Megatrends in electronic business: An analysis of the impacts on SMEs. In S. Nasir (Ed.), *Modern entrepreneurship and e-business innovations* (pp. 12–27). Hershey, PA: Business Science Reference; doi:10.4018/978-1-4666-2946-2.ch002

Özcan, O., & Reeves, K. A. (2011). The firm boundary decision for sustainability-focused companies. *International Journal of Applied Logistics*, *2*(2), 49–68. doi:10.4018/jal.2011040104

Öztayşi, B., & Kahraman, C. (2014). Quantification of corporate performance using fuzzy analytic network process: The case of e-commerce. In P. Vasant (Ed.), *Handbook of research on novel soft computing intelligent algorithms: Theory and practical applications* (pp. 385–413). Hershey, PA: Information Science Reference; doi:10.4018/978-1-4666-4450-2.ch013

Palmer, D. E. (2010). The transformative nature of e-business: Business ethics and stakeholder relations on the internet. In D. Palmer (Ed.), *Ethical issues in e-business: Models and frameworks* (pp. 1–14). Hershey, PA: Business Science Reference; doi:10.4018/978-1-61520-615-5.ch001

Pańkowska, M. (2014). Frameworks of IT prosumption for business development (pp. 1-347). doi:10.4018/978-1-4666-4313-0

Pelet, J. É., & Papadopoulou, P. (2013). The effect of e-commerce websites' colors on customer trust. In I. Lee (Ed.), *Mobile applications and knowledge advancements in e-business* (pp. 167–185). Hershey, PA: Business Science Reference; doi:10.4018/978-1-4666-1960-9.ch011

Pennington, R. (2012). Enhanced social presence through ebranding the consumer in virtual communities. In A. Kapoor & C. Kulshrestha (Eds.), *Branding and sustainable competitive advantage: Building virtual presence* (pp. 189–206). Hershey, PA: Business Science Reference; doi:10.4018/978-1-61350-171-9.ch012

Peslak, A. R. (2012). Industry variables affecting ERP success and status. *International Journal of Enterprise Information Systems, 8*(3), 15–33. doi:10.4018/jeis.2012070102

Peterson, D., & Howard, C. (2012). Electronic payment systems evaluation: A case study to examine system selection criteria and impacts. *International Journal of Strategic Information Technology and Applications, 3*(1), 66–80. doi:10.4018/jsita.2012010105

Pflügler, C. (2012). Fostering networked business operations: A framework for B2B electronic intermediary development. *International Journal of Intelligent Information Technologies, 8*(2), 31–58. doi:10.4018/jiit.2012040103

Pillai, K., & Ozansoy, C. (2013). Web-based digital habitat ecosystems for sustainable built environments. In P. Ordóñez de Pablos (Ed.), *Green technologies and business practices: An IT approach* (pp. 185–199). Hershey, PA: Information Science Reference; doi:10.4018/978-1-4666-1972-2.ch011

Pinto, M., Rodrigues, A., Varajão, J., & Gonçalves, R. (2011). Model of funcionalities for the development of B2B e-commerce solutions. In M. Cruz-Cunha & J. Varajão (Eds.), *Innovations in SMEs and conducting e-business: Technologies, trends and solutions* (pp. 35–60). Hershey, PA: Business Science Reference; doi:10.4018/978-1-60960-765-4.ch003

Pires, J. A., & Gonçalves, R. (2011). Constrains associated to e-business evolution. In M. Cruz-Cunha & J. Varajão (Eds.), *E-business issues, challenges and opportunities for SMEs: Driving competitiveness* (pp. 335–349). Hershey, PA: Business Science Reference; doi:10.4018/978-1-61692-880-3.ch019

Polovina, S., & Andrews, S. (2011). A transaction-oriented architecture for structuring unstructured information in enterprise applications. In V. Sugumaran (Ed.), *Intelligent, adaptive and reasoning technologies: New developments and applications* (pp. 285–299). Hershey, PA: Information Science Reference; doi:10.4018/978-1-60960-595-7.ch016

Potocan, V., Nedelko, Z., & Mulej, M. (2011). What is new with organization of e-business: Organizational viewpoint of the relationships in e-business. In M. Cruz-Cunha & J. Varajão (Eds.), *E-business issues, challenges and opportunities for SMEs: Driving competitiveness* (pp. 131–148). Hershey, PA: Business Science Reference; doi:10.4018/978-1-61692-880-3.ch009

Potocan, V., Nedelko, Z., & Mulej, M. (2011). What is new with organization of e-business: Organizational viewpoint of the relationships in e-business. In M. Cruz-Cunha & J. Varajão (Eds.), *E-business issues, challenges and opportunities for SMEs: Driving competitiveness* (pp. 131–148). Hershey, PA: Business Science Reference; doi:10.4018/978-1-61692-880-3.ch009

Pucihar, A., & Lenart, G. (2011). eSME Slovenia: Initiative and action plan for the accelerated introduction of e-business in SMEs. In Global business: Concepts, methodologies, tools and applications (pp. 995-1022). Hershey, PA: Business Science Reference. doi::10.4018/978-1-60960-587-2.ch409

Quan, J. (2011). E-business strategy and firm performance. In *Global business: Concepts, methodologies, tools and applications* (pp. 56–66). Hershey, PA: Business Science Reference; doi:10.4018/978-1-60960-587-2.ch105

Quente, C. (2010). Brand driven mobile marketing: 5 theses for today and tomorrow. In K. Pousttchi & D. Wiedemann (Eds.), *Handbook of research on mobile marketing management* (pp. 468–483). Hershey, PA: Business Science Reference; doi:10.4018/978-1-60566-074-5.ch025

Qureshil, S., Kamal, M., & Wolcott, P. (2011). Information technology interventions for growth and competitiveness in micro-enterprises. In M. Tavana (Ed.), *Managing adaptability, intervention, and people in enterprise information systems* (pp. 106–137). Hershey, PA: Information Science Reference; doi:10.4018/978-1-60960-529-2.ch006

Rabaey, M. (2014). Complex adaptive systems thinking approach to enterprise architecture. In P. Saha (Ed.), *A systemic perspective to managing complexity with enterprise architecture* (pp. 99–149). Hershey, PA: Business Science Reference; doi:10.4018/978-1-4666-4518-9.ch003

Rahman, H., & Ramos, I. (2012). Trends of open innovation in developing nations: Contexts of SMEs. In H. Rahman & I. Ramos (Eds.), *Cases on SMEs and open innovation: Applications and investigations* (pp. 65–80). Hershey, PA: Business Science Reference; doi:10.4018/978-1-61350-314-0.ch004

Rahman, H., & Ramos, I. (2013). Implementation of e-commerce at the grass roots: Issues of challenges in terms of human-computer interactions. *International Journal of Information Communication Technologies and Human Development*, *5*(2), 1–19. doi:10.4018/jicthd.2013040101

Rajagopal, D. (2010). Customer value and new product retailing dynamics: An analytical construct for gaining competetive advantage. In *Business information systems: Concepts, methodologies, tools and applications* (pp. 1998–2014). Hershey, PA: Business Science Reference; doi:10.4018/978-1-61520-969-9.ch121

Rajagopal, D. (2010). Internet, reengineering and technology applications in retailing. In *Business information systems: Concepts, methodologies, tools and applications* (pp. 1324–1342). Hershey, PA: Business Science Reference; doi:10.4018/978-1-61520-969-9.ch082

Rajagopal, D. (2011). Marketing strategy, technology and modes of entry in global retailing. In *Global business: Concepts, methodologies, tools and applications* (pp. 1–27). Hershey, PA: Business Science Reference; doi:10.4018/978-1-60960-587-2.ch101

Rajagopal, D. (2012). Convergence marketing. In *Systems thinking and process dynamics for marketing systems: Technologies and applications for decision management* (pp. 274–290). Hershey, PA: Business Science Reference; doi:10.4018/978-1-4666-0969-3.ch011

Rajagopal, D. (2012). Product development and market governance. In *Systems thinking and process dynamics for marketing systems: Technologies and applications for decision management* (pp. 88–117). Hershey, PA: Business Science Reference; doi:10.4018/978-1-4666-0969-3.ch004

Rajagopal, D. (2012). Systems thinking and cognitive process in marketing. In *Systems thinking and process dynamics for marketing systems: technologies and applications for decision management* (pp. 170–197). Hershey, PA: Business Science Reference; doi:10.4018/978-1-4666-0969-3.ch007

Rajagopal, D. (2013). Pricing for new products. In *Marketing decision making and the management of pricing: Successful business tools* (pp. 56–74). Hershey, PA: Business Science Reference; doi:10.4018/978-1-4666-4094-8.ch003

Ramayah, T., Popa, S., & Suki, N. M. (2013). Key dimensions on B2C e-business: An empirical study in Malaysia. *International Journal of Human Capital and Information Technology Professionals*, *4*(2), 43–55. doi:10.4018/jhcitp.2013040104

Rambo, K., & Liu, K. (2011). Culture-sensitive virtual e-commerce design with reference to female consumers in Saudi Arabia. In B. Ciaramitaro (Ed.), *Virtual worlds and e-commerce: Technologies and applications for building customer relationships* (pp. 267–289). Hershey, PA: Business Science Reference; doi:10.4018/978-1-61692-808-7.ch016

Ratnasingam, P. (2010). The evolution of online relationships in business to consumer e-commerce. In M. Khosrow-Pour (Ed.), *E-commerce trends for organizational advancement: New applications and methods* (pp. 167–176). Hershey, PA: Information Science Reference; doi:10.4018/978-1-60566-964-9.ch010

Ratnasingam, P. (2010). The impact of e-commerce customer relationship management in business-to-consumer e-commerce. In M. Hunter (Ed.), *Strategic information systems: Concepts, methodologies, tools, and applications* (pp. 2099–2111). Hershey, PA: Information Science Reference; doi:10.4018/978-1-60566-677-8.ch132

Razavi, A. R., Krause, P., & Moschoyiannis, S. (2010). Digital ecosystems: Challenges and proposed solutions. In N. Antonopoulos, G. Exarchakos, M. Li, & A. Liotta (Eds.), Handbook of research on P2P and grid systems for service-oriented computing: Models, methodologies and applications (pp. 1003-1031). Hershey, PA: Information Science Reference. doi::10.4018/978-1-61520-686-5.ch043

Regazzi, J. J. (2014). *Infonomics and the business of free: Modern value creation for information services*. Hershey, PA: IGI Global; doi:10.4018/978-1-4666-4454-0

Riaz, N., & Rehman, M. (2013). Negotiation by software agents in electronic business: An example of hybrid negotiation. In E. Li, S. Loh, C. Evans, & F. Lorenzi (Eds.), *Organizations and social networking: Utilizing social media to engage consumers* (pp. 327–349). Hershey, PA: Business Science Reference; doi:10.4018/978-1-4666-4026-9.ch017

Roberti, G., & Marinelli, A. (2012). Branding identity: Facebook, brands and self construction. In F. Comunello (Ed.), *Networked sociability and individualism: Technology for personal and professional relationships* (pp. 147–168). Hershey, PA: Information Science Reference; doi:10.4018/978-1-61350-338-6.ch008

Rodrigues, D. E. (2012). Cyberethics of business social networking. In M. Cruz-Cunha, P. Gonçalves, N. Lopes, E. Miranda, & G. Putnik (Eds.), *Handbook of research on business social networking: Organizational, managerial, and technological dimensions* (pp. 314–338). Hershey, PA: Business Science Reference; doi:10.4018/978-1-61350-168-9.ch016

Roos, G. (2013). The role of intellectual capital in business model innovation: An empirical study. In P. Ordóñez de Pablos, R. Tennyson, & J. Zhao (Eds.), *Intellectual capital strategy management for knowledge-based organizations* (pp. 76–121). Hershey, PA: Business Science Reference; doi:10.4018/978-1-4666-3655-2.ch006

Rowley, J., & Edmundson-Bird, D. (2013). Brand presence in digital space. *Journal of Electronic Commerce in Organizations, 11*(1), 63–78. doi:10.4018/jeco.2013010104

Rusko, R. (2013). The redefined role of consumer as a prosumer: Value co-creation, coopetition, and crowdsourcing of information goods. In P. Renna (Ed.), *Production and manufacturing system management: Coordination approaches and multi-site planning* (pp. 162–174). Hershey, PA: Engineering Science Reference; doi:10.4018/978-1-4666-2098-8.ch009

Sahi, G., & Madan, S. (2013). Developing a website usability framework for B2C e-commerce success. *International Journal of Information Communication Technologies and Human Development, 5*(1), 1–19. doi:10.4018/jicthd.2013010101

Sainz de Abajo, B., de la Torre Díez, I., & López-Coronado, M. (2010). Analysis of benefits and risks of e-commerce: Practical study of Spanish SME. In I. Portela & M. Cruz-Cunha (Eds.), *Information communication technology law, protection and access rights: Global approaches and issues* (pp. 214–239). Hershey, PA: Information Science Reference; doi:10.4018/978-1-61520-975-0.ch014

Samanta, I., & Kyriazopoulos, P. (2011). Can global environment influence B2B relationships? In P. Ordóñez de Pablos, M. Lytras, W. Karwowski, & R. Lee (Eds.), *Electronic globalized business and sustainable development through IT management: Strategies and perspectives* (pp. 54–69). Hershey, PA: Business Science Reference; doi:10.4018/978-1-61520-623-0.ch004

Sambhanthan, A., & Good, A. (2012). Implications for improving accessibility to e-commerce websites in developing countries: A study of hotel websites. *International Journal of Knowledge-Based Organizations*, *2*(2), 1–20. doi::10.4018/ijkbo.2012040101

Sampaio, L., & Figueiredo, J. (2011). E-sourcing electronic platforms in real business. In M. Cruz-Cunha & J. Varajão (Eds.), *E-business managerial aspects, solutions and case studies* (pp. 185–205). Hershey, PA: Business Science Reference; doi:10.4018/978-1-60960-463-9.ch011

Seetharaman, A., & Raj, J. R. (2011). Evolution, development and growth of electronic money. In S. Sharma (Ed.), *E-adoption and socio-economic impacts: Emerging infrastructural effects* (pp. 249–268). Hershey, PA: Information Science Reference; doi:10.4018/978-1-60960-597-1.ch013

Sengupta, A., & Glavin, S. E. (2013). Predicting volatile consumer markets using multi-agent methods: Theory and validation. In B. Alexandrova-Kabadjova, S. Martinez-Jaramillo, A. Garcia-Almanza, & E. Tsang (Eds.), *Simulation in computational finance and economics: Tools and emerging applications* (pp. 339–358). Hershey, PA: Business Science Reference; doi:10.4018/978-1-4666-2011-7.ch016

Serpico, E., Aquilani, B., Ruggieri, A., & Silvestri, C. (2013). Customer centric marketing strategies: The importance and measurement of customer satisfaction – Offline vs. online. In H. Kaufmann & M. Panni (Eds.), *Customer-centric marketing strategies: Tools for building organizational performance* (pp. 315–357). Hershey, PA: Business Science Reference; doi:10.4018/978-1-4666-2524-2.ch016

Shareef, M. A., & Kumar, V. (2012). Prevent/control identity theft: Impact on trust and consumers' purchase intention in B2C EC. *Information Resources Management Journal*, *25*(3), 30–60. doi:10.4018/irmj.2012070102

Sherringham, K., & Unhelkar, B. (2011). Business driven enterprise architecture and applications to support mobile business. In *Enterprise information systems: Concepts, methodologies, tools and applications* (pp. 805–816). Hershey, PA: Business Science Reference; doi:10.4018/978-1-61692-852-0.ch316

Shin, N. (2011). Information technology and diversification: How their relationship affects firm performance. In N. Kock (Ed.), *E-collaboration technologies and organizational performance: Current and future trends* (pp. 65–79). Hershey, PA: Information Science Reference; doi:10.4018/978-1-60960-466-0.ch005

Sidnal, N., & Manvi, S. S. (2010). Service discovery techniques in mobile e-commerce. In I. Lee (Ed.), *Encyclopedia of e-business development and management in the global economy* (pp. 812–823). Hershey, PA: Business Science Reference; doi:10.4018/978-1-61520-611-7.ch081

Sidnal, N., & Manvi, S. S. (2013). English auction issues in mobile e-commerce. In K. Tarnay, S. Imre, & L. Xu (Eds.), *Research and development in e-business through service-oriented solutions* (pp. 208–223). Hershey, PA: Business Science Reference; doi:10.4018/978-1-4666-4181-5.ch010

Singh, S. (2010). Usability techniques for interactive software and their application in e-commerce. In T. Spiliotopoulos, P. Papadopoulou, D. Martakos, & G. Kouroupetroglou (Eds.), *Integrating usability engineering for designing the web experience: Methodologies and principles* (pp. 81–102). Hershey, PA: Information Science Reference; doi:10.4018/978-1-60566-896-3.ch005

Söderström, E. (2010). Guidelines for managing B2B standards implementation. In E. Alkhalifa (Ed.), *E-strategies for resource management systems: Planning and implementation* (pp. 86–105). Hershey, PA: Business Science Reference; doi:10.4018/978-1-61692-016-6.ch005

Sood, S. (2012). The death of social media in start-up companies and the rise of s-commerce: Convergence of e-commerce, complexity and social media. *Journal of Electronic Commerce in Organizations*, *10*(2), 1–15. doi:10.4018/jeco.2012040101

Soto-Acosta, P. (2010). E-business and the resource-based view: Towards a research agenda. In I. Lee (Ed.), *Encyclopedia of e-business development and management in the global economy* (pp. 336–346). Hershey, PA: Business Science Reference; doi:10.4018/978-1-61520-611-7.ch033

Sourouni, A. M., Mouzakitis, S., Kourlimpini, G., Askounis, D., & Psarras, J. (2010). Ontology-based registries: An e-business transactions' registry. In E. Alkhalifa (Ed.), *E-strategies for resource management systems: Planning and implementation* (pp. 106–117). Hershey, PA: Business Science Reference; doi:10.4018/978-1-61692-016-6.ch006

Srinivasan, S., & Barker, R. (2012). Global analysis of security and trust perceptions in web design for e-commerce. *International Journal of Information Security and Privacy*, *6*(1), 1–13. doi:10.4018/jisp.2012010101

Su, Q., & Adams, C. (2012). Consumers' attitudes toward mobile commerce: A model to capture the cultural and environment influences. In A. Scupola (Ed.), *Innovative mobile platform developments for electronic services design and delivery* (pp. 1–20). Hershey, PA: Business Science Reference; doi:10.4018/978-1-4666-1568-7.ch001

Swilley, E., Hofacker, C. F., & Lamont, B. T. (2012). The evolution from e-commerce to m-commerce: Pressures, firm capabilities and competitive advantage in strategic decision making. *International Journal of E-Business Research*, *8*(1), 1–16. doi:10.4018/jebr.2012010101

Swimm, N., & Andriole, S. J. (2010). Business technology strategy for an energy management company. *Journal of Information Technology Research*, *3*(3), 54–65. doi:10.4018/jitr.2010070105

Tadjouddine, E. M. (2011). E-commerce systems for software agents: Challenges and opportunities. In M. Cruz-Cunha & J. Varajão (Eds.), *E-business issues, challenges and opportunities for SMEs: Driving competitiveness* (pp. 20–29). Hershey, PA: Business Science Reference; doi:10.4018/978-1-61692-880-3.ch002

Taylor, P. R. (2014). Enterprise architecture's identity crisis: New approaches to complexity for a maturing discipline. In P. Saha (Ed.), *A systemic perspective to managing complexity with enterprise architecture* (pp. 433–453). Hershey, PA: Business Science Reference; doi:10.4018/978-1-4666-4518-9.ch013

Tella, A. (2012). Determinants of e-payment systems success: A user's satisfaction perspective. *International Journal of E-Adoption*, *4*(3), 15–38. doi:10.4018/jea.2012070102

Terjesen, A. (2010). Anonymity and trust: The ethical challenges of e-business transactions. In D. Palmer (Ed.), *Ethical issues in e-business: Models and frameworks* (pp. 40–57). Hershey, PA: Business Science Reference; doi:10.4018/978-1-61520-615-5.ch004

Tijsen, R., Spruit, M., van de Ridder, M., & van Raaij, B. (2011). BI-FIT: Aligning business intelligence end-users, tasks and technologies. In M. Cruz-Cunha & J. Varajao (Eds.), *Enterprise information systems design, implementation and management: Organizational applications* (pp. 162–177). Hershey, PA: Information Science Reference; doi:10.4018/978-1-61692-020-3.ch011

Toka, A., Aivazidou, E., Antoniou, A., & Arvanitopoulos-Darginis, K. (2013). Cloud computing in supply chain management: An overview. In D. Graham, I. Manikas, & D. Folinas (Eds.), *E-logistics and e-supply chain management: Applications for evolving business* (pp. 218–231). Hershey, PA: Business Science Reference; doi:10.4018/978-1-4666-3914-0.ch012

Tran, Q., Huang, D., & Zhang, C. (2013). An assessment method of the integrated e-commerce readiness for construction organizations in developing countries. *International Journal of E-Adoption*, *5*(1), 37–51. doi:10.4018/jea.2013010103

Tung, H., Kung, H., Lawless, D. S., Sofge, D. A., & Lawless, W. F. (2011). Conservation of information and e-business success and challenges: A case study. In M. Cruz-Cunha & J. Varajão (Eds.), *E-business managerial aspects, solutions and case studies* (pp. 254–269). Hershey, PA: Business Science Reference; doi:10.4018/978-1-60960-463-9.ch015

Unhelkar, B. (2011). *Handbook of research on green ICT: Technology, business and social perspectives*. Hershey, PA: IGI Global; doi:10.4018/978-1-61692-834-6

Unhelkar, B., Ghanbary, A., & Younessi, H. (2010). Collaborative business process engineering (CBPE) model. In B. Unhelkar, A. Ghanbary, & H. Younessi (Eds.), *Collaborative business process engineering and global organizations: Frameworks for service integration* (pp. 98–120). Hershey, PA: Business Science Reference; doi:10.4018/978-1-60566-689-1.ch004

Unhelkar, B., Ghanbary, A., & Younessi, H. (2010). Emerging technologies for business collaboration. In B. Unhelkar, A. Ghanbary, & H. Younessi (Eds.), *Collaborative business process engineering and global organizations: Frameworks for service integration* (pp. 37–64). Hershey, PA: Business Science Reference; doi:10.4018/978-1-60566-689-1.ch002

Unhelkar, B., Ghanbary, A., & Younessi, H. (2010). Fundamentals of collaborative business. In B. Unhelkar, A. Ghanbary, & H. Younessi (Eds.), *Collaborative business process engineering and global organizations: Frameworks for service integration* (pp. 1–36). Hershey, PA: Business Science Reference; doi:10.4018/978-1-60566-689-1.ch001

Van Huy, L., Rowe, F., Truex, D., & Huynh, M. Q. (2012). An empirical study of determinants of e-commerce adoption in SMEs in Vietnam: An economy in transition. *Journal of Global Information Management*, *20*(3), 23–54. doi:10.4018/jgim.2012070102

Vannoy, S. A. (2011). A structured content analytic assessment of business services advertisements in the cloud-based web services marketplace. *International Journal of Dependable and Trustworthy Information Systems, 2*(1), 18–49. doi:10.4018/jdtis.2011010102

Vasconcelos, V., & Campos, P. (2012). The role of social networks in distributed informal information systems for innovation. In J. Varajão, M. Cruz-Cunha, & A. Trigo (Eds.), *Organizational integration of enterprise systems and resources: Advancements and applications* (pp. 60–75). Hershey, PA: Business Science Reference; doi:10.4018/978-1-4666-1764-3.ch004

Venkatraman, R., Venkatraman, S., & Asaithambi, S. P. (2013). A practical cloud services implementation framework for e-businesses. In K. Tarnay, S. Imre, & L. Xu (Eds.), *Research and development in e-business through service-oriented solutions* (pp. 167–198). Hershey, PA: Business Science Reference; doi:10.4018/978-1-4666-4181-5.ch008

Verkasalo, H. (2011). Analysis of the forces reshaping the mobile internet business. In M. Bartolacci & S. Powell (Eds.), *Interdisciplinary and multidimensional perspectives in telecommunications and networking: Emerging findings* (pp. 19–45). Hershey, PA: Information Science Reference; doi:10.4018/978-1-60960-505-6.ch003

Verma, A. (2013). Effects of phishing on e-commerce with special reference to India. In R. Khurana & R. Aggarwal (Eds.), *Interdisciplinary perspectives on business convergence, computing, and legality* (pp. 186–197). Hershey, PA: Business Science Reference; doi:10.4018/978-1-4666-4209-6.ch017

Walker, B., & Posey, E. (2013). Digital El Paso: A public-private business model for community wireless networks. In A. Abdelaal (Ed.), *Social and economic effects of community wireless networks and infrastructures* (pp. 94–111). Hershey, PA: Information Science Reference; doi:10.4018/978-1-4666-2997-4.ch006

Wan, Y., Clegg, B., & Dey, P. K. (2013). A framework for enabling dynamic e-business strategies via new enterprise paradigms and ERP solutions. In *Enterprise resource planning: Concepts, methodologies, tools, and applications* (pp. 1561–1595). Hershey, PA: Business Science Reference; doi:10.4018/978-1-4666-4153-2.ch083

Wang, F., Lupton, N., Rawlinson, D., & Zhang, X. (2012). EBDMSS: A web-based decision making support system for strategic e-business management. In P. Zaraté (Ed.), *Integrated and strategic advancements in decision making support systems* (pp. 265–284). Hershey, PA: Information Science Reference; doi:10.4018/978-1-4666-1746-9.ch019

Wenyin, L., Liu, A., Li, Q., & Huang, L. (2011). Business models for insurance of business web services. In H. Leung, D. Chiu, & P. Hung (Eds.), *Service intelligence and service science: Evolutionary technologies and challenges* (pp. 261–272). Hershey, PA: Information Science Reference; doi:10.4018/978-1-61520-819-7.ch014

Wiedmann, K., Reeh, M., & Schumacher, H. (2010). Employment and acceptance of near field communication in mobile marketing. In K. Pousttchi & D. Wiedemann (Eds.), *Handbook of research on mobile marketing management* (pp. 190–212). Hershey, PA: Business Science Reference; doi:10.4018/978-1-60566-074-5.ch011

Williams, J. G., & Premchaiswadi, W. (2011). On-line credit card payment processing and fraud prevention for e-business. In *Global business: Concepts, methodologies, tools and applications* (pp. 699–717). Hershey, PA: Business Science Reference; doi:10.4018/978-1-60960-587-2.ch312

Wilms, A., & Andriole, S. J. (2010). Business technology strategy for a specialty chemicals company. *Journal of Information Technology Research, 3*(3), 11–18. doi:10.4018/jitr.2010070102

Winkler, U., & Gilani, W. (2012). Business continuity management of business driven IT landscapes. In S. Reiff-Marganiec & M. Tilly (Eds.), *Handbook of research on service-oriented systems and non-functional properties: Future directions* (pp. 381–399). Hershey, PA: Information Science Reference; doi:10.4018/978-1-61350-432-1.ch017

Wollenberg, A. (2013). Optimizing international joint venture (IJV) ownership structures: A technology and knowledge transfer-linked productivity growth perspective. In B. Christiansen, E. Turkina, & N. Williams (Eds.), *Cultural and technological influences on global business* (pp. 142–164). Hershey, PA: Business Science Reference; doi:10.4018/978-1-4666-3966-9.ch009

Wood, A. M., Moultrie, J., & Eckert, C. (2010). Product form evolution. In A. Silva & R. Simoes (Eds.), *Handbook of research on trends in product design and development: Technological and organizational perspectives* (pp. 499–512). Hershey, PA: Business Science Reference; doi:10.4018/978-1-61520-617-9.ch027

Wresch, W., & Fraser, S. (2011). Persistent barriers to e-commerce in developing countries: A longitudinal study of efforts by Caribbean companies. *Journal of Global Information Management, 19*(3), 30–44. doi:10.4018/jgim.2011070102

Wresch, W., & Fraser, S. (2013). Persistent barriers to e-commerce in developing countries: A longitudinal study of efforts by Caribbean companies. In F. Tan (Ed.), *Global diffusion and adoption of technologies for knowledge and information sharing* (pp. 205–220). Hershey, PA: Information Science Reference; doi:10.4018/978-1-4666-2142-8.ch009

Xiao, X., Liu, Y., & Zhang, Z. (2012). The analysis of the logistics mode decision to e-commerce. *Journal of Electronic Commerce in Organizations*, *10*(4), 57–70. doi::10.4018/jeco.2012100105

Xu, L. (2010). Outsourcing and multi-party business collaborations modeling. In K. St.Amant (Ed.), *IT outsourcing: Concepts, methodologies, tools, and applications* (pp. 558–577). Hershey, PA: Business Science Reference; doi:10.4018/978-1-60566-770-6.ch033

Xu, M., Rohatgi, R., & Duan, Y. (2010). Engaging SMEs in e-business: Insights from an empirical study. In *Business information systems: Concepts, methodologies, tools and applications* (pp. 115–134). Hershey, PA: Business Science Reference; doi:10.4018/978-1-61520-969-9.ch009

Yermish, I., Miori, V., Yi, J., Malhotra, R., & Klimberg, R. (2010). Business plus intelligence plus technology equals business intelligence. *International Journal of Business Intelligence Research*, *1*(1), 48–63. doi::10.4018/jbir.2010071704

Yeung, W. L. (2013). Specifying business-level protocols for web services based collaborative processes. In A. Loo (Ed.), *Distributed computing innovations for business, engineering, and science* (pp. 137–154). Hershey, PA: Information Science Reference; doi:10.4018/978-1-4666-2533-4.ch007

Z arour, M., Abran, A., & Desharnais, J. (2014). Software process improvement for small and very small enterprises. In *Software design and development: Concepts, methodologies, tools, and applications* (pp. 1363-1384). Hershey, PA: Information Science Reference. doi:10.4018/978-1-4666-4301-7.ch066

Zerenler, M., & Gözlü, S. (2012). Issues influencing electronic commerce activities of SMEs: A study of the Turkish automotive supplier industry. In *Human resources management: Concepts, methodologies, tools, and applications* (pp. 1035–1055). Hershey, PA: Business Science Reference; doi:10.4018/978-1-4666-1601-1.ch064

# Compilation of References


Abdullah, M., Ahmad, R., Peck, L. S., Kasirun, Z. M., & Alshammari, F. (2014). Benefits of CMM and CMMI-based software process improvement. In *Software design and development: Concepts, methodologies, tools, and applications* (pp. 1385–1400). Hershey, PA: Information Science Reference; doi:10.4018/978-1-4666-4301-7.ch067

Abu-Shanab, E., & Ghaleb, O. (2012). Adoption of mobile commerce technology: An involvement of trust and risk concerns. *International Journal of Technology Diffusion*, *3*(2), 36–49. doi:10.4018/jtd.2012040104

Acar, E., Kocak, L., Sey, Y., & Arditi, D. (2005). Use of information and communication technologies by small and medium-sized enterprises (SMEs) in building construction. *Construction Management and Economics*, *23*(7), 713–722. doi:10.1080/01446190500127112

Adapa, S. (2013). Electronic retailing of prepared food in Australia. In K. Tarnay, S. Imre, & L. Xu (Eds.), *Research and development in e-business through service-oriented solutions* (pp. 280–292). Hershey, PA: Business Science Reference; doi:10.4018/978-1-4666-4181-5.ch014

Adizes, I. (1979). Organizational passages: Diagnosing and treating life cycle problems in organizations. *Organizational Dynamics*, *8*(1), 3–24. doi:10.1016/0090-2616(79)90001-9

Adler, P., & Kwon, S. (1999). Social capital: The good, the bad, and the ugly. In E. L. Lesser (Ed.), *Knowledge and Social Capital*. Boston, MA: Butterworth-Heinemann. doi:10.2139/ssrn.186928

Adner, R., & Zemsky, P. (2006). A demand-based perspective on sustainable competitive advantage. *Strategic Management Journal*, *27*(3), 215–239. doi:10.1002/smj.513

Agarwal, R., & Prasas, J. (2000). A field study of the adoption of software process innovations by information system professionals. *IEEE Transactions on Engineering Management*, *47*(3), 295–308. doi:10.1109/17.865899

Ahlstrom, D., & Bruton, G. D. (2006). Venture capital in emerging economics: Network and institutional change. *Entrepreneurship Theory and Practice*, *30*(2), 299–320. doi:10.1111/j.1540-6520.2006.00122.x

Ahuja, G., & Katila, R. (2004). Where do resources come from? The role of idiosyncratic situations. *Strategic Management Journal*, *25*(89), 887–904. doi:10.1002/smj.401

Aklouf, Y., & Drias, H. (2011). An adaptive e-commerce architecture for enterprise information exchange. In *Enterprise information systems: Concepts, methodologies, tools and applications* (pp. 329–345). Hershey, PA: Business Science Reference; doi:10.4018/978-1-61692-852-0.ch202

Alavi, M. T., & Karami, A. (2009). Managers of small and medium enterprises: Mission statement and enhanced organizational performance. *Journal of Management Development*, *28*(6), 555–562. doi:10.1108/02621710910959729

Alavi, M., & Leidner, D. E. (2001). Review: Knowledge management and knowledge management systems: Conceptual foundations and research issues. *Management Information Systems Quarterly*, *25*(1), 107–136. doi:10.2307/3250961

Alavi, S. (2013). Collaborative customer relationship management-co-creation and collaboration through online communities. *International Journal of Virtual Communities and Social Networking*, *5*(1), 1–18. doi:10.4018/jvcsn.2013010101

Alavi, S., & Ahuja, V. (2013). E-commerce in a web 2.0 world: Using online business communities to impact consumer price sensitivity. *International Journal of Online Marketing*, *3*(2), 38–55. doi:10.4018/ijom.2013040103

Alawneh, A., Al-Refai, H., & Batiha, K. (2011). E-business adoption by Jordanian banks: An exploratory study of the key factors and performance indicators. In A. Tatnall (Ed.), *Actor-network theory and technology innovation: Advancements and new concepts* (pp. 113–128). Hershey, PA: Information Science Reference; doi:10.4018/978-1-60960-197-3.ch008

Albadvi, A., Keramati, A., & Razmi, J. (2007). Assessing the impact of information technology on firm performance considering the role of intervening variables: Organizational infrastructures and business processes reengineering. *International Journal of Production Research*, *45*(12), 2697–2734. doi:10.1080/00207540600767780

Albertao, B. M., & Fernando, L. L. (2007). A firm-level analysis of determinants of ICT adoption in Spain. *Technovation*, *27*(6/7), 352–366.

Albuquerque, S. L., & Gondim, P. R. (2012). Applying continuous authentication to protect electronic transactions. In T. Chou (Ed.), *Information assurance and security technologies for risk assessment and threat management: Advances* (pp. 134–161). Hershey, PA: Information Science Reference; doi:10.4018/978-1-61350-507-6.ch005

Aldrich, H. (1999). *Evolving Organizations*. London: Sage Publications.

Alfahl, H., Sanzogni, L., & Houghton, L. (2012). Mobile commerce adoption in organizations: A literature review and future research directions. *Journal of Electronic Commerce in Organizations*, *10*(2), 61–78. doi:10.4018/jeco.2012040104

Allison, C. W., & Hayes, J. (1996). The cognitive styles index: A measure of intuition-analysis for organizational research. *Journal of Management Studies*, *33*(1), 119–135. doi:10.1111/j.1467-6486.1996.tb00801.x

Al-Nawayseh, M. K., Alnabhan, M. M., Al-Debei, M. M., & Balachandran, W. (2013). An adaptive decision support system for last mile logistics in e-commerce: A study on online grocery shopping. *International Journal of Decision Support System Technology*, *5*(1), 40–65. doi:10.4018/jdsst.2013010103

Aloini, D., Dulmin, R., & Mininno, V. (2013). E-procurement: What really matters in B2B e-reverse auctions. In P. Ordóñez de Pablos, J. Lovelle, J. Gayo, & R. Tennyson (Eds.), *E-procurement management for successful electronic government systems* (pp. 87–113). Hershey, PA: Information Science Reference; doi:10.4018/978-1-4666-2119-0.ch006

Al-Qirim, N. (2007). The adoption of e-commerce communications and applications technologies in small business in New Zealand. *Electronic Commerce Research and Applications: Intelligent Agents in E-services*, *6*(4), 462–473. doi:10.1016/j.elerap.2007.02.012

Alshawi, S., Missi, F., & Irani, Z. (2010). Organizational, technical and data quality factors in CRM adoption: SMEs perspective. *Industrial Marketing Management*, *40*(3), 376–383. doi:10.1016/j.indmarman.2010.08.006

Al-Somali, S. A., Clegg, B., & Gholami, R. (2013). An investigation into the adoption and implementation of electronic commerce in Saudi Arabian small and medium enterprises. In *Small and medium enterprises: Concepts, methodologies, tools, and applications* (pp. 816–839). Hershey, PA: Business Science Reference; doi:10.4018/978-1-4666-3886-0.ch040

Al-Somali, S. A., Gholami, R., & Clegg, B. (2013). An investigation into the adoption of electronic commerce among Saudi Arabian SMEs. In M. Khosrow-Pour (Ed.), *E-commerce for organizational development and competitive advantage* (pp. 126–150). Hershey, PA: Business Science Reference; doi:10.4018/978-1-4666-3622-4.ch007

Amer, M., & Gómez, J. M. (2010). Measuring B2C quality of electronic service: Towards a common consensus. In I. Lee (Ed.), *Encyclopedia of e-business development and management in the global economy* (pp. 135–143). Hershey, PA: Business Science Reference; doi:10.4018/978-1-61520-611-7.ch014

Amer, M., & Gómez, J. M. (2012). Measuring quality of electronic services: Moving from business-to-consumer into business-to-business marketplace. In E. Kajan, F. Dorloff, & I. Bedini (Eds.), *Handbook of research on e-business standards and protocols: Documents, data and advanced web technologies* (pp. 637–654). Hershey, PA: Business Science Reference; doi:10.4018/978-1-4666-0146-8.ch029

Andries, P., & Debackere, K. (2006). Adoption of new technology-based ventures: Insights at the company level. *International Journal of Management Reviews*, *8*(2), 91–112. doi:10.1111/j.1468-2370.2006.00122.x

Andriole, S. J. (2010). Business technology strategy for an energy information company. *Journal of Information Technology Research*, *3*(3), 19–42. doi::10.4018/jitr.2010070103

Andriole, S. J. (2010). Templates for the development of business technology strategies. *Journal of Information Technology Research*, *3*(3), 1–10. doi:10.4018/jitr.2010070101

Ang, J. (1991). Small business uniqueness and the theory of financial management. *The Journal of Small Business Finance*, *1*(1), 1–13.

Ang, J. (1992). On the theory of finance for privately held firms. *The Journal of Small Business Finance*, *1*(3), 185–203.

Ang, J., Cole, R., & Lin, J. (2000). Agency costs and ownership structure. *The Journal of Finance*, *55*(1), 81–106. doi:10.1111/0022-1082.00201

Anonymous, . (2006). How to succeed in small business. *Maclean's*, *119*(40), 9, 49–57.

Apulu, I., & Latham, A. (2011). Drivers for information and communication technology adoption: A case study of Nigerian small and medium sized enterprises. *International Journal of Business and Management*, *6*(5), 51–60. doi:10.5539/ijbm.v6n5p51

Archer, N. (2010). Electronic marketplace support for B2B business transactions. In *Electronic services: Concepts, methodologies, tools and applications* (pp. 85–93). Hershey, PA: Information Science Reference; doi:10.4018/978-1-61520-967-5.ch007

Archer, N. (2010). Management considerations for B2B online exchanges. In *Business information systems: Concepts, methodologies, tools and applications* (pp. 1740–1747). Hershey, PA: Business Science Reference; doi:10.4018/978-1-61520-969-9.ch105

Ardichivli, A., Cardozo, R., & Ray, S. (2003). A theory of entrepreneurial opportunity identification and development. *Journal of Business Venturing*, *18*(1), 105–123. doi:10.1016/S0883-9026(01)00068-4

Arduini, D., Nascia, L., & Zanfei, A. (2012). Complementary approaches to the diffusion of innovation: Empirical evidence on e-services adoption in Italy. *International Journal of E-Services and Mobile Applications*, *4*(3), 42–64. doi:10.4018/jesma.2012070103

Argiles, J. M., & Slof, E. J. (2003). The use of financial accounting information and firm performance: An empirical quantification for farms. *Accounting and Business Review*, *33*(4), 251–273. doi:10.1080/00014788.2003.9729653

Arh, T., Dimovski, V., & Blažic, B. J. (2011). ICT and web 2.0 technologies as a determinant of business performance. In M. Al-Mutairi & L. Mohammed (Eds.), *Cases on ICT utilization, practice and solutions: Tools for managing day-to-day issues* (pp. 59–77). Hershey, PA: Information Science Reference; doi:10.4018/978-1-60960-015-0.ch005

Arikpo, I., Osofisan, A., & Eteng, I. E. (2012). Enhancing trust in e-commerce in developing IT environments: A feedback-based perspective. In A. Usoro, G. Majewski, P. Ifinedo, & I. Arikpo (Eds.), *Leveraging developing economies with the use of information technology: Trends and tools* (pp. 193–203). Hershey, PA: Information Science Reference; doi:10.4018/978-1-4666-1637-0.ch011

Armstrong, S. J., & Hird, A. (2009). Cognitive style and entrepreneurial drive of new and mature business owner-managers. *Journal of Business and Psychology*, *24*(4), 419–430. doi:10.1007/s10869-009-9114-4

Arregle, J., Hitt, M. A., Sirmon, D. G., & Very, P. (2007). The development of organizational social capital: Attributes of family firms. *Journal of Management Studies*, *44*(1), 73–95. doi:10.1111/j.1467-6486.2007.00665.x

Aryanto, V. D., & Chrismastuti, A. A. (2013). Model for digital economy in Indonesia. In I. Oncioiu (Ed.), *Business innovation, development, and advancement in the digital economy* (pp. 60–77). Hershey, PA: Business Science Reference; doi:10.4018/978-1-4666-2934-9.ch005

Ash, C. G., & Burn, J. M. (2003). A strategic framework for the management of ERP enabled e-business change. *European Journal of Operational Research*, *146*(2), 374–387. doi:10.1016/S0377-2217(02)00556-8

Asim, M., & Petkovic, M. (2012). Fundamental building blocks for security interoperability in e-business. In E. Kajan, F. Dorloff, & I. Bedini (Eds.), *Handbook of research on e-business standards and protocols: documents, data and advanced web technologies* (pp. 269–292). Hershey, PA: Business Science Reference; doi:10.4018/978-1-4666-0146-8.ch013

Askool, S., Jacobs, A., & Nakata, K. (2013). A method of analysing the use of social networking sites in business. In *IT policy and ethics: Concepts, methodologies, tools, and applications* (pp. 794–813). Hershey, PA: Information Science Reference; doi:10.4018/978-1-4666-2919-6.ch036

Association, I. R. (2013). Enterprise resource planning: Concepts, methodologies, tools, and applications (Vols. 1–3). Hershey, PA: IGI Global; doi:10.4018/978-1-4666-4153-2

Astrachan, J. H., & Shanker, M. C. (2003). Family businesses contributions to the US economy: A closer look. *Family Business Review*, *15*(3), 211–219.

Austin, J., Stevenson, H., & Wei-Skillern, J. (2006). Social and commercial entrepreneurship: Same, different, or both? *Entrepreneurship Theory and Practice*, *30*(1), 1–22. doi:10.1111/j.1540-6520.2006.00107.x

Avram, D. O., & Kuhne, S. (2008). Implementing responsible business behavior from a strategic management perspective: Developing a framework for Austrian SMEs. *Journal of Business Ethics*, *82*(2), 463–475. doi:10.1007/s10551-008-9897-7

Azab, N., & Khalifa, N. (2013). Web 2.0 and opportunities for entrepreneurs: How Egyptian entrepreneurs perceive and exploit web 2.0 technologies. In N. Azab (Ed.), *Cases on web 2.0 in developing countries: Studies on implementation, application, and use* (pp. 1–32). Hershey, PA: Information Science Reference; doi:10.4018/978-1-4666-2515-0.ch001

Azevedo, S. G., & Carvalho, H. (2012). RFID technology in the fashion supply chain: An exploratory analysis. In T. Choi (Ed.), *Fashion supply chain management: Industry and business analysis* (pp. 303–326). Hershey, PA: Information Science Reference; doi:10.4018/978-1-60960-756-2.ch017

Bahaddad, A. A., AlGhamdi, R., & Houghton, L. (2012). To what extent would e-mall enable SMEs to adopt E-commerce? *International Journal of Business and Management*, *7*(22), 123–132. doi:10.5539/ijbm.v7n22p123

Baird, L., & Meshoulam, I. (1988). Managing two fits of strategic human resource management. *Academy of Management Review*, *13*(1), 116–126.

Bakos, J. Y., & Treacy, M. E. (1986). Information technology and corporate strategy: A research perspective. *Management Information Systems Quarterly*, *10*(2), 107–119. doi:10.2307/249029

Balderson, D. W. (2011). *Canadian Entrepreneurship and Small Business Management* (8th ed.). Toronto: McGraw-Hill Ryerson.

Baldwin, T. T., Danielson, C., & Wiggenhorn, W. (1997). The evolution of learning strategies in organizations: From employee development to business redefinition. *The Academy of Management Executive*, *11*(4), 47–58.

Balje, S. H., & Waasdorp, P. M. (1999). High growth companies in The Netherlands. In B. C. M. Alder (Ed.), *The Formula for High Growth Companies: A Question of Smart Competition? TNO Report STB-98-32*.

Baltzan, P., Phillips, A., & Detlor, B. (2011). *Business Driven Information Systems* (2nd Canadian Edition). Toronto, Ontario: McGraw-Hill Ryerson.

Bandura, A. (1997). *Self-efficacy: The Exercise of Control*. New York: W. H. Freeman & Co.

Baporikar, N. (2013). ICT challenge for ebusiness in SMEs. *International Journal of Strategic Information Technology and Applications*, *4*(1), 15–26. doi:10.4018/jsita.2013010102

Barach, J. A., Gantisky, J., Carson, J. A., & Doochin, B. J. (1988). Entry of the next generation: Strategic challenge for family business. *Journal of Small Business Management*, *26*(2), 49–56.

Barbin Laurindo, F. J., Monteiro de Carvalho, M., & Shimizu, T. (2010). Strategic alignment between business and information technology. In M. Hunter (Ed.), *Strategic information systems: Concepts, methodologies, tools, and applications* (pp. 20–28). Hershey, PA: Information Science Reference; doi:10.4018/978-1-60566-677-8.ch002

Barjis, J. (2012). Software engineering security based on business process modeling. In K. Khan (Ed.), *Security-aware systems applications and software development methods* (pp. 52–68). Hershey, PA: Information Science Reference; doi:10.4018/978-1-4666-1580-9.ch004

Barkham, R. J. (1994). Entrepreneurial characteristics and the size of the new firm: A model and an econometric test. *Small Business Economics*, *6*(2), 117–126. doi:10.1007/BF01065184

Barki, H., & Hartwick, J. (1994). Measuring User Participation, User Involvement, and User Attitude. *Management Information Systems Quarterly*, *18*(1), 59–82. doi:10.2307/249610

Barnes, D., & Hinton, M. (2011). The benefits of an e-business performance measurement system. In N. Shi & G. Silvius (Eds.), *Enterprise IT governance, business value and performance measurement* (pp. 158–169). Hershey, PA: Information Science Reference; doi:10.4018/978-1-60566-346-3.ch011

Barney, J. (1986). Strategic factor markets: Expectations, luck, and business strategy. *Management Science*, *32*(10), 1231–1241. doi:10.1287/mnsc.32.10.1231

Barney, J. (1991). Firm resources and sustained competitive advantage. *Journal of Management*, *17*(1), 99–120. doi:10.1177/014920639101700108

Barney, J. (2001). Resource-based theories of competitive advantage: A ten-year retrospective on the resource-based view. *Journal of Management*, *27*(6), 643–650. doi:10.1177/014920630102700602

Barney, J. B. (1995). Looking inside for competitive advantage. *The Academy of Management Executive*, *9*(4), 49–61.

Barney, J. B. (1996). The resource-based theory of the firm. *Organization Science*, *7*(5), 469. doi:10.1287/orsc.7.5.469

Barney, J., Wright, M., & Ketchen, D. J. (2001). The resource-based view of the firm: Ten years after 1991. *Journal of Management*, *27*(6), 625–641. doi:10.1177/014920630102700601

BarNir, A., Gallaugher, J. M., & Auger, P.BarNir. (2003). Business process digitization, strategy, and the impact of firm age and size: The case of the magazine publishing company. *Journal of Business Venturing*, *18*(6), 789–814. doi:10.1016/S0883-9026(03)00030-2

Baron, R. A. (1998). Cognitive mechanisms in entrepreneurship: Why and when entrepreneurs think differently than other people. *Journal of Business Venturing*, *13*(4), 275–294. doi:10.1016/S0883-9026(97)00031-1

Baron, R. A., & Markman, G. D. (2000). Beyond social capital: The role of social competence in entrepreneurs' success. *The Academy of Management Executive*, *14*(1), 106–116.

Barrett, R., & Mayson, S. (2007). Human resource management in growing small firms. *Journal of Small Business and Enterprise Development*, *14*(2), 307–320. doi:10.1108/14626000710746727

Barringer, B. R., & Jones, F. F. (2004). Achieving rapid growth – revisiting the managerial capacity problem. *Journal of Developmental Entrepreneurship*, *9*(1), 73–87.

Barringer, B. R., & Jones, F. F. (2004). Achieving rapid growth: Revisiting the managerial capacity problem. *Journal of Developmental Entrepreneurship*, *9*(1), 73–86.

Bask, A., Lipponen, M., & Tinnilä, M. (2012). E-commerce logistics: A literature research review and topics for future research. *International Journal of E-Services and Mobile Applications*, *4*(3), 1–22. doi:10.4018/jesma.2012070101

Bask, A., & Tinnilä, M. (2013). Impact of product characteristics on supply chains: An analytical literature review. *International Journal of Applied Logistics*, *4*(1), 35–59. doi:10.4018/jal.2013010103

Basu, S. (2012). Direct taxation and e-commerce: Possibility and desirability. In E. Druicã (Ed.), *Digital economy innovations and impacts on society* (pp. 26–48). Hershey, PA: Information Science Reference; doi:10.4018/978-1-4666-1556-4.ch003

Bates, T. (1995). A comparison of franchise and independent small business survival rates. *Small Business Economics*, *7*(5), 377–388. doi:10.1007/BF01302738

Bates, T., & Nucci, A. (1989). An analysis of small business size and rate of discontinuance. *Journal of Small Business Management*, *27*(4), 1–7.

Beattie, R. (1999). The creative entrepreneur: A study of the entrepreneur's creative processes. www.babson.edu/entrep/fer/papers/99/III/III_B/IIIB%20Text.htm

Beaver, G. (2003). Small business: Success and failure. *Strategic Change, 12*(3), 115–122. doi:10.1002/jsc.624

Beaver, G., & Jennings, P. (2005). Competitive advantage and entrepreneurial power: The dark side of entrepreneurship. *Journal of Small Business and Enterprise Development, 12*(1), 9–23. doi:10.1108/14626000510579617

Beaver, G., & Prince, C. (2004). Management, strategy and policy in UK small business sector: A critical review. *Journal of Small Business and Enterprise Development, 11*(1), 34–49. doi:10.1108/14626000410519083

Becker, G. S. (1975). *Human Capital* (2nd ed.). New York: Columbia University Press.

Beckinsale, M. (2011). eBusiness among ethnic minority businesses: Ethnic entrepreneurs' ICT adoption and readiness. In S. Sharma (Ed.), E-adoption and socio-economic impacts: Emerging infrastructural effects (pp. 168-189). Hershey, PA: Information Science Reference. doi::10.4018/978-1-60960-597-1.ch009

Beckinsale, M. (2010). E-business among ethnic minority businesses: The case of ethnic entrepreneurs. In B. Thomas & G. Simmons (Eds.), *E-commerce adoption and small business in the global marketplace: Tools for optimization* (pp. 187–207). Hershey, PA: Business Science Reference; doi:10.4018/978-1-60566-998-4.ch010

Bedeian, A. (1990). Choice and determination: A comment. *Strategic Management Journal, 11*(7), 571–573. doi:10.1002/smj.4250110707

Bedini, I., Gardarin, G., & Nguyen, B. (2011). Semantic technologies and e-business. In E. Kajan (Ed.), *Electronic business interoperability: Concepts, opportunities and challenges* (pp. 243–278). Hershey, PA: Business Science Reference; doi:10.4018/978-1-60960-485-1.ch011

Beedle, J., & Wang, S. (2013). Roles of a technology leader. In S. Wang & T. Hartsell (Eds.), *Technology integration and foundations for effective leadership* (pp. 228–241). Hershey, PA: Information Science Reference; doi:10.4018/978-1-4666-2656-0.ch013

Belhajjame, K., & Brambilla, M. (2013). Ontological description and similarity-based discovery of business process models. In J. Krogstie (Ed.), *Frameworks for developing efficient information systems: Models, theory, and practice* (pp. 30–50). Hershey, PA: Engineering Science Reference; doi:10.4018/978-1-4666-4161-7.ch002

Belich, T. J., & Dubinsky, A. J. (1999). Information processing among exporters: An empirical examination of small firms. *Journal of Marketing Theory and Practice, 7*(4), 45–58.

Bennett, J., Polkinghorne, M., Pearce, J., & Hudson, M. (1999). Technology transfer for SMEs. *Engineering Management Journal*, (April): 75–80.

Bennett, R., & McCoshan, A. (1993). *Enterprise and Human Resource Development.* London: Paul Chapman Publishing Ltd.

Benou, P., & Bitos, V. (2010). Developing mobile commerce applications. In M. Khosrow-Pour (Ed.), *E-commerce trends for organizational advancement: New applications and methods* (pp. 1–15). Hershey, PA: Information Science Reference; doi:10.4018/978-1-60566-964-9.ch001

Bergeron, F., & Raymond, L. (•••). (19920. Planning of information systems to gain a competitive advantage. *Journal of Small Business Management, 30*(1), 21–26.

Berisha-Namani, M. (2013). Information systems usage in business and management. In I. Oncioiu (Ed.), *Business innovation, development, and advancement in the digital economy* (pp. 48–59). Hershey, PA: Business Science Reference; doi:10.4018/978-1-4666-2934-9.ch004

Berman, P. (1997). *Small business and entrepreneurship*. Scarborough, Ontario: Prentice Hall.

Berman, P. (1997). *Small Business and Entrepreneurship*. Scarborough, Ontario: Prentice Hall.

Bermúdez, G. M., & Rojas, L. A. (2013). Model-driven engineering for electronic commerce. In V. Díaz, J. Lovelle, B. García-Bustelo, & O. Martínez (Eds.), *Progressions and innovations in model-driven software engineering* (pp. 196–208). Hershey, PA: Engineering Science Reference; doi:10.4018/978-1-4666-4217-1.ch007

Bernardino, J. (2013). Open business intelligence for better decision-making. *International Journal of Information Communication Technologies and Human Development, 5*(2), 20–36. doi:10.4018/jicthd.2013040102

Berry, L. L. (1983). Relationship marketing. Chapter. In L. L. Berry, G. L. Shostack, & G. D. Upah (Eds.), *Emerging Perspectives on Service Marketing*. Chicago, IL: American Marketing Association.

Berzins, M. (2012). Scams and the Australian e-business environment. In K. Mohammed Rezaul (Ed.), *Strategic and pragmatic e-business: Implications for future business practices* (pp. 156–175). Hershey, PA: Business Science Reference; doi:10.4018/978-1-4666-1619-6.ch007

Bessant, J., Burkinshaw, J., & Delbridge, R. (20040. Innovation as usual. *Business Strategy Review*, 15(3), 32-35.

Beugelsdijk, S. (2007). Entrepreneurial culture, regional innovativeness and economic growth. *Journal of Evolutionary Economics, 17*(2), 187–210. doi:10.1007/s00191-006-0048-y

Bhagwat, R., & Sharma, M. K. (2007). Information system architecture: A framework for a cluster of small and medium-sized enterprises (SMEs). *Production Planning and Control, 18*(4), 283–296. doi:10.1080/09537280701248578

Bharadwaj, A. S. (2000). A resource-based perspective on information technology capability and firm performance: An empirical investigation. *Management Information Systems Quarterly, 24*(1), 169–196. doi:10.2307/3250983

Bharadwaj, A. S., & Soni, R. G. (2007). E-commerce usage and perception of e-commerce issues among small firms: Results and implications from an empirical study. *Journal of Small Business Management, 45*(4), 501–521. doi:10.1111/j.1540-627X.2007.00225.x

Bharati, P., & Chaudhury, A. (2010). IT adoption in small and medium-sized enterprises: The role of knowledge acquisition. *Proceedings of Americas Conference on Information Systems*, Lima, August, 12-15.

Bhatt, G. D., & Grover, V. (2005). Types of information technology capabilities and their role in competitive advantage: An empirical study. *Journal of Management Information Systems*, *22*(2), 253–277.

Bidgoli, H. (2013). *MIS3*. Boston, MA: Course Technology, Cengage Learning.

Binsaleh, M., & Hassan, S. (2011). Systems development methodology for mobile commerce applications. *International Journal of Mobile Computing and Multimedia Communications*, *3*(4), 36–52. doi:10.4018/jmcmc.2011100103

Binsaleh, M., & Hassan, S. (2013). Systems development methodology for mobile commerce applications. In I. Khalil & E. Weippl (Eds.), *Contemporary challenges and solutions for mobile and multimedia technologies* (pp. 146–162). Hershey, PA: Information Science Reference; doi:10.4018/978-1-4666-2163-3.ch009

Birley, S. (1986). The role of new firms: Births, deaths, and job creation. *Strategic Management Journal*, *7*(4), 361–376. doi:10.1002/smj.4250070406

Birley, S. (1996). The start-up. In P. Burns & J. Dewhurst (Eds.), *Small Business and Entrepreneurship*. Basingstoke: Macmillan.

Bjerke, B. (2007). *Understanding Entrepreneurship*. Cheltenham and Northampton, MA: Edward Elgar.

Bjuggren, P., & Sund, L. (2002). A transaction cost rationale for transition of the firm within the family. *Small Business Economics*, *19*(2), 123–134. doi:10.1023/A:1016289106477

Blake, R., Gordon, S., & Shankaranarayanan, G. (2013). The role of case-based research in information technology and systems. In P. Isaias & M. Baptista Nunes (Eds.), *Information systems research and exploring social artifacts: approaches and methodologies* (pp. 200–220). Hershey, PA: Information Science Reference; doi:10.4018/978-1-4666-2491-7.ch011

Blili, S., & Raymond, L. (1993). IT: Threats and opportunities for SMEs. *International Journal of Information Management*, *13*, 439–448. doi:10.1016/0268-4012(93)90060-H

Block, J. H., & Wagner, M. (2010). Necessity and opportunity entrepreneurs in Germany: Characteristics and earnings differential. *Small Business Review*, *62*, 154–174.

Bluedorn, A. C., & Martin, G. (2008). The time frames of entrepreneurs. *Journal of Business Venturing*, *23*(1), 1–20. doi:10.1016/j.jbusvent.2006.05.005

Boateng, R., Heeks, R., Molla, A., & Hinson, R. (2013). Advancing e-commerce beyond readiness in a developing country: Experiences of Ghanaian firms. In M. Khosrow-Pour (Ed.), *E-commerce for organizational development and competitive advantage* (pp. 1–17). Hershey, PA: Business Science Reference; doi:10.4018/978-1-4666-3622-4.ch001

Bonfatti, F., Monari, P. D., & Martinelli, L. (2011). Business document exchange between small companies. In E. Kajan (Ed.), *Electronic business interoperability: Concepts, opportunities and challenges* (pp. 482–510). Hershey, PA: Business Science Reference; doi:10.4018/978-1-60960-485-1.ch020

Boone, C., de Brabander, B., & Hellemans, J. (2000). Research note: CEO locus of control and small firm performance. *Organization Studies, 21*(3), 641–646. doi:10.1177/0170840600213007

Boot, A. (2000). Relationship banking: What do we know? *Journal of Financial Intermediation, 9*(1), 7–25. doi:10.1006/jfin.2000.0282

Bosma, N., van Praag, M., Thurik, R., & de Wit, G. (2004). The value of human and social capital investments for the business performance of startups. *Small Business Economics, 23*(3), 227–236. doi:10.1023/B:SBEJ.0000032032.21192.72

Boswell, J. (1971). Corporate planning in small manufacturing firms. *Journal of Business Policy, 2*(1), 49–53.

Boucadair, M., & Binet, D. (2014). Issues with current internet architecture. In M. Boucadair & D. Binet (Eds.), *Solutions for sustaining scalability in internet growth* (pp. 1–16). Hershey, PA: Information Science Reference; doi:10.4018/978-1-4666-4305-5.ch001

Bouras, A., Gouvas, P., & Mentzas, G. (2009). A semantic service-oriented architecture for business process fusion. In I. Lee (Ed.), *Electronic business: Concepts, methodologies, tools, and applications* (pp. 504–532). Hershey, PA: Information Science Reference; doi:10.4018/978-1-60566-056-1.ch032

Brady, A., & Voss, B. (1995). Small is as small does. *The Journal of Business Strategy, 16*(2), 44–52. doi:10.1108/eb039690

Braun, P. (2011). Advancing women in the digital economy: eLearning opportunities for meta-competency skilling. In *Global business: Concepts, methodologies, tools and applications* (pp. 1978–1990). Hershey, PA: Business Science Reference; doi:10.4018/978-1-60960-587-2.ch708

Breen, A., Burton-Houle, T., & Aron, C. (2002). Applying the theory of constraints in health care: Part 1 – the philosophy. *Quality Management in Health Care, 10*(3), 40–46. doi:10.1097/00019514-200210030-00010 PMID:12512464

Bridge, J., & Peel, M. (1999). Research note: A study of computer usage and strategic planning in the SME sector. *International Small Business Journal*, Jul-Sep, 82-87.

Bridge, J., & Peel, M. J. (1999). A study of computer usage and strategic planning in the SME sector. *International Small Business Journal, 17*(4), 82–87. doi:10.1177/0266242699174005

Brockhaus, R. H. (1980). Risk taking propensity of entrepreneurs. *Academy of Management Journal, 23*(3), 509–520. doi:10.2307/255515

Brockner, J. (1992). The Escalation of Commitment to a failing Course of Action: Toward Theoretical Progress. *Academy of Management Review, 17*(1), 39–61.

Brouwer, M. T. (2002). Weber, Schumpeter and Knoght on entrepreneurship and economic development. *Journal of Evolutionary Economics, 12*(1-2), 83–105. doi:10.1007/s00191-002-0104-1

Brown, D. H., & Kaewkitipong, L. (2009). Relative size and complexity: E-business use in small and medium sized tourism enterprises in Thailand. *Journal of Enterprise Information Management, 22*(1/2), 212–231. doi:10.1108/17410390910932849

Brown, D. H., & Lockett, N. (2004). Potential of critical e-applications for engaging SMEs in e-business: A provider perspective. *European Journal of Information Systems, 13*(1), 21–34. doi:10.1057/palgrave.ejis.3000480

Brown, M., & Garson, G. (2013). Organization behavior and organization theory. In *Public information management and e-government: Policy and issues* (pp. 160–195). Hershey, PA: Information Science Reference; doi:10.4018/978-1-4666-3003-1.ch007

Brown, M., & Garson, G. (2013). The information technology business model. In *Public information management and e-government: Policy and issues* (pp. 76–98). Hershey, PA: Information Science Reference; doi:10.4018/978-1-4666-3003-1.ch004

Brown, R. B., & Coverly, R. (1999). Succession planning in family businesses: A study from East Anglia, UK. *Journal of Small Business Management, 37*(1), 93–97.

Brown, S. (2007). Seven Skills for the Aspiring Entrepreneur. *Business and Economic Review, 53*(2), 16–18.

Bruderl, J., Preisendorfer, P., & Ziegler, R. (1992). Survival chances of newly founded business organizations. *American Sociological Review, 57*(2), 227–242. doi:10.2307/2096207

Brun de Pontet, S., Wrosch, C., & Gagne, M. (2007). An exploration of the generational differences in levels of control held among family businesses approaching succession. *Family Business Review, 20*(4), 337–354. doi:10.1111/j.1741-6248.2007.00103.x

Brush, C. G., Manolova, T. S., & Edelman, L. E. (2008). Properties of emerging organizations: An empirical test. *Journal of Business Venturing, 23*(5), 547–566. doi:10.1016/j.jbusvent.2007.09.002

Bryant, P. (2009). Self-regulation and moral awareness among entrepreneurs. *Journal of Business Venturing, 24*(6), 505–518. doi:10.1016/j.jbusvent.2008.04.005

Bull, C. (2003). Strategic issues in customer relationship management (CRM) implementation. *Business Process Management Journal, 9*(5), 592–602. doi:10.1108/14637150310496703

Burca, S., Fynes, B., & Marshall, D. (2005). Strategic technology adoption: Extending ERP across the supply chain. *Journal of Enterprise Information Management, 18*(4), 427–440. doi:10.1108/17410390510609581

Burete, R., Badica, A., Badica, C., & Moraru, F. (2011). Enhanced reputation model with forgiveness for e-business agents. *International Journal of Agent Technologies and Systems, 3*(1), 11–26. doi:10.4018/jats.2011010102

Burgess, S. (2003). *A definition of small business*. Information Resources Management Association Special Research Cluster on Small Business and Information Technology. Retrieved from www.businessandlaw.vu.edu.au/sbirit/research_issue_Results.htm

Burgess, S., & Trethowan, P. (2002). GP's and their web sites in Australia: Doctors as small businesses. *Proceedings of ISOneWorld Conference, Las Vegas, Nevada.*

Burlingham, B. (2006). In search of small giants. *Inc. Magazine*, *28*(2), 84–87.

Burt, R. S. (1992). *Structural Holes: The Social Structure of Competition*. Cambridge: Harvard University Press.

Burt, R. S. (1997). The Contingent Value of Social Capital. *Administrative Science Quarterly*, *42*(2), 339–363. doi:10.2307/2393923

Business Research and Case Center. (2011). *Cases on business and management in the MENA region: New trends and opportunities*. Hershey, PA: IGI Global; doi:10.4018/978-1-60960-583-4

Bwalya, K. J. (2011). E-commerce penetration in the SADC region: Consolidating and moving forward. In M. Cruz-Cunha & J. Varajão (Eds.), *E-business managerial aspects, solutions and case studies* (pp. 235–253). Hershey, PA: Business Science Reference; doi:10.4018/978-1-60960-463-9.ch014

Byers, C. R., & Blume, D. (1994). Tying Critical Success Factors to Systems Development. *Information & Management*, *26*(1), 51–61. doi:10.1016/0378-7206(94)90006-X

Caldeira, M. M., & Ward, J. M. (2002). Understanding the successful adoption and use of IS/IT in SMEs: An explanation for Portuguese manufacturing industries. *Information Systems Journal*, *12*(2), 121–152. doi:10.1046/j.1365-2575.2002.00119.x

Caldeira, M. M., & Ward, J. M. (2003). Using resource-based theory to interpret the successful adoption and use of information systems and technology in manufacturing small and medium-sized enterprises. *European Journal of Information Systems*, *12*(2), 127–141. doi:10.1057/palgrave.ejis.3000454

Calkins, J. D., Farello, M. J., & Shi, C. S. (2000). From retailing to e-tailing. *The McKinsey Quarterly*, *1*, 4–11.

Campbell, A. J. (1998). Embracing electronic data interchange now will keep your company in step with the competition. *Business America*, *119*(6), 28–30.

Canadian Federation of Independent Business. (1999). Results of members' opinion surveys #37-42, http://www.cfib.ca/research/98internet.asp

Canadian Federation of Independent Business. (1999). Results of members' opinion surveys #37-42, http://www.cfib.ca/research/98internet.asp (August 29, 2000).

Canadian Federation of Independent Business. (1999). Results of Members' Opinion Surveys #37-42, http://www.cfib.ca/research/98internet.asp (August 29, 2000).

Cardwell, M. (1994). *Customer Care Strategy for the '90s*. Cheltenham, England: Thomas.

Carland, J. C., & Carland, J. W. (1992). Managers, small business owners and entrepreneurs: The cognitive dimension. *Journal of Business and Entrepreneurship*, *4*(2), 55–66.

Carland, J. C., Carland, J. W., & Stewart, W. H. Jr. (2000). The indefatigable entrepreneur: A study of the dispositions of multiple venture founders. *Journal of Business and Entrepreneurship*, *12*(1), 1–18.

Carland, J. W., Carland, J. C., & Ensley, M. (2002). Hunting the heffalump: The theoretical Basis and dimensionality of the Carland entrepreneurial index. *Academy of Entrepreneurship Journal*, *7*(2), 51–84.

Carland, J. W., Hoy, F., Bolton, W. R., & Carland, J. A. (1984). Differentiating entrepreneurs from small business owners: A conceptualization. *Academy of Management Review*, *9*(2), 354–359.

Carland, J. W., Hoy, F., & Carland, J. A. (1988). Who is an entrepreneur? Is a question worth asking. *American Journal of Small Business*, *12*(4), 33–39.

Carneiro, A. (2007). What is required for growth? *Business Strategy Series*, *8*(1), 51–57. doi:10.1108/17515630710686888

Carr, N. G. (2003). IT doesn't matter. *Harvard Business Review*, *81*(5), 41–49. PMID:12747161

Carson, D., & Gilmore, A. (2000). SME marketing management competencies. *International Business Review*, *9*(3), 363–382. doi:10.1016/S0969-5931(00)00006-8

Casson, M. (2003). Entrepreneurship, business culture and the theory of the firm, in Handbook of Entrepreneurship Research: An Interdisciplinary Survey and Introduction, Editors Acs, Z. J. & Audretch, D. B. Dordretch: Kluwer Academic Publishers, 223-246.

Chaganti, R. W., & Chaganti, R. (1983). A profile of profitable and not-so-profitable small businesses. *Journal of Small Business Management*, *21*(3), 126–137.

Chaganti, R. W., Cook, R. G., & Smeltz, W. J. (2002). Effects of styles, strategies and systems on the growth of small businesses. *Journal of Developmental Entrepreneurship*, *7*(2), 175–193.

Chandler, G. N., & Lyon, D. W. (2001). Issues of research design and construct measurement in entrepreneurship research. *Entrepreneurship Theory and Practice*, *25*(4), 101–113.

Chan, Y. E., Huff, S. L., Barclay, D. W., & Copeland, D. G. (1997). Business strategic orientation, information systems orientation and strategic alignment. *Information Systems Research*, *8*(2), 125–150. doi:10.1287/isre.8.2.125

Chao, C. A., & Chandra, A. (2012). Impact of owner's knowledge of information technology (IT) on strategic alignment and IT adoption in US small firms. *Journal of Small Business and Enterprise Development*, *19*(1), 114–131. doi:10.1108/14626001211196433

Chapman, P., James-Moore, M., Szczygiel, M., & Thompson, D. (2000). Building internet capabilities in SMEs. *Logistics Information Management*, *13*(6), 353–361. doi:10.1108/09576050010355662

Charbaji, R., Rebeiz, K., & Sidani, Y. (2010). Antecedents and consequences of the risk taking behavior of mobile commerce adoption in Lebanon. In H. Rahman (Ed.), *Handbook of research on e-government readiness for information and service exchange: Utilizing progressive information communication technologies* (pp. 354–380). Hershey, PA: Information Science Reference; doi:10.4018/978-1-60566-671-6.ch018

Chaston, I. (1997). Small firm performance: Assessing the interaction between entrepreneurial style and organizational structure. *European Journal of Marketing*, *31*(11/12), 814–831. doi:10.1108/03090569710190550

Chatterjee, D., Grewal, R., & Sambamurthy, C. (2002). Shaping up for e-commerce: Institutional enablers of the organizational assimilation of web technologies. *Management Information Systems Quarterly*, *26*(2), 65–89. doi:10.2307/4132321

Chaturvedi, N. (2013). Collaborative web for natural resources industries. In *Supply chain management: Concepts, methodologies, tools, and applications* (pp. 601–614). Hershey, PA: Business Science Reference; doi:10.4018/978-1-4666-2625-6.ch035

Chau, P. Y. K., & Hui, K. L. (2001). Determinants of small business EDI adoption: An empirical investigation. *Journal of Organizational Computing and Electronic Commerce*, *11*(4), 229–252. doi:10.1207/S15327744JOCE1104_02

Chau, Y. K., & Jim, C. F. (2002). Adoption of electronic data interchange in small and medium enterprises. *Journal of Global Information Management*, *10*(4), 61–85. doi:10.4018/jgim.2002100104

Chen, C. C., Greene, P. G., & Crick, A. (1998). Does entrepreneurial self-efficacy distinguish entrepreneurs from managers? *Journal of Business Venturing*, *13*(4), 295–316. doi:10.1016/S0883-9026(97)00029-3

Chen, C., & Yang, S. C. (2008). E-commerce and mobile commerce application adoptions. In A. Becker (Ed.), *Electronic commerce: Concepts, methodologies, tools, and applications* (pp. 826–836). Hershey, PA: Information Science Reference; doi:10.4018/978-1-59904-943-4.ch068

Chen, J. C., & Williams, B. C. (1993). The impact of microcomputer systems on small business: England, 10 years later. *Journal of Small Business Management*, (July): 96–102.

Chen, Q., & Zhang, N. (2013). IT-supported business performance and e-commerce application in SMEs. *Journal of Electronic Commerce in Organizations*, *11*(2), 41–52. doi:10.4018/jeco.2013040104

Chen, T. F. (2011). Emerging business models: Value drivers in e-business 2.0 and towards enterprise 2.0. In T. Chen (Ed.), *Implementing new business models in for-profit and non-profit organizations: Technologies and applications* (pp. 1–28). Hershey, PA: Information Science Reference; doi:10.4018/978-1-60960-129-4.ch001

Chen, T. F. (2011). The critical success factors and integrated model for implementing e-business in Taiwan's SMEs. In *Global business: Concepts, methodologies, tools and applications* (pp. 1109–1133). Hershey, PA: Business Science Reference; doi:10.4018/978-1-60960-587-2.ch416

Chew, E., & Gottschalk, P. (2013). Critical success factors of IT strategy. In *Knowledge driven service innovation and management: IT strategies for business alignment and value creation* (pp. 185–220). Hershey, PA: Business Science Reference; doi:10.4018/978-1-4666-2512-9.ch006

Chew, E., & Gottschalk, P. (2013). Strategic alignment and IT-enabled value creation. In *Knowledge driven service innovation and management: IT strategies for business alignment and value creation* (pp. 141–184). Hershey, PA: Business Science Reference; doi:10.4018/978-1-4666-2512-9.ch005

Chew, E., & Gottschalk, P. (2013). Theories and models of service-oriented firms. In *Knowledge driven service innovation and management: IT strategies for business alignment and value creation* (pp. 1–34). Hershey, PA: Business Science Reference; doi:10.4018/978-1-4666-2512-9.ch001

Chiang, L. (2010). Digital confidence in business: A perspective of information ethics. In M. Pankowska (Ed.), *Infonomics for distributed business and decision-making environments: Creating information system ecology* (pp. 288–300). Hershey, PA: Business Science Reference; doi:10.4018/978-1-60566-890-1.ch017

Chiasson, M., & Saunders, C. (2005). Reconsiling diverse approaches to opportunity research using the structuration theory. *Journal of Business Venturing*, *20*(6), 747–767. doi:10.1016/j.jbusvent.2004.07.004

Chibelushi, C. (2008). Learning the hard way? Issues in the adoption of new technology in small technology oriented firms. *Education + Training*, 50(8/9), 725-736.

Childers, J. S., & Offstein, E. (2007). Building entrepreneurial E-commerce competitive advantage: A blending of theory and practice. *Advances in Competitiveness Research*, *15*(1/2), 41–53.

Chircu, A. M., & Kauffman, R. J. (2000). Limits to value in electronic commerce-related IT investments. *Journal of Management Information Systems*, 17(20), 59-80.

Chircu, A. M., & Kauffman, R. J. (2000). Limits to value in electronic commerce-related IT investments. *Journal of Management Information Systems*, *17*(2), 59–80.

Choi, S. Y., Lee, H., & Yoo, Y. (2010). The impact of information technology and transitive memory systems on knowledge sharing, application and team performance: A field study. *Management Information Systems Quarterly*, *34*(4), 855–870.

Chong, A. Y.-L., Ooi, K.-B., Lin, B., & Tang, S. Y. (2009). Influence of interorganizational relationships on SMEs' e-business adoption. *Internet Research*, *19*(30), 313–331. doi:10.1108/10662240910965379

Chong, S. (2008). Success in electronic commerce implementation: A cross-country study of small and medium-sized enterprises. *Journal of Enterprise Information Management*, *21*(5), 469–492. doi:10.1108/17410390810904247

Chong, S., & Pervan, G. (2007). Factors influencing the extent of deployment of electronic commerce for small and medium-sized enterprises. *Journal of Electronic Commerce in Organizations*, *5*(10), 1–29. doi:10.4018/jeco.2007010101

Choo, C. W., & Bontis, M. (2002). *Strategic Management of Intellectual Capital and Organizational Knowledge*. New York: Oxford University Press.

Choran, I. (1969). *The Manager of a Small Company*, unpublished MBA thesis, Montreal, Quebec: McGill University.

Chrisman, J. J., Chua, J. H., & Litz, R. A. (2004). Comparing the agency costs of family and non-family firms: Conceptual issues and exploratory evidence. *Entrepreneurship Theory and Practice*, *28*(4), 335–354. doi:10.1111/j.1540-6520.2004.00049.x

Chugh, R., & Gupta, P. (2011). A unified view of enablers, barriers, and readiness of small to medium enterprises for e-business adoption. In M. Cruz-Cunha & J. Varajão (Eds.), *E-business issues, challenges and opportunities for SMEs: Driving competitiveness* (pp. 291–312). Hershey, PA: Business Science Reference; doi:10.4018/978-1-61692-880-3.ch017

Churchill, B. C. (1952). Survival Patterns of the Postwar Business Population. *Survey of Current Business*, *32*(12), 12–19.

Churchill, N. C., & Lewis, V. L. (1983). The five stages of small business growth. *Harvard Business Review*, *61*(3), 30–50.

Chwelos, P., Benbasat, I., & Dexter, A. S. (2001). Empirical test of an EDI adoption model. *Information Systems Research*, *12*(3), 304–321. doi:10.1287/isre.12.3.304.9708

Clark, D. N. (2010). Innovation management in SMEs: Active innovators in New Zealand. *Journal of Small Business and Entrepreneurship*, *23*(4), 601–619. doi:10.1080/08276331.2010.10593504

Clear, F., Woods, A., & Dickson, K. (2013). SME adoption and use of ICT for networked trading purposes: The influence of sector, size and age of firm. In *Small and medium enterprises: Concepts, methodologies, tools, and applications* (pp. 774–791). Hershey, PA: Business Science Reference; doi:10.4018/978-1-4666-3886-0.ch038

Clemons, E. K., & Row, M. C. (1991). Sustaining IT advantage: The role of structural differences. *Management Information Systems Quarterly*, *15*(3), 275–294. doi:10.2307/249639

Cochran, A. B. (1981). Small business mortality rates: A review of the literature. *Journal of Small Business Management*, *19*(4), 50–59.

Coghlan, D. (2001). An intervals perspective of OD in IT enabled change. *Organization Development Journal*, *19*(1), 49–56.

Cohen, W. (2006). *The entrepreneur and Small Business Problem Solver* (2nd ed.). Hoboken, NJ: John Wiley & Sons.

Cohen, W., & Levinthal, D. (1990). Absorptive capacity: A new perspective on learning and innovation. *Administrative Science Quarterly*, *35*(1), 128–152. doi:10.2307/2393553

Cole, R. A., & Wolken, J. D. (1996). Bank and nonbank competition for small business credit: Evidence from the 1987 and 1993 national surveys of small business finances. *Federal Reserve Bulletin*, November, 983-995.

Coleman, J. S. (1988). Social capital in the creation of human capital. *American Journal of Sociology*, *94*(s1), 95–120. doi:10.1086/228943

Collins, J. (2002). Chinese entrepreneurs: The Chinese diaspora in Australia. *International Journal of Entrepreneurial Behaviour & Research*, *8*(1/2), 113–133. doi:10.1108/13552550210423750

Companys, Y. E., & McMullen, J. S. (2007). Strategic entrepreneurs at work: The nature, discovery, and exploitation of entrepreneurial opportunities. *Small Business Economics*, *28*(4), 301–322. doi:10.1007/s11187-006-9034-x

Connolly, R. (2013). eCommerce trust beliefs: Examining the role of national culture. In P. Isaias & M. Baptista Nunes (Eds.), Information systems research and exploring social artifacts: Approaches and methodologies (pp. 20-42). Hershey, PA: Information Science Reference. doi::10.4018/978-1-4666-2491-7.ch002

Cooper, A. C., Dunkelberg, W. C., & Woo, C. Y. (1988). Survival and Failure: A Longitudinal Study, Wellesley, MA, Frontiers of Entrepreneurship Research, Babson College.

Corbett, L. M., & Campbell-Hunt, C. (2002). Grappling with a gusher! Manufacturing's response to business success in small and medium enterprises. *Journal of Operations Management*, *20*(5), 495–517. doi:10.1016/S0272-6963(02)00026-8

Cormican, K. (2013). Collaborative networks: Challenges for SMEs. In *Small and medium enterprises: Concepts, methodologies, tools, and applications* (pp. 1638–1653). Hershey, PA: Business Science Reference; doi:10.4018/978-1-4666-3886-0.ch083

Corso, M., Martini, A., Pellegrini, L., & Paolucci, E. (2003). Technological and organizational tools for knowledge management: In search of configurations. *Small Business Economics*, *21*(4), 397–408. doi:10.1023/A:1026123322900

Costante, E., Petkovic, M., & den Hartog, J. (2013). Trust management and user's trust perception in e-business. In *IT policy and ethics: Concepts, methodologies, tools, and applications* (pp. 64–83). Hershey, PA: Information Science Reference; doi:10.4018/978-1-4666-2919-6.ch004

Costin, Y. (2012). Adopting ICT in the mompreneurs business: A strategy for growth? In C. Romm Livermore (Ed.), *Gender and social computing: Interactions, differences and relationships* (pp. 17–34). Hershey, PA: Information Science Publishing; doi:10.4018/978-1-60960-759-3.ch002

Cox, S. (2013). E-business planning in morphing organizations: Maturity models of business transformation. In E. Li, S. Loh, C. Evans, & F. Lorenzi (Eds.), *Organizations and social networking: Utilizing social media to engage consumers* (pp. 286–312). Hershey, PA: Business Science Reference; doi:10.4018/978-1-4666-4026-9.ch015

Cragg, P. B. (2002). Benchmarking information technology practices in small firms. *European Journal of Information Systems*, *11*(4), 267–282. doi:10.1057/palgrave.ejis.3000430

Cragg, P. B., & King, M. (1993). Small-firm computing: Motivators and inhibitors. *Management Information Systems Quarterly*, *17*(1), 47–60. doi:10.2307/249509

Cragg, P. B., King, M., & Hussin, H. (2002). IT alignment and performance in small manufacturing firms. *The Journal of Strategic Information Systems, 11*(2), 109–132. doi:10.1016/S0963-8687(02)00007-0

Cragg, P. B., & Mills, A. (2011). IT support for business processes in SMEs. *Business Process Management Journal, 17*(5), 697–710. doi:10.1108/14637151111166141

Cragg, P., Mehrtens, J., & Mills, A. (2001). A model of internet adoption by SMEs. *Information & Management, 39*(3), 165–176. doi:10.1016/S0378-7206(01)00086-6

Craig, J., & Dibrell, C. (2006). The natural environment, and firm performance: A comparative study. *Family Business Review, 19*(4), 275–288. doi:10.1111/j.1741-6248.2006.00075.x

Crawford, J., Leonard, L. N. K., & Jones, K. (2011). The human resource's influence in shaping IT competence. *Industrial Management & Data Systems, 111*(2), 164–183. doi:10.1108/02635571111115128

Cressy, R. (2006). Why do most firms die young? *Small Business Economics, 26*(2), 103–116. doi:10.1007/s11187-004-7813-9

Crick, D. (2011). Enterprising individuals and entrepreneurial learning. *International Journal of Entrepreneurial Behaviour & Research, 17*(2), 203–218. doi:10.1108/13552551111114941

Cromie, S. (2000). Assessing entrepreneurial inclinations: Some approaches and empirical evidence. *European Journal of Work and Organizational Psychology, 9*(1), 7–30. doi:10.1080/135943200398030

Cruz-Cunha, M. M., Moreira, F., & Varajão, J. (2014). *Handbook of research on enterprise 2.0: Technological, social, and organizational dimensions*. Hershey, PA: IGI Global; doi:10.4018/978-1-4666-4373-4

Curran, J. (1986). *Bolton 15 Years on: A Review and Analysis of Small Business Research in Britain 1977-1986*. London: Small Business Research Trust.

Curran, J., & Blackburn, R. A. (2001). *Researching the Small Enterprise*. London: SAGE Publications.

D'Aubeterre, F., Iyer, L. S., Ehrhardt, R., & Singh, R. (2011). Discovery process in a B2B emarketplace: A semantic matchmaking approach. In V. Sugumaran (Ed.), *Intelligent, adaptive and reasoning technologies: New developments and applications* (pp. 80–103). Hershey, PA: Information Science Reference; doi:10.4018/978-1-60960-595-7.ch005

D'Intino, R. S., Goldsby, M. G., Houghton, J. D., & Neck, C. P. (2007). Self-leadership: A process for entrepreneurial success. *Journal of Leadership & Organizational Studies, 13*(4), 105–130. doi:10.1177/107179190701300401 01

Dabbagh, R. A. (2011). E-business: Concepts and context with illustrative examples of e-business and e-commerce in education. In A. Al Ajeeli & Y. Al-Bastaki (Eds.), *Handbook of research on e-services in the public sector: E-government strategies and advancements* (pp. 450–462). Hershey, PA: Information Science Reference; doi:10.4018/978-1-61520-789-3.ch033

Daft, R., & Weick, K. (1984). Toward a model of organizations as interpretations systems. *Academy of Management Review*, *9*(2), 284–295.

Dalley, J., & Hamilton, R. T. (2000). Knowledge, context and learning in the small business. *International Small Business Journal*, *18*(3), 51–59. doi:10.1177/0266242600183003

Damsgaard, J., & Lyytinen, K. (1998). Contours of diffusion of electronic data interchange in Finland: Overcoming technological barriers and collaborating to make it happen. *The Journal of Strategic Information Systems*, *7*(4), 275–297. doi:10.1016/S0963-8687(98)00032-8

Dandrige, T., & Levenburg, N. M. (2000). High-tech potential? An exploratory study of very small firms' usage of the internet. *International Small Business Journal*, *18*(2), 81–91. doi:10.1177/0266242600182004

Davidsson, P., & Delmar, F. (1997). High-growth firms: Characteristics, job contribution and method observations. Paper presented at RENTXI Conference, Mannheim.

Davidsson, P. (1991). Continued Entrepreneurship: Ability, need, and opportunity as determinants of small firm growth. *Journal of Business Venturing*, *6*(6), 405–429. doi:10.1016/0883-9026(91)90028-C

Davidsson, P., Delmar, F., & Wiklund, J. (2002). Entrepreneurship as growth: Growth as entrepreneurship. In M. A. Hitt, R. D. Ireland, S. M. Camp, & D. L. Sexton (Eds.), *Strategic Entrepreneurhsip: Creating a New Mindset* (pp. 328–340). Oxford: Blackwell.

Davidsson, P., & Honig, B. (2003). The role of social and human capital among nascent entrepreneurs. *Journal of Business Venturing*, *18*(3), 301–331. doi:10.1016/S0883-9026(02)00097-6

Davidsson, P., Hunter, E., & Klofsten, M. (2006). Institutional forces: The invisible hand that shapes venture ideas? *International Small Business Journal*, *24*(2), 115–131. doi:10.1177/0266242606061834

Davidsson, P., & Klofsten, M. (2003). The business platform: Developing an instrument to gauge and to assist the development of young firms. *Journal of Small Business Management*, *41*(1), 1–26. doi:10.1111/1540-627X.00064

Davis, C. H., & Vladica, F. (2006). Use of internet technologies and e-business solutions: A structural model of sources of business value among Canadian micro-enterprises. *Proceedings of the 39th Annual HICCS Conference*, Hawaii. doi:10.1109/HICSS.2006.519

Davis, G. B., Lee, A. S., Nickles, K. R., Chatterjee, S., Hartung, R., & Wu, Y. (1992). Diagnosis of an information system failure - a framework and interpretive process. *Information & Management*, *23*(5), 293–318. doi:10.1016/0378-7206(92)90059-O

Davis, J. H., Schoorman, F. D., & Donaldson, L. (1997). Toward a stewardship theory of management. *Academy of Management Review*, *22*(1), 20–47.

De Clercq, D., Menzies, T. V., Diochan, M., & Gasse, Y. (2009). Explaining nascent entrepreneurs' goal commitment: An exploratory study. *Journal of Small Business and Entrepreneurship*, *22*(2), 123–140. doi:10.1080/08276331.2009.10593446

De Geus, A. (2002). *The Living Company: Habits for Survival in a Turbulent Environment*. Boston, MA: Harvard Business School Press.

De Guinea, O. A., Kelly, H., & Hunter, M. G. (2005). Information systems effectiveness: Extending a Singapore model in Canada. *Journal of Global Information Management*, *13*(2), 55–79. doi:10.4018/jgim.2005070104

Deakins, D., & Freel, M. (1998). Entrepreneurial learning and growth processes in SMEs. *The Learning Organization*, *5*(3), 144–156. doi:10.1108/09696479810223428

Deakins, D., Morrison, A., & Galloway, L. (2002). Evolution, financial management and learning in the small firm. *Journal of Small Business and Enterprise Development*, *9*(1), 7–16. doi:10.1108/14626000210419446

Decker, M., Schiefer, G., & Bulander, R. (2006). Specific challenges for small and medium-sized enterprises in m-business: A SME-suitable framework for mobile services. *Proceedings of the International Conference on E-Business*, 169-174.

Deeks, J. (1973). The small firm – asset or liability? *Journal of Management Studies*, *10*(1), 25–47. doi:10.1111/j.1467-6486.1973.tb00499.x

Degryse, H., & Van Cayseele, P. (2000). Relationship lending within a bank-based system: Evidence from European small business data. *Journal of Financial Intermediation*, *9*(1), 90–109. doi:10.1006/jfin.1999.0278

Dekimpe, M. G., & Morrison, D. G. (1991). A modeling framework for analyzing retail store durations. *Journal of Retailing*, *67*(1), 68–92.

Delmar, F., & Davidsson, P. (2000). Where do they come from? Prevalence and characteristics of nascent entrepreneurs. *Entrepreneurship and Regional Development*, *12*(1), 1–23. doi:10.1080/089856200283063

Delone, W. H. (1988). Determinants of success for computer usage in small business. *Management Information Systems Quarterly*, *12*(1), 51–61. doi:10.2307/248803

Delvecchio, S., & Anselmi, K. (2006). Sales force automation tools for small business. *Journal of Small Business Strategy*, *16*(2), 15–27.

Dembla, P., Palvia, P., & Krishnan, B. (2007). Understanding the adoption of web-enabled transaction processing by small business. *Journal of Electronic Commerce Research*, *8*(1), 1–17.

Demirkan, H., & Spohrer, J. C. (2012). Servitized enterprises for distributed collaborative commerce. In S. Galup (Ed.), *Technological applications and advancements in service science, management, and engineering* (pp. 70–83). Hershey, PA: Business Science Reference; doi:10.4018/978-1-4666-1583-0.ch005

Denison, D., Lief, C., & Ward, J. L. (2004). Culture in family-owned enterprises: Recognizing and leveraging unique strengths. *Family Business Review*, *17*(1), 61–70. doi:10.1111/j.1741-6248.2004.00004.x

Denno, P. (2013). Trade collaboration systems. In *Supply chain management: Concepts, methodologies, tools, and applications* (pp. 615–633). Hershey, PA: Business Science Reference; doi:10.4018/978-1-4666-2625-6.ch036

Department for Business and Innovation Skills. (2013). *Small Business: Great Ambition. Business Population Estimates for the UK and Regions*. Retrieved from https://www.gov.uk/government/uploads/system/uploads/attachment_data/file/266212/bis-13-1313-small-business-great-ambition-FINAL.pdf. Retrieved January 8, 2014.

Derickx, L., & Cool, K. (1989). Asset stock accumulation and the sustainability of competitive advantage. *Management Science*, *35*(12), 1504–1511. doi:10.1287/mnsc.35.12.1504

Deshpande, S., & Golhar, D. (1994). HRM practices in large and small manufacturing firms: A comparative study. *Journal of Small Business Management*, *32*(2), 49–56.

DeThomas, A. R., & Fredenberger, W. B. (1985). Account need of a very small business. *The CPA Journal*, *55*(10), 14–23.

Devaraj, S., Krajewski, L., & Wei, J. C. (2007). Impact of e-business technologies on operational performance: The role of production information integration in the supply chain. *Journal of Operations Management*, *25*(6), 1199–1216. doi:10.1016/j.jom.2007.01.002

Dewar, R. D., & Dutton, J. E. (1986). The adoption of radical and incremental innovations: An empirical analysis. *Management Science*, *32*(11), 1422–1433. doi:10.1287/mnsc.32.11.1422

Dholakia, R. R., & Kshetri, N. (2004). Factors impacting the adoption of the internet among SMEs. *Small Business Economics*, *23*(4), 311–322. doi:10.1023/B:SBEJ.0000032036.90353.1f

Diochan, M., Menzies, T. V., & Gasse, Y. (2008). Exploring the nature and impact of gestation-specific human capital among nascent entrepreneurs. *Journal of Developmental Entrepreneurship*, *13*(2), 151–165. doi:10.1142/S1084946708000909

Dixit, A. K., & Prakash, O. (2011). A study of issues affecting ERP implementation in SMEs. *International Refereed Research Journal*, *2*(2), 77–85.

Dixon, T., Thompson, B., & McAllister, P. (2002). *The value of ICT for SMEs in the UK: A critical review of literature. Report for the Small Business Research Programme*. Reading: The College of Estate Management.

Djoleto, W. (2013). eCommerce and organisational leadership. In Electronic commerce and organizational leadership: Perspectives and methodologies (pp. 99-121). Hershey, PA: Business Science Reference. doi::10.4018/978-1-4666-2982-0.ch005

Djoleto, W. (2013). eCommerce: An overview. In Electronic commerce and organizational leadership: Perspectives and methodologies (pp. 74-98). Hershey, PA: Business Science Reference. doi::10.4018/978-1-4666-2982-0.ch004

Djoleto, W. (2011). E-business efficacious consequences the etiquettes and the business decision making. In O. Bak & N. Stair (Eds.), *Impact of e-business technologies on public and private organizations: Industry comparisons and perspectives* (pp. 278–295). Hershey, PA: Business Science Reference; doi:10.4018/978-1-60960-501-8.ch017

Djoleto, W. (2013). Cloud computing and ecommerce or ebusiness: "The now it way" – An overview. In *Electronic commerce and organizational leadership: Perspectives and methodologies* (pp. 239–254). Hershey, PA: Business Science Reference; doi:10.4018/978-1-4666-2982-0.ch010

Djoleto, W. (2013). Empirical analyses of ecommerce: The findings – A mixed methodology perspective. In *Electronic commerce and organizational leadership: Perspectives and methodologies* (pp. 150–189). Hershey, PA: Business Science Reference; doi:10.4018/978-1-4666-2982-0.ch007

Djoleto, W. (2013). Future endeavours. In *Electronic commerce and organizational leadership: Perspectives and methodologies* (pp. 269–280). Hershey, PA: Business Science Reference; doi:10.4018/978-1-4666-2982-0.ch012

Djoleto, W. (2013). Information technology and organisational leadership. In *Electronic commerce and organizational leadership: Perspectives and methodologies*. Hershey, PA: IGI Global; doi:10.4018/978-1-4666-2982-0.ch003

Djoleto, W. (2013). Information technology: The journey. In *Electronic commerce and organizational leadership: Perspectives and methodologies* (pp. 32–54). Hershey, PA: Business Science Reference; doi:10.4018/978-1-4666-2982-0.ch002

Dobbs, M., & Hamilton, R. T. (2007). Small business growth: Recent evidence and new directions. *International Journal of Entrepreneurial Behaviour and Research*, *13*(5), 296–322. doi:10.1108/13552550710780885

Donaldson, L., & Davis, J. H. (1989). CEO governance and shareholder returns: Agency theory and stewardship theory. Academy of Management Annual Meeting, Washington, DC.

Donaldson, L., & Davis, J. H. (1991). Stewardship theory or agency theory: CEO governance and shareholder returns. *Australian Journal of Management*, *16*(1), 49–64. doi:10.1177/031289629101600103

Dongen, J., Maitland, C., & Sadowski, B. (2002). Strategic use of the internet by small and medium-sized companies: An exploratory study. *Information Economics and Policy*, *14*(1), 75–93. doi:10.1016/S0167-6245(01)00054-3

Donnelly, R. (1964). The Family Business. *Harvard Business Review*, *42*(2), 93–105.

Doolin, B., & Ali, E. I. (2012). Mobile technology adoption in the supply chain. In *Wireless technologies: Concepts, methodologies, tools and applications* (pp. 1553–1573). Hershey, PA: Information Science Reference; doi:10.4018/978-1-61350-101-6.ch603

Doukidis, G. L., Smithson, S., & Lybereas, T. (1994). Trends in information technology in small businesses. *Journal of End User Computing*, *6*(4), 15–25.

Downing, S. (2005). The social construction of entrepreneurship: Narratives and dramatic processes in the coproduction of organizations and identities. *Entrepreneurship Theory and Practice*, *29*(2), 185–204. doi:10.1111/j.1540-6520.2005.00076.x

Downs, A. (1967). The life cycle of bureaus. In A. Downs (Ed.), *Inside Bureaucracy*. San Francisco, CA: Little Brown & Co. and Rand Corporation.

Drew, S. (2003). Strategic uses of e-commerce by SMEs in the east of England. *European Management Journal, 21*(1), 79–88. doi:10.1016/S0263-2373(02)00148-2

Drucker, P. F. (1998). The discipline of innovation. *Harvard Business Review, 76*(5), 143–159. PMID:10187245

DTI. (2003). *The Small Business Services; National Statistics*, Department of Trade and Industry. www.sbs.gov.uk

Duberley, J., & Walley, P. (1995). Assessing the adoption of HRM by small and medium sized manufacturing organizations. *International Journal of Human Resource Management, 6*(4), 891–909. doi:10.1080/09585199500000052

Duin, H., & Thoben, K. (2011). Enhancing the preparedness of SMEs for e-business opportunities by collaborative networks. In M. Cruz-Cunha & J. Varajão (Eds.), *E-business issues, challenges and opportunities for SMEs: Driving competitiveness* (pp. 30–45). Hershey, PA: Business Science Reference; doi:10.4018/978-1-61692-880-3.ch003

Dulai, T., Jaskó, S., & Tarnay, K. (2013). IOTP and payments protocols. In K. Tarnay, S. Imre, & L. Xu (Eds.), *Research and development in e-business through service-oriented solutions* (pp. 20–56). Hershey, PA: Business Science Reference; doi:10.4018/978-1-4666-4181-5.ch002

Dun & Bradstreet. (1991). Press Release June.

Duncan, W. J., Ginter, P. M., & Swayne, L. E. (1998). Competitive advantage and internal organizational assessment. *The Academy of Management Executive, 12*(3), 6–16.

Duncombe, R. A., & Heeks, R. B. (2001). Information and communication technologies and small enterprise development in Africa: Lessons from Botswana. *Institute for Development Policy and Management, 16*, 66–87.

Dunn, B. (1995). Success themes in Scottish family enterprises: Philosophies and practices through the generations. *Family Business Review, 8*(1), 17–28. doi:10.1111/j.1741-6248.1995.00017.x

Dunne, T., Roberts, M. J., & Samuelson, L. (1989). The growth and failure of U.S. manufacturing plants. *The Quarterly Journal of Economics, 104*(4), 672–698. doi:10.2307/2937862

Dutta, S., & Evrard, P. (1999). Information technology and organisation within European small enterprises. *European Management Journal, 17*(3), 239–251. doi:10.1016/S0263-2373(99)00003-1

Dyer, W. G. (2006). Examining the 'family effect' on firm performance. *Family Business Review, 19*(4), 253–273. doi:10.1111/j.1741-6248.2006.00074.x

Dyer, W. G. Jr. (1997). Organisation development in the entrepreneurial firm. *The Journal of Applied Behavioral Science, 33*(2), 190–208. doi:10.1177/0021886397332008

Dyt, R., & Halabi, A. K. (2007). Empirical evidence examining the accounting information systems and accounting reports of small and micro business in Australia. *Small Enterprise Research, 15*(2), 1–9. doi:10.5172/ser.15.2.1

Dza, M., Fisher, R., & Gapp, R. (2013). Service-dominant logic and supply network management: An efficient business mix? In N. Ndubisi & S. Nwankwo (Eds.), *Enterprise development in SMEs and entrepreneurial firms: Dynamic processes* (pp. 376–389). Hershey, PA: Business Science Reference; doi:10.4018/978-1-4666-2952-3.ch021

Earl, M. J. (1989). *Management strategies for information technology*. New York: Prentice-Hall.

Eckhardt, J., & Shane, S. (2003). The importance of opportunities to entrepreneurship. *Journal of Management, 29*(3), 333–349. doi:10.1016/S0149-2063(02)00225-8

E-Commerce Times. (2008). US B2B to Reach $6 Trillion by 2005. www.ecommercetimes.com

Edvinsson, L., & Malone, M. S. (1997). *Intellectual Capital: Realizing Your Company's True Value by Finding its Hidden Brainpower*. New York, NY: Harper Collins Business.

Ehsani, E. (2011). Defining e-novation in action. In H. Pattinson & D. Low (Eds.), *E-novation for competitive advantage in collaborative globalization: Technologies for emerging e-business strategies* (pp. 58–74). Hershey, PA: Business Science Reference; doi:10.4018/978-1-60566-394-4.ch005

Ekong, U. O., Ifinedo, P., Ayo, C. K., & Ifinedo, A. (2013). E-commerce adoption in Nigerian businesses: An analysis using the technology-organization-environmental framework. In *Small and medium enterprises: Concepts, methodologies, tools, and applications* (pp. 840–861). Hershey, PA: Business Science Reference; doi:10.4018/978-1-4666-3886-0.ch041

El Louadi, M. (1998). The relationship among organizational structure, information technology and information processing in small Canadian firms. *Canadian Journal of Administrative Sciences, 15*(2), 180–199. doi:10.1111/j.1936-4490.1998.tb00161.x

eMarketer. (2005). E-Commerce in the US. www.eMarketer.com

Emens, S. (2010). The new paradigm of business on the internet and its ethical implications. In D. Palmer (Ed.), *Ethical issues in e-business: Models and frameworks* (pp. 15–27). Hershey, PA: Business Science Reference; doi:10.4018/978-1-61520-615-5.ch002

Eriksson, P., Henttonen, E., & Meriläinen, S. (2011). Managing client contacts of small KIBS companies: Turning technology into business. *International Journal of Innovation in the Digital Economy, 2*(3), 1–10. doi:10.4018/jide.2011070101

Escofet, E., Rodríguez-Fórtiz, M. J., Garrido, J. L., & Chung, L. (2012). Strategic e-business/IT alignment for SME competitiveness. In *Computer engineering: Concepts, methodologies, tools and applications* (pp. 1427–1445). Hershey, PA: Engineering Science Reference; doi:10.4018/978-1-61350-456-7.ch604

Esteve-Perez, S., & Manez-Castillejo, J. A. (2008). The resource-based theory of the firm and firm survival. *Small Business Economics, 30*(3), 231–249. doi:10.1007/s11187-006-9011-4

Ettlie, J. E. (1990). What makes a manufacturing firm innovative? *The Academy of Management Executive, 4*(4), 7–20. doi:10.5465/AME.1990.4277195

*European Parliament*. (2002). Retrieved from www.europarl.eu.int/dg4/factsheets/en/4_14_0.htm

European Parliament. (2002). www.europarl.eu.int/dg4/factsheets/en/4_14_0.htm (07/06/2002).

Ewusi-Mensah, K. (1997). Critical Issues in Abandoned Information Systems Development Projects. *Communications of the ACM*, *40*(9), 74–80. doi:10.1145/260750.260775

Ewusi-Mensah, K., & Przasnyski, Z. H. (1991). On Information Systems Project Abandonment: An Exploratory Study of Organizational Practices. *Management Information Systems Quarterly*, *15*(1), 67–86. doi:10.2307/249437

Eze, U. C., & Poong, Y. S. (2013). Consumers' intention to use mobile commerce and the moderating roles of gender and income. In I. Lee (Ed.), *Strategy, adoption, and competitive advantage of mobile services in the global economy* (pp. 127–148). Hershey, PA: Information Science Reference; doi:10.4018/978-1-4666-1939-5.ch007

Eze, U. C., & Poong, Y. S. (2013). The moderating roles of income and age in mobile commerce application. *Journal of Electronic Commerce in Organizations*, *11*(3), 46–67. doi:10.4018/jeco.2013070103

Fairchild, G. B. (2009). Residential segregation influences on the likelihood of ethnic self-employment. *Entrepreneurship Theory and Practice*, *33*(2), 373–395. doi:10.1111/j.1540-6520.2009.00295.x

Fama, E. F., & Jensen, M. C. (1983). Agency problems and residual claims. *The Journal of Law & Economics*, *26*(2), 327–349. doi:10.1086/467038

*Federation of Small Businesses*. (2013). Retrieved from http://www.fsb.org.uk/stats

Fehér, P. (2012). Integrating and measuring business and technology services in the context of enterprise architecture. In V. Shankararaman, J. Zhao, & J. Lee (Eds.), *Business enterprise, process, and technology management: Models and applications* (pp. 148–163). Hershey, PA: Business Science Reference; doi:10.4018/978-1-4666-0249-6.ch008

Feindt, S., Jeffcoate, J., & Chappell, C. (2002). Identifying success factors for rapid growth in SME E-commerce. *Small Business Economics*, *19*(1), 51–62. doi:10.1023/A:1016165825476

Feja, S., Witt, S., & Speck, A. (2014). Tool based integration of requirements modeling and validation into business process modeling. In *Software design and development: Concepts, methodologies, tools, and applications* (pp. 285–309). Hershey, PA: Information Science Reference; doi:10.4018/978-1-4666-4301-7.ch016

Fengel, J. (2012). Semantic alignment of e-business standards and legacy models. In E. Kajan, F. Dorloff, & I. Bedini (Eds.), *Handbook of research on e-business standards and protocols: Documents, data and advanced web technologies* (pp. 676–704). Hershey, PA: Business Science Reference; doi:10.4018/978-1-4666-0146-8.ch031

Ferreira, M. P. (2013). SMEs and e-business: Implementation, strategies and policy. In *Small and medium enterprises: Concepts, methodologies, tools, and applications* (pp. 97–117). Hershey, PA: Business Science Reference; doi:10.4018/978-1-4666-3886-0.ch006

Fiegener, M. K., Brown, B. M., Prince, R. A., & File, K. M. (1996). Passing on strategic vision: Favored modes of successor preparation by CEOs of family and non-family firms. *Journal of Small Business Management*, *34*(3), 15–26.

Filley, A. C., & House, R. J. (1969). Managerial process and organisational behaviour. Glenview, Il: Scott Foresman and Company.

Fitzgerald, M. A., Haynes, G. W., Schrank, H. L., & Danes, S. M. (2010). Socially responsible processes of small family business owners: Exploratory evidence from the national family businesss survey. *Journal of Small Business Management*, *48*(4), 524–551. doi:10.1111/j.1540-627X.2010.00307.x

Fitzsimmons, J. R., & Douglas, E. J. (2011). Interaction between feasibility and desirability in the formation of entrepreneurial intentions. *Journal of Business Venturing*, *26*(4), 431–440. doi:10.1016/j.jbusvent.2010.01.001

Floren, H. (2006). Managerial work in small firms: Summarising what we know and sketching a research agenda. *International Journal of Entrepreneurial Behaviour and Research*, *12*(5), 272–288. doi:10.1108/13552550610687646

Fluvià, M., & Rigall-I-Torrent, R. (2013). Public sector transformation and the design of public policies for electronic commerce and the new economy: Tax and antitrust policies. In N. Pomazalová (Ed.), *Public sector transformation processes and internet public procurement: Decision support systems* (pp. 32–57). Hershey, PA: Engineering Science Reference; doi:10.4018/978-1-4666-2665-2.ch003

Fombrun, C. J. (1996). *Reputation: Realizing Value from the Corporate Image*. Boston: Harvard Business School.

Foong, S. Y. (1999). Effect of end user personal and systems attributes on computer based information systems success in Malaysian SMEs. *Journal of Small Business Management*, *37*(3), 81–87.

Forsman, H. (2008). Business development success in SMEs: A case study approach. *Journal of Small Business and Enterprise Development*, *15*(3), 606–622. doi:10.1108/14626000810892382

Francalanci, C., & Morabito, V. (2008). IS integration and business performance: The mediation effect of organizational absorptive capacity in SMEs. *Journal of Information Technology*, *23*(4), 297–312. doi:10.1057/jit.2008.18

Franquesa, J., & Brandyberry, A. (2009). Organizaitonal slack and information technology innovation adoption in SMEs. *International Journal of E-Business Research*, *5*(1), 25–48. doi:10.4018/jebr.2009010102

Franquesa, J., & Brandyberry, A. (2011). Organizational slack and information technology innovation adoption in SMEs. In I. Lee (Ed.), *E-business applications for product development and competitive growth: emerging technologies* (pp. 25–48). Hershey, PA: Business Science Reference; doi:10.4018/978-1-60960-132-4.ch002

Fredland, E. J., & Morris, C. E. (1976). A cross-section analysis of small business failure. *American Journal of Small Business*, *1*(1), 7–18.

Freeman, J., Caroll, G. R., & Hannan, M. T. (1983). The liability of newness: Age dependence in organizational death rates. *American Sociological Review*, *48*(5), 692–710. doi:10.2307/2094928

Frese, M. (2007). Towards a psychology of entrepreneurship: An action theory perspective. *Foundations and Trends in Entrepreneurship*, *5*(6), 437–496. doi:10.1561/0300000028

Friedman, S. (1989). Conflict inherited: Sibling rivalry in family firms. paper presented at the Academy of Management Meetings, Washington, DC.

Friedman, S. (1989). Conflict inherited: Sibling rivalry in family firms. Paper presented at the Academy of Management Meetings, Washington, DC.

Fries, T. P. (2014). Reengineering structured legacy system documentation to UML object-oriented artifacts. In *Software design and development: Concepts, methodologies, tools, and applications* (pp. 749–771). Hershey, PA: Information Science Reference; doi:10.4018/978-1-4666-4301-7.ch036

Fuller-Love, N. (2006). Management development in small firms. *International Journal of Management Reviews*, *8*(3), 175–190. doi:10.1111/j.1468-2370.2006.00125.x

Fuller, T. (1996). Fulfilling IT needs in small businesses: A recursive learning model. *International Journal of Small Business*, *14*(4), 25–44. doi:10.1177/0266242696144002

Galbraith, J. R. (1973). *Designing complex organizations*. Reading, MA: Addison-Wesley.

Galinski, C., & Beckmann, H. (2014). Concepts for enhancing content quality and eaccessibility: In general and in the field of eprocurement. In *Assistive technologies: Concepts, methodologies, tools, and applications* (pp. 180–197). Hershey, PA: Information Science Reference; doi:10.4018/978-1-4666-4422-9.ch010

Galliers, R. (1994). Choosing Information Systems Research Approaches. In Information Systems Research - Issues, Methods and Practical Guidelines. Henley-on-Thames, UK: Alfred Waller Ltd.

Galliers, R. D., & Sutherland, A. R. (1999). Informaiton systems management and strategy formation: Applying and extending the "stages of growth" concept. In R. D. Galliers, D. E. Leidner, & D. S. H. Baker (Eds.), *Strategic information management: Challenges and strategies in managing information systems* (2nd ed.). Oxford: Butterworth-Heinemann.

Ganguly, P. (Ed.). (1985). *U.K. Small Business Statistics and International Comparisons*. London: Harper and Row.

Gan, J., & Gutiérrez, J. A. (2011). Viable business models for m-commerce: The key components. In M. Cruz-Cunha & F. Moreira (Eds.), *Handbook of research on mobility and computing: Evolving technologies and ubiquitous impacts* (pp. 837–852). Hershey, PA: Information Science Reference; doi:10.4018/978-1-60960-042-6.ch052

Garcia-Parra, M., Simo, P., Sallan, J. M., & Mundet, J.Garcia-Parra. (2009). Intangible liabilities: Beyond models of intellectual assets. *Management Decision*, *47*(5), 819–830. doi:10.1108/00251740910960141

Garito, M. (2012). Mobile business and mobile TV: Available technologies, future opportunities and new marketing trends. In E-marketing: Concepts, methodologies, tools, and applications (pp. 1240-1251). Hershey, PA: Business Science Reference. doi::10.4018/978-1-4666-1598-4.ch072

Gartner, W. B. (1989). Who is an entrepreneur? Is the wrong question. *Entrepreneurship, Theory and Practice*, summer, 47-68.

Gersick, C. (1991). Revolutionary change theories: A multilevel exploration of the punctuated equilibrium paradigm. *Academy of Management Review*, *16*(1), 10–36.

Gersick, K. E., Davis, J. A., Hampton, M. M., & Lansberg, I. (1997). *Generation to Generation: Life Cycles of the Family Business*. Boston: Harvard Business School Press.

Ghobakhloo, M., & Zulkifli, N. (2013). Adoption of mobile commerce: The impact of end user satisfaction on system acceptance. *International Journal of E-Services and Mobile Applications*, *5*(1), 26–50. doi:10.4018/jesma.2013010102

Gibb, A. (1998). Entrepreneurial core capabilities, competitiveness and management development in the 21st Century.*8th Annual Conference of Internationalizing Entrepreneurship Education and Training, Schloss Reichartshausen Oestrich-Winkel*, Germany.

Gibb, A. A., & Davies, L. (1990). Pursuit of frameworks for the development of growth models of the small business. *International Small Business Journal*, *9*(1), 15–31.

Gibb, A., & Webb, T. (1980). *Policy Issues in Small Business Research*. Andover: Teakfield.

Gibbs, J. L., & Kramer, K. L. (2004). A cross-country investigation of the determinants of scope of e-commerce use: An institutional approach. *Electronic Markets*, *14*(2), 124–137. doi:10.1080/10196780410001675077

Gibrat, R. (1931). *Les Inegalites Economiques*. Paris: Librairie du Recueil.

Gill, A. Q., & Bunker, D. (2014). SaaS requirements engineering for agile development. In *Software design and development: Concepts, methodologies, tools, and applications* (pp. 351–380). Hershey, PA: Information Science Reference; doi:10.4018/978-1-4666-4301-7.ch019

Gimenez, J. (2014). Reflections of professional practice: Using electronic discourse analysis networks (EDANs) to examine embedded business emails. In H. Lim & F. Sudweeks (Eds.), *Innovative methods and technologies for electronic discourse analysis* (pp. 327–345). Hershey, PA: Information Science Reference; doi:10.4018/978-1-4666-4426-7.ch015

Gionis, G. A., Schroth, C., & Janner, T. (2011). Advancing interoperability for agile cross-organisational collaboration: A rule-based approach. In Y. Charalabidis (Ed.), *Interoperability in digital public services and administration: Bridging e-government and e-business* (pp. 238–253). Hershey, PA: Information Science Reference; doi:10.4018/978-1-61520-887-6.ch013

Giroux, I. (2009). Problem solving in small firms: An interpretive study. *Journal of Small Business and Enterprise Development*, *16*(1), 167–184. doi:10.1108/14626000910932944

Gnoni, M. G., & Rollo, A. (2011). A content analysis for evaluating RFID applications in supply network management. In I. Mahdavi, S. Mohebbi, & N. Cho (Eds.), *Electronic supply network coordination in intelligent and dynamic environments: Modeling and implementation* (pp. 93–112). Hershey, PA: Business Science Reference; doi:10.4018/978-1-60566-808-6.ch004

Goel, S., & Karri, R. (2006). Entrepreneurs, effectual logic, and over-trust. *Entrepreneurship Theory and Practice*, *30*(4), 477–493. doi:10.1111/j.1540-6520.2006.00131.x

Goldratt, E. M. (1994). *It's not luck, Croton-on-Hudson*. New York: North River Press, Inc.

Gonçalves, A., Serra, N., Serra, J., & Sousa, P. (2011). How to use information technology effectively to achieve business objectives. In M. Cruz-Cunha & J. Varajao (Eds.), *Enterprise information systems design, implementation and management: Organizational applications* (pp. 21–37). Hershey, PA: Information Science Reference; doi:10.4018/978-1-61692-020-3.ch002

Goode, S. (2002). Management attitudes towards the world wide web in Australian small business. *Information Systems Management*, *19*(1), 45–48. doi:10.1201/1078/43199.19.1.20020101/31475.6

Gordini, N., & Veglio, V. (2014). Customer relationship management and data mining: A classification decision tree to predict customer purchasing behavior in global market. In P. Vasant (Ed.), *Handbook of research on novel soft computing intelligent algorithms: Theory and practical applications* (pp. 1–40). Hershey, PA: Information Science Reference; doi:10.4018/978-1-4666-4450-2.ch001

Gottschalk, P. (2007). The CIO developing e-business. In P. Gottschalk (Ed.), *CIO and corporate strategic management: Changing role of CIO to CEO* (pp. 148–185). Hershey, PA: Idea Group Publishing; doi:10.4018/978-1-59904-423-1.ch007

Goutam, S. (2010). Analysis of speedy uptake of electronic and digital signatures in digital economy with special reference to India. In E. Adomi (Ed.), *Frameworks for ICT policy: Government, social and legal issues* (pp. 76–88). Hershey, PA: Information Science Reference; doi:10.4018/978-1-61692-012-8.ch005

Grandon, E., & Pearson, J. (2004). E-commerce adoption: Perceptions of managers/owners of small and medium-sized firms in Chile. *Communications of the Association for Information Systems*, *13*, 81–102.

Grandon, E., & Pearson, J. (2004). Electronic commerce adoption: An empirical study of small and medium US businesses. *Information & Management*, *42*(97), 216.

Grandon, E., & Pearson, J. M. (2003). Strategic value and adoption of electronic commerce: An empirical study of Chilean small and medium businesses. *Journal of Global Information Technology Management*, *6*(3), 22–43. doi:10.1080/1097198X.2003.10856354

Grandy, G., & Wicks, D. (2008). Competitive advantage as a legitimacy-creating process. *Qualitative Research in Organizations and Management*, *3*(1), 21–41. doi:10.1108/17465640810870373

Graves, C., & Thomas, J. (2006). Internationalization of Australian family businesses: A managerial capabilities perspective. *Family Business Review*, *19*(3), 207–224. doi:10.1111/j.1741-6248.2006.00066.x

Greiner, L. E. (1972). Evolution and revolution as organizations grow. *Harvard Business Review*, *76*(3), 55–68. PMID:10179654

Grieger, M., Hartmann, E., & Kotzab, H. (2011). E-markets as meta-enterprise information e systems. In *Enterprise information systems: Concepts, methodologies, tools and applications* (pp. 638–647). Hershey, PA: Business Science Reference; doi:10.4018/978-1-61692-852-0.ch306

Grundry, L. K., & Welsch, H. P. (2001). The ambitious entrepreneur: High growth strategies of women-owned enterprises. *Journal of Business Venturing*, *16*(5), 453–470. doi:10.1016/S0883-9026(99)00059-2

grzonkowski, s., ensor, b. d., & mcdaniel, b. (2013). applied cryptography in Electronic Commerce. In *IT policy and ethics: Concepts, methodologies, tools, and applications* (pp. 368-388). Hershey, PA: Information Science Reference. doi:10.4018/978-1-4666-2919-6.ch017

Gunasekaran, A., & Ngai, E. W. T. (2005). E-commerce in Hong Kong: An empirical perspective and analysis. *Internet Research*, *15*(2), 141–159. doi:10.1108/10662240510590333

Haber, S., & Reichel, A. (2007). The cumulative nature of the entrepreneurial process: The contribution of social capital, planning and environment resources to small venture performance. *Journal of Business Venturing*, *22*(1), 119–145. doi:10.1016/j.jbusvent.2005.09.005

Hadaya, P. (2006). Determinants of the future level of use of electronic marketplaces: The case of Canadian firms. *Electronic Commerce Research*, *6*(2), 173–185. doi:10.1007/s10660-006-6956-y

Hage, J., & Aiken, M. (1967). Relationship of centralization to other structural properties. *Administrative Science Quarterly*, *12*(1), 72–93. doi:10.2307/2391213

Ha, H. (2012). Online security and consumer protection in ecommerce an Australian case. In K. Mohammed Rezaul (Ed.), *Strategic and pragmatic e-business: Implications for future business practices* (pp. 217–243). Hershey, PA: Business Science Reference; doi:10.4018/978-1-4666-1619-6.ch010

Ha, H., Coghill, K., & Maharaj, E. A. (2012). Current measures to protect e-consumers' privacy in Australia. In *Cyber crime: Concepts, methodologies, tools and applications* (pp. 1728–1755). Hershey, PA: Information Science Reference; doi:10.4018/978-1-61350-323-2.ch806

Halabi, A. K., Barrett, R., & Dyt, R. (2010). Understanding financial information used to assess small firm performance. *Qualitative Research in Accounting and Management*, *7*(2), 163–179. doi:10.1108/11766091011050840

Halas, H., & Klobucar, T. (2011). Business models and organizational processes changes. In *Global business: Concepts, methodologies, tools and applications* (pp. 192–205). Hershey, PA: Business Science Reference; doi:10.4018/978-1-60960-587-2.ch113

Hall, G. (1995). *Surviving and Prospering in the Small Firm Sector*. London: Routledge.

Hall, R. (1992). The strategic analysis of intangible resources. *Strategic Management Journal*, *13*(2), 135–144. doi:10.1002/smj.4250130205

Hamel, G., & Prahalad, C. K. (1994). *Competing on the Future*. Boston, MA: Harvard Business School Press.

Hamilton, B. (1984). Entry and exit of business in Scotland. In J. Lewis, J. Stanworth, & A. Gibb (Eds.), *Success and Failure in Small Business* (pp. 57–69). Aldershot, England: Gower.

Han, B. (2012). I play, I pay? An investigation of the user's willingness to pay on hedonic social network sites. *International Journal of Virtual Communities and Social Networking*, *4*(1), 19–31. doi:10.4018/jvcsn.2012010102

Handler, W. C. (1991). Key interpersonal relationships of next-generation family members in family firms. *Journal of Small Business Management*, *29*(3), 21–32.

Hankinson, A., Bartlett, D., & Ducheneaut, B. (1997). The key factors in the small profiles of small-medium enterprise owner-managers that influence business performance. The UK (Rennes) SME survey 1995-97: An international research project survey. *International Journal of Entrepreneurial Behaviour and Research*, *3*(3), 168–175. doi:10.1108/13552559710190421

Hanks, S. (1990). Am empirical examination of the organizaitonal life cycle in high technology firms. Doctoral dissertation, University of Utah: Salt Lake City, Utah.

Harnesk, D. (2011). Convergence of information security in B2B networks. In E. Kajan (Ed.), *Electronic business interoperability: Concepts, opportunities and challenges* (pp. 571–595). Hershey, PA: Business Science Reference; doi:10.4018/978-1-60960-485-1.ch023

Harrison, D. A., Mykytyn, P. P., & Rienenschneider, C. K. (1997). Executive decisions about IT adoption in small business: Theory and empirical tests. *Information Systems Research*, *8*(2), 171–195. doi:10.1287/isre.8.2.171

Hart, P. J., & Saunders, C. S. (1998). Emerging electronic partnerships: Antecedents and dimensions of EDI use from the supplier's perspective. *Journal of Management Information Systems*, *14*(4), 87–111.

Harwood, T. (2012). Emergence of gamified commerce: Turning virtual to real. *Journal of Electronic Commerce in Organizations*, *10*(2), 16–39. doi:10.4018/jeco.2012040102

Hashim, J. (2007). Information technology adoption among small and medium enterprise owners in Malaysia. *The International Journal of Business and Information*, *2*(2), 221–240.

Hashmi, M., & Cuddy, J. (1990). Strategic initiatives for introducing CIM technologies. In Faria, L. (Editor), *Computer Integrated Manufacturing – Proceedings of the 6th CIM-Europe Conference*, Lisbon: Spring Verlag.

Haug, A., Pedersen, S. G., & Arlbjorn, J. S. (2011). IT readiness in small and medium-sized enterprises. *Industrial Management & Data Systems*, *111*(4), 490–508. doi:10.1108/02635571111133515

Haugh, H. (2007). Community-led social venture creation. *Entrepreneurship Theory and Practice*, *31*(2), 161–182. doi:10.1111/j.1540-6520.2007.00168.x

Hayes, T. P. (2012). Predicting information technology adoption in small businesses: An extension of the technology acceptance model. *Academy of Information and Management Sciences Journal*, *15*(1), 37–46.

Hay, M., & Kamshad, K. (1994). Small firm growth: Intentions, implementation and impediments. *Business Strategy Review*, *5*(3), 49–68. doi:10.1111/j.1467-8616.1994.tb00166.x

Headd, B. (2003). Redefining business success: Factors leading to surviving and closing successfully. *Small Business Economics*, *21*(1), 51–61. doi:10.1023/A:1024433630958

Hebert, R. F., & Link, A. N. (1989). In search of the meaning of entrepreneurship. *Small Business Economics*, *1*(1), 39–49. doi:10.1007/BF00389915

Heneman, H., & Berkley, R. (1999). Applicant attraction practices and outcomes among small businesses. *Journal of Small Business Management*, *37*(1), 53–74.

Heravi, B. R., & Lycett, M. (2012). Semantically enriched e-business standards development: The case of ebXML business process specification schema. In E. Kajan, F. Dorloff, & I. Bedini (Eds.), *Handbook of research on e-business standards and protocols: Documents, data and advanced web technologies* (pp. 655–675). Hershey, PA: Business Science Reference; doi:10.4018/978-1-4666-0146-8.ch030

Herbert, R. F., & Link, A. N. (1988). *The Entrepreneur – Mainstream Views and Radical Critiques*. New York: Praeger.

Hill, D. S. (2012). An examination of standardized product identification and business benefit. In E. Kajan, F. Dorloff, & I. Bedini (Eds.), *Handbook of research on e-business standards and protocols: Documents, data and advanced web technologies* (pp. 387–411). Hershey, PA: Business Science Reference; doi:10.4018/978-1-4666-0146-8.ch018

Hinson, R., & Sorenson, O. (2006). E-business and small Ghanaian exporters: Preliminary micro firm explorations in the light of a digital divide. *Online Information Review*, *30*(2), 116–138. doi:10.1108/14684520610659166

Hisrich, R. (2004). *Small Business Solutions*. New York, NY: McGraw-Hill.

Hisrich, R. D., & Peters, M. P. (2002). *Entrepreneurship*. Boston Burr Ridge, IL: McGraw-Hill.

Hitt, M. A., Ireland, R. D., Camp, M. S., & Sexton, D. L. (2001). Special introduction to the special issue on strategic entrepreneurship: Entrepreneurial strategies for wealth creation. *Strategic Management Journal*, *22*(6-7), 479–491. doi:10.1002/smj.196

Hitt, M. A., Ireland, R. D., Camp, M. S., & Sexton, D. L. (2002). Strategic entrepreneurship: Integrating entrepreneurial and strategic management perspectives. In M. Hitt, R. Ireland, M. Camp, & D. Sexton (Eds.), *Strategic Entrepreneurship: Creating a New Mindset* (pp. 1–13). Oxford: Blackwell. doi:10.1111/b.9780631234104.2002.00015.x

Hitt, M. A., Ireland, R. D., & Hoskisson, R. E. (2001). *Strategic Management: Competitiveness and Globalization*. Cincinnati, Ohio: South-Western College.

Ho, C. T. (2009). The relationship between knowledge management enablers and performance. *Industrial Management & Data Systems*, *109*(1), 98–117. doi:10.1108/02635570910926618

Hoffman, J., Hoelscher, M., & Sorenson, R. (2006). Achieving sustained competitive advantage: A family capital theory. *Family Business Review*, *19*(2), 135–145. doi:10.1111/j.1741-6248.2006.00065.x

Hollander, A. S., Cherrington, J. O., & Denna, E. L. (2000). *Accounting, Information Technology, and Business Solutions*. Boston, MA: McGraw-Hill.

Honjo, Y. (2000). Business failure of new firms: An empirical analysis using a multiplicative hazards model. *International Journal of Industrial Organization*, *18*(4), 557–574. doi:10.1016/S0167-7187(98)00035-6

Hoogstra, G. J., & van Dijk, J. (2004). Explaining firm employment growth: Does location matter? *Small Business Economics*, *22*(3/4), 179–190. doi:10.1023/B:SBEJ.0000022218.66156.ac

Hoops, D. S. (2011). Legal issues in the virtual world and e-commerce. In B. Ciaramitaro (Ed.), *Virtual worlds and e-commerce: Technologies and applications for building customer relationships* (pp. 186–204). Hershey, PA: Business Science Reference; doi:10.4018/978-1-61692-808-7.ch010

Hornsby, J., & Kuratko, D. (2003). Human resource management in US small business: A replication and extension. *Journal of Developmental Entrepreneurship*, *8*(1), 73–92.

Horton, T. P. (1986). Managing in a family way. *Management Review*, *75*(2), 3.

Hua, G. B. (2013). *Implementing IT business strategy in the construction industry.* Hershey, PA: IGI Global; doi:10.4018/978-1-4666-4185-3

Huang, C. J., & Liu, C. J. (2005). Exploraiton for the relationship between innovation, IT and performance. *Journal of Intellectual Capital*, *6*(2), 237–252. doi:10.1108/14691930510592825

Huang, J., & Dang, J. (2011). Context-sensitive ontology matching in electronic business. In E. Kajan (Ed.), *Electronic business interoperability: Concepts, opportunities and challenges* (pp. 279–301). Hershey, PA: Business Science Reference; doi:10.4018/978-1-60960-485-1.ch012

Huang, Z., Janz, B. D., & Frolick, M. N. (2008). A comprehensive examination of internet-eDI adoption. *Information Systems Management*, *25*(3), 273–286. doi:10.1080/10580530802151228

Hua, S. C., Rajesh, M. J., & Theng, L. B. (2011). Determinants of e-commerce adoption among small and medium-sized enterprises in Malaysia. In S. Sharma (Ed.), *E-adoption and socio-economic impacts: Emerging infrastructural effects* (pp. 71–89). Hershey, PA: Information Science Reference; doi:10.4018/978-1-60960-597-1.ch005

Huggins, R., & Weir, M. (2007). Intellectual assets and public policy. *Journal of Intellectual Capital*, *8*(4), 708–720. doi:10.1108/14691930710830855

Hughes, P., & Morgan, R. E. (2008). Fitting strategic resources with product-market strategy: Performance implications. *Journal of Business Research*, *61*(4), 323–331. doi:10.1016/j.jbusres.2007.06.023

Hunaiti, Z., Tairo, D., Sedoyeka, E., & Elgazzar, S. (2010). Factors facing mobile commerce deployment in United Kingdom. In W. Hu & Y. Zuo (Eds.), *Handheld computing for mobile commerce: Applications, concepts and technologies* (pp. 109–123). Hershey, PA: Information Science Reference; doi:10.4018/978-1-61520-761-9.ch007

Hung, H. (2006). Formation and survival on new ventures. *International Small Business Journal*, *24*(4), 359–378. doi:10.1177/0266242606065508

Hung, W. J., Tsai, C., Hung, S., McQueen, R., & Jou, J. (2011). Evaluating web site support capabilities in sell-side B2B transaction processes: A longitudinal study of two industries in New Zealand and Taiwan. *Journal of Global Information Management*, *19*(1), 51–79. doi:10.4018/jgim.2011010103

Hunter, M. G. (2003). Information systems and small business: What's in the wind in L, A.? ISOneWorld, April 23-25, Las Vegas, Nevada.

Hunter, M. G. (2003). Information systems and small business: What's in the wind in L, A.? ISOneWorld, April 23-25, Las Vegas, NV.

Hunter, M. G. (2005). International information systems and small business project: A western Canadian perspective, Chapter 5 in Hunter, M. G., Burgess, S. & Wenn. A. (Editors). Small Business and Information Technology: Research Issues and International Case Studies, Heidelberg Press, Melbourne, Australia. ISBN: 1-920889-04

Hunter, M. G. (2008). Information systems and small business, Chapter in Khosrow-Pour, M. (Editor). Encyclopedia of Information Science and Technology, Volume I-V, Idea Group Publishing, Hershey, PA.

Hunter, M. G. (2011). Small Business Orientation: A Preliminary Investigation into Variety in Canadian Small Business. Management Report prepared for The Monieson Centre, Queen's University School of Business.

Hunter, M. G. (2002). Information systems development outcomes: The case of song book music. In S. Burgess (Ed.), *Managing Information Technology in Small Business: Challenges and Solutions*. Hershey, PA: Idea Group Publishing. doi:10.4018/978-1-930708-35-8.ch003

Hunter, M. G. (2013). The duality of information technology roles: A case study. In C. Howard (Ed.), *Strategic adoption of technological innovations* (pp. 38–49). Hershey, PA: Information Science Reference; doi:10.4018/978-1-4666-2782-6.ch003

Hunter, M. G., Diochon, M., Pugsley, D., & Wright, B. (2002). Unique challenges for small business adoption of information technology: The case of the Nova Scotia ten. In S. Burgess (Ed.), *Managing Information Technology in Small Business: Challenges and Solutions*. Hershey, PA: Idea Group Publishing. doi:10.4018/978-1-930708-35-8.ch006

Hunter, M. G., & Kazakoff, D. (2008). *Little Empires: Multi-Generation Small Business in Southern Alberta, Canada*. Melbourne, Australia: Heidelberg Press.

Hunter, M. G., & Kazakoff, D. (2008). *Little Empires: Multi-Generation Small Business in Southern Alberta, CANADA*. Melbourne, Australia: Heidelberg Press.

Hunter, M. G., & Kazakoff, D. (2012). Multi-generation small business response to the recent financial crisis. *Journal of Applied Management and Entrepreneurship*, *17*(1), 37–51.

Hunter, M. G., & Long, W. A. (2003). Adopting the Entrepreneurial Process in the Study of Information Systems and Small Business. In G. Gingrich (Ed.), *Managing Information Technology in Government, Business, and Communities*. Hershey, PA: IRM Press.

Hunt, S. D. (1999). The strategic imperative and sustainable competitive advantage: Public policy implications of resource-advantage theory. *Journal of the Academy of Marketing Science*, *27*(2), 144–159. doi:10.1177/0092070399272003

Huoivinen, S., & Pasanen, M. (2010). Entrepreneurial and management teams: What makes the difference? *Journal of Management & Organization*, *16*(3), 436–453. doi:10.5172/jmo.16.3.436

Huq, N., Shah, S. M., & Mihailescu, D. (2012). Why select an open source ERP over proprietary ERP? A focus on SMEs and supplier's perspective. In R. Atem de Carvalho & B. Johansson (Eds.), *Free and open source enterprise resource planning: Systems and strategies* (pp. 33–55). Hershey, PA: Business Science Reference; doi:10.4018/978-1-61350-486-4.ch003

Hussin, H., King, M., & Cragg, P. (2002). IT alignment in small firms. *European Journal of Information Systems*, *11*(2), 108–127. doi:10.1057/palgrave/ejis/3000422

Hutchinson, R. G., Hutchinson, A. R., & Newcomer, M. (1938). A study in business mortality. *The American Economic Review*, *28*(3), 497–514.

Hu, W., Zuo, Y., Kaabouch, N., & Chen, L. (2010). A technological perspective of mobile and electronic commerce systems. In M. Khosrow-Pour (Ed.), *E-commerce trends for organizational advancement: New applications and methods* (pp. 16–35). Hershey, PA: Information Science Reference; doi:10.4018/978-1-60566-964-9.ch002

Huybrechts, J., Voordeckers, W., Lybaert, N., & Vandemaele, S. (2011). The distinctiveness of family-firm intangibles: A review and suggestions for future research. *Journal of Management & Organization*, *17*(2), 268–287. doi:10.5172/jmo.2011.17.2.268

Iacovou, C., Benbasat, I., & Dexter, A. (1995). Electronic data interchange and small organizations: Adoption and impact of technology. *Management Information Systems Quarterly*, *19*(4), 465–485. doi:10.2307/249629

Ifinedo, P. (2011). Internet/e-business technologies acceptance in Canada's SMEs: An exploratory investigation. *Internet Research*, *21*(3), 255–281. doi:10.1108/10662241111139309

Industry Canada. (2010). *Key Small Business Statistics (Catalogue No. Iu186-1/2010-2E)*. Ottawa: Canadian Government Publishing Centre.

Industry Canada. (2010). *Key Small Business Statistics*, (Catalogue No. Iu186-1/2010-2E), ISSN 1718-3456, Ottawa: Canadian Government Publishing Centre.

Ingvaldsen, J., & Gulla, J. (2010). Semantic business process mining of SAP transactions. In M. Wang & Z. Sun (Eds.), *Handbook of research on complex dynamic process management: Techniques for adaptability in turbulent environments* (pp. 416–429). Hershey, PA: Business Science Reference; doi:10.4018/978-1-60566-669-3.ch017

Ingvaldsen, J., & Gulla, J. (2011). Semantic business process mining of SAP transactions. In *Enterprise information systems: Concepts, methodologies, tools and applications* (pp. 866–878). Hershey, PA: Business Science Reference; doi:10.4018/978-1-61692-852-0.ch320

Internetworldstats.com. (2007). Internet users by world region. www.internetworldstats.com

Ioannou, M. (2013). Customer relationship management (CRM): A one-size-fits-all philosophy? In H. Kaufmann & M. Panni (Eds.), *Customer-centric marketing strategies: Tools for building organizational performance* (pp. 150–170). Hershey, PA: Business Science Reference; doi:10.4018/978-1-4666-2524-2.ch008

Ireland, R. D., Hitt, M. A., Camp, S. M., & Sexton, D. L. (2001). Integrating entrepreneurship and strategic management actions to create firm wealth. *The Academy of Management Executive*, *15*(1), 49–64. doi:10.5465/AME.2001.4251393

Ireland, R. D., Hitt, M. A., & Simon, D. G. (2003). A model of strategic entrepreneurship: The construct and its dimensions. *Journal of Management*, *29*(6), 963–989. doi:10.1016/S0149-2063(03)00086-2

Islam, M. S., & Scupola, A. (2013). E-service research trends in the domain of e-government: A contemporary study. In A. Scupola (Ed.), *Mobile opportunities and applications for e-service innovations* (pp. 152–169). Hershey, PA: Information Science Reference; doi:10.4018/978-1-4666-2654-6.ch009

Jack, S., Dodd, S. D., & Anderson, A. J. (2008). Change and the development of entrepreneurial networks over time: A processual perspective. *Entrepreneurship and Regional Development*, *20*(2), 125–159. doi:10.1080/08985620701645027

Jackson, P., & Harris, L. (2003). E-business and organizational change. *Journal of Organizational Change Management*, *16*(5), 497–511. doi:10.1108/09534810310494900

Jailani, N., Patel, A., Mukhtar, M., Abdullah, S., & Yahya, Y. (2010). Concept of an agent-based electronic marketplace. In I. Lee (Ed.), *Encyclopedia of e-business development and management in the global economy* (pp. 239–251). Hershey, PA: Business Science Reference; doi:10.4018/978-1-61520-611-7.ch024

James, H. S. Jr. (1999). Owner as manager, extended horizons and the family firm. *International Journal of the Economics of Business*, *6*(1), 41–55. doi:10.1080/13571519984304

Jarzabkowski, P. (2002). Centralized or decentralized? Strategic implications of resource allocation models. *Higher Education Quarterly*, *56*(1), 5–32. doi:10.1111/1468-2273.00200

Jenkins, M. (2010). Technological discontinuities and competitive advantage: A historical perspective on Formula 1 motor racing 1950-2006. *Journal of Management Studies*, *47*(5), 884–910. doi:10.1111/j.1467-6486.2010.00928.x

Jennings, P. A., & Beaver, G. (1997). The performance and competitive advantage of small firms: A management perspective. *International Small Business Journal*, *15*(2), 63–75. doi:10.1177/0266242697152004

Jensen, M. C., & Luthans, F. (2006). Relationship between entrepreneurs' psychological capital and their authentic leadership. *Journal of Managerial Issues*, *18*(2), 254–273.

Jensen, M. C., & Meckling, W. (1976). The theory of the firm: Managerial behaviour, agency costs, and ownership structure. *Journal of Financial Economics*, *3*(4), 305–360. doi:10.1016/0304-405X(76)90026-X

Jeon, B. N., Han, K. S., & Lee, M. J. (2006). Determining factors for the adoption of e-business: The case of SMEs in Korea. *Applied Economics*, *38*(16), 1905–1916. doi:10.1080/00036840500427262

Jeyaraj, A., Rottman, J. W., & Lacity, M. C. (2006). A review of the predictors, linkages, and biases in IT innovation adoption research. *Journal of Information Technology*, *21*(1), 1–23. doi:10.1057/palgrave.jit.2000056

Johnson, M. (2010). Barriers to innovation adoption: A study of e-markets. *Industrial Management & Data Systems*, *110*(2), 157–174. doi:10.1108/02635571011020287

Johns, R. (2011). Technology, trust and B2B relationships: A banking perspective. In O. Bak & N. Stair (Eds.), *Impact of e-business technologies on public and private organizations: Industry comparisons and perspectives* (pp. 79–96). Hershey, PA: Business Science Reference; doi:10.4018/978-1-60960-501-8.ch005

Johnston, D. A., Wade, M., & McClean, R. (2007). Does e-business matter to SMEs? A comparison of the financial impacts of internet business solutions on European and North American SMEs. *Journal of Small Business Management*, *45*(3), 354–361. doi:10.1111/j.1540-627X.2007.00217.x

Jones, O. (2003). Competitive advantage in SMEs: Towards a conceptual framework. In O. Jones & F. Tilley (Eds.), *Competitive Advantage in SMEs: Organising for Innovation and Change* (pp. 15–33). Chichester: Wiley.

Joshi, S. (2013). E-supply chain collaboration and integration: Implementation issues and challenges. In D. Graham, I. Manikas, & D. Folinas (Eds.), *E-logistics and e-supply chain management: Applications for evolving business* (pp. 9–26). Hershey, PA: Business Science Reference; doi:10.4018/978-1-4666-3914-0.ch002

Joyce, P., & Woods, A. (2003). Managing for growth: Decision making, planning, and making changes. *Journal of Small Business and Enterprise Development*, *10*(2), 144–151. doi:10.1108/14626000310473175

Julien, P., & Raymond, L. (1994). Factors of new technology adoption in the retail sector. *Entrepreneurship Theory and Practice*, Summer, 79-90.

Julien, P. (1995). New technologies and technological information in small businesses. *Journal of Business Venturing*, *10*(6), 459–475. doi:10.1016/0883-9026(95)00084-L

Jutla, D., Bodorik, P., & Dhaliqal, J. (2002). Supporting the e-business readiness of small and medium-sized enterprises: Approaches and metrics. *Internet Research: Electronic Networking Applications and Policy*, *12*(2), 139–164. doi:10.1108/10662240210422512

Kagan, A., Lau, K., & Nusgart, K. R. (1990). Information system usage within small business firms. *Entrepreneurship Theory and Practice*, Spring, 25-37.

Kamal, M., Qureshil, S., & Wolcott, P. (2013). Promoting competitive advantage in micro-enterprises through information technology interventions. In *Small and medium enterprises: Concepts, methodologies, tools, and applications* (pp. 581–606). Hershey, PA: Business Science Reference; doi:10.4018/978-1-4666-3886-0.ch030

Kamel, S. (2012). Electronic commerce prospects in emerging economies: Lessons from Egypt. In *Regional development: Concepts, methodologies, tools, and applications* (pp. 1104–1115). Hershey, PA: Information Science Reference; doi:10.4018/978-1-4666-0882-5.ch604

Kamoun, F., & Halaweh, M. (2012). User interface design and e-commerce security perception: An empirical study. *International Journal of E-Business Research*, *8*(2), 15–32. doi:10.4018/jebr.2012040102

Kangasharju, A. (2000). Growth of the smallest: Determinants of small firm growth during strong macroeconomic fluctuations. *International Small Business Journal*, *19*(1), 28–43. doi:10.1177/0266242600191002

Kannabiran, G., & Dharmalingam, P. (2012). Enablers and inhibitors of advanced information technologies adoption by SMEs: An empirical study of auto ancillaries in India. *Journal of Enterprise Information Management*, *25*(2), 186–209. doi:10.1108/17410391211204419

Karagozoglu, N., & Lindell, M. (2004). Electronic commerce strategy, operations, and performance in small and medium-sized enterprises. *Journal of Small Business and Enterprise Development*, *11*(3), 290–301. doi:10.1108/14626000410551555

Karakaya, F. (2012). Business-to-consumers ecommerce: How companies use the internet in marketing products and services to consumers. In N. Delener (Ed.), *Service science research, strategy and innovation: Dynamic knowledge management methods* (pp. 227–244). Hershey, PA: Business Science. doi:10.4018/978-1-4666-0077-5.ch014

Karakaya, F. (2013). B2B ecommerce: Current practices. In *Supply chain management: Concepts, methodologies, tools, and applications* (pp. 497–510). Hershey, PA: Business Science Reference; doi:10.4018/978-1-4666-2625-6.ch029

Karakaya, F., & Stahl, M. J. (2009). After market entry barriers in E-commerce markets. *Journal of Electronic Commerce Research*, *10*(3), 130–143.

Karimov, F. P. (2013). Factors influencing e-commerce growth: A comparative study of central Asian transition economies. In S. Sharma (Ed.), *Adoption of virtual technologies for business, educational, and governmental advancements* (pp. 1–17). Hershey, PA: Information Science Reference; doi:10.4018/978-1-4666-2053-7.ch001

Kart, F., Moser, L. E., & Melliar-Smith, P. M. (2010). An automated supply chain management system and its performance evaluation. *International Journal of Information Systems and Supply Chain Management*, *3*(2), 84–107. doi:10.4018/jisscm.2010040105

Kartiwi, M., & MacGregor, R. C. (2007). Electronic commerce adoption barriers in small to medium-sized enterprises in developed and developing countries: A cross-country comparison. *Journal of Electronic Commerce in Organizations*, *5*(3), 35–51. doi:10.4018/jeco.2007070103

Kaynak, H. (2003). The relationship between total quality management practices and their effects on firm performance. *Journal of Operations Management, 21*(4), 405–435. doi:10.1016/S0272-6963(03)00004-4

Kazanjian, R. (1988). Relation of dominant problems to stages of growth in technology-based new ventures. *Academy of Management Journal, 31*(2), 257–279. doi:10.2307/256548

Keil, M., & Mixon, R. (1993). Laboratory Studies of IS Failures as Escalating Commitment to a Failing Course of Action: Overcoming the Obstacles", *Proceedings of the Fourteenth International Conference on Information Systems*, DegrossJ.I.BostromR. P.RobeyD. (Editors), New York: ACM.

Kelarev, A. V., Brown, S., Watters, P., Wu, X., & Dazeley, R. (2011). Establishing reasoning communities of security experts for internet commerce security. In J. Yearwood & A. Stranieri (Eds.), *Technologies for supporting reasoning communities and collaborative decision making: Cooperative approaches* (pp. 380–396). Hershey, PA: Information Science Reference; doi:10.4018/978-1-60960-091-4.ch020

Kelley, D. J., & Nakosteen, R. A. (2005). Technology resources, alliances, and sustained growth in new, technology-based firms. *IEEE Transactions on Engineering Management, 52*(3), 292–300. doi:10.1109/TEM.2005.851272

Kelliher, F., & Henderson, J. B. (2006). A learning framework for the small business environment. *Journal of European Industrial Training, 30*(7), 512–528. doi:10.1108/03090590610704385

Kelliher, F., & Reinl, L. (2009). A resource-based view of micro-firm management practice. *Journal of Small Business and Enterprise Development, 16*(3), 521–532. doi:10.1108/14626000910977206

Kendall, J. D., Tung, L. L., Chua, K. H., Hong, C., Ng, D., & Tan, S. M. (2001, September). (20010. Receptivity of Singapore's SMEs to electronic commerce adoption. *The Journal of Strategic Information Systems, 10*(3), 223–242. doi:10.1016/S0963-8687(01)00048-8

Kerr, D., Gammack, J. G., & Boddington, R. (2011). Overview of digital business security issues. In D. Kerr, J. Gammack, & K. Bryant (Eds.), *Digital business security development: Management technologies* (pp. 1–36). Hershey, PA: Business Science Reference; doi:10.4018/978-1-60566-806-2.ch001

Kerr, D., Gammack, J. G., & Bryant, K. (2011). *Digital business security development: Management technologies*. Hershey, PA: IGI Global; doi:10.4018/978-1-60566-806-2

Kett, H. (2013). A business model approach for service engineering in the internet of services. In P. Ordóñez de Pablos & R. Tennyson (Eds.), *Best practices and new perspectives in service science and management* (pp. 228–236). Hershey, PA: Business Science Reference; doi:10.4018/978-1-4666-3894-5.ch013

Khan, M. R., & Rocha, J. R. (1982). Recurring management problems in small business. *American Journal of Small Business, 7*, 50–58.

Khurana, R., & Aggarwal, R. (2013). *Interdisciplinary perspectives on business convergence, computing, and legality*. Hershey, PA: IGI Global; doi:10.4018/978-1-4666-4209-6

Kickul, J., Gundry, L. K., Barbosa, S. D., & Whitcanack. Intuition versus analysis? Testing differential models of cognitive style on entrepreneurial self-efficacy and the new venture creation. *Entrepreneurship Theory and Practice*, 33(2), 439-453.

Kickul, J. (2001). Promises made, promises broken: An explanation of employee attraction and retention practices in small business. *Journal of Small Business Management, 39*(4), 320–335. doi:10.1111/0447-2778.00029

Kienan, B. (2000). *Small Business Solutions: E-Commerce*. Redmond, WA: Microsoft Press.

Kim, G., & Suh, Y. (2012). Building semantic business process space for agile and efficient business processes management: Ontology-based approach. In V. Shankararaman, J. Zhao, & J. Lee (Eds.), *Business enterprise, process, and technology management: Models and applications* (pp. 51–73). Hershey, PA: Business Science Reference; doi:10.4018/978-1-4666-0249-6.ch004

King, K. P., & Foley, J. J. (2012). 21st century learning opportunities for SME success: Maximizing technology tools and lifelong learning for innovation and impact. In *Human resources management: Concepts, methodologies, tools, and applications* (pp. 731–752). Hershey, PA: Business Science Reference; doi:10.4018/978-1-4666-1601-1.ch045

King, W. R. (2005). Communication and information processing as a critical success factor in the effective knowledge organization. *International Journal of Business Information Systems, 1*(1/2), 31–52. doi:10.1504/IJBIS.2005.007399

Kipp, A., & Schubert, L. (2011). E-business interoperability and collaboration. In E. Kajan (Ed.), *Electronic business interoperability: Concepts, opportunities and challenges* (pp. 153–184). Hershey, PA: Business Science Reference; doi:10.4018/978-1-60960-485-1.ch008

Kirbey, D., & Turner, M. (1993). IT and the small retail business. *International Journal of Retail & Distribution Management, 21*(7), 20–27.

Kirkwood, J. (2009). To grow or not? Growing small service firms. *Journal of Small Business and Enterprise Development, 16*(3), 485–503. doi:10.1108/14626000910977189

Kirschenhofer, F., & Lechner, C. (2012). Performance drivers of serial entrepreneurs. *International Journal of Entrepreneurial Behaviour & Research, 18*(3), 305–329. doi:10.1108/13552551211227693

Kirton, M. J. (1976). Adaptors and innovators: A description and measure. *The Journal of Applied Psychology, 61*(5), 622–629. doi:10.1037/0021-9010.61.5.622

Kirzner, I. (1973). *Competition and Entrepreneurship*. Chicago: Chicago University Press.

Kirzner, I. (1992). *The Meaning of the Market Process*. London: Routledge. doi:10.4324/9780203004456

Kirzner, I. (1997). Entrepreneurial discovery and the competitive market process: An Austrian approach. *Journal of Economic Literature*, *35*(1), 60–85.

Klein, H. (1991). Further evidence of the relationship between goal setting and expectancy theories. *Organizational Behavior and Human Decision Processes*, *49*(2), 230–257. doi:10.1016/0749-5978(91)90050-4

Klink, S., & Weiß, P. (2011). Social impact of collaborative services to maintain electronic business relationships. In *Virtual communities: Concepts, methodologies, tools and applications* (pp. 2011–2040). Hershey, PA: Information Science Reference; doi:10.4018/978-1-60960-100-3.ch609

Kmieciak, R., Michna, A., & Meczynska, A. (2012). Innovativeness, empowerment and IT capability: Evidence from SMEs. *Industrial Management & Data Systems*, *112*(5), 707–728. doi:10.1108/02635571211232280

Kobia, M., & Sikalieh, D. (2010). Towards a search for the meaning of entrepreneurship. *Journal of European Industrial Training*, *34*(2), 110–127. doi:10.1108/03090591011023970

Kohli, A. K., & Jaworski, B. J. (1990). Market orientation: The construct, research propositions, and managerial implications. *Journal of Marketing*, *54*(2), 1–18. doi:10.2307/1251866

Kohli, A. S., & Gupta, M. (2010). Improving operations strategy: Application of TOC principles in a small business. *Journal of Business & Economics Research*, *8*(4), 37–45.

Koh, S. C. L., & Maguire, S. (2004). Identifying the adoption of e-business and knowledge management within SMEs. *Journal of Small Business and Enterprise Development*, *11*(3), 338–348. doi:10.1108/14626000410551591

Konorti, E. (2010). The relationship between wealth cration and professional management in small-medium enterprises. *The Journal of American Academy of Business*, *16*(1), 11–23.

Konorti, E. (2010). The relationship between wealth creation and professional management in small-medium enterprises. *The Journal of American Academy of Business*, *16*(1), 11–23.

Koontz Traverso. (2001). *The Small Business Owner's Guide to a Good Night's Sleep: Preventing and Solving Chronic and Costly Problems*. Princeton, NJ: Bloomberg Press.

Korchak, R., & Rodman, R. (2001). Ebusiness adoption among US small manufacturers and the role of manufacturing extension. *Economic Development Review (Schiller Park, Ill.)*, *17*(3), 20–25.

Korper, S., & Ellis, J. (2001). *The E-Commerce Book*. San Diego, CA: Academic Press.

Korunka, C., Frank, H., Lueger, M., & Mugler, J. (2003). The entrepreneurial personality in the context of resources, environment, and the startup process – A configurational approach. *Entrepreneurship Theory and Practice*, *28*(1), 23–42. doi:10.1111/1540-8520.00030

Koshy, P. (2011). *Adoption of information and communications technology in rural micro and small enterprises. Paper 2, Institute for Development Studies and Enterprise Research*. Kerala: Samadhan Foundation.

Kotey, B., & Sheridan, A. (2001). Gender and the practice of HRM in small business. *Asia Pacific Journal of Human Resources*, *39*(3), 23–40. doi:10.1177/103841110103900303

Koumpis, A., & Protogeros, N. (2010). Doing business on the globalised networked economy: Technology and business challenges for accounting information systems. In M. Cruz-Cunha (Ed.), *Social, managerial, and organizational dimensions of enterprise information systems* (pp. 81–92). Hershey, PA: Business Science Reference; doi:10.4018/978-1-60566-856-7.ch004

Kritchanchai, D., Tan, A. W., & Hosie, P. (2010). An empirical investigation of third party logistics providers in Thailand: Barriers, motivation and usage of information technologies. *International Journal of Information Systems and Supply Chain Management*, *3*(2), 68–83. doi:10.4018/jisscm.2010040104

Kritchanchai, D., Tan, A. W., & Hosie, P. (2012). An empirical investigation of third party logistics providers in Thailand: Barriers, motivation and usage of information technologies. In J. Wang (Ed.), *Information technologies, methods, and techniques of supply chain management* (pp. 272–288). Hershey, PA: Business Science Reference; doi:10.4018/978-1-4666-0918-1.ch016

Krueger, M. E. (2004). Creativity and innovation in the entrepreneurship domain. Unpublished PhD Thesis in Entrepreneurship, University of Pretoria, Pretoria.

Krueger, N. F., Reilly, M. D., & Carsrid, A. L. (2000). Competing models of entrepreneurial intentions. *Journal of Business Venturing*, *15*(5/6), 411–432. doi:10.1016/S0883-9026(98)00033-0

Kuan, K., & Chau, P. Y. K. (2001). A perception-based model for EDI adoption in small businesses using a technology-organized environment framework. *Information & Management*, *38*(8), 507–521. doi:10.1016/S0378-7206(01)00073-8

Kula, V., & Tatoglu, E. (2003). An exploratory study of internet adoption by SMEs in an emerging market economy. *European Business Review*, *15*(5), 324–333. doi:10.1108/09555340310493045

Kumar, M. (2011). Role of web interface in building trust in B2B e-exchanges. In S. Chhabra & H. Rahman (Eds.), *Human development and global advancements through information communication technologies: New initiatives* (pp. 63–74). Hershey, PA: Information Science Reference; doi:10.4018/978-1-60960-497-4.ch005

Kumar, M., & Sareen, M. (2012). Trust theories and models of e-commerce. In *Trust and technology in B2B e-commerce: Practices and strategies for assurance* (pp. 58–77). Hershey, PA: Business Science Reference; doi:10.4018/978-1-61350-353-9.ch003

Kumar, M., Sareen, M., & Chhabra, S. (2013). Technology related trust issues in SME B2B e-commerce. In S. Chhabra (Ed.), *ICT influences on human development, interaction, and collaboration* (pp. 243–259). Hershey, PA: Information Science Reference; doi:10.4018/978-1-4666-1957-9.ch015

Kung, M. T., & Zhang, Y. (2011). Creating competitive markets for small businesses with new media and e-business strategy. *International Journal of E-Business Research*, *7*(4), 31–49. doi:10.4018/jebr.2011100103

Kuo, D., Wong, D., Gao, J., & Chang, L. (2013). A 2D barcode validation system for mobile commerce. In W. Hu & S. Mousavinezhad (Eds.), *Mobile and handheld computing solutions for organizations and end-users* (pp. 1–19). Hershey, PA: Information Science Reference; doi:10.4018/978-1-4666-2785-7.ch001

Kuratko, D. F., Hornsby, J. S., & Naffziger, D. (1993). The adverse impact of public policy on micro-enterprises: An exploratory study of owners' perceptions. *Journal of Developmental Entrepreneurship*, *4*(1), 81–92.

Kuratko, D. F., Ireland, R. D., Covin, J. G., & Hornsby, J. S. (2005). A model of middle-level managers' entrepreneurial behavior. *Entrepreneurship Theory & Practice*, *29*(6), 699–716. doi:10.1111/j.1540-6520.2005.00104.x

Kyobe, M. (2004). Investigating the strategic utilization of IT resources in small and medium-sized firms of the Eastern Free State Province. *International Small Business Journal*, *22*(2), 131–158. doi:10.1177/0266242604041311

Kyobe, M. (2010). E-crime and non-compliance with government regulations on e-commerce: Barriers to e-commerce optimization in South African SMEs. In B. Thomas & G. Simmons (Eds.), *E-commerce adoption and small business in the global marketplace: Tools for optimization* (pp. 47–66). Hershey, PA: Business Science Reference; doi:10.4018/978-1-60566-998-4.ch003

Lai, F., Wang, J., Hsieh, C. T., & Chen, J. C. V. (2007). On network external, e-business adoption and information asymmetry. *Industrial Management & Data Systems*, *107*(5), 728–746. doi:10.1108/02635570710750453

Lai, F., Zhao, X., & Wang, Q. (2006). The impact of information technology on the competitive advantage of logistics firms in China. *Industrial Management & Data Systems*, *106*(9), 1249–1263. doi:10.1108/02635570610712564

Laudon, K. C., & Laudon, J. P. (1998). *Management Information Systems – New Approaches to Organization and Technology*. Upper Saddle River, NJ: Prentice Hall, Inc.

Laudon, K. C., Laudon, J. P., & Brabston, M. E. (2015). *Management Information Systems* (7th Canadian Edition). Don Mills, Ontario: Pearson Canada Inc.

Laudon, K., & Laudon, J. (2007). *Essentials of Business Information Systems* (7th ed.). Englewood Cliffs, NJ: Prentice-Hall.

Laurence, G. (2001). *Fast Growth: How to Attain it, How to Sustain it*. Chicago, IL: Kaplan Professional Company.

Lauzen, L. (1985). Small business failures are controllable. *Corporate Accounting*, *3*(3), 34–38.

Lawrence, J. E. (2011). The growth of e-commerce in developing countries: An exploratory study of opportunities and challenges for SMEs. *International Journal of ICT Research and Development in Africa*, *2*(1), 15–28. doi:10.4018/jictrda.2011010102

Lawrence, J. E. (2013). Barriers hindering ecommerce adoption: A case study of Kurdistan region of Iraq. In A. Zolait (Ed.), *Technology diffusion and adoption: Global complexity, global innovation* (pp. 152–165). Hershey, PA: Information Science Reference; doi:10.4018/978-1-4666-2791-8.ch010

Lawson, R., Alcock, C., Cooper, J., & Burgess, L. (2003). Factors affecting adoption of electronic commerce technologies by SMEs: An Australian study. *The Electronic Journal on Information Systems in Developing Countries*, *14*(1), 1–9.

Lazear, E. P. (2002). Entrepreneurship. Working paper, National Bureau of Economic Research, Cambridge MA.

Le Breton-Miller, I., & Miller, D. (2006). Why do some family businesses out-compete? Governance, long-term orientations and sustainable capability. *Entrepreneurship: Theory and Practice*, *30*(6), 731–746.

LeBrassuer, R., Zanibbi, L., & Zinger, T. J. (2003). Growth momentum in early stages of small business start-ups. *International Small Business Journal*, *21*(3), 315–330. doi:10.1177/02662426030213004

Lederer, A. L., & Nath, R. (1991). Managing Organizational Issues in Information Systems Development. *Journal of Systems Management*, *42*(11), 23–39.

Lee, D. Y., & Tsang, E. W. K. (2001). The effects of entrepreneurial personality: Background and network activities on venture growth. *Journal of Management Studies*, *38*(4), 583–602. doi:10.1111/1467-6486.00250

Lee, I. (2012). B2B e-commerce, online auction, supply chain management, and e-collaboration. In *Electronic commerce management for business activities and global enterprises: Competitive advantages* (pp. 249–299). Hershey, PA: Business Science Reference; doi:10.4018/978-1-4666-1800-8.ch007

Lee, I. (2012). B2C online consumer behavior. In *Electronic commerce management for business activities and global enterprises: competitive advantages* (pp. 166–201). Hershey, PA: Business Science Reference; doi:10.4018/978-1-4666-1800-8.ch005

Lee, I. (2012). Introduction to e-commerce in the global economy. In *Electronic commerce management for business activities and global enterprises: Competitive advantages* (pp. 1–46). Hershey, PA: Business Science Reference; doi:10.4018/978-1-4666-1800-8.ch001

Lee, I. (2012). Mobile commerce. In *Electronic commerce management for business activities and global enterprises: Competitive advantages* (pp. 300–338). Hershey, PA: Business Science Reference; doi:10.4018/978-1-4666-1800-8.ch008

Lee, I. (2012). Online payment systems. In *Electronic commerce management for business activities and global enterprises: Competitive advantages* (pp. 340–365). Hershey, PA: Business Science Reference; doi:10.4018/978-1-4666-1800-8.ch009

Lee, J., & Runge, J. (2001). Adoption of information technology in small business: Testing drivers of adoption for entrepreneurs. *Journal of Computer Information Systems*, *42*(1), 44–57.

Lee, Y. C., Chu, P. Y., & Tseng, H. T. (2011). Corporate performance of ICT-enabled business process re-engineering. *Industrial Management & Data Systems*, *111*(5), 735–754. doi:10.1108/02635571111137287

Lefebvre, L. A., & Lefebvre, E. (1993). Competitive positioning and innovative efforts in SMEs. *Journal of Small Business Economics*, *5*(4), 297–305. doi:10.1007/BF01516250

Leitner, K. H., & Guldenberg, S. (2010). Generic strategies and firm performance in SMEs: A longitudinal study of Austrian SMEs. *Small Business Economics*, *35*(2), 169–189. doi:10.1007/s11187-009-9239-x

Leonard, L. N. (2010). C2C mobile commerce: Acceptance factors. In I. Lee (Ed.), *Encyclopedia of e-business development and management in the global economy* (pp. 759–767). Hershey, PA: Business Science Reference; doi:10.4018/978-1-61520-611-7.ch076

Lertpittayapoom, N., & Paul, S. (2010). The roles of online intermediaries in collective memory-supported electronic negotiation. In *Electronic services: Concepts, methodologies, tools and applications* (pp. 1831–1847). Hershey, PA: Information Science Reference; doi:10.4018/978-1-61520-967-5.ch112

Lesjak, D., & Lynn, M. (2000). Small Slovene firms and strategic information technology usage. *Proceedings of the Eighth European Conference on Information Systems*, 63-70.

Lester, D. L., & Tran, T. T. (2008). Information technology capabilities: Suggestions for SME growth. Institute of Behavioral and Applied Management, 72-88.

Lester, D. L., & Parnell, J. A. (2006). The complete life cycle of a family business. *Journal of Applied Management and Entrepreneurship*, *11*(3), 3–22.

Lester, D. L., & Parnell, J. A. (2008). Firm size and environmental scanning pursuits across organizational life cycle stages. *Journal of Small Business and Enterprise Development*, *15*(3), 540–554. doi:10.1108/14626000810892337

Lester, D. L., Parnell, J. A., & Carraher, S. (2003). Organizational life cycle: A five-stage empirical scale. *The International Journal of Organizational Analysis*, *11*(4), 339–354. doi:10.1108/eb028979

Lester, D. L., Parnell, J. A., Crandall, W. R., & Menefee, M. L. (2008). Organizational life cycle and performance among SMEs: Generic strategies for high and low performers. *International Journal of Commerce and Management*, *18*(4), 313–330. doi:10.1108/10569210810921942

Levy, M., & Powell, P. (1998). SME flexibility and the role of information systems. *Journal of Small Business Economics*, *11*(2), 183–196. doi:10.1023/A:1007912714741

Levy, M., & Powell, P. (2000). Information systems strategy for small and medium sized enterprises: An organisational perspective. *The Journal of Strategic Information Systems*, *9*(1), 63–84. doi:10.1016/S0963-8687(00)00028-7

Levy, M., Powell, P., & Yelton, P. (2002). The dynamics of SME information systems. *Small Business Economics*, *19*(4), 341–354. doi:10.1023/A:1019654030019

Levy, M., Powell, P., & Yetton, P. (2001). SMEs: Aligning IS and the strategic context. *Journal of Information Technology*, *16*(3), 133–144. doi:10.1080/02683960110063672

Lewis, R., & Cockrill, A. (2002). Going global, remaining local: The impact of e-commerce on small retail firms in Wales. *Journal of International Information Management*, *22*(3), 195–215. doi:10.1016/S0268-4012(02)00005-1

Liao, J., Welsch, H., & Moutray, C. (2008/2009). Start-up resources and entrepreneurial discontinuance: The case of nascent entrepreneurs. *Journal of Small Business Strategy*, *19*(2), 1–15.

Liao, J., Welsch, H., & Stoica, M. (2003). Organizaitonal obsorptive capacity and responsiveness: An empirical investigation of growth-oriented SMEs. *Entrepreneurship Theory and Practice*, *28*(1), 133–144. doi:10.1111/1540-8520.00032

Liao, Q., Luo, X., & Gurung, A. (2011). Trust restoration in electronic commerce. In S. Clarke & A. Dwivedi (Eds.), *Organizational and end-user interactions: New explorations* (pp. 72–88). Hershey, PA: Information Science Reference; doi:10.4018/978-1-60960-577-3.ch003

Liberato, N. A., Varajão, J. E., Correia, E. S., & Bessa, M. E. (2011). Location based e-commerce system: An architecture. In M. Cruz-Cunha & F. Moreira (Eds.), *Handbook of research on mobility and computing: Evolving technologies and ubiquitous impacts* (pp. 881–892). Hershey, PA: Information Science Reference; doi:10.4018/978-1-60960-042-6.ch055

Lichtenstein, B. B., Dooley, K. J., & Lumpkin, G. T. (2006). Measuring emergence in the dynamics of new venture creation. *Journal of Business Venturing*, *21*(2), 153–175. doi:10.1016/j.jbusvent.2005.04.002

Li, J., Merenda, M., & Venkatachalam, A. R. (2009). Business process digitization and new product development: An empirical study of small and medium-sized manufacturers. *International Journal of E-Business Research*, *5*(1), 49–64. doi:10.4018/jebr.2009010103

Li, L., Liu, C., Zhao, X., & Wang, J. (2011). Transactional properties of complex web services. In H. Leung, D. Chiu, & P. Hung (Eds.), *Service intelligence and service science: Evolutionary technologies and challenges* (pp. 21–34). Hershey, PA: Information Science Reference; doi:10.4018/978-1-61520-819-7.ch002

Lim, S. Y., & Wong, S. F. (2012). Impact of applying aggregate query processing in mobile commerce. *International Journal of Business Data Communications and Networking*, *8*(2), 1–17. doi:10.4018/jbdcn.2012040101

Lin, B., Vassar, J., & Clack, L. (1993). Information technology strategies for small business. *Journal of Applied Business Research*, *9*(2), 25–29.

Lin, C. Y. Y. (1998). Success factors of small and medium sized enterprises in Taiwan: An analysis of cases. *Journal of Small Business Management*, *36*(4), 43–57.

Lin, C., Huang, Y. A., & Stockdale, R. (2011). Developing a B2B web site effectiveness model for SMEs. *Internet Research*, *21*(3), 304–325. doi:10.1108/10662241111139327

Lin, C., & Jalleh, G. (2013). Key issues and challenges for managing and evaluating B2B e-commerce projects within the Australian pharmaceutical supply chain. In *Supply chain management: Concepts, methodologies, tools, and applications* (pp. 1083–1100). Hershey, PA: Business Science Reference; doi:10.4018/978-1-4666-2625-6.ch064

Lin, C., Jalleh, G., & Huang, Y. (2013). E-business investment evaluation and outsourcing practices in Australian and Taiwanese hospitals: A comparative study. In K. Tarnay, S. Imre, & L. Xu (Eds.), *Research and development in e-business through service-oriented solutions* (pp. 244–266). Hershey, PA: Business Science Reference; doi:10.4018/978-1-4666-4181-5.ch012

Lin, C., Lin, H. K., Jalleh, G., & Huang, Y. (2011). Key adoption challenges and issues of B2B e-commerce in the healthcare sector. In M. Cruz-Cunha & F. Moreira (Eds.), *Handbook of research on mobility and computing: Evolving technologies and ubiquitous impacts* (pp. 175–187). Hershey, PA: Information Science Reference; doi:10.4018/978-1-60960-042-6.ch011

Lin, C., Pervan, G., Lin, H. C., & Tsao, H. (2008). An investigation into business-to-business electronic commerce organizations. *Journal of Research and Practices in Information Technology*, *40*(1), 3–18.

Lin, H. F., & Lee, G. G. (2005). Impact of organizational learning and knowledge management factors on e-business adoption. *Management Decision*, *43*(2), 171–188. doi:10.1108/00251740510581902

Link, A. N., & Bozeman, B. (1991). Innovative behavior in small-sized firms. *Small Business Economics*, *3*(3), 179–184. doi:10.1007/BF00400023

Linton, D. J., & Walsh, S. T. (2008). Acceleration and extension of opportunity recognition for nanotechnologies and other emerging technologies. *International Small Business Journal*, *26*(1), 83–99. doi:10.1177/0266242607084660

Lippitt, G., & Schmidt, W. (1967). Crises in developing organizations. *Harvard Business Review*, *45*(6), 102–112.

Littunen, H. (2000). Entrepreneurship and the characteristics of the entrepreneurial personality. *International Journal of Entrepreneurial Behaviour and Research*, *6*(6), 295–309. doi:10.1108/13552550010362741

Littunen, H., & Niittykangas, H. (2010). The rapid growth of young firms during various stages of entrepreneurship. *Journal of Small Business and Enterprise Development*, *17*(1), 8–31. doi:10.1108/14626001011019107

Li, X., & Lin, J. (2011). Call u back: An agent-based infrastructure for mobile commerce. *International Journal of E-Entrepreneurship and Innovation*, *2*(2), 1–13. doi:10.4018/jeei.2011040101

Liyanage, J. P. (2011). Copying with dynamic change: Collaborative business interfacing for SMEs under intergated eoperations. In M. Cruz-Cunha & J. Varajão (Eds.), *E-business managerial aspects, solutions and case studies* (pp. 136–147). Hershey, PA: Business Science Reference; doi:10.4018/978-1-60960-463-9.ch008

Liyanage, J. P. (2012). Hybrid intelligence through business socialization and networking: Managing complexities in the digital era. In M. Cruz-Cunha, P. Gonçalves, N. Lopes, E. Miranda, & G. Putnik (Eds.), *Handbook of research on business social networking: organizational, managerial, and technological dimensions* (pp. 567–582). Hershey, PA: Business Science Reference; doi:10.4018/978-1-61350-168-9.ch030

Loeser, F., Erek, K., & Zarnekow, R. (2013). Green IT strategies: A conceptual framework for the alignment of information technology and corporate sustainability strategy. In P. Ordóñez de Pablos (Ed.), *Green technologies and business practices: An IT approach* (pp. 58–95). Hershey, PA: Information Science Reference; doi:10.4018/978-1-4666-1972-2.ch004

Longnecker, J., Moore, C., & Petty, J. (1997). *Small Business Management*. Cincinnati, OH: South-Western College Printing.

Long, W. A. (1983). The meaning of entrepreneurship. *American Journal of Small Business*, *8*(2), 47–56.

Long, W. A., & McMullan, W. E. (1984). Mapping the opportunity identification process. In J. A. Hornaday et al. (Eds.), *Frontiers of Entrepreneurship Research*. Wellesley, MA: Babson College.

Looi, H. C. (2005). E-commerce adoption in Brunei Darussalam: A quantitative analysis of factors influencing its adoption. *Communications of the Association for Information Systems*, *15*(3), 61–81.

Love, P. E. D., & Irani, Z. (2004). An exploratory study of information technology evaluation and benefits management practices of SMEs in the construction industry. *Information & Management*, *42*(1), 227–242. doi:10.1016/j.im.2003.12.011

Love, P. E. D., Irani, Z., Li, H., Cheng, E. W. L., & Tse, R. Y. C. (2001). An empirical analysis of the barriers to implementing e-commerce in small-medium sized construction contractors in the state of Victoria, Australia. *Construction Innovation*, *1*(1), 31–41. doi:10.1108/14714170110814497

Lowe, J., McKenna, J., & Tibbits, G. (1991). Small firm growth and failure: Public policy issues and practical problems. *Economic Papers*, *10*(2), 69–81. doi:10.1111/j.1759-3441.1991.tb00858.x

Low, M., & MacMillan, I. C. (2001). Entrepreneurship: Past research and future challenges. *Journal of Management*, *14*(2), 139–161. doi:10.1177/014920638801400202

Lubatkin, M., Schulze, W., Ling, Y., & Dino, R. (2005). The effects of parental altruism on the governance of family-managed firms. *Journal of Organizational Behavior*, *26*(3), 313–330. doi:10.1002/job.307

Luftman, J. N., Papp, R., & Brier, T. (1999). Enablers and inhibitors of business-IT alignment. *Communications of the Association for Information Systems*, *1*(11), 1–32.

Lussier, R. N. (1995). A nonfinancial business success versus failure prediction model for young firms. *Journal of Small Business Management*, *33*(1), 8–20.

Lussier, R. N., & Halabi, C. E. (2010). A three-country comparison of business success versus failure prediction model. *Journal of Small Business Management*, *48*(3), 360–377. doi:10.1111/j.1540-627X.2010.00298.x

Lymer, A., Johnson, R., & Baldwin, A. (1997). The internet and small businesses: A study of impacts.*Fifth European Conference on Information Systems*, Cork Publishing, Cork. 145-163.

Maamar, Z., Faci, N., Mostéfaoui, S. K., & Akhter, F. (2011). Towards a framework for weaving social networks into mobile commerce. *International Journal of Systems and Service-Oriented Engineering*, *2*(3), 32–46. doi:10.4018/jssoe.2011070103

MacGregor, R. C. (2004). Factors associated with formal networking in regional small business: Some findings from a study of Swedish SMEs. *Journal of Small Business and Enterprise Development*, *11*(1), 60–74. doi:10.1108/14626000410519100

MacMillan, I. (1986). To really learn about entrepreneurship, let's study habitual entrepreneurs. *Journal of Business Venturing*, *1*(3), 241–243. doi:10.1016/0883-9026(86)90001-7

Ma, H. (2002). Competitive advantage: What's luck got to do with it? *Management Decision*, *40*(6), 525–536. doi:10.1108/00251740210433927

Mahmood, M. A., Gemoets, L., Hall, L. L., & López, F. J. (2011). Building business value in e-commerce enabled organizations: An empirical study. In *Global business: Concepts, methodologies, tools and applications* (pp. 229–253). Hershey, PA: Business Science Reference; doi:10.4018/978-1-60960-587-2.ch201

Mahran, A. F., & Enaba, H. M. (2013). Exploring determinants influencing the intention to use mobile payment service. In R. Eid (Ed.), *Managing customer trust, satisfaction, and loyalty through information communication technologies* (pp. 288–309). Hershey, PA: Business Science Reference; doi:10.4018/978-1-4666-3631-6.ch017

Maiga, A. S., & Jacobs, F. A. (2009). Performance impacts of extent of information technology usage. *Journal of International Technology and Information Management*, *18*(3/4), 277–298.

Makadok, R. (2001). Toward a synthesis of the resource-based and dynamic-capability views of rent creation. *Strategic Management Journal*, *22*(5), 387–401. doi:10.1002/smj.158

Malone, S. (1985). Computerizing small business information systems. *Journal of Small Business Management*, *23*(2), 10–16.

Maltz, E., & Kohli, A. K. (1996). Market intelligence dissemination across functional boundaries. *JMR, Journal of Marketing Research*, *33*(1), 177–201. doi:10.2307/3152012

Maman, D. (2000). Who accumulates directorships of big business firms in Israel? Organizational structure, social capital and human capital. *Human Relations*, *53*(5), 603–630. doi:10.1177/0018726700535001

Man, T., Lau, T., & Chan, K. F. (2002). The competitiveness of small and medium enterprises: A conceptualization with focus on entrepreneurial competencies. *Journal of Business Venturing*, *17*(2), 123–142. doi:10.1016/S0883-9026(00)00058-6

Manthey, R., & Balhoff, W. E. (2002). Pass the baton without missing a beat. *Journal of Accountancy*, *193*(3), 43–48.

Marimuthu, M., Omar, A., Ramayah, T., & Mohamad, O. (2013). Readiness to adopt e-business among SMEs in Malaysia: Antecedents and consequence. In S. Sharma (Ed.), *Adoption of virtual technologies for business, educational, and governmental advancements* (pp. 18–36). Hershey, PA: Information Science Reference; doi:10.4018/978-1-4666-2053-7.ch002

Markman, G. D., & Baron, R. A. (2003). Person – entrepreneurship fit: Why some people are more successful as entrepreneurs than others. *Human Resource Management Review*, *13*(2), 281–301. doi:10.1016/S1053-4822(03)00018-4

Marriott, N., & Marriott, P. (2000). Professional accountants and the development of a management accounting service for the small firm: Barriers and possibilities. *Management Accounting Research*, *11*(4), 475–492. doi:10.1006/mare.2000.0142

Martin, L. M., & Matlay, H. (2003). Innovative use of the internet in established small firms: The impact of knowledge management and organizational learning in assessing new opportunities. *Qualitative Market Research: An International Journal*, *6*(1), 18–26. doi:10.1108/13522750310457348

Martin, L. M., & Wright, L. T. (2005). No gender in cyberspace? Women empowered in innovation and entrepreneurship by ICT. *International Journal of Entrepreneurship Behaviour & Research*, *11*(2), 162–178. doi:10.1108/13552550510590563

Marvel, M. R., & Lumpkin, G. T. (2007). Technology entrepreneurs' human capital and its effects on innovation radicalness. *Entrepreneurship Theory and Practice*, *31*(6), 807–828. doi:10.1111/j.1540-6520.2007.00209.x

Mata, F. J., Fuerst, W. L., & Barney, J. B. (1995). Information technology and sustained competitive advantage: A resource-based analysis. *Management Information Systems Quarterly*, *19*(4), 487–507. doi:10.2307/249630

Matlay, H. (1999). Employee relations in small firms: A micro-business perspective. *Employee Relations*, *21*(3), 285–295. doi:10.1108/01425459910273125

Mayes, P. (2014). Interactive advertising: Displays of identity and stance on YouTube. In H. Lim & F. Sudweeks (Eds.), *Innovative methods and technologies for electronic discourse analysis* (pp. 260–284). Hershey, PA: Information Science Reference; doi:10.4018/978-1-4666-4426-7.ch012

Mazzarol, T., Reboud, S., & Soutar, G. N. (2009). Strategic planning in growth oriented small firms. *International Journal of Entrepreneurial Behaviour & Research*, *15*(4), 320–345. doi:10.1108/13552550910967912

McAdam, R., Reid, R., & Mitchell, N. (2010). Longitudinal development of innovation implementation in family-based SMEs: The effects of critical incidents. *International Journal of Entrepreneurial Behaviour & Research*, 437-456.

McClelland, D. (1961). *The Achieving Society*. Princeton, New Jersey: Van Nostrand Reinhold. doi:10.1037/14359-000

McCline, R. L., Bhat, S., & Baj, P. (2000). Opportunity recognition: An exploratory investigation of a component of the entrepreneurial process in the context of the health care industry. *Entrepreneurship Theory & Practice*, *25*(2), 81–94.

McClure, D. L. (2000). Statement of David L. McClure, US General Accounting Office, before the Subcommittee on Government Reform, House of representatives, www.gao.gov

McComb, D., & Smith, J. Y. (1991). System Project Failure: The Heuristics of Risk. *Journal of Information Systems Management*, *8*(1), 25–34. doi:10.1080/07399019108964967

McDonagh, P., & Prothero, A. (2000). Euroclicking and the Irish SME: Prepared for e-commerce and the single currency. *Irish Marketing Review*, *13*(1), 21–33.

McEvoy, G. (1984). Small Business personnel practices. *Journal of Small Business Management*, *22*(4), 1–8.

McGrath, T. (2012). The reality of using standards for electronic business document formats. In E. Kajan, F. Dorloff, & I. Bedini (Eds.), *Handbook of research on e-business standards and protocols: Documents, data and advanced web technologies* (pp. 21–32). Hershey, PA: Business Science Reference; doi:10.4018/978-1-4666-0146-8.ch002

McKelvie, A., & Cedere, A. (2001). Network pollination: Habitual entrepreneurship and incubators. Paper presented at BKERC 2001, Jonkoping.

McKelvie, B. (2004). Towards a complexity science of entrepreneurship. *Journal of Business Venturing*, *19*(3), 313–341. doi:10.1016/S0883-9026(03)00034-X

McKenna, R. (1991). *Relationship Marketing: Successful Strategies for the Age of the Customer*. Reading, MA: Addison-Wesley.

McMahon, R. G. P. (1998). Stage models of SME growth reconsidered. *Small Business Research: The Journal of SEAANZ*, *6*(2), 20–35.

McMahon, R. G. P. (2001). Business growth and performance and the financial reporting practices of Australian manufacturing SMEs. *Journal of Small Business Management*, *39*(2), 152–165. doi:10.1111/1540-627X.00014

McMullan, W. E., & Long, W. A. (1990). *Developing New Ventures: The Entrepreneurial Option*. San Diego, CA: Harcourt Brace Jovanovich, Publishers.

McNight, C. (1990). Business and bankruptcy: A review. *The Journal of Finance*, *16*(3), 43–51.

Mellahi, K., & Wilkinson, A. (2004). Organizational failure: A critique of recent research and a proposed integrative framework. *International Journal of Management Reviews*, *5-6*(1), 21–41. doi:10.1111/j.1460-8545.2004.00095.x

Mendo, F. A., & Fitzgerald, G. (2005). A multidimensional framework for SME e-business progression. *Journal of Enterprise Information Management*, *18*(15), 678–696. doi:10.1108/17410390510628382

Meredith, J., & Potter, J. (2014). Conversation analysis and electronic interactions: Methodological, analytic and technical considerations. In H. Lim & F. Sudweeks (Eds.), *Innovative methods and technologies for electronic discourse analysis* (pp. 370–393). Hershey, PA: Information Science Reference; doi:10.4018/978-1-4666-4426-7.ch017

Michma, J., & Bednarz, L. M. (2006). Small Business in the USA. *International Journal of Entrepreneurship and Innovation Management*, *6*(1/2), 4–17. doi:10.1504/IJEIM.2006.008202

Migdadi, M. (2008). Knowledge management enablers and outcomes in the small-and-medium sized enterprises. *Industrial Management & Data Systems*, *109*(6), 840–858. doi:10.1108/02635570910968072

Miles, R., & Snow, C. (1978). *Organizational Strategy, Structure, and Process*. New York, NY: McGraw-Hill.

Miller, S. M. (1996). Monitoring and blunting of threatening information: Cognitive interference and facilitation in the coping process. In Sarason, I. G., Pierce, G. R., & Sarason, B. R. (Editors), Cognitive Interference: Theory, Methods, and Findings (175-190). Mahwahm NJ: Lawrence Erlbaum Associate Publishers.

Miller, D., & Freisen, P. H. (1982). Innovation in conservation and entrepreneurial firms. *Strategic Management Journal*, *3*(1), 1–25. doi:10.1002/smj.4250030102

Miller, D., & Friesen, P. (1984). A longitudinal study of corporate life. *Management Science*, *30*(10), 1161–1183. doi:10.1287/mnsc.30.10.1161

Miller, D., & Le Breton-Miller, I. (2003). The challenges and advantages of family business. *Strategic Organization*, *1*(1), 127–134. doi:10.1177/1476127003001001222

Miller, D., & Le Breton-Miller, I. (2006). Priorities, practices and strategies in successful and failing family businesses: An elaboration and test of the configuration perspective. *Strategic Organization*, *4*(4), 379–407. doi:10.1177/1476127006069575

Millman, C., & El-Gohary, H. (2011). New digital media marketing and micro business: A UK perspective. *International Journal of Online Marketing*, *1*(1), 41–62. doi:10.4018/ijom.2011010104

Mintzberg, H. (1984). Power and organization life cycles. *Academy of Management Review*, *9*(2), 207–224.

Mirchandani, A. A., & Motwani, J. (2001). Understanding small business electronic commerce adoption: An empirical analysis. *Journal of Computer Information Systems*, *41*(3), 70–73.

Mishra, B., & Shukla, K. K. (2014). Data mining techniques for software quality prediction. In *Software design and development: Concepts, methodologies, tools, and applications* (pp. 401–428). Hershey, PA: Information Science Reference; doi:10.4018/978-1-4666-4301-7.ch021

Misra, H., & Rahman, H. (2013). *Managing enterprise information technology acquisitions: Assessing organizational preparedness*. Hershey, PA: IGI Global; doi:10.4018/978-1-4666-4201-0

Mitchelmore, S., & Rowley, J. (2010). Entrepreneurial competencies: A literature review and development agenda. *International Journal of Entrepreneurial behaviour & Research*, 16(2), 92-111.

Mithas, S., Ramsubbu, N., & Sambamurthy, V. (2011). How information management capability influences firm performance. *Management Information Systems Quarterly*, *35*(1), 237–256.

Mohammadi, S., Golara, S., & Mousavi, N. (2012). Selecting adequate security mechanisms in e-business processes using fuzzy TOPSIS. *International Journal of Fuzzy System Applications*, *2*(1), 35–53. doi:10.4018/ijfsa.2012010103

Möhlenbruch, D., Dölling, S., & Ritschel, F. (2010). Interactive customer retention management for mobile commerce. In K. Pousttchi & D. Wiedemann (Eds.), *Handbook of research on mobile marketing management* (pp. 437–456). Hershey, PA: Business Science Reference; doi:10.4018/978-1-60566-074-5.ch023

Molla, A., & Peszynski, K. (2013). E-business in agribusiness: Investigating the e-readiness of Australian horticulture firms. In S. Chhabra (Ed.), *ICT influences on human development, interaction, and collaboration* (pp. 78–96). Hershey, PA: Information Science Reference; doi:10.4018/978-1-4666-1957-9.ch004

Monsanto, C., & Andriole, S. J. (2010). Business technology strategy for a major real estate and mortgage brokerage company. *Journal of Information Technology Research*, *3*(3), 43–53. doi:10.4018/jitr.2010070104

Montazami, A. R. (1998). Factors affecting information satisfaction in the context of small business environment. *Management Information Systems Quarterly*, *12*(2), 239–256. doi:10.2307/248849

Montes, J. A., Gutiérrez, A. C., Fernández, E. M., & Romeo, A. (2013). Reality mining, location based services, and e-business opportunities: The case of city analytics. In S. Nasir (Ed.), *Modern entrepreneurship and e-business innovations* (pp. 87–99). Hershey, PA: Business Science Reference; doi:10.4018/978-1-4666-2946-2.ch007

Montserrat, E. (2002). The impact of the alignment of strategy and managerial characteristics on Spanish SMEs. *Journal of Small Business Management*, *40*(3), 260–271. doi:10.1111/1540-627X.00056

Moodley, S. (2003). The challenge of e-business for South African apparel sector. *Technovation*, *23*(7), 557–570. doi:10.1016/S0166-4972(02)00002-0

Moqbel, A., Yani-De-Soriano, M., & Yousafzai, S. (2012). Mobile commerce use among UK mobile users: An experimental approach based on a proposed mobile network utilization framework. In A. Zolait (Ed.), *Knowledge and technology adoption, diffusion, and transfer: International perspectives* (pp. 78–111). Hershey, PA: Information Science Reference; doi:10.4018/978-1-4666-1752-0.ch007

Morse, E. A., Fowler, S. W., & Lawrence, T. B. (2007). The impact of virtual embeddedness on new venture survival: Overcoming the liabilities of newness. *Entrepreneurship Theory & Practice*, *31*(2), 139–159. doi:10.1111/j.1540-6520.2007.00167.x

Movahedi, B. M., Lavassani, K. M., & Kumar, V. (2012). E-marketplace emergence: Evolution, developments and classification. *Journal of Electronic Commerce in Organizations*, *10*(1), 14–32. doi:10.4018/jeco.2012010102

Mowday, R., Porter, L., & Steers, R. (1982). *Organizational Linkages: The Psychology of Commitment, Absenteeism, and Turnover*. New York: Academic Press.

Mpufu, C., & Watkins-Mathys, L. (2011). Understanding ICT adoption in the small firm sector in southern Africa. *Journal of Systems and Information Technology*, *13*(2), 179–199. doi:10.1108/13287261111136007

Mugge, R., & Schoormans, J. P. (2010). Optimizing consumer responses to mass customization. In C. Mourlas & P. Germanakos (Eds.), *Mass customization for personalized communication environments: Integrating human factors* (pp. 10–22). Hershey, PA: Information Science Reference; doi:10.4018/978-1-60566-260-2.ch002

Muir, I., & Langford, D. (1994). Managerial behaviour in two small construction organizations. *International Journal of Project Management*, *12*(4), 244–253. doi:10.1016/0263-7863(94)90049-3

Mullen, M. R., Budeva, D. G., & Doney, P. M. (2009). Research methods in the leading small business – entrepreneursip journals: A critical review with recommendations for future research. *Journal of Small Business Management*, *47*(3), 287–307. doi:10.1111/j.1540-627X.2009.00272.x

Musso, F. (2012). Technology in marketing channels: Present and future drivers of innovation. *International Journal of Applied Behavioral Economics*, *1*(2), 41–51. doi:10.4018/ijabe.2012040104

Mustaffa, S., & Beaumont, N. (2004). The effect of electronic commerce on small Australian enterprises. *Technovation*, *24*(2), 85–95. doi:10.1016/S0166-4972(02)00039-1

Mutula, S. M. (2010). Digital economy components. In S. Mutula (Ed.), *Digital economies: SMEs and e-readiness* (pp. 29–38). Hershey, PA: Business Science Reference; doi:10.4018/978-1-60566-420-0.ch003

Mutula, S. M. (2010). Trends and best practices in the digital economy. In S. Mutula (Ed.), *Digital economies: SMEs and e-readiness* (pp. 283–301). Hershey, PA: Business Science Reference; doi:10.4018/978-1-60566-420-0.ch017

Myers, I. B. (1962). *The Myers-Briggs Type Indicator*. Princeton, NJ: Educational Testing Service. doi:10.1037/14404-000

Nachtigal, S. (2011). E-business: Definition and characteristics. In O. Bak & N. Stair (Eds.), *Impact of e-business technologies on public and private organizations: Industry comparisons and perspectives* (pp. 233–248). Hershey, PA: Business Science Reference; doi:10.4018/978-1-60960-501-8.ch014

Nahapiet, J., & Ghoshal, S. (1998). Social capital, intellectual capital, and the organizational advantage. Academy of Management Review, 23(20, 242-266.

Nahapiet, J., & Ghoshal, S. (1998). Social capital, intellectual capital, and the organizational advantage. *Journal of Corporate Finance*, *13*(5), 829–858.

Nah, F. F., Hong, W., Chen, L., & Lee, H. (2012). Information search patterns in e-commerce product comparison services. In K. Siau (Ed.), *Cross-disciplinary models and applications of database management: Advancing approaches* (pp. 131–145). Hershey, PA: Information Science Reference; doi:10.4018/978-1-61350-471-0.ch006

Nair, P. R. (2010). Benefits of information technology implementations for supply chain management: An explorative study of progressive Indian companies. In S. Parthasarathy (Ed.), *Enterprise information systems and implementing IT infrastructures: Challenges and issues* (pp. 323–343). Hershey, PA: Business Science Reference; doi:10.4018/978-1-61520-625-4.ch021

Narva, R. L. (2003). Financing transitions: Managing capital and liquidity in the family business. *Family Business Review*, *16*(2), 153–154.

Naylor, J., & Williams, J. (1994). Successful use of IT in SMEs. *European Journal of IS*, *3*(1), 48–56.

Ndou, V., Del Vecchio, P., Passiante, G., & Schina, L. (2013). Web-based services and future business models. In P. Papajorgji, A. Guimarães, & M. Guarracino (Eds.), *Enterprise business modeling, optimization techniques, and flexible information systems* (pp. 1–13). Hershey, PA: Business Science Reference; doi:10.4018/978-1-4666-3946-1.ch001

Ndou, V., & Sadguy, N. (2013). Digital marketplaces as a viable model for SME networking. In *Supply chain management: Concepts, methodologies, tools, and applications* (pp. 275–288). Hershey, PA: Business Science Reference; doi:10.4018/978-1-4666-2625-6.ch016

Nfuka, E. N., & Rusu, L. (2011). The effect of critical success factors on IT governance performance. *Industrial Management & Data Systems*, *111*(9), 1418–1448. doi:10.1108/02635571111182773

Nguyen, T., Sherif, J., & Newby, M. (2007). Strategies for successful CRM implementation. *Information Management & Computer Security*, *15*(2), 102–115. doi:10.1108/09685220710748001

Nicholson, N. (2008). Evolutionary psychology and family business: A new synthesis for theory, research, and practice. *Family Business Review*, *21*(1), 103–118. doi:10.1111/j.1741-6248.2007.00111.x

Nickell, G., & Seado, P. (1986). The impact of attitudes and experiences on small business computer use. *American Journal of Small Business*, *10*(1), 37–48.

Nielsen, S. L., & Lassen, A. H. (2012). Images of entrepreneurship: Towards a new categorization of entrepreneurship. *The International Entrepreneurship and Management Journal*, *8*(1), 35–53. doi:10.1007/s11365-010-0159-7

O'Connell, B. (2004). The FastTrac to Success – Why do some small businesses handle change better than others? *Baylor Business Review*, *22*(1), 26–27.

O'Farrell, P. N., & Hitchens, D. M. W. N. (1988). Alternative theories of small firm growth: A critical review. *Environment & Planning*, *20*(3), 1365–1383. doi:10.1068/a201365

O'Gorman, C. (2001). The sustainability of growth in small and medium sized enterprises. *International Journal of Entrepreneurship Behaviour & Research*, *7*(2), 60–71. doi:10.1108/13552550110396095

O'Gorman, C., Bourke, S., & Murray, J. A. (2005). The nature of managerial work in small growth-oriented small businesses. *Small Business Economics*, *25*(1), 1–16. doi:10.1007/s11187-005-4254-z

O'Regan, N., Ghobadian, A., & Gallear, D. (2006). In search of the drivers of high growth in manufacturing SMEs. *Technovation*, *26*(1), 30–41. doi:10.1016/j.technovation.2005.05.004

O'Regan, N., Ghobadian, A., & Sims, M. (2006). Fast tracking innovation in manufacturing SMEs. *Technovation*, *26*(2), 251–261. doi:10.1016/j.technovation.2005.01.003

O'Reilly, C., & Chatman, J. (1986). Organizational commitment and psychological attachment: The effects of compliance, identification, and internalization on prosocial behavior. *The Journal of Applied Psychology*, *71*(3), 492–499. doi:10.1037/0021-9010.71.3.492

Obloj, T., Obloj, K., & Pratt, M. G. (2010). Dominant logic and entrepreneurial firms' performance in a transition economy. *Entrepreneurship Theory and Practice*, *34*(1), 151–170. doi:10.1111/j.1540-6520.2009.00367.x

Ochara, N. M., & Krauss, K. (2012). Towards a collaborative e-business vision for Africa. In K. Mohammed Rezaul (Ed.), *Strategic and pragmatic e-business: Implications for future business practices* (pp. 396–414). Hershey, PA: Business Science Reference; doi:10.4018/978-1-4666-1619-6.ch018

Olson, P. D., & Bokor, D. W. (1995). Strategy process-content interaction: Effects on growth performance in small start-up firms. *Journal of Small Business Management, 33*(1), 34–44.

Oncioiu, I. (2013). *Business innovation, development, and advancement in the digital economy*. Hershey, PA: IGI Global; doi:10.4018/978-1-4666-2934-9

Ondimu, K. O., Muketha, G. M., & Ondago, C. O. (2013). E-business adoption framework in the hospitality industry: The case of Kenyan coast. In K. Tarnay, S. Imre, & L. Xu (Eds.), *Research and development in e-business through service-oriented solutions* (pp. 225–243). Hershey, PA: Business Science Reference; doi:10.4018/978-1-4666-4181-5.ch011

Ong, J. W., Ismail, H. B., & Goh, G. G. G. (2010). The competitive advantage of small and medium enterprises (SMEs): The role of entrepreneurship and luck. *Journal of Small Business and Entrepreneurship, 23*(3), 373–391. doi:10.1080/08276331.2010.10593491

Ongori, H., & Migiro, S. O. (2010). Information and communication technology adoption in SMEs: A literature review. *Journal of Chinese Entrepreneurship, 2*(1), 93–104. doi:10.1108/17561391011019041

Orser, B. J., Hogarth-Scott, S., & Riding, A. L. (2000). Performance, firm size, and management problem solving. *Journal of Small Business Management, 38*(4), 42–58.

Ovaskainen, M., & Tinnilä, M. (2013). Megatrends in electronic business: An analysis of the impacts on SMEs. In S. Nasir (Ed.), *Modern entrepreneurship and e-business innovations* (pp. 12–27). Hershey, PA: Business Science Reference; doi:10.4018/978-1-4666-2946-2.ch002

Özcan, O., & Reeves, K. A. (2011). The firm boundary decision for sustainability-focused companies. *International Journal of Applied Logistics, 2*(2), 49–68. doi:10.4018/jal.2011040104

Öztayşi, B., & Kahraman, C. (2014). Quantification of corporate performance using fuzzy analytic network process: The case of e-commerce. In P. Vasant (Ed.), *Handbook of research on novel soft computing intelligent algorithms: Theory and practical applications* (pp. 385–413). Hershey, PA: Information Science Reference; doi:10.4018/978-1-4666-4450-2.ch013

Packalen, K. (2010). ICT capabilities and possibilities in micro-firms: A study of micro-firms in the Aland Islands archipelago. 23rd Bled e-Conference on e-Trust, Slovenia.

Packham, G. (2002). Competitive advantage and growth: The challenge for small firms. *International Journal of Management and decision Making*, 3(2), 165-179.

Packham, G., Brooksbank, D., Miller, C., & Thomas, B. (2005). Climbing the mountain: Management practice adoption in growth oriented firms in Wales. *Journal of Small Business and Enterprise Development*, *12*(4), 482–497. doi:10.1108/14626000510628171

Palmer, D. E. (2010). The transformative nature of e-business: Business ethics and stakeholder relations on the internet. In D. Palmer (Ed.), *Ethical issues in e-business: Models and frameworks* (pp. 1–14). Hershey, PA: Business Science Reference; doi:10.4018/978-1-61520-615-5.ch001

Palvia, P., Mearns, D. B. Jr, & Jackson, W. M. (1994). Determinants of computing in very small businesses. *Information & Management*, *27*(3), 161–174. doi:10.1016/0378-7206(94)90044-2

Pańkowska, M. (2014). Frameworks of IT prosumption for business development (pp. 1-347). doi:10.4018/978-1-4666-4313-0

Parnell, J. A. (2005). Managing paradoxes in strategic decision-making. *International Journal of Management and Decision Making*, *7*(6), 708–724. doi:10.1504/IJMDM.2006.011078

Parnell, J. A., & Dent, E. B. (2009). The role of luck in the strategy-performance relationship. *Management Decision*, *47*(6), 1000–1021. doi:10.1108/00251740910966703

Parnell, J. A., & Lester, D. L. (2007). Reevaluating the entrepreneurship-management conundrum: Challenges and solutions. *Journal of Applied Management and Entrepreneurship*, *12*(4), 74–88.

Parnell, J., & Carraher, S. (2002). The role of effective resource utilization in strategy's impact on performance. *International Journal of Commerce and Management*, *13*(3), 1–34.

Parrott, G., Roomi, M. A., & Holliman, D. (2010). An analysis of marketing programmes adopted by regional small and medium-sized enterprises. *Journal of Small Business and Enterprise Development*, *17*(2), 184–203. doi:10.1108/14626001011041201

Patrakosol, B., & Lee, S. (2009). IT capabilities, interfirm performance and the state of economic development. *Industrial Management & Data Systems*, *109*(9), 1231–1247. doi:10.1108/02635570911002298

Patterson, K. A., Grimm, C. M., & Corsi, T. M. (2003). Adopting new technologies for supply chain management. *Transportation Research Part E, Logistics and Transportation Review*, *39*(2), 95–121. doi:10.1016/S1366-5545(02)00041-8

Pavic, S., Koh, S. C. L., Simpson, M., & Padmore, J. (2007). Could e-business create a competitive advantage in UK SMEs? *Benchmarking: An International Journal*, *14*(3), 320–351. doi:10.1108/14635770710753112

Pavlou, P. A. (2003). Consumer acceptance of electronic commerce: Integrating trust and risk with the technological acceptance model. *International Journal of Electronic Commerce*, *7*(3), 101–134.

Pavlou, P. A., & El Sawy, O. A. (2006). From IT leveraging competence to competitive advantage in turbulent environments: The case of new product development. *Information Systems Research*, *17*(3), 198–227. doi:10.1287/isre.1060.0094

Pelet, J. É., & Papadopoulou, P. (2013). The effect of e-commerce websites' colors on customer trust. In I. Lee (Ed.), *Mobile applications and knowledge advancements in e-business* (pp. 167–185). Hershey, PA: Business Science Reference; doi:10.4018/978-1-4666-1960-9.ch011

Penn, D. W., Angiwa, W., Forster, R., Heydon, G., & Rishardson, S. J. (1998). Learning in small organisations. *The Learning Organization*, *5*(3), 128–137. doi:10.1108/09696479810223400

Pennington, R. (2012). Enhanced social presence through ebranding the consumer in virtual communities. In A. Kapoor & C. Kulshrestha (Eds.), *Branding and sustainable competitive advantage: Building virtual presence* (pp. 189–206). Hershey, PA: Business Science Reference; doi:10.4018/978-1-61350-171-9.ch012

Penrose, E. T. (1959). *The Theory of the Growth of the Firm*. New York: John Wiley & Sons.

Perez-Arostegui, M. N., Benitez-Amado, J., & Tamayo-Torres, J. (2012). Information technology-enabled quality performance: An exploratory study. *Industrial Management & Data Systems*, *112*(3), 502–518. doi:10.1108/02635571211210095

Perez-Lopez, S., & Alegre, J. (2012). Information technology competency, knowledge processes and firm performance. *Industrial Management & Data Systems*, *112*(4), 644–662. doi:10.1108/02635571211225521

Peslak, A. R. (2012). Industry variables affecting ERP success and status. *International Journal of Enterprise Information Systems*, *8*(3), 15–33. doi:10.4018/jeis.2012070102

Peterson, D., & Howard, C. (2012). Electronic payment systems evaluation: A case study to examine system selection criteria and impacts. *International Journal of Strategic Information Technology and Applications*, *3*(1), 66–80. doi:10.4018/jsita.2012010105

Peterson, R. A., Kozmetsky, G., & Ridgway, N. M. (1983). Perceived causes of small business failures: A research note. *American Journal of Small Business*, *8*(1), 15–19.

Pett, T. L., & Wolff, J. A. (2012). SME identity and homogeneity – are there meaningful differences between micro, small, and medium-sized enterprises? *Journal of Marketing Development and Competitiveness*, *6*(2), 48–59.

Pflughoeft, K., Ramamurthy, K., Soofi, E., Yasai-Ardekani, M., & Zahedi, F. (2003). Multiple conceptualizations of small business web use and benefit. *Decision Sciences*, *34*(3), 467–512. doi:10.1111/j.1540-5414.2003.02539.x

Pflügler, C. (2012). Fostering networked business operations: A framework for B2B electronic intermediary development. *International Journal of Intelligent Information Technologies*, *8*(2), 31–58. doi:10.4018/jiit.2012040103

Phillips, B. D., & Kirchoff, B. A. (1989). Formation, growth and survival: Small firm dynamics in the U.S. economy. *Small Business Economics*, *1*(1), 65–74. doi:10.1007/BF00389917

Phillipson, J., Bennett, K., Lowe, P., & Raley, M. (2004). Adaptive responses and asset strategies: The experience of rural micro-firms and foot and mouth disease. *Journal of Rural Studies*, *20*(2), 227–243. doi:10.1016/j.jrurstud.2003.08.006

Pierce, J. L., & Delbecq, A. L. (1977). Organizational structure, individual attitudes and innovation. *Academy of Management Review*, *2*(1), 27–37.

Pierce, J. L., & Delbecq, A. L. (1977). Organizational structure: Individual attitudes and innovation. *Academy of Management Review*, *2*(1), 27–37.

Pillai, K., & Ozansoy, C. (2013). Web-based digital habitat ecosystems for sustainable built environments. In P. Ordóñez de Pablos (Ed.), *Green technologies and business practices: An IT approach* (pp. 185–199). Hershey, PA: Information Science Reference; doi:10.4018/978-1-4666-1972-2.ch011

Pinto, M., Rodrigues, A., Varajão, J., & Gonçalves, R. (2011). Model of funcionalities for the development of B2B e-commerce solutions. In M. Cruz-Cunha & J. Varajão (Eds.), *Innovations in SMEs and conducting e-business: Technologies, trends and solutions* (pp. 35–60). Hershey, PA: Business Science Reference; doi:10.4018/978-1-60960-765-4.ch003

Pires, G. D., & Stanton, J. (2005). A research framework for the electronic procurement adoption process: Drawing from Australian evidence. *Journal of Global Business and Technology*, *1*(2), 12–20.

Pires, J. A., & Gonçalves, R. (2011). Constrains associated to e-business evolution. In M. Cruz-Cunha & J. Varajão (Eds.), *E-business issues, challenges and opportunities for SMEs: Driving competitiveness* (pp. 335–349). Hershey, PA: Business Science Reference; doi:10.4018/978-1-61692-880-3.ch019

Pitt, L. F., & Kannemeyer, R. (2000). The role of adaptation in microenterprise development: A marketing perspective. *Journal of Developmental Entrepreneurship*, *5*(2), 137–155.

Pitt, L., Van der Merwe, R., Brethon, P., Salehi-Sanagari, E., & Barnes, B. R. (2006). Swedish biotech SMEs: The veiled values in online networks. *Technovation*, *26*(5/6), 553–560. doi:10.1016/j.technovation.2005.09.009

Politis, D., & Gabrielsson, J. (2009). Entrepreneurs' attitudes towards failure: An experiential learning approach. *International Journal of Entrepreneurial Behaviour & Research*, *15*(4), 364–383. doi:10.1108/13552550910967921

Pollard, C., & Hayne, S. (1998). The changing faces of information systems issues in small firms. *International Small Business Journal*, *16*(3), 70–87. doi:10.1177/0266242698163004

Polovina, S., & Andrews, S. (2011). A transaction-oriented architecture for structuring unstructured information in enterprise applications. In V. Sugumaran (Ed.), *Intelligent, adaptive and reasoning technologies: New developments and applications* (pp. 285–299). Hershey, PA: Information Science Reference; doi:10.4018/978-1-60960-595-7.ch016

Poon, S., & Swatman, P. (1999). An exploratory study of small business internet commerce issues. *Information & Management*, *35*(1), 9–18. doi:10.1016/S0378-7206(98)00079-2

Porter, M. (1980). *Competitive Strategy*. New York, NY: Free Press.

Porter, M. E. (1980). *Competitive Strategy: Techniques for Analyzing Industries and Competitors*. New York: Free Press.

Porter, M. E. (1980). *Competitive strategy: Techniques for Analyzing Industries and Competitors*. New York: Macmillan Publishing Co.

Porter, M. E. (1985). *Competitive Advantage*. New York: The Free Press.

Porter, M. E. (1985). *Competitive Advantage: Creating and Sustaining Superior Performance*. New York, NY: The Free Press.

Porter, M. E. (1998). *The Competitive Advantage of the Nation*. New York: The Free Press.

Potocan, V., Nedelko, Z., & Mulej, M. (2011). What is new with organization of e-business: Organizational viewpoint of the relationships in e-business. In M. Cruz-Cunha & J. Varajão (Eds.), *E-business issues, challenges and opportunities for SMEs: Driving competitiveness* (pp. 131–148). Hershey, PA: Business Science Reference; doi:10.4018/978-1-61692-880-3.ch009

Poutsma, E. F., Van Uxem, F. W., & Walravens, A. H. C. M. (1987). *Process Innovation and Automation in Small and Medium Sized Business*. Delft, Netherlands: Delft University Press.

Powell, T. C., & Dent-Micallef, A. (1997). Information technology as competitive advantage: The role of human, business, and technology resources. *Strategic Management Journal*, *18*(5), 375–405. doi:10.1002/(SICI)1097-0266(199705)18:5<375::AID-SMJ876>3.0.CO;2-7

Prahalad, C. K., & Hamel, G. (1990). The core competence of the corporation. *Harvard Business Review*, *68*(3), 79–91.

Premkumar, G. (2003). A meta-analysis of research on information technology implementation in small business. *Journal of Organizational Computing and Electronic Commerce*, *13*(2), 91–121. doi:10.1207/S15327744JOCE1302_2

Premkumar, G., & Roberts, M. (1999). Adoption of new information technologies in rural small businesses. *Omega: International Journal of Management Science*, *27*(4), 467–484. doi:10.1016/S0305-0483(98)00071-1

Pretorius, M., Millard, S. M., & Kruger, M. E. (2006). The relationship between implementation, creativity and innovation in small business ventures. *Management Dynamics*, *15*(1), 2–13.

Price, R. (1984). *Small Business Management for Small Business Owner/Managers*. Melbourne: Wadsworth.

Pucihar, A., & Lenart, G. (2011). eSME Slovenia: Initiative and action plan for the accelerated introduction of e-business in SMEs. In Global business: Concepts, methodologies, tools and applications (pp. 995-1022). Hershey, PA: Business Science Reference. doi::10.4018/978-1-60960-587-2.ch409

Pugsley, D., Wright, B., Diochon, M., & Hunter, M. G. (2000). Information technology and small business: Listening to voices from the field. *Proceedings of the Administrative Sciences Association of Canada (ASAC) Conference*. Montreal, Canada: ASAC.

Purao, S., & Campbell, S. (1998). Critical concerns for small business electronic commerce: Some reflections based on interviews of small business owners.*Proceedings of the AIS Conference*, Baltimore, MD.

Putnam, R. D. (1993). The prosperous community: Social capital and public life. *The American Prospect*, *13*, 35–42.

Quaddus, M., & Hofmeyer, G. (2007). An investigation into the factors influencing the adoption of B2B trading exchanges in small businesses. *European Journal of Information Systems*, *16*(3), 202–215. doi:10.1057/palgrave.ejis.3000671

Quan, J. (2011). E-business strategy and firm performance. In *Global business: Concepts, methodologies, tools and applications* (pp. 56–66). Hershey, PA: Business Science Reference; doi:10.4018/978-1-60960-587-2.ch105

Quente, C. (2010). Brand driven mobile marketing: 5 theses for today and tomorrow. In K. Pousttchi & D. Wiedemann (Eds.), *Handbook of research on mobile marketing management* (pp. 468–483). Hershey, PA: Business Science Reference; doi:10.4018/978-1-60566-074-5.ch025

Quinn, J. B. (1979). Technological innovation, ownership, and strategy. *Sloan Management Review*, *20*(2), 19–30.

Quinn, R., & Cameron, K. (1983). Organizational life cycles and shifting criteria of effectiveness: Some preliminary evidence. *Management Science*, *29*(1), 33–41. doi:10.1287/mnsc.29.1.33

Qureshil, S., Kamal, M., & Wolcott, P. (2009). Information technology interventions for growth and competiveness in micro-enterprises. *International Journal of E-Business Research*, *5*(1), 117–139. doi:10.4018/jebr.2009010106

Qureshil, S., Kamal, M., & Wolcott, P. (2011). Information technology interventions for growth and competitiveness in micro-enterprises. In M. Tavana (Ed.), *Managing adaptability, intervention, and people in enterprise information systems* (pp. 106–137). Hershey, PA: Information Science Reference; doi:10.4018/978-1-60960-529-2.ch006

Rabaey, M. (2014). Complex adaptive systems thinking approach to enterprise architecture. In P. Saha (Ed.), *A systemic perspective to managing complexity with enterprise architecture* (pp. 99–149). Hershey, PA: Business Science Reference; doi:10.4018/978-1-4666-4518-9.ch003

Rahman, H., & Ramos, I. (2012). Trends of open innovation in developing nations: Contexts of SMEs. In H. Rahman & I. Ramos (Eds.), *Cases on SMEs and open innovation: Applications and investigations* (pp. 65–80). Hershey, PA: Business Science Reference; doi:10.4018/978-1-61350-314-0.ch004

Rahman, H., & Ramos, I. (2013). Implementation of e-commerce at the grass roots: Issues of challenges in terms of human-computer interactions. *International Journal of Information Communication Technologies and Human Development*, *5*(2), 1–19. doi:10.4018/jicthd.2013040101

Rajagopal, D. (2010). Customer value and new product retailing dynamics: An analytical construct for gaining competetive advantage. In *Business information systems: Concepts, methodologies, tools and applications* (pp. 1998–2014). Hershey, PA: Business Science Reference; doi:10.4018/978-1-61520-969-9.ch121

Rajagopal, D. (2010). Internet, reengineering and technology applications in retailing. In *Business information systems: Concepts, methodologies, tools and applications* (pp. 1324–1342). Hershey, PA: Business Science Reference; doi:10.4018/978-1-61520-969-9.ch082

Rajagopal, D. (2011). Marketing strategy, technology and modes of entry in global retailing. In *Global business: Concepts, methodologies, tools and applications* (pp. 1–27). Hershey, PA: Business Science Reference; doi:10.4018/978-1-60960-587-2.ch101

Rajagopal, D. (2012). Convergence marketing. In *Systems thinking and process dynamics for marketing systems: Technologies and applications for decision management* (pp. 274–290). Hershey, PA: Business Science Reference; doi:10.4018/978-1-4666-0969-3.ch011

Rajagopal, D. (2012). Product development and market governance. In *Systems thinking and process dynamics for marketing systems: Technologies and applications for decision management* (pp. 88–117). Hershey, PA: Business Science Reference; doi:10.4018/978-1-4666-0969-3.ch004

Rajagopal, D. (2012). Systems thinking and cognitive process in marketing. In *Systems thinking and process dynamics for marketing systems: technologies and applications for decision management* (pp. 170–197). Hershey, PA: Business Science Reference; doi:10.4018/978-1-4666-0969-3.ch007

Rajagopal, D. (2013). Pricing for new products. In *Marketing decision making and the management of pricing: Successful business tools* (pp. 56–74). Hershey, PA: Business Science Reference; doi:10.4018/978-1-4666-4094-8.ch003

Ramachandran, J., Mukherji, S., & Sud, M. (2006). Strategic entrepreneurship in a globalising economy: Evidence from emerging economies. *IIMB Management Review*, *28*(3), 291–302.

Ramayah, T., Popa, S., & Suki, N. M. (2013). Key dimensions on B2C e-business: An empirical study in Malaysia. *International Journal of Human Capital and Information Technology Professionals*, *4*(2), 43–55. doi:10.4018/jhcitp.2013040104

Rambo, K., & Liu, K. (2011). Culture-sensitive virtual e-commerce design with reference to female consumers in Saudi Arabia. In B. Ciaramitaro (Ed.), *Virtual worlds and e-commerce: Technologies and applications for building customer relationships* (pp. 267–289). Hershey, PA: Business Science Reference; doi:10.4018/978-1-61692-808-7.ch016

Ramdani, B., Kawalek, P., & Lorenzo, O. (2009). Predicting SMEs' adoption of enterprise systems. *Journal of Enterprise Information Management*, *22*(1/2), 10–24. doi:10.1108/17410390910922796

Rao, S. S., Metts, G., & Mora-Monge, C. A. (2003). Electronic commerce development in small and medium sized enterprises; A stage model and its implications. *Business Process Management Journal*, *9*(1), 11–32. doi:10.1108/14637150310461378

Ratnasingam, P. (2001). Electronic commerce adoption in Australia and New Zealand. *Malaysian Journal of Computer Sciences*, *4*, 223–242.

Ratnasingam, P. (2010). The evolution of online relationships in business to consumer e-commerce. In M. Khosrow-Pour (Ed.), *E-commerce trends for organizational advancement: New applications and methods* (pp. 167–176). Hershey, PA: Information Science Reference; doi:10.4018/978-1-60566-964-9.ch010

Ratnasingam, P. (2010). The impact of e-commerce customer relationship management in business-to-consumer e-commerce. In M. Hunter (Ed.), *Strategic information systems: Concepts, methodologies, tools, and applications* (pp. 2099–2111). Hershey, PA: Information Science Reference; doi:10.4018/978-1-60566-677-8.ch132

Rauch, A., & Frese, M. (2000). Psychological approach to entrepreneurial success: A general model and an overview of findings. In Cooper, C. L. & Robertson, I. T. (Editors), International review of Industrial and Organizational Psychology, 101-142. Chichester, Wiley.

Ray, G., Muhanna, W., & Barney, J. B. (2005). Information technology and the performance of the customer service process: A resource-based analysis. *Management Information Systems Quarterly*, *29*(4), 625–652.

Raymond, L. (2001). Determinants of web site implementation in small businesses. *Internet Research*, *11*(5), 411–422. doi:10.1108/10662240110410363

Raymond, L., & Bergeron, F. (2008). Enabling the business strategy on SMEs through e-business capabilities: A strategic alignment perspective. *Industrial Management & Data Systems*, *108*(5), 577–595. doi:10.1108/02635570810876723

Raymond, L., Pare, G., & Bergeron, F. (1995). Matching information technology and organizational structure: An empirical study with implications for performance. *European Journal of Information Systems*, *4*(1), 3–16. doi:10.1057/ejis.1995.2

Razavi, A. R., Krause, P., & Moschoyiannis, S. (2010). Digital ecosystems: Challenges and proposed solutions. In N. Antonopoulos, G. Exarchakos, M. Li, & A. Liotta (Eds.), Handbook of research on P2P and grid systems for service-oriented computing: Models, methodologies and applications (pp. 1003-1031). Hershey, PA: Information Science Reference. doi::10.4018/978-1-61520-686-5.ch043

Read, S., Song, M., & Smit, W. (2009). A meta-analytical review of effectuation and venture performance. *Journal of Business Venturing*, *24*(6), 573–587. doi:10.1016/j.jbusvent.2008.02.005

Regazzi, J. J. (2014). *Infonomics and the business of free: Modern value creation for information services*. Hershey, PA: IGI Global; doi:10.4018/978-1-4666-4454-0

Reich, B. H., & Benbasat, I. (1996). Measuring the linkage between business and information technology objectives. *Management Information Systems Quarterly*, *20*(1), 3–16. doi:10.2307/249542

Reid, G., & Jacobsen, C. (1988). *The Small Entrepreneurial Firm*. Aberdeen: Aberdeen University Press.

Reynolds, J. (2000). *The Complete E-Commerce Book*. Berkley, CA: Publishers Group West.

Reynolds, P. D. (1987). New firms' societal contribution versus survival potential. *Journal of Business Venturing*, *2*(3), 231–246. doi:10.1016/0883-9026(87)90011-5

Reynolds, P., Camp, S. M., Bygrave, W. D., Autio, E., & Hay, M. (2002). *Global Entrepreneurship Monitor 2001 Executive Report. Babson Park/London.* Babson College and London Business School.

Riaz, N., & Rehman, M. (2013). Negotiation by software agents in electronic business: An example of hybrid negotiation. In E. Li, S. Loh, C. Evans, & F. Lorenzi (Eds.), *Organizations and social networking: Utilizing social media to engage consumers* (pp. 327–349). Hershey, PA: Business Science Reference; doi:10.4018/978-1-4666-4026-9.ch017

Rice, G. H., & Hamilton, R. E. (1979). Decision theory and the small business. *American Journal of Small Business*, *6*(4), 1–9.

Rivard, S., Boisvert, C., & Talbot, J. (1988). Key management issues in IS: A comparative analysis.*Proceedings of the Annual Conference of the ASAC*.

Robbins, S. P., Coulter, M., Leach, E., & Kilfoil, M. (2012). *Management* (10th Canadian Edition). Don Mills, Ontario: Pearson, Canada, Inc.

Roberti, G., & Marinelli, A. (2012). Branding identity: Facebook, brands and self construction. In F. Comunello (Ed.), *Networked sociability and individualism: Technology for personal and professional relationships* (pp. 147–168). Hershey, PA: Information Science Reference; doi:10.4018/978-1-61350-338-6.ch008

Roberts, M., & Wood, M. (2001). The strategic use of computerised information systems by a micro enterprise. *Logistics Information Management*, *15*(1/2), 115–125.

Robey, D., Smith, L. A., & Vijayasarathy, L. R. (1993). Perceptions of Conflict and Success in Information Systems Development Projects. *Journal of Management Information Systems*, *10*(1), 123–139.

Rodgers, J. A., Yen, D. C., & Chou, D. C. (2002). Developing e-business: A strategic approach. *Information Management & Computer Security*, *10*(4), 184–192. doi:10.1108/09685220210436985

Rodrigues, D. E. (2012). Cyberethics of business social networking. In M. Cruz-Cunha, P. Gonçalves, N. Lopes, E. Miranda, & G. Putnik (Eds.), *Handbook of research on business social networking: Organizational, managerial, and technological dimensions* (pp. 314–338). Hershey, PA: Business Science Reference; doi:10.4018/978-1-61350-168-9.ch016

Rogers, E. M. (1983). *Diffusion of Innovation* (3rd ed.). New York: Free Press.

Rogers, E. M. (1983). *Diffusion of Innovations 3rd*. New York: Free Press.

Romanelli, E., & Tushman, M. L. (1994). Organizational transformation as punctuated equilibrium: An empirical test. *Academy of Management Journal*, *37*(5), 1141–1166. doi:10.2307/256669

Romano, A., Passiante, G., & Elia, V. (2001). New sources of clustering in the digital economy. *Journal of Small Business and Enterprise Development*, *8*(1), 19–27. doi:10.1108/EUM0000000006813

Roos, G. (2013). The role of intellectual capital in business model innovation: An empirical study. In P. Ordóñez de Pablos, R. Tennyson, & J. Zhao (Eds.), *Intellectual capital strategy management for knowledge-based organizations* (pp. 76–121). Hershey, PA: Business Science Reference; doi:10.4018/978-1-4666-3655-2.ch006

Roos, J., Roos, G., Dragonetti, N. C., & Edvinsson, L. (1997). *Intellectual capital: Navigating the New Business Landscape*. London: Macmillan Press.

Rosen, A. (2000). *The Commerce: A Survival Guide for Business Managers*. New York, NY: AMA Publishers.

Ross, S. A. (1973). The economic theory of agency: The principal's problem. *The American Economic Review*, *63*(2), 134–139.

Rotefoss, B., & Kolvereid, L. (2005). Aspiring, nascent, and fledgling entrepreneurs: An investigation of the business start-up process. *Entrepreneurship and Regional Development*, *17*(2), 109–127. doi:10.1080/08985620500074049

Rotter, J. B. (1966). Generalized expectancies for internal versus external control of reinforcement. *Psychological Monographs*, *609*(80), 1–28. doi:10.1037/h0092976 PMID:5340840

Rowley, J., & Edmundson-Bird, D. (2013). Brand presence in digital space. *Journal of Electronic Commerce in Organizations*, *11*(1), 63–78. doi:10.4018/jeco.2013010104

Rumelt, R. P. (1984). Towards a strategic theory of the firm. In R. R. Lamb (Ed.), *Competitive Strategic Management*. Upper Saddle River, NJ: Prentice Hall.

Rusko, R. (2013). The redefined role of consumer as a prosumer: Value co-creation, coopetition, and crowdsourcing of information goods. In P. Renna (Ed.), *Production and manufacturing system management: Coordination approaches and multi-site planning* (pp. 162–174). Hershey, PA: Engineering Science Reference; doi:10.4018/978-1-4666-2098-8.ch009

Rutherford, M. W., McMullen, P., & Oswald, S. (2001). Examining the issue of size and the small business: A self-organising map approach. *The Journal of Business and Economic Studies*, *7*(2), 64–81.

Sabherwal, R., Jeyaraj, A., & Chowa, C. (2006). Information system success: Individual and organizational determinants. *Management Science*, *52*(12), 849–864. doi:10.1287/mnsc.1060.0583

Sahi, G., & Madan, S. (2013). Developing a website usability framework for B2C e-commerce success. *International Journal of Information Communication Technologies and Human Development*, *5*(1), 1–19. doi:10.4018/jicthd.2013010101

Sainz de Abajo, B., de la Torre Díez, I., & López-Coronado, M. (2010). Analysis of benefits and risks of e-commerce: Practical study of Spanish SME. In I. Portela & M. Cruz-Cunha (Eds.), *Information communication technology law, protection and access rights: Global approaches and issues* (pp. 214–239). Hershey, PA: Information Science Reference; doi:10.4018/978-1-61520-975-0.ch014

Salojarvi, S., Furu, P., & Sveiby, K. E. (2005). Knowledge management and growth in Finnish SMEs. *Journal of Knowledge Management*, *9*(2), 103–122. doi:10.1108/13673270510590254

Samanta, I., & Kyriazopoulos, P. (2011). Can global environment influence B2B relationships? In P. Ordóñez de Pablos, M. Lytras, W. Karwowski, & R. Lee (Eds.), *Electronic globalized business and sustainable development through IT management: Strategies and perspectives* (pp. 54–69). Hershey, PA: Business Science Reference; doi:10.4018/978-1-61520-623-0.ch004

Sambhanthan, A., & Good, A. (2012). Implications for improving accessibility to e-commerce websites in developing countries: A study of hotel websites. *International Journal of Knowledge-Based Organizations*, *2*(2), 1–20. doi::10.4018/ijkbo.2012040101

Sampaio, L., & Figueiredo, J. (2011). E-sourcing electronic platforms in real business. In M. Cruz-Cunha & J. Varajão (Eds.), *E-business managerial aspects, solutions and case studies* (pp. 185–205). Hershey, PA: Business Science Reference; doi:10.4018/978-1-60960-463-9.ch011

Sanchez-Rodriquez, C., & Martinez-Lorente, A. R. (2011). Effect of IT and quality management on performance. *Industrial Management & Data Systems*, *111*(6), 830–848. doi:10.1108/02635571111144937

Schafer, S. (1995). How information technology is leveling the playing field. *Inc. Technology (Elmsford, N.Y.)*, *17*(4), 92–96.

Schein, E. H. (1992). The role of the CEO in the management of change: The case of information technology. In T. A. Kochan & M. Useem (Eds.), *Transforming Organizations*. Oxford: Oxford University Press.

Schlemmer, F., & Webb, B. (2009). The internet as a complementary resource for SMEs: The interaction effect of strategic assets and the internet. *International Journal of E-Business Research*, *5*(1), 1–24. doi:10.4018/jebr.2009010101

Schlenkar, L., & Crocker, N. (2003). Building an e-business scenario for small business: The IBM SME Gateway project. *Qualitative Market Research*, *6*(1), 7–17. doi:10.1108/13522750310457339

Schneider, G. P., & Perry, J. T. (2000). *Electronic Commerce*. Cambridge, MA: Course Technology.

Scholes, L., Westhead, P., & Burrows, A. (2008). Family firm succession: The Management buy-out and buy-in routes. *Journal of Small Business and Enterprise Development*, *15*(1), 8–30. doi:10.1108/14626000810850829

Schulze, W. S., Lubatkin, M., & Dino, R. H. (2003). Exploring the agency consequences of ownership dispersion among the directors of private family firms. *Academy of Management Journal*, *46*(2), 179–194. doi:10.2307/30040613

Schulze, W. S., Lubatkin, M., Dino, R. H., & Buchholtz, A. K. (2001). Agency relationships in family firms: Theory and evidence. *Organization Science*, *12*(2), 99–116. doi:10.1287/orsc.12.2.99.10114

Schumpeter, J. A. (1934). The Theory of Economic Development. New Brunswick, NP: Transaction Publishers.

Schumpeter, J. A. (1934). *The Theory of Economic Development*. Cambridge, MA: Harvard University Press.

Scott, M., & Bruce, R. (1987). Five stages of growth in small business. *Long Range Planning*, *20*(3), 45–52. doi:10.1016/0024-6301(87)90071-9

Scupola, A. (2003). The adoption of internet commerce by SMEs in the south of Italy: An environmental, technological and organizational perspective. *Journal of Global Information Technology Management*, *6*(1), 52–71. doi:10.1080/1097198X.2003.10856343

Seetharaman, A., & Raj, J. R. (2011). Evolution, development and growth of electronic money. In S. Sharma (Ed.), *E-adoption and socio-economic impacts: Emerging infrastructural effects* (pp. 249–268). Hershey, PA: Information Science Reference; doi:10.4018/978-1-60960-597-1.ch013

Sekhar, S. C. (2001). E-commerce and two popular business-level typologies: A competitive analysis. *Global Competitiveness*, *9*(1), 525–543.

Sengupta, A., & Glavin, S. E. (2013). Predicting volatile consumer markets using multi-agent methods: Theory and validation. In B. Alexandrova-Kabadjova, S. Martinez-Jaramillo, A. Garcia-Almanza, & E. Tsang (Eds.), *Simulation in computational finance and economics: Tools and emerging applications* (pp. 339–358). Hershey, PA: Business Science Reference; doi:10.4018/978-1-4666-2011-7.ch016

Serpico, E., Aquilani, B., Ruggieri, A., & Silvestri, C. (2013). Customer centric marketing strategies: The importance and measurement of customer satisfaction – Offline vs. online. In H. Kaufmann & M. Panni (Eds.), *Customer-centric marketing strategies: Tools for building organizational performance* (pp. 315–357). Hershey, PA: Business Science Reference; doi:10.4018/978-1-4666-2524-2.ch016

Serwer, A. E. (1995). Paths to wealth: In the new economy. *Fortune*, (20), February, 57-62.

Seyal, A. H., Awais, M. M., Shamail, S., & Abbas, A. (2004). Determinants of electronic commerce in Pakistan: Preliminary evidence from small and medium enterprises. *Electronic Markets*, *14*(4), 372–387. doi:10.1080/10196780412331311801

Seyal, A. H., Noah Abd Rahman, M., & Awg Yussof Hj Awg Mohammad, H. (2007). A quantitative analysis of factors contributing electronic data interchange adoption among Bruneian SMEs. *Business Process Management Journal*, *13*(5), 728–746. doi:10.1108/14637150710823183

Shackle, G. (1962). Concluding comment. Chapter in Carter, Meredith, C. G., & Shackle, G., (Editors), Uncertainty and Business Decisions, Liverpool: Liverpool University Press.

Shane, S. (2007). *A General Theory of Entrepreneurship: The Individual-Opportunity Nexus*. Aldershot: Edward Elgar.

Shane, S., & Venkataraman, S. (2000). The promise of entrepreneurship as a field of research. *Academy of Management Review*, *26*(1), 13–17. doi:10.5465/AMR.2001.27879269

Shareef, M. A., & Kumar, V. (2012). Prevent/control identity theft: Impact on trust and consumers' purchase intention in B2C EC. *Information Resources Management Journal*, *25*(3), 30–60. doi:10.4018/irmj.2012070102

Sharma, M. K., & Bhagwat, R. (2006). Performance measurements in the implementation of information systems in small and medium-sized enterprises: A framework and empirical analysis. *Measuring Business Excellence*, *10*(4), 8–21. doi:10.1108/13683040610719245

Sharma, S., & Rai, A. (2003). An assessment of the relationship between ISD leadership characteristics and IS innovation adoption in organizations. *Innovation & Management*, *40*(5), 391–401.

Shaver, K. G., & Scott, L. R. (1991). Person, process, choice: The psychology of new venture creation. *Entrepreneurship Theory and Practice*, *16*(2), 23–45.

Shepherd, D. A., Wiklund, J., & Haynie, J. M. (2009). Moving forward: Balancing the financial and emotional costs of business failure. *Journal of Business Venturing*, *24*(2), 134–148. doi:10.1016/j.jbusvent.2007.10.002

Shepherd, D., & Haynie, M. J. (2009). Family business, identity conflict and an expedited entrepreneurial process: A process of resolving identity conflict. *Entrepreneurship Theory and Practice*, *33*(6), 1245–1264. doi:10.1111/j.1540-6520.2009.00344.x

Sherringham, K., & Unhelkar, B. (2011). Business driven enterprise architecture and applications to support mobile business. In *Enterprise information systems: Concepts, methodologies, tools and applications* (pp. 805–816). Hershey, PA: Business Science Reference; doi:10.4018/978-1-61692-852-0.ch316

Shim, J. S., & Min, B. K. (2002). Organizational factors associated with expert systems implementation. *Journal of Computer Information Systems*, *42*(4), 71–76.

Shin, N. (2011). Information technology and diversification: How their relationship affects firm performance. In N. Kock (Ed.), *E-collaboration technologies and organizational performance: Current and future trends* (pp. 65–79). Hershey, PA: Information Science Reference; doi:10.4018/978-1-60960-466-0.ch005

Shleifer, A., & Vishny, R. W. (1997). A survey of corporate governance. *The Journal of Finance*, *52*(2), 759–783. doi:10.1111/j.1540-6261.1997.tb04820.x

Sidnal, N., & Manvi, S. S. (2010). Service discovery techniques in mobile e-commerce. In I. Lee (Ed.), *Encyclopedia of e-business development and management in the global economy* (pp. 812–823). Hershey, PA: Business Science Reference; doi:10.4018/978-1-61520-611-7.ch081

Sidnal, N., & Manvi, S. S. (2013). English auction issues in mobile e-commerce. In K. Tarnay, S. Imre, & L. Xu (Eds.), *Research and development in e-business through service-oriented solutions* (pp. 208–223). Hershey, PA: Business Science Reference; doi:10.4018/978-1-4666-4181-5.ch010

Siggelkow, N., & Leventhal, D. (2005). Escaping real (non-benign) competency trap: Linking the dynamics of organizational structure to the dynamics of search. *Strategic Organization*, *3*(1), 85–115. doi:10.1177/1476127005050521

Simpson, B. (2001). Innovation and the micro-enterprise. *International Journal of Services Technology and Management*, *2*(3/4), 377–387. doi:10.1504/IJSTM.2001.001610

Simpson, M., & Doherty, A. J. (2004). E-commerce adoption support and advice for UK SMEs. *Journal of Small Business and Enterprise Development*, *11*(3), 315–328. doi:10.1108/14626000410551573

Singh, J. V. (1986). Performance, slack, and risk taking in organizational decision making. *Academy of Management Journal*, *29*(4), 562–585. doi:10.2307/256224

Singh, R. K., Garg, S. K., & Deshmukh, S. G. (2006). Strategy development by Indian SMEs in plastic sector: An empirical study. *Singapore Management Review*, *28*(2), 65–83.

Singh, R. K., Garg, S. K., & Deshmukh, S. G. (2008). Strategy development by SMEs for competitiveness: A review. *Benchmarking: An International Journal*, *15*(5), 525–547. doi:10.1108/14635770810903132

Singh, S. (2010). Usability techniques for interactive software and their application in e-commerce. In T. Spiliotopoulos, P. Papadopoulou, D. Martakos, & G. Kouroupetroglou (Eds.), *Integrating usability engineering for designing the web experience: Methodologies and principles* (pp. 81–102). Hershey, PA: Information Science Reference; doi:10.4018/978-1-60566-896-3.ch005

Sirmon, D. G., & Hitt, M. (2003). Managing resources: Linking unique resources, management and wealth creation in family firms. *Entrepreneurship Theory and Practice*, *27*(4), 339–358. doi:10.1111/1540-8520.t01-1-00013

Slater, S. F., & Narver, J. C. (1995). Market orientation and the learning organization. *Journal of Marketing*, *59*(3), 63–74. doi:10.2307/1252120

Small Business Administration. (2010). SBA website www.sba.gov, retrieved July 19, 2011.

Small Business Administration. (2010). *SBA website*. Retrieved from www.sba.gov

Smallbone, D., & Wyer, P. (2000). Growth and development in the small firm. Chapter in Carter, S. and D. James-Evans (Editors), Enterprise and Small Business. Harlow: Prentice Hall.

Smallbone, D., Leigh, R., & North, D. (1995). The characteristics and strategies of high growth SME's. *International Journal of Entrepreneurial Behaviour and Research*, *1*(3), 44–62. doi:10.1108/13552559510100657

Smallbone, D., & Wyer, P. (2000). Growth and development in the small firm. In *Enterprise and small business*. Harlow, MA: Prentice Hall.

Smith, B., & Simon, M. (2009). How data integration systems affect strategic decision making in small firms. *Journal of Small Business Strategy*, *20*(1), 35–51.

Smith, C. A., Organ, D., & Near, J. (1983). Organizational citizenship behavior: Its nature and antecedents. *The Journal of Applied Psychology*, *68*(4), 653–663. doi:10.1037/0021-9010.68.4.653

Smith, K., Mitchell, T., & Summer, C. (1985). Top level management priorities in different stages of the organizational life cycle. *Academy of Management Journal*, *28*(4), 799–820. doi:10.2307/256238

Smith, M. J. (2004). Steward leadership in the public sector. *Global Virtue Ethics Review*, *5*(3), 120–150.

Söderström, E. (2010). Guidelines for managing B2B standards implementation. In E. Alkhalifa (Ed.), *E-strategies for resource management systems: Planning and implementation* (pp. 86–105). Hershey, PA: Business Science Reference; doi:10.4018/978-1-61692-016-6.ch005

Somuyiwa, A. O., & Adewoye, J. O. (2010). Managing logistics information system: Theoretical underpinnings. *Asian Journal of Business Management*, *2*(2), 41–47.

Somuyiwa, A., & Adebayo, T. (2011). Analysis of information and communication technologies (ICT) usage on logistics activities of manufacturing companies in Southwestern Nigeria. *Journal of Emerging Trends in Economics and Management Science*, *2*(1), 68–74.

Sood, S. (2012). The death of social media in start-up companies and the rise of s-commerce: Convergence of e-commerce, complexity and social media. *Journal of Electronic Commerce in Organizations*, *10*(2), 1–15. doi:10.4018/jeco.2012040101

Soto-Acosta, P. (2010). E-business and the resource-based view: Towards a research agenda. In I. Lee (Ed.), *Encyclopedia of e-business development and management in the global economy* (pp. 336–346). Hershey, PA: Business Science Reference; doi:10.4018/978-1-61520-611-7.ch033

Sourouni, A. M., Mouzakitis, S., Kourlimpini, G., Askounis, D., & Psarras, J. (2010). Ontology-based registries: An e-business transactions' registry. In E. Alkhalifa (Ed.), *E-strategies for resource management systems: Planning and implementation* (pp. 106–117). Hershey, PA: Business Science Reference; doi:10.4018/978-1-61692-016-6.ch006

Southern, A., & Tilley, F. (2000). Small firms and information and communication technologies (ICTs): Toward a typology of ICTs usage. *New Technology, Work and Employment*, *15*(2), 138–154. doi:10.1111/1468-005X.00070

Spanos, Y. E., Zaralis, G., & Lioukas, S. (2004). Strategy and industry effects on profitability: Evidence from Greece. *Strategic Management Journal*, *25*(2), 139–165. doi:10.1002/smj.369

Srinivasan, S., & Barker, R. (2012). Global analysis of security and trust perceptions in web design for e-commerce. *International Journal of Information Security and Privacy*, *6*(1), 1–13. doi:10.4018/jisp.2012010101

Stake, R. E. (1994). Case Studies. In N. K. Denzin & Y. S. Lincoln (Eds.), *Handbook of Qualitative Research*. Thousand Oaks, USA: Sage Publications, Inc.

Standing, C., & Lin, C. (2007). Organizational evaluation of the benefits, constaints and satisfaction with business-to-business electronic commerce. *International Journal of Electronic Commerce*, *11*(3), 107–153. doi:10.2753/JEC1086-4415110304

Stanworth, J. (1995). Penetrating the mists surrounding franchise failure rates: Some old lessons for new businesses. *International Small Business Journal*, *13*(2), 59–63. doi:10.1177/0266242695132005

Stanworth, J., & Curran, J. (1986). Growth and the small firm. In J. Curran, J. Stanworth, & D. Watkins (Eds.), *The Survival of the Small Firm* (Vol. 2). Aldershot: Gower.

Steier, L., & Greenwood, R. (2000). Entrepreneurship and the evolution of angel financial networks. *Organization Studies*, *21*(1), 163–192. doi:10.1177/0170840600211002

Steinmetz, L. L. (1969). Critical stages of small business growth: When they occur and how to survive them. *Business Horizons*, *12*(1), 29–36. doi:10.1016/0007-6813(69)90107-4

Sternberg, R., Brixy, U., & Schlapfner, J. F. (2006). *Global Entrepreneurship Monitor. Landerbericht Deutschland 2005*. Hanover, Bonn: University of Hanover and IAB.

Stevenson, H. H. (1999). A perspective of entrepreneurship, in Stevenson, H. H., H. I. Grousebeck, M. J. Roberts and A. Bhide (Eds.). New Business Ventures and the Entrepreneur, 3-17. Boston: Irwin McGraw-Hill.

Stevenson, H. H. (1999). A perspective of entrepreneurship. In H. H. Stevenson, I. Grousebeck, M. J. Roberts, & A. Bhide (Eds.), *New Business Ventures and the Entrepreneur* (pp. 3–17). Boston: Irwin McGraw-Hill.

Stewart, H., & Gallagher, C. (1986). Business death and firm size in the U.K. *International Small Business Journal*, *4*(1), 42–57. doi:10.1177/026624268500400104

Stewart, W. H. Jr, Carland, J. C., Carland, J. W., Watson, W. E., & Sweo, R. (2003). Entrepreneurial dispositions and goal orientations: A comparative exploration of United States and Russian entrepreneurs. *Journal of Small Business Management*, *14*(1), 27–46. doi:10.1111/1540-627X.00065

Stewart, W. H., & Roth, P. L. (2007). A meta-analysis of achievement motivation differences between entrepreneurs and managers. *Journal of Small Business Management*, *45*(4), 401–421. doi:10.1111/j.1540-627X.2007.00220.x

Stockdale, R., & Standing, C. (2004). Benefits and barriers of electronic marketplace participation: An SME perspective. *Journal of Enterprise Information Management*, *17*(4), 301–311. doi:10.1108/17410390410548715

Stockdale, R., & Standing, C. (2006). A classification model to support SME e-commerce adoption initiatives. *Journal of Small Business and Enterprise Development*, *13*(3), 381–394. doi:10.1108/14626000610680262

Stokes, A. (2000). Small and medium-sized enterprises and the environment: Business imperatives. *International Small Business Journal*, *19*(1), 100–102. doi:10.1177/0266242600191007

Storey, D. J., & Cressy, R. (1996). Small business risk – a firm bank perspective. Working paper: The Centre for Small & Medium-sized Enterprises (CSME), Warwick Business School, 39, 1-16.

Storey, D. J. (1994). *Understanding the Small Business Sector*. London: Routledge.

Straub, D., & Klein, R. (2001). E-competitive transformations. *Business Horizons*, *44*(3), 3–12. doi:10.1016/S0007-6813(01)80029-X

Street, C. T., & Meister, D. B. (2004). Small business growth and internal transparency: The role of information systems. *Management Information Systems Quarterly*, *28*(3), 473–506.

Strowbridge, L. (1999). Wired. *Atlantic Progress*, *6*(7), 41–50.

Su, Q., & Adams, C. (2012). Consumers' attitudes toward mobile commerce: A model to capture the cultural and environment influences. In A. Scupola (Ed.), *Innovative mobile platform developments for electronic services design and delivery* (pp. 1–20). Hershey, PA: Business Science Reference; doi:10.4018/978-1-4666-1568-7.ch001

Sveiby, K. E. (1997). *The New Organizational Wealth: Managing and Measuring Knowledge Based Assets*. San Francisco, CA: Berrett-Koehler.

Sveiby, K. E. (2001). A knowledge-based theory of the firm to guide in strategy formulation. *Journal of Intellectual Capital*, *2*(4), 344–358. doi:10.1108/14691930110409651

Swilley, E., Hofacker, C. F., & Lamont, B. T. (2012). The evolution from e-commerce to m-commerce: Pressures, firm capabilities and competitive advantage in strategic decision making. *International Journal of E-Business Research*, *8*(1), 1–16. doi:10.4018/jebr.2012010101

Swimm, N., & Andriole, S. J. (2010). Business technology strategy for an energy management company. *Journal of Information Technology Research*, *3*(3), 54–65. doi:10.4018/jitr.2010070105

Szajna, B., & Scamell, R. W. (1993). The Effects of Information System User Expectations on Their Performance and Perceptions. *Management Information Systems Quarterly*, *17*(4), 493–516. doi:10.2307/249589

Tadjouddine, E. M. (2011). E-commerce systems for software agents: Challenges and opportunities. In M. Cruz-Cunha & J. Varajão (Eds.), *E-business issues, challenges and opportunities for SMEs: Driving competitiveness* (pp. 20–29). Hershey, PA: Business Science Reference; doi:10.4018/978-1-61692-880-3.ch002

Tagiuri, R., & Davis, J. A. (1996). Bivalent attributes of the family firm. *Family Business Review*, *9*(2), 199–208. doi:10.1111/j.1741-6248.1996.00199.x

Tan, J., Fischer, E., Mitchell, R., & Phan, P. (2009). At the center of action: Innovation and technology strategy research in the small business setting. *Journal of Small Business Management*, *47*(3), 233–262. doi:10.1111/j.1540-627X.2009.00270.x

Tan, K. S., Chong, S., Lin, B., & Eze, U. (2009). Internet-based ICT adoption: Evidence from Malaysian SMEs. *Industrial Management & Data Systems*, *109*(2), 224–244. doi:10.1108/02635570910930118

Tan, K. S., & Eze, U. (2008). An empirical study of internet-based ICT adoption among Malaysian SMEs. *Communications of IBIMA Malaysia*, *1*(1), 1–12.

Tan, Z., & Wu, Q. (2003). Globalization and e-commerce I: Factors affecting e-commerce diffusion in China. *Communications of the Association for Information Systems*, *10*(2), 25–35.

Tauzell, J. (1982). Survival of Minnesota new businesses: 1977-1980. *Review of Labour and Economic Conditions*, *9*(2), 10–17.

Taylor, J. (1999). Fitting enterprise software in smaller companies. *Management Accounting*, *80*(8), 36–39.

Taylor, P. R. (2014). Enterprise architecture's identity crisis: New approaches to complexity for a maturing discipline. In P. Saha (Ed.), *A systemic perspective to managing complexity with enterprise architecture* (pp. 433–453). Hershey, PA: Business Science Reference; doi:10.4018/978-1-4666-4518-9.ch013

Teece, D. J. (1992). Foreign investment and technological development in Silicon Valley. *California Management Review*, *34*(2), 88–106. doi:10.2307/41166695

Tella, A. (2012). Determinants of e-payment systems success: A user's satisfaction perspective. *International Journal of E-Adoption*, *4*(3), 15–38. doi:10.4018/jea.2012070102

Teo, T. S. H., & Pian, Y. (2003). A contingency perspective on internet adoption and competitive advantage. *European Journal of Information Systems*, *12*(2), 78–92. doi:10.1057/palgrave.ejis.3000448

Terjesen, A. (2010). Anonymity and trust: The ethical challenges of e-business transactions. In D. Palmer (Ed.), *Ethical issues in e-business: Models and frameworks* (pp. 40–57). Hershey, PA: Business Science Reference; doi:10.4018/978-1-61520-615-5.ch004

Theng, L. G., & Boon, J. L. W. (1996). An exploratory study of factors affecting the failure of local small and medium enterprises. *Asia Pacific Journal of Management*, *13*(2), 47–61. doi:10.1007/BF01733816

Thomason, S. J., Simendinger, E., & Kiernan, D. (2013). Several determinants of successful coopetition in small business. *Journal of Small Business and Entrepreneurship*, *26*(1), 15–28. doi:10.1080/08276331.2012.761800

Thompson, D. V., & Rust, R. T. (2005). The business of value of e-government for small firms. *International Journal of Service Industry Management*, *16*(4), 385–407. doi:10.1108/09564230510614022

Thompson, J. L. (1999). A strategic perspective of entrepreneurship. *International Journal of Entrepreneurial Behavior & Research*, *5*(6), 279–296. doi:10.1108/13552559910306105

Thompson, V. A. (1969). *Bureaucracy and Innovation*. Huntsville: University of Alabama Press.

Thomson, A., & Gray, C. (1999). Determinants of management development in small businesses. *Journal of Small Business and Enterprise Development*, *6*(2), 113–127. doi:10.1108/EUM0000000006676

Thong, J. (2001). Resource constraints and information system implementation in Singaporean small businesses. *OMEGA International Journal of Management science*, 29(2), 143-156.

Thong, J. Y. L. (1999). An integrated model of information systems adoption in small businesses. *Journal of Management Information Systems*, *15*(4), 187–214.

Thong, J. Y. L., & Yap, C. S. (1995). CEO characteristics, organizational characteristics, and information technology adoption in small business. *Omega*, *23*(4), 429–442. doi:10.1016/0305-0483(95)00017-I

Thong, J. Y. L., Yap, C. S., & Raman, K. S. (1996). Top management support, external expertise and information systems implementation in small business. *Information Systems Research*, *7*(2), 248–267. doi:10.1287/isre.7.2.248

Thong, J., Yap, C., & Raman, K. (1994). Engagement of external expertise in information systems implementation. *Journal of Management Information Systems, 11*(2), 209–223.

Thornhill, S., & White, R. E. (2007, May). (20070. Strategic purity: A multi-industry evaluation of pure vs. hybrid business strategies. *Strategic Management Journal, 28*(5), 553–561. doi:10.1002/smj.606

Tijsen, R., Spruit, M., van de Ridder, M., & van Raaij, B. (2011). BI-FIT: Aligning business intelligence end-users, tasks and technologies. In M. Cruz-Cunha & J. Varajao (Eds.), *Enterprise information systems design, implementation and management: Organizational applications* (pp. 162–177). Hershey, PA: Information Science Reference; doi:10.4018/978-1-61692-020-3.ch011

Timmons, J. A. (1999). *New Venture Creation* (5th ed.). Boston: Irwin McGraw-Hill.

Tippins, M. J., & Sohi, R. S. (2003). IT competency and firm performance: Is organizational learning a missing link? *Strategic Management Journal, 24*(8), 745–761. doi:10.1002/smj.337

Todd, P. R., & Javalgi, R. (2007). Internationalization of SMEs in India. Fostering entrepreneurship by leveraging information technology. *International Journal of Emerging Markets, 2*(2), 160–188.

Toftoy, C. N., & Chaterjee, J. (2004). Mission statements and the small business. *Business Strategy Journal, 15*(3), 41–44. doi:10.1111/j.0955-6419.2004.00326.x

Toka, A., Aivazidou, E., Antoniou, A., & Arvanitopoulos-Darginis, K. (2013). Cloud computing in supply chain management: An overview. In D. Graham, I. Manikas, & D. Folinas (Eds.), *E-logistics and e-supply chain management: Applications for evolving business* (pp. 218–231). Hershey, PA: Business Science Reference; doi:10.4018/978-1-4666-3914-0.ch012

Tornatzky, L. G., & Klein, K. J. (1982). Innovation characteristics and innovation adoption implementation: A meta-analysis of findings. *IEEE Transactions on Engineering Management, 29*(1), 28–45. doi:10.1109/TEM.1982.6447463

Tran, Q., Huang, D., & Zhang, C. (2013). An assessment method of the integrated e-commerce readiness for construction organizations in developing countries. *International Journal of E-Adoption, 5*(1), 37–51. doi:10.4018/jea.2013010103

Tung, H., Kung, H., Lawless, D. S., Sofge, D. A., & Lawless, W. F. (2011). Conservation of information and e-business success and challenges: A case study. In M. Cruz-Cunha & J. Varajão (Eds.), *E-business managerial aspects, solutions and case studies* (pp. 254–269). Hershey, PA: Business Science Reference; doi:10.4018/978-1-60960-463-9.ch015

Turban, E., MacLean, E., & Wetherbe, L. (2002). *Information Technology for Management: Transforming Business in the digital Economy*. New York: Wiley.

Tushman, M. L., & Romanelli, E. (1985). Organizational evolution: A metamorphosis model of convergence and reorientation. In B. M. Shaw (Ed.), *Research in Organizational Behavior* (Vol. 7, pp. 171–222). Greenwich, CT: JSL Press.

Ucbasaran, D., Westhead, P., & Wright, M. (2008). Opportunity identification and pursuit: Does an entrepreneur's human capital matter? *Small Business Economics*, *30*(2), 153–173. doi:10.1007/s11187-006-9020-3

Unhelkar, B. (2011). *Handbook of research on green ICT: Technology, business and social perspectives*. Hershey, PA: IGI Global; doi:10.4018/978-1-61692-834-6

Unhelkar, B., Ghanbary, A., & Younessi, H. (2010). Collaborative business process engineering (CBPE) model. In B. Unhelkar, A. Ghanbary, & H. Younessi (Eds.), *Collaborative business process engineering and global organizations: Frameworks for service integration* (pp. 98–120). Hershey, PA: Business Science Reference; doi:10.4018/978-1-60566-689-1.ch004

Unhelkar, B., Ghanbary, A., & Younessi, H. (2010). Emerging technologies for business collaboration. In B. Unhelkar, A. Ghanbary, & H. Younessi (Eds.), *Collaborative business process engineering and global organizations: Frameworks for service integration* (pp. 37–64). Hershey, PA: Business Science Reference; doi:10.4018/978-1-60566-689-1.ch002

Unhelkar, B., Ghanbary, A., & Younessi, H. (2010). Fundamentals of collaborative business. In B. Unhelkar, A. Ghanbary, & H. Younessi (Eds.), *Collaborative business process engineering and global organizations: Frameworks for service integration* (pp. 1–36). Hershey, PA: Business Science Reference; doi:10.4018/978-1-60566-689-1.ch001

United Nations. (2004). *E-Commerce and Development Report*. Geneva: United Nations.

Van de Ven, H. (1993). The development of an infrastructure for entrepreneurship. *Journal of Business Venturing*, *8*(3), 211–230. doi:10.1016/0883-9026(93)90028-4

Van der Deen, M. (2005). Measuring e-business adoption in SMEs. In W. During, R. Oakley, & S. Kauser (Eds.), *New technology-based Firms in the New Millennium* (Vol. 5). Amsterdam: Elsevier.

Van Gelder, J.-L., de Vries, R. E., Frese, M., & Goutbeek, J.-P. (2007). Differences in psychological strategies of failed and operational business owners in the Fiji Islands. *Journal of Small Business Management*, *45*(3), 388–400. doi:10.1111/j.1540-627X.2007.00219.x

Van Hooft, F. P. C., & Stegwee, R. A. (2001). E-business strategy: How to benefit from a hype. *Logistics Information Management*, *14*(1/2), 44–53. doi:10.1108/09576050110360223

Van Huy, L., Rowe, F., Truex, D., & Huynh, M. Q. (2012). An empirical study of determinants of e-commerce adoption in SMEs in Vietnam: An economy in transition. *Journal of Global Information Management*, *20*(3), 23–54. doi:10.4018/jgim.2012070102

Van Praag, C., & Cramer, J. (2001). The roots of entrepreneurship and labour demand: Individual ability and low risk aversion. *Economica*, *68*(269), 45–62. doi:10.1111/1468-0335.00232

Vannoy, S. A. (2011). A structured content analytic assessment of business services advertisements in the cloud-based web services marketplace. *International Journal of Dependable and Trustworthy Information Systems*, *2*(1), 18–49. doi:10.4018/jdtis.2011010102

Vargas, D. M., & Rangel, R. G. T. (2007). Development of internal resources and capabilities as sources of differentiation of SME under increased global competition: A field study in Mexico. *Technological Forecasting and Social Change*, *74*(1), 90–99. doi:10.1016/j.techfore.2005.09.007

Vasconcelos, V., & Campos, P. (2012). The role of social networks in distributed informal information systems for innovation. In J. Varajão, M. Cruz-Cunha, & A. Trigo (Eds.), *Organizational integration of enterprise systems and resources: Advancements and applications* (pp. 60–75). Hershey, PA: Business Science Reference; doi:10.4018/978-1-4666-1764-3.ch004

Venkataraman, S. (1997). The distinctive domain of entrepreneurship research. *Entrepreneur Theory and Practice*, *4*(7), 34–45.

Venkataraman, S., & Sarasvathy, S. D. (2001). Strategy and entrepreneurship: Outlines of an untold story. In M. A. Hitt, E. Freeman, & J. S. Harrison (Eds.), *Handbook of Strategic Management* (pp. 650–668). Oxford: Blackwell. doi:10.2139/ssrn.275186

Venkatesh, V., & Brown, S. A. (2001). A longitudinal investigation of personal computers in homes: Adoption determinants and emerging challenges. *Management Information Systems Quarterly*, *25*(1), 71–102. doi:10.2307/3250959

Venkatraman, R., Venkatraman, S., & Asaithambi, S. P. (2013). A practical cloud services implementation framework for e-businesses. In K. Tarnay, S. Imre, & L. Xu (Eds.), *Research and development in e-business through service-oriented solutions* (pp. 167–198). Hershey, PA: Business Science Reference; doi:10.4018/978-1-4666-4181-5.ch008

Verheul, I., Uhlaner, L., & Thurik, R. (2005). Business accomplishments, gender and entrepreneurial self-image. *Journal of Business Venturing*, *20*(4), 483–518. doi:10.1016/j.jbusvent.2004.03.002

Verkasalo, H. (2011). Analysis of the forces reshaping the mobile internet business. In M. Bartolacci & S. Powell (Eds.), *Interdisciplinary and multidimensional perspectives in telecommunications and networking: Emerging findings* (pp. 19–45). Hershey, PA: Information Science Reference; doi:10.4018/978-1-60960-505-6.ch003

Verma, A. (2013). Effects of phishing on e-commerce with special reference to India. In R. Khurana & R. Aggarwal (Eds.), *Interdisciplinary perspectives on business convergence, computing, and legality* (pp. 186–197). Hershey, PA: Business Science Reference; doi:10.4018/978-1-4666-4209-6.ch017

Villalonga, B., & Amit, R. (2006). How do family ownership, control and management affect firm value? *Journal of Financial Economics*, *80*(2), 385–417. doi:10.1016/j.jfineco.2004.12.005

Vinten, G. (1999). Corporate communication in small and medium-sized enterprises. *Industrial and Commercial Training*, *31*(3), 112–119. doi:10.1108/00197859910269220

Voordeckers, W., Steijivers, T., & Peeters, L. (2010). The ownership-performance relationship: Agency issues in private family firms. paper presented at the Annual European Academy of Management, (EURAM) Conference, May 19-22, Rome Italy.

Vroom, V. (1964). *Work and Motivation*. New York: Wiley.

Wade, M., Johnston, D., & McClean, R. (2004). Exploring the net impact of internet business solution adoption of SME performance. *International Journal of Electronic Business*, *2*(4), 336–350. doi:10.1504/IJEB.2004.005637

Wagner, J. (2004). What a difference a Y makes – female and male nascent entrepreneurs in Germany. IZA Discussion Paper No. 1134, Bonn: Institute for the Study of Labour.

Wagner, J. (2004). What a difference a Y makes – female and male nascent entrepreneurs in Germany. IZA Discussion Paper No. 1134, Institute for the Study of Labour, Bonn.

Wagner, B., Fillis, I., & Johansson, U. (2003). An empirical investigation into e-business adoption in the Scottish smaller firm. *International Journal of Electronic Business*, *1*(4), 408–422. doi:10.1504/IJEB.2003.004113

Wainwright, D., Green, G., Mitchell, E., & Yarrow, D. (2005). Toward a framework for benchmarking ICT practice, competence and performance in small firms. *The International Journal for Library and Information Sciences*, *6*(1), 39–52.

Walczuch, R., van Braven, G., & Lundgran, H. (2000). Internet adoption barriers for small firms in The Netherlands. *European Management Journal*, *18*(5), 561–572. doi:10.1016/S0263-2373(00)00045-1

Waldman, D. A., Ramirez, G. G., House, R. J., & Puranam, P. (2001). Does leadership matter? CEO leadership attributes and profitability under conditions of perceived environmental uncertainty. *Academy of Management Journal*, *44*(1), 134–143. doi:10.2307/3069341

Walker, B., & Posey, E. (2013). Digital El Paso: A public-private business model for community wireless networks. In A. Abdelaal (Ed.), *Social and economic effects of community wireless networks and infrastructures* (pp. 94–111). Hershey, PA: Information Science Reference; doi:10.4018/978-1-4666-2997-4.ch006

Walley, K. (2007). Coopetition: An introduction to the subject and an agenda for research. *International Studies of Management & Organization*, *37*(2), 11–31. doi:10.2753/IMO0020-8825370201

Wang, F., Lupton, N., Rawlinson, D., & Zhang, X. (2012). EBDMSS: A web-based decision making support system for strategic e-business management. In P. Zaraté (Ed.), *Integrated and strategic advancements in decision making support systems* (pp. 265–284). Hershey, PA: Information Science Reference; doi:10.4018/978-1-4666-1746-9.ch019

Wan, Y., Clegg, B., & Dey, P. K. (2013). A framework for enabling dynamic e-business strategies via new enterprise paradigms and ERP solutions. In *Enterprise resource planning: Concepts, methodologies, tools, and applications* (pp. 1561–1595). Hershey, PA: Business Science Reference; doi:10.4018/978-1-4666-4153-2.ch083

Ward, J. L. (1987). *Keeping the family business healthy*. San Fransico: Jossey Boss.

Ward, J. L. (1987). *Keeping the Family Business Healthy*. San Fransico: Jossey Boss.

Ward, J. L. (2004). *Perpetuating the Family Business*. New York: Palgrave MacMillan. doi:10.1057/9780230505995

Ward, J. L., & Aronoff, C. E. (1991). The power of patient capital. *Nation's Business*, *79*(9), 48–49.

Ward, J. L., & Lief, C. (2005). Unconventional wisdom: Counterintuitive insights for family business success. *Perspectives for Managers*, *120*, 1–4.

Ward, T. B. (2004). Cognition, creativity, and entrepreneurship. *Journal of Business Venturing*, *19*(2), 173–188. doi:10.1016/S0883-9026(03)00005-3

Waters, J. (2000). Living in the world 24x7. *Software Magazine*, *20*(1), 53–57.

Watson, J., & Everett, J. E. (1999). Small business failure rates: Choice of definition and industry effects. *International Small Business Journal*, *17*(2), 33–49. doi:10.1177/0266242699172002

Watson, K., Hogarth-Scott, S., & Wilson, N. (1998). Small business start-ups: Success factors and support implications. *International Journal of Entrepreneurial Behaviour & Research*, *4*(3), 217–238. doi:10.1108/13552559810235510

Watters, J., Jackson, F., & Russell, I. (2006). Capturing intangibles for improved IA management and benchmarking. *Journal of Intellectual Capital*, *7*(4), 549–567. doi:10.1108/14691930610709167

Weinrauch, J. D., Man, K., Robinson, P. A., & Pharr, J. (1991). Dealing with limited financial resources: A marketing challenge for small business. *Journal of Small Business Management*, *29*(4), 4–54.

Welsch, J. A., & White, J. F. (1981). A small business is not a little big business. *Harvard Business Review*, *59*(4), 18–32.

Wenyin, L., Liu, A., Li, Q., & Huang, L. (2011). Business models for insurance of business web services. In H. Leung, D. Chiu, & P. Hung (Eds.), *Service intelligence and service science: Evolutionary technologies and challenges* (pp. 261–272). Hershey, PA: Information Science Reference; doi:10.4018/978-1-61520-819-7.ch014

Wernerfelt, B. (1984). A resource-based view of the firm. *Strategic Management Journal*, *5*(2), 171–180. doi:10.1002/smj.4250050207

Westhead, P., Ucbasaran, D., & Wright, M. (2005). Decisions, actions, and performance: Do novice, serial, and portfolio entrepreneurs differ? *Journal of Small Business Management*, *43*(4), 393–417. doi:10.1111/j.1540-627X.2005.00144.x

Westhead, P., Ucbasaran, D., & Wright, M. (2005). Experience and Cognition: Do Novice, Serial and Portfolio Entrepreneurs Differ? *International Small Business Journal*, *23*(1), 72–98. doi:10.1177/0266242605049104

Westhead, P., Ucbasaran, D., Wright, M., & Binks, M. (2005). Novice, serial, and portfolio entrepreneur behavior and contributions. *Small Business Economics*, *25*(2), 109–132. doi:10.1007/s11187-003-6461-9

Westhead, P., & Wright, M. (1999). Contributions of novice, portfolio and serial founders located in rural and urban areas. *Regional Studies*, *33*(2), 157–173.

Whaley, A. M. (2003). Study of information systems integration into micro-enterprises. *Proceedings of the Fourth Conference in the Department of Computing*, University of central Lancashire, Preston.

Whiteley, D. (2000). *E-commerce – Strategy, Technologies and Applications*. Maidenhead: McGraw-Hill Publishing Company.

Wickham, P. A. (2001). *Strategic Entrepreneurship: A Decision-Making Approach to New Venture Creation and Management*, 2nd Edition, London: Financial Times Pitman Publishing.

Wiedmann, K., Reeh, M., & Schumacher, H. (2010). Employment and acceptance of near field communication in mobile marketing. In K. Pousttchi & D. Wiedemann (Eds.), *Handbook of research on mobile marketing management* (pp. 190–212). Hershey, PA: Business Science Reference; doi:10.4018/978-1-60566-074-5.ch011

Wiklund, L., & Shepherd, D. (2003). Aspiring for, and achieving growth: The moderating role of resources and opportunities. *Journal of Management Studies, 40*(8), 1919–1941. doi:10.1046/j.1467-6486.2003.00406.x

Willcocks, L., Reynolds, P., & Feeny, D. (2007). Evolving IS capabilities to leverage the external IT services market. *MIS Quarterly Executive, 6*, 127–145.

Williams, J. G., & Premchaiswadi, W. (2011). On-line credit card payment processing and fraud prevention for e-business. In *Global business: Concepts, methodologies, tools and applications* (pp. 699–717). Hershey, PA: Business Science Reference; doi:10.4018/978-1-60960-587-2.ch312

Wilms, A., & Andriole, S. J. (2010). Business technology strategy for a specialty chemicals company. *Journal of Information Technology Research, 3*(3), 11–18. doi:10.4018/jitr.2010070102

Wiltshire Committee. (1971). *Report of the Committee on Small Business*. Canberra, Australia: The Government Printer of Australia.

Winborg, J., & Landstrom, H. (2001). Financial bootstrapping in small businesses: Examining small business managers' resource acquisition behaviors. *Journal of Business Venturing, 16*(3), 235–254. doi:10.1016/S0883-9026(99)00055-5

Windrum, P., & de Berranger, P. (2003). *Factors affecting the adoption of intranets and extranets by SMEs: A UK study. Research Memoranda*. Maastricht: Maastricht Economic Research Institute on Innovation and Technology.

Winkler, U., & Gilani, W. (2012). Business continuity management of business driven IT landscapes. In S. Reiff-Marganiec & M. Tilly (Eds.), *Handbook of research on service-oriented systems and non-functional properties: Future directions* (pp. 381–399). Hershey, PA: Information Science Reference; doi:10.4018/978-1-61350-432-1.ch017

Winston, E., & Dologite, D. (2002). How does attitude impact IT implementation: A study of small business owners. *Journal of End User Computing, 14*(2), 16–29. doi:10.4018/joeuc.2002040102

Winter, S. J., Gaglio, C. M., & Rajagopalan, H. K. (2009). The value of information systems to small and medium-sized enterprises: Information and communications technologies as signal and symbol of legitimacy and competitiveness. *International Journal of E-Business Research, 5*(1), 65–91. doi:10.4018/jebr.2009010104

Wollenberg, A. (2013). Optimizing international joint venture (IJV) ownership structures: A technology and knowledge transfer-linked productivity growth perspective. In B. Christiansen, E. Turkina, & N. Williams (Eds.), *Cultural and technological influences on global business* (pp. 142–164). Hershey, PA: Business Science Reference; doi:10.4018/978-1-4666-3966-9.ch009

Wood, A. M., Moultrie, J., & Eckert, C. (2010). Product form evolution. In A. Silva & R. Simoes (Eds.), *Handbook of research on trends in product design and development: Technological and organizational perspectives* (pp. 499–512). Hershey, PA: Business Science Reference; doi:10.4018/978-1-61520-617-9.ch027

Wresch, W., & Fraser, S. (2011). Persistent barriers to e-commerce in developing countries: A longitudinal study of efforts by Caribbean companies. *Journal of Global Information Management*, *19*(3), 30–44. doi:10.4018/jgim.2011070102

Wresch, W., & Fraser, S. (2013). Persistent barriers to e-commerce in developing countries: A longitudinal study of efforts by Caribbean companies. In F. Tan (Ed.), *Global diffusion and adoption of technologies for knowledge and information sharing* (pp. 205–220). Hershey, PA: Information Science Reference; doi:10.4018/978-1-4666-2142-8.ch009

Wyer, P. (1997). Small business integration with the external operating environment – the role of strategic management and planning in the small business. Paper presented at Small Business and Enterprise Development Conference, Sheffield.

Wyer, P., Donohue, S., & Matthews, P. (2010). Fostering strategic learning capability to enhance creativity in small service businesses. *Service Business*, *4*(1), 9–26. doi:10.1007/s11628-009-0086-2

Wymer, S., & Regan, E. (2005). Factors influencing e-commerce adoption and use by small and medium businesses. *Electronic Markets*, *15*(4), 412–438. doi:10.1080/10196780500303151

Xiao, X., Liu, Y., & Zhang, Z. (2012). The analysis of the logistics mode decision to e-commerce. *Journal of Electronic Commerce in Organizations*, *10*(4), 57–70. doi::10.4018/jeco.2012100105

Xu, L. (2010). Outsourcing and multi-party business collaborations modeling. In K. St.Amant (Ed.), *IT outsourcing: Concepts, methodologies, tools, and applications* (pp. 558–577). Hershey, PA: Business Science Reference; doi:10.4018/978-1-60566-770-6.ch033

Xu, M., Rohatgi, R., & Duan, Y. (2010). Engaging SMEs in e-business: Insights from an empirical study. In *Business information systems: Concepts, methodologies, tools and applications* (pp. 115–134). Hershey, PA: Business Science Reference; doi:10.4018/978-1-61520-969-9.ch009

Yao, L. j., Sutton, S. G., & Chan, S. H. (2010). Wealth creation from information technology investments using the eva. *Journal of Computer Information Systems*, *50*, 42–48.

Yap, C., Soh, C., & Raman, K. (1992). Information systems success factors in small business. *Omega*, *20*(5-6), 597–609. doi:10.1016/0305-0483(92)90005-R

Yermish, I., Miori, V., Yi, J., Malhotra, R., & Klimberg, R. (2010). Business plus intelligence plus technology equals business intelligence. *International Journal of Business Intelligence Research*, *1*(1), 48–63. doi::10.4018/jbir.2010071704

Yetton, P., Johnston, K., & Craig, J. (1994). Computer-aided architects: A case study of IT and strategic change. *Sloan Management Review*, *35*(4).

Yeung, W. L. (2013). Specifying business-level protocols for web services based collaborative processes. In A. Loo (Ed.), *Distributed computing innovations for business, engineering, and science* (pp. 137–154). Hershey, PA: Information Science Reference; doi:10.4018/978-1-4666-2533-4.ch007

Yin, R. K. (1994). *Case Study Research – Design and Methods*. Thousand Oaks, USA: Sage Publications, Inc.

York, G. J., & Venkataraman, S. (2010). The entrepreneur-environment nexus: Uncertainty, innovation and allocation. *Journal of Business Venturing*, *25*(5), 449–463. doi:10.1016/j.jbusvent.2009.07.007

Yulong, L. (2001). ERP adoption in Chinese small enterprise: An exploratory case study. *Journal of Manufacturing Technology Management*, *22*(4), 489–505.

Z arour, M., Abran, A., & Desharnais, J. (2014). Software process improvement for small and very small enterprises. In *Software design and development: Concepts, methodologies, tools, and applications* (pp. 1363-1384). Hershey, PA: Information Science Reference. doi:10.4018/978-1-4666-4301-7.ch066

Zachary, R. K., & Mishra, C. S. (2010). Entrepreneurship research today and beyond: Hidden in plain sight. *Journal of Small Business Management*, *48*(4), 471–474. doi:10.1111/j.1540-627X.2010.00304.x

Zahra, S. A., & George, G. (2002). Absorptive capacity: A review, reconceptualization, and extension. *Academy of Management Review*, *27*(2), 185–203.

Zahra, S. A., Hayton, J. C., & Salvato, C. (2004). Entrepreneurship in family vs. non-family firms: A resource-based analysis of the effect of organizational culture. *Entrepreneurship: Theory and Practice*, *28*(4), 363–381.

Zahra, S., & Dess, G. G. (2001). Entrepreneurship as a field of research: Encouraging dialogue and debate. *Academy of Management Review*, *26*(1), 8–10. doi:10.5465/AMR.2001.4011916

Zaltman, G., Duncan, R., & Holbek, J. (1973). *Innovations and Organizations*. New York: John Wiley.

Zerbinati, S., & Souitaris, V. Entrepreneurship in the public sector: A framework of analysis in European local governments. *Entrepreneurship and Regional Development*, 17(1), 43-64.

Zerenler, M., & Gözlü, S. (2012). Issues influencing electronic commerce activities of SMEs: A study of the Turkish automotive supplier industry. In *Human resources management: Concepts, methodologies, tools, and applications* (pp. 1035–1055). Hershey, PA: Business Science Reference; doi:10.4018/978-1-4666-1601-1.ch064

Zhang, K., Li, H., & Ziegelmayer, J. L. (2009). Resource or capability? A dissection of SMEs' IT infrastructure flexibility and its relationship with IT responsiveness. *Journal of Computer Information Systems*, *50*, 46–53.

Zhuang, Y., & Lederer, A. L. (2003). An instrument for measuring the business benefits of e-commerce retailing. *International Journal of Electronic Commerce*, *7*(3), 65–99.

Zhu, K., Kraemer, K., & Xu, S. (2003). Electronic business adoption by European firms: A cross-country assessment of the facilitators and inhibitors. *European Journal of Information Systems*, *12*(4), 251–268. doi:10.1057/palgrave.ejis.3000475

Zhu, K., Kraemer, K., & Xu, S. (2006). The process of innovation assimilation by firms in different countries: A technology diffusion perspective on e-business. *Management Science*, *52*(10), 1557–1576. doi:10.1287/mnsc.1050.0487

Zhu, Y., Basil, D. Z., & Hunter, M. G. (2009). The extended website stage model: A study of Canadian winery websites. *Canadian Journal of Administrative Sciences*, *26*(4), 286–300. doi:10.1002/cjas.118

Zinger, J. T., Huguette, B., Zanibbi, L., & Mount, J. (1996). An empirical study of the small business support network – the entrepreneurs' perspective. *Canadian Journal of Administrative Sciences*, *13*(4), 347–357. doi:10.1111/j.1936-4490.1996.tb00743.x

Zinger, J., LeBrasseur, T. R., & Zanibbi, L. R. (2001). Factors influencing early stage performance in Canadian microenterprises. *Journal of Developmental Entrepreneurship*, *6*(2), 129–150.

Zontanos, G., & Anderson, A. R. (2004). Relationships, marketing and small business: An exploration of links in theory and practice. *Qualitative Market Research*, *7*(3), 228–236. doi:10.1108/13522750410540236

Zuboff, S. (1988). *In the Age of Smart Machine: The Future of Work and Power*. New York, NY: Basic Books.

# About the Author

**M. Gordon Hunter** is Professor of Information Systems in the Faculty of Management at The University of Lethbridge, Alberta, Canada. He has also been appointed Visiting Professor, Faculty of Business, Computing and Information Management, London South Bank University. Gordon has previously held academic positions at universities in Canada, Hong Kong, and Singapore. He has held visiting positions at universities in Australia, England, Germany, Monaco, New Zealand, Poland, Turkey, and USA. In 2012 Gordon received the Lloyd Houlden Research Fellowship from the Canadian Insolvency Foundation. From April to July of 2009 Gordon was a Fellow at the University of Applied Sciences, Munich, Germany. During July and August of 2005 Gordon was an Erskine Fellow at the University of Canterbury, Christchurch, New Zealand. He has a Bachelor of Commerce Degree from the University of Saskatchewan in Saskatoon, Saskatchewan, Canada; and a Ph.D. from Strathclyde Business School, University of Strathclyde in Glasgow, Scotland. Gordon has also obtained a Certified Management Accountant (CMA) designation from the Society of Management Accountants of Canada and was appointed a Fellow of the Society in 2010. In 2011 Gordon was appointed CMA Distinguished Scholar by CMA Alberta. He is a Chartered Information Technology Professional (CITP) and a Chartered Member of the British Computer Society. Gordon is also a member of the Canadian Information Processing Society (CIPS), where he has obtained designations including Information Systems Professional (ISP), Canadian Information Technology Professional (CITP), and International Information Technology Professional (IITP). At the University of Lethbridge Gordon is the Director of the Small Business Institute which investigates small business issues; and is the Committee Chair of the Burns Endowment Fund which supports visiting academics and business professionals. He has extensive experience as a systems analyst and manager in industry and government organizations in Canada. He is a member of the Advisory Board for the *Journal of Information, Information Technology, and Organizations*. Gordon is an Associate Editor of *the International Journal of Qualitative Information Systems Research, the Journal of Global Information Technology Management, the International Journal of Transcultural Tech-*

*nology Transfer, and the International Journal on Innovation in the Digital Economy*, and *the International Journal of Sociotechnology and Knowledge Development.* He serves on the Editorial Review Board of several journals. Gordon has published articles in *MIS Quarterly; Information Systems Research; The Journal of Strategic Information Systems; Information Systems Journal; Information, Technology and People; The Journal of Global Information Management; Canadian Journal of Administrative Sciences; International Journal of Strategic Information Technology and Applications; The International Journal of Sociotechnology and Knowledge Development; The Journal of Information, Information Technology, and Organizations; and Journal of Applied Management and Entrepreneurship.* He has conducted over 100 seminar presentations in Australia, Canada, England, Germany, Hong Kong, New Zealand, Poland, Singapore, Taiwan, Turkey, and USA. Gordon's research approach takes a qualitative perspective employing Personal Construct Theory and Narrative Inquiry to conduct in-depth interviews. He applies qualitative techniques in interdisciplinary research such as small business, agricultural management, and cross-cultural investigations. His current research interests in the information systems (IS) area include the effective management of IS with emphasis on the personnel component; the role of Chief Information Officers; and the use of IS by small business.

# Index

## F



## G



## H



## I



## K



## L



## M

## T



## U



## V



## W

www.ingramcontent.com/pod-product-compliance
Lightning Source LLC
Chambersburg PA
CBHW080501051126
54379CB00005B/135